Kurt E. Free, Ph. D.

THE
PSYCHOTHERAPEUTIC
TECHNIQUES
OF
RICHARD A. GARDNER

THE PSYCHOTHERAPEUTIC TECHNIQUES OF RICHARD A. GARDNER

RICHARD A. GARDNER, M.D.

Clinical Professor of Child Psychiatry
Columbia University, College of Physicians and Surgeons

Creative Therapeutics
P.O. Box R, Cresskill, New Jersey 07626-0317

© 1986 by Creative Therapeutics
155 County Road, Cresskill, New Jersey 07626–0317

PRINTED IN THE UNITED STATES OF AMERICA

10   9   8   7   6   5   4   3   2   1

Library of Congress Cataloging-in-Publication Data

Gardner, Richard A.
   The psychotherapeutic techniques of Richard A.
Gardner.

   Bibliography: p. 861
   Includes index.
   1. Child psychotherapy.   2. Gardner, Richard A.
I. Title.   [DNLM: 1. Psychotherapy—methods.
WM 420 G228p]
RJ504.G344   1986   618.92′8914   86–11531
ISBN 0–933812–14–0

To Patricia Ann

> You and this book
> both represent
> a culmination and
> a commencement

Other Books by Richard A. Gardner

The Boys and Girls Book About Divorce
Therapeutic Communication with Children:
    The Mutual Storytelling Technique
Dr. Gardner's Stories About the Real World, Volume I
Dr. Gardner's Stories About the Real World, Volume II
Dr. Gardner's Fairy Tales for Today's Children
Understanding Children: A Parents Guide to Child Rearing
MBD: The Family Book About Minimal Brain Dysfunction
Psychotherapeutic Approaches to the Resistant Child
Psychotherapy with Children of Divorce
Dr. Gardner's Modern Fairy Tales
The Parents Book About Divorce
The Boys and Girls Book About One-Parent Families
The Objective Diagnosis of Minimal Brain Dysfunction
Dorothy and the Lizard of Oz
Dr. Gardner's Fables for Our Times
The Boys and Girls Book About Stepfamilies
Family Evaluation in Child Custody Litigation
Separation Anxiety Disorder:
    Psychodynamics and Psychotherapy
Child Custody Litigation:
    A Guide for Parents and Mental Health Professionals
Psychotherapy of Psychogenic Learning Disabilities

Contents

ACKNOWLEDGMENTS   xix

INTRODUCTION   xxi

1   Theoretical and Developmental Foundations
     of the Author's Techniques   1

   ELEMENTARY AND JUNIOR HIGH SCHOOL
     [1936-1945] 2
   HIGH SCHOOL [1945-1948] 2
   COLLEGE [1948-1952] 3
   MEDICAL SCHOOL [1952-1956] 5
   INTERNSHIP [1956-1957] 7
   RESIDENCY TRAINING
     [PART I, GENERAL PSYCHIATRY, 1957-1959] 8
   RESIDENCY TRAINING
     [PART II, CHILD PSYCHIATRY, 1959-1960] 12
   MILITARY SERVICE [1960-1962] 18
   RESIDENCY TRAINING
     [PART III, CHILD PSYCHIATRY, 1962-1963] 20
   PSYCHOANALYTIC TRAINING [1959-1960,
     1962-1966] 21
   PRIVATE PRACTICE 27
   1963–1965 27   1965–1970 30   1970–1975 33   1975–1980 34
   1980–1986 35

2   Historical Considerations Regarding
    Child Psychotherapeutic Techniques   36

    CHILD PSYCHOANALYSIS 36
    PSCHOANALYTIC PLAY THERAPY 39
    COMMUNICATION AT THE SYMBOLIC LEVEL 41
    The Play Interview 41
    Active Play Therapy 42
    DOLL PLAY 43
    ALLEN'S "RELATIONSHIP THERAPY" 44
    ROGERS' "NONDIRECTIVE"
        OR "CLIENT-CENTERED THERAPY" 46
    RELEASE THERAPY 49
    FANTASIES CREATED AROUND DRAWINGS 50
    DIRECT INTERPRETATION OF THE DRAWING 53
    FINGER PAINTS, CLAY, BLOCKS, AND WATER 54
    Finger Paints 54
    Clay 55
    Blocks 57
    Water Play 58
    Further Comments on Finger Painting, Clay, Blocks,
        and Water Play 59
    PUPPETS AND MARIONETTES 60
    DRAMATIZATION 61
    "PARAVERBAL THERAPY" 63
    TRADITIONAL COMPETITIVE BOARD GAMES 63
    CONCLUDING COMMENTS 64

3   Central Elements
    in the Psychotherapeutic Process   66

    THE ORIGIN OF SYMPTOMS 67
    THERAPY AS A WAY OF OPENING UP
        NEW OPTIONS 73
    COMMENTS ON TIME-LIMITED THERAPY 74
    THE THERAPIST-PATIENT RELATIONSHIP 76
    Genuine Respect vs. Idealization and/or Idolization
        of the Therapist 76
    Receptivity to the Therapist's Messages 77
    Identification with and Emulation of the
        Therapist 78
    Trying to Help Patients vs. Helping Patients 82
    THERAPY—AN EDUCATIONAL EXPERIENCE 84
    The Therapist as Teacher 85
    The Levels of Therapeutic Learning 85
    Intellectual and Emotional Learning 85   The Metaphor 86
    Conceptualizations and Abstractions vs. Concrete Examples 87
    The Experience 88
    CONCLUDING COMMENTS 90

4   The Therapist-Patient Relationship   **91**

THE THERAPIST'S PERSONALITY 91
Language Limitations 92
Liking Children 93
Projection of Oneself into the Child's Position 93
Treatment of the Projected Self 94
Memory of One's Own Childhood 95
Excitation 96
The Inner Warmth Response 97
Childlike Personality Characteristics 98
"On the Same Wavelength" 99
A Strong Parental Instinct 99
Frustration Tolerance 100
Flexibility and Creativity 101
The Therapist as Parent 103
Boredom 104
Comfort with Therapeutic Failure 104
FACTORS IN THE THERAPIST-PATIENT RELATIONSHIP
** CONDUCIVE TO BRINGING**
** ABOUT THERAPEUTIC CHANGE 105**
Introduction 105
Time Alone Together 106
The Therapist's Affection for the Patient 107
Taking the Child's Side in His or Her Conflict
** with the Parents 109**
Child Talk 111
The Resolution of the Transference Neurosis 114
The Transference Cure 115
The Corrective Emotional Experience 117
Identification with the Therapist 118
The Therapist as Educator 120
Intimacy and Self-Revelation 126
The Role of Seduction 129
Fun 131   Humor 132   Candy and Other Foods 133
Magic Tricks 134   The Peabody Picture Vocabulary Test (PPVT) 135
CLINICAL EXAMPLES 138
The Case of George
** ["Can I Call You Dick?"] 138**
The Case of Henry
** [An Attempt on the Therapist's Life] 139**
The Case of Harry
** [Rebuking the Patient] 141**
The "Amotivational Syndrome" 144
The Passive-Aggressive Child 145
The Case of Carol
** [The Hostile Parent] 146**
The Case of Greg
** [Death of a Boy's Father] 147**
The Case of Timmy
** [Revelation of the Therapist's Defect] 149**
Other Assorted Examples
** of a Good Therapist-Patient Relationship 150**

5   The Initial Screening Evaluation   153

WHO SHALL BE SEEN
  IN THE INITIAL CONSULTATION 154
THE INITIAL TELEPHONE CALL 157
THE QUESTIONNAIRE 162
Basic Data 164
Pregnancy 167
Delivery 169
Post-Delivery Period [While in the Hospital] 171
The Infancy-Toddler Period 174
Developmental Milestones 175
Coordination 178
Comprehension and Understanding 179
School 179
Peer Relationships 181
Home Behavior 183
Interests and Accomplishments 183
Medical History 185
Present Medical Status 187
Family History—Mother 187
Family History—Father 189
Psychological Symptoms 189
Siblings 194
Names and Addresses
  of Other Professionals Consulted 194
INTERVIEWING THE CHILD
  AND PARENTS TOGETHER 196
INTERVIEW WITH THE PARENTS ALONE 208
INTERVIEW WITH THE CHILD ALONE 210
The Freely-Drawn Picture 211
Draw-a-Person 213
The Make-a-Picture Story Test 215
Additional Diagnostic Instruments 216
Final Comments 222
CRITERIA FOR DECIDING WHETHER TREATMENT
  IS WARRANTED 223
School 224
The Neighborhood 225
The Home 225
DSM-III 227
PRESENTING THE INITIAL
  RECOMMENDATIONS 228
Should the Child Be Present? 228
When Therapy Is Not Warranted 229
When A Decision Regarding Therapy Has Not
  Yet Been Made 230
When Psychotherapy Is Warranted 231
Discussion of Fees 233
The Question of Payment for Missed Sessions 236
CONCLUDING COMMENTS 237

6   The Intensive Diagnostic Evaluation   239

THE EVALUATION OF THE MOTHER 240
The Initial Inquiry 241
Inquiry into the Causes
  of the Child's Difficulties 244
Inquiry Regarding Parental Dealings
  with the Child 245
Description of the Marriage 248
History of Psychiatric Treatment 250
Background Information 250
Family Background 250   The First Memory Question 253
School Life 256   Work History 257
The Premarital Relationship with the Father 257
Projective Questions 257
        Five Wishes 258, Verbal Projective Questions 262,
        Draw-a-Person and Draw-a-Family 265, Dreams 270
THE EVALUATION OF THE FATHER 275
The Initial Inquiry 275
Description of the Marriage 276
History of Psychiatric Treatment 276
Background Information 277
Military Service 277   The First Memory Question 278
School Life 280   Work History 280
The Premarital Relationship with the Mother 281
Projective Questions 281
        Five Wishes 281, Verbal Projective Questions 283,
        Draw-a-Person and Draw-a-Family 290, Dreams 294
Concluding Comments 296
EVALUATION OF THE CHILD 296
Introduction 296
Direct Verbal Inquiry with the Child 298
Three Wishes 304
First Memory 306
Free Picture 309
Draw-a-Person and Draw-a-Family 314
Verbal Projective Questions 318
Dreams 324
Concluding Comments 340
JOINT INTERVIEW WITH THE PARENTS 341
The Correction of Distortions
  and Other Kinds of False Data 341
"The Whole May Be Greater Than the Sum
  of Its Parts" 345
The Marriage 348
Dealing with the Children 350
Concluding Comments 352
THE FAMILY INTERVIEW 353
PREPARATION OF THE PRESENTATION 356
PRESENTATION OF THE FINDINGS
  TO THE PARENTS 359

7   Parental Involvement
      in the Child's Treatment   364

      **THE ISSUE OF CONFIDENTIALITY
        AS IT RELATES TO THE PARENTS' INVOLVEMENT
        IN THE CHILD'S TREATMENT 366**
      Confidentiality in Adult Therapy 366
      Confidentiality in Adolescent Therapy 368
      Confidentiality in Child Psychotherapy 369
      **REASONS FOR PARENTAL AMBIVALENCE
        REGARDING A CHILD'S TREATMENT 372**
      **WAYS IN WHICH PARENTS [USUALLY THE MOTHER]
        CAN BE USEFUL IN A CHILD'S THERAPY 375**
      **SITUATIONS IN WHICH THE PARENTAL PRESENCE
        IS CONTRAINDICATED 379**
      CLINICAL EXAMPLES 384
      **Freud's Case of Little Hans
        [The Boy Who Feared Horses] 384**
      **The Case of Jack
        ["Daddy, please take me fishing"] 391**
      **The Case of Howie
        [Nude Bathing in New Zealand] 393**
      **The Case of Walter
        ["Stop touching the walls"] 397**
      **The Case of Tara
        ["Your brother's in heaven"] 398**
      **The Case of Mack
        [The Baseball Hall of Fame] 401**
      CONCLUDING COMMENTS 403

8   The Mutual Storytelling Technique   404

      HISTORICAL BACKGROUND 404
      THE BASIC TECHNIQUE 408
      **SPECIFIC TECHNIQUE
        FOR ELICITING SELF-CREATED STORIES 410**
      FUNDAMENTALS OF STORY ANALYSIS 413
      CLINICAL EXAMPLES 415
      **The Case of Martin
        [The Bear and the Bees] 415**
      **The Case of Mark
        [The Farmer and the Stone] 417**
      **The Case of Evan
        [The Killed Guide
        and the Grilled-Cheese Sandwiches] 429**
      **The Case of Todd
        [The Club of Mean Tigers] 430**
      **The Case of David
        [The Family with Sixteen Children] 437**
      **The Case of Harry
        [Valentine Day's Candy from a Loving Mother] 444**

The Case of Frank
 [The Nutcracker and the Three Peanuts] 451
Freud's Theory of the Oedipus Complex 451
Freud's Theory of the Resolution of the Oedipus Complex 452
The Author's View of the Oedipus Complex 452
The Author's Approach to the Alleviation of Oedipal Problems 454
The Case of Frank 456
CONCLUDING COMMENTS 464

9   Dramatized Storytelling   465

INTRODUCTION 465
CLINICAL EXAMPLES 468
The Case of Adam
 ["Can a Dead Frog Be Brought Back to Life?"] 468
The Case of Frank
 ["Gonga Wants Too Much"] 470
The Case of George
 ["This Damn Magic Wand Is No Good"] 498

10   Mutual Storytelling Derivative Games   519

INTRODUCTION 519
THE BOARD OF OBJECTS GAME 523
Clinical Example 527
The Case of Norman
 (The Cowboy Whose Gun Was Missing) 527
THE THREE GRAB-BAG GAMES 532
The Bag of Toys Game 532
Clinical Example: The Case of Bernard
 (Let Sleeping Dogs Lie, But Give Him a Bone) 533
Clinical Example: The Case of Tom
 (The Bed That Dumped Its Occupants) 539
The Bag of Things Game 543
Clinical Example: The Case of Betty ("Get Off My Back") 544
Clinical Example: The Case of Ronald
 (The Robot Baby Who Receives Unconditional Positive Regard) 548
The Bag of Words Games 550
Clinical Example: The Case of Marc
 (The Man Who Picked the Big Coconuts Off the Palm Tree) 553
SCRABBLE FOR JUNIORS 558
Clinical Examples 561
The Case of Cary (The Frog and the Seal) 561
The Case of Timothy (The Seal and the Cat) 565
THE FEEL AND TELL GAME 570
Clinical Example 572
The Case of Mary (The Kangaroo in the Mother's Pouch) 572
THE ALPHABET SOUP GAME 577
Clinical Example 579
The Case of Larry (The Boy Who Felt His Mother's Breasts) 579

THE PICK-A-FACE GAME **589**
Clinical Example **591**
The Case of Gloria (Make Believe There's No Trouble,
  and You Won't Be Bothered by Things) 591
THE MAKE-A-PICTURE STORY CARDS **595**
Diagnostic Utilization **595**
Therapeutic Utilization **598**
Clinical Example: The Case of Ruth (The Army of Babysitters) 598
CONCLUDING COMMENTS **607**

11 The Talking, Feeling, and Doing Game 609

THE BASIC FORMAT OF THE TALKING, FEELING,
  AND DOING GAME **610**
EXAMPLES OF CARD RESPONSES **616**
Talking Cards **616**
Feeling Cards **629**
Doing Cards **639**
EXAMPLES OF THERAPIST-PATIENT INTERCHANGES **646**
The Case of Frank
  [Dealing with a Psychopathic Partner] **646**
The Case of Andy
  [The Boy with Hypospadias] **652**
The Case of Morton
  [Therapists Also Get Rejected] **669**
The Case of Harry
  [Getting Therapeutic Mileage from an Auto Mechanic] **671**
CONCLUDING COMMENTS **683**

12 Bibliotherapy 685

INTRODUCTION **685**
THE EXPOSITORY BOOK **687**
MBD: The Family Book About Minimal Brain Dysfunction **688**
The Boys and Girls Book About Divorce **689**
The Boys and Girls Book About One-Parent Families **693**
The Boys and Girls Book About Stepfamilies **695**
The Parents Book About Divorce **695**
Understanding Children—A Parents Guide
  to Child Rearing **696**
REALITY-ORIENTED STORIES **698**
FABLES **701**
FAIRY TALES **705**
Introduction **705**
Reasons Why Fairy Tales Are Extremely Attractive
  to Children [of All Ages] **706**
What Should We Do with Fairy Tales? **710**
Fairy Tales for Today's Children **711**
Modern Fairy Tales **712**
Dorothy and the Lizard of Oz **715**
CONCLUDING COMMENTS **720**

13 Psychoanalytically Oriented
    Child Psychotherapy   722

   **THE SO-CALLED DISCIPLINE
     OF CHILD PSYCHOANALYSIS 722**
   **REASONS WHY ADULT PSYCHOANALYTIC TECHNIQUES
     CANNOT GENERALLY BE APPLIED TO CHILDREN 726**
   "Where There Is Unconscious, There Shall Conscious Be" 726
   The Denial Mechanism 727
   **Transference and the Resolution
     of the Transference Neurosis 728**
   Free Association and the Blank Screen 731
   Analysis of the Childhood Roots of the Symptoms 733
   The Freudian Stages of Psychosexual Development 734
   The Superego and Intrapsychic Conflict 735
   **PSYCHOANALYTICALLY ORIENTED
     CHILD PSYCHOTHERAPY 736**
   The Development and Utilization of Insight 737
   **What Psychoanalytically Oriented Child Therapy Is,
     and What It Is Not 738**
   **Some Common Ways in Which the Therapist
     Uses Psychodynamic Information 739**
   **THE USE OF THE TALKING, FEELING, AND DOING GAME
     IN FACILITATING PSYCHOANALYTIC INQUIRY 740**
   DREAM PSYCHOANALYSIS 744
   The Purpose of Dreams 745
   The Dream as a Vehicle for Wish Fulfillment 748
   The Dream as a Vehicle for Alerting the Individual to Danger 748
   The Dream as a Method of Desensitization to a Trauma 754
   The Nightmare 755   The Panic Dream 758
   The Dream as a Mechanism for Providing Brain Cell Stimulation 759
   Teaching Children How to Psychoanalyze Dreams 760
   Children Who Are Candidates for Dream Analysis 760
   Fundamental Principles of Dream Analysis 762
   Explaining the Theory of Dream Formation and Analysis to a Child 765
   Clinical Examples 769
   The Case of Sean (The Monks, the Spanish Inquisitors, and the Lions) 769
   The Case of Timothy ("A Boy Eats His Belt and His Mother Gets Angry") 773
   CONCLUDING COMMENTS 787

14 Family Therapy   789

   THEORETICAL CONSIDERATIONS 789
   What Is the Normal Family? 790
   The Family Psychiatrist 792
   The Procrustean Bed 793
   "Life Is a Rorschach Test" 793
   Providing Experiences 794
   Hospitalization 795
   **Is Family Therapy Only Marital Counseling
     with the Children Observing? 796**

**COMMON SITUATIONS IN WHICH FAMILY THERAPY
   IS INDICATED   796**
Basic Requirements   796
Communication Problems   797
Antisocial Behavior   798
Separation Anxiety Disorder   799
Marital Conflict   799
Post-Marital Conflict   801
**SITUATIONS IN WHICH FAMILY THERAPY
IS CONTRAINDICATED   801**
**Those "Identified Patients" Who Do Indeed Need
   "Individual Attention"   801**
The Mutual Storytelling Technique and Derivative Games   802
Separation Anxiety Disorder 803   Antisocial Adolescents 803
The Intellectually Normal Child with a Very Bright Sibling(s)   804
Exaggerated Reaction to the Birth of a Sibling 804
The Child with a Sibling Who Suffers
   with a Neurologically Based Learning Disability 805
A Child Dealing with the Impending Death of a Parent 805
Borderline or Psychotic Family Members   806
Fixed and Unchangeable Family Subsystems   806
**EVALUATING AND PREPARING FAMILIES
   FOR FAMILY THERAPY   807**
Assessment in the Evaluative Sessions   807
**Who Shall Be Prepared for Involvement
   in Family Therapy   809**
Separated and Divorced Parents   810
Family Therapy with Stepfamilies   812
Involvement of Other Parties in the Family's Treatment   813
**COMMON PSYCHODYNAMIC PATTERNS
   IN FAMILY PSYCHOPATHOLOGY   814**
Complementary Psychopathology in the Marital Dyad   814
**Use of the Child to Fulfill Pathological
   Parental Expectations   816**
**The Constructive and Cohesive Factors
   in Pathological Interactions   818**
The Family of the Schizophrenic Patient   822
**TECHNICAL CONSIDERATIONS WHEN CONDUCTING
   FAMILY THERAPY   823**
Conducting the Treatment in the Home   823
Team Therapists   824
**The Utilization of Other Parties
   in the Family's Treatment   826**
**Changing the Family's Concept
   of the "Designated Patient"   827**
The Therapeutic Ally   828
"Letting It All Hang Out"   830
Transferential Reactions   831
The Family Therapy–Individual Therapy Combination   832
The Talking, Feeling, and Doing Game in Family Therapy   833
Clinical Example   834
CONCLUDING COMMENTS   838

15 Concluding Comments   841

    THE EFFICACY OF CHILD PSYCHOTHERAPY 842
    TERMINATION 843
    THE FUTURE OF THE FIELD
      OF CHILD PSYCHOTHERAPY 845
    The Ever-Burgeoning Psychopathy in American Society 845
    Payment of Fees 846
    Malpractice Suits 847
    The Craze for Quick Cures 849
    Training in Child Psychiatry 850
    Prepaid Treatment Plans 852
    The Dehumanization of Psychiatric Care 856
    CHILD PSYCHOTHERAPY
      IN NONMEDICAL DISCIPLINES 858
    FINAL COMMENTS 859

References   861

Index   873

Acknowledgments

I deeply appreciate the dedication of my secretaries Linda Gould, Carol Gibbon, and Susan Monti to the typing of this manuscript in its various forms. Once again, I am grateful to Barbara Christenberry for her diligence in editing the manuscript. She provided useful suggestions and, at the same time, exhibited respect for my wishes regarding style and format. I am grateful to Colette Conboy for her valuable input into the production of this book, from edited manuscript to final volume. My greatest debt, however, is to those children and families who have taught me so much over the years about the development and alleviation of psychopathology. What I have learned from their sorrows and grief will, I hope, contribute to the prevention and alleviation of such unfortunate experiences by others.

Introduction

Over the years many have asked that I write a book that presents a comprehensive statement of my work. This volume has been prepared in response to these requests. It is basically a distillation of over 200 publications (books, articles, audiotapes, and videotapes) as well as hundreds of lectures given over the past 25 years. In addition, it includes much material that has not thus far been published. This book should not, however, be considered an overview. It is far more detailed than the word "overview" implies. Rather, I have attempted to provide an in-depth description of my contributions to therapeutic technique, both at the theoretical and the practical levels. As was the case for my previous publications, my aim has been to provide readers with enough details to allow them to implement my techniques themselves. Accordingly, my clinical examples are often presented verbatim, with frequent explanatory interruptions that enable the reader to know exactly why I have handled the situation as described. Many of these clinical vignettes have been taken directly from video- and audiotape transcripts.

The title of this book, *The Psychotherapeutic Techniques of Richard A. Gardner*, is actually a compromise of many possible names that came to mind. The word *of* in the title basically means *used by* and includes both techniques introduced by me and those that I have selected from others. The word *of* does not mean *entirely created by*. If I were to be 100% certain that the reader would not misinterpret my title, I would have called the book: *The Psychotherapeutic Techniques Used by Richard A. Gardner, Both Those Originated by Him and Those He Has Selected From Others.* Although an accurate title, it is obviously not one that is viable. My choice then was to choose between a completely accurate and non-misleading title that was lengthy and cumbersome or a shorter form that was reasonable but might introduce a slight misconception. I chose the latter title with the understanding that I would clarify its meaning in the introduction to the book. The reader should appreciate that I do not claim to have devised all the methods and techniques presented in this book. Rather, it is a collection of the various methods that I utilize. Throughout, I have given credit to the work of others that I have incorporated into my therapeutic program. And I do not even consider my own techniques to be entirely of my own invention. I am a product of my heritage and my work derives from others, some known and some unknown.

On occasion I have been asked what "school of thought" I belong to. I find this an impossible question to answer. I belong to no particular school of thought or therapeutic persuasion. Rather, I consider myself genuinely eclectic. I recognize that just about everyone considers him- or herself eclectic. No one says: "I rigidly subscribe to one theoretical therapeutic system and have no flexibility regarding changing my opinions or bringing in the ideas of others." (I believe that, in spite of their claims to be eclectic, there are therapists who are just that inflexible.) There are, however, some people who are more eclectic than others, and I believe myself to be in the more flexible category. This does not mean that I do not have firm convictions on any subject, nor do I consider myself wishy-washy. Rather, when I have come upon worthy ideas that work well, I stick with them, and these are the approaches that I describe in this book.

I begin the book by detailing the personal experiences in my background and training that served as the foundation for the development of my ideas, with special emphasis on those individuals who had the greatest impact on me. In the next chapter I trace historically the various techniques in child psychotherapy that have influenced my thinking. Next, I describe in detail what I consider to be the central processes by which psychogenic symptoms are formed and the basic ways in which psychotherapy brings about clinical change. Then, I discuss the therapist-patient relationship and the special techniques by which the therapist can contribute to the development of a good relationship with the patient. This is a crucial area because without a solid relationship meaningful therapy is not likely to take place. The chapters on the initial screening interview and the intensive diagnostic evaluation are designed to provide therapists with an evaluative format that can serve optimally as a foundation for effective treatment. Next, I discuss parental involvement in the child's treatment, with particular emphasis on the importance of the therapist's having a good relationship with the child's parents if treatment is to be effective. The next three chapters are devoted to the *mutual storytelling technique.* The first presents the basic technique; the second, dramatic utilization of the stories; and the third, the use of derivative games— games that have been devised to increase the likelihood that resistant children will be able to enjoy the benefits of the method. The next chapter describes the use of *The Talking, Feeling, and Doing Game,* both with resistant and more cooperative children. This is followed by a chapter on bibliotherapy in which I discuss the rationale for and utilization of the therapeutic children's books I have written. Although trained as an adult psychoanalyst, I do not consider myself a child psychoanalyst. In fact, as discussed in this book, I do not see the purpose for such a field. However, I do on occasion what can reasonably be called psychoanalytically oriented child psychotherapy, and so I have devoted a chapter to this type of treatment. The last chapter deals with family therapy, which is differentiated from my individual work with children (which I prefer to call: "individual child psychotherapy with parental observation and intermittent participation"). In my concluding statement I describe what I consider to be the present state of the field of child psychotherapy and the not particularly judicious direction (to put it euphemistically) in which we are headed. Throughout, I present clinical vignettes, many of which are verbatim and provide specific examples of the methods I utilize.

Although we have no "proof" that child psychotherapy "works" (if we are to use formal statistical confirmation), I believe that it is an effective tool not only for the alleviation of childhood psychogenic disorders, but for preventing the development of adult psychopathology. Most therapists attempt to learn about the mistakes that parents made in the lives of their patients during childhood. Most would agree that if their patients had been handled differently in childhood, the adult difficulties might not have arisen or would have appeared in less virulent form. The child psychiatrist has the opportunity to interrupt such psychopathological processes *in statu nascendi*. The child therapist is there when the pathology is beginning to exhibit itself and is therefore in a better position to interrupt the process. When the patient comes to the child therapist, the psychiatric difficulties have generally existed for shorter periods than the presenting problems in the adult patient. It is well known that the more chronic the problem, the less likely it will be amenable to psychotherapeutic intervention (or any other type of intervention, for that matter). The child therapist is in a better position to alter the patient's environment. The parents' child-rearing procedures can be improved upon, schools changed, extra tutoring provided, parental psychopathology reduced, et cetera. Adult patients' situations are generally less flexible, and they are usually involved in a rigid life structure related to career and marriage. Changes in these areas, although certainly possible, are not effected without significant consequences. It is because he or she faces a more flexible situation that the child therapist is in a better position to effect change and thereby prevent the development of psychopathology in adulthood.

Psychotherapy, either in children or in adults, has not convincingly proved itself to be an effective therapeutic measure, but most would agree that the information that we have gained from our patients has served to prevent the development of psychopathology in subsequent generations. Although we may not have made certain patients significantly better, what we have learned from their difficulties has enabled us to reduce the likelihood that the psychopathology will be transmitted down to the next generation. Herein probably lies the greatest benefit to be gained from dynamically oriented psychotherapy. Guidebooks for parents often rely heavily on psychodynamic principles derived from our understanding of patients with a wide variety of psychiatric disturbances. In addition, the knowledge gained from the treatment of such patients has enabled writers of children's books to provide youngsters with entertaining stories that are developmentally sound and therapeutically useful. The psychotherapist generally suffers with the frustration that he or she can treat only a small fraction of all those who need therapy. The number of people who can be helped in our professional lifetime is far smaller than those that our colleagues in other branches of medicine can help. We do well, however, to acknowledge that our medical colleagues generally treat a specific number of patients who have finite lifetimes; the number of people who can be helped by one physician, even though vast, is still specific. In contrast, the benefits derived by our psychotherapy patients may be passed down to their progeny. Because our help may extend down the generations, there is no telling how long-lived our influence may be.

ONE

Theoretical and Developmental Foundations of the Author's Techniques

The Child is father of the Man.

William Wordsworth

Every man's work, whether it be literature or music or pictures or architecture, or anything else, is always a portrait of himself, and the more he tries to conceal himself, the more clearly will his character appear in spite of him.

Samuel Butler

On occasion, I have been asked if I have ever published a description of the evolution of my concepts, especially in regard to the various people who have influenced my thinking. To date, there has been no such publication, although I have occasionally spoken on the subject. Accordingly, I thought that a good place to provide such background information would be in the first chapter of this book. I believe it will enable the reader to place my concepts in better perspective. I suspect that it will come as a surprise to some readers that many of my ideas emerged not so much from the influence of individual mentors or teachers, but from institutional philosophies.

Of course, there must have been human beings who taught these philosophies and created institutions that implemented and promulgated them. Although their names are either unknown to me or have been lost in memory, their influence has been formidable.

ELEMENTARY AND JUNIOR HIGH SCHOOL (1936–1945)

My educational experiences at the elementary and junior high school levels were not particularly unique. I was born (1931) and raised in the Bronx in New York City. My educational background was much more rigorous and disciplined than that which is generally obtained now in the same schools (unfortunately at all levels). My parents provided strong support for my education, but were deprived of significant educational opportunities themselves. This was especially the case for my father, who was born in Eastern Europe in 1898 and emigrated to this country in 1906—at which point his formal education ended. What little education he did have ended at the third-grade level in his Jewish parochial school (Chadah). My mother's older siblings also emigrated from Eastern Europe but she was born in the United States. She graduated from a public high school on the lower east side of Manhattan, in New York City.

HIGH SCHOOL (1945–1948)

It was my good fortune, however, to gain admission to *The Bronx High School of Science,* one of the select public high schools in New York City, where I received what I consider to have been a superb education. I consider myself to have a lifelong debt to Dr. Morris Meister, the founder and first principal of the school. The teachers at Bronx Science were, with rare exception, highly dedicated and proud to have been given the opportunity to teach at the school. And the students were, with rare exception, similarly appreciative of the wonderful opportunity to study there. Students who were held in the highest esteem were those who were most successful academically. The school had some athletic teams, but "jocks" were not particularly held in high regard unless, of course, they were simultaneously able to distinguish themselves academically. The atmosphere was one of deep intellectual curiosity, love of learning, and commitment to the advancement of human knowledge. Accordingly, it provided what I consider to be the optimum educational atmosphere. Rote memorization was discouraged; rather, we were encouraged to actively inquire as to the reasons behind most of what we were taught and read. These influences exist with me to this day and have played an important role in my subsequent investigations and research.

COLLEGE (1948–1952)

Following graduation from high school, I also had the good fortune to gain admission to Columbia College in New York City. In a way, it was like another four years of high school. Instead of taking the train northward to Bronx Science, I took trains southward to Columbia College. There, too, I found the same wonderfully stimulating academic environment. Columbia College prided itself on being "a small college in a large university," and this is exactly what it was. The vast majority of classes were quite small (with 10 to 15 students), yet many were taught by senior faculty people. The school prided itself upon the fact that prestigious professors did not confine themselves to their research and graduate students, but were selected because of their commitment to teaching undergraduates as well. Accordingly, I often had the opportunity to have individual guidance and supervision from people who were giants in their fields. At the same time, we had access to the wealth of knowledge that was available from a wide variety of graduate faculties.

One of the most important things I learned at Columbia College was this: Listen with receptivity, but not with gullibility, to those who you have good reason to believe are worthy of being attended to. If you find reasonable what they say, then incorporate their ideas into your repertoire of information about the world. If you don't agree, then it isn't enough just to say you don't agree. Rather, you do well to think about *why* you don't agree and make every reasonable attempt to come up with a better explanation or solution. Although it was recognized that one might not be able to provide better solutions ("So vast is art, so narrow human wit" [Alexander Pope]), at least one should recognize that there may be better explanations and that those who make advances in human knowledge are generally those who have dedicated themselves to finding them. At Columbia College a student might get a passing grade for reading the assigned material and regurgitating it back on an examination. However, for merely doing that the grade was likely to be low. The difference between a low grade and a high grade was generally what the student himself (there were no "herselves" at Columbia College in those days) could bring to the material, either in support or refutation.

And this principle has been a guiding dictum for me throughout my professional career. Whenever I find myself criticizing the work of others (something that the field of psychiatry easily lends itself to), I almost reflexly ask myself, "What would be a better way?" This book, in a sense, is a collection of some of the alternatives that I have come up with over the years—alternatives that have emerged from my disagreements with things that I was taught. As the years have passed, I have become increasingly appreciative of this aspect of my Columbia College education. I believe that it is no exaggeration to state that the overwhelming majority of students, at all levels of education, in the United States and abroad, are basically regurgitators. And it makes me uncomfortable to see people doing the same with my work.

On a number of occasions people have said to me, "It's really good to hear you speak. It gives me support for what I've been doing." And some will go even further and say, "I must be doing it right if that's the way you do it." I do not view this to be the optimum attitude of the student. I believe students in the mental health professions (and most other professions, as well) do better to view themselves (and their professors) like the blind men and the elephant. We are all groping to make sense out of things that are vastly complex and often incomprehensible. The best we can hope for is to arrive at something that *tentatively* appears reasonable, but to recognize that it subsequently may not appear to be so. Accordingly, readers of this book would do well to follow the aforementioned dictum, namely, to read this book with receptivity (and reading this book suggests such receptivity), but not with gullibility, and to incorporate into their own amalgam and potpourri that which appears reasonable. They would also do well to reject that which appears unreasonable and try, if possible, to come up with better solutions.

MEDICAL SCHOOL (1952-1956)

I attended medical school at the State University of New York, Downstate Medical Center in Brooklyn. With rare exception, we were a group of extremely hardworking, upwardly mobile young-sters from lower and middle class homes. Most of our parents had not gone beyond high school, and many not beyond elementary school. I recall during my first week at medical school, while three classmates of mine and I were involved in the traditional dissection of a human cadaver, a professor coming over to our table and say-ing to us, "You fellows are still in the 'gee-whiz' phase of medi-cine." To which I replied, "I hope I never leave the 'gee-whiz' phase of medicine." I would like to believe that I still haven't left the gee-whiz phase of medicine. Healthy human children, even at the in-fancy level, gain great joy from the gratification of their intellectual curiosity. Unfortunately, stultifying home and school environments often squelch these propensities at the earliest levels of develop-ment. Those individuals who are fortunate enough to have escaped such suppressive exposures have much richer lives. In addition, the residua into adulthood of the childhood gee-whiz attitude toward learning contribute significantly to advances in human knowledge. It is the driving force behind the desire to learn more about the world and contribute to its betterment. I feel fortunate that I still have this feeling.

The psychiatry program at Downstate was primarily under the influence of an affiliated classical psychoanalytic institute. With-out realizing what was going on, we were led to believe that this approach to the understanding of human psychological processes was superior to any other that had thus far been proposed and that as a method of treatment for psychiatric disorders it was clearly the best and the most likely to produce lasting change. We didn't realize at the time that other ideas were not being given "equal time." I was enthralled and fascinated by psychoanalytic theory. Although bothered, on occasion, by the grandiosity and aloofness of many of the psychoanalysts, I was not at the time able to put into proper perspective my subsequent appreciation that these at-titudes were basically defensive. Their self-assuredness and pom-posity served to protect them from the realization that they were basically sitting on top of a house of cards. But these realizations came later. I was so enthralled by what they taught me that I decided then to become a psychiatrist and go on to become a psychoanalyst. Psychoanalysis not only promised to provide the best insights into most forms of psychogenic psychopathology (if not all forms) but also appeared to provide explanations for a wide variety of other phenomena in life such as literature, art, music, poetry, philosophy, and whatever else one wanted to apply it to. Accordingly, it gave me the feeling that here was a medical specialty which would allow me to gratify my interests in a wide variety of areas while, at the same time, not neglect my medical commitment. In the other specialties in medicine, one had to neglect these other areas if one was to keep up in one's field. And this was an important consideration in my decision to become a psychiatrist. The reader should remember that I am speaking here about the 1950s, when psychoanalysis was still in its heyday in American medicine. Just about every departmental chairman was analytically trained and the failure to have such background generally precluded one's appointment to such a position (as well as other important positions on the academic faculty).

At about the time that I made my decision to become a psychiatrist I also sought personal therapy through the school's student health service—which served as a rich source of patients for candidates in training at the Downstate Psychoanalytic Institute. It wasn't too long before I was on the couch, talking at the ceiling. The analyst said practically nothing, but vigorously took notes. He was a good student at the Institute and dutifully took care to say very little (so as not to contaminate the "blank screen") and take copious notes (to provide him with detailed data for his supervisory sessions). As I look back on that two-year experience in classical psychoanalysis, I realize that from the psychotherapeutic point of view it was a total waste of time. Even worse, it might have been detrimental. His cockiness made me feel small (I didn't realize then that it was defensive). He didn't relate to me as a human being, but as a source of data for him which was presumably going to bring about (ultimately) important insights for me that would be to my therapeutic benefit. But "ultimately" never came. I personally experienced no benefit, but he must have progressed along in his studies with the information I was providing him.

However, some good did come from it. I learned firsthand what it means to be on a couch and how cold, impersonal, and even inhumane is the classical psychoanalytic approach. A part of me felt this then, but I was so enraptured by analysis that I did not allow myself to verbalize these objections. I appreciated subsequently that the procedure robbed both individuals of forming a genuine human relationship, the only kind that can serve as the foundation for meaningful treatment. I realized later that this fantasized relationship, in which the analyst is often idealized (seen as perfect) and even idolized (worshipped as a God), is antitherapeutic. The absence of this human relationship is a heavy price to pay for the greater purity of the free associations provided on the couch. Much more is lost than gained—it is a sorry and simple-minded trade-off.

I realized later that the people who were most likely to gravitate toward being therapists of this persuasion were those who themselves had serious deficiencies in forming healthy human relationships and were most comfortable in one in which they were given sanction to be withdrawn, isolated, intellectualized, and unemotional. I also learned later that Freud's decision to use the couch in psychoanalysis derived from his earlier experiences with hypnotherapy. Here, it appeared that the patient's lying in the supine position, without being in direct view of the analyst, did facilitate induction into the hypnotic trance. Analysis was, in part, the result of Freud's appreciation that hypnotherapy had significant limitations as a therapeutic modality. But after Freud went beyond hypnotherapy, he still retained the practice of keeping patients in the supine position, out of view of the analyst. And Freud has given us the reason why he retained the couch: the prospect of seeing patients face-to-face made him uncomfortable, especially sitting with a series of patients in this manner throughout the course of the day. What arose as a psychopathological maneuver by Sigmund Freud became standard practice for his followers and disciples.

INTERNSHIP (1956–1957)

I interned at Montefiore Hospital in the Bronx, in New York City. I was finally a doctor. It was grueling work. Generally, I worked over 100 hours a week, for which I was paid $12 (plus "free" room and board). I can't say I learned very much *directly* about psychiatry during that program (with the exception of a four-week elective at the affiliated New York State Psychiatric Institute at the Columbia-Presbyterian Medical Center). I did learn much about human suffering and the ravages to the human psyche that disease causes. I was also becoming a better human being from the important and humane services I was providing. So indirectly I was building a foundation to be a good psychiatrist. My one month at the New York State Psychiatric Institute (PI) confirmed my decision that I wanted to be a psychiatrist and that the place where I wanted to train was PI.

RESIDENCY TRAINING [PART I, GENERAL PSYCHIATRY, 1957–1959]

I had the good fortune to take my residency at the New York Psychiatric Institute at the Columbia-Presbyterian Medical Center. Fortunately, the chairman of the department at that time was Dr. Lawrence C. Kolb. He provided a program that was genuinely eclectic. In retrospect I have come to appreciate that most individuals consider themselves to be "eclectic." I have also come to appreciate that *nobody* wants to consider him- or herself "rigid" or "narrow" in his or her thinking—but obviously some people are more eclectic than others. Lawrence Kolb provided a truly eclectic program. There was room in his house of worship for all psychoanalytic religions. As a result, I had the opportunity to learn firsthand about other psychoanalytic schools and came to appreciate that there were ways of looking at the world other than through Freud's eyes, and that other psychoanalytic schools (which I had not even heard of in my medical school days) might have something worthwhile to say. Biological psychiatry was also taught in those days; however, I believe it was put in proper perspective. At this point the biological approach is very much in vogue, with psychoanalytically oriented therapy somewhat in disrepute. While Downstate gave too much credence to analysis, most programs today give too little. Lawrence Kolb provided us with a reasonable balance, a balance that I like to believe I still have to this day.

It would be an error for the reader to conclude that I have rejected totally all of classical Freudian teachings. This would be a grievous misinterpretation of my position. I still view Freud to be a pioneer whose contributions are formidable. What I object to is reflex acceptance of most if not all of his work. Specifically, I believe his elucidation of the defense mechanisms to be a monumental contribution, especially in regard to the way in which unconscious processes bring them about. It is in the area of certain psychodynamic explanations (for example, the Oedipus complex, castration anxiety, the psychosexual developmental levels, and the libido theory) that I have strong doubts and criticisms. In addition, the classical psychoanalytic model of therapy is also one that I believe does more harm than good in most cases.

I realized during my residency days that the sickest patients were being treated by the most inexperienced people and that, conversely, the healthiest were being treated by the most experienced. We residents were treating in-patients, most of whom were psychotic. And such treatment would often begin on the first day of residency. In contrast, the senior training psychoanalysts, in their outside offices, were sought after by those who could afford to pay their high fees. Although wealth and mental health cannot necessarily be equated, it is reasonable to say that there is at least *some* relationship. Unfortunately, this situation exists to this day. Now I too, from my private office, treat the healthiest patients, and the residents are still treating the sickest. I assuage my guilt about this situation in two ways. First, for many years, I have supervised residents in the treatment of indigent patients, often seeing them directly as part of the treatment program. In addition, I believe that my writings and lectures enable therapists to treat patients more effectively. In this way, I also help the indigent.

During my general residency training I attended a number of conferences conducted by Dr. Nathan Ackerman, one of the early workers in the field of family therapy. I was impressed with his emphasis on intrafamilial psychodynamics as an important way of understanding patients' problems. I was particularly impressed with the Grand Rounds format that Nathan Ackerman utilized. The traditional routine was that during a one-and-a-half hour conference, the first half-hour was devoted to a presentation of the case by the resident. During the second half-hour the visiting dignitary would interview the patient. And during the third half-hour, the patient would leave and the visitor would present his or her observations and conclusions to the staff, during which time questions would be discussed. Afterwards, the resident would discuss the conference with the patient during the next session. Ackerman departed from this format by requesting that the patient be allowed to be present throughout all three segments of the conference. Although I do not recall his exact reasons for conducting the conference in this way, I considered it to be a valuable innovation which, unfortunately, is rarely utilized, even today.

There are many arguments in favor of this approach. The resident's discussing the patient with the group, while the patient is sitting outside, cannot but compromise the therapist-patient relationship in that it implies that the doctor has secrets about the patient, which he or she can tell to others but not to the patient him- or herself. It also contributes to the idealization of the therapist in that it implies that he or she has some kind of superior knowledge that the patient is "not yet ready for." The same situation prevails in the post-interview conference when the patient is again sitting outside while the whole staff is discussing him or her. This approach, however, should not be used for fragile patients, especially those who are borderline or psychotic. (Occasionally there are even patients in this category who might be still better off with the Ackerman approach than the traditional one.) Unfortunately, the traditional approach still prevails, but I make every attempt to utilize Ackerman's method when I have the opportunity.

During my residency I had the opportunity to do group therapy, which also impressed me with the importance of interpersonal psychodynamics in understanding psychopathology. My supervisor was Dr. Jack Sheps. He was not generally viewed as one of the more distinguished members of the faculty because, although psychoanalytically trained, he was not one who could spout forth at length complex and intricate psychodynamic speculations about the meaning of a particular symptom, comment, gesture, or behavioral manifestation. However, he was a warm, genuine, and devoted psychiatrist who, I realize now, probably did more good for his patients than those who looked down upon him (a common attitude in psychoanalytic circles). I was particularly impressed with the therapeutic combination of individual and group therapy, wherein one could enjoy the benefits to be derived from both types of treatment. And this is a combination that I try to provide when indicated and when possible. I have found it immensely useful for adolescents who need individual treatment (in order to help them separate from their families), but who also need group therapy (because they are so dependent on group opinion and feel so comfortable in a group situation).

A supervisor who had a profound effect on me was Dr. Hilda Bruch. Although trained in Germany, under a rigid educational program, she, unlike most of the European trained psychoanalysts, was more flexible in regard to her psychiatric techniques. Her main area of interest was the treatment of patients with anorexia/bulimia in the days before this disease entity was in vogue. One of the most important things I learned from her was that the therapist does well to be in the position of the "ignorant interrogator." The word ignorant here was not used in the sense of being stupid, but rather in the sense of not knowing and being curious to learn. I also learned from her that mere intellectual understanding of one's psychodynamics is not enough.

There was an anorexic adolescent boy in the hospital at that time. His was an unusual "case" because of the rarity of anorexia in males. (Although anorexia among female adolescents is now an "in" condition to have, it is still relatively rare in males.) This patient had been in the hospital about five years and had been seen by a series of residents (one every six-to-twelve months), all under Dr. Bruch's supervision. The patient was a walking textbook on the psychodynamics of anorexia, especially in the male. At conferences he would expound to the faculty his knowledge about the factors that underlay his condition. Even senior faculty people often took notes, so informed was he on this subject. I consider it reasonable to say that this young boy could have made lecture tours to professional audiences and might have even been paid for his contributions. However, he had lost all his hair and eyebrows, was gaunt, lean, and his bones were prominent. His eyes were sunken and his skin, pale and dark. He looked like a concentration camp victim. At times he was on the brink of death. He reached a point where intravenous feeding was no longer useful (one cannot indefinitely keep a person alive on intravenous feeding). As a last resort his food was ground in a blender and he was forced fed through a wide naso-gastric tube.

I learned two things from this boy. First, I learned much about the psychodynamics of anorexia nervosa, especially in the male. Second, but certainly not less important, I learned that there is more to treatment than bringing into conscious awareness that which is unconscious and that insight per se is not likely to bring about therapeutic change. I realized later that Dr. Bruch did not appreciate that basic human compassion is far more important than psychodynamics in bringing about therapeutic change. I am not saying that she lacked compassion entirely, only that her emphasis on understanding underlying psychodynamics and elucidating them for the patient was given so much emphasis that the basic human factors were ignored, both at the experiential and intellectual levels.

Another thing I learned in my general residency was the psy-

chologically detrimental effects of the frequent turnover of therapists. The model of psychiatric training was based on the medical
model in other training programs in which therapists rotated from
one service to the next. This is probably an excellent arrangement
for medical training, but it is detrimental for psychiatric patients.
It loses sight, again, of the fundamental building block of therapy,
namely, the therapist-patient relationship. The therapy of most patients under these circumstances was essentially divided into two
phases: the initial introductory phase and termination. There was
no middle phase because it wasn't long after the relationship began
to be established that both the therapist and the patient began planning for the termination and the changeover to a new therapist.
Out of some recognition of the drawbacks of this arrangement, we
did have some "long-term" patients, but the majority were seen in
accordance with the rapid turnover program. In this way, we had
the opportunity to have experience with a larger variety of patients,
but there was little appreciation given to the detrimental effects of
the turnover on the patients. One common rationalization for the
arrangement was that sick patients would be threatened by ongoing
relationships and are basically much more comfortable with the
turnover. I view this as a crass rationalization. The people who were
teaching it were actually involving themselves in long-term treatment (especially psychoanalysis) in their private practices. In fact,
some of these analyses would go on for as long as a quarter of a
century and even more! Unfortunately, the situation still prevails
in most residency programs and even more so under the influence
of the biological psychiatrists, most of whom have little if any appreciation of the importance of the relationship in their treatment.

RESIDENCY TRAINING [PART II, CHILD PSYCHIATRY, 1959–1960]

My original plans were to do a three-year residency in general psychiatry, which would include limited child psychiatric experiences
during the second year. My original plans also were to devote my
third year to research. However, with about one month left in my
second year of residency, Dr. William Langford, the chairman of
the department of child psychiatry at Columbia, informed me that
The American Board of Psychiatry and Neurology had just set up
training requirements for certification in the subspecialty of child

psychiatry. He was pleased to inform me that the Columbia program had been approved and that such training could begin in one month. He also invited me to serve as the program's first chief resident. I had no particular intentions of going into child psychiatry at that point. However, my limited experiences in the field had been positive in that one of the patients I had been treating had done quite well. I attributed this to the fact that he was young and therefore more malleable than my adult patients, whose problems had become entrenched over many years. In addition, the relative ease with which I was able to change this child's environment (via counseling with his parents) played an important role in the changes that were brought about. Adult patients, in contrast, generally presented with their pathology deeply entrenched, and they were more often fixed in some rigid situation, such as job and marriage.

However, I had certain reservations about the field in regard to the difficulty one had engaging children in treatment, especially psychoanalytic therapy (which I still believed was the supreme form of psychotherapeutic intervention). Because of this ambivalence I did not immediately accept Dr. Langford's invitation. After a few days, however, I decided to commit myself to one year of the two-year training program because of my uncertainty as to whether I wanted to go into the field. One of the factors that contributed to my positive (albeit tentative) decision was my appreciation of the fact that psychiatrists (and especially psychoanalysts) were routinely delving into the childhood roots of their adult patients' psychopathology without any particular training in child development and therapy. This was often being done by people who not only had never had any clinical experience treating children but who never even had children of their own. Yet they felt free to speculate about various psychological processes that were allegedly going on in children's minds. My hope was that training in child psychiatry would provide me with firsthand information and experiences in this area that could not but prove useful in my work with adults (which is what I was primarily interested in anyway, at that time).

In that first year of residency I suddenly found myself assuming formidable obligations. I was *the* resident child psychiatrist. I did the emergency room consultations and consultations on the ward at the Babies Hospital. I treated in-patients and out-patients. I taught residents, medical students, student nurses, social workers, and occupational therapists. I participated in teaching conferences, presented and discussed cases. And, of course, as chief resident, there were administrative duties as well. I believe that the intensive experience I had at that time served as a good foundation for my subsequent work in the field of child psychiatry. Although I did have some supervision (but not from anyone who sticks in my memory as having been a formidable influence), it was primarily "on the job" training.

The treatment structure then was that the resident, as the physician, was the primary therapist, and work with the parents was done by the social worker. The two then would communicate with one another regarding what went on in each other's sessions. Even then, I considered this to be an inefficient system which was somewhat divisive for the family. My recognition of the drawbacks of this arrangement ultimately resulted in my working directly with all family members, in all combinations as warranted. (This aspect of my work will be elaborated upon in Chapter Seven in which I discuss the details of my involvement of the parents in the child's treatment.) Unfortunately, many residency programs today still use the psychiatrist and the social worker combination treatment method.

In my work with children my supervisors routinely presented the psychoanalytic approach as the optimum one. When I complained that the patients I was seeing were not particularly good candidates for such insight therapy, I was told that this was because they were primarily inner-city indigent children (in New York City, primarily black and hispanic) who did not have much capability for insightful thinking. However, I was reassured that once I got into private practice I would have many analytic-type patients. This promise never came to be realized. I subsequently learned, when reading Piaget, that children are not cognitively capable of involving themselves in psychoanalytic introspection until about 11 years of age, the age at which they reach Piaget's level of *formal operations*. It is only then that the child can cognitively separate a symbol from the object it denotes and switch back and forth intellectually between the two. (Although children can *form* unconsciously symbols of objects, they cannot consciously involve themselves in the intellectual process of appreciating to a significant degree the relationship between the two until about the age of 11.) This resulted in my appreciation of the fact that my failure to see analytic-type children had nothing to do with their coming from the inner-city, but was more related to the fact that they were not cognitively capable of involving themselves to a significant degree in this kind of mental operation.

I did find, however, an occasional child (younger than 10 or 11) who was indeed interested in psychoanalytic inquiry. Such a child was generally quite bright and therefore, although younger in age, was intellectually functioning at the 10-to-11 year level. In addition, the child often came from a home environment in which people were continually speculating about the underlying meanings of what they were thinking, feeling, and doing. This was especially the case if the parents were in psychoanalysis themselves over many years and deeply committed to the process. But these represented only a small fraction of all my patients (perhaps one percent). The rest were not particularly interested in such inquiry on an ongoing basis. They showed some occasional spark of interest and capability for such inquiry, but not to the point where I could call their treatment analytic. Accordingly, there is no chapter in this book on child psychoanalysis. I do, however, have a chapter on psychoanalytically oriented psychotherapy, wherein some level of conscious understanding is attempted.

An alternative therapeutic model that was very much in vogue in child therapy at that time was the application of Carl Rogers' work to children. Probably the most well-known therapist to do this was V. Axline (1947, 1964). The theory here was that there resides within all of us basic knowledge about what is best for us, but that social inhibitions suppress and repress the expression of these healthy forces. The primary goal of treatment is to help people bring about a state of "self-actualization" via which the blocked impulses are given free expression. The optimum atmosphere in which to realize this goal is one in which the therapist is basically nondirective and provides the patient with "unconditional positive regard." Technically, this is best accomplished by the therapist serving a catalytic role in which the last fragments of the patient's statement are repeated back to him or her. If one looks at psychology textbooks of the 1950s and 1960s and turns to the chapter on psychotherapy, Rogerian treatment is often presented as psychotherapy per se—often with few alternative psychotherapeutic methods described. At that time, psychoanalysis was viewed as the supreme form of treatment by psychiatrists and Rogerian therapy as the optimum form of treatment by psychologists. One element in this development probably related to the fact that the classical psychoanalytic institutes were not permitting psychologists admission—a situation that still exists, with rare exception, to this day. However, this too is changing as fewer physicians are demonstrating interest in psychoanalytic training. This new receptivity to psychologists has not been brought about by true insight into the contributions psychology can provide; rather, it stems from the desire for self-preservation. Without such input most analytic institutes would be defunct from lack of new recruits and acolytes.

Although Rogerian therapists claimed that the treatment was quite complex and not simply one in which the therapist, in parrot-like fashion, repeated the last fragments of the patient's statement, in practice this is what generally went on. I recall an anecdote that was making the rounds at that time about the man who went to a Rogerian analyst. The following interchange took place:

> *Patient:* Boy, I'm feeling depressed today.
> *Therapist:* So, you're feeling depressed today.
> *Patient:* I'm feeling so depressed, I feel like killing myself.
> *Therapist:* So you're feeling so depressed, you feel like killing yourself.
> *Patient:* I'm feeling so depressed, I could jump right out of that window, even though we're on the 23rd floor.
> *Therapist:* You're feeling so depressed, you could jump right out of that window, even though we're on the 23rd floor.
> *Patient:* Yes, that's how I feel. (At this point, the patient gets up, walks to the window, opens it up, and stands on the window sill.)
> *Therapist* (Now looking at the patient, who is standing on the ledge of the open window): So that's how you feel.
> *Patient:* (Now leaps off the ledge and a few seconds later the sound of his body is heard as it splatters on the sidewalk.)
> *Therapist* (Now walks to the window and peers out, looking down at the sidewalk): Splat!

The reader may say that the above anecdote is a mockery of Rogerian treatment and that it is a *reductio ad absurdum*, that only the most simple-minded therapists would respond in this manner. I am in agreement that most Rogerian therapists would not go so far as to let the patient jump out the window. However, I do believe that the overwhelming majority of Rogerian therapists were not doing much more than "splat therapy."

Not only was I in disagreement with the technical maneuver

of catalyzing the patient's comments by repeating the last fragment, but I had other disagreements with the Rogerian approach as well. First, I did not have the conviction for the notion of the existence of a pool of information and feelings which is basically healthy, the suppression of which brings about psychopathology. In fact, when people who had completed such treatment were "self-actualized" they appeared to be quite similar to others who had self-actualized themselves at the same time. In the 1960s this often took the form of going to Vermont, joining a commune, and engaging oneself in eating natural foods and weaving baskets.

Furthermore, I was not in agreement with the notion that a therapist should provide a patient with "unconditional positive regard." I considered this to be a disservice in that it ill equips the patient to function in a world where this is rarely if ever provided. In fact, one's mother does not even give one unconditional positive regard. Providing this must involve some fabrication and/or suppression of the therapist's thoughts and feelings, and I believe that the therapist, rather than being nondirective and providing unconditional positive regard, should be more directive and should provide "negative regard," when such is warranted. One must differentiate between criticism given benevolently and criticism given malevolently. Patients need benevolent criticism and direction to help them in life. If they cannot get it from their therapists, then who else is going to provide it in as objective and hopefully benevolent way.

There was a third approach that was taught to me, which was not given any specific name, nor was there any particular reference to those who might have utilized the techniques. I am referring to a form of play therapy in which the therapist responds to the child at the symbolic level, utilizing the same characters used by the child. For example, if the child tells a story about a cat's biting a dog and shows little interest in finding out, or ability to ascertain, who the dog and cat symbolize, then one merely responds with questions such as, "Why did the cat bite the dog?" and "Was there a better way the cat could have handled that problem with the dog, other than to bite the dog?" I subsequently learned that these techniques were first described in the literature in the 1930s in articles by J.C. Solomon (1938, 1940, 1951, 1955) and J.H. Conn (1939, 1941a, 1941b, 1948, 1954).

During my residency training I went into analysis for the second time. This time I chose someone who was more appeciative of the social and cultural factors in the development of psychopa-thology, yet I was still on the couch. He talked much more than my first analyst, but to the back of my head. I learned a few things from him about doing therapy because I would often bring up problems that related to the patients I was seeing in the hospital. He made, however, what I considered to have been a serious technical error in my treatment. I was involved in a conflict with a member of my extended family and requested a joint interview in the hope that the problem might be resolved. He insisted upon seeing that person alone and absolutely refused the joint interview. This compromised significantly the rest of the treatment in that he would frequently come up with what I considered to be misinformation derived from the other source. This was one of the places where I learned about the value of joint interviews and so I believe that I gained some-thing from the experience. Although I believe he taught me some things about how to do therapy, he certainly was of no help in solv-ing the family problem (in fact, I believe he made it worse). Whether the advantages outweighed the disadvantages, I cannot say.

MILITARY SERVICE (1960–1962)

By all usual criteria, the war in which I should have been involved was the Korean War. It broke out when I was 19 and ended when I was 22. Fortunately for me, premedical students were given pref-erential deferments, as were those who scored highest on a nation-wide competitive examination. (If there was one thing that students at The Bronx High School of Science loved, it was nationwide com-petitive examinations.) I did not question the wisdom of these crite-ria for deferment at the time; they were not utilized subsequently during the Vietnam War (during which time I had already served in the military). Accordingly, I was fortunate enough to have been able to fulfill my military commitment by subscribing to the old advice: "serve between wars."

Because I entered with one year of formal training in child psychiatry and because, at that time, that was the most possible formal training anyone could have had, I was in a unique position regarding my assignment. Having never been to Europe before, I requested service there and was assigned to the U.S. Army Hospital in Frankfurt am Main, Germany. My chief was unreceptive to the idea of an army psychiatrist doing child psychiatry. His basic position was: "At no time in the history of mankind has an army seen fit to have an officer spend time trying to find out why the sergeant's kid pisses in bed." He recognized, however, in compliance with the old army tradition that "orders is orders," he was required to let me do some child psychiatry. He decided, however, to confine me to the last two hours of each day, so that my most efficient time would be utilized working with adult soldiers. It wasn't too long before word spread through the military medical network in Germany that there was a child psychiatrist in Frankfurt. Because the treatment was free, I quickly built up a practice. My chief, however, insisted that all work be confined to my prescribed two hours a day and that everybody be seen at least once. Although this was quite early in my military career, I recognized that there would be only two solutions to this problem. The first was to voluntarily extend my military service. The other was to confine every person to one hour of "treatment." Not coming from a family with a strong military tradition (a number of relatives of mine at the grandparental level deserted from the Russian army), I chose the latter course. Accordingly, I gave the appointment sargeant instructions to inform all subsequent referrals that I would be giving them one hour and one hour only. I suggested that he inform the caller that I want to see *simultaneously* the child, both parents, and any other individuals whom the family thought could provide me with useful information.

For approximately two years this was the program I followed. Most often both parents and the child came for the consultation. On occasion, another party was present such as a maid or grandparent. The first three-quarters of an hour were spent obtaining as much data as I could and the last 15 minutes was spent making a therapeutic recommendation and discussing these with the family. Early in the course of this program, I made a vow that I would never again (that is, after discharge from the service) allow anyone to dictate to me how much time I could spend with a patient or family. No one dictated to surgeons how much time they should spend in the OR nor was anyone else in the service being ordered to confine their treatment to a specific time slot. And I have kept this vow. Schools have long since given up on me because they know I will not do a consultation in which I am confined to a certain number of sessions or a fixed amount of money. The vast majority of school reports I have seen that were done under these circumstances have been defective. It is clear that the psychiatric consultant has spent about 10 or 15 minutes reviewing the child's chart, 10 or 15 minutes interviewing the child, and 15 or 20 minutes dictating a report. What the schools are getting is worth what they are paying. Over the years I have also seen reports based on one-hour consultations given by prominent people in our field. These "hot shot," "shoot from the hip" consultations are also a disservice to our profession. They stem from a medical tradition of some senior guru making snap diagnoses on the basis of limited data. This often impresses medical students, but it does not impress me. It may get more people to watch the TV series "MASH," but it serves as a poor model for good medical treatment. I generally have the reputation of doing evaluations that are more expensive than my other colleagues in private practice. Accordingly, I am certain that I have lost many referrals. However, I also believe that I have a reputation of doing very fine work. I cannot imagine myself doing things differently. I am indebted to the U.S. Army for having taught me this valuable lesson.

Over time my referrals in the service came from ever greater distances. Some came from Italy and England, and a few radio wave consultations were conducted from Turkey. As was true in my residency, I was thrust into a position of being the expert, with limited earlier experience. By the time I was discharged I had had three years of high pressured learning on the job experiences as a child psychiatrist.

RESIDENCY TRAINING (PART III, CHILD PSYCHIATRY, 1962–1963)

After my two years in the military service, I decided to return to Columbia for a fourth year of residency (my second year of child psychiatry training) in order to fulfill the basic training requirements for board certification. On my return, I found that there were now eight people (four at the first-year level and four at the second) who were doing what I had done alone three years previously. (One was assigned to the emergency room, one to do ward consultations, one on the in-patient service, and so on.) It was during this second year of residency that I began to think seriously about what I could do to rectify the criticisms I was making of many of the therapeutic techniques utilized in the field. It was in the context of these deliberations that I came upon the procedure which I ultimately termed *the mutual storytelling technique.* Children obviously like telling stories and they also enjoy listening to stories. Stories of general therapeutic value were being introduced, such as those for children entering the hospital. However, I viewed these like penicillin in the drinking water in that they were only applicable to a small fraction of children, namely those who happened to need that particular kind of story at that moment. I wondered whether creating a story designed to direct its attention to the specific issues in the story the child had just told might be more beneficial therapeutically. I did not believe that I had come upon a new idea. I asked Dr. William Langford, my chief, if he could give me some references of articles written on this method. He told me that he knew of none but suspected, as did I, that there must have been some written because it seemed like such an obvious idea. Neither I nor the librarian were able to find any such references in the literature. Accordingly, I started to collect data and my first publication on the technique appeared about five years later (1968a) and my book three years after that (1971a).

PSYCHOANALYTIC TRAINING (1959–1960, 1962–1966)

During the year prior to my entering the service and the four following my discharge, I received psychoanalytic training at the William A. White Psychoanalytic Institute in New York City. I found the emphasis on interpersonal elements in the development and treatment of psychopathology to be more consistent with my views than the classical psychoanalytic approach. Although classical theory was also taught, there was a heavy emphasis on the contributions of people such as Harry Stack Sullivan, Frieda Fromm-Reichmann, and Erich Fromm. It was then that I entered into analysis for the third (and last) time. This time, however, I told the analyst in the first session that I would, under no circumstances, use the couch and that if he wished to discharge me as a patient for my position on the subject he was free to do so. Of course, I recognized that it would be good technique on his part to explore with me my reasons for this decision and we did so. Accordingly, we sat face-to-face (a very human way of doing things). When I did wish to free associate, I had no trouble looking downward or sideways, and sometimes closing my eyes.

In the course of my analytic therapy, I suggested to my analyst that it might be a good idea to have an interview with my parents. Although his approach was not one in which much time was spent delving into the childhood roots of my difficulties, there was still some time spent in that area. He recognized the value of such an interview but did not generally recommend it for his analytic candidates. My parents, of course, would have liked to have subscribed to the myth that this was a "training analysis" and not a therapeutic one, that is, it was only necessary for me to be in analysis as part of my training program, but it did not in any way suggest that I might have bona fide psychiatric problems. I informed them that I did not believe in the existence of a training analysis and that anybody who could spend three or four days a week, for four or five years, talking about him- or herself had to have some problems or he or she wouldn't be there. Although they still saw absolutely nothing wrong with me, they joined me in the interview. I considered it to have been a turning point in my analysis in that a number of useful things came out of the interview. My analyst saw firsthand the people I was talking about and got a better grasp of the things that occurred in my childhood. A few dreams emerged after the interview, the analysis of which also proved valuable. Although in retrospect I have some criticisms of the man (a good thing, in that in a successful analysis one does not walk away with a view of the person as perfect), I believe that the advantages far outweighed the disadvantages.

Of my three supervisors in analytic training, the one who made the greatest impression on me was a unique woman named Dr. Anna Gourevitch. She may have taught me the most important thing I learned in analytic training, namely, that one of the most important things in life, and in analysis (which is only one slice of life), is good human relationships—relationships in which there are sympathy, empathy, benevolence, sensitivity to the feelings of others, and treating people in ways that are uniquely human. Many times over, when faced with a dilemma regarding how to conduct myself in a situation in analysis (and in life), I have asked myself the question, "What is the *human* thing to do here?"

I recall one incident that demonstrates this point quite well. It occurred while Dr. Gourevitch was supervising me as part of a class supervisory experience. The patient in supervision was a young woman in her early twenties. On the day in which the incident under discussion took place, she was my last patient. At the end of the session she left my office (which was then in an apartment house in New York City). About ten minutes later, I too left the office. On my arrival at the front entrance, she was standing under the awning, waiting for the rain to stop. The rain was coming down so heavily that one would be instantaneously drenched if one were foolish enough to walk in it. My car was parked only a few feet from the awning. My first thought was to offer to give her a lift to the subway station. I immediately stopped myself with thoughts of my ten colleagues criticizing me for removing myself from the analytic position, involving myself in a "social" activity with her, engendering oedipal fantasies in her, being seductive, psychologically raping her, etc. My next thought was "What is the human thing to do here?" And my answer to myself: "Not only is it the human thing to offer her a lift, but it is inhuman to leave her standing in the rain—who knows for how long? If I were just to leave her there, it would be a unique situation in human relationships. It's not the way to treat someone I know and like." Accordingly, I invited the young woman into my car and drove her the five blocks to the subway station.

As was expected, the entire class came down heavily on me with all of the aforementioned accusations (and more). By that time, I had had an additional session with the patient and she made no mention of feelings of having been seduced, raped, or treated in any way that was injudicious or improper. Rather, at the beginning of the session she thanked me once again for having dropped her off and went on to much more important matters. My colleagues only responded that she was suppressing all the fantasies that were engendered by my invitation. My final response was that I considered it the human thing to do and that their arguments did not convince me otherwise. As expected, Gourevitch supported my position. I cannot even say that my taking this woman to the subway station played an important role in entrenching our relationship. I am not mentioning it here for that reason. Rather, I mention it because of Gourevitch's influence on me—an influence that remains to this day. Anna Gourevitch is now dead, but what she has taught me will remain with me in good stead throughout my professional career and I believe throughout my life.

It was during my analytic training that I decided to add group therapy to the individual analysis of one of my controlled patients (a patient treated by a candidate under the supervision of the training analyst). Although others were using the term "adjunctive therapy," I did not view group therapy to be an adjunct to the individual work, but an additional therapeutic modality that could be as valuable as individual therapy. (With some patients it was more valuable, with other patients it was less.) I did this unself-consciously without any consideration of "getting permission from the authorities." After the woman was in group therapy about two months, I happened to mention to one of the Institute's secretaries (to whom I was handing my progress report) how useful I was finding group therapy for her along with the individual work. Little did I realize what a bomb I was dropping that day.

About a week later, in my class with the Director of the Institute, he opened up the meeting with the grave announcement that *someone* in the Institute (he knows that person would not want his or her name mentioned publicly) was doing group therapy with an analytic control patient. He reminded us that this was a *Psychoanalytic Institute* and that, although he had no particular criticisms of group therapy, it could not but be a contamination of the psychoanalysis. The person in question, then, should cease engaging in this sinful combination immediately or risk the displeasure of the Institute. Accordingly, I passively and sheepishly (of all the types of human beings, there is nothing closer to the sheep than the psychoanalytic candidate) submitted and regretfully told the patient that the powers at the Institute had decided that group therapy would contaminate her treatment and that she would have to leave the group. Although all the members of the group considered this absurd, and although I agreed with them that it was so, she left the group. In retrospect, the patient might have done well to have left me as well because I was basically serving as a poor model for self-assertion. I was submitting to a policy for which I had absolutely no conviction. I suspect, however, that in spite of this defect of mine, she was still deriving benefit from the treatment (at least I would like to think that). Three years later, when she had reached the number of sessions that she was promised by the Institute, she became a fully private patient of mine, no longer under the Institute's "blessings." And so I put her back in the group. Her treatment then began to proceed much more rapidly. This experience in analytic training taught me about the value of group therapy, a lesson that remains with me to this day.

On the one hand, I still feel indebted to people at the White Institute for the genuinely eclectic psychoanalytic training program that they provided me. In addition, their emphasis in the human and interpersonal aspects of therapy influenced me formidably. On the other hand, the structure of the analytic training program (at the White Institute and elsewhere) still leaves a bitter taste in my mouth. If there ever was an educational training program whose structure is designed to defeat the educational purpose, it is the psychoanalytic training program. Mention has already been made of the sheepishness of the candidates. This is especially the case where they view the graduation certificate to be one of the most coveted awards any human being can possibly aspire to. To the degree that they hold this belief, to *that* degree will they be at the mercy of the faculty. A central problem in the training program is the feeling of impotency the student often has when confronted with a deficiency. In every other scientific discipline, the instructor can generally detail exactly what the student's deficiencies are and prescribe a particular program which, if followed, provides promise of rectifying them. A third-grade teacher tells Johnny that his multiplication skills are weak. He does well up to the four-times table, but the rest of the class is up to the six-times table. She points to the multiplication table in Johnny's mathematics book and directs him to memorize specifically the deficient levels. The high-school chemistry teacher tells Mary that she is weak on the theory of basic chemical equations and that she should review carefully the chapters in her textbook devoted to that topic. The college biology teacher advises Harry to read again the chapter on DNA.

In contrast, the psychoanalytic supervisor tells Mary that she's "exhibiting hostile countertransferential reactions" and that she should discuss these with her analyst. Bob's analytic supervisor tells him that "It appears that female patients make you anxious and until you work through this problem, you're not going to be successful working with women." These confrontations have quite complex and confusing implications. There are two possibilities here: the criticism is valid or it is not. If the supervisor is right, how does one rectify this deficiency? The method of psychoanalytic treatment is at best nebulous and the course to the alleviation of these problems unpredictable. This places the candidate in a precarious position, with grave feelings of impotence. Or, the supervisor may be providing an erroneous criticism. The subjectivity of the assessment criteria results in many misguided recommendations. The criticism may be more related to the supervisor's own projections onto the candidate than what is actually going on between the candidate and the patient. Supervisors are known to see the same problems in many of their candidates, just as candidates are known to see similar problems in their patients.

In all previous training the course for rectification of educational deficiencies was clear cut: here it is just the opposite, often to the point where it may appear impossible. Most candidates, because they are so beholden to the graduation certificate, regress to levels of slavish dependency and anxious compliance with their supervisors. They select the "easiest" cases in order to insure that they will "progress." They espouse the supervisor's theories in order not to jeopardize their progression. Although independent thinking and self-assertion are officially promulgated, in actuality the student who deviates too much from the mainstream is likely to find him- or herself placed on probation and then dropped from the program entirely. There are many other criticisms I have of formal analytic training, but it goes beyond the scope of this chapter to discuss them.

After five-and-one-half years of training, which had many rough spots, I was awarded my certificate. At the dinner dance held to celebrate our graduation, I found myself preoccupied with a passage from Archibald MacLeish's poem-play *J.B.* (1956). The play was written as a modern-day variation on the biblical book of Job. At one point J.B. castigates himself for having pleaded obsequiously to God in the attempt to understand the reasons why so many calamities befell him. So regretfully he mutters, "I will not duck my head again. I will not duck my head again." I had no previous plan to think about the play that evening. But I recognized immediately the reason why this passage kept coming to mind. I was now past 35 years and, with the exception of my pre-kindergarten years and my two years in the military service, I had continually been involved in a formal educational program. A certain amount of head ducking was necessary, but there was very little of it at Bronx Science and Columbia College. At the White Institute, genuflecting was a full-time program, even though there was less of it than in the classical analytical institutes. But that night I was finished and I vowed that I would never duck my head again. I believe that I haven't. I believe that there is not one word in any of my voluminous writings that has been changed because I feared alienating someone or because I wanted to ingratiate myself to anyone. Nor have I compromised myself in my lectures. Although there are many who would disagree with my opinions, there are very few who consider me to be lacking in forthrightness. Similarly, in my academic work at both the White Institute and Columbia, I consider myself to be genuinely independent. After supervising a number of trembling candidates at the White Institute, I decided to resign rather than be party to the perpetuation of an educational system that had such grave deficiencies. At Columbia, as well, especially in the recent years in which biological psychiatry reigns supreme, my views are often met with disfavor. It may be that learning not to duck my head was one of the most valuable things I learned from psychoanalytic training. I believe this lesson has played an important role in my professional contributions.

I generally do not advise younger colleagues to pursue a formal course in psychoanalytic training. Rather, if they feel the need for therapy, they should select an analyst whose orientation they are comfortable with and whose writings and lectures suggest that he or she would make a skilled therapist. I advise them as well to see two or three people before making a selection. I recommend, also, that they engage privately two or three supervisors, over a four- or five-year period. I impress upon them the fact that universities were founded by students who hired the professors to teach them. Somehow, over the centuries, things got turned upside down and students have often been at the mercy of their professors and school administrators (although things have improved somewhat since the 1960s). One can "fire" one's private supervisor if one finds the teaching deficient or does not get along with him or her. Such dismissal of a supervisor at an analytic institute is often viewed as a manifestation of psychopathology on the candidate's part. With regard to the courses that I took in analytic training, most agree that they were primarily a waste of time. Rather, I recommend that the individual read selected works, especially those recommended by supervisors and one's analyst. Although following this course will not result in admission to any private clubs, the individual will come away with a much richer and more useful educational experience. I genuinely believe that if I had the opportunity to do it all over again, this is the program I would subscribe to.

PRIVATE PRACTICE

1963–1965 In 1963, after my second year of child psychiatry training (and fourth year of residency), I entered private practice and began teaching at the Columbia Medical Center in New York City. At the time of this writing (1985), I am still involved in both of these activities. When I started my private practice, I immediately saw myself as having the freedom to make changes that were not easily made within the institutional structure. For example, as mentioned, I recognized during my residency days that my seeing the child patient and a social worker seeing the parents produced an artificial schism in the family and, in the overwhelming majority of families, was more detrimental than beneficial. As the reader will come to see, throughout the years, I gradually modified this with the result that there was ever increasing joint work with parents. I find it amazing that at the Columbia Medical Center they are still doing this the way they did it in my training a quarter of a century ago. (My efforts to change this practice have proved futile.)

In my training I was taught to bring the child alone into the consultation room at the beginning of the first session. In this way one can ascertain whether the child has "separation anxiety." On a number of occasions, I observed therapists struggling with children who were panicked over the prospect of being dragged off into a room alone with a strange person who was referred to by the mother as a "nice lady" who was going to discuss with the child his or her "problems." I appreciated then that the child who did *not* have so-called separation anxiety under these circumstances was the one who was sick. It suggested a child who had not bonded with any human being and so couldn't care less whether or not it was mother, father, or a stranger. With this introduction into treatment, I cannot imagine a therapist then having a meaningful therapeutic relationship with a child. After such an initial exposure, meaningful treatment is either entirely impossible or only possible after a long uphill struggle has taken place. Accordingly, in my private practice I immediately began doing consultations in which both parents and the child were brought together from the waiting room into the consultation room. In addition, because of the one-hour restrictions I had in the military service, I began to initiate two-hour initial consultations. During such consultations I could more leisurely assess the presenting problem and interview the various parties in any combination I considered fit.

I was also taught in residency that I should never see in treatment the sibling of a child patient. I was taught that it would be bad for the first child's treatment to see the sibling. After a couple of years of doing this, I gradually came to appreciate how absurd was this advice. Actually, it was parents who first convinced me of the absurdity of this rule. A mother, for example, would ask me to see her other son. When I informed her that this would be psychologically detrimental to both boys, she might reply, "But my husband and I are very pleased with how well Billy's doing with you. We really don't want to start over with someone else for Tom. We don't know if we can easily find someone and besides, even if we do, the person will have to start from scratch all over again." These arguments seemed to make sense and so I started seeing siblings and found that neither's treatment was compromised by my seeing the other. In fact, the treatment of the second was enhanced by the increased knowledge of the family that I had prior to the onset of the second child's therapy. Surprisingly, no child complained about my seeing the other. The children, after all, went to the same pediatrician and no one said, "I want my own pediatrician!" In retrospect, I feel guilty about the people I turned away at that time, people whose children might have enjoyed a good therapeutic experience because a positive relationship with the family had already been established. Also I am somewhat embarrassed to think now about how much of a parrot I too was at that time. I really believed what I had been taught without thinking too seriously about the system's obvious flaws.

It was also at about that time that I began to break the rule about seeing a parent in individual therapy at the same time that I was seeing a child. No one (parent or child) got insanely jealous about my seeing the other and if someone did, I would use it as a point of departure for therapeutic inquiry. To want me exclusively to oneself, without my seeing any of the family members, is a manifestation of pathological jealousy, unless proven otherwise. In short, my position is that the thrust of the therapist's approach to the family should be one of starting with the assumption that any and all family members, in any combination, can be seen by the therapist and only if special situations warrant an exception to this rule, should referral to another therapist be considered. This is the exact reverse of the traditional rule that each family member should have his or her own therapist. This principle was especially prevalent among classical psychoanalysts, some of whom still practice in this way to this day. By the mid-1960s I was already viewing myself as a family doctor who would see whichever members of the family needed treatment, alone or in combination. It would be an error for the reader to conclude that I never recommend that a family member see another therapist. The criteria that I utilize for such referrals will become more apparent throughout the course of this book—especially in the discussions of my work with parents (Chapter Seven) and in my discussion of family therapy (Chapter Fourteen).

1965–1970   By 1965 I was still treating children individually, for the most part. I did counseling with the parents and some individual work with the parents. In a typical session the mother or father (usually the mother, who was generally more available to bring the patient) would come into the room at the outset and the child, mother, and I would talk together for a few minutes about what had gone on since the previous session. Then I would send the mother to sit in the waiting room throughout most of the session. On occasion, during the last few minutes, I would invite the mother in and give her some advice. Generally, this was done quite quickly because my next patient was waiting. Not surprisingly, there was little follow-through after this advice. The mother, not having observed the situation from which the advice emerged, was less likely to have conviction for it. This was one of the considerations that led me to work more actively with parents.

It was also around that time that I began to appreciate how unreliable children were in regard to following through with my therapeutic recommendations. I remember specifically a boy who complained bitterly in each session about the fact that his father would insist upon his eating every single morsel of food on the plate and leave not a scrap behind. I advised him to assert himself with his father and to express his complaints directly to him. Each week the boy would come back to the session with a rationalization for not speaking with his father. For example, he feared that his father would beat him mercilessly. I reassured him that I knew his father well and that I was quite confident that his father would not do such a thing. However, in spite of my reassurances, he came back to each session without having spoken to his father. He would not bring up the issue himself. When I brought it up, he would say, "I forgot" or "I had too much homework." (This was a boy who came for treatment because he was not attending properly to his homework.) Finally, I brought the father and mother in and suggested that the boy speak directly to his father about this problem. In the session with me, with my implied protection, he did so and we were able to resolve this issue. This experience also contributed to my decision to work more actively with parents and bring them more intimately into the treatment.

Around 1966, at which time I was using the audio tape recorder when playing the mutual storytelling technique game, a girl in treatment asked me if it was all right for her to bring her own tape recorder so that she could listen to the stories at home. I told her that I welcomed the idea because I thought "homework for therapy was a good thing to do." About a week later she came in and told me that her father and mother had also listened to the tapes and her father had said, "Well, I'm finally finding out what I've been paying for." Furthermore, she told me that the issues brought up on the tape had served as a point of departure for family discussions. It was for these and other reasons (to be described in detail in Chapter Seven) that I began to work much more actively with parents. I call what I do "individual child psychotherapy with parental observation and intermittent participation." This is not family therapy. I do family therapy as well and this will be described in detail in Chapter Fourteen.

It was in the middle 1960s that I saw a patient who played an important role in the development of my career as a writer. Prior to that time I never had any interest in writing and never considered myself to have any particular talents in this area. In fact, I was not a particularly distinguished English student and always considered it to be one of my weakest subjects in school. The boy was 12 years old and had what was then called "brain injury." (Today we would say that this child has a neurologically based learning disability.) The diagnosis had been made by a number of prominent neurologists. He was referred to me because during the three months prior to my initial consultation, he had developed psychotic symptomatology which included his sitting on the floor and flapping his hands, clapping, staring into space, and responding to hallucinations. In the course of my evaluation, I learned that the parents had told the child nothing about the nature of his disorder and had strictly refrained from doing so at the recommendation of the highest authorities in the field of neurology.

After an intensive evaluation of the child and parents, I informed them that it was my belief that an important factor in the child's regression into psychosis related to the fact that he was being deprived of vital information about his condition and I advised them to discuss it with him at a level commensurate with his ability to understand. The parents were initially aghast over my recommendation, having been warned by distinguished professors that such information could not but be extremely detrimental. I explained to them the reasons for my difference of opinion and told them that I would certainly be available to discuss this disorder with them and the child subsequent to their divulgence and that I was not just suggesting that they tell him and not return.

Somewhat reluctantly they followed my advice. Over the next month or so, there was a progressive diminution in the secondary symptomatology. After another five weeks or so the child was completely free of the secondary psychotic symptomatology. He did, of course, exhibit the primary manifestations of his neurological disorder. The father was very grateful and suggested that I write a book for children describing the disorder to them. In 1966 my book, *The Child's Book About Brain Injury* (1966), was published by the New York Association for Brain Injured Children (subsequently called the New York Association for Children with Learning Disabilities). The book subsequently was updated in 1973 with *MBD: The Family Book About Minimal Brain Dysfunction* (1973a).

In the late 1960s I began seeing children of divorce at an ever-increasing rate. The divorce rate was already starting to increase, and I suspected that there would be an increasing demand for a book for children on the subject of divorce. Accordingly, I began collecting data on this subject and in 1970 my *The Boys and Girls Book About Divorce* appeared (paperback edition, 1971b). It has been a source of great gratification in that the book was so well received and still continues to be used.

In the late 1960s I also began to appreciate how individual therapy of a person involved in a marital conflict might be more detrimental than useful to the marriage. And this, of course, was the traditional psychoanalytical approach. Each partner was seen by a separate analyst, each of whom might strictly warn the patient not to discuss anything that went on in the treatment with the spouse. And the analysts would not talk to each other either. In the context of such therapy, the patient's delusions were being taken on by the therapist. I began to appreciate that in analytic therapy a mutual admiration society evolved between the patient and the therapist. First, the patient feels flattered over the fact that the therapist is so interested, sympathetic, empathic, sensitive, and so forth. And the therapist feels flattered over the fact that of the billions of people on earth he or she has been selected to be the only person to whom these special divulgences are made. The patient, sensing the analyst's respect, feels even more admiring of the analyst. And the analyst, sensing the patient's increasing idealization, becomes even more enamored of the patient. And so there is an upward spiraling of respect and admiration in the context of which the analyst is not likely to view with objectivity the patient's complaints about the spouse.

I began to appreciate that the psychoanalytic position in this area was an extremely grandiose one. It made the assumption that one need not hear both sides of a story in order to ascertain what is really happening. To the best of my knowledge this is the first time in the history of mankind that an individual has taken the position that he or she needs to hear only one side of a story to make judgments about what is going on. The analyst's retort that the reality is not important, but only the patient's fantasy or view of it, is absurd. Both are important: the reality and the patient's view of it. And one is not going to learn much about the reality by hearing only one side of the story. Accordingly, from the recognition of the way in which classical psychoanalysis can be detrimental to marriages (I saw many divorces which I considered to be the direct result of such a preposterous treatment approach), I began actively working in conjoint marital therapy.

1970–1975   It was in 1970 that I switched from the audio tape recorder to the video tape recorder when playing the mutual storytelling game. At that time the large reel-to-reel equipment was just coming into use. It was far more cumbersome and expensive than our present video cassette equipment. It proved to be a valuable instrument. The tapes I made provided children with the opportunity to watch themselves involved in the various therapeutic modalities and this proved useful therapeutically. In addition, I began showing the tapes at conferences and this enhanced significantly the value of my presentations in that conference participants were now able to see exactly what I was doing. My hope then was that the day might come when an instrument would be devised which would enable children to watch their tapes at home, but I could not envision then what the instrument might be.

By 1970 I had been using the mutual storytelling technique for about seven or eight years. I had found it very useful and was on the verge of publishing my book on the subject (*Therapeutic Communication with Children*, 1971a). However, there were children who were not particularly receptive to freely fantasizing and providing me with self-created stories. I began thinking about creating board games that might enhance the likelihood that children would tell stories. These involved token reinforcement, prizes, and other aspects of board game play. These games are described in Chapter Ten. However, even then, there were some children who were too resistant and/or inhibited to provide meaningful stories. Accordingly, I began to think about other kinds of games that might prove useful in the treatment of such difficult children. And it was for them that I devised *The Talking, Feeling, and Doing Game* (1973b). This game proved successful in engaging such children, especially because it did not rely heavily upon their providing fantasies, but rather used verbal projective material, such as, "A boy has something on his mind that he's ashamed to tell his mother. What is it?" "Name three things that could make a person sad," and "If the walls of your house could talk, what would they say about your family?" The game also proved useful as an additional therapeutic modality for those children who were comfortable telling stories but could utilize other therapeutic approaches as well. The game is described in detail in Chapter Eleven.

During this period I began appreciating also the value of bibliotherapy as a therapeutic modality. *The Boys and Girls Book About Divorce* was written at the didactic level. I began writing in other genres, including reality-oriented stories (*Stories About the Real World*, 1972a) and modified fairy tales (*Fairy Tales for Today's Children*, 1974a; *Modern Fairy Tales*, 1977a). I also began writing books for parents, as an adjunct to my parent counseling (*Understanding Children: A Parents Guide to Child Rearing*, 1973c).

1975–1980   It was in this period that I began to appreciate the importance of bringing together both parents and stepparents into a child's treatment. The suggestion that the parents and the stepparents meet together at the same time was initially met with horror and amazement, but I began to get useful results with this therapeutic modality. Although there were some situations in which the hostilities were so formidable that I feared for the physical well-being of one or more of the participants (and so the therapy had to be discontinued), there were many situations in which it proved quite valuable. In fact, I came to view stepfamily therapy as one of the primary indications for family therapy.

Although I had occasionally done custody evaluations prior to this period, in the mid-1970s I began to do them with increasing frequency. This related to the fact that the "tender years presumption," under which mothers were automatically considered to be the preferable parents, came to be considered intrinsically "sexist" by fathers, and they began to litigate more frequently for custody. Furthermore, in the late 1970s and early 1980s we saw the beginning of the increased popularity of the joint custodial concept. This too contributed to the burgeoning of custody litigation. This prompted my collecting data for my *Family Evaluation in Child Custody Litigation* (1982).

1980–1986 In 1981 I replaced my reel-to-reel videotape recorder with a video cassette recorder, the same kind that people have in their homes. This proved to be a therapeutic boon. Children, with increasing frequency, now have the opportunity to view their tapes in their home themselves (along with family members). More recently, I have two video cassette recorders running simultaneously. My tape is in one and the patient's tape (which is brought to the session) is placed in the other. For some patients the whole session is taped, for others, selected segments. And these too are watched at home. At no extra cost the child is provided with additional therapeutic exposure. The dream that could only be hoped for in vague form in the early 1970s came to be realized far sooner than I had imagined.

Probably the most important change I have observed in the field of child psychiatry during this period has been the marked swing to a biological orientation, to the point where many training programs provide only minimal training in child psychotherapy. I consider this to be an unfortunate situation. I believe that a swing away from the classical analytic position was warranted, but a swing this far in the opposite direction is replacing one extreme theory with another. Because funding for biological research is much more readily available than for research in the psychodynamic realm, I do not see much hope for a swing back to a more moderate position in the immediate future. I would like this prediction to prove to be false!

TWO

Historical Considerations Regarding Child Psychotherapeutic Techniques

There is but one way left to save a classic; to give up revering him and use him for our own salvation--that is, to lay aside his classicism, to bring him close to us, to make him contemporary, to set his pulse going again with an injection of blood from our own veins, whose ingredients are our passions . . . and our problems.

Ortega y Gasset on Goethe

CHILD PSYCHOANALYSIS

To the best of my knowledge, the first article ever published on the psychotherapeutic treatment of a child was Sigmund Freud's case of Little Hans, published in 1909. Hans was a five year old who suffered with a fear of horses. His father, Max Graf, was a Viennese music publisher with an interest in a variety of cultural matters, including psychoanalysis. He was one of a group of friends and colleagues who met with Freud once a week to discuss Freud's analytic work. When Freud heard about Hans' fear, he concluded that the boy was suffering with a phobia, a psychoneurotic symptom, that should be amenable to psychoanalytic therapy. It would have been consistent with Freud's previous approach to such problems to have suggested that Max Graf bring his son to Freud's office and to have Hans lie down on the couch and free associate in the hope that the insights so gained would be useful for Hans in curing his phobia. However, Freud did no such thing. Rather than treat the child himself, he decided to have the father serve as the therapist and Freud would be the supervisor. The reason for this decision is described in the very first paragraph of this article (page 149):

> No one else, in my opinion, could possibly have prevailed upon the child to make any such avowels; the special knowledge by means of which he was able to interpret the remarks made by his five-year-old son was indispensable, and without it, the technical difficulties in the way of conducting a psychoanalysis on so young a child would have been insuperable.

In short, Freud did not believe that Hans would be comfortable enough with him to provide the kinds of personal information that would be necessary for a successful psychoanalysis, and so he chose the father to be the therapist. One might question here why Freud did not choose the mother. Was this a manifestation of male chauvinism on his part? In Freud's defense, we do know that the mother had been a patient of his. Perhaps this was a reason why he chose the father. We know, as well, that the father had been schooled in psychoanalytic theory, and perhaps this was the reason. In any case, Freud did not treat the child himself and the approach was straight psychoanalytic. The theory behind Hans' treatment was that "cure" (a word Freud used freely, a word that I do not use in regard to any form of psychotherapy) of Hans' neurosis would be brought about via the process of Hans' gaining conscious awareness into the unconscious processes that were contributing to the development of his symptom. The fundamental dictum of psychoanalytic treatment was applied to Hans: "Where there is unconscious, there shall conscious be." At no point was there any mention of play therapy. Actually, this concept was outside of Freud's scheme of things. Hans did enjoy an alleviation of his symptoms. Freud believed that this was the result of Hans' gaining insight into the unconscious processes that underlay his neurosis. Elsewhere (1972b) I have described what I consider to have been more important factors that brought about the alleviation (I do not use the word "cure" here) of Hans' symptoms.

If Freud's report is accurate, Hans' was an "easy case." The child appears to have willingly involved himself in the psychoanalytic process. Most child therapists would agree that the vast majority of children are not so receptive to psychotherapy, whether it be psychoanalytic or any other kind of psychiatric treatment. Children are not coming to us voluntarily, stating that they wish to delve into the unconscious processes that they suspect are at the roots of their psychoneurotic problems in the hope that the insights so gained will bring about an alleviation (or "cure") of their symptomatology.

Most children are referred against their will, have little motivation to change themselves, and do not appreciate how their therapeutic experiences will fit into their life patterns. Commonly, the only things children want from the therapist is that he or she be instrumental in getting their parents, teachers, and others who are dissatisfied with their behavior "off their backs." Even those children who have some insight into the fact that they do have problems, and may exhibit some motivation to change things, will often still prefer to play with friends, watch television, or just hang around doing nothing. Children are basically hedonistic and avoid unpleasant thoughts and feelings, the toleration of which is vital for meaningful therapy. Children basically prefer to live in the present. They do not take a long range view of things in which they are willing to give up present pleasures (or suffer present discomforts) for future gains or rewards. Rather than introspect, children tend to act out. Rather than view themselves as contributors to their difficulties, they prefer to externalize and consider their problems as caused by forces in the environment. Rather than see themselves as initiating their difficulties, they frequently see themselves as innocent victims. And this view only lessens even further the likelihood of the child's being motivated for therapy, especially one that relies on their gaining insight into their unconscious processes. If child therapy is to succeed with children who are less motivated for treatment than little Hans—and this would include about 99 percent of all child patients—then other techniques have to be devised to engage them. I discuss here, roughly in chronological order, the various methods that have been devised to engage children meaningfully in psychotherapy.

PSYCHOANALYTIC PLAY THERAPY

L. Kanner (1957) credits H. von Hug-Hellmuth with having published in 1913 the first article describing the introduction of play into psychoanalysis. Her 1921 article appears to be the first in the English language on the use of play techniques in child psychoanalytic treatment. Hug-Hellmuth ascribed meaning to just about every act and verbalization of the child, and tended to interpret the child's behavior along strictly classical Freudian lines. Although one might disagree with her specific interpretations, her observation that the child's play fantasies and activities can be a valuable source of information about his or her psychodynamics was a formidable contribution to the field.

Although S. Freud (1959), as early as 1908, commented briefly on one psychological aspect of play (The "opposite of play is not serious occupation, but reality"), it was von Hug-Hellmuth's work that stimulated an interest in play as a tool in child therapy—an interest that persists to the present. In the 1920s M. Klein and A. Freud began using play in child psychoanalysis. M. Klein (1932) considered the fantasies that the child wove around his or her play to be the equivalent of the adult patient's free associations and the resistances revealed in such verbalization to be susceptible to analysis. She directly confronted children as young as one to two years of age with what she regarded to be the psychodynamic meaning of their play and considered children capable of understanding her interpretations and utilizing therapeutically the insights so gained. M. Klein's critics are generally dubious about the ability of such young children to comprehend the formulations she presented them and consider many of her interpretations to express the content of her own mind rather than the child's (L. Kanner, 1940).

A. Freud (1946, 1965) was generally more cautious than Klein in applying adult psychoanalytic technique to children. She recognized play as a valuable source of information about the child's psychodynamics (although she did not consider play verbalization to be the exact equivalent of adult free association) and as a useful tool in helping the child overcome resistance to treatment. She utilized play in the early phase of therapy to facilitate the child's forming a close and trusting relationship with the analyst; in later phases, she attempted to involve the child in analyzing the play verbalizations (including resistance fantasies). However, her approach to such analysis was always more cautious than Klein's. In general, she approached children through their defenses and tried to get them to derive insights on their own rather than presenting them with the Kleinian kinds of direct interpretations.

Although M. Klein and A. Freud differed in regard to the interpretations they would give to children's play fantasies, they both worked very much within the classical Freudian framework. Specifically, they both believed that a primary goal of therapy was to help the child gain conscious awareness of the unconscious processes that were at the foundation of his or her symptoms. They subscribed to the dictum: "Where there is unconscious, there shall conscious be." They believed that such insight was central to the therapeutic process and that without it, any clinical improvement was not as likely to be as enduring as that which was obtained by this method—an assumption that I take issue with. As will be described so many times over in this book, I believe that more important factors are involved in the therapeutic process and, furthermore, that insight is one of the *least* effective ways of bringing about therapeutic change in children (and even in many adults). M. Klein's and A. Freud's work is based on the assumption that children are cognitively capable of gaining and utilizing psychoanalytic insights at very young ages. I disagree with this hypothesis and have Piaget's support for my position. It is not until children reach the age of 10 or 11, that is, the level of cognitive development that Piaget referred to as "formal operations," that children are cognitively capable of separating an object and the symbol that denotes it, and then moving back and forth between the two. And such capacity is central to the ability to engage in meaningful psychoanalytic treatment. Although some highly intelligent children can do this earlier, most cannot. A. Freud and M. Klein appeared to have been oblivious to this obvious developmental fact. I suspect that they may have reported on their most obvious successes with highly intelligent children or (and this was especially the case for M. Klein) described more their own projections than that which went on in the minds of their child patients.

M. Klein's and A. Freud's studies stimulated an intensive interest in the psychology of children's play that persists to the present. In 1933 Waelder described the value of play as a medium for the child's wish fulfillments, parental emulation, gratification of regressive needs, and dealing with traumatic events (through desensitization and identification with the traumatizer, for example, the dentist).

COMMUNICATION AT THE SYMBOLIC LEVEL

Recognizing that the child's self-created fantasies are a valuable source of information about the child's psychodynamics has resulted in therapists' giving the highest priority to the child's expressing such material in the session. Therapists found, however, that most child patients resisted revealing themselves in this way, often from an awareness (at some level) that even the symbolic representations may reveal material they do not wish divulged. Many of the techniques to be described subsequently were designed to overcome such resistance. To varying degrees, they have also attempted to solve the problem of how to make therapeutic use of the rich information that children's fantasies so often provide us. They are all essentially attempts to deal with the problem of how to utilize the child's play fantasies as a vehicle for bringing about therapeutic change.

The Play Interview

One of the earliest modifications of psychoanalytic doll-play therapy was described by J. Conn, who referred to his approach as the "Play Interview" (1939, 1941a, 1941b, 1948, 1954). Conn considered the fantasies that children wove around their doll play to be highly valuable sources of information about their basic problems. He defined these primarily, however, as direct reality problems. He believed that the child's gaining insight into these here-and-now issues was more important than inquiries into the "classical" psychoanalytic conflicts of the past. His therapeutic approach focused on children's gaining a more objective view of themselves, appreciating their own role in bringing about their difficulties, and acquiring more adaptive ways of handling life's conflicts. He frequently urged children to suppress everyday anxieties and to desensitize themselves to them while entering the anxiety-provoking situation. He took an active role in the play, asked many questions, and often set up specific situations that would channel the child's attention into specific areas that Conn considered to be important. Whereas classical psychoanalysts at that time considered catharsis to be an important therapeutic modality, Conn did not have a high opinion of the value of catharsis in the treatment of most psychological disorders, whether such release was obtained from doll play or in other ways. He worked actively with parents in the attempt to change environmental contributions to the child's difficulties.

Active Play Therapy

During the same period J. Solomon, a student of Conn, described a somewhat similar therapeutic approach which he referred to as "Active Play Therapy" (1938, 1940, 1951, 1955). He considered his more structured and active therapeutic approach to be indicated when the child exhibited resistance to verbalizing in association with free play. He believed that doll-play catharsis could be salutary especially, for hostile release. He viewed his approach as a modality through which the therapist could reduce guilt, provide therapeutic suggestions, and encourage desensitization through repetition. Although he too emphasized the importance of focusing on present problems, he considered attention to the past to have a definite, albeit less important, role to play in therapy. As he saw it, the child did not necessarily need to gain insight in order to achieve therapeutic change. He observed that what the therapist transmitted through the doll play had therapeutic value even when it was directed only to the dolls and not ostensibly to the child him- or herself. In fact, keeping the discussion at the third person (or animal) level was, in his view, one of the most efficacious ways to diminish children's resistance to self-revelation. For more receptive children, he advised helping them relate the doll fantasies to themselves; however, he warned against encouraging such inquiry too rapidly as it might cause the child to become so anxious that he or she would resist completely any further work through doll-play fantasy.

I consider Solomon's work to represent a landmark contribution in the field of child psychotherapy. His belief that it was not necessary for the patient to gain insight to bring about therapeutic change and that one could provide therapeutic communications at the symbolic level represents a breakthrough. For example, if the child, who is not particularly receptive to analyzing his or her self-created stories (the usual case), tells a story about a cat who bites a dog, the therapist, instead of trying to help the child analyze the story, might respond with such questions as, "Why did the cat bite the dog?" and "Is there a better way the cat could have handled that problem with the dog, other than biting the dog?" He recognized that children were most comfortable communicating at the symbolic level and was comfortable himself communicating with them at the same level. I consider my mutual storytelling technique to be a direct derivative of Solomon's work. I consider myself to be sitting on his shoulders.

DOLL PLAY

Figurines representing various family members have traditionally been among the mainstays of the child therapist's playroom. Many consider such dolls to be among the most valuable items in the child therapist's armamentarium—facilitating as they do the production of fantasies that concern the individuals most involved in the child's difficulties. However, there is an intrinsic contaminating aspect to them, a contaminant that exists in all ready-made objects used as foci for the production of the child's fantasies. Because they have a specific form, they are likely to suggest particular fantasies, thereby altering the purer fantasy that might have been elicited from a less recognizable object or from one that the child him- or herself had created (Woltmann, 1964a). A preferable "doll" would be one that is more nondescript—a lump of clay on the top of a pencil, for example. To carry this principle further, the ideal "doll" would be no doll at all—because then there would be no contamination of the natural fantasies. The worst kind of doll for therapeutic use is an elaborate, and often expensive, one which presents multiple stimuli that not only restrict fantasies but may be focused upon by the child in the service of resistance. In spite of their potential for fantasy contamination, such dolls are still useful for the child who is too inhibited to verbalize without them. In addition, it is likely that the pressure of impulses to express themselves in fantasies related to the child's unconscious complexes is far greater than the power of the external facilitating stimulus to alter significantly the elicited fantasies.

The therapist does well not only to listen to the stories that the child creates around the dolls, but to observe the child's movements as well. The child's various nonverbal activities and the ways in which he or she physically structures the doll play can provide additional information of considerable value. Such structuring, however, may be used in the service of resistance. Most therapists have had the experience of a child's spending significant time placing various family members in even rows and then repeatedly becoming dissatisfied with each new arrangement. Or the child may endlessly rearrange the furniture in the dollhouse, never seeming able to get to the story. Accordingly, it seems wiser not to have furniture displayed on the therapist's toy shelves. One may, however, keep certain items in a closet such as a bed and a toilet which, in special circumstances, can be introduced into the play. Similarly, dolls such as soldiers, cowboys, and Indians tend to elicit stereotyped, age-appropriate play ("war," fighting, etc.) that is not particularly revealing. The reason for this is that the normal fantasies so produced are difficult to differentiate from the pathological. Such figurines usually elicit hostile fantasies in normal children as well as those who have hostile acting-out problems. Accordingly, such dolls are best left in the closet and only brought out if the therapist wishes to use them for specific therapeutic purposes. More will be said about doll therapy throughout the course of this chapter.

ALLEN'S "RELATIONSHIP THERAPY"

F.H. Allen considered certain transactions in the therapist-patient relationship to be the crucial elements in successful treatment. He referred to his approach as "Relationship Therapy" (1942). Allen considered the experiences of the present, especially those that occurred in the therapeutic situation, to be the most important focus for therapeutic attention. Accordingly, he did not concern himself with helping the child gain insight into past events. He assumed that the child would repeat past pathological behavior in the session, and worked with the present repetition. He considered this to be the most efficacious way of alleviating the child's symptoms because then "living and understanding became one." Allen believed the child's problems to stem primarily from environmental repressive forces, the reduction of which he considered to be salutary. Providing the child "freedom" was a paramount element in Allen's approach: ". . . the therapeutic value of talking lies less in the content and more in the freedom to talk." In his view, the child has the innate capacity to discover healthy values and capabilities;

the therapist's task is to provide the kind of accepting environment that would allow for their expression. However, Allen still understood that the therapist had to place reasonable controls on the child. The child was aware that these limitations would protect him or her from the untoward consequences of total abandonment to free expression. Given such controls, children would then be more comfortable in expressing themselves. Allen suggested that the therapist concentrate more on what the child is attempting to accomplish with verbalizations in the therapeutic relationship than on the verbal content per se. For example, the child may be talking about his or her difficulties not so much in the attempt to resolve them, but in the hope that the therapist will magically cure his or her problems. Allen appears to be less concerned than many other therapists with the problem of dealing with resistances. What were often considered to be obstructions to treatment by others were viewed by Allen as healthy expression and self-assertion. For Allen, these were manifestations of the child's trying to overthrow the restrictive environmental influences that were the primary source of his or her pathology.

Although Allen referred to his treatment as "Relationship Therapy," there is little in his work suggesting that he gave proper appreciation to the importance of the therapist-patient relationship as the foundation on which I believe effective treatment is built. Accordingly, I believe the name he gave to his treatment approach is misleading. It is more a cathartic type of therapy and is based on the belief that there lies within all children an inner knowledge of what is best for them and one need only provide them with freedom of expression and disinhibition and the healthy forces will express themselves. I am not in agreement with this view. I cannot agree that we are born with some inner knowledge as to what is healthy or unhealthy for us, with the exception of certain biological survival reactions such as fight and flight. Also, Allen's focus on the freedom to talk as opposed to focusing on the content of what is being said is an unfortunate emphasis. I believe that *both* are important and therapists who do not give proper attention to verbal content are depriving themselves of vital information. I suspect also that Allen's approach contributed to the perpetuation of antisocial acting out, in that he tended to interpret such expressions in the interview as healthy attempts to overthrow social repression, rather than as possible displacement of pathological anger onto the therapist.

ROGERS' "NONDIRECTIVE"
OR "CLIENT-CENTERED THERAPY"

C. Rogers referred to his approach as "Nondirective or Client-centered Therapy" (1951, 1967). To Rogers, the term "patient" implied inferior status, whereas "client" connoted responsibility. I am in disagreement with Rogers on this point. The word "patient" does not have any intrinsic connotation of inferiority. Some words may, but the word "patient" is not one of them. If a person who works with a therapist has feelings of inferiority because the word *patient* is used to refer to him or her, it is generally a manifestation of some problem on the patient's part. One could argue that the word "client" has an intrinsic derogatory connotation. Many nonmedical therapists, however, welcome the word "client" because it protects them from potential litigation. If they were to refer to an individual as a patient, then the therapist might be brought up on charges of practicing medicine without a license. However, if one does not use the word patient, then a nonphysician therapist may protect him- or herself from such an allegation. Rogers' referring to his treatment as "client-centered" has the implication that other therapists are not focusing enough attention on their patients. There is a definite note of superiority here. It is reminiscent of the advertising campaign of some politicians who claim that they are supportive of the needs of widows and orphans—with the implication that their opponents are just the opposite.

Rogers considers there to be a "self-actualizing" drive present in all human beings from birth. He believes that there exists within all of us some knowledge of what is healthy and useful for us and what is not. He considers that there is some potpourri of thoughts and feelings in which there is some knowledge, at birth, about what would be in our best interests. Repression by social forces of these impulses produces various types of discontent—one type of which is psychopathology. Again, I am in disagreement with Rogers on this point. I do not believe that we are born with some pool of knowledge of what is in our best interests. Rather, we have to learn these things from our culture and society, and each individual's milieu differs with regard to the input in this area. I have found it of interest, even to the point of its being humorous, that many of the patients who undergo Rogerian therapy, when they are self-actualized, look very much like many other people who have been similarly self-actualized. In the 1960s and 1970s, it was common for these people to decide to move to a commune in Vermont, weave baskets, grow natural foods, and remove themselves from society in general. In their so-called nonconformity they were slavishly conformative in imitation of others who self-actualized themselves in compliance with an identical personality pattern.

The purpose of the treatment is to foster full expression of one's self-actualizing impulses. This is said to be most efficaciously accomplished when therapists exhibit certain important attitudes in their relationships with their clients. They must have an attitude of what Rogers called "unconditional positive regard" for the client, that is, they should be completely free of judgments, both positive and negative. It is only in such a permissive attitude that the patient will be willing to drop resistances to self-expression and self-actualization. Again, I am in disagreement with Rogers on this point. I cannot imagine any human being taking an attitude of unconditional positive regard on an ongoing basis. Inevitably, in any human relationship, there must be some times when one of the parties is going to do something that will irritate the other. And the therapeutic relationship is no exception. For a therapist to maintain a position of "unconditional" regard requires duplicity. It requires the therapist to withhold critical thoughts and feelings about the patient that must be experienced from time to time. Strictly refraining from the expression of such reactions deprives the patient of important therapeutic input and is therefore a disservice to the patient.

A number of years ago, the *Listerine* mouthwash company ran an advertisement about a young woman who had bad breath and her best friends didn't tell her. The primary caption was: "Your Best Friends Won't Tell You." Accordingly, she was lonely and dateless. After she started using *Listerine*, the phone didn't stop ringing. I believe that the therapist should be better than a best friend. The therapist should tell patients things that a best friend might hesitate telling. However, crucial here is that the therapist's motivation be benevolent, rather than malevolent. A friend criticizes benevolently. One's own mother does not give one "unconditional positive regard." Therapists who claim to be providing their patients with this attitude are deceiving themselves (if they believe that they are) or their patients (if they know that they aren't). In either case it is a fabrication and an unhealthy situation for the patient. In addition, Rogers recommends that the therapist not pass judgments. He apparently is a subscriber to the advice that one should not judge one's patients. I find this impossible to imagine. We are continually judging other people in our human relationships. We are always making decisions as to whether or not the other person's thoughts, feelings, or actions are good, bad, right, or wrong. We must do so if we are to interact properly and decide in what way we are going to involve ourselves with others. Therapists should not only be comfortable making therapeutic judgments but should be willing to share them at the proper time with their patients. One has to differentiate between therapeutic judgments transmitted benevolently and those that are transmitted malevolently. When the former is the case, then one has an extremely useful therapeutic situation; when the latter is true, it is likely that the treatment will be detrimental.

Rogers suggests that the therapist assume a completely passive and nondirective role. He refers to his technique as "nondirective therapy." It is only in such an atmosphere that the patient will be willing to drop resistances to self-expression and self-actualization. Rogers considers individuals, even children, to have both the innate capacity and the strength to devise the proper steps toward mature behavior, especially when placed in this unguided and nondirective milieu. The therapist attempts to help the patient by reflecting back the latter's verbalizations and feelings in such a way that self-awareness is accomplished. This often involves repeating the last segment of the patient's statement. However, therapists were also instructed to intuitively make guesses as to what the patient might be feeling and express these emotions as well, for example, "That must have made you feel very sad." The highly skilled therapist should be able to intuitively ascertain what the patient's unconscious processes are and help bring these into self-awareness. The overwhelming majority of therapists, I believe, do not possess such insights and intuition. Accordingly, in practice, the therapy often degenerates into the therapist's providing parrot-like mimicry of the last fragments of the patient's comment and merely reflects back the obvious thoughts and feelings the patient is expressing.

In line with Rogers' view that the child has the ability to assume responsibility for his or her own actions, and that what the child does is generally in the child's best interests, the concept of resistance takes a different form. Traditional therapists would view the child's obstructionistic attitude toward treatment to be a manifestation of pathological processes. Rogers would more likely view such behavior as a manifestation of the child's desire to actualize him- or herself. Traditional resistances then are viewed as healthy expressions of the child's inner needs and they no longer appear to be an obstruction to the therapeutic process. The child is then viewed to be freer to grow in directions natural to him or her. Because of the significant overlap between symptoms and resistances (the same psychodynamic mechanisms are often used in both), I suspect that Rogerian therapists often promulgated psychopathology with the nondirective approach. V.M. Axline (1947, 1964) is probably the most well known therapist to have applied Rogerian techniques to the treatment of children.

RELEASE THERAPY

D.M. Levy held that catharsis in certain situations could be therapeutic and referred to his techniques for promoting emotional expression in these situations as "Release Therapy" (1939, 1940). Levy described three types of release therapy. In the first, simple release, a child is allowed free expression of inhibited impulses (usually regressive or hostile): spilling, throwing, aggressive outbursts, and so forth. This form of treatment is indicated for children whose parents will not or cannot allow such release. In the second type, the child is encouraged to express inhibited feelings which are derived from standard situations such as sibling rivalry and curiosity about nudity. For such children the doll material and the therapist's remarks are so structured that comments in these specific areas are likely to be evoked from the child. The third type is designed for children who are reacting pathologically to a specific trauma and whose untoward behavior relates to their having suppressed or repressed recollection of the event. In the treatment of such conditions, the dolls are set up to resemble the situation in which the trauma occurred; the therapist's comments are then designed to elicit responses related to the event. Generally, the technique works best for children who are relatively healthy prior to the traumatic event and for whom the symptoms are of short duration. One danger of Levy's method is that the children may be led prematurely to deal with issues with which they are not ready to cope. Great anxiety will then be produced and they may become even more resistant to therapeutic work. However, for the situation for which the third type of release therapy is in fact indicated (admittedly a small segment of the children who are brought for therapy), the technique may prove useful.

FANTASIES CREATED AROUND DRAWINGS

In the 1920s and 1930s, therapists primarily used dolls as the objects on which children projected their fantasies. In the 1940s therapists began experimenting with other children's play equipment in the hope that they would prove useful in therapy. The child's self-created drawing then became a therapeutic standby. Actually, it is superior to doll play in that the child's picture is self-created and does not have any significant external contamination such as is the case with doll play. The doll has an obvious size, shape, sex, and is often clothed. All of these items provide potentially contaminating stimuli. The only restriction that the self-created drawing has is that it has a border and generally confines the child with regard to what can be placed therein. However, even then, the therapist can generally advise the child to tell a story that goes beyond the borders of the page and to introduce whatever else the child wishes. The picture as well as the stories created around it can be a rich source of psychodynamic information. The self-created picture generally portrays external projections of various aspects of the child's personality.

In order to facilitate the child's drawing such pictures, the therapist does well to create an atmosphere that is likely to produce the freest and most uncontaminated pictures and accompanying fantasies. I have found a useful opening for this purpose to be: "Here's a piece of drawing paper and some crayons. I'd like you to draw a picture, a made-up picture." To a child who shows some initial reluctance, I might say, "I'd like to see how good you are at drawing pictures." I introduce a slightly competitive element ("See how good you are") in order to enhance the child's motivation. I have no problem with benevolently motivated competition. It is the malevolent kind that we have to avoid. This point is an important one. Those who would attempt to remove competition entirely because of the destructive type would deprive us of an important motivational enhancement. For the child who is more resistant and says that he or she can't draw well, I will generally impress upon the child that this is not an art contest. The child may reveal resistances by drawing a design. I might then encourage the child to draw something "more interesting," something that would be enjoyable to talk about. I might replace the paper with another blank one and say that "designs don't count."

After the child has completed the picture I will then ask the child to tell me something about the picture, especially a story. I request first a description because it is easier to do and may not be as anxiety provoking as telling a self-created story. To the child who exhibits some hesitation telling a story, I might respond, "Every picture has a story. What's the story about this one? I want to see how good you are at making up stories." A common resistance maneuver is for the child to tell a story that is mundane and basically nonrevealing. An example of such a story would be one that itemizes the events of the day—when the child got up in the morning, what was eaten for breakfast, what occurred in school with regard to the various subjects studied, and what happened after school. In such cases, I will generally tell the child that that was kind of an uninteresting or boring story and encourage him or her to tell one that is more interesting or exciting.

When a child has difficulty telling a story, I may draw cartoon-style balloons over the heads of each of the figures and ask the child to write in the balloon what the figures are saying. Of course, generally only key words will fit and a certain amount of erasing may be necessary. Using a blackboard and chalk facilitates this procedure because of the ease with which the messages can be erased. I have found this approach particularly useful for children with neurologically based learning disabilities or linguistic problems. They may have difficulty verbalizing and may do better writing down their thoughts. This technique enables them to do so, and they then provide meaningful psychodynamic material. Furthermore, because of auditory receptive linguistic problems, many of these children have trouble retaining what they hear, but have less difficulty retaining what they read.

L. Bender (1952) was one of the first to describe in detail the ways in which children's self-created fantasies around drawings could provide useful psychodynamic material. However, her interpretations were generally along strict classical psychoanalytic lines. She tended to interpret especially the sexual and aggressive impulses revealed therein. She also gave emphasis to the motor release aspect of stories and drawings, as well as the psychological significance of the configurational elements.

D.W. Winnicott (1968, 1971) devised a projective drawing technique that he called the "Squiggles Game." The therapist scribbles something formless with pencil on a blank sheet of paper. The child is asked to add lines in order to convert the "squiggle" into some recognizable form. The child then draws his or her own squiggle and the therapist transforms it into something distinguishable. Back and forth the game goes. Each drawing serves as a point of departure for a therapeutic interchange. Generally, Winnicott tried to guide the conversation in a direction in which the child was helped to gain insight (usually along classical psychoanalytic lines) into what the squiggles and the associated verbalizations revealed. The game was designed primarily for situations when only a short-term therapeutic process was possible; however, it can prove useful as a tool in long-term therapy as well. It is certainly a technique with which the child therapist should be familiar. However, it is likely that many of the dramatic cures which Winnicott attributed to the Squiggles Game (often accomplished in one or two interviews) were less related to the interpretations Winnicott provided than they were to the effect of certain aspects of Winnicott's personality and of the situation in which the consultations occurred. When reading Winnicott's material I am often dubious about how much his interpretations actually "sink in." Often obtruse psychoanalytic interpretations are presented to the child in rapid order. I doubt whether much was comprehended by the child under such circumstances. Also, Winnicott did not seem to appreciate the importance of the child's trying to derive his or her own insights into the meaning of the story; rather Winnicott typically spoon fed his interpretations to the child. Because I am dubious about the validity of many of these interpretations, I am less impressed with Winnicott's work than many. Having seen Winnicott personally a few years before he died, I suspect that other factors were operative in the improvements that he described, factors related to his personality. In Chapter Four I will discuss this factor in Winnicott's treatment in greater detail.

R.C. Burns and S.H. Kaufman (1970) have developed a technique which they call "Kinetic Family Drawings." When utilizing this method, the child is asked to draw a picture of the various members of the family—with each person *doing* something. It is not simply a test in which the child is asked to draw a family. Of importance here is the fact that the child is asked to have the family member *do* something. They claim that this technique provides more information than the less directive approaches. My experience with the instrument has been that the drawings so produced do not provide as much useful information as those created around more freely drawn pictures. I found that the child's stories tend to be more stereotyped and mundane.

J.N. Buck (1948) and E.F. Hammer (1960) used the "House-Tree-Person Technique." The child is asked to draw these three entities and to tell stories about what has been drawn. An attempt is made to score objectively some of the items, but I am not impressed with the utilization of these drawings for that purpose. However, as a focus for self-created stories, they can be useful. Others who have described the use of children's drawings as a vehicle for projective material in therapy are P. Elkisch (1960), M.L. Rambert (1964), and R. Kellogg and S. O'Dell (1967).

DIRECT INTERPRETATION
OF THE DRAWING

In the previous section I have described the use of the child's self-created drawing as a focus on which the child is asked to project a story. The story is then used as a source of understanding of the child's underlying psychodynamics and as a point of departure for various types of psychotherapeutic interchange. However, one can also use the drawing per se as a source of information about underlying psychodynamics. Of course, one can do both. In each situation there is a certain amount of speculation. K. Machover (1949, 1951, 1960) was one of the early investigators in this area. She appears to have been an acute interpreter of such drawings and has provided a wealth of information about how to interpret them. Her most well-known work was with the Draw-a-Person Test in which a child is simply asked to draw a person without any specific statements regarding the age, sex, or any other aspects of the person to be drawn. Then the child is asked to draw a person of opposite sex to the one depicted in the first picture. The body parts and coverings are separately analyzed: hair, eyes, ears, nostrils, mouth, shirt, dress, jewelry, etc. The interpretations are not based on any standardized data, but rather Machover's own personal clinical experiences and speculations. Eyes glancing sideways are said to suggest suspiciousness or avoidance mechanisms. Eyes closed suggests denial. Areas blackened are those about which there may be anxiety. The interpretations appear reasonable. My main objection to her work is the speculation involved and the paucity of confirmatory clinical data. One does not have to confine oneself to the drawings per se. One can use the drawings in the context of the clinical interview as well as in a setting in which associated fantasies, discussion, and stories are obtained. The conclusions that one then derives are more likely to be valid. For this instrument to be useful the child must be free enough to draw more than stick figures, because such figures are not likely to provide as much information as those pictures that depict richer material.

A child begins to draw recognizable human figures between the ages of three and four. Most often the earliest figures include a head with some facial characteristics and the extremities, typically emanating from the face. The head and the body may be depicted as one circle or oval. With increasing age the child's drawing of the human figure becomes more complex and accurate. F. Goodenough (1926) was the first to provide a scoring system to assess the child's developmental and intellectual level from the sophistication of the drawings of the human figure. D.B. Harris, in 1963, updated and refined Goodenough's scoring system. It cannot be denied that children's drawings become more complex, sophisticated, and accurate as they grow older. However, the Goodenough and Harris scales do not differentiate between the drawing that is immature because of intellectual impairment and the one that is below the chronological age level because of psychological immaturity. This is one of this technique's greatest defects, a deficiency not often appreciated by some examiners.

FINGER PAINTS, CLAY, BLOCKS, AND WATER

Finger Paints

Finger painting is generally pleasurable to young children. Such paintings, like drawings, can serve as a source of information about underlying psychodynamics—both with regard to the picture per se and the fantasies woven around it. Finger painting can provide regressive gratifications because of the smearing and messing outlets that they provide. Some therapists believe that this is a valuable aspect of finger painting because such regression is necessary before the child can then progress to higher levels of developmental functioning. The theory goes that one must allow the child to experience past gratifications that he or she may have been deprived of at that particular stage of development. Having then gratified these desires, the child is presumably in a better position to mature. I am dubious about this theory. I am more of the persuasian that what is past is past and that, although one may learn from history, one cannot go back in time and change it. This utilization of finger painting is based on the theory that one can. Accordingly, I generally do not encourage regression in my therapeutic work. There are, however, times when a child may regress in the face of some particular psychological trauma. Regression then provides a certain amount of solace, but I do not encourage it on an ongoing basis. Rather, after permitting a reasonable degree of regression, I will encourage a child to proceed along the developmental track to higher levels of functioning.

Finger painting can also be useful for inhibited children from homes where such free expression is neither encouraged nor tolerated. The pictures created with crayons are less easily changed; those produced with finger paints can be altered significantly before the final picture has dried. Accordingly, they allow for a richer elaboration of fantasies. The process of drawing the picture provides the child with tactile, kinesthetic, and visual gratifications that may have some therapeutic value. Lastly, drawing such a picture can provide the child with creative gratifications. Because less skill is necessary than drawing with crayons, the younger less accomplished child is more likely to gravitate toward finger painting (P.J. Napoli, 1951). I, personally, have never used finger paints in my therapeutic work with children. This relates in part to the inevitable mess that I would not be comfortable with. Furthermore, I view them as being more *play* than *therapy*, with significant nontherapeutic time spent in the physical activity.

Clay

One of the advantages of using clay as a focus for self-created stories is its malleability. Whereas a drawing is a relatively fixed stimulus for such fantasies, clay can be altered. Drawings have two dimensions whereas clay obviously has three. The medium almost asks the child to do things with it. It thereby expands the possibilities for the child's projected fantasies (A.G. Woltmann, 1964a). Of course, less technical skill is required to work with clay than to draw. It is appealing therefore to younger children, especially those who are less skilled.

Because clay almost invites the child to pound it, it is viewed by many therapists as a useful vehicle for the expression and release of tensions and hostility (M.R. Haworth and A.I. Rabin, 1960). I do not have much respect for therapeutic techniques that provide for such gratifications. All too often the therapist views such hostile release as a therapeutic end in itself. That is, the therapist believes a primary goal in therapy is to provide a vehicle for the release of pent-up hostility. Such therapists often lose sight of the fact that a more judicious goal of therapy, a goal that is more likely to help the person deal with real-life situations, is to help patients (regardless of age) to deal with their anger at the earliest moment and to direct it toward the source of frustration and irritation. The purpose of anger is to help increase the patient's efficiency in removing a noxious stimulus, the stimulus that is bringing about the anger in the first place. So removed, there will be little anger to express. Therefore, this use of clay, although a common one, is in my opinion misguided.

Clay resembles feces and therefore allows certain children regressive manifestations. Children can get messy with it and can smear with it in a manner that is approved of rather than forbidden. Therapists who believe that this can be therapeutically useful are likely to introduce clay into the child's play. I personally am not too enthusiastic about this use of clay, nor, as mentioned, am I enthusiastic about encouraging patients to regress.

Classical Freudian analysts are often quick to see sexual symbols in the objects that a child makes with clay. If a child rolls a piece of clay, it is difficult to imagine something coming out that doesn't resemble a snake. Many therapists of this persuasian reflexly assume that the child has then formed a penis with the clay. Under such circumstances, just about all children will receive the same interpretation, not a very therapeutically convincing thing for a therapist to do. Or the child is likely to roll the clay into a ball. The same therapists may automatically assume that the child is now creating a breast or testicle. Again, such "rubber stamp" interpretations are not very convincing to me. These therapists would do well to consider the possibility that there is absolutely no symbolic significance at all to many play activities and that the clay modality lends itself extremely well to the creation of objects of these shapes.

It is only with additional self-created fantasies that one is in a position to determine whether or not the therapist's own fantasies about the meaning of the clay figures are valid.

My experience has been that one of the important drawbacks of clay as a therapeutic vehicle is its pliability and lack of cohesiveness. Frequently a figure's arms and legs fall off, especially when it is moved. The child then spends an inordinate amount of time trying to get the extremities to stick to the body of the figurine. This wastes valuable therapeutic time. Because I am a somewhat obsessive and orderly person, and am not comfortable with the child's dirtying up my office with clay, I keep it in the closet and only bring it out for special purposes. I may not be the optimum therapist for children who come from homes which are extremely uptight. However, most of the children I see have problems because they are too loose, disorganized, and just the opposite of obsessive. Accordingly, I believe that for the vast majority of children, my personality type is preferable. All therapists should recognize the areas in which they can be helpful and those in which they cannot and should refer patients with pathology in certain areas to other therapists. We cannot be all things to all people. If our personality styles are such that we cannot be of help to certain patients, it is only ethical to refer them elsewhere.

Blocks

Many therapists have blocks in their play rooms. Proponents of their use describe them as providing valuable outlets for suppressed and repressed hostility. The child can throw them, drop them as "bombs," and so on. I am dubious about the therapeutic value of such hostile play. In fact, it may even encourage such acting out in that the therapist is catalyzing expression of hostility. Furthermore, anger, like other emotions has a way of "getting out of bounds." This unbridled expression of angry feelings may bring about a situation in which the expression of feelings becomes an end in itself and a vicious cycle spirals upward. This phenomenon has not been given the attention it deserves by therapists. For example, a murderer stabs a person in the heart. Most would agree that one or two such stabs will suffice to kill the individual. However, occasionally a murderer may stab the dead person 10 or 15 times in association with the homicidal act. Clearly, one or two stabs is enough to kill the individual. The additional stabs do not seem to serve any useful purpose. But they do serve a purpose. They allow for the release of the anger that is generated by the earlier anger. The anger then seems to build up in its own right, beyond the original purpose of its formation. Teachers know this phenomenon well. Children in classes can get out of control. They know they must try to interrupt the process early or everyone else goes wild. Therapists should not be encouraging their patients to "go wild."

Children enjoy building houses, castles, and other edifices which give them a sense of achievement and power. Such structures can be used to satisfy regressive fantasies by the children's building cozy retreats in which they can withdraw in womb-like fashion. E.H. Erickson (1950) has emphasized the importance of the configurational aspects of the structures that the child builds with blocks. He considers these to be of diagnostic value as well as useful points of departure for therapeutic interchanges.

Water Play

Water play has not been as popular as some of the aforementioned therapeutic modalities. In part, this probably relates to the fact that most therapists don't enjoy the mess of puddles of water all over their offices. Proponents of its use (Hartley et al., 1964) consider it to be the most flexible play medium that therapists can use—the most fluid of the various therapeutic modalities used in the playroom. Some child psychoanalysts claim that water stimulates play that involves urination, just as clay stimulates play that involves bowel movements. I am dubious about the symbolization here, but even if such interpretations are valid, I would often have a hard time translating such play into useful therapy. The use of water and clay for these purposes is based on the theory that symbolically playing with one's urine and feces can be therapeutically useful in that it provides gratifications that may not have been provided at earlier developmental levels. I have already expressed my opinion of such utilization of play materials, namely, that the past is dead, one cannot relive it, and doing so serves little if any therapeutic purpose.

Water is also used as a medium for the release of pent-up hostile feelings. By spitting, splashing, throwing, and spilling water, one releases anger. As mentioned, I am dubious about the use of catharsis as a therapeutic modality. A child who comes from a restrained and restrictive home may find playing with water a useful release from which he or she can gain a sense of freedom. I think swimming would provide more of a sense of freedom than the therapist's office, and it is far less costly and impractical.

Further Comments on Finger Painting, Clay, Blocks, and Water Play

When utilizing clay, finger paints, water, and blocks (and to a lesser degree, other play materials), the therapist does well to differentiate *psychotherapy* from that which is *psychotherapeutic*. Psychotherapy is a process that requires the talents and skills of a person trained in the treatment of psychological disturbances. However, a child can have many experiences that are psychotherapeutic—without the participation of a psychotherapist. Most healthy pleasurable activities are ego-enhancing and thereby contribute to the alleviation of psychological disturbance. The gratifications that flow from creative activity are in general psychologically beneficial. Physical activities can reduce tension and serve to release pent-up aggression. Sexual encounters can reduce tension, give pleasure, and facilitate benevolent human interchanges—all of which can be psychologically salutary. Because individuals can gain psychotherapeutic benefit alone or from interactions with others who are not trained therapists, it behooves the therapist to provide patients with something *beyond* what can be obtained elsewhere.

Clay, finger paints, water, and blocks along with other traditional toys used in therapy create the possibility that play therapy with them may be more *play* than *therapy*. Mention has been made of their value in providing the child with a greater sense of freedom and in reducing inhibitions. Obviously, such an experience is not valuable for all child patients; there are many children who need just the opposite. Their main problems relate to the fact that they are too uninhibited. Providing them with a therapeutic approach that encourages release and free expression may be antitherapeutic and merely frighten them or entrench their pathology. The aforementioned modalities have been described as providing the child with opportunities for regressive satisfactions: with return-to-the-womb gratifications and opportunities for symbolic play with urine and feces. Some hold that such regressive gratifications can be therapeutic, especially for the child who has been deprived of them; however, there is danger in providing too much such satisfaction and thereby entrenching regressive symptomatology. Finally, the value of these modalities in releasing hostility is often a naive approach to the treatment of hostility problems. I like to use the analogy here of anger as a kettle of boiling water with the flames under it symbolizing the anger generating frustrations and noxious stimuli. The person who needs anger release is viewed as someone who has a cork or plug in the spout of the kettle. Therapists of such a patient might consider their job to be that of pulling the cork out of the spout of the boiling kettle. This, in my opinion, is an oversimplification of the therapist's role. The therapist must not only help the patient pull the cork out but help the patient connect a tube from the spout to the underlying flames in order to extinguish the fires that are causing the water to boil in the first place. The therapist's role is to help the patient him- or herself pull the cork out and then connect a pipe from the spout to the flames that are generating the anger. If he or she is successful in this regard, the flames will be extinguished and there will be no anger generated—at least with regard to that particular issue.

PUPPETS AND MARIONETTES

Puppets and marionettes, like dolls, are used to stimulate fantasies (A.G. Woltmann, 1951, 1964b). My own experience with puppets is such that I rarely use them in therapeutic work. When children are given two puppets, one on each hand, it is likely that they will bang their heads together or engage them in some kind of aggressive play. The equipment almost asks for such utilization. The therapist then is not in a good position to know whether significant pent-up hostility is being expressed by such play or whether the puppet is serving as a vehicle for the expression of normal playful activity. Although one may have a large number of puppets, the human being has only two hands. Accordingly, the medium has an intrinsic restricting element in that one can only utilize two figures at a time.

Marionettes are occasionally used in child therapy. I have limited experience with them, mainly because I discarded them years ago. A significant amount of time was spent on untangling the strings, obviously a waste of therapeutic time. The fact that only one figure can be used at a time is also a serious detriment. L.

Bender (1952) and A.G. Woltmann (1972) tried a therapeutic technique in which hospitalized children were presented with puppet shows that were designed to elicit material of psychological significance. Puppets and marionettes were utilized in these theatrical performances and the issues presented in the plays were used as points of departure for analytically oriented group discussions. My main criticism of this technique is that the stories, although selected to cover a wide variety of life situations, were intrinsically restricting of the child's fantasies and so had a contaminating potential in the psychotherapeutic process. I have much greater commitment to the encouragement of free and self-created fantasies. The Bender and Woltmann stories are just the opposite.

DRAMATIZATION

Most children love plays and will welcome the opportunity to act in them. Children spontaneously play act their fantasies, the traditional game of "house" being one of the more common examples. In such games, the child entrenches adult identifications, reflects relationships and experiences, gratifies wishes, releases unacceptable impulses, and attempts to work through various problems and experiences (R.E. Hartley, L.K. Frank, and R.M. Goldenson, 1952). Play acting a theme of psychological significance provides the child with a far richer experience than merely talking about it and possibly emoting over it. With dramatization, various other sensory elements are brought into the experience: kinesthetic, tactile, an enhancement of the visual, and occasionally the olfactory and gustatory. This multisensory stimulation provides greater input than a single sensory modality and increases the likelihood that the experience will be remembered and incorporate itself into the child's psychic structure. Encouraging children to play act their fantasies enables the therapist to gain a deeper appreciation of their social interactional processes; it may help children as well to see more clearly how they relate to others. Through play acting, children can desensitize themselves to an anxiety-provoking situation, one that is either experienced or anticipated.

I. Marcus (1966) found children's donning costumes to be a useful device in helping some children overcome their resistances to revealing their fantasies. Wearing a costume appears to encourage children to "act" and hence reveal themselves. Marcus has found a box of hats to be similarly useful. He found that passive children tend to become more active and less defensive when wearing the costume. The material so elicited is used for psychoanalytic inquiry. The child has the opportunity to choose from a variety of costumes and an assortment of hats. One drawback to this technique is that it provides intrinsic contaminants to the child's productions in that the hats and costumes serve as foci for the fantasies that might otherwise be more freely self-created. However, a contaminated fantasy is generally more valuable than no fantasy at all (because the child often introduces idiosyncratic material), and for some children a costume or hat may enable them to provide material that would not otherwise have been obtained.

R.B. Hass and J.L. Moreno (1951) have utilized what they call the "Projection Action Test." They describe both diagnostic and therapeutic utilization of this instrument. When using this technique, children are encouraged to involve themselves in a series of structured dramatic situations from which projective material is likely to emerge. For example, a child may be asked to imagine him- or herself on a stage with an imaginary person. A series of questions is then asked about who the person is and what the child is doing with that person. The material so derived then becomes a focus for therapeutic discussion. In Chapter Eight I will discuss the mutual storytelling technique, a therapeutic device in which self-created stories are elicited from the child followed by the examiner's creating stories of his or her own that are specifically tailored to the psychological needs of the child. In Chapter Nine I will discuss the dramatization of these stories as an enhancement of the original technqiue.

Dance can also be a useful aspect of therapeutic dramatizations. L. Bender (1952) considered dance to be an excellent way to lower children's inhibitions. She considered it therapeutic in other ways: it provides pleasure (which in itself is often therapeutic), it can be ego-enhancing (as the child gains confidence in it), it reduces tension, and it serves to sublimate sexual desires. Hartley et al. (1952) emphasized the therapeutic role of dance in lessening tensions, providing primitive pleasure (especially kinesthetic), inducing spontaneity, and as a release for hostility. I am less enthusiastic about the hostility release element here, but I cannot deny that it serves the other purposes.

"PARAVERBAL THERAPY"

E. Heimlich (1965, 1972, 1973) uses a technique which she refers to as "paraverbal therapy." As a therapeutic modality she attempts to unite the therapeutic aspects of music (listening, singing, playing instruments, mime, dance, and finger painting). In her techniques, she sings with the child a song that is likely to touch upon issues relevant to his or her pathology. Her purpose is not only to provide strong and dramatic carthartic release but to use the issues in the song as points of departure for therapeutic discussions. There is no question that music, properly utilized, can be an extremely useful therapeutic modality. The most resistant and withdrawn children are likely to be engaged in musical activities, both verbal and along with musical instruments. It touches something primitive in all of us. If one adds words to music, there is a greater likelihood that the words will be heard—they seem to float on top of the music into the brain. Messages transmitted verbally are less likely to be incorporated into the psychic structure than those which utilize the musical vehicle of transmission. Heimlich adds to these mime, dance, and other elements of physical movement, all of which attempt to enhance the efficacy of the therapeutic communications. The method is especially useful for children who have proven resistant to other modes of treatment, but it should not be viewed simply for them. It can also be utilized for more cooperative children.

TRADITIONAL COMPETITIVE BOARD GAMES

Many child therapists have available traditional board games for utilization in therapy with children. I am very dubious about the basic therapeutic value of most of these instruments. I am not claiming that they have no therapeutic benefit at all; only that they are of limited therapeutic value and that most of the other instruments described in this chapter are much more efficient. One cannot deny that, while playing a traditional competitive board game with a child, many aspects of the child's personality will be revealed without the child's appreciating what is happening. A child's reactions to winning and losing, how competitive a child is, if a child is prone to cheat, if a child plays aggressively or passively, and if the child shows forethought and planning may be revealed in the course of playing the game (Gardner, 1969a, 1986a). Games may also be fun and therefore therapeutic in their own right in that pleasure is generally therapeutic. These benefits notwithstanding, the disadvantages of the utilization of these games generally far outweighs their advantages. The time during which useful information is being gained about the child often represents an extremely small fraction of the therapeutic session. The rest of the time is just spent playing a game. When most of the other instruments described in this chapter are utilized, there is often a higher frequency of meaningful material being provided.

For many therapists the utilization of traditional competitive board games is essentially a "cop out." They require little therapeutic talent or skill, and the therapist can rationalize that useful therapy is being accomplished when, in actuality, all the therapist is doing is whiling away the time with the child by playing games. Obviously, more uncooperative and inhibited children are likely to be engaged by such instruments. The hope of some therapists is that after some period spent on this relatively low-key activity, the child will be groomed for deeper, more introspective treatment. The danger of such an approach is that after many months, and even years, this goal may never be reached (the usual situation). Other more predictably successful resistance-reducing approaches (mentioned throughout this book), might have been utilized with a better chance of a positive therapeutic outcome. Play therapy should be much more *therapy* than play. The use of these games is often much more *play* than therapy.

CONCLUDING COMMENTS

Most of the therapeutic instruments described in this chapter are designed to elicit fantasies from children. Such utilization is based on the theory that self-created fantasies may be a rich source of psychodynamic information about the processes that underly the child's symptomatology. The therapist must appreciate, however, that eliciting this material too quickly, especially in the very guarded, fragile, and borderline child, may frighten the child and thereby induce resistances to self-revelation that would not have occurred if the therapist had proceeded more cautiously. Therefore, therapists do well to hold off encouraging such inhibited children to reveal themselves until later in treatment, after a trusting relationship has been established.

Most of the techniques described in this chapter are basically those that I was familiarized with during the course of my residency during the late 1950s. I have discussed what I consider to be the advantages and drawbacks to most of them. As mentioned in Chapter One, my educational background was such that I was strongly encouraged to attempt to provide improvements of work of which I was critical. The rest of this book, in a sense, can be viewed as an attempt to rectify the deficiencies and drawbacks of the techniques described in this chapter. In addition, it represents an attempt to enrich and expand upon those therapeutic modalities that I consider worthy of utilization and perpetuation.

THREE

Central Elements in the Psychotherapeutic Process

A good man is one who knows what he feels, says what he means, and means what he says.

Hasidic saying

A teacher affects eternity; he can never tell where his influence stops.

Henry Brooks Adams

The theoretical principles presented here regarding the origin of symptoms and the central elements in the psychotherapeutic process are applicable to children, adolescents, and adults. Although the general principles presented here apply to all three age categories, there are differences in the therapeutic application of these principles regarding the degree to which the therapist relies on the patient to make active contributions to the treatment. The younger the child, the more it behooves the therapist to actively elicit, encourage, and even suggest the ways in which the child should respond to particular life situations that are causing difficulties. The older the patient the more the therapist should encourage (and at times require) the patient to contribute him- or herself to the solutions to these life problems. But even with the most mature and healthy patient, a certain amount of suggestion and introduction of behavioral solutions are warranted.

THE ORIGIN OF SYMPTOMS

I view symptoms to represent maladaptive and inappropriate ways of dealing with the problems of life with which we are all confronted. The patient's selections of solutions to these problems have originally been devised because they appeared to be the most judicious. What we refer to as psychodynamics are basically the pathways and processes by which these problems produce symptoms. Symptoms then can be viewed as the "tip of the iceberg"—the most superficial manifestations of the disease process. At the base of the iceberg are the fundamental problems of life for which the symptom represents an injudicious solution. Between the base and the tip of the iceberg are the processes by which the symptomatic solution is created. These processes are called psychodynamics.

The iceberg analogy holds because most of the etiological processes that are operative in the symptoms' formation are not apparent to conscious awareness; it is as if they were submerged. (In the case of the iceberg, six-sevenths is under water.) What is above the surface is well viewed to be the conscious material (what is readily observable), and what is below the surface is well considered to be subconscious (not immediately in conscious awareness, but readily available to such scrutiny) and unconscious (not readily available to conscious awareness, but potentially so via such procedures as psychoanalytic therapy, especially dream psychoanalysis).

As an example of the above let us take Bob's situation. Bob is eight years old and in the third grade. His teacher has informed the class that there will be a big test the next day. Bob is quite upset about this because he was looking forward to watching his favorite television program. The problem then for Bob is whether he should watch his program or study for the test. If he indulges himself and watches the TV program he may get a low grade on the next day's examination. A good grade might only be obtained by his depriving himself of the television program. Bob is being confronted here with one of the common dilemmas of just about all schoolchildren. Bob is facing one of the fundamental problems of life which, like all such problems, lends itself well to the utilization of maladaptive solutions.

Bob decides to watch the program in the hope that he will be lucky enough to know the answers to the questions his teacher selects to give on the test (already we sense trouble, that is, a maladaptive solution). On the next day, as luck would have it, Bob finds that he doesn't know the answers to most of the questions. In order to protect himself from the embarrassments and discomfort of getting a poor grade, he decides to copy from the paper of the little girl sitting next to him. Such behavior is called *cheating*, a symptom. Like all symptoms, it is an inappropriate adaptation and may result in more trouble and discomfort for Bob than that which he would have suffered had he studied for the test and deprived himself of the gratifications of watching his favorite television program.

Now let us consider the possible outcomes of Bob's symptomatic resolution of this conflict. One outcome is that the teacher will catch him cheating, scold him, give him a failing grade, and possibly report the event to his parents. He may then suffer further disapprobation at home. Perhaps the teacher won't catch him but his classmates observe what he is doing. He may suffer from them a certain amount of criticism and alienation. Or, the girl from whom he is cheating may get angry at him, cover her paper, and then may reject him subsequently as a "cheater." Perhaps none of these occur and he appears to be "successful." However, when the grades come back, and Bob sees that he has gotten a high one, if he has anything approaching healthy superego development, he is likely to feel less proud of his high grade than he would have had he come by it honestly. In his heart he knows that it was not deserved and so he cannot enjoy the gratification he otherwise would have had he achieved his high grade by honest effort.

All of these outcomes are examples of the principle that the selection of the symptomatic solution generally results in the individual's suffering with more difficulties than he or she would have if the more judicious and healthy solution had been utilized. In this case it would have been Bob's deciding to forego the pleasures of television and appreciating that such deprivation would ultimately be less painful than the discomforts and embarrassments associated with the consequences of his cheating.

However, the possibility still remains that Bob could have cheated and *not* suffered any of the above difficulties. Let us suppose there was no negative feedback from any of the aforementioned individuals (that is, "he got away with it") and his superego development was so limited that he suffered no guilt or remorse over his behavior—behavior that would generally be considered unacceptable in the classroom. But even then there would be the untoward effect of his not having gained the optimum benefit from his educational process. His failure to study would have deprived him of the information learned by those who had studied. Although this outcome might not have caused Bob any immediate discomfort, in the long run, especially if this pattern were repeated, Bob's education would suffer. Thus, the aforementioned principle still holds.

Another example: A boy does not have friends because of personality problems. However, he learns that he need not suffer loneliness very long if he provides peers with candy, toys, and other presents. His utilization of *bribery* (the name of the symptom) is seemingly successful in that he now finds himself more popular. He enjoys thereby an alleviation of the painful feelings of loneliness. However, his pleasure is compromised by the inner knowledge that his friends are being bought and that they would not be there if he did not have the wherewithal to pay them off. In addition, his position is a precarious one because he does not have a steady supply of bribes to insure that he will not once again be lonely. And this unstable feeling also compromises his pleasure. At some level he probably senses that his "friends" do not basically respect him, and this cannot but lower his feelings of self-worth. Last, if and when he does run out of bribes (the usual case), he cannot but feel "used." Bribing, the psychopathological symptom, was devised in an attempt to deal with the common human problem of loneliness. Ostensibly, it served its purpose of providing friends; however, it was an injudicious selection. As is usually the case when psychopathological symptoms are used to resolve a problem, the individual usually ends up being worse off than he or she was before.

Jim is afraid to join *Little League*. He fantasizes public humiliation if he strikes out at bat or if he drops a ball in the course of the game's action. Jim is a well-coordinated boy, and there is no reason to believe that he would humiliate himself to a significant degree. He chooses to take the safe course and doesn't try out for *Little League* and thereby protects himself from his anticipated humiliations. The solution that Jim has chosen does "work" in that he doesn't suffer the tensions he would have experienced had he joined. However, he suffers even worse repercussions as a result of his withdrawal. He becomes somewhat lonely in that when his friends are playing baseball, he has little to do. But more important, he has deprived himself of the ego-enhancing gratifications that he would have gained as the result of his participation. He has deprived himself of the joys of playing well in an area in which he has every reason to believe he would have been competent.

There is an extremely important principle demonstrated here that pervades many aspects of living. Most new things are anxiety provoking. The healthy person tolerates such fear with the knowledge that it is usually transient and that the benefits to be derived outweigh the loss of joy and ego-enhancement to be suffered from failure to act. The philosophy is epitomized in the aphorism: *Nothing ventured, nothing gained.* All individuals can choose the safe course and avoid risk and anxiety. In the extreme, the individual psychologically digs a hole in the ground, hides therein, thereby protecting him- or herself from the vast majority of life's rejections, disappointments, indignities, and traumas. However, a heavy price is paid for such "safety." One leads an extremely boring existence, and one is deprived of the ego-enhancement that comes from accomplishment. Again, the psychopathological solution to this problem causes the individual more difficulty than he or she would have suffered had the healthier course been pursued.

Here is another example common to childhood. While playing alone with a ball, Jane accidentally breaks a neighbor's window. To the best of her knowledge, no one has observed the incident. A conflict is immediately set up. On the one hand, she would like to run away as fast as she can and thereby avoid any responsibility or repercussions for the damage. On the other hand, part of her appreciates that such flight would be "wrong" and that she would not respect herself for doing so. Furthermore, she might be observed and then would suffer punishment for having "run from the scene of the crime." Jane decides to take her chances and run as fast as she can. She gets home and breathes a sigh of relief. To the best of her knowledge she was unobserved, and she feels that she has "gotten away with it." However, there is some lingering guilt and fear that she might have been seen and that word of her misdeed will ultimately get to her parents. So even at this stage the pathological course is not without its negative repercussions. She is enjoying the pleasure of not having to own up to her responsibility for her transgression, but her pleasure is compromised by her guilt and fear of disclosure. Of course, if her superego development has been impaired, she will not suffer this guilt and she truly will have "gotten away with it." Last, if she were observed, and the incident is reported to her parents, then she is likely to suffer repercussions for her flight.

Had she gone to the neighbor and reported the incident, she would probably have been respected and even praised for her honesty, even though the neighbor might have been angry as well. If she offered to pay for the window, she would have to suffer the privations attendant to such payment. However, this negative element would have been offset by the ego-enhancement that comes with the knowledge that one is doing the "right" thing. In addition, she might have been praised by others for her honesty, and this could further enhance feelings of self-worth. She would have avoided the guilt and fear of detection that she might have suffered following the commission of her "crime." The ancient aphorism *honesty is the best policy* is not trite. There is great wisdom in it. The honest course usually (though certainly not always) is the best course because its advantages usually outweigh its disadvantages. People who utilize psychopathological mechanisms for resolving disputes may not be aware of this ancient truth.

Now, some examples from adult life. A man is very dissatisfied with his boss. He dreads going to work most days because of the indignities he suffers in his office. He is a somewhat timid person who fears expressing resentment. He feels that if he were to assert himself with his employer he might lose his job. In addition, even if he were not to lose his job, he is afraid of his boss's anger. These fears contribute significantly to his failure to assert himself and to discuss in a civilized manner the problems he has with his employer. Most often (but not always) such failure to assert oneself is pathological. It is a heavy price to pay for job security and protection from the possible resentment of the person to whom a complaint is directed.

A healthier course for this man would be to assert himself and make reasonable attempts to resolve the conflict with his boss. If he is successful in this regard, he will have accomplished his goal of a better work relationship with his boss. In addition, he will have reduced, if not eliminated, his loathing of work as well as the self-loathing that comes with repression and suppression of pent-up resentment. He will enjoy the sense of well-being that comes with successful resolution of a problem. However, such assertion could conceivably result in his being fired. This repercussion will have to be taken into consideration before he decides to assert himself. Having made the decision to act, he must bear this risk. He might even have to suffer the discomforts of trying to find another job, and he might not even be able to find one. He has to consider the discomforts and loss of self-worth that come with unemployment and being a public charge. Although these are certainly formidable negative repercussions of self-assertion, the man would at least be free from the self-loathing and the painful effects of not expressing his resentments.

Another example from adult life. A teller in a bank makes an error. Although some discrepancy will ultimately be detected in the accounting process, the person who caused the error may not readily be identified. The teller knows that if she reveals the error, there might be some criticism and reprimand. However, her position is such that it is extremely unlikely that she would lose her job. Moreover, if she says nothing, there may be no repercussions because the process of detecting the person who made the error is so cumbersome that the company accountants may not wish to go to the trouble. Or, another person might be falsely implicated. She decides to say nothing. During the ensuing days she hears talk about the repercussions of her mistake and the resentment felt by her superiors toward the individual (still unknown) who could have been so careless. Although "innocent," she suffers with the fear of disclosure and some guilt. Had she admitted the error, there would have been some criticism, but no job loss and no ongoing fear of disclosure. The pathological way seemed easier at first but ended up being the more difficult course.

I do not claim that the examples given above explore in great depth all the ramifications of a psychological act. They focus on the symptom as a manifestation of the individual's attempt to find the solution to a common, if not universal, life problem. They demonstrate how the pathological solution causes the individual more trouble than the healthy one. The examples have not focused on complex psychodynamic factors that play a role in determining whether the individual chooses the healthy or pathological adaptation to the conflict. Nor have I elucidated the psychodynamic pattern by which the fundamental conflict brings about the symptomatic solution.

THERAPY AS A WAY
OF OPENING UP NEW OPTIONS

Therapy involves helping people learn better ways of dealing with these inevitable conflicts and problems. Therapy must open up new options—options that may not have been considered by the patient previously, options that may not have been part of his or her repertoire. The utilization of these more adaptive solutions *over time* lessens the likelihood that the patient will have to resort to the maladaptive, symptomatic solutions. In Bob's case (the boy who cheated on the test), the therapist might have tried to help him appreciate in advance how short-sighted was his decision to indulge himself in television viewing without giving serious consideration to the potential consequences of his utilizing the cheating solution. In the course of such a discussion, the therapist might have asked Bob if he could think of any other solution to his dilemma. If Bob's family owned a video cassette recorder, then the option of making a videotape of the program and studying at the same time could have been discussed. Then, he could watch the program on the weekend and so both television watching and studying would have been accomplished. Or, if Bob himself doesn't own a video cassette recorder, he could be asked if he had a friend who might be prevailed upon to tape the program for him. The videotape recorder resolution, then, becomes a new option—an option that may not have previously been considered by Bob. Once utilized, this solution might become an automatic consideration for Bob when confronted in the future with this conflict. Although this new option originated in treatment, it can now become a part of Bob's repertoire of options.

In each of the other examples, the therapist could have helped the patient consider healthier options. The boy who used bribes "to gain friendships" could have been helped to appreciate the precariousness of his situation and the lowered feeling of self-worth that comes from being so utilized. Jim, the boy who was afraid to join *Little League*, could have been helped to appreciate the wisdom of "nothing ventured, nothing gained"—that those who do not venture forth will often lead very lonely and unrewarding lives. Jane, the girl who accidentally broke a neighbor's window, could have been helped to appreciate that it was ultimately to her benefit to take the initially painful but more courageous course of admitting her guilt. And the man who was dissatisfied with his boss could be helped to appreciate that the security and ego-enhancement potentially derived from healthy and civilized self-assertion are much more likely to outweigh the risks and disadvantages associated with passive submission. The teller in the bank could have been helped to appreciate the wisdom of the "honesty is the best policy" aphorism.

COMMENTS ON TIME-LIMITED THERAPY

The reader may recall that in the above discussion on therapy as a way of opening up new options, the words *over time* are italicized. My purpose here is to emphasize the point that meaningful therapeutic changes are not likely to take place quickly. Although there are rare occasions when a brief encounter with the therapist can bring about long-term therapeutic results, such situations are unusual. Therapy first requires the establishment of a meaningful therapist-patient relationship (to be discussed in detail in Chapter Four). In the context of such a relationship, therapeutic messages are received by the patient with receptivity and therapeutic experiences take place that, when repeated over time, bring about personality change. Freud feared that psychoanalysis would degenerate in the United States because of the lack of patience that Americans had for solutions that might require a long-term investment of time and energy. He feared that the method would be bastardized by a wide variety of quick and seemingly attractive short cures. And he was right. Short-term methods of treatment have sprung up everywhere and promise better, more rapid, and less expensive results than long-term psychoanalytic therapy or psychoanalysis. I consider this to be a deplorable development. It is not that I do not have criticisms of psychoanalytic treatment (many have been and will continue to be presented in this book); it is only that I am critical of quick methods of treatment, especially those that promise results in a prescribed period of time, even before the patient's problems are known.

Short-term and brief psychotherapies are very much in vogue. Often a specific time limit is imposed upon the patient from the outset. Ten to fifteen sessions is a common figure. The selection of such a number demonstrates complete ignorance of what I consider to be a crucial requirement of meaningful psychotherapy. One cannot possibly know how long it will take to develop the kind of relationship in which meaningful therapy is most likely to be productive. Furthermore, the imposed time limits are likely to compromise significantly the nature of the work accomplished in each of the sessions. If the patient is watching the clock, is pressured into working quickly, and is trying to figure out a solution to a particular problem within time limitations, it is likely that the solutions so derived will be injudiciously selected.

If a boy were to call up a girl and ask her to go out with him for ten dates and then break up, he would be considered strange. If a man asked a woman to marry him for twelve days, weeks, months, or even years—and then to divorce—he would probably be considered by the woman to be insane. Yet the same kind of arrangement is frequently made between therapists and patients, and there are many who do not consider this absurd. It is not that I do not do brief psychotherapy. I do it all the time, but I only do it in situations where happily it takes place. It occurs in situations where I cannot know beforehand how long the treatment will take, and in some cases it does indeed turn out to be brief. But I have never promised it would be brief at the outset because I could not know the degree to which the parties would cooperate, whether or not a relationship would be established, whether there would be receptivity to what I had to say, and what things would come up in the course of the treatment.

Psychotherapy in which a patient is told at the outset that a specific number of sessions is all that will be required is basically a "rip off" by clinical administrators on a gullible public. It is one way of rationalizing giving a little therapy to a lot of people rather than a lot of therapy to a select few. If one is going to do this, then one should at least be honest and let people know that they are getting a watered-down form of treatment. Time-limited therapy is mainly for the poor, who often have little choice. People who are in better financial positions most often get as much treatment as they need. And those rich people who do opt for brief psychotherapy are often the naive and gullible ones, those who, despite their financial positions, are still simple-minded enough to be attracted to this absurd form of treatment.

THE THERAPIST-PATIENT RELATIONSHIP

If patients are to experience an alleviation (the reader should note that I did not use the word *cure* here) of the presenting symptomatology, it is highly desirable that both the therapist and the patient possess certain qualities. The importance of the therapist-patient relationship in therapy is often spoken of. However, the specific personality qualities that are important for each to possess and the ways in which these bring about symptomatic alleviation and therapeutic change are not often elaborated upon. The main reason for this, I believe, is that these issues have not been studied to the degree that is warranted. I present here a few of the important elements that I consider necessary to be present in each party if therapy is to be meaningful. Only basic principles will be presented here. In Chapter Four I will discuss these principles in greater detail, especially as they apply to child psychotherapy.

Genuine Respect vs. Idealization and/or Idolization of the Therapist

The patient should be reasonably respectful of the therapist because of *actual* qualities that the therapist has that engender such respect. Idealization (viewing the therapist as perfect) and idolizing (viewing as God-like, worthy of worship) of the therapist is antitherapeutic in that it creates unfavorable comparisons with the therapist that are ego-debasing to the patient and makes it unlikely that the patient will relate realistically to other human beings who will inevitably reveal their deficits. The classical analytic model, especially, is likely to result in such distortions of the therapist. One might argue that the kind of "blank screen" created by the analyst sitting behind the couch will provide him or her with the "purest" kinds of free associations, associations that are less likely to be contaminated by input from the analyst. However, whatever benefits there are to be derived from this approach (and I do not deny that they exist), there is a heavy price to be paid for them—a price that far outweighs the benefits. As stated, one of the prices is that the patient, having been studiously deprived of vital information about the therapist, is likely to view him or her as being perfect or close to it. This is intrinsically ego-debasing because it produces unfavorable comparisons between the patient and the therapist. Feelings of low self-worth are intrinsically associated with most (if not all) forms of psychogenic psychopathology. Idealizing and idolizing the therapist only adds to this disparity. Furthermore, this unreal atmosphere interferes with the patient's relating to others in the world who will inevitably reveal their deficits and who will not provide the patient with the same kind of accepting and tolerant environment that the therapist provides.

We live in a world where certain conspiracies of silence are prevalent. When speaking with someone in a social situation it is generally considered inappropriate to criticize directly the individual's spouse or analyst. A woman, for example, may meet someone at a cocktail party who tells her that she is in treatment with Dr. X. The listener may know that Dr. X's general reputation at the hospital is that everyone of his five wives despised him. In addition, two of them might have been personal friends of hers so she knows first-hand that this is the case. Yet, she may not reveal any of this information to Dr. X's patient, lest she "rock the boat" and/or compromise the treatment. I believe that it would be far better for the listener to present the information that she knows even at the risk of its being somewhat distorted. The information would certainly serve as "grist for the mill" during the next session. As a result of the patient's confronting her therapist with this information, there could be one of two outcomes. The patient might decide to leave the therapist, from the recognition that his personality deficiencies are so grave that it is not likely he can be of help to her. Or, she might decide to stay in treatment because of the appreciation that Dr. X still has enough on the positive side to warrant his remaining an effective therapist. In either case she is less likely to view him as a perfect person, and this cannot but be therapeutic.

Receptivity to the Therapist's Messages

The patient should be receptive to the therapist's comments, but not to the point of gullibility. If there has been no idealization or idolizing of the therapist, then there is less likely to be gullibility. If there is a good relationship and genuine respect, that is, respect based on genuine qualities that the therapist possesses and exhibits (as opposed to fantasized ones), then there is a greater likelihood that there will be healthy receptivity. Respect must be earned, and healthy respect is not likely to be earned in a fantasized relationship. Healthy respect is based on knowledge of both a person's assets and liabilities. When there is healthy respect, the balance tips in favor of those qualities that engender respect in others. In such situations people recognize another's liabilities but consider them small in comparison to assets. It is only by judicious revelation of deficiencies (to be discussed in detail in various parts of this book) that such genuine respect is likely to evolve.

Identification with and Emulation of the Therapist

There should be a reasonable desire to emulate qualities in the therapist that would serve the person well in life. (This may be conscious or unconscious.) As a result of such emulation, there will be some identification with the therapist's traits and values. I do not believe that there is any psychotherapeutic interchange that does not involve some attempt on the therapist's part to transmit his or her own values to the patient. It is hoped that the values and qualities so taken on will be in the patient's best interests.

There are many who take issue with what I have just said about identification with the therapist's traits and values. Many have been taught in their training that one should strictly avoid doing or saying anything, either implicitly or explicitly, that involves the communication of, let alone imposition of, the therapist's values on the patient. I believe that this is well-meaning but injudicious advice. I cannot imagine a psychotherapeutic interchange that does not involve, at some level, the process of transmission of the therapist's values to the patient. Even in silence such imposition is taking place. Implicit in the therapist's silence is the message: "What you're saying is all right with me. I don't think it warrants any comment on my part. I don't have any books that say it is unhealthy, inappropriate, unreasonable, or otherwise maladaptive."

When we use the word "values" we refer to that which we consider to be good and bad, right and wrong. The therapist is continually making such judgments. At times, however, the term sick and healthy may be utilized. But even here, values are intrinsically present in that what we refer to as psychopathological is basically an opinion regarding whether or not the behavior is good or bad, right or wrong. And this is very much determined by the "eye of the beholder." A mother brings a seven-year-old boy to the psychotherapist with the complaint that, although of superior intelligence, the child shows little academic motivation or curiosity. The therapist, after detailed inquiry into the family life, decides that the child has psychological problems that stem from family difficulties. The therapist recommends a therapeutic approach in which the child is treated individually along with active work with the family. The goal here is to reduce those family tensions and pressures that are contributing to the child's difficulties. The goal, as well, is to help the child himself deal with these family stresses in such a way that academic performance returns to the expected level.

By the therapist's agreeing to treat this patient, he or she is implicitly subscribing to the value judgment that education is a "good" thing and that those who do not avail themselves of their educational opportunities are doing a "bad" thing. One could argue that this is only the therapist's personal opinion. One could say (as many in our society do) that all one needs to do in life is to learn how to sign an X on one's welfare check. Under these circumstances, one will receive (in cash, goods, and services) almost as much as the average working man or woman (especially woman) or perhaps 10 to 15% less. By agreeing to treat this child and help this child reach his academic potential, the therapist is implicitly subscribing to the parents' value judgment that education is a "good" thing. I personally happen to share this value, but I am very clear that it is a value nevertheless.

Another example: A 35-year-old man enters treatment with complaints of depression and excessive drinking. He fears that he may become an alcoholic. In the course of the history taking, the therapist learns that the man's father died when he was in grade school and that he is an only child. Although 35, he still lives with his mother. He does not consider this to be a problem, rather he states that he and his mother have agreed that both would be unreceptive to any therapeutic approach that might ultimately result in his leaving home. It may be the therapist's opinion (supported by many books in his library) that this man has an "unresolved Oedipus complex" and that he is far too old to be living with his mother. Consistent with this opinion, one of the aims of therapy should be to help this man "resolve his Oedipus complex," move out of the house, meet a woman, get married, and have children—like other normal, healthy human beings. Although I am in agreement with this goal (even though I might not agree that the man's problems relate to the so-called "Oedipus complex") I recognize that my position on this subject is still a value judgment. An anthropologist might say that there is an island in the South Pacific where people do this routinely. (There is always an island in the South Pacific where one can justify practically any conclusion regarding human behavior!) Again, my point here is that the therapist cannot take a position on a therapeutic issue without an implicit attempt to impose his or her own values on the patient. In short we must be honest about the fact that we are "brainwashing" our patients. We must also accept the fact that in the context of such brainwashing, many patients have been done terrible disservices and much grief has been caused by such impositions.

Accordingly, therapy is a very "risky business." This problem of value imposition is further compounded by the fact that whether or not one sees something as good or bad is highly individualized and strongly determined by what the therapist brings to the situation, that is, his or her own anticipations, hopes, and even neurotic distortions. The point is well made by the anecdote of the rabbi who dies and finds himself in the hereafter, but he doesn't know whether he's in heaven or hell. He's not experiencing very much pain, so he decides he's probably not in hell. But he's not enjoying very much pleasure either, so he concludes that he's probably not in heaven. As he's groping about, trying to determine where he is, he suddenly sees coming out of the distant clouds none other than Rabbi Isaac Cohen (his mentor from the Talmudic Academy, dead now these 30 years). Rabbi Cohen, he well recalls, was one of the most religious and pious men he ever knew. In his 87 years in life he never broke one rule, so pious was he. Happily, he runs toward his old mentor. He then notices that standing next to the old, stooped man's side is a beautiful, young, voluptuous woman—obviously the old rabbi's companion. The two rabbis embrace, tears running down their cheeks, happy to see one another after all these years.

At this point, the younger rabbi states: "Rabbi Cohen, it's so good to see you here. I've been roaming about, lost. I didn't know whether I was in heaven or hell. But it's obvious that if *you* are here, this must be heaven! A more religious and pious man never lived. It's obvious, also, that this beautiful, young voluptuous woman is God's reward to you for all the good works you've done on earth!"

To which the old rabbi replies: "I'm sorry to have to tell you, rabbi, two things. First, this is not heaven, this is *hell*. And second, this beautiful, gorgeous, voluptuous woman is *not* God's reward to me. I am her punishment!"

The anecdote demonstrates my point that the aspirations and hopes that one brings to a situation are going to be an important determinant of how one interprets it. Shakespeare's Hamlet put it well: "There's nothing either good or bad, but thinking makes it so." The point is demonstrated again in a wonderful scene from the Woody Allen movie, *Annie Hall*. In a split-screen vignette, Woody Allen is on one side complaining to his psychoanalyst; and Diane Keaton is on the other side, complaining to her analyst. Woody is complaining bitterly about Diane's lack of sexual receptivity to him. He complains about how "up tight" she is and how painful is his ongoing state of sexual frustration. The deprivation is driving him crazy and he's practically tearing his hair out so distraught is he over his sexual privation. When the analyst asks him how often he is having sexual relations, he replies, "Imagine, only two or three times a week."

At the same time, Diane Keaton is complaining that Woody is continually bothering her with his sexual advances, from the moment he gets up in the morning, throughout the course of the day, until the moment he goes to sleep at night. He rarely gives her any peace. In the course of her complaining she refers to him as an animal. After further complaints about Woody's insatiable lust, her analyst asks Diane how frequently she is having sexual relations. To which she replies, "Imagine, two to three times a week, the beast." The vignette demonstrates well my point regarding the role of "the eye of the beholder" in determining whether something is good or bad, right or wrong. Therapists are no exception. Our value judgments are colored by our own experiences, anticipations, and aspirations. And these inevitably will be transmitted to our patients. Let us hope that we don't do too much damage.

Most have heard at some time or other anecdotes about people who are looking for "the secret of life"—the one great wisdom under which is encompassed all the meaning of life's experiences. The jokes and/or stories often involve seeking the secret from some guru, often seated in some mountain cave in India or high in the Himalayas. Finally after a long circuitous route, during which time the individual may be exposed to many dangers, the wise man is finally confronted with the question: "What is the secret (or meaning) of life?" Well, I have the answer here for the reader. (Remember, it was I who told it to you.) The secret of life is this: *Life is a Rorschach test!* Yes, that's it. Life is a Rorschach test. Under this dictum one can subsume all the experiences in life. In every experience there is the reality and there is the interpretation that we make of it, depending upon our own psychic structure. There is the Rorschach inkblot, and there is the patient's projection which gives meaning to the inkblot. There is the external reality, and there is the interpretation we give to it. There is the glass of water, and there is our interpretation as to whether it is half empty or half full, or whatever other meaning we want to give to it. The reality then is not simply an external entity. Rather, it is a *combination* of an external entity and the meaning and interpretation that our internal psychic structure gives to it. Then the two together determine our thoughts, feelings, and actions. Let us hope that our projections and our interpretations of what is good and bad for our patients will serve them well.

Trying to Help Patients vs. Helping Patients

The therapist should have a genuine desire to help the patient. There should be a reasonable degree of sympathy (an intellectual process) and empathy (an emotional resonance) with the patient. Therapists should have a reasonable capacity to identify with their patients, that is, put themselves in their patients' positions to view situations from their vantage point. The therapist's goal should be that of *trying* to help the patient, but he or she should not feel that the failure to do so represents a failure in him- or herself. I have emphasized the word *trying* because many therapists consider it their goal to "cure" patients or to bring about significant improvements. Many such therapists suffer with what I call *The Statue of Liberty syndrome.* This name is derived from a poem, written by Emma Lazarus, a poem that was placed at the base of the statue when it arrived in this country in 1886. It says:

> Give me your tired, your poor,
> Your huddled masses yearning to breathe free,
> The wretched refuse of your teaming shore,
> Send these, the homeless,
>   the tempest-tossed to me.
> I lift my lamp beside the golden door.

These lines are certainly inspiring. With the exception of those who are American Indians and those who trace their heritage to pre-Columbian days in South America, all of us are either immigrants ourselves or are the descendants of immigrants, either recent or remote. This principle, however, is extended by many mental health professionals to:

> Give me your chronic hebephrenic schizophrenics,
> Your alcoholics, your drug addicts, your criminals,
> Your psychopaths, your prostitutes,
> And all your other rejects from society.
> I will give them sympathy, empathy, and understanding.
> With analytically oriented psychotherapy,
> I will help them gain insight into the underlying psychological
>   processes that cause their disorders.
> And with such treatment I will raise them to new heights of
>   mental health.

Those therapists who exhibit manifestations of *The Statue of Liberty syndrome*, whether they realize it or not, are placing terrible demands upon themselves. They are doomed to suffer frustration because their claims are impossible to achieve. The pathology that we deal with (even the less severe types) is generally generations in the making, and it is therefore grandiose on the part of anyone to believe that he or she can help more than a small fraction of those who come our way.

We generally interview parents of our child patients, and often get information about grandparents. But we rarely get information about earlier generations. Yet, it is naive to assume that the influences of these ancestors have not played a role in our patients' pathology. Furthermore, we are often impotent to change the formidable social and cultural factors that are likely to have played a role in the development of our patients' psychopathology. Accordingly, therapists do well to have very modest goals in regard to the treatment of their patients. We should be comfortable with small changes. To believe that we can do more is to impose upon ourselves goals that may be extremely frustrating for us. The therapist's goal should be that of *trying*. The therapist should be able to say, after a failure, that he or she has worked to the best of his or her ability. That is all that we can ask of ourselves and that is all that our patients should be asking of us.

Those who are afflicted with *The Statue of Liberty syndrome* are welcomed by various individuals in our society. Jails are overcrowded and judges are happy to learn about people who claim that they will bring about the prevention of criminal recidivism. School principals are happy to "get off the hook" by telling complaining parents that a troublemaking child is "in therapy." Even worse is the principal who tells parents that if their child does not go into therapy he or she will be discharged from the school. (This is an extremely misguided statement and compromises significantly the likelihood of the child's being helped by treatment.) Last, therapists who try too hard are likely to defeat their own purposes because the pressures placed on the patient are apt to lessen the likelihood that treatment will be effective.

I have discussed here, somewhat briefly, some of the elements that I consider central to the meaningful therapist-patient relationship. In Chapter Four I will elaborate upon these and discuss in detail other factors I consider to be important. Throughout the course of this book I will provide examples of the implementation of these principles.

THERAPY—AN EDUCATIONAL EXPERIENCE

In the context of a good therapist-patient relationship, the therapist helps the patient learn better how to deal with the fundamental problems and conflicts of life with which we all are confronted and must deal in the course of our existence. After a detailed study of the factors operative in bringing about change in psychoanalysis (one form of psychotherapy), H. Strupp (1975) concluded that the most important elements in bringing about therapeutic change were the "lessons in constructive living" that the patient learned. I am in full agreement with Strupp on this point. The more judiciously and intelligently a person deals with the problems of life, the less likely it is that the individual will resort to pathological modes of adaptation. Therapy, more than anything else, should enhance one's capacity to deal with life's challenges. Therapy, more than anything else, involves helping people learn how to deal with these inevitable problems. The younger the patient, the more guidance, advice and instruction the therapist should be willing to provide, and the older the patient, the more the therapist should facilitate the patient's finding his or her own solutions to these problems. However, even with the most mature adults, some guidance and instruction is warranted *after* the patient has made every reasonable attempt to resolve the problem him- or herself. Accordingly, the therapeutic process is very similar to the educational.

The Therapist as Teacher

This similarity between the educational and therapeutic processes goes further. An important determinant of whether a student will learn from the teacher relates to whether the student will identify with the teacher. Teachers who are bored with teaching or unmotivated and watch the clock throughout the day are not likely to teach their students very much. In contrast, teachers who are enthusiastic, who genuinely enjoy learning and teaching what they themselves have learned, are much more likely to impart knowledge to their students. The former teach little, the latter are likely to create an atmosphere in which their students are swept up in the learning process. An important factor in this process is that of identification with the teacher. Children in the classrooms of the enthusiastic teacher want to "join in on the fun," and they thereby imitate the teacher in order to derive similar enjoyments. We learn best from those we admire and respect, and we are going to learn little from those who produce little desire for identification and emulation. Worse yet is the teacher who is feared. She not only teaches her students little, if anything, but may contribute to a generalized distaste and revulsion of the educational process and the development of psychopathology as well.

The Levels of Therapeutic Learning

Intellectual and Emotional Learning The therapeutic learning process occurs at many levels. I believe that the *least* efficacious is the intellectual. An intellectual insight acquired by the patient is, however, more useful than one provided by the therapist. Classical analytic treatment focuses heavily on the intellectual. It is based on the theory that the primary way of bringing about clinical change is to help the patient gain conscious insight into the unconscious processes that are bringing about the psychopathology: "Where there is unconscious, there shall conscious be." As will be discussed in detail throughout this book, I believe that this focus on intellectualization robs both the therapist and the patient of more predictably therapeutic experiences. When emotions are associated with intellectual learning, there is a greater likelihood of change. Classical analysts appreciate this and recognize that an emotional loading adds clout to an intellectual insight and is more likely to be remembered.

The Metaphor   Metaphorical communications are especially potent. Aristotle recognized this long ago and considered the metaphor to be the richest and most valuable form of verbal communication (Poetics, 1459a):

> The greatest thing by far is to be a master of the metaphor; it is the one thing that cannot be learned from others; and it is also a sign of genius, since a good metaphor implies an intuitive perception of the similarity in the dissimilar.

A metaphor is basically a figure of speech in which two entities, which have no intrinsic relationship with one another, are equated. An example of a metaphor would be: "He is a rock!" There is no intrinsic relationship between a rock and a particular man. However, when one equates them, one provides a statement that is richer than the two separate entities that are being equated. The whole here is indeed greater than the sum of its parts. "She is a flower" is another example of a metaphor. Probably the greatest creator of metaphors in the English language was William Shakespeare. One of my favorites is from *MacBeth*. One could say that life is transient and that before you know it, it's over. However, one could also say, as does MacBeth (v, 5):

> Out, out brief candle!
> Life's but a walking shadow, a poor player
> That struts and frets his hour upon the stage
> And then is heard no more: it is a tale
> Told by an idiot full of sounds and fury,
> Signifying nothing.

The same message, but obviously Shakespeare's way of putting it makes the initial statement weak and sterile. I do not believe that the creation of metaphors can be taught. The ability to see linkages where others do not and to make the proper selections so that rich metaphors are formed is a talent that I believe to be inborn. Of course, we therapists do not have the creative capacity of William Shakespeare, and our ability to form metaphors is far more limited. However, to the degree that we can utilize them in our work, to that degree we will enhance the efficacy of our therapeutic communications.

Metaphors become even more enriched when incorporated into the context of allegories, anecdotes, and other narrative forms. This is not only true of children who traditionally enjoy stories, but of adults as well in that they will often learn better from a well-selected anecdote or the relating of an experience by the therapist. M. Erikson (J. Haley, 1973) was especially appreciative of the value of the metaphor in therapy. My main criticism of his work, however, is that the metaphors he would often present to his patients appeared to be "pulled out of the sky" and were not, I suspect, as carefully tailored to the needs of the patient as he professed. I say this because the information upon which he would often select his metaphor was often miniscule and, accordingly, his metaphorical presentations often had a high degree of speculation.

Conceptualizations and Abstractions vs. Concrete Examples
Conceptualizations and abstractions are far less potent vehicles for clarifying issues than specific concrete examples, especially examples that relate to the patient's immediate experiences. Many therapeutic interchanges are quite sterile and therapeutically unproductive because the therapist and the patient are speaking at abstract levels. It is much harder to pay attention to an abstraction, which cannot be visualized, than a concrete example, which can. One of the reasons why philosophy textbooks are so boring to students is that they dwell to a significant degree on abstractions. In contrast, the traditional detective story is very specific and concrete regarding the details it provides and is therefore much more likely to maintain the reader's interest. If a patient, for example, talks about being depressed, the patient is speaking at a conceptual level. The therapist does well, in response, to ask the patient what he or she is specifically depressed about, what in concrete terms are the exact thoughts and feelings that the patient is experiencing and, even more important, to focus on the specific situations that have brought about the depressed feelings. The best way to alleviate the psychogenic components in the depression is to focus in detail on the specific concrete events that have contributed to it.

The Experience The most potent mechanism for modifying behavior is the experience. The old proverb, "A picture is worth a thousand words," is well known. I would add to this, however, that "An experience is worth a million pictures." To the degree that the therapist can provide experiences, to that degree will he or she be able to bring about clinical change. This hierarchy of the efficacy of the various forms of learning is well epitomized by the following comparisons. Let us take, for example, the experience of reading a play. Reading the play is purely a visual experience, both at the level of reading the written page and the visual imagery that is engendered by such reading. It is primarily an intellectual experience, although some emotions may certainly be engendered. Let us compare this with attending a theatre and observing the play being acted. It is likely that the individual will be more affected by the play because an auditory modality of input has now been added to the visual experience associated with reading the play. If one becomes an actor in the play, then one is even more likely to remember its messages. The reason for this is that one is now adding physical action to the visual and auditory modalities of input. With each additional modality, there is a greater likelihood that the story will have an impact. However, the emotions being exhibited in the play are feigned. No matter how convincing the actor is, the emotions are still turned on and off in accordance with the dictates of the script. The actor is still play acting. Compare this with emotions that are caused by an actual experience. Here, the reactions are engendered by reality and are even more likely to be recalled in the future.

Therapy, more than anything else, should be an experience. It is an experience that is one slice of life. It is a living experience in which one has an ongoing encounter with a person who is more honest than any other individual with whom one may be involved in one's lifetime. Our best friends may hesitate to criticize us, lest they hurt our feelings. Therapists criticize benevolently with the purpose of helping remove those behavioral manifestations that alienate others and that interfere with our dealing most effectively with the problems in life with which we are all confronted.

Although the therapist's specific knowledge and experience may increase the likelihood that an involvement with him or her will be therapeutic, such encounters were taking place long before Sigmund Freud was born. Let us take, for example, a young woman, in her late twenties, who comes to therapy because she is not yet married and is concerned that she may never meet a man with whom she will have a satisfactory marital relationship. Let us assume that the therapist is a man in his late fifties, approximately the age of her father. Let us assume further that she reports early in treatment that her father was particularly cruel and rejecting and that she learns in therapy that her anticipation of similar rejection from young men is playing a role in her avoidance and rejection of them. In the course of her treatment she discusses with the therapist her male relationships, and this insight helps her avoid a repetition of her childhood experiences. The therapist is sympathetic, understanding, sensitive, and kind. At no point does he treat her in a way similar to her father. Let us assume that her treatment was successful and she ultimately marries a man with whom she has a stable and rewarding relationship.

I believe that the *insights* this woman gained in her therapy were far less important in bringing about the therapeutic change than the *experience* she had with the benevolent and sympathetic therapist. Without necessarily having any conscious insight into the process, the experience with the therapist enabled her to reduce and possibly even remove her generalization that all men would treat her similarly. Similarly, the therapist's discouraging her from involving herself in the same pathological pattern with other young men increased the likelihood that she would have *experiences* with men who were more kindly disposed to her. In short, then, I believe that the major elements in bringing about change in this woman had less to do with intellectual insights and more to do with the quality of the therapist and the men that she subsequently encountered. Had the therapist been aloof, cool, and unsympathetic, she probably would not have changed—all her insights notwithstanding. I would speculate further that this experience was had by a multiplicity of women long before Sigmund Freud's birth. With similar upbringing they too had difficulties in their relationships with young men. However, if they had the good fortune to form a relationship with an older man (an uncle, teacher, or mentor, etc.), then this might have modified their views of men and lessened the likelihood that they would carry the generalization over into their courting patterns. All this may have occurred without conscious awareness and was certainly much more likely to have taken place outside of conscious awareness in the days prior to psychoanalysis. In short, it was the experience that was the best teacher, not the insight.

CONCLUDING COMMENTS

The material presented in this chapter represents a statement of my views regarding the basic factors that contribute to the development of psychogenic symptoms and the fundamental elements operative in the psychotherapeutic process. This "blind man" sees the elephant this way in the mid-1980s. It was not the way I saw things in the mid-1950s, 1960s, and 1970s. I have learned things over the years, and I suspect some modifications of my present position by the 1990s. My purpose here has been to present a relatively short statement of my views on these issues. Throughout the course of this book, however, I will be elaborating on all of these points with many clinical examples. Throughout this book, as well, I will be making reference to these principles because they are the basic foundation of just about everything that is described herein.

There is an old Hasidic saying: "A good man is one who knows what he feels, says what he means, and means what he says." The statement could very well serve as a central therapeutic goal. Although less applicable to children's than to adult's therapy, it epitomizes the kinds of qualities that therapy attempts to engender in patients. We want our patients to know what their feelings are and to be able to use them judiciously. We want them to be forthright and express themselves honestly. And we want them to be viewed as credible human beings who have the courage to follow through with their convictions. Therapists who possess these qualities themselves are more likely to engender them in their patients. Passive therapists, those who hide behind "blank screens," those who are fearful of appropriately revealing themselves, and those who are vague and/or indecisive, are not likely to be of much assistance in helping their patients reach these goals.

FOUR

The Therapist-Patient Relationship

There is no psychotherapy without a genuine relationship. For a relationship to be genuine it must be human. Therapy without humanity is a farce, a caricature, an act, a waste of time for both— even though one party may derive some financial gain from the charade.

R. A. Gardner

THE THERAPIST'S PERSONALITY

The therapist's personality, probably more than any other factor, is the ultimate determinant as to whether therapy will be successful. The personality qualities that contribute to one therapist's being successful with children and another's failing are vital to understand and yet we know little about them. To the best of my knowledge, there is a paucity of articles in the psychiatric and psychological literature describing in depth this crucial entity—especially with regard to the factors that bring about a good therapist-patient relationship and how it can be achieved. Yet we continue to neglect what may very well be the most important focus for our investigations. Many believe that the reason why therapists of different persuasions can report successes is not that the techniques utilized are so valuable or that one technique is better than another, but that subtle personality characteristics of the therapist have been the crucial elements in bringing about the described improvements. Thus, we are ill-equipped to evaluate and compare the efficacy of various therapeutic techniques if we remain ignorant of the personality characteristics of the therapists who have been using them.

Language Limitations

In this chapter I will attempt to delineate some of the personality qualities that contribute to a good therapist-patient relationship. I recognize that in attempting to do so I am handicapped not only by our ignorance of the processes but by the limitations of our language, which does not have specific words for many of the characteristics I will attempt to delineate. Our English language, the richest on earth, with almost five hundred thousand words, is still inadequate to define certain phenomena accurately. For example, my dictionary defines *déja vu* as "the illusion of having previously experienced something actually being experienced for the first time." It informs me, as well, that in French *déjà vu* means "already seen." Most of us have had, at some time or other, a *déjà vu* experience. And we know how insufficient that definition is. There are other qualities in the experience that make the words *already seen* banal to the point of being misleading. The dictionary says nothing of the *uncanniness* of the experience, the altered state of consciousness, the futile quest for the time and place of the alleged original experience, and the frustration in not being able to pinpoint it. Even my description of these other elements in the phenomenon does not convey accurately what it is actually like to a person who never had the experience. It does not enable him or her *really* to know what I am talking about. My term *uncanny* is in itself too vague, too inaccurate, to convey truly the feelings.

Our language is replete with words that only purport to describe the phenomena they are labeling. When people use such words, we get fooled into thinking that they are talking about the same thing. Take the word *orgasm*, for example. In interviewing a woman suspected of frigidity, a therapist generally does not rely on a yes or no answer to the question of whether she has ever achieved orgasm. He goes by the *quality* of her response—by whether the affirmative answer communicates: "I know exactly what you're talking about." If she says, "I think so," or "Maybe," then the therapist knows that she hasn't. There are many other examples of such words: *beautiful, schizophrenia, cool, rapport, irony,* and *love.*

I recognize that the qualities that I will attempt to describe are not those that a therapist can easily acquire. With some, the recognition of their absence may be a step toward their acquisition. Others may have to accept their deficiencies. However, this need not mean that they must necessarily discontinue doing child therapy. No therapist can possibly have *all* the qualities that one should ideally possess to be an effective child therapist. However, therapists who possess few of these qualities are not likely to work successfully with children.

Liking Children

The first, and possibly most important quality, is that of genuinely liking children. I cannot imagine someone's involving him- or herself meaningfully and effectively in the field of child therapy without basically liking children. I am not suggesting that he or she needs to like children *all the time;* in fact, I would be distrustful of anyone who claimed that he or she did. (Children inevitably cause us periods of resentment and exasperation.) Rather, I am only suggesting that a significant percentage of therapeutic experiences with them should be benevolent and moderately enjoyable.

Projection of Oneself into the Child's Position

Therapists must have the capacity to project themselves into the child's situation, to see the world through the child's eyes—and probably to feel the way the child feels. We know little of this phenomenon. Why is it easy for some and for others impossible? Piaget's panoramas (in which the child is asked to determine which card shows the view that the little model man in the center of the panorama sees as his position is changed) could give us information about this quality. Some would easily be able to see the view of the model, and others would have trouble. But this is only part of the phenomenon. It describes only a *visual-mechanical* aspect of the projective process; the *human elements* are far more complex. We use such terms as *sympathy* and *empathy* in our feeble attempt

to describe this quality, but we still have much to learn about it—
its mechanics, its psychodynamics, and the factors that play a role
in its development. Does an accurate memory of one's own childhood play a role in this capacity? I think so, but as far as I know
this has not been tested. And, indeed, it might be hard to evaluate
accurately. *Egocentrism* (another one of those umbrella terms) may
inhibit this quality. But we still have to define how. Therapists who
lack this capacity to a significant degree are ill-equipped to help
their patients. If they cannot view the world through their patients'
eyes (not necessarily agree with their patients, however), then they
are handicapped in helping them.

Treatment of the Projected Self

This phenomenon has broad implications for many aspects of treatment, for both the patient and the therapist, and has not been given
the attention it deserves. For example, adults in individual therapy,
who tend to see all others as harboring or exhibiting certain alienating qualities, are usually denying these same characteristics in
themselves by projecting them on to others. Similarly, those who
do group therapy frequently observe patient A suggest an interpretation of patient B's behavior that is totally irrelevant to B, but a
clear statement of A's difficulties. This defense is well known to
therapists and we most often have little difficulty detecting it. It is
when we ourselves utilize the mechanism that we are less likely to
be aware of it. I believe that all of us use it to varying degrees. When
properly utilized, it can enhance the efficacy of our work; improp-
erly used, it can seriously interfere with it.

Practically every therapist has been asked at some time or
other, "How can you listen to that stuff all day long?" If the question is benevolently asked (and it often isn't) and if the therapist is
inclined to respond seriously (and he is not often so inclined), one
of the answers, if he or she is to be completely honest, is: "In treating my patients, I treat vicariously my projected self, and this is an
important determinant of my interest." Although many factors certainly contribute to one's choice of psychotherapy as a profession,
one that is central for most, if not all, is the desire to cure one's
own pathology. Rarely is personal analysis, or other forms of therapy which the therapist may experience, enough to accomplish this
goal. We are still at too primitive a level in our knowledge to use
comfortably the word *cure*; at best, we usually strive toward sig-

nificant alleviation of our own and our patients' difficulties. And whether previously treated or not, the therapist, I believe, continually attempts to lessen his or her own psychological problems through psychotherapeutic endeavors (whatever other purposes they serve). Without this factor operative, I do not think the therapist would maintain for long interest in the psychological minutiae that patients in treatment can often endlessly discuss. In fact, if one could indeed *cure* a prospective therapist of all neurotic problems (whatever that really means), then I question whether he or she would continue on as a therapist—so vital do I believe this mechanism to be as a motivating factor for those who do psychotherapy. There are certainly other motivating factors operative—and many of these are far less self-serving—but it is a vital one that is not given the attention it deserves. The child therapist is, in all likelihood, treating vicariously childhood problems that have yet to be resolved.

If therapists are using patients to treat themselves vicariously, may this not be detrimental to the patient? Doesn't this interfere with the patient's therapy? Does not this tendency result in the therapist's seeing things in the patient that do not exist? The questions are rhetorical. They describe real dangers in the therapeutic situation—dangers that we have not studied enough to enable us to avoid them effectively. Yet, if what I have said is true—that a certain amount of this need is necessary if the therapist is to be meaningfully interested in the patient—what is the solution to this problem? It lies, I believe, in determining that level at which the salutary use of the therapist's treatment of the projected self ends and the pathological begins. How can we learn then to make this important distinction between the helpful and detrimental use of this mechanism? It is not within the scope of this book to discuss in detail possible methods that we might utilize to make this important distinction. Elsewhere (1973d) I have proposed some techniques by which we might be able to differentiate between healthy and pathological treatment of the projected self.

Memory of One's Own Childhood

The ability to remember one's own childhood experiences deserves further emphasis. There are people who will say with all honesty that they cannot remember a thing about their lives before the age of eight, or ten, or even twelve. The person who is so repressed regarding memories of his or her childhood experiences is not likely to be an effective child therapist. Therapists have to recall how it was when they were the same age their child patient is at the time of treatment, if they are to appreciate optimally the child's situation. Child therapists have to be able to put themselves in the positions of their patients if they are to be successful. They need to be able to project themselves back in time. In addition, child therapists must be able to involve themselves in both processes, both present and past projections. Their task, therefore, is much more difficult than that of the adult therapist.

Charles Dickens, in his *The Personal History of David Copperfield* (1850), stated this phenomenon well:

> This may be fancy, though I think the memory of most of us can go farther back into such times than many of us suppose; just as I believe the power of observation in numbers of very young children to be quite wonderful for its closeness and accuracy. Indeed, I think that most grown men who are remarkable in this respect, may with greater propriety be said not to have lost the faculty, than to have acquired it; the rather, as I generally observe such men to retain a certain freshness, and gentleness, and capacity of being pleased, which are also an inheritance they have preserved from their childhood.

Excitation

I introduce discussion of the next quality anecdotally. As mentioned in Chapter One, when I was a freshman medical student, an instructor once commented to a small group of us, "You fellows are still in the 'gee whiz' phase of medicine." To which I replied, "I hope I never get out of that phase." (I would like to think I haven't.) Many gifted child therapists carry this quality with them throughout life. One such person was the late British child psychiatrist D.W. Winnicott, who exhibited many of the qualities I describe in this chapter. I had the good fortune to hear him speak on a few occasions a number of years ago and served on a panel of his discussions. To say he was enthusiastic and interested in what he was doing when he was with child patients is an understatement. There was a certain "wow" quality (I cannot describe it any better, but that's close to it) to him which he shared with his child patients. This was not loudly stated; he did not seem the kind of man who would loudly say, "Wow!" Rather it came through in the tonal qualities of his voice. There were intonations of excitement and of slight breathlessness—all subtle, but nevertheless there. These qualities, of course, are exhibited by all but the most sick children, and Donald Winnicott retained them to the end of his life. They must have contributed to his patients' thinking, at some level, "He's one of us, even though he's a grown-up. He gets excited about the same kinds of things we get excited about."

How this quality contributes to therapeutic change is speculative. But I shall speculate. With such a person children cannot but feel better about themselves. Here is an adult who enjoys being with them—and this cannot but raise the child's self-esteem. Because most, if not all, psychogenic symptoms are formed, at least in part, to adapt to or bolster a low self-esteem, this esteem-enhancing experience with Dr. Winnicott was salutary.

The Inner Warmth Response

The next quality of Donald Winnicott's that I wish to describe is also best introduced anecdotally—this with an incident that occurred during my residency training. I was seeing a little boy of four who had what I can best describe as an *infectious personality* (another one of those vague terms). When I would walk down the hall with him from the waiting room to my office, adults who passed us would look at him and smile. There was a *cuteness* (another one of those words) about him which engendered a heart-warming feeling in adults. I cannot say exactly what it was about the child that produced this response. I know it had something to do with his smile, his seriousness, and his little-man-trying-to-act-big quality as he strutted down the hall. Once, in the midst of a session with him, a schizophrenic woman mistakenly came to my office earlier than the appointed time. She opened the door, saw that I was still with the boy, and with a stony facial expression closed the door. I was struck by the fact that she did not smile. Although rivalrous feelings with another patient and disappointment that she could not see me exactly when she wanted may have contributed to her reaction, I believe that she was incapable of the "inner warmth" response that other adults almost invariably had to this child. (I even thought half-seriously that with this episode I might have come upon a good test for schizophrenia.)

Donald Winnicott had this "warm inner glow" response. Those who have had it know exactly what I am talking about. Those who have not may never appreciate what I am saying. We use the term *heartwarming* to describe the phenomenon. It does feel as if it comes from the chest, but this may be socially induced. We are taught that love comes from the heart, yet to the best of our knowledge the brain and often the genitalia seem to have something to do with it as well. There must be physiological correlates to the experience that can be measured: changes in blood pressure, cardiac rate, and biochemical reactions. These have yet to be identified. When with a person who enjoys such a response to him or her, the child cannot but feel: "He(she) likes me. I am likable. I give him (her) pleasure. I am worthwhile." And such responses contribute to the child's improvement.

Childlike Personality Characteristics

M.M.R. Khan (1972) describes Dr. Winnicott as having had: "A childlike clownish spontaneity (that) imbued his movements." All of us retain some childlike, even childish (the pejorative term), qualities. Some of these are probably necessary to preserve our sanity. When someone retains, as an adult, too many childhood characteristics, we call him or her "immature," "fixated at infantile levels of development," or "regressed." Where does one draw the line? Where does the normal, healthy degree end and the pathologic being? D.W. Winnicott had, without question, more than the average degree of childlike qualities. Since they were obviously so constructively used, one cannot label them pathological. Effective child therapists have, in my opinion, more such childhood residua than their adult counterparts, and these can serve them well in their work. These residua enable therapists to play unself-consciously (or less self-consciously) on the floor with their patients. They contribute to the pleasure of their work. They are a dangerous asset, these childhood residua, in that therapists may go too far in this regard when they do play therapy and accomplish more *play* than *therapy*. Where one ends and the other begins is still a relatively unexplored area. My hope is that the readers of this book—whose play therapy has been more play than therapy—will shift the balance and conduct a play therapy that is more *therapy* than *play*.

"On the Same Wavelength"

An analogy from the physical sciences may be of help in describing my next point. When a vibrating tuning fork is placed next to a nonvibrating fork of the same intrinsic frequency of vibration, the second will begin to vibrate along with the first. We know that there are people with whom we "vibrate," and there are others with whom we do not. We say, "I can't really talk to her; he understands me," or "There are times when we don't even have to say certain things; we just know what one another is thinking," or "We think alike; we're on the same track." Many young people today even use the term *vibrate* to describe this phenomenon. D.W. Winnicott vibrated with children. He was on the same wavelength as most of them. And this, I am sure, contributed to his therapeutic efficacy. But what is this phenomenon? We know so little about it. Why do we experience it with some people and not with others? Does some form of extrasensory perception have something to do with it? It is another important element in the therapeutic process that is yet to be understood. Certainly, we are more likely to be on the same wavelength with people who resemble significant figures in our early upbringing, especially our parents. I am sure that sexual attraction plays a role in many adults. Similar educational experiences are also probably operative in that our cognitive processes are very much affected by our educational experiences.

A Strong Parental Instinct

Then there are the so-called *instincts.* We speak in psychiatry and psychoanalysis about maternal instincts, but far less about paternal instincts. Dr. Winnicott, most would agree, exhibited toward his patients what appeared to be a strong paternal instinct. M.M.R. Khan (1972), refers to him as "a caring and concerned mother." What is this instinct? Why do some exhibit it more than others? Is this merely biological variation? Or can environmental factors significantly influence its expression? And how does this play a role in the child therapist's work with patients? The term *parental instinct* is only a rubric, subsumed under which are a host of qualities and personality characteristics. Feeding, protecting, touching, cleaning, loving, guiding, and enjoying are only some of these elements. Khan refers to D.W. Winnicott's generosity to his regressed patients and at times his exaggerated need in this regard. He refers to Mrs. Winnicott's reference to her husband's "illusions of munificence."

How therapeutic was Winnicott's tendency to give? When was it excessive? And by what criteria? Therapists have to be giving to some degree if they are to help their patients. But how far should they go? Where do we draw the line? There is still much we have to learn in this area. The reader interested in further comments of mine regarding qualities in D.W. Winnicott that I consider operative in his therapeutic successes should refer to my article on him (1972c) and my review of two of his books (1973e). And the reader who is interested in reading about the work of Edgar Baldock, another man whom I consider to possess qualities similar to Winnicott's, may wish to refer to his article on the therapeutic relationship (1974).

Frustration Tolerance

There are certain frustrations that child therapists must be willing to tolerate that their adult counterparts need not contend with. One such potential problem is the child's parents. They often feel threatened by the therapeutic process. Having a child in therapy may be considered proof of the parents' failure, and many defenses may be utilized to avoid coming to terms with this notion. Many parents come not because they have seen the problems themselves (they have often been denied for months to years), but because some outside agency (most often the school) has suggested psychiatric consultation. Such parents often hope to hear the child is completely normal and that the referrer was in error. Once the child is in therapy, their ambivalence may manifest itself through forgotten appointments, lateness, cancellations with meager excuses, withholding payment of bills, failure to follow through with recommendations, hostility toward the therapist, and other gambits that are consciously or unconsciously designed to undermine the treatment. Sudden withdrawal of the child from treatment is common.

At any particular time the child therapist has to keep three people involved: a child who would prefer to be playing with friends; a mother whose life is hectic enough caring for the house and other children without having to bring the patient to the therapist; and a father who could find much better ways to spend his money. If, at any point, any one of these three develops significant psychological resistances, the others are dragged down and the project fails. I often feel like I'm juggling three greasy balls and that when one of them drops, the whole act is over. Some therapists get fed up and gradually confine themselves to adult work. When in residency, one of the definitions we had of a child psychiatrist was: "someone who used to do child psychiatry." The humor stemmed from the recognition that many of our supervisors were no longer doing child therapy, merely supervising it. The general consensus was that people got tired of doing such therapy after the age of 40 or so. I passed that landmark uneventfully (with regard to my enthusiasm for child therapy) and also passed the age 50 landmark. As I write this, I am 54 and starting to get tired. Perhaps it's my age, perhaps the frustrations of the field are finally getting to me. At the same time, my interest still appears to be quite high.

However, the frustrations may be more than counterbalanced by certain gratifications that the adult therapist may not so frequently enjoy. The satisfactions of therapeutic success are more easy to come by in child work than in adult therapy. The child's problems are generally of shorter duration than the adult's and may be less deeply imbedded in his or her psychic structure. In addition, more change can be effected in the child's environment. The deleterious influences to which the child is exposed can be altered more readily—parental attitudes modified; misconceptions rectified; management advice provided; and schools, clubs, and camps recommended. Adults who come for treatment are usually deeply entrenched in their life situations. They may be locked into a bad marriage from which it is difficult to remove themselves because of children and the financial privations attendant to a divorce. And their work situation may be similarly rigid in that quitting a job or changing one's field may not be a viable option for them.

Flexibility and Creativity

Child psychiatrists must be capable of utilizing a wider variety of therapeutic techniques than those used by adult therapists and must be flexible enough to alter these at a moment's notice. They are often requested to make specific recommendations for immediate action. The child therapist may be required to take action on the spur of the moment—much more frequently than the adult therapist. The parents who ask what to do about a child's fire setting cannot be told that no immediate or specific suggestions can be given and that the child must work this through in the therapeutic sessions. The therapist must be able to say: "On the basis of what I know thus far, I suggest we try this. If it doesn't work out, there are other options. As I learn more, I hope to be in a better position to advise you." They must be comfortable providing tentative advice.

The child therapist who has had adult psychoanalytic training may be faced with a conflict. The analytic training emphasizes the importance of a very passive role, whereas in child work such passivity can be antitherapeutic and even, at times, dangerous. Accordingly, such a therapist must be able to switch readily between the two orientations. At times the two types of training may tend to contaminate one another. The analytic training may result in the therapist's being too passive in his or her work with children; and the child therapy training causes the therapist to be too active in his or her work with adults. I would not, however, recommend that the child therapist avoid psychoanalytic training (especially the modified type I have recommended in Chapter One) in order to avoid these problems. The enrichment that psychoanalytic training can provide the child therapist far outweighs its disadvantages.

Child therapy and adult therapy differ in regard to the predictability of the process. Although there is a universe of possible communications between the adult patient and the psychiatrist, in adult treatment the participants talk to one another and there is little action. This is not the case in child therapy, where there are many more possibilities. There is much greater unpredictability, as the child is less likely to "follow the rules"of treatment. Child therapists, then, must be ever on their toes and, in addition, generally need to be much more flexible and even creative than their adult counterparts. (This is not to say that such qualities are not desirable in the adult therapist, but they are much more continually demanded of the child therapist by the patient.)

Most adult therapists find group therapy to be a useful experience for their patients. In such groups, interactions that could not be observed in individual sessions become observable to the therapist. Much more firsthand information becomes available to the therapist. Child therapists cannot generally avail themselves of this therapeutic modality. Children do not generally sit quietly in a circle and talk about their problems, especially with an orientation toward gaining insight. Rather, such discussions are predictably interrupted by horseplay, joking, and the children's general restlessness. *The Talking, Feeling, and Doing Game,* (1973b) (described in detail in Chapter Eleven) provides the kind of structure that may facilitate the therapist's doing group therapy with children. Some of the difficulties of group therapy with children are somewhat obviated with this tool.

Similarly, family therapy generally entails much more conversation between the adults and teenagers than with younger children. The latter appear to have low frustration for such meetings, may easily become restless, and are not generally interested in prolonged discussions centering on why people do the things they do. Although such family discussions can certainly be useful for children with psychiatric problems, the therapeutic benefit comes not so much from the child's direct involvement with the treatment as from the changes in the adults that such meetings bring about. In short, because group therapy and family therapy are of less value to children (especially younger ones), the child therapist cannot often use these techniques with children and must utilize a variety of other modalities.

The Therapist as Parent

The question is sometimes raised as to whether it is necesary for child therapists to have had children of their own. It is certainly possible to be an effective and accomplished child psychotherapist without having had such experiences, but I believe that the lack may compromise one's therapeutic abilities. The child, when seen in an office setting, is in an artificial situation. The childless therapist has not had the experience of living and growing with children in their natural setting; fathering and mothering; worrying and scolding; changing diapers; seeing them through physical illness; handling their fights with siblings and peers; and of involving themselves in the thousands of other activities that enrich one's knowledge and appreciation of children. Childless therapists, no doubt, gain many of these experiences vicariously through their patients. They may, indeed, be able to involve themselves with their patients to a greater degree than therapists who have children of their own. These considerations notwithstanding, I believe that having one's own children enhances one's efficacy as a child therapist.

Boredom

If the therapist lacks enthusiasm and interest in his or her work, the patient will sense these feelings and will respond similarly. I cannot imagine effective therapy being done in such an atmosphere. I am not suggesting that the therapist should *never* be bored during the session (I myself get bored at times); we can't possibly be on a "high" all the time. Rather, I am suggesting that when therapists occasionally find themselves bored, they should try to look into the reasons why and attempt to rectify the situation—both for their own sakes and that of the patient. Therapists do well to avoid involving themselves in therapeutic activities that they basically do not like. To do so inevitably produces resentment which will be picked up by the child. A child cannot, in my opinion, possibly gain anything therapeutic at a time when the therapist is in such a state of mind. Some of the games and therapeutic activities I will be describing in this book have served to reduce such antitherapeutic reactions in me, and my hope is that they will serve the reader similarly.

I wish to emphasize that we cannot be all things to all people; that the personality characteristics we possess will inevitably attract some and alienate others. There have been many patients with whom, in spite of my best efforts, I have been unable to relate to in a way that I would consider therapeutically beneficial. My practice in such cases has been to inform the child and parents my belief that things are not proceeding well, and I suggest that we all together try to find out what the difficulties are and try to rectify them. At times we have been able to improve things, and at other times referral to another therapist or discontinuation of treatment has been necessary.

Comfort with Therapeutic Failure

Last, it is important that therapists be comfortable with therapeutic failure. Therapists who think that it behooves them to alleviate the difficulties of all (or most of) those who come to them, will suffer significant frustration and a deep sense of failure. Children often present with a total life of exposure (even though only three to four years old) to the detrimental influences that have contributed to their difficulties. Their parents generally have been living with their own problems for many years as well. But things do not stop there.

Not only may the pathological processes have been transmitted down numerous generations, but social and cultural processes have usually contributed as well. It is therefore grandiose of therapists to consider themselves capable of rectifying all these pathological influences, and they are assuming unrealistic obligations if they consider it their responsibility to do so. The best attitude therapists can take is that they will commit themselves to the therapeutic process and try their best to do what they can. If they can say to themselves, with regard to the unsuccessful case, that they have tried their best and possibly learned a few things that will serve them in good stead in the future, they should be able to accept therapeutic failure without undue guilt and self-recrimination. I have spoken previously (Chapter Three) about *The Statue of Liberty syndrome*. Therapists should ask themselves whether they are exhibiting manifestations of this disorder. If they are, they do well to cure themselves as soon as possible; otherwise, they are doomed to lead very frustrating lives.

FACTORS IN THE THERAPIST-PATIENT RELATIONSHIP CONDUCIVE TO BRINGING ABOUT THERAPEUTIC CHANGE

Introduction

Possessing certain qualities requisite to doing effective work with children is of little value if these qualities are not utilized in building a good relationship with the child. A good therapist-patient relationship is crucial to successful therapy. It is the focal point around which the various therapeutic experiences occur, and I cannot imagine therapy's being successful if the relationship is not a good one.

A meaningful relationship with other human beings is vital to survival. Provide a newborn infant with food, clothing, and shelter, but deprive it of the tender loving care of a mother (or her substitute) and the child will lose its appetite, become unresponsive to the environment, and may actually waste away and die. Others similarly deprived may survive infancy but may develop such severe withdrawal from others that they become effectively nonfunctioning individuals, living in their own mental worlds, and gaining whatever little gratification they can from their fantasies. The deprivation need not be overt (such as physical abandonment) but can result from psychological rejection in the form of parental withdrawal, hostility, uninvolvement, or other kinds of detrimental interaction with the child. In short, it is only through meaningful and gratifying involvement with others that we develop into human beings; without such exposure we may survive, but we cannot then be called truly human.

Meaningful relationships with others are the stuff of life. More than anything else they enrich us; without them we become shells—mere imitations of living individuals. From the moment we are born until the time of our death we need others—necessary times for solitude notwithstanding. The child in treatment has generally suffered some difficulties in the ability to form and gain gratifications from involvement with others. It is hoped that therapy will help the child accomplish this. But I cannot imagine its being successful if a meaningful relationship hasn't been accomplished between the therapist and the patient.

Time Alone Together

I can conceive of an experiment in which all patients coming to a mental health clinic were divided into three groups which were matched for age, sex, socioeconomic status, and diagnosis. Children in the first group would receive the full course of treatment indicated for their particular problems. Children in the second group would come to the clinic with a parent at a frequency that would be indicated for the treatment of their problems. However, instead of receiving therapy, the parent and child would merely sign in and then immediately return home. No therapy would be given. Those in the third group would not come to the clinic at all and receive no therapy at home either. Then, at the end of a prescribed period (such as two years), all three groups of children would be reevaluated with particular emphasis on whether there had been any improvement in the presenting problems. I believe that those children in the first group would exhibit the most improvement; those in the second group some improvement as well (but less than those in the first group), and those in the third group, least of all. I suspect that the second group would *not* be half way between the other two in regard to the degree of improvement, but closer to the first group than the third. In addition, if one studied the second group in detail to determine if there was any relationship between the distance traveled to the clinic and the amount of clinical improvement, I believe a positive correlation would be found. In other words, the longer the child had to travel to get to the clinic the greater would be the improvement. Furthermore, I would guess that the same would hold true for those in the first group as well.

We have not given proper attention to the therapeutic effects of the parent's (usually the mother's) time alone with the child as they travel to and from the therapist. Often, it may be the only time the child and mother may be able to be alone together. At home, the child must vie with siblings for mother's time and attention; when traveling to the therapist, she is a captive audience. Often the mother may bring books and games along in order to entertain the child. Sometimes they may talk together in depth, and such discussions can be extremely therapeutic. Most children's symptoms are, in part, the result of some degree of deprivation of parental affection. Spending time alone with a parent while engaged in pleasurable activities is the most specific therapy for such deprivation. Similarly, enjoyable time spent by the child with the therapist can also be therapeutic. Accordingly, even if all the child does is play games (and unfortunately this is all that does happen in some children's therapy), he or she can derive some therapeutic benefit. (This is one of the reasons, I believe, why practitioners of a wide variety of therapeutic techniques claim that their methods produce clinical improvement.) It is to be hoped that the play therapy will involve more therapy than that which can be derived from play. It is the purpose of this book to provide the therapist with some methods of enhancing this likelihood.

The Therapist's Affection
for the Patient

The therapist's affection for the child can serve to compensate for some of the privations the patient may have experienced in relationships with others. However, there are significant limitations in the degree to which the therapist can do this. After all, although the parents may exhibit formidable deficiencies, they most often are providing the child with food, clothing, shelter, protection, and guidance. Even though they may have serious psychological problems, they are in all likelihood more bonded with the child than the therapist and probably will always be. The child who has been severely deprived, so much so that there are and there never will be any bonds established with any human being, is not likely to benefit from the therapist's affection. It is the child who has suffered *some* (but not formidable) deprivation in this area who will be most likely to profit from the therapist's affection. Such affection can be ego-enhancing to the child and therefore therapeutic. In a way, it is easier for the therapist to provide the child with unadulterated affection than the parents and others may be able to give. The therapeutic situation is so structured that therapists need not have to do much of the "dirty work" entailed in raising children. Therapists don't have to change diapers, get dawdling children dressed in the morning, bring them to emergency rooms in the middle of the night, worry about them when they are not home on time, and so on. They, like the grandparents, can enjoy children in the most relaxed and nondemanding situations—when few demands and restrictions are placed on any of the parties—and so there is less chance that there will be conflicts, power struggles, and other difficulties.

I am not suggesting that the therapist should like the child all the time. It is unrealistic to expect anyone to like anyone else more than a significant percentage of the time. Children will do things at times that will irritate their therapists, bore them, and alienate them in a variety of ways. It is hoped that the therapist will use these negative reactions in constructive and therapeutic ways. I do not agree with those who hold that therapists should have "unconditional positive regard" for their patients. Those who claim that they do are either lying or just not in touch with the inevitable frustrations and irritations we experience in our relationships with all human beings—patients included. Patients who are told that the therapist "accepts" them (a condescending remark if there ever was one) regardless of what they do or say, will distrust the therapist (and justifiably so). They will recognize the duplicity inherent in such an attitude and this must be antitherapeutic. Accordingly, the optimum experience children can have in regard to their therapist's affection is that they view the therapist as someone who likes them most of the time and that when they do things that alienate the therapist, the latter will use his or her negative reactions in the service of helping them.

Intimately associated with the affection the therapist has for the child is the feeling of pleasure that the therapist may experience with the child. The child's appreciation, at some level, that he or she is capable of providing another individual with pleasure on a continual (but not necessarily uninterrupted) basis is gratifying and ego-enhancing. And this is yet another element in the therapist-patient relationship that can be therapeutic.

Taking the Child's Side in His or Her Conflict with the Parents

There are therapists who believe that taking the child's side against parents or other authority figures is a good way of engaging the child in treatment and entrenching the therapeutic relationship. One of the earliest and most well-known proponents of this approach was August Aichhorn, a Viennese schoolmaster who tried to apply Freudian psychoanalytic techniques to the treatment of delinquent boys. In his classic *Wayward Youth* (1925) he described the difficulties that arose in such boys' treatment because they were very defiant of authority and tended to see him as another authority against whom to rebel. He found however, that if he looked at the world from their vantage point and identified with them in their antisocial attitudes, he could form a relationship with them. In words, but not in act, he expressed sympathy for their antisocial behavior. He would become a psychological ally in order to win their confidence. Once such a relationship was established he would gradually shift his position and attempt to bring about a stronger superego in the youngsters. His hope was that their desire to maintain their relationship with him would motivate them to follow along with him as he encouraged and became a model for pro-social behavior.

There is an obvious duplicity involved in such an approach, and I myself would not be comfortable utilizing it. I think that most youngsters would sense the therapist's artificiality and would thereby lose respect for him or her—and this could not but be antitherapeutic. Most therapists today would not utilize this approach.

There are therapists, however, who consider themselves to be the protectors of their child patients against the indignities they suffer at the hands of their parents. Such a position has a divisive effect on the family. It puts the child in between the therapist and the parents in a tug-of-war—and thus is antitherapeutic. To a lesser degree there are therapists who feel that they should try to take their child patients' positions whenever possible and tend to side with them in order to engage them in treatment and entrench the therapeutic relationship. I think this is an error. Children, at some level, will appreciate that the therapist's reflex support of their positions is not provided with full conviction and this will compromise the relationship. They will sense the therapist's dishonesty here.

I believe that the ideal therapeutic situation is one in which children come to view their therapists as impartial, as criticizing them benevolently when such criticism is warranted, and equally ready to criticize the parents when the therapist considers them to be in error. In the context of such impartiality, the therapist can still serve to protect child patients from irrational and inappropriate attitudes and reactions they may be exposed to. In such situations children may feel quite helpless; having someone whom the parents respect (and the ways in which this can be brought about will be discussed in Chapter Seven) and who can bring about a reduction and even elimination of parental detrimental exposures can be most salutary for the child. It reduces tension and anxiety, takes a heavy burden off the child, and removes environmental influences that may be significantly contributory to the child's symptoms.

Ideally, the therapist's position should be one of providing information and advice to both parents and children. It is hoped that the parents will be receptive to the therapist's recommendations. If not, therapists should listen with receptivity to the parents' disagreements. If modification is justified, the therapist should be comfortable doing so. If the therapist remains unconvinced that his or her suggestion should be altered, the following statement should be made: "Well, this is what I think would be in the best interests of your child. Perhaps one of us may change his or her opinion in the future."

Therapists should not be viewed by the child as the manipulator of the parents but as someone who provides advice and information for them. Children should not view the therapist as someone who controls the parents, but rather as someone who provides advice and information and leaves it up to the parents to decide whether or not they wish to accept the therapist's opinions and implement his or her recommendations. If the therapist is seen as the manipulator of the parents and if the child sees the parents as being unduly dependent on the therapist, as people who hang on the therapist's every word and put them into action—this situation can compromise the parent-child relationship. In addition, such a situation may produce in the child some discomfort with the therapist because he or she is jeopardizing the respect that the child has for the parents.

Ideally, both parents and the child should come to view the therapist as truly impartial, as attempting to be as objective as possible and as not favoring anyone. They should come to view the therapist as someone who sides with healthy behavior—regardless of who exhibits it—and benevolently criticizes unhealthy behavior—regardless of who manifests it. Generally, the criticisms tend to balance out and no one tends to feel that the therapist is prejudiced against him or her. In such an atmosphere, both the child and parents will generally come to respect the therapist. In contrast, when therapists attempt to favor the child, they will alienate the parents and lose the respect of the child, who senses the duplicity—a situation that is definitely antitherapeutic.

Child Talk

There are those (both therapists and nontherapists) who tend to use "baby talk" with children in the obvious attempt to ingratiate themselves to them. Although infants may like this sort of thing, the average child of five to six and above gets turned off by it. Children want to believe that they are more mature than they actually are; therefore, communicating with them with babyish intonations and language is alienating.

Generally, therapists should speak to a child patient as they would to an adult—with the important exception that they avoid using words that they suspect the child will not understand. Such an approach can in itself be therapeutic. Speaking to the child in this manner helps enhance self-esteem (enhancing self-esteem is one of the universal antidotes to most, if not all, forms of psychogenic pathology). It makes the child feel bigger and more mature. Avoiding the use of words children will not understand protects them from the ego-debasing experience of being talked to with words they cannot comprehend. Such exposure may result in the child's thinking: "How stupid I am. I can't understand what he(she) is saying."

To avoid using words that children cannot understand and to speak at their level, I have found certain words and expressions particularly useful. They are terms that the child is generally familiar with and they not only enhance communication but improve the therapist-patient relationship. When referring to the child's psychological difficulties I usually prefer to use words such as *worries*, *troubles*, or *problems*. One does better to use the word *scared* rather than *afraid* and *mad* rather than *angry*. Other useful words are: *mean* (rather than *cruel*), *brave* ("That was very brave of you"), *silly* (instead of *foolish*), *dirty trick*, *grown-up* (instead of *adult*), *kind* ("That was a very kind thing to do"), *big* (rather than *large*), *make believe*, *manners* ("That was very bad manners"), *mistake* ("That was a big mistake"), *pick on*, *polite* ("That wasn't very polite"), *proud* ("That must have made you very proud"), *student* (rather than *pupil*), *scold*, *scary*, *really* ("He smiled but he was really very sad inside"), *share*, *smart*, *tease*, *teenager* (the incarnation of all the desirable traits the child may aspire to acquire), *treat*, *trick*, *cry* (not *weep*), and *whisper*. When referring to other children's behavior or to a figure in a story (who may symbolically represent the patient), I have found useful such words as: *brat*, *spoiled brat*, *dumb*, *bully*, *crybaby*, *stupid*, *bad* (rather than *naughty*), *stingy*, *teacher's pet*, *temper tantrum*, *selfish*, *sissy*, *stupid*, *sore loser*, and *scaredy-cat*.

While playing a game with a child I may say such things as "Ooooh, are *you* lucky," "You're a lucky stiff," or "Boy, is this your lucky day." When things go badly for me I may exclaim: "Rats!" or "Gee, this is *really* your lucky day." And when the child wins: "And you thought you weren't good. You're really a very good player," or (while shaking the child's hand) "Congratulations. Excellent game. You played beautifully." Shaking the child's hand provides an extra dramatic touch that strengthens the effect of the message.

When a child hesitates to tell me something or tells his or her mother not to tell me, I incredulously reply: "What, keeping a secret from your *own* psychiatrist?" Emphasizing the word *own* introduces an ego-enhancing element to counterbalance the possible esteem-lowering effects of the statement. However, there is an associated quality of good humor (communicated by my gesture, facial expression, and intonations) that conveys to the child that I am not bitterly condemning him for any embarrassment over the "transgression." A stance of incredulity can help the child express thoughts and feelings that he or she might otherwise have difficulty talking about. For example, "You mean never in your *whole life* — in the seven years that you have been alive—you not once had hateful feelings toward your brother?" Emphasizing the words *whole life* tends to add a subtle dramatic quality that the children often utilize in their own talk. It is important that the therapist not be excessively condemning when expressing such surprised disbelief. It is the *quality* of the communication, more than its *content*, that will determine whether or not the message will be ego-debasing.

In a conversation in which the child expresses something that I consider maladaptive but which he or she does not recognize as such, I may say, "Do you want to know what *my* opinion is about what Robert did?" Emphasizing the word *my* tends to imply that I am not necessarily right—only that I am expressing an alternative view. The therapist's always being "right" (which is usually the case) tends to undermine the child's self-esteem and is an anti-therapeutic element in even the most well-conducted therapy engaged in by the most sensitive therapist. It is hoped that other ego-enhancing experiences will outweigh this untoward effect of the treatment. If after the ensuing discussion the child and I still differ, I do not push the point—I do not get into an argument. Rather, I say, "Well, I guess we have different opinions on that. Perhaps sometime one of us may change his(her) mind. Why don't we go on to something else?"

When a mother reports that the child has exhibited an important clinical breakthrough and is no longer exhibiting a particular pathological pattern, I will often ask the child to sit next to me (and even in my seat if he or she is small enough) and observe as I slowly and emphatically write in the chart: "I am very happy to learn that three weeks have passed now and Ronald hasn't once picked on another boy or girl. I am very proud of him and he must be very proud of himself." I may then ask him to fetch a pen from my desk (such as a Flair pen or a Magic Marker) and I then dramatically encircle the note. Sometimes I will have the child read the message aloud for further reinforcement. Similarly, when a child exhibits what I consider particularly dangerous or pathological behavior I may say, "I'm very sorry, James, but I'm going to have to write that in your chart." I will then emphatically write: "James was once again found playing with matches. I hope that I never have to write this in his chart again." These dramatically written notations serve as an added touch to whatever therapeutic approaches are being used. They add additional positive and negative reinforcement. The closer the relationship the therapist has with the child, the greater effectiveness they will have.

The Resolution
of the Transference Neurosis

Of the innumerable patterns of human interaction each person tends to select a few favorites. From earliest childhood (primarily as the result of our interaction with our parents) we develop a constellation of patterns of relating to others that are unique. As we grow older these patterns become strengthened and we tend to utilize them in preference to others that may be either absent from our repertoire or have lower priority for utilization. Some of these patterns of interaction are healthy and enhance our effectiveness in life. Others are maladaptive and often cause us significant difficulty, both personally and in our interaction with others. These patterns are strongly repetitive—almost reflexly so. Accordingly, in new situations we tend to use the old patterns even though we may suffer significantly because of our injudicious reactions.

Using psychoanalytic terminology, we tend to *transfer* onto others reactions that we had toward our parents in infancy and childhood. We tend to interact with others in a manner similar to the way we interacted with our parents. When these modes of interaction are neurotic and they exhibit themselves in the therapeutic relationship they are termed *transference neuroses*. Specifically, patients try to involve the therapist in the same pathological patterns in which they were involved with their parents and in which they try to involve others as well. Those who comply with these requests (because of their own pathological needs) maintain their relationships with the patient (they may call such individuals their "friends"); those who do not comply with the psychopathological request avoid or sever ties (and may be regarded as "unfriendly"). When the therapist refuses to involve him- or herself in the pathological pattern, the patient will generally react with resentment, anxiety, or other unpleasant thoughts and emotions. At such a point the patient may leave therapy and consider the therapist uncaring, unloving, disinterested, hostile, and so on. Or, he or she may choose to try to gain insight into what is going on and attempt to change the maladaptive pattern. Such working through is referred to as the *resolution of the transference neurosis* and is an important step in the alleviation of the patient's difficulties. It is to be hoped that once the pathological pattern of interaction is alleviated in the patient's relationship with the therapist, he or she will exhibit healthier modes of interaction in relationships with others as well.

Although child analysts differ regarding whether a child can exhibit what can justifiably be termed a transference neurosis (M. Klein, 1932; A. Freud, 1965), I believe that most children will do so if they get involved with the therapist. In other words, the deeper the child's relationship with the therapist the greater the likelihood the child will exhibit the pathological patterns of inter- action and the greater the chance the child will try to involve the therapist in them. For example, a little girl who uses coyness and seductivity to get her way with adults may try to involve the ther- apist similarly. In response to the therapist's failure to react with the expected "affection," she may become angry, consider him or her to be mean and unfriendly, and refuse to return. However, if such a child can be engaged (and it is the purpose of this book to help the therapist accomplish this), she may be helped to appreciate and experience that there are more effective and predictably grat- ifying ways of relating to others. Similarly, the therapist who does not give in to a child's temper tantrums, or allow him- or herself to be bribed, or coax the pouting child, is helping the child resolve the transference neurosis.

If a good relationship is not established, the child will be less willing to tolerate the frustrations attendant to the therapist's re- fusal to comply with pathological requests. And the child will thereby be less likely to gain this important therapeutic benefit that can be derived from the relationship.

The Transference Cure

When patients, very early in treatment, exhibit a sudden and dra- matic alleviation (and even cure) of the presenting symptoms, they are described by psychoanalysts as having exhibited a *transference cure*. Specifically, because the patient hasn't delved into the un- conscious roots of the neurosis and worked out the basic problems that underlie it (something that generally takes a long time to do), the therapeutic change is usually considered specious. When this occurs extremely early in therapy (such as after the first or second session), it is understood to reflect the patient's resistance to en- tering into treatment:

> *Patient:* You are, without doubt, the most brilliant doctor I've ever met. Since I saw you last time, I'm one hundred percent better. I'm

feeling so good that I'm wondering whether I need any more treatment.

   Therapist: But all I did was ask you some questions about your problems and get some background history.

   Patient: Oh, it was much more than that, doctor. There was something about the way you asked me those questions—I don't know what it was—that made me feel so much better.

When the "cure" occurs a little later in treatment, it often relates to an attempt by patients to get the therapist to like or even love them. After all, if the primary goal of the therapist is to cure the patient then it is reasonable to assume that the therapist will love someone who helps him or her achieve quickly this goal. Of course, both of the aforementioned factors may be operating simultaneously, and others as well. Rarely is there a simple explanation for anything that occurs in psychoanalytic treatment—or any other kind of psychotherapy as well.

   These specious kinds of cure are well known to most psychotherapists. Because they are generally manifestations of a pathological pattern, the term *transference cure* is generally spoken of with a certain amount of derision. This, I believe, is unfortunate because there is a useful, and often unappreciated, element in the transference cure. All patients, I believe, change partly in the attempt to ingratiate themselves to the therapist. From the very first encounter the patient has with the therapist he or she wants to be liked. (This doesn't differ in any way from all other first encounters with nontherapists.) The anxiety the patient experiences in the first session is, in part, a manifestation of the fear that he or she will be considered loathesome and unworthy because of the things that will be revealed to the therapist. As the relationship intensifies, there is usually an even greater need to be liked by the therapist. The patient has invested much time and (often) money in the project, and the reliance on the therapist to help with his or her difficulties is great.

   I believe that *one* element that plays a role in patients' exhibiting therapeutic change is the desire to get the therapist to like them. Others are certainly operative. But this factor is, I believe, an important one in the early phases of alleviation of a symptom. Patients know that when they tell their therapists that improvement has occurred, the therapists cannot but feel good about themselves for their contribution to the success. (Some therapists, in accor-

dance with their theoretical position, deny having any such gratification. I don't believe them.) If the patient has it within his or her
power to make the therapist feel good, then it follows that the therapist will like the patient. After all, we generally like most those
who have the good sense to provide us with the gratifications we
seek. It is to be hoped that the new mode of adaptation will become
more deeply entrenched as the patient gains greater insights into
the causes of the symptoms and has the experience that the newer
way is the more judicious and gratifying. Then, the patient is likely
to maintain the healthier adaptation because, through knowledge
and/or experience, he or she will have developed the inner conviction that it is the preferable alternative. Ideally, the patient will then
no longer need to maintain the symptom in order to please the therapist (whom he or she will probably never see again anyway after
the treatment is over—psychological ties, fond memories, gratitude,
and other positive feelings notwithstanding).

The younger the patient the greater the likelihood he or she
will change behavior in order to please the therapist. Children are
constantly concerning themselves with the approbations of parents, teachers, and other authorities. They are constantly being told
about whether what they do and say is "good" or "bad," "right"
or "wrong." And the therapist is just another authority from whom
they usually wish to gain acceptance. It behooves the child therapist to make use of this phenomenon. It can enhance significantly
the efficacy of the treatment. Accordingly, the therapist does well
to praise the child (often profusely) for newly gained healthier
modes of behavior. It is hoped that this will help the child reach
the point where he or she engages in the healthier adaptations, both
from the inner conviction and the experience that life is much more
gratifying when he or she does so.

The Corrective Emotional Experience

In the process of working through or resolving the transference
neurosis a particularly effective therapeutic phenomenon that may
occur is the corrective emotional experience (F. Alexander and T.
French, 1946; F. Alexander, 1950). Essentially, the patient has a living
experience (often associated with a significant upheaval of emotional reaction) that alters significantly a previous pattern. For example, a girl whose father has been very punitive may generalize
and expect similar treatment from all men, including her male ther-

apist. For the therapist to tell such a child that he or she will treat her differently will not generally be very effective because intellectual processes only are involved in the communication. However, if the child has the living experience, over an extended period of time, that the therapist indeed does not react punitively then her view of men may indeed change. Her fearful reactions lessen and relaxation and trust gradually replace them. It is this combination of insight, feeling, and experience that brings about some of the most meaningful changes that can occur in psychotherapy.

When a boy cheats during a game I may say: "You know, it's no fun for me to play this game when you cheat. If you do that again I'm going to stop playing and we'll do something else." To simply discuss why the patient cheats may have some value. However, if this discussion takes place in a setting in which the patient experiences some frustration over the alienation his symptom causes, the conversation is more likely to be therapeutically meaningful. In such a discussion we might talk about whether this might be one of the reasons why children don't like to play with him, or about the futility of this way of trying to compensate for feelings of inadequacy, or about other aspects of the problem which may be of psychological significance. But, without the emotional reactions attendant to the threat of alienating the therapist and/or interrupting an enjoyable experience, such discussions are not likely to be very effective.

Identification with the Therapist

Just as children imitate their parents and acquire many of their traits (both adaptive and maladaptive), they will tend to identify with the therapist if the relationship is a good one. It is to be hoped that the personality qualities that children acquire in this way will serve them in good stead. There are those who believe that what I am saying is risky business—that such a process is dangerous and antitherapeutic. They would hold that therapists must do everything possible to present themselves as a blank screen upon which the patient's fantasies can be projected. Some believe that the therapist should encourage the child's realizing his or her "true self." Central to such a theory is that there exists such an entity—that each individual has within him- or herself a personality pattern that is blocked from free expression and that such blockage is central to psychopathological behavior. They hold that an important aspect of treatment involves helping the individual express freely these hidden personality characteristics.

Although I certainly agree that many people who are in treatment are repressed and need to be helped to express themselves (although there are many who need some repression more than anything else), I believe most people usually need to express some *specific* pent-up thoughts or feelings. I am somewhat dubious about the concept of a whole personality being hidden inside, knocking for release. Rather, I believe that certain aspects of our personality may be genetically determined (such as certain temperamental patterns as activity level, assertiveness, passivity, and curiosity); but most are environmentally induced (and even the genetic ones are subject to significant environmental modification). I see core *potentials* not core personalities. Most of our character traits, I believe, are derived from the environment—more specifically from what we learn from those in the world around us and what we acquire by imitation of significant individuals in our lives. The therapist becomes another in the series of individuals whom the child may copy, emulate, and identify with. Even the kind of therapist described above, who tries to provide the patient with a neutral atmosphere to facilitate "self-actualization," sends many subtle cues that encourage the patient to proceed in specific directions. In addition, the therapist still has a personality, and no matter how much he or she may try to suppress it, much is still revealed—much that the patient can identify with.

As mentioned, it is obviously preferable that the qualities of the therapist that patients identify with will serve them well. For example, a boy's father may have operated in accordance with the principle that admitting any deficiencies to his children will lessen their respect for him. The child, then, may take on this similar maladaptive pattern and find himself having trouble with his classwork because he cannot tolerate admitting errors. If his therapist, however, is the kind of person who can, without discomfort, admit errors when they naturally arise (to do so in a contrived situation is not only therapeutically worthless but may be antitherapeutic because it is basically dishonest), and the patient comes to see that this is a desirable and effective pattern, he may take on the quality himself. Another example. A girl may have acquired the pattern of lying (in both subtle and overt ways) as a significant part of her interactional repertoire. Observing the therapist to be one who is consistently honest and experiencing, as well, that such honesty makes the therapist's life simpler, enables him or her to enjoy the esteem of others, and has numerous other benefits, may result in the child's attempting to acquire this valuable asset herself.

Therapists traditionally encourage their patients to express their pent-up thoughts and feelings in appreciation that such expression, properly directed and utilized (not often the case [Gardner, 1968b, 1973c]), can be therapeutic. However, many therapists attempt to do this in a setting where they do little if any such expression themselves. They thereby serve as poor models for their patients and so impede the process they are attempting to achieve. Therapists who express themselves in situations where such expression is appropriate and in the best interests of the patient (and, as mentioned, without artificiality) have a much better chance of getting their patients to do so as the latter identify with them. Therapists who assert themselves and do not allow themselves to be taken advantage of serve as good models for patients who are inhibited in these areas. And it is only in the context of a good patient-therapist relationship that such salutary identifications can occur. As mentioned in Chapter Three, such identification can be risky, especially because it involves identification with the therapist's values. It is to be hoped that the therapist's values will be healthy, otherwise the therapy will do the patient more harm than good (a not uncommon occurrence, unfortunately).

The Therapist as Educator

We learn best from those we respect and admire. Disliked, hated, or disrespected teachers will teach their students little of educational value (although they may teach them something about having to tolerate a despised person in certain situations). If the therapist is basically respected, there is much that he or she can teach patients that can be of therapeutic value. One does well to compare the relationship between a therapist and a child with that between a teacher and a pupil. A teacher who is enthusiastic about his or her work and genuinely enjoys teaching will communicate to the child the message that learning can be fun. The child will thereby emulate the teacher and attempt to gain the same gratifications. In such a setting, the child will be willing to tolerate the frustrations and drudgery that are necessary if one is to truly learn. The identification with the teaching person is a central element in the healthy educational process. A teacher who basically dislikes the work is not likely to serve as such a model for children and is not likely to teach them very much. Even worse, a teacher who instills anger and fear in children not only is going to teach them little, but may very well contribute to the development of psychopathology. I believe that therapy, more than anything else, is an educational process. Although we certainly try to help our patients learn as much as they can on their own, we are also providing a significant amount of information in the course of the therapeutic process.

A. Freud (1965) strictly warned therapists against submitting to the temptation to provide child patients with information and educational communications. Such advice is like warning an internist not to submit to the temptation to provide patients with penicillin. I am in full agreement with H. Strupp (1975), who considers the central element in adult psychoanalytic therapy (and other forms of psychotherapy as well) to be what he calls "lessons in constructive living." The more competent one is in dealing with the problems in life, the less likely one will be to form symptoms in an attempt to resolve the inevitable conflicts and problems with which we are all confronted. Whether a child therapist provides such communications directly, symbolically, or through the insights into the unconscious that he or she helps the patient gain, the educational element regarding more effective living is ever there. When a therapist is admired and respected, the child will be receptive to what he or she has to say and treatment is more likely to succeed. When the therapist is bored, just putting in time to get payment, or otherwise going through the motions, little is likely to happen.

As part of the educational process the therapist helps the patient alter distortions. For example, all of us carry with us into adult life distorted concepts of the world that we blindly accept. Adherence to these dicta may cause us many difficulties and yet they may never be questioned. It is one of the purposes of treatment to help patients examine (sometimes for the first time in their lives) these premises that guide their behavior. Some of the more common ones that adult (and often child) therapists must deal with are: "No one is to be trusted," "Sex is bad," "Fun is sinful," "I must do everything to avoid criticism because all negative comments about me must be correct," "I must do everything possible to avoid anyone's getting angry at me," and "If there's a choice between another person's being inconvenienced and my being so, rather it be me." Some common dicta of childhood (which may continue throughout life) are: "Mother and father are always right," "Nice boys and girls never have hateful thoughts toward their parents," "Thoughts can harm, that is, wishing that something bad will happen to someone can make it happen," "If my mother and/or father doesn't love me very much, I can't be very good and no one can ever love me," "One fault makes you totally worthless," "There are perfect people who never make mistakes and never do anything wrong or bad," and "An unacceptable thought is as bad as an unacceptable act."

I believe that emotions related to fight and flight follow cognition and that many feelings of guilt, fear, anger, etc. can be alleviated if notions such as the aforementioned are corrected. A. Ellis (1963) holds that the correction of such cognitive distortions are the basic issues to be focused upon in psychotherapy and has coined the term *Rational-Emotive Psychotherapy* for this type of therapeutic approach. I am in agreement with Ellis that emphasis on this element is important in practically everyone's treatment, regardless of age. However, I believe that things are more complex and that many other factors contribute to symptom formation. (Although Ellis admits to other facts, he considers them far less important than cognitive distortions in producing psychopathology.)

From the earliest days of psychoanalysis S. Freud (1895) considered reducing the patient's guilt to be one of the analyst's most important tasks. With less guilt, there is less repression and hence symptoms are less likely to persist. Although his subsequent experience convinced him that things were far more complex (some have yet to read his later work), the concept is certainly still valid if one considers it to be one of the possible contributing factors in *some* patients' difficulties. Partly by virtue of the therapist's position of authority and his or her experience in matters of things such as guilt, patients become convinced that their urges are very common, if not universal, and that the difference between themselves and others is not so much that they have the particular thoughts and feelings, but that they feel guilty over them. In essence the analyst communicates to the patient: "You're still acceptable to me, even though you have those ideas." (Condescending elements in the communication notwithstanding, the message is often helpful.)

In my work with children who need some loosening up of their superegos I will make such comments as: "Most children I know would get very angry when something like that happens. I guess you must have been pretty mad also," "I can't believe that somewhere, someplace, you weren't a little bit angry when that happened," "So what's so terrible about *wanting* to do that? You know wanting is not the same as doing."

Many children I see, however, do not need any loosening up of their consciences. They have what A.M. Johnson (1949, 1959) called "super-ego lacunae," that is, like Swiss cheese they seem to have holes in the part of the brain where the superego is (I speak figuratively, of course). Again, as part of the therapy of such children cognitive changes have to be made. Some comments that I may make in the service of this goal: "That's terrible. She really must have felt bad after you ripped up her new kite," and "I really don't think you could have felt very good about yourself getting 100% on that test after copying most of the answers from the children around you."

Most psychopathological symptoms are developed, in part, in an attempt to enhance and compensate for feelings of low self-worth. However, they are misguided solutions and usually result in the individual's feeling even worse about him- or herself than before—temporary ego-enhancement notwithstanding. The boy who feels unpopular may attempt to gain respect and admiration by boasting about various exploits, travels, etc. However, the fear of exposure and possible guilt he may feel generally result in his feeling even worse about himself than before. And if (as is often the case) others learn of his duplicity, his social position is further worsened. As part of the therapy of such symptoms the therapist does well to inform the child of the injudiciousness of his mode of compensation. For the lonely child who "clowns" in the classroom, I might say: "I know you think that clowning around in class gets the kids to like you. And I know you think that their laughing at you proves this. However, I believe that although you're good for laughs, they really don't like you in other ways. They still don't seem to invite you to parties nor do they seem to want to see you after school." To the bully, I might say: "I know you think you're quite a big shot when you beat up those little kids. But deep down inside, you know that there's nothing so great about it and that must make you feel kind of bad about yourself," "You think the kids think you're hot stuff when you go around beating up lots of kids. Some of them may; but others, I am sure, don't like you at all. They feel sorry for the children you're hitting and I'm sure you've noticed how they stay away from you." Although these comments can be very bitter medicine to swallow, they are accepted if the patient has a good relationship with the therapist. In addition, as mentioned, the therapist's attitude is more important than the content in determining whether his or her comments will alienate a patient. When benevolently communicated in the context of a firm relationship the most painful confrontations may be accepted.

All patients, regardless of their age, have to be helped in treatment to gain a clearer view of their parents. As children, we tend to operate on the principle: "If it's good enough for them, it's good enough for me." We tend to incorporate most if not all of their traits—healthy and unhealthy. We swallow the whole bag, without separating the good from the bad. Therapy, in part, involves making (often very belatedly) these vital discriminations. And the child therapist has the opportunity to provide this at a time when it can do the most good, at a time before the deleterious results of such indiscriminating incorporation and acceptance have had a chance to become deeply entrenched. Children have to be helped to appreciate that their parents, like all other human beings (including the therapist), are not perfect. We all have our deficits. Helping children become clear regarding which personality traits of their parents are assets and which are liabilities can be very useful. And the therapist is in a unique position to provide such information. (This, of course, may require some advance work with the parents; but if the relationship with them is a good one [and I will discuss in Chapter Seven the ways that may help bring this about], their cooperation can often be relied upon.)

The phobic child of a phobic mother can be told: "You know that your mother has many fears that she herself realizes are not real. She knows that there's nothing to be afraid of in elevators or crowded places, but she just can't help herself. She'd prefer not to have these fears and that's why she's seeing a psychiatrist." Ideally, it can be helpful to get the mother herself to verbalize to the child comments such as these. (The reader interested in a detailed account of such parental divulgences in the therapy of a phobic child may wish to refer to Chapter Sixteen of my text *Therapeutic Communication with Children* [1971a]). The child of divorce can be told: "Your father can be counted upon to give your mother the money she needs to take care of herself and the children. However, as you know, he's not very reliable when it comes to showing up for appointments on visiting days. This doesn't mean that he doesn't love you at all. It does mean that he has less love for you than a father has who does show up all the time. This doesn't mean that you are unlovable or that no one else can love you more. You still have many people who like being with you and you can spend time with them when your father doesn't show up."

I introduce my next point anecdotally. A number of years ago Listerine mouthwash was advertised with the slogan "Your best friend won't tell you." In the typical pitch a young girl cannot understand why dates persistently reject her even though she is bright, pretty, etc. Finally, she realizes that *bad breath* is driving them away! Happily, she chances on Listerine, washes her mouth with it, and the boys come flocking. I believe that therapists should be better than one's best friend. They should be able to tell their patient things that even their best friends will hesitate to reveal. And if the therapist's motivation is benevolent and his or her timing judicious, he or she should be able to do so with only occasional difficulty or hesitation.

To put it another way. Robert Burns (1786) once wrote:

'O wad some Pow'r the giftie [small gift] gie [give] us
To see oursels as others see us!"

It is the therapist's job to help patients see themselves as others see them. And this is one of the significant benefits that all patients, regardless of age, can derive from treatment. Patients should be able to gain, as well, what Harry Stack Sullivan (1953) called "consensual validation" of their views of the world. For example, a child can be told: "You think that the kids really like you when they play with you after you give them candy. If you think about it, I think you'll agree that they don't play with you *unless* you give them candy. I suspect you're doing things that turn them off." And if the patient agrees: "I wonder what those things might be?"

Another can be told: "You always seem to want your way when you're here in the office. You always seem to want to do only those things you want. You never seem to care about what your mother or father or I would like to do or talk about. If you act this way with friends, perhaps that's why they don't want to play with you." Another example: "You say you're sorry in the hope that a person will no longer be bothered or angry about what you've done. Although people may *say* that they accept your apology and that they're not angry, *deep down inside they really still are.* Even though you've told your father that you're sorry that you broke the television set, I think he's still angry that it's cost him all that money to fix it." (I often suggest that children who utilize this common manipulative device [invariably taught by parents] read my story "Say You're Sorry" in my book of psychologically oriented children's stories, *Dr. Gardner's Stories About the Real World* [1972a].)

Part of the confrontational process involves helping children gain a more accurate picture of their assets and liabilities (both inborn and acquired). The child with a neurologically based coordination deficit should be discouraged from intensive involvement in competitive sports (although special training and exercises preparing for minimal to moderate involvement may be indicated). In the earliest years children's views of themselves are acquired from what H.S. Sullivan called "reflected appraisals" (P. Mullahy, 1970). In essence, children come to view themselves in accordance with information about them provided by significant figures in their lives, especially their parents. A four-year-old boy runs into the house crying, "Mommy, the kids all call me stupid." Mother replies, "You're not stupid. You're very smart. Although you're four you can write your name, count to 25, and you know nickels, dimes, and quarters. He's the one who's stupid, if he calls you stupid." The child leaves the house reassured. As he grows older the child generally gathers information from others (teachers, neighbors, peers, etc.) that may modify and expand this information—which become his criteria for judging his self-worth. It is to be hoped that his data will be accurate and it is one of the therapist's jobs to help correct any distortions that may have arisen.

Last, it is part of the therapeutic educational process to introduce to children alternative modes of adaptation to those pathological and self-defeating ones that they may be utilizing. These options may never have occurred to the child, nor may he or she ever have been introduced to them. For example, in a boy's family, denial of or flight from awareness of one's deficiencies may have been the only reactions. Such a child must be helped to appreciate the value of dealing directly with one's deficits and he must be encouraged to try this alternative to see for himself its advantages.

Intimacy and Self-Revelation

When we use the term *intimacy*, we are generally referring to a close personal relationship. I consider a central element in the intimate relationship to be the revelation of personal thoughts and feelings which one would generally not reveal indiscriminately to others. The revelation, however, is made in a situation where one anticipates a benevolent and/or understanding response by the listener. Without the freedom for such self-revelation the term intimacy, in my opinion, does not apply. Intimate revelations tend to bring people closer. The one to whom the information is divulged generally feels flattered by the revelation, especially because he or she has been selected from many possible listeners. Also, intimacy cannot be a one-way arrangement. Both individuals must feel comfortable with such revelations. Unilateral revelation is not properly called intimate. Accordingly, many, if not most, therapist-patient relationships are not, by the above definition, intimate. They are generally one-way arrangements in which the patient reveals all (the ideal to be achieved) and some therapists believe that it behooves them to reveal nothing (or as close to nothing as is humanly possible). Whatever benefits may be derived from such an arrangement (and I do not deny that there are some), it cannot reasonably be referred to as an intimate relationship.

This situation presents dilemmas for therapists. If they reveal more of themselves, in order to enhance the intimacy of the relationship, they are going to contaminate blank-screen associations. In addition, there is the risk that the patient's time will be used more for the benefit of the therapist than the patient, especially if the revelations focus on problems of the therapist's. This easily becomes exploitive of the patient. I believe there is some point between these two extremes where there is a proper balance of self-revelation by the therapist and self-revelation by the patient. The vast majority of the revelations should be made by the patient, but not every revelation provided by the therapist need be viewed as unnecessary utilization of the patient's time or exploitation of the patient by the therapist. Such revelations by the therapist—judiciously provided—can be therapeutically beneficial. They bring the two individuals closer, entrench the relationship, and thereby strengthen the foundation upon which therapy rests.

It is difficult to state specifically when the revelations are judicious and when they are not. There are some guidelines, however. As mentioned, a revelation made by the therapist—whose primary purpose is to use the patient for assistance in dealing with the therapist's own problems—is clearly contraindicated. Also, if a significant amount of the patient's time is used for such therapist revelations, then this too is exploitive of the patient. One of the best guidelines is that the revelation should have immediate benefit to the patient's treatment. A personal experience of the therapist's that may help the patient gain insight into his or her problems at that point would be in this category. As mentioned in Chapter Three, metaphorical, anecdotal, and experiential communications often provide a useful vehicle for communicating important therapeutic messages. And the experiences and anecdotal material provided by the therapist can very much be in this category.

Another guideline is that the divulgence of such material should not be contrived or artificial. Rather, it should flow from the natural course of the material provided in the session. Obviously, this guideline is not being followed if the therapist initiates such divulgences at the beginning of the session. *The Talking, Feeling, and Doing Game* (1973b), to be described in detail in Chapter Eleven, provides therapists with many opportunities to divulge information about themselves in a noncontrived manner. After all, the card provides the opportunity to make such revelations and, in accordance with the rules of the game, if the therapist doesn't answer the question, he or she does not get a reward chip!

There is another aspect to the therapeutic benefits of the therapist's self-revelations that is particularly applicable to child therapy. Children generally enjoy thoroughly hearing details about events that occurred in their parents' lives during their childhood. A child will commonly ask a parent, "Mommy, tell me about how things were with you when you were my age and living with grandma and grandpa." Such information is generally of great interest to children and the divulgence of it strengthens the parent-child bond. Similarly, therapists who judiciously provide such information about their own childhoods can also strengthen the therapist-patient relationship with such revelations. What is lost by the resultant contamination of the blank screen is more than counterbalanced, I believe, by the therapeutic advantages related to the strengthening of the therapist-patient bond that such divulgences create. Furthermore, the therapist is thereby serving as a model for the child to reveal his or her own feelings and will thus increase the likelihood that the child will be freer to provide such revelations. Last, when such revelations involve the therapist's describing shortcomings and deficiencies, this too can be therapeutic. It helps reduce the idealization and idolization of the therapist that can be so antitherapeutic. It makes the therapist more of a real human being who has both assets and liabilities—just like the rest of the world. Viewing the therapist as perfect will contribute to patients' lowering of feelings of self-worth as they invariably compare themselves unfavorably with their perfect, or nearly perfect, therapists. This too is antitherapeutic. And children, especially, already feeling so impotent in their relationships with adults, are more likely to benefit from such revelations.

The Role of Seduction

Generally, at some point during the introductory lecture of one of my courses on child psychotherapy, I ask the students if they are familiar with two main forms of reasoning: *inductive* and *deductive*. They usually are. I then tell them that in doing child psychotherapy one must utilize a third form of reasoning: *seductive* reasoning.

Children (and to a lesser extent, adults) do not come to therapy motivated to gain insight into the psychodynamic processes that underlie their problems. In fact, they generally do not consider themselves to have difficulties. It is the parents, teachers, and other powerful authority figures who have decided that the child has them. If one were to ask the average child who comes to treatment what he or she *really* wants of the therapist, he or she would probably say: "Well, doctor, if you really want to know what I want, I'll tell you. First of all, please get those teachers off my back. Tell them to stop hounding me to do my homework and tell them to stop getting angry at me when I don't turn it in. And if I do turn it in, and it's sloppy or has food stains on it, tell them to still accept it and give me a good grade. Also, tell them to stop disciplining me when I horse around in the classroom and don't cooperate. Tell them not to punish me by making me stay after school and tell them not to send me to the principal's office when I fool around in the classroom. Get my mother and father off my back also. Tell them to stop bugging me about turning off the television set and doing my homework. Tell them not to punish me when I start fights with my brother and sister. Tell them not to make me go to bed when they want me to and let me stay up as late as I want, watching television or doing anything else I want. Tell them to stop calling me in off the street to eat supper. Tell them to stop making me take baths and showers. Tell them to stop making me go for religious training after school, to take music lessons, and other things like that. And then, doctor, when you've done all those things for me, tell them to stop taking me here."

Of course, there is no child who is going to be so honest, nor will most children be so articulate. However, every single cell in the child's body is giving me this message. We child therapists are continually competing with after school activities, playing with friends, television, or just "hanging around doing nothing." The competition is formidable and it behooves us to rise to the challenge and to recognize the enormous competition against which we are working. The seductive process is in the service of this goal.

But even those children who do recognize that they do have some problems do not clearly appreciate how the things we want them to do in our offices are going to bring about an alleviation of their troubles. This is not surprising, because we ourselves are not clear about the relationship between our therapeutic approaches and the changes we hope to effect with them. This book is an attempt to present my ideas about this relationship but, as mentioned, we still do best to view ourselves like the blind men and the elephant, groping for some understanding in what is a very mysterious process.

The child therapist does well to avoid trying to derive a statement from the child about the exact nature of his or her difficulties, let alone extracting a vow on the child's part regarding his or her desire to alleviate them. A. Freud (1965) considered it important to get children to the point where they had insight into the fact that they had problems before they could be considered candidates for psychoanalysis. Furthermore, once they had gained insight into this fact, she then proceeded to the step of helping them gain motivation to analyze their difficulties. She did not consider analysis to be possible before these two steps were accomplished. I am dubious about her reported successes in these areas. I suspect that many of the children who had presumably gained such insight and motivation were parroting what they believed she wanted to hear. And this, of course, is antitherapeutic in that the child is basically lying to the therapist. I do not attempt to obtain testimonials from children regarding their insight into their problems and motivations for treatment. Even when I do get such testimonials, I do not take them too seriously. Generally, I view them to be attempts on the child's part to ingratiate him- or herself to me or to comply with parental requests. One should be thankful that the child is coming and hope that, in the course of the therapeutic experience, some benefit will be derived.

Fun　If children aren't coming primarily to alleviate their problems, then why else are they coming to the therapist's office? The word that answers that question better than any other is *fun*. I believe that the therapist who does not provide a significant amount of fun for the child patient (I refer only to the prepubertal child in this discussion; much of what I say here is *not* applicable to the adolescent) is not likely to keep the child in therapy for very long; or, if the child does continue to come, little will be accomplished. Children are extremely hedonistic; they are not particularly renowned for their willingness to suffer discomforts in the present in the hope of enjoying future rewards. (Adults are not particularly famous in this department either, but many of us do acquire the capacity.) In addition, the therapist is often competing for the patient's time with the child's friends and enjoyable after school recreational activities. It behooves therapists, then, to make the sessions as enjoyable as possible. This does not mean that they should reduce themselves to the level of clowns or function as playground directors. (The observer should not be able to ask: "To do this, he (she) had to become a doctor?") Rather, they must weave the therapy into the play and other enjoyable experiences provided the child. They must make the therapy an intrinsic part of the enjoyable experience. The therapy and pleasurable experience must be the warp and woof of the same fabric. They must so sweeten the medicine that there is little, if any, evidence of its sour taste. ("Just a spoon full of sugar helps the medicine go down.") If they use play therapy, it should be both *play* and *therapy*, but more therapy than play. All too often it is only *play* rationalized as therapy. It is the necessity to combine art and science (more art than science) that is child therapists' greatest challenge, but it can also provide them with their greatest gratifications.

I refer to these factors that attract children into involving themselves in the therapeutic activities as the *seductive* elements in child therapy. They not only serve to keep the child coming but, in addition, enrich the therapy and make it far more likely that the child will find the experiences with the therapist meaningful. If we compare pure intellectual insight to the words of a play on the printed page, then the true therapeutic experience would be analogous to actually having the experience. Other analogies come to mind: the difference between seeing the blueprints of a building and actually viewing and walking through the edifice, or between reading a musical score and actually listening to the music played by an orchestra, or between hearing about a sexual act and actually engaging in it oneself. To provide our patients with insight alone is to give them a relatively sterile experience compared with the deeper impact we possibly can offer them. Fromm-Reichmann put it well when she said, "The patient doesn't need an insight. He needs an experience."

Many forms of therapy attempt to provide the child with such enriching experiences. This is particularly true of the various forms of play therapy. When storytelling is a part of such therapy (whether the stories be told by the child and/or the therapist) one can gain the benefit of allegorical communication—so universally enjoyable to the child. (I will discuss this in greater detail in Chapter Eight.) Dramatization of one's therapeutic messages is a most efficacious way of communicating them, especially with younger children. This requires of therapists the ability to be somewhat of a "ham," as well as some degree of comfort with involving themselves in floor play, animal noises, various forms of childlike physical activity, etc. Therapists who are comfortable enough to allow themselves such regressive behavior, can provide the child with highly valuable therapeutic exposures. (This will be discussed further in Chapter Nine.)

Humor   Child therapists should commit to memory a collection of jokes that are traditionally enjoyed by children. Riddles are probably the most common form of such humor. Some examples: *Question* "Why does a humming bird hum?" *Answer* "Because it doesn't know the words." *Question* "What's *Smokey the Bear's* middle name?" *Answer* "the." *Question* "What looks like a box, smells like lox, and has wings?" *Answer* "A flying lox box." Some of these may even have a mildly scatological element. For example: *Question* "What's invisible and smells like worms?" *Answer* "A bird's fart." (Jokes such as these are a statement of the levels to which child therapists must stoop if they are to engage successfully their patients.) Humor serves many purposes. It is a pleasurable distraction from some of the heavier material often focused on in treatment. Laughing is ego enhancing, and this in itself is therapeutic. The jokes that the child learns from the therapist may be useful in improving relationships with children outside the office. They make the therapist more attractive to the child (the seductive element) and thereby increase the likelihood that the child will want to come to the office. Last, they can contribute to an entrenchment of the therapist-patient relationship via their contribution to the child's liking the therapist's personality.

The ability to introduce these elements into the child's therapeutic situation requires the acquisition of talents far above those required of the adult therapist—who need only devote his or her life to the overwhelming task of acquiring competence in helping patients gain insight and providing them with the array of other traditional therapeutic experiences.

Candy and Other Foods There are therapists who claim that having candy and other foods available is very helpful in establishing a good relationship with the child—especially because food is so often a symbol of love (M.R. Haworth and M.J. Keller, 1964). I believe that it is important that therapists appreciate that they can provide the child with some affection (that may even be very deep), but the parents of their patients—whatever their problems, whatever their deficiencies, and whatever deprivations the child may have suffered because of them—are generally more loving of the child than they. They are the ones who are providing the child with food, clothing, and shelter. They are the ones who continually devote themselves to him or her. Generally, at least one of them is continually available to protect, guide, educate, nurse, discipline, and involve him- or herself in whatever else may be necessary to the children's welfare. The parents are the ones who suffer all the discomforts and sacrifices attendant to the children's upbringing—parental gratifications from the process notwithstanding. Their bringing their child to therapy—involving as it does sacrifices of time and money—is in itself another manifestation of their love. The therapist is getting, therefore, a selected population. Parents who have little, if any, affection for their children are not bothering, not suffering the discomforts of bringing them to treatment. It is the parents who are changing the diapers in the middle of the night, sitting with their sick children, worrying about their being scapegoated, et cetera, who bring their children for therapy. Therapists do not have these obligations. It is easier for them, therefore, to exhibit affection; but it is naive of them to think that they can provide a degree of love anywhere close to that which most of the parents of their patients are providing.

At best the therapist can provide the child with some affection in compensation for some of the privations he or she may have suffered. This, if it is in any way to be meaningful, must evolve from an ever-deepening relationship. At best, candy can play an insignificant role in bringing about such a relationship. The therapist must appreciate that food is a *symbol* for love; it is not a *replacement* for love. It is not the real thing. There are therapists who are somewhat deficient in providing that degree of affection optimum in the therapeutic situation and who may try to compensate for their deficiencies in this regard by providing food. Such therapists may be entrenching a common parental problem in which the parent uses food to compensate for deficiencies in providing genuine affection.

Central to the success of treatment is that a good relationship be established with the child. If this exists there will be no need to provide substitutes or symbols. I myself *occasionally* have lollipops or other candy available for their minor seductive value and that's all. I do not provide other foods. I would not say that providing more food is necessarily therapeutically contraindicated; rather, I believe that it doesn't help significantly and that there is a danger that it can be used, as described, in an antitherapeutic way. In short, I think that there are more disadvantages than advantages to using food as a method of engaging the child and entrenching the therapeutic relationship.

Magic Tricks   One of the most predictable ways to make oneself attractive to children is to show them a few magic tricks. It is a rare child who is so recalcitrant, uncooperative, distractible, et cetera who will not respond affirmatively to the therapist's question: "Would you like to see a magic trick?" Although not generally useful as primary, high-efficiency therapeutic tools, magic tricks can be extremely useful in facilitating the child's involvement with the therapist. Only five minutes spent in such activities can make a significant difference regarding the success of the session. The anxious child will generally be made less tense and will then be freer to engage in higher-order therapeutic activities. The child who is very resistant often becomes less so after such an "icebreaker." The uninvolved or distractible child will usually become quite interested in them and will then be more readily shifted into more efficient therapeutic activities.

In short, they facilitate attention and involvement. In addition, because they make the therapist more fun to be with and more attractive to the child, they contribute to a deepening of the therapeutic relationship which, as already emphasized, is the mainstay of the therapeutic process.

The therapist does well to gradually build a small collection of the kinds of card tricks, magic boxes and cups, secret mazes, et cetera readily purchased in many toy stores (preferably those specializing in "magic"). This small investment of time and money may have significant therapeutic dividends. My previous warning that therapists should not reduce themselves to the level of clowns still holds. I am not suggesting that the therapist become a magician for the child; rather, he or she should use such tricks on occasion, for short periods of time, for their value in facilitating more highly efficient therapeutic interchanges. The therapist interested in an excellent discussion of the use of such tricks in therapy should refer to Moskowitz's article (1973) in which he describes the aforementioned uses of magic as well as its more extensive value as a therapeutic modality.

Following the therapist's presenting a *really* good trick, a child may ask, "How did you do that trick?" To which I will generally reply, "Well, I usually don't tell people how I do my tricks. Perhaps I'll tell you, perhaps I won't. It depends on how much you're going to cooperate." I have no hesitation in utilizing such a bribe. When I talk about the utilization of seductive techniques in child psychotherapy, I can guiltlessly say that, "The end justifies the means." The child who is sitting silently refusing to talk, may be approached with a deck of cards that are fanned directly under his or her nose. To such a child I might say, "Go ahead, pick a card. You'll see I'll be able to tell you what card it was." I have never yet seen a child who will not rise to this challenge. It is difficult to imagine a child's just sitting there adamantly refusing to draw the card. Again, if the child expresses the wish to know how I did the trick, I will suggest that I may tell him or her how, depending on the degree of cooperation.

The Peabody Picture Vocabulary Test (PPVT)   The Peabody Picture Vocabulary Test (L.M. Dunn, 1965) can be a valuable "icebreaker" for involving the child who refuses to speak. The instrument tests word knowledge, which is roughly correlated with the verbal section of the WISC. The patient is presented with a series of plates, on each of which are four pictures. The examiner presents a word and the patient is asked to point to the picture that is most closely associated with the presented word. The words, of course, become progressively more difficult. The instrument is designed to assess word knowledge from age three through adulthood.

Let us take, for example, a seven-year-old boy who is sitting in my office in stony silence. This is his first session with his parents and he has informed me that he will absolutely not say a word. To such a child I might say, "You know, if you don't want to talk here, you don't have to talk here. Have you ever heard of the Constitution of the United States?" The child will generally nod affirmatively or, if not, I may take a few minutes to explain to the child the importance of this document. I will then say, "The Constitution of the United States guarantees, that means promises, that every person in the United States will have freedom of speech. And that means that a person is free to speak and say anything he or she wants. However, that doesn't mean that a person can yell 'Fire' in a crowded theater or speak in such a way that people's lives will be in danger. Anyway, freedom of speech also means freedom *not to speak*. So, if you don't want to speak, I respect your right *not* to speak, and under the Constitution of the United States you have the right not to speak!" In this way, I undermine the child's passive-aggressive gratifications which he had hoped to enjoy by thwarting me in my attempts to get him to speak.

I then proceed: "Now, because we're both in agreement that you're not going to speak, I'm going to give you this test that does not require you to speak. This is a test to see how smart you are. All you have to do is point to the picture that is closest to the word that I will say to you. Now here's the first picture." At that point I turn to the first plate of the booklet, the sample that is used for the youngest children. Generally, the instructions indicate that the examiner turns to the plate that is commensurate with the child's age and level of sophistication. My reason for starting with this first plate is to insure that the words I will be giving will not only be readily understandable to the child but significantly *below* the child's age level. The first plate (Example A) portrays a crib, an adult woman, a kitten, and a spoon. I will then say to the boy, "Please point to the *kitten*." True to form the child will sit there silently, adamantly refusing to point. I will then say, "You don't know which one is the kitten? You know, a little baby pussy cat. A little kitty cat that says 'Meow, meow.'" At this point I will utilize baby talk. As mentioned, the utilization of baby talk is contraindicative in child therapy. However, this is one exception to that rule. Here I want to *demean* the child into pointing. If the child still refuses to respond, I will incredulously say, "Gee, he doesn't know kitty cat." And then I will dramatically place a cross mark on the examiner's score sheet.

I then proceed to the second plate (Example B) on which is depicted a chair, a banana, a man hammering a nail, and a fish. Proceeding with the examination, I will say: "Now, I'm sure you'll get this one, everyone does. This is *really* an easy one. Please point to the *fish*." Again, the child will adamantly refuse to point. At which time I will shake my head, again incredulously, "Come on, you know which one is the fish. You know, a little fishy that swims around in a pond." Again, I purposely use baby talk in order to embarrass the patient into responding. If there is still no response, I will say, "Wow, seven years old and doesn't know fish. Are you sure you're really seven?" At which point the patient may nod that he really is seven. I will then turn to the parents and somewhat incredulously say, "Is that right? Is he *really* seven years old?" Again, after the parents' confirmation, I may say, "Gee, this is really something. I haven't seen anything like this in a long time. Seven years old and doesn't know fish." Then I will again dramatically place a large cross on the score sheet.

I now turn to the third plate (Example C) on which is depicted a comb, a table, a little doll, and a car. I then proceed: "I know, for sure, you'll get this one because this is *really* easy. Okay now, please point to the *doll*." Again, after no response from the patient, I will incredulously say, "Of course you know which one is the doll, a little baby dolly, that little girls play with." Again, I will utilize baby talk.

By this point, the patient is likely to say, "Wait a minute, what's going on here? What's happening?"

To which I will reply, "Well, as I told you before, this is a test to see how *smart* you are. And to be very truthful with you, you're not doing too well!"

At this point, the patient is likely to say, "Wait a minute, I know which one is the doll. That's the doll." And the patient will then point to the doll.

I will then say, "Oh, very good, I was really surprised when you said you didn't know which one was the doll. You know you're allowed to change your answers." And then I'll erase the cross and turn back to the fish and to the kitten, giving the patient another opportunity to give the answer. I have never yet seen a child who has the guts to sit there while I repeatedly and dramatically give him or her cross after cross. To date, *all*—even the most adamantly silent—have succumbed. We then proceed with the test and I get some idea about the child's word knowledge which, as mentioned, is roughly correlated with the verbal section of the WISC. With this instrument, the child is likely to involve him- or herself in the further activities. I recommend this instrument highly for its value in this regard. I also recommend it as a quick way of gaining some information about the child's general level of intelligence. (In the above example I utilize the original PPVT. In 1981 the revised edition (PPVT-R) was published [L.M. Dunn and L.M. Dunn] and although the pictures are different, it can be used in an identical manner.)

CLINICAL EXAMPLES

In the following clinical examples I demonstrate what I consider to have been good and bad therapeutic relationships that I have had with my child patients. In each case I will try to identify those factors that contributed to the kind of relationship that evolved.

The Case of George ["Can I Call You Dick?"]

When eight-year-old George's divorced mother called to make his first appointment, she told me that he was not attending to his studies and that he was fighting so excessively with peers that he had no friends. Her former husband was living in South America and although he often wrote George letters professing his intense love for him and promising future visits, the latter rarely materialized. Accordingly, George's life was fraught with frustration and disillusionment.

At the time of their first visit, when I entered the waiting room to greet George and his mother, he told me that his name was George, but that his friends called him Jojo. I asked him which name he preferred I use with him and he answered, "Jojo. What do your friends call you?" "Dick," I replied. "Can I call you Dick?" he asked. "Of course," I answered. It was clear that George was craving a close, friendly relationship. To have insisted that he call me "Dr. Gardner" or to have inquired as to the reasons why he wished to call me by my first name would have squelched him at this vital point and lessened the possibility of our forming a good relationship. (It is of interest that about three months later George began calling me Dr. Gardner. I think that he was basically uncomfortable with this "egalitarianism" and was able to give up the contrived symbol of friendliness when we had the real thing going for us.)

Following the interchange in which we decided what names we would use with one another, George presented me with a clay figurine that he had made for me in school. "I made this present for you, Dick," he said. I admired the piece of work, told him how proud he must be to have made such a thing, and thanked him warmly for the gift. Although there was a pathetic quality in George's intense craving for me to like him (even to the point where one has to consider there may have been a bribing element in the gift), there was also a warmth and optimism communicated as he gave me the present. To have hesitated to take the gift and/or to have conducted a psychoanalytic inquiry into his motivations would have compromised our already budding relationship, because such an inquiry would have robbed us of the warm feelings being engendered in both of us. But worse, it would have been inhumane. I am not suggesting that one never question a gift given by a patient. Rather, I am only saying that for this patient, at this time, such a reaction would definitely have been antitherapeutic.

The Case of Henry
[An Attempt on the Therapist's Life]

Henry, a 14-year-old boy, was referred for treatment because of delinquent behavior. His defiance of authority was ubiquitous. His father was an extremely rigid and punitive person who made Henry feel quite impotent. From ages ten to twelve he had worked with another therapist without too much success. Unfortunately, this therapist had died a year previously.

When he entered his first session he smugly looked around and said, "You shrinks are all the same . . . same stupid couch . . . same stupid diplomas on the walls . . . same damn pictures of your family on the desk." I understood Henry to be trying to lessen his anxiety in this new situation. By finding similarities between my office and that of his previous therapist he was reducing his feelings of strangeness. In addition, he was trying to identify me with his former therapist in order that I could better serve as his replacement. The hostile veneer was also anxiety alleviating; acting like a tough guy is a typical teenage defense against fear. Although anger displaced from his father onto me was also contributing to Henry's hostility, I considered the anxiety-alleviating factor to be the most important at that time. To have delved into the hostility at that point would have missed the aforementioned important issues and would have robbed the patient of his defenses at a time when he was very much in need of them. Appreciating his need for reassurance that his therapist and I did indeed have many similarities, I replied, "Yes, we psychiatrists often have much in common." These comments made Henry less tense and less hostile.

In spite of a promising beginning, I cannot say that Henry and I had a very good relationship during the subsequent months. This was primarily due to the fact that I could not identify well with him when he engaged in antisocial behavior—especially when it took on dangerous proportions. I was, however, making some headway when the father angrily stated in a joint session that he was fed up with Henry's long hair and that he wanted him to cut it shorter. (This occurred in the mid-to-late 1960s when the long hair vogue [and its antisocial value] had reached a peak.) I tried to dissuade the father from putting pressure on Henry and tried to explain to him that it was one of the most innocuous forms of rebellion ever invented and he should be happy that Henry was resorting more to it and less to the more destructive and violent forms. The father was deaf to my advice. Following the session he took Henry to a barber shop. There he and a barber held Henry down while another barber gave him a very short haircut. Following this, Henry completely refused to attend school. (During the course of the therapy he had gotten to the point of attending most of the time.) In subsequent sessions it became apparent that Henry considered himself to have been castrated by his father and his rage was enormous.

About two weeks after this incident Henry came to my office with a teenage friend and asked if the latter could wait for him in the waiting room. The session was not particularly eventful. During my session with the patient who followed, she thought she smelled smoke. I didn't smell anything and neither of us thought it was necessary to investigate. At the end, when we walked out into the waiting room, I was horrified to see that attempts had been made to set my waiting room on fire. Fortunately, the curtains were made of fire-resistant material and so did not completely ignite. The bathroom toilet tissue and paper hand towels had all burned, but fortunately the flames did not spread to the walls. Had the waiting room caught on fire, my only exit would have been out the 13th-story window.

I summoned Henry and his family back for a session at the end of my day. When I asked Henry about the incident, he admitted that he and his friend were responsible. When I asked him if he appreciated that I might have been killed, he smugly replied, "Doc, you gotta die sometime." I concluded that this was not a time for analytic inquiry. Since I was discharging Henry from treatment, such inquiry would have served little, if any, purpose. Besides, I was not particularly interested in spending time helping Henry to gain insight into such things as his act being a reflection of rage felt toward his father being displaced onto me. I was just interested in getting rid of him as quickly and efficiently as possible. I called his parents in, told them about the fire incident, explained that I could not effectively treat anyone who had tried to kill me, and refused their request that I recommend them to someone else—explaining that I had too much concern for my respected colleagues to refer someone such as Henry to them. Although I recognized that this rejection might help Henry appreciate that there could be untoward repercussions to his dangerous behavior, this was not my motivation in discharging him. My intent was not to provide him with any kind of therapeutic "corrective emotional experience"; rather, I just wanted to get rid of him.

Before they left I suggested the parents give me the name of Henry's friend, so I could call his parents and inform them about what their son had done. I called the boy's father, a lawyer, whose immediate response was, "Can you prove it?" I replied, "You and your son deserve one another." And I hung up. A more blatant example of a parent's sanctioning a son's antisocial behavior (so often the case) would be hard to find.

The Case of Harry [Rebuking the Patient]

Harry entered treatment at the age of fourteen because of poor school performance, in spite of extremely high intelligence, and profound shyness. Both of his parents were professional scientists and highly unemotional and intellectualized. Their pressures on Harry to perform well in the academic area were formidable. Harry's poor school performance was, in part, a rebellion against his parents' coercions. In addition, they had a condescending attitude toward practically everyone and little meaningful involvement with anyone outside their family. Harry's shyness and uninvolvement with others was a reflection of his parents' attitudes. The family was Catholic, very religious, and puritanical in their attitudes about profanity, sex, and pleasurable activities.

After about a year of therapy, Harry joined his parochial school's computer club, where he immediately became recognized as the most knowledgeable and enthusiastic member. The activity well suited him because of his very high intelligence and his interest in activities that did not involve emotional expression. A few months after joining he began to report in session his club's new project: computerized matching of boys in his school with the girls of a nearby Catholic school. All students in both schools were to fill out a questionnaire describing various basic physical characteristics, interests, personality preferences in members of the opposite sex, et cetera. All these data were to be fed into a computer and every boy and girl would be matched to three others. A large dance was to be held, everyone was to be assigned a number, and at prescribed times each student would dance with the partner assigned by the computer.

For weeks Harry excitedly spoke of the details of this project. I was most pleased about it not only because of his enthusiasm (a rare quality for Harry to express) but because it would provide Harry with the opportunity to involve himself with girls in a way that would produce less anxiety than some of the more traditional methods of boy-girl meeting. When the week came for the students to fill out their questionnaires, Harry spoke animatedly about the large number of questionnaires being received and how happy he was that everything pointed to the program's being a success. In the context of this discussion I casually asked Harry what answers he had written on his questionnaire. Harry replied, "Oh, I'm not putting in any questionnaire. My job is to organize the whole thing and make sure that everything works well with the computer." I was astonished. For weeks we had spoken about this activity and not once did I ever consider the possibility that Harry himself would not enter. The session took place the day before the deadline for the submission of the questionnaires. There was little time to work things out, to help Harry assuage his anxieties, and to help Harry appreciate what he was doing.

Speaking more as a frustrated father than as a therapist, I told Harry that I was flabbergasted that he wasn't submitting his own questionnaire. I told him that he was making a grave error, that everybody gets nervous in such situations, and that he has to push through his anxieties if he is to enjoy the rewards of a new situation. I spoke quickly and somewhat heatedly—ending with the warning that if he came back to the next session without having submitted his questionnaire I would not only be very disappointed in him but very irritated with him as well.

One could argue that my approach was extremely antitherapeutic. I was coercing this boy; I was pushing him into an anxiety-provoking situation; I would be producing unnecessary guilt and self-loathing if he did not comply with my request; and I was jeopardizing the therapeutic relationship by such coercive and antitherapeutic tactics. I agree completely with these criticisms and I was completely aware of these dangers as I spoke to Harry. My hope was that this risk would be more than counterbalanced by Harry's appreciation, at some level, that my frustration, anger, and coercion came from a deep sense of concern; that only an uninvolved therapist could sit calmly by and allow him to pass by this wonderful opportunity. (I am reminded at this point of a psychiatric ward nurse who once reported to me overhearing a conversation among three children. The first said, "My mother's a bitch." The second, "My father's always hitting me." And the third, "My father never even hits me!" Obviously the third's situation was the worst. Having a father who never even bothers to discipline and even punish is a severe deprivation indeed.) I hoped also that the general strength of our relationship was such that he not only would comply, but that he would appreciate that I was being basically benevolent.

Harry did submit his questionnaire. On the night of the dance he "could not find" one of the girls with whom he was matched and the second "didn't show up." However, he did spend some time with the third. But because he didn't know how to dance (and forgot my suggestion that he ask her to teach him a few steps), they talked awhile and then went their separate ways. I was not surprised that no great romance developed from this first encounter with a female. One cannot expect a patient to overcome lifelong inhibitions in one evening. However, the ice was broken. Had I not reacted as I had, I believe that Harry would not have taken this step and I would have therefore been somewhat remiss in my obligation to him. I saw no evidence that Harry's relationship with me had in any way suffered because of my coercion; in fact, I believe that it strengthened. However, this improvement could not have taken place if the coercion had not occurred at a time after a good relationship had already formed. To have used such an approach very early in treatment might very well have destroyed, or seriously compromised, our relationship.

The "Amotivational Syndrome"

It is sometimes said that the patient who has been a failure in most areas of his life is likely to be a failure in therapy as well. Unfortunately, this has been my experience. I cannot say that I have had much success salvaging patients who present with massive difficulties in most areas of functioning. My best successes have been with those who have proved themselves capable of succeeding in at least some areas of functioning. One group of such difficult patients are those who present with the parents' complaint that they just aren't interested in anything—a total "amotivational syndrome." They sit in school and couldn't care less. They forget homework assignments, hand in sloppy work, daydream in class, and are generally tuned out. These are not psychotic children nor are they significantly depressed or unhappy. They just plod along. They have little, if any, interest in playing with friends. They do not seem to be in much pain and can be quite content to spend all their free time watching television. Usually they are of average intelligence (but on occasion may be a little higher or lower).

In the therapy sessions they act similarly. They just sit there—having little to talk about. There is no spontaneity, no dreams to be recalled, nothing of interest to report to the therapist. They will often go along passively with playing games, but their lack of interest becomes infectious and the therapist soon finds him- or herself yawning. I have had the feeling at times when working with such children that I have been "turning myself inside out" or "standing on my head" to draw them out—but to no avail. They may even tell stories, but their stories are often short, stereotyped, and not particularly revealing of significant psychodynamic material. One gets the feeling that they are telling the story, drawing the picture, playing the game, et cetera, in order to comply with the therapist's request as fast as possible. It is as if their main message to parents, teachers, and the therapist is: "Just leave me alone. I'm perfectly content with myself the way I am. I'm getting food, clothing, and shelter from my parents; what else should anyone want in life?" But even this "statement" is made in such a way that both patient and therapist find themselves on the verge of falling asleep as it is being said. Although I have been able, in most of these cases, to delineate those factors which I believe have contributed to the formation of this type of personality disturbance, I have been uniformly unsuccessful in helping such children.

The Passive-Aggressive Child

The aforementioned children are not passive-aggressive, that is, they are not particularly angry nor using obstructionism as a way of expressing their hostility. The passive-aggressive represent another category of children who are extremely difficult to engage. They are basically very angry children who express their anger by thwarting those around them. They seem to operate in accordance with the principle: "What he wants me to do is the very thing I will not do." The request becomes the cue for not doing. It provides the child with his or her weapon. It tells the child exactly what particular kind of refusal will be most effective at that particular time. Home life provides a continuous opportunity for such negativistic expression: they dawdle in practically everything, they forget to do what's expected of them, they won't eat or eat very slowly or messily. Everything quickly turns into a power struggle. In school also, where things are expected of them, they do not comply. They exasperate the teacher who finds them fighting her at every point—always silently and passively. And it is no surprise that they react similarly in the session with the therapist. The child is asked to talk; so the child has nothing to say. The therapist asks the child to play games; the reply: "not interested," "can't think of a story," "I don't like to draw," et cetera.

The therapist who is willing to spend weeks, months, and perhaps even years sitting silently and not falling into the child's trap of reaching out and then being thwarted may be providing such a child with a therapeutically beneficial experience. I, however, like myself too much to endure such boredom for the sake of a patient. In fact, the resentment I would feel in such sessions could not but be antitherapeutic. In addition, my experience has been that the child who is willing to sit silently as a gratification of passive-aggressive needs knows that the therapy is costing his or her parents money and so the therapist's participation in such sessions makes him or her an ally in the child's acting out—an obviously antitherapeutic situation. I have sometimes tried to work with such children in family sessions. I take the tack: "We are talking here about you and it behooves you to participate in this discussion because we'll be making decisions that concern you." I try to draw such children into the discussion to get their opinions—especially when it may behoove them to talk in order to argue against a decision's being made that may make them uncomfortable. Again, I cannot say that this approach has been particularly successful either.

The Case of Carol [The Hostile Parent]

The parent who is actively antagonistic to the therapist and who still brings the child (for a variety of pathological reasons) impedes and even prevents formation of a working therapist-patient relationship. Torn between the two, the child usually sides with the one who is most important: the parent. A good example of such interference occurred with Carol, a nine-and-a-half-year-old girl with stuttering, insomnia, and poor peer relationships, who was placed in just such a difficult bind quite early in treatment. Her mother, a very angry woman, became increasingly hostile toward me and tried to get the patient to side with her against me. She would interrogate the patient after each session in an attempt to point out what she considered to be my defects. On one occasion, after two months of treatment, the following dialogue—related by the patient and confirmed by the mother—took place:

> *Mother:* (in a tone of biting sarcasm): So what did you and Dr. Gardner talk about today?
> *Patient:* We talked about a nightmare I had. I dreamed monsters were chasing me.
> *Mother:* And what did *he* think about *that?*
> *Patient:* He thought I had a lot of anger in me that I was scared to let out.
> *Mother:* I think he's full of shit!

Following similar reports by the patient, I arranged an interview with the parents. I told them that the likelihood of therapy succeeding was small as long as the mother continued to try to undermine Carol's relationship with me. My invitation to the mother to air her complaints to me directly, in the hope that at least some of the difficulties might be resolved, was greeted with a barrage of invective. Attempts to help her gain insight into her reactions were futile. She did agree, however, to consult with another therapist regarding treatment for herself. It was also decided that if, after another month, there was still no appreciable difference in the mother's attitude, treatment would be discontinued.

One month later the mother, although in treatment, was as hostile as ever toward me, and it was agreed that there was no point to my working further with the child, who had been in treatment for three months. The parents also decided not to seek treatment elsewhere for the child at that time.

The Case of Greg [Death of a Boy's Father]

This 11-year-old boy's father died suddenly of a heart attack at the age of 39, two days after my initial two-hour evaluation. Over the next few months, every session with Greg was spent talking about his father and helping him work through his reactions to this tragedy. The sessions were deep and meaningful to both of us, and I believe that his involvement with me at that time contributed significantly to his adjustment to the loss.

During his seventh week of treatment he presented me with a piece of paper and stated that he had written a poem about me. We sat down together and read the poem (errors retained):

> I KNOW A MAN
> written in honor of
> Doctor Richard Gardner
>
> I know a man that
> tries to help others
> as much as he Poss-
> ibly can, With a
> desire to find and
> see out you're prob-
> lem, and cure it
> to the best of his
> ability. His quest;
> to follow through on
> his everlasting path
> overcoming all obstac-
> les in his way. His
> kind and understand-
> ing personality, and

        self convidence,
        with a mind that
        expresses great
        contributions
        towrd his feild.
        wich all help to
        guide him through
        lifes endless
        passage, accomp-
        lishing more than
        most any man
        could ever dream.

Following my reading of the poem I told him how touched I was by it and how pleased I was that he had taken the trouble to write it for me. I told him that I was glad to see that he appreciated that I can only *help* people with their problems to the *best of my ability*, but that their help is important also if their problems are to be reduced. I then asked him if he would like to read a poem that I had written which was hanging on the wall. We went over and he began to read:

        To Children

            whose infectious joie de vivre
        elates us,
            whose ingenuousness
        refreshes us,
            whose guilelessness
        embarrasses and teaches us,
            whose undiscriminating love
        flatters us,
            whose optimism
        gives us hope,
            and who, as our progeny,
        provide us with our most meaningful
        link to immortality.

There were a number of words that the patient did not understand and I explained their meaning to him. When we got to the end we discussed the last line: "and who, as our progeny, provide us with our most meaningful link to immortality." I then said to him: "This last line reminds me of your father. Although he is dead,

I am sure that when he was alive you were a great source of pride to him. When people have such fine, bright, and good-natured children it makes it easier for them to die because they know that they are leaving something good and wonderful behind—something that they have helped to create—something that they have helped to grow."

Both the patient and I found the experience quite meaningful. There was an extra dimension to the experience that went beyond our discussing his father and our feelings about one another. The interchange—especially the feelings that existed between us while talking—created a closeness that I find extremely difficult to describe exactly. There was a mutual sense of respect and admiration. We were joined together in our sorrowful feelings over the loss of his father. This mutual experience in which we both felt the same emotion at the same time contributed to the richness of the experience. I believe that such experiences are among the most ego-enhancing that an individual can have, and they serve as the most powerful antidote to psychopathological processes and the most effective prophylactic against their formation.

The Case of Timmy
[Revelation of the Therapist's Defect]

During my initial consultation in which I discussed the treatment of Timmy, a ten-year-old boy, I informed the parents that they should contact me if they knew that they could not keep any of their appointments. I told them that if I could fill the session there would be no charge; however, if I was unable to do that I would charge them. In addition, I told them that I usually spend about three hours collating all the data from my intensive evaluation of themselves and their child, as well as reports from the schools, psychological tests, and so on. For this time, I informed them, I charge for two sessions.

One morning, about a half hour prior to the patient's final evaluative session, the mother called me and told me that she would be unable to bring her son for his session. With such short notice it was impossible to fill the appointment. Accordingly, at the end of the month there was a charge for the missed session, as well as the two sessions' time for the preparation of my final report. A few days after sending out the bill I received an angry note from the father asking me why I could not have used his son's session time toward the preparation of my final presentation. The letter arrived on a morning when I was under great pressure taking care of many last minute details prior to leaving on a lecture tour to the west coast. I quickly dictated a letter to my secretary angrily informing the father that I charge for my time, that his son had not shown up for his session, that it was too late for me to fill it, and that my bill still held.

When I returned from my trip full payment had been sent with another angry letter from the father claiming that he still felt that his criticism was justified. I found myself getting angry at the man and then began questioning myself very seriously as to whether there was some justification for his complaint. I had to admit that I had used his son's time for telephone calls and that there *was* some justification for his complaint.

Accordingly, during the next interview in which I was to see the patient *with* his parents and two brothers, I took the opportunity to apologize to the father for having charged him and explained that I'd been somewhat greedy in doing so. Although I described the pressure of my final preparations for my trip to have contributed, I openly admitted that I was not for one minute claiming that this was a justifiable excuse. The apology was made at a point in the discussion when the patient's older brother was describing how Timmy was unable to tolerate deficiencies. Timmy suffered with a mild learning disability and reacted violently whenever his learning deficiencies were exposed. Following this discussion I apologized to the father. We then discussed the father's feelings about me, and he described admiration for my willingness to admit a deficiency. Of course, as part of my apology, I informed the father that he would be credited for the cost of the charged session in his next bill. In a subsequent discussion, I believe that Timmy was helped to appreciate that admitting a deficiency might bring one more respect than covering it up. The fact that I, his therapist, could have a deficiency was also of therapeutic value to Timmy, in that it contributed to his feeling less loathesome about his own defects.

Other Assorted Examples of a Good Therapist-Patient Relationship

Some children have collected the prizes that they have won playing *The Talking, Feeling, and Doing Game* (1973b) (Chapter Eleven) and the *mutual storytelling technique* derivative games (Chapter Ten). Some children will amass collections, others merely save special prizes that have particular significance. A number of children have developed special psychological relationships with certain books of mine. This is especially the case for *The Boys and Girls Book About Divorce* (1970a, 1971b). On occasion, I will see parents who are contemplating separation or divorce in order to counsel them regarding the best way to tell their children about the forthcoming separation. In the course of the consultation, I will recommend that they give the children a copy of the book as a present from me. I am especially prone to do this when I suspect a child might become involved in therapy. Reading the book provides a useful transition in that a relationship is already established via the book.

My *Stories About the Real World* (1972a) has also proven a useful vehicle for entrenching the relationship. A number of children have related so strongly to the book that they develop a psychological tie with it and actually put it under their pillows when going to sleep. One boy with many fears took the book along with him when he went for his swimming lesson. He was particularly absorbed with the story of Helen (the girl who wouldn't try, a girl who was fearful of entering new situations). He actually took the book along to his swimming lessons, clutched it as he approached the pool, and gave it to his mother just before he entered the pool. It clearly served as a kind of security blanket.

Joel lived in the same town as I and belonged to the same community swim club. One day, as I was walking at the edge of the pool, he yelled from the other side of the pool to a boy in the water, about halfway between us: "Hey, Benjy, look over there (pointing to me). That's Dr. Gardner. He's my psychiatrist!" Although the boy's mother (who was standing next to him) cringed beyond description, he beamed with pride as many in the pool looked at me as I waved to Joel. About one year after the completion of his treatment Joel, then age ten, came up to me at the pool one day and said: "Dr. Gardner, I know you're off duty. But I had this dream last night that bothers me. Would you help me analyze it? I don't have much money; but I can pay you fifty cents." I told him that there was no charge for postgraduate dream analyses and we sat down together and discussed the dream.

Michael, whose divorced father rarely visited, when he sat opposite me often put his feet up on the ottoman between us—in obvious imitation of me. At times, he would place the soles of his feet against the soles of mine and we would continue talking in this way. This was never discussed. To have done so would have robbed the experience of some of its beauty and import. There are certain times in therapy when talking about something robs it of therapeutic benefit—and this is one such example.

One day, Bernard, during his sixth month of treatment, saw a clock in my wastepaper basket. When he asked if he could have it I told him yes, but informed him that it was broken and that was why I had thrown it away. Two years later, during our last session, his mother said to me: "Doctor, do you remember that clock from the wastepaper basket you once let Bernard have?" Since it had never been mentioned again, I had a little difficulty recalling it, but the patient soon refreshed my memory by describing the incident in which I had given it to him. "Well," she continued, "I don't know whether you know it or not but he sleeps with that broken clock under his pillow every night."

One girl asked if she could bring her own cassette tape recorder and tape her sessions—especially the stories we told—so she could bring them home and listen to them. I readily agreed, and it was from this request that I ultimately suggested that all patients do so because it provides such a good opportunity for reiteration of the therapeutic messages and in many cases an entrenchment of the relationship with me.

Sally came to the session the day after Christmas and wanted to take my picture with her new camera so that she could show all her friends what I looked like. Helen, age 12, came to her second session with a notebook entitled: "Secret Things to Tell Dr. Gardner." And Susan's younger sister is reported to have told her mother, "I wish that I had a problem so that I could go and see Dr. Gardner too."

As is obvious, forming a good relationship with the child has more benefits than just helping the child's therapy. It can be extremely gratifying for the therapist in its own right. My hope is that the methods described in this book will prove useful to therapists in helping them form such satisfying and enriching relationships themselves.

FIVE

The Initial
Screening Evaluation

Let's start at the very beginning—a very good place to start.

Maria Trapp, *The Sound of Music*

In my discussion of my military service in Chapter One, I mentioned the frustrations I experienced when confined to one-hour evaluations of children and their parents. I promised myself then that I would never allow myself to work under such artificial and stringent conditions. And I believe that I have kept that promise. Accordingly, my initial screening interview is two hours. This generally gives me the opportunity to get enough of a "feel" for the situation to provide me with guidelines regarding how I should proceed further. At that point, I not only make a decision on the basis of information acquired during the interview but on information obtained from an extensive questionnaire (to be discussed in detail below) that the parent brings to the first interview. If, however, by the end of the two hours I still do not have enough information to come to a definite decision, I have no hesitation scheduling a third. I feel no inner compulsion to pressure myself into coming to a conclusion under any kind of time restraints. If therapy is warranted,

I will generally recommend the more extensive evaluation, which I will discuss in Chapter Six.

WHO SHALL BE SEEN IN THE INITIAL CONSULTATION?

There are many ways to conduct the initial screening interview. Various combinations of child and/or parent(s) in different sequences, with one or more interviewers, may be utilized. For example, the child may be seen alone, the parent(s) alone, the child and parent(s) together, or a total family interview may be held. There may be one interviewer for all or separate interviewers seeing one or more individuals at a time. Of all the possible approaches, I personally prefer the first interview to be conducted with the child and parents together, individually and in varying combinations—as warranted. All things considered, I believe this arrangement to have the greatest number of advantages and the fewest drawbacks as compared to the other commonly used methods. Moreover, I believe that the clinical interviews are best conducted by one person.

Those who first see the parents alone claim that it provides an atmosphere in which information can be obtained without the child's distractions, and the parents need not be inhibited for fear that they may needlessly embarrass or otherwise harm the child by their open disclosures of his or her problems.

I consider the child's "distractions" to be a potentially rich source of information that is lost when the child is not there. Also, I have found that the direct confrontation has been more therapeutic than not. It helps crystallize in the child's mind (and also in the parents') the nature of the problems and this may be the first step toward their alleviation. If what is said is too painful the child's defenses can be relied upon to protect him or her. One can be quite sure that the child has been confronted many times before with the manifestations of the difficulties, but to do so again in the accepting and sympathetic environment of the therapist's office may be salutary. Such discussion fosters healthy communication between parents and child, and this kind of open conversation is often lacking in families in which children suffer psychological problems.

The three person interview also provides the therapist with the opportunity to observe directly interactions between the parents and the child. Seeing the parents alone in the initial interview deprives the therapist of first-hand observation of the patient. No matter how astute the parents may be in describing their child, they cannot provide the interviewer with as accurate a picture as his or her actual presence can.

In such an interview, I usually encourage hesitant parents to speak up. I tell them that my experience has been that it is in their child's best interests to discuss openly what directly pertains to the child in his or her presence and that we will have the opportunity later to talk about their own (the parents') personal matters which are less directly concerned with the child. Knowing that they will have subsequent time alone with me often makes it easier for them to discuss the child's problems in his or her presence.

There are some who take great pains to keep the child-therapist dyad completely separate from all therapeutic work and/or contact with the parents. From the outset, they will arrange for the parents to be counseled by a colleague, with whom there are occasional conferences. Proponents of this approach claim that the child's relationship with the therapist will be diluted and contaminated by any contact the therapist may have with the parents; that the patient will not have the feeling of having the therapist all to him- or herself and the treatment will thereby suffer. There are some therapists who take this so far that they will have absolutely no contact at all with the parents at any time.

I have formidable criticisms of this approach. It deprives the therapist of the opportunity of seeing the parents first-hand. No matter how accurate the child's description, he or she most often has distortions, which may be clarified via direct contact with the parents. And the colleague working with the parents is likely to have distortions about the child because information about him or her has been filtered through the parents. The child's problems are inextricably involved with the family's, and the therapist, by isolating the dyad, removes it from the field within which the problems have arisen and taken place and within which they must be worked through. Furthermore, the arrangement precludes joint interviews with the parents that can be a valuable source of information about family dynamics and interpersonal relations.

I have not found that my relationships with my child patients have suffered because of contact with parents (and these have varied from occasional interviews to actual stimultaneous therapy with one of the parents, usually the mother). In fact, such contacts and involvements have most often deepened my relationship with the child. The child will follow the parents. If the latter have respect for and faith enough in the therapist to consult him or her themselves, this enhances the child's involvement; whereas when the opposite is true, when there is no contact, the child's loyalty becomes divided between the therapist and the parents. In such a situation therapy can be deeply undermined, if not made entirely impossible.

There are some who feel quite strongly that the child should be seen alone in the first interview, but they will work subsequently with the parents in varying degrees. They reason that such an approach communicates to the child, from the very beginning, that *he* or *she* is the patient; they hold that this is vital if subsequent work is to be successful. I do not consider this to be such an important consideration because, more often than not, I see the parents as equally worthy of my clinical attention. I prefer to communicate to all that they are each to be clinically evaluated and that the greatest concentration is yet to be determined—therefore, the three person interview.

In addition, proponents of this method claim that taking the child away from the parents in the waiting room provides a direct opportunity to observe the child's reaction to separation—with special regard to the degree of separation anxiety. The assumption here is that there are children who do not have such anxiety. It is hard for me to imagine any child who would not be fearful going off alone in a room with an adult stranger in a setting which is probably unlike anything he or she has ever seen before. Not only is nothing learned when such separation is demanded but worse, the resulting fears interfere with the therapist's obtaining information about the child—all for the purpose of observing how he or she reacts under extreme tension. I would go further and say that such enforced separation often interferes with or delays the formation of the warm, friendly, trusting relationship which is a *sine qua non* of treatment. Another disadvantage of this approach is that it may place the therapist in the position of having to force or drag the child into his or her office. This is probably the only *never* I mention in this book, but I use it here without hesitation. This should *never* be. Such a struggle is totally antithetical to the process and goals of therapy, and adherence to the dictum of seeing the child alone in the beginning of the first session merely invites such a deplorable situation. In Chapter Seven I will discuss in greater detail what I consider to be the optimum kind of involvement the therapist should have with the parents.

It is for these reasons, and others to be discussed in detail in Chapters Seven and Fourteen, that my initial two-hour interview is one in which all three parties are invited, that is, the child and both the parents. During that time they are seen in any combination that one can imagine, either individually or jointly. Generally, younger children (below the age of 11 or so) are invited to come into my consultation room together with their parents. Adolescents (13 and above) are first brought in alone, and the parents join us subsequently. In this way, I provide the adolescent with a separate experience from the parents, which is important for youngsters of this age to have. However, the parents are still brought in, which gets across the message that I am going to involve them in the treatment as well. (Some adolescents object to parental involvement, usually as a manifestation of specious independence or as a way of preventing parental disclosures. There is rarely a good reason.) Regarding children between ages 11 to 13, I utilize a number of criteria to decide how I will structure the initial invitation. If the youngster appears to be a mature individual, I may treat him or her like an adolescent and invite the child in first. In contrast, if the youngster appears to be younger and immature, I will invite the parents to join us. And, if I have any doubts about which way to go, I will ask the child how he or she would like to structure the interview, that is, whether the child wishes to accompany me alone or to be joined by the parents. Sometimes the discussion that takes place in the waiting room over this issue can, in itself, provide useful information about the family.

THE INITIAL TELEPHONE CALL

Although one of my secretaries almost invariably answers my telephone, they make no appointments—whether it be the first appointment or any other appointment in the total course of the treatment. When a person calls to make an appointment, he or she is informed that I will be available to speak during certain call times, during which period I can generally speak in a more leisurely manner regarding the appointment. If the day is particularly tight (often the case), I will converse with the parent during the evening. I generally find a ten-minute conversation necessary before setting up the initial appointment. My purpose here is to get some information about the nature of the child's problems in order that I may be in a better position to deal with unexpected events that may occur during the initial consultation. Because of the unpredictability of children, therapists who work with them must be prepared to deal with many more "surprises" than those who treat adults.

But there are other reasons for my acquiring more information before making the initial appointments. Sometimes, an appointment might not be necessary. A parent might call requesting a consultation regarding how to tell the children about an impending separation. In such cases I may refer the caller to my *The Parents Book About Divorce* (1977b, 1979a) to read the section on telling children about an impending separation. I am careful, however, to reassure such callers that I am not turning them away; rather, I am trying to save them money in that the cost of the pocket edition of my book is far less than a consultation. I inform them also that if this does not prove sufficient, then I will be happy to set up an appointment for a consultation. On a number of occasions I have received calls from distraught parents at the time of a sudden death of a spouse, and there is a family argument regarding whether or not children should attend the funeral services and burial. Often I can provide meaningful advice in a short time, and no consultation is necessary.

Sometimes the symptoms described are short-lived and the parent is not aware of the fact that all children exhibit at times transient symptomatology such as tics, gastrointestinal complaints, or a wide variety of fears. On occasion symptomatic reactions to parental divorce may be the reason for the parent's call. In many such situations I will advise the parents to wait awhile because such symptoms are predictable and are usually transient. The authors of DSM-III are most appreciative of this phenomenon, and this is reflected in the stipulation that time considerations must be taken into account before many childhood diagnoses are warranted.

Some parents who anticipate custody litigation may call requesting therapy in the hope that they can then use the therapist as an advocate in the litigation. It behooves the therapist to "smell these out" over the telephone in order to avoid sticky and compromising situations. (I consider myself to have an excellent sense of smell in these situations.) If there is any doubt about such a caller's true motives, I will inform the individual that a decision must be made *before the first interview* as to whether my services are requested for the purpose of *litigation* or for *therapy*. I inform such callers that I am receptive to following either path; however, once one course is chosen I will not switch to the other and I will be asking that the appropriate document be signed—*again before the first interview*—which strictly confines me to a particular path. The reasons for my rigidity on this point relate to important legal issues (Gardner, 1982, 1986b).

On one occasion a mother called to make the initial appointment and, after telling me the presenting problems, told me that I would have to promise her something before she would make the first appointment. I immediately smelled something foul, but I didn't know what it would be. She then told me that her child was adopted and that I must promise her that under no circumstances would I ever reveal this to him. I told her that I would make no such promise and that I cannot imagine the child's therapy proceeding without this topic being discussed at some point in the treatment. I reassured her that I would not scream the fact in the child's face as soon as he entered the room, but I would not agree to such a restriction throughout the whole course of the treatment. She advised me that other doctors had agreed to this restriction. I advised her then to consult these other doctors and that I was giving her my opinion on the subject.

Another mother, again after telling me her daughter's problems, also asked me to make a promise. (Again, smelly odors emanated through the telephone wires.) This time the mother informed me that the child was diagnosed as having a learning disability at the age of three and the parents were advised to start the child in school a year later than they had originally planned. In order to protect the child from the psychological trauma of such late commencement into the educational process, they told the girl that she was one year younger than she really was. Again, I informed the mother that I would not confront the child with this fact during the first minute of my first session, but I would not agree to be part of this conspiracy throughout the whole course of the treatment. The mother informed me that the school principal, all the teachers, and all the extended family members on both sides had agreed to withhold this information from the child. I informed the mother that I considered her not to have learned the lesson that Richard Nixon sadly learned, namely, that it is unreasonable to expect a few hundred people to keep a secret. And so we too parted ways.

A common problem that can easily be obviated in the initial telephone call is the one in which a divorced mother sets up an appointment and informs the therapist that her former husband will be paying her bills and that the therapist should be billing him directly. In response to such callers I generally respond that I will be happy to do so if her former husband will call me and tell me directly that he will be paying for my services. Often I will get the response that he is required to pay all medical bills as a stipulation of the divorce decree and that if I have trouble getting the money from him she is sure that the court will order him to pay. Any therapist who is naive or gullible enough to accept a patient under these circumstances does not get my pity.

A divorced mother will call asking for a consultation. I inform her that my usual procedure is to see both parents and the child, in varying combinations, during a two-hour consultation. The mother informs me that she is divorced, with the implication that that fact in itself is justification for my not involving her former husband in the therapy. I will generally then ask if the child's father still maintains some involvement with him or her. If the answer is in the affirmative, I then recommend that the mother consult with the father and invite him to join us during the first interview. I generally do this before a specific appointment is made. This insures that the mother will at least invite the father (who, of course, may or may not accept). My experience is that they most often do. The mother may argue that it would not be a good idea to have her former husband join us because "all we'll do is fight." My response to such a mother goes along these lines: "It is certainly not my goal to get you to fight. However, this I can tell you: I already know that as long as you and your husband cannot be in the same room together without fighting, your child will continue to have problems. I cannot imagine helping your son(daughter) with his(her) problems, as long as there is such severe animosity between you and your ex-husband. I can tell you now that one of my goals in therapy will be to help the two of you to reduce the hostilities. If that wasn't one of my goals, I wouldn't be qualified to help your child. Also, although the fighting is certainly unpleasant, I will probably learn some important things from it that will be useful in your child's treatment." Here again I have most often been successful in getting both parties to attend the initial interview.

On occasion, the calling mother may respond to my request for the father's involvement with "My husband doesn't believe in psychiatry. He told me that if I want to take Sally to a psychiatrist, it's okay with him but he doesn't want to get involved. To which I will replay, "Please tell your husband that my experience has been that the more involvement I have on the part of both parents, the greater the likelihood the treatment will be successful. If your husband refuses to involve himself entirely, I will do the best I can, but please inform him that I'll be working under compromised circumstances." I call this the "ball-is-in-your-court-baby principle." I basically say to the husband that the choice is his; if he wants me to conduct therapy under optimum circumstances, he will involve himself. If he doesn't do so, there will be less of a likelihood that the treatment will be successful, and he will have thereby contributed to its failure. Again, most often husbands appear when this message is transmitted to them. I might say here parenthetically, for those readers in private practice, that those husbands who do not *believe in* psychiatry are not famous for their *paying for* psychiatry. Doing everything reasonable to bring both parents into the initial interview establishes also a certain precedent, namely, that their involvement in the child's treatment is important and my urging them both to be present at the outset is a clear statement of this.

During this initial telephone conversation some parents ask my fee. Without hesitation I give my response. At the time of this writing my answer is this: "My standard fee is $90 for 45-minute sessions and $120 for full-hour sessions. The fee for the initial two-hour consultation, therefore, will be $240. Following that, there is a possibility of some lowering, but not below $75 for 45-minute sessions and $100 for full-hour sessions. This can be determined at the time of the consultation on the basis of your financial situation and insurance coverage." I know of many therapists who refuse to discuss fees over the telephone. This is not only injudicious but alienating. It cannot but engender distrust on the patient's part. It is reasonable for a patient to conclude from such an answer that "I guess he's going to try and get as much as he can." And such a conclusion is warranted. The argument that the discussion may have psychoanalytic significance is not justified. The caller is not an analytic patient; he or she is just a parent who is entitled to know what the therapist charges. Later in this chapter, I will discuss further the issue of fees.

Before closing, I inform the caller that I will be sending a questionnaire that I would like both parents to fill out. As will be discussed below, this questionnaire is quite comprehensive and provides me with a significant amount of "upfront" information at the time of the initial consultation. Attached to the questionnaire is a face letter (Figure 5.1) which I consider to be quite important. For parents who have not asked about the fees, they are provided this information with the questionnaire so that there is no disappointment, incredulity, amazement, or other reactions that may result in nonpayment of the fees. It also informs the parents that they will have the obligation themselves to pay me and that I will not pursue third parties for payment. (Many patients feel no guilt over doctors' doing this.)

THE QUESTIONNAIRE

I have found my questionnaire extremely valuable for the large majority of consultations. It provides the therapist with an immense amount of information in a few minutes, information that might take hours to obtain via direct questioning. The questionnaire provides information useful in ascertaining for the presence of psychogenic disturbances as well as diagnosing children who suffer with what I refer to as the Group of Minimal Brain Dysfunction Syndromes (GMBDS). I prefer to use this term over MBD because MBD implies a single disease entity. Rather, we are dealing here with a group of syndromes. It is unreasonable to attempt to assess for both psychogenic problems and the presence of GMBDS in a single two-hour interview. The questionnaire helps the examiner determine which are the areas that should most appropriately be focused on in the initial consultation. It tells the examiner where the "smoke" is so that he or she can know where to look for the "fires."

Furthermore, it has certain fringe benefits. It is detailed and thorough, thereby creating a good impression with many parents. This "good impression" helps establish a good relationship with the parents, which can ultimately contribute to the child's having a better relationship with the therapist. Furthermore, it provides examiners with a well-organized format on which to base their re-

Figure 5.1

Dear

Attached please find the questionnaire I would like you to fill
out about your child. Please bring it with you at the time of
your first appointment. In addition, I would appreciate your
bringing copies of any other material that you suspect might be
useful to me, e.g. reports from psychologists, psychiatrists,
child study teams, learning disability consultants, teachers,
etc. Please make copies of these reports so that I can have
them for my files.

My fee for consultations is $120/60-minute session. Unlike
reports from other medical specialists, child psychiatric reports
are generally quite lengthy and time consuming to prepare.
Accordingly, if a written report is desired, there is an additional charge for its preparation, dictation, and review, which
is prorated at the aforementioned rate. My fee for treatment
ranges from $90/45-minute session down to $75/45-minute session,
the exact fee to be determined at the time treatment is instituted.
Payment is due at the time services are rendered.   hours have
been set aside for the initial consultation with your child. I
would appreciate your paying my secretary the $ fee at the
time of the consultation. My secretary will be happy to provide
receipts and assist in the preparation of forms for subsequent
reimbursement to you by insurance companies and other third
party payers.

Please know that I will do everything possible to be helpful to
your child. If you have any questions regarding the above, please
do not hesitate to call my office.

                           Sincerely,

                           Richard A. Gardner, M.D.
                           Clinical Professor of
                             Child Psychiatry
                           Columbia University, College
                             of Physicians and Surgeons

RAG/lg
encl.

ports. When dictating a report the examiner merely peruses the questionnaire and dictates information directly from it. The organization is already there and the examiner is saved the trouble of thumbing through notes, shifting back and forth, etc.

Basic Data

Most questionnaires request name, address, telephone number, etc. for the child and then for each of the parents. With the burgeoning divorce rate in recent years, fewer children are living in homes with both natural parents. Many other combinations are being seen and it is important that the examiner have a clear idea of the child's family structure and the exact nature of his or her relationships with the various adults who are involved in the child's care. Therefore, immediately after I get basic information about where the child is living (address, telephone number, school), the parent is asked to place checks in the appropriate places in the present placement table (Figure 5.2) to indicate the child's relationships with the adults with whom he or she is living (column A), as well as those who are involved in his or her care but living elsewhere (column B). For example, a boy might be living with his natural mother and stepfather. Checks for these individuals would be placed in column A. His natural father might be living with his new wife, the child's stepmother. Checks for these individuals would be placed in column B. The parent would then place numbers 1 and 2 next to the checks in column A for the natural mother and stepfather and the number 3 next to the check for the natural father in column B. More data on the nonresidential stepmother would generally not be obtained here (unless the situation specifically warranted its inclusion). Because the home address for the natural mother and stepfather has already been obtained, only their business addresses are requested. Then information about the natural father's home and business is requested. Although this type of inquiry may appear cumbersome at first, it is ultimately easier than the explanations that parents are required to provide when the questionnaire asks simply for data about the mother and father. In addition, columns A and B provide at-a-glance information about present placement.

Information about the referral source is then requested (Figure 5.3) as well as the reasons for the consultation. Just a few lines are available for this because I only wish the parent to make a brief

Figure 5.2

PLEASE BRING THIS COMPLETED FORM WITH YOU AT THE TIME OF YOUR FIRST APPOINT-

MENT ON_____AT_____

IT IS PREFERABLE THAT BOTH PARENTS ACCOMPANY THE CHILD TO THE CONSULTATION.

Child's name_____ Birth date_____ Age___ Sex_____
           last   **first**   middle
Home address_____
           street   city   state   zip
Home telephone number_____
                   area code   number
Child's school_____
              name   address   **grade**
Present placement of child (place check in appropriate bracket):

	Column A Adults with whom child is living	Column B Non-residential adults involved with child
Natural mother	( ) ___	( ) ___
Natural father	( ) ___	( ) ___
Stepmother	( ) ___	( ) ___
Stepfather	( ) ___	( ) ___
Adoptive mother	( ) ___	( ) ___
Adoptive father	( ) ___	( ) ___
Foster mother	( ) ___	( ) ___
Foster father	( ) ___	( ) ___
Other (specify)	_____ ___	_____ ___

Place the number 1 or 2 next to each check in Column A and provide the
following information about each person:

  1. Name_____Occupation_____
          last   first
     Business name_____Business address_____

     _____Business tel. No. ( )_____

  2. Name_____Occupation_____
          last   first
     Business name_____Business address_____

     _____Business tel. No. ( )_____

Place the number 3 next to the person checked in Column B who is most involved
with the child and provide the following information:

  3. Name_____Home address_____
                                        street
     _____Home tel. No. ( )_____
     city   state   zip
     Occupation_____Business name_____

Figure 5.3

Business address_____Bus. Tel. No. (   )_____

Source of referral: Name_____Address_____

_____Tel. No. (   )_____

Purpose of consultation (brief summary of the main problems):_____

_____

_____

_____

_____

PREGNANCY
  Complications:
    Excessive vomiting_____hospitalization required_____

    Excessive staining or blood loss_____

    Threatened miscarriage_____

    Infection(s) (specify)_____

    Toxemia_____

    Operation(s) (specify)_____

    Other illness(es) (specify)_____

  Smoking during pregnancy_____average number of cigarettes per day_____

  Alcoholic consumption during pregnancy_____describe, if beyond an occa-

    sional drink_____

  Medications taken during pregnancy_____

  X-ray studies during pregnancy_____

  Duration_____weeks

DELIVERY
  Type of labor: Spontaneous_____Induced_____
  Forceps: high_____mid_____low_____
  Duration of labor_____hours

  Type of delivery: Vertex (normal)_____breech_____Caesarean_____

  Complications:
    cord around neck_____

    cord presented first_____

    hemorrhage_____

statement here. To provide more space would probably result in a repetition of material to be obtained subsequently.

Pregnancy

It is probable that many, if not most, of the causes of the GMBDS exert their effects during pregnancy. Although genetic factors and those related to delivery and afterwards are certainly seen, it is probable that most of the cases of MBD are the result of interferences that occurred during the gestational period.

One should get further information about any of the complications of pregnancy that may have been checked off on the questionnaire. Most women stain during pregnancy. If, however, prolonged periods of bed rest were required, or hospitalization was necessary, then one could assume that this complication was in the pathological range. It is probable that many children's MBD is the result of maternal infections that get transmitted to the embryo and fetus. Sometimes such infections are subclinical and so we have no information about them. When they produce clinical symptoms, especially if severe, then the likelihood of their being of etiological significance is greater. The maternal infections that have most conclusively been demonstrated to produce fetal brain dysfunction are cytomegalic inclusion disease, toxoplasmosis, rubella, herpes simplex, and syphilis. Toxemia has been associated with the GMBDS. One should, therefore, inquire about high blood pressure, seizures, and proteinuria. Most women vomit during pregnancy. Vomiting can cause dehydration that might result in fluid and nutriment deprivation for the fetus. The crucial question is how much vomiting is necessary to cause fetal deprivation? If hospitalization was required, especially for intravenous fluid replacement, then it is possible that vomiting was the cause of the child's MBD. However, it would only be under suspicion as an etiological factor.

A standard warning on many drug labels is that safe administration during pregnancy has not been established. Accordingly, any medication that was taken over time during the pregnancy should be noted by the examiner. Thalidomide has probably been one of the more widely publicized causes of congenital anomalies and intellectual impairment. Other drugs that have been known to cause brain dysfunction include aminopterin, diphenylhydantoin, methotrexate, and high doses of vitamin D. And there are probably many other drugs, as yet unimplicated, that will ultimately be shown to have such effects.

Exposure to X-radiation has also been implicated. The most common story is of a woman who presents with nausea, vomiting, and other gastrointestinal symptoms. Pregnancy may not have been suspected, especially if the woman is single or over 40. The patient may undergo a number of radiological examinations (GI series, gall bladder studies, barium enema, et cetera) in the attempt to ascertain the cause of the vomiting. By the time the correct diagnosis is made, the woman may have been exposed to significant amounts of X-radiation. Most radiologists now inquire into the recent menstrual history to be sure that they are not exposing a pregnant woman to X-rays.

Smoking during pregnancy has been associated with low birth weight, increased fetal and neonatal death rate, and impairments in the child's physical, neurological, and intellectual growth. And there appears to be a correlation between the amount of smoking and the incidence of these effects. Excessive alcoholic ingestion can cause what has been referred to as the *fetal alcohol syndrome.* These babies exhibit alterations in growth, facial dysmorphism and other disturbances of body morphogenesis, as well as low birth weight. The GMBDS and mental retardation have been described in these children.

One also wants to learn about the duration of the pregnancy. Traditionally the mother's report on this has not been too reliable because many mothers do not know exactly when they became pregnant. One definition of prematurity (a term falling into disuse) used to be that a child whose gestation was less than 37 weeks was considered premature. Because of the unreliability of this figure, the child's birth weight was subsequently used and children under 2500 grams (5.5 pounds) were considered premature. But, this criterion has also been found wanting because there were some babies below this weight who showed none of the traditional manifestations of prematurity. Accordingly, new criteria (the *gestational age*) are being used to determine if the infant's birth weight is indeed a problem, and these will be presented below when I discuss the significance of the birth weight. The duration of pregnancy figure, however, can still serve as a clue (admittedly a poor one) as to whether there were problems regarding the pregnancy's duration. It is more significant if the gestational age (see below) has been determined by the physician, using recently developed physiological and neurological criteria. Only babies born after the early 1970s were so examined. In time, all knowledgeable mothers may refer to the child's gestational age at birth rather than the duration of the pregnancy.

Delivery

The delivery is another period when the child may be exposed to factors that can produce MBD. Inducing labor runs certain risks for the child, more so in the past than in the present. The physician may miscalculate the pregnancy's duration (especially if he or she relies too heavily on the mother's estimate) and deliver the baby before it can thrive optimally in the extrauterine environment. In the past oxytocin, the drug most commonly used to initiate and maintain uterine contractions, was administered by buccal tablet. One had no control over the duration of its action. Accordingly, uterine contractions might persist after it was determined that cephalopelvic disproportion was present and the fetus was being traumatized. In addition, drugs such as oxytocin can produce tetanic contractions of the uterus. These can cut off blood circulation from the placenta to the fetus and thereby cause anoxia in the child. In recent years such drugs can be given by intravenous drip, which can be carefully controlled. Once trouble is suspected, the oxytocin is immediately discontinued. Because there is no reserve of the drug present in the body (as is the case with buccal tablets) uterine contractions due to the drug can be quickly interrupted. The mother who was spontaneously delivered does not run the risk of these complications.

High forceps delivery is practically unknown today. Just about all obstetricians recognize the danger of its producing trauma to the infant. It is generally agreed among obstetricians that low forceps delivery is without danger, but mid-forceps delivery may cause some trauma. Most obstetricians will choose to do a Caesarean section rather than expose the child to the traumatic risks of mid-forceps delivery.

Mothers may not be completely reliable regarding the accuracy of their reports on the duration of labor. Considering all the things they have to think about during this time, they cannot be seriously faulted for such impairment in their recollection. Strictly speaking, labor is considered to begin when the cervix starts to dilate, and is considered to be continuing as long as there is progressive cervical dilation. Most women enter the hospital already partially dilated, so cervical observation and the more objective reporting of the onset is no longer possible. The clinical definition of the onset is the time when contractions begin to occur at a frequency greater than one every five minutes. Labor is considered to be going on as long as such contractions are *regular and continuous*. Normally, the duration of labor for the first pregnancy is 12–14 hours. Labors more than 16 hours should be considered prolonged, with an increased risk for fetal damage. The normal duration of second and subsequent labors is 8–10 hours, with more than 12 hours being considered prolonged. Of course, there is no exact cutoff point for defining prolonged labors. The longer beyond these figures the labor goes, the greater likelihood there will be fetal distress and damage.

Head trauma incurred during labor is a common cause of brain damage. The most common manifestations of birth trauma that may be associated with brain injury are cephalhematoma, facial nerve paralysis, brachial palsy, phrenic nerve paralysis, fracture of the clavicle, and hematoma of the sternocleidomastoid muscle.

Breech deliveries are generally more traumatic than vertex. Caesarean sections, especially those that are resorted to because of complications that have interfered with delivery via the birth canal, have also been associated with the GMBDS. It is probable that it was not the Caesarean section *per se* that caused the MBD, but the complications that caused the obstetrician to utilize this method of delivery. When a child is born with the umbilical cord around the neck, there may have been some compromise of blood circulation from the placenta to the fetal brain. When the cord presents first, there may be compression of the blood circulation to the child, with resultant impairment of circulation to the infant's brain. Excessive blood loss during labor may also reduce the amount of blood reaching the infant.

As mentioned, birth weight is no longer considered to be the criterion of prematurity. In fact, most neonatologists discourage the use of the term prematurity. Low-birth-weight babies, that is, those weighing less than 2500 grams, are divided into two categories: (1) those whose birth weights are appropriate for their gestational age (AGA) and (2) those whose weights are low, that is, they are small for gestational age (SGA). As mentioned above, we now have objective physiological and neurological criteria for determining gestational age and do not have to rely on a mother's recollection of when she thinks she became pregnant. The babies in these two groups are quite different. Consider, for example, two babies whose birth weight is 1500 grams. One baby is found to have a gestational age of 31 weeks and the other 37 weeks. Because 1500 grams is about normal for 31 week fetuses, the first baby would be considered AGA. The second would be considered SGA. The assumption is made that the second baby has only grown to the 31 week size in a 37 week pregnancy. Something has happened to retard the child's growth. The second child is more likely to exhibit difficulties that would include GMBDS. The first is more likely to develop normally in that nothing serious is considered to have happened to it, although its low birth weight is still an abnormality that may cause difficulty. The questionnaire asks the parent for the birth weight as well as whether it was an AGA or SGA baby. Many parents are not familiar with these terms, but in time knowledge of them should become more widespread.

Babies of large size (over 9 pounds) are also at greater risk for the development of MBD, in that their deliveries are more likely to be traumatic. Babies of long gestation (over 42 weeks) are also likely to have complications such as MBD because the aging placenta becomes more inefficient in its functioning and meconium aspiration is also more likely in such infants.

Post-Delivery Period
[While in the Hospital]

The healthy child breathes spontaneously at birth. At most, the child requires some clearing of the nasal passages. The traditional slap on the buttocks to get the child breathing is considered by most obstetricians to be unnecessary. The usual nasopharyngeal aspiration provides enough stimulation to induce breathing. The longer the delay in breathing the greater the likelihood the child will suffer with cerebral anoxemia. The normal infant spontaneously cries at birth. A delayed cry is also an index of infant depression, especially of respiration and bodily response to stimulation. A fairly objective statement about the newborn's overall physical condition at the time of birth is the Apgar score (Figure 5.4). At one, two, and five minutes after birth, the child is given a score of 0, 1, or 2 on five items. The five physiological functions evaluated are heart rate, respiratory effort, muscle tone, reflex irritability, and general color. With a maximum score of 2 in each category, the maximum score

Figure 5.4

infant injured during delivery_____

other (specify)_____

Birth Weight_____
  Appropriate for gestational age (AGA)_____
  Small for gestational age (SGA)_____

POST-DELIVERY PERIOD (while in the hospital)
  Respiration: immediate_____delayed (if so, how long)_____

  Cry: immediate_____delayed (if so, how long)_____

  Mucus accumulation_____

  Apgar score (if known)_____

  Jaundice_____

  Rh factor_____transfusion_____

  Cyanosis (turned blue)_____

  Incubator care_____number of days_____

  Suck: strong_____weak_____

  Infection (specify)_____

  Vomiting_____diarrhea_____

  Birth defects (specify)_____

  Total number of days baby was in the hospital after the delivery_____

INFANCY-TODDLER PERIOD
  Were any of the following present--to a significant degree--during the
  first few years of life? If so, describe.

    Did not enjoy cuddling _____

    Was not calmed by being held and/or stroked _____

    Colic_____

    Excessive restlessness_____

    Diminished sleep because of restlessness and easy arousal _____

    Frequent headbanging_____

    Constantly into everything_____

    Excessive number of accidents compared to other children_____ is 10. A score of 1, 2, or 3 is considered severe depression; 4, 5, 6, or 7 is moderate depression; and 8, 9, or 10 is no depression. Most mothers are not aware of the existence of this figure, and many who are do not know what recording was made on their child. When the figure can be obtained, it is a valuable bit of information.

About 40% of newborns exhibit a transient physiologic jaundice (icterus neonatorum). There are two causes of this type of jaundice: 1) Increased destruction of red blood cells in order to reduce the high fetal red cell concentration (necessary for intrauterine existence) to the lower levels necessary after birth. 2) The immature liver is inefficient in its capacity to metabolize bilirubin and other products of red blood cell destruction. Generally, the jaundice appears on the second to fourth day and ends betweeen the seventh and fourteenth. Jaundice due to Rh incompatibility (erythroblastosis fetalis) or ABO incompatability (icterus praecox) usually begins during the first 24 hours and is severer. Whereas transfusions are not necessary for physiological jaundice, they are for the treatment of Rh incompatability and severe forms of ABO incompatability. Recently developed immunological treatment with RhoGAM (an anti-Rh + antibody globulin) can prevent Rh incompatibility disorder in mothers who have not yet been sensitized. Less common causes of jaundice in the newborn are congenital obliteration or obstruction of the bile ducts, septicemia, hepatitis, and a variety of blood dyscrasias. The most common examples of brain damage caused by high bilirubin levels is the kernicterus resulting from icteric degeneration of the basal ganglia as well as other cerebral centers.

Cyanosis is a concomitant of anoxia, which may cause cerebral ischemia and nerve cell dysfunction and degeneration. Anoxia may be seen in prematurity in association with the respiratory distress syndrome (hyaline membrane disease), maternal toxemia, and any other condition in which the neonate is under stress. Intracranial hemorrhage (most often caused by birth trauma and hemorrhagic disease of the newborn), congenital atalectasis, hyaline membrane disease, and various congenital heart diseases can also cause cyanosis. The need for incubator care may be a clue to the presence of apnea, cyanosis, and a variety of diseases affecting respiration and circulation.

The normal baby has a strong suck. A weak suck at birth is generally suggestive of some pathological process. Often it is one manifestation of general neurological depression. Meningitis may be the result of infections in the newborn. Generally it is caused by organisms found in the mother's vagina infecting the fetus and producing septicemia in the newborn infant. Infected circumcisions, umbilical stumps, and otitis media, once common causes of meningitis, are less common today.

A variety of congenital anomolies may be associated with neurophysiological impairment. This is especially true of those disorders that directly involve the central nervous system and/or the tissues and bones in which it is encased. The most common disorders in this category are meningocele, meningomyelocele, meningoencephalocele, hydrocephalus, and spina bifida. Cogenital cardiac anomalies may also be associated with cerebral nerve cell degeneration. This is especially true of the cyanotic forms that are associated with hypoxic spells such as the tetralogy of Fallot. If the child was in the hospital for more than five days, one should inquire about the reasons. Usually, a stay beyond that time was necessitated by some physical disorder that may be associated with the GMBDS.

The Infancy-Toddler Period

The normal human infant enjoys being hugged and caressed. This desire is present from birth and the child who is deprived of such gratification may become listless, lose his or her appetite, withdraw interest from the environment, become marantic, and even die. If a child, from the day of birth, does not respond to stroking and cuddling, then some interfering factor is usually present. Sometimes the mother herself is impaired in her desire and/or capacity to fondle her baby. Or she does so with such tension that the child does not find it a gratifying experience. Such mothers may consider breast feeding "disgusting" and may show other signs of inhibition in maternal capacity. Such a mother will generally react similarly to her other children. The child's hyporeactivity in such situations should be considered psychogenic.

If, however, the child is described as not having reacted to cuddling and stroking from birth and the siblings are described as having done so, then it is more likely that the child's impairment is due to some physical disease such as mental retardation, autism, and brain dysfunction. At times the GMBDS child may be differentiated from the retarded and autistic by its hyperreactivity to such stimulation. The autistic and retarded child may be described as lying in the mother's arms limp and unresponsive "like a sack of potatoes." The GMBDS child, however, may respond to stroking by becoming irritable, crying, and fighting off such stimulation. These reactions may be a manifestation of the same mechanisms that produce hyperactivity and impulsivity.

A history of colic is often described by parents of MBD children. They may look back upon the first year or two of the child's life as a nightmare in which they hardly slept. The cry of such children is often shrill and piercing, described by parents as "a sound like a siren," "an animal in acute distress," and "the high thin note of static on the radio."

These children are often described as the "last to go to sleep at night and the first to get up in the morning." Their restlessness in bed may interfere with the sleep of others in the household. They may frequently knock themselves against the sides of their cribs or bang their heads. After they begin to walk, they are constantly into everything and their curiosity is even greater than that of the normal toddler (whose curiosity is usually insatiable). Some parents say of MBD children that "their terrible twos started at nine months." They are heedless to danger and are accident prone. This does not appear to be on a psychogenic basis. They are not compelled by some deep psychopathological self-destructive need to harm themselves. Rather their accident proneness is the result of their neurophysiological impairments: their inability to learn well from experience, their intellectual deficits, their problems in adequately processing incoming stimuli, etc. They may be well known to the doctors at the nearby emergency room, and they may have a number of scars which serve to remind observers of their accidents but not themselves.

Developmental Milestones

Parents are not renowned for the accuracy of their recollections regarding the times at which their children reached the various developmental milestones (Figure 5.5). Many parents, rather than saying that they do not recall, provide a figure that is no more than a guess. Obviously, such information is of little value to the examiner. Yet it is important for the examiner to get such data because developmental lags are commonly seen in children with the GMBDS. Furthermore, the data provide vital information regarding the presence of the developmental type of soft neurological sign. The ques-

Figure 5.5

DEVELOPMENTAL MILESTONES
If you can recall, record the age at which your child reached the following developmental milestones. If you cannot recall, check item at right.

	age	I cannot recall exactly, but to the best of my recollection it occurred		
		early	at the normal time	late
Smiled				
Sat without support				
Crawled				
Stood without support				
Walked without assistance				
Spoke first words besides "ma-ma" and "da-da"				
Said phrases				
Said sentences				
Bowel trained, day				
Bowel trained, night				
Bladder trained, day				
Bladder trained, night				
Rode tricycle				
Rode bicycle (without training wheels)				
Buttoned clothing				
Tied shoelaces				
Named colors				
Named coins				
Said alphabet in order				
Began to read				

COORDINATION
Rate your child on the following skills:

	Good	Average	Poor
Walking			
Running			
Throwing			
Catching			
Shoelace tying			
Buttoning			
Writing			
Athletic abilities			

tionnaire allows the parent the face-saving "out" of being able to say that the information has been forgotten. In addition, three categories of response can be provided under the "I cannot recall exactly" heading: it occurred 1) early, 2) at the normal time, and 3) late. When developmental questions are so posed, the information the examiner does get is more likely to be useful.

The normal times at which the milestones occur is subject to significant variation, but the later beyond the normal range the capacity is reached the greater the likelihood that pathology is present. Smiling usually occurs by two months, sitting with support at six–seven months, crawling at seven months, standing without support at 10–11 months, and walking without support at 12–14 months. There is greater variability regarding the normal range for the onset of speech.

The words *ma-ma* and *da-da* are poor criteria for determining the age of speech onset because parents are likely to hear such articulations in the normal babbling sounds of the infant. (This is especially true for first babies.) Accordingly, the question for determining the age of onset of first words asks for words other than these. Nine to 14 months is generally the time for the appearance of single words. The appearance of first phrases and first sentences is very variable. First phrases appear at about 18 months and short sentences at about 24 months, but the normal range is so variable that the age of onset of these functions is of limited diagnostic value. However, it is important for the examiner to appreciate that there are children who do not speak at all until three and even four years of age who do not have any neurological impairment. I believe that the failure to speak between two and four, when there is no demonstrable organic cause (such as MBD, severe hearing loss, retardation, autism or schizophrenia) is a manifestation of psychogenic problems. The period between four and five appears to be a crucial one for the onset of speech. My experience has been that if a child does not start to speak by four it may or may not be a sign of organic pathology. However, if a child does not utilize *intelligible* speech by five years of age it is almost invariably a sign of severe pathology. In such cases I generally consider mental retardation and autism or other forms of childhood schizophrenia. The GMBDS children, although sometimes lagging with regard to the time of speech onset, are not generally so late that they do not start until five or after. In addition, the child who has not started to utilize intelligible speech by five may never do so. Such children must be differentiated from those with elective mutism. The latter know how to speak, but generally confine themselves to communicating verbally with certain people (usually their parents).

The general assumption is made that children cannot voluntarily control their bowel movements until they are old enough to walk. Accordingly, the parent who states that a child was bowel trained at six months and started to walk at 12 months is not providing valid information. One possibility here is that the child had a fairly regular schedule and the parent caught him or her at the right moment for placement on the potty or toilet. Bowel training for day and night usually occurs between two and three years of age. Bladder training occurs later and is more variable. Many children are bladder trained during the day (commonly established by two-three years of age) before nocturnal control is achieved. So great is the normal variation for nighttime wetting that there is no good cutoff point in childhood which can be used to define the pathological. It is a disservice to a child to automatically assume that nighttime wetting after the age of five or six, for example, is automatically a manifestation of psychiatric problems. It may be the result of neurophysiological immaturity or physiological hyperirritability. When bowel and bladder training are late in the GMBDS child, a number of factors may be operative: neurophysiological lag, hyperirritability, impaired attention to internal stimuli, and intellectual deficit.

Children of two to three generally pedal a tricycle and by six or seven ride a bicycle without training wheels. The ability to button clothing generally occurs at three to four and tying shoelaces at five to six. At four most children can name the majority of colors and by five to six name a few coins. Most can repeat the letters of the alphabet at four to five years and start to read between five and six. It is in the area of reading that the GMBDS child may exhibit his or her problems most dramatically.

Coordination

The evaluation of coordination may be quite subjective. This is true not only for the parent, but for the examiner as well. The parents' views, however, often do have merit, especially if they are only asked to state whether the child is "good," "average," or "poor" compared to others with regard to the ability to perform certain functions that depend upon coordination capacity. The questionnaire (Figure 5.5) focuses on such functions that involve fine and/ or gross motor coordination.

Comprehension and Understanding

The questions in this section of the questionnaire (Figure 5.6) attempt to provide the examiner with information about the child's general level of intelligence. This may be a very highly charged area for the parents of the GMBDS child. They generally will view the child to be brighter than he or she may be. They may use rationalizations such as, "His intelligence is really normal but he's *slower* to understand than other children." Others may even describe the child as "basically very bright" even though there is little if any evidence that this is the case. The parents may hold to the statement made by some professionals that "MBD children's intelligence is in the normal range." I do not believe that the average child who is correctly diagnosed as having MBD is of normal intelligence. Although there are many GMBDS children with above average and even superior IQs, there are many more in the low average and borderline range. The average GMBDS child in my experience has an IQ of about 90, that is, at the bottom of the normal range. The professional who says that the average MBD child has a normal IQ is ignoring all we know about the ways in which such children's deficits impair them on most, if not all, of the WISC-R subtests, the very test used to assess these children's intelligence.

The first question in this section of the questionnaire (Figure 5.6) is essentially directed to parents who are defensive about or denying their child's possible intellectual impairment. The second asks more directly about intelligence.

School

It is in school, more than anywhere else, that the GMBDS child's deficits may reveal themselves. Many GMBDS children are not recognized as being different from others until they attend school. There the teacher has the opportunity to compare the child to others his or her age, and is generally knowledgeable enough about what is age appropriate to be able to recognize atypical behavior quite readily. In addition, it is in school that the learning impairments, so commonly seen in GMBDS, may first become apparent.

Figure 5.6

COMPREHENSION AND UNDERSTANDING
    Do you consider your child to understand directions and situations as well as other children his or her age?_____If not, why not?_____

    How would you rate your child's overall level of intelligence compared to other children? Below average_____Average_____Above average_____

SCHOOL
    Rate your child's school experiences related to <u>academic learning</u>:

	Good	Average	Poor
Nursery school			
Kindergarten			
Current grade			

To the best of your knowledge, at what grade level is your child functioning: reading_____spelling_____arithmetic_____

Has your child ever had to repeat a grade? If so, when_____

Present class placement: regular class_____special class (if so, specify)

Kinds of special therapy or remedial work your child is currently receiving

Describe briefly any academic school problems_____

Rate your child's school experience related to <u>behavior</u>:

	Good	Average	Poor
Nursery school			
Kindergarten			
Current grade			

Does your child's teacher describe any of the following as significant classroom problems?
    Doesn't sit still in his or her seat_____
    Frequently gets up and walks around the classroom_____
    Shouts out. Doesn't wait to be called upon _____
    Won't wait his or her turn_____

Lastly, it is in the school, more than anywhere else, that the child's capacity for self-inhibition is tested, and it is in school, therefore, that the GMBDS child's impulsivity is likely to cause him or her the most difficulty.

The questionnaire sections that refer to school (Figures 5.6 and 5.7) are divided into two categories: academic learning and behavior. In the academic section the questions attempt to provide the examiner with specific information regarding the child's level of academic performance. The questions have been designed to focus on information that will provide the examiner with as accurate a picture as possible of the child's academic functioning: specific grade levels in reading, spelling, and arithmetic; history of grade repeat; type of class (regular or special); and special therapy or remedial work.

The second section is devoted to school behavior. Again, the aim is to get information that is as specific as possible. The checklist in the middle of this section focuses on many of the most common complaints made by teachers about GMBDS children. These problems are manifestations of their hyperactivity (Doesn't sit still in his or her seat); impulsivity (Shouts out. Won't wait his or her turn); impaired concentration (Typically does better in a one-to-one relationship); and impaired ability to project oneself into another's situation (Doesn't respect the rights of others). Finally, both sections provide the parent with the opportunity to describe other school problems that may not have been referred to in the questions previously posed.

Peer Relationships

Information about peer relationships is less useful than school behavior, but more useful than home behavior in diagnosing GMBDS. The requirement for self-restraint is greatest in school, least at home, and somewhere in the middle of these with peers. Teachers will tolerate the least degree of antisocial behavior, parents the most, and peers an amount between these two. The questions posed about peer relationships (Figure 5.7) attempt to focus specifically on the most common problems with friends that GMBDS children have. The most sensitive indices of whether the GMBDS child is relating well to peers is his or her degree of reaching out to them and whether they are seeking the child. The age of playmates (younger, older, same age) also tells something about the child's de-

Figure 5.7

Does not cooperate well in group activities_____
Typically does better in a one-to-one relationship_____
Doesn't respect the rights of others_____
Doesn't pay attention during storytelling_____

Describe briefly any other classroom behavioral problems_____

_____

_____

PEER RELATIONSHIPS
Does your child seek friendships with peers?_____

Is your child sought by peers for friendship?_____

Does your child play primarily with children his or her own age?_____

    younger_____older_____

Describe briefly any problems your child may have with peers_____

_____

_____

HOME BEHAVIOR
All children exhibit, to some degree, the kinds of behavior listed below.
Check those that you believe your child exhibits to an excessive or ex-
aggerated degree when compared to other children his or her age.

    Hyperactivity (high activity level)_____
    Poor attention span_____
    Impulsivity (poor self control)_____
    Low frustration threshold_____
    Temper outbursts_____
    Sloppy table manners_____
    Interrupts frequently_____
    Doesn't listen when being spoken to_____
    Sudden outbursts of physical abuse of other children_____
    Acts like he or she is driven by a motor_____
    Wears out shoes more frequently than siblings_____
    Heedless to danger_____
    Excessive number of accidents_____
    Doesn't learn from experience_____
    Poor memory_____
    More active than siblings_____

182

gree of success with friends. Also, the quality of the friendships is important to learn about, whether the children are normal or atypical, whether they are sought after or in the fringe group.

Home Behavior

Home behavior is a poor criterion on which to determine whether a child's behavior is pathological. Practically all siblings fight. At what level does the normal degree of rather fierce sibling rivalry end and the pathological begin? All children exhibit poor table manners at times. Where does one draw the line between normal table sloppiness and the pathological? And, as mentioned, parents will tolerate greater degrees of atypical behavior than teachers and peers. Yet pathology can certainly manifest itself in the home. In order to ascertain whether the child's home behavior may be pathological, the parent is asked to check those items (Figure 5.7) in which the child's behavior is exaggerated or excessive when compared to other children the child's age. Included here again are those behavioral patterns that relate to some of the primary manifestations of GMBDS, viz., hyperactivity, poor attention span, impulsivity, and memory impairments.

Interests and Accomplishments

Most of the previous items have focused on the child's deficits. Such emphasis may be upsetting to the parent who is filling out the questionnaire. For the parents' well-being, as well as providing the examiner with a more balanced picture of the child, a section (Figure 5.8) is devoted to the child's assets. An inquiry into hobbies, interests, and accomplishments may provide useful diagnostic information. Reading is obviously not likely to be the favorite pastime of the GMBDS child. Watching TV or listening to music may be (I don't claim these to be pathognomonic for the disorder). A GMBDS child may have deep involvement in sports and do well in them. Success in this area, then, provides information about the child's coordination. Others may do well in school but are abysmally poor in sports. In short, the areas of interest and pleasure may provide information about the child's healthy areas of neurophysiological functioning.

Figure 5.8

INTERESTS AND ACCOMPLISHMENTS
What are your child's main hobbies and interests?_____

_____

What are your child's areas of greatest accomplishment?_____

_____

What does your child enjoy doing most?_____

_____

What does your child dislike doing most?_____

_____

MEDICAL HISTORY
If your child's medical history includes any of the following, please note
the age when the incident or illness occurred and any other pertinent information.

    Childhood diseases (describe any complications)_____

_____

    Operations_____

_____

    Hospitalizations for illness(es) other than operations_____

_____

    Head injuries_____

    _____with unconsciousness_____without unconsciousness_____
    Convulsions_____

    _____with fever_____without fever_____
    Coma_____
    Meningitis or encephalitis_____
    Immunization reactions_____
    Persistent high fevers_____highest temperature ever recorded_____
    eye problems_____
    ear problems_____
    poisoning_____

184

Medical History

In this section of the questionnaire (Figure 5.8), an attempt is made to learn about any illnesses that occurred after the newborn child left the hospital, illnesses that might have been of etiological importance in the child's MBD. The traditional childhood diseases, such as measles and mumps, were occasionally associated with central nervous system complications such as encephalitis. Fortunately, with the advent of new vaccines, we are seeing much less of these disorders. A history of coma and/or seizures associated with such an illness is suggestive of central nervous system involvement even though medical attention may not have been sought. Operations may provide a clue to the etiology. For example, the child with frequent bouts of otitis media requiring myringotomies is suspect for hearing impairment which may interfere with speech and learning. There is hardly a child who does not sustain occasional head trauma. But when it is associated with unconsciousness or coma, then brain dysfunction (not necessarily permanent) must be suspected.

There was a time when a child who only had seizures with fever was considered to be neurologically normal. Such children were considered to have "febrile seizures," which were not taken as seriously as those that occurred in the afebrile state. One reflection of this relaxed attitude toward febrile convulsions was the view that such seizures did not warrant anticonvulsant medication. The traditional treatment of such seizures was to warn the mother to give the child elixir phenobarbital (or other anticonvulsant medication) as soon as the child showed signs of illness—especially a febrile illness. Unfortunately, children have a way of spiking fevers so rapidly that mothers were often unaware that the child was getting sick and so did not often give the anticonvulsant in time to prevent the convulsion. Many pediatric neurologists today take such seizures more seriously. They hold also that in addition to the basic pathology that causes the seizures, a seizure *per se* can result in superimposed damage to the brain. A grand mal seizure includes an apneic phase and this can cause cerebral hypoxia. Accordingly, a child with febrile seizures may be placed on maintenance anticonvulsant medication if there is a family history of seizures, signs of organic cerebral dysfunction, or other factors indicative of a high risk of further brain dysfunction. I have seen a few children with MBD who had febrile seizures that went untreated because they were "only febrile." I believe that the extent of their brain dysfunction would have been far less had they been on medication to prevent their convulsions.

Meningitis and encephalitis, especially when associated with coma, is highly correlated with residual brain damage and is one of the more generally accepted causes of GMBDS. Encephalitides are also known to be a concomitant of untoward immunization reactions. There are some children who easily run persistently high fevers with practically any infection. Others may manifest such fevers without known cause. Children with fevers of unknown etiology may have some kind of neurophysiological dysfunction which is akin to and possibly a symptom of GMBDS. The same factors that have produced neurophysiological abnormalities in other parts of the brain may be causing impaired functioning of temperature regulatory mechanisms.

Reading difficulties can be the result of pathological processes anywhere along the pathway from the eye to the occipital cortex (as well as in neurological systems that are interconnected). Strabismus, squinting, tearing, holding the book at a distance, holding the book too close, inclining the head to the side while reading, and easy reading fatigability are all suspicious signs of ocular problems that can contribute to reading difficulties—problems that can usually respond to optometric and/or ophthalmological treatment. Such considerations are all too often neglected in the GMBDS workup and the parent's indicating a history of eye problems should alert the examiner to their presence.

Ear disorders, such as chronic infections, can involve the brain. The child who has trouble hearing or trouble understanding what he or she hears may not only have some disorder of the external ear but of the central auditory processing mechanisms as well. Auditory examination is all too often neglected in the GMBDS workup. The parents' recording a history of ear problems should warrant the examiner's further investigation.

Although lead has been implicated more than other substances as an etiological factor in GMBDS, the ingestion of other substances must be considered. The impulsivity, poor judgment, and intellectual impairment of children makes them more likely to ingest drugs, poisons, and other dangerous substances. Accordingly, poisons should not only be viewed as primary etiological agents, but as potentially causing superimposed brain damage as well.

Last, my experience has been that a specific etiological factor cannot be found in the vast majority of GMBDS children. These are the children, I believe, whose only etiological factor is the fact that they are at the 15th-25th percentile level on the normal bell-shaped curve and are considered, in our society, to have a disease.

Present Medical Status

Most of the examiners for whom this book is written do not have scales in their offices for the purpose of measuring height and weight. Accordingly, it is useful to get these figures (Figure 5.9). They are not as likely to be significantly distorted by the parents as some of the other information provided, and the examiner, by merely looking at the child, can generally determine whether the figures provided are roughly accurate.

It is also important for the examiner to know whether the child is presently suffering with any illnesses, because the symptoms of such disorders can affect one's findings. For example, acute allergic reactions can cause the kind of agitation that can sometimes be confused with hyperactivity. The allergic child, however, will manifest other signs of allergy (sniffling, rash, conjunctivitis, etc.) to help the examiner in the differential diagnosis. The medications a child is taking are also important to know about. We have a long way to go in learning about the various factors that can produce GMBDS. It is possible, and even probable, that long-term use of certain medications might cause nerve cell dysfunction. In addition, the drugs a child is taking may affect performance on the diagnostic tests that are given. A child taking phenobarbital as an anticonvulsant is not likely to be as alert when taking the WISC-R, for example, as the child who is not taking barbiturates.

Family History—Mother

One is interested in the mother's age at the time of the pregnancy with the patient because the older the mother the greater the likelihood she will give birth to a child with various kinds of anomalies and malformations. One is also interested in the past history of spontaneous abortion because it is reasonable to assume that if the mother tends to lose and reject embryos and fetuses, those that are retained may be subject to the same kinds of rejection processes. Accordingly, there may be a greater likelihood of impairment in such mothers' retained fetuses than in fetuses of mothers with no previous history of spontaneous abortion. This is especially the case when chromosomal malfunctions habitually cause the abortions. In

Figure 5.9

PRESENT MEDICAL STATUS

  Present height_____Present weight_____

  Present illness(es) for which child is being treated_____

  _____

  Medications child is taking on an ongoing basis_____

  _____

FAMILY HISTORY - MOTHER

  Age_____ Age at time of pregnancy with patient_____

  Number of previous pregnancies_____Number of spontaneous abortions

  (miscarriages)_____Number of induced abortions_____

  Sterility problems (specify)_____

  School: Highest grade completed_____

    Learning problems (specify)_____grade repeat_____

    Behavior problems (specify)_____

  Medical problems (specify)_____

  Have any of your blood relatives (not including patient and siblings) ever

  had problems similar to those your child has? If so, describe_____

  _____

  _____

FAMILY HISTORY - FATHER

  Age_____Age at the time of the patient's conception _____

  Sterility problems (specify)_____

  School: Highest grade completed_____

    Learning problems (specify)_____grade repeat_____

    Behavior problems (specify)_____

  Medical problems (specify)_____

  Have any of your blood relatives (not including patient and siblings) ever

  had problems similar to those your child has? If so, describe_____

  _____

188

addition, one is also interested in the past history of induced abortions. A mother with a history of sterility problems may be rejecting fertilized eggs and providing an intrauterine environment that is not optimally conducive to the healthy growth and development of the fertilized ovum. It is reasonable to speculate that the embryo that does finally grow to maturity is being exposed to the same detrimental influences and has a greater likelihood of being malformed.

One does well to inquire into the presence of significant medical problems because many maternal illnesses (infectious, metabolic, toxic, etc.) can have a significant effect on the developing embryo and fetus. Lastly, one wants to learn if blood relatives of the mother had symptoms similar to the child's when they were younger. As mentioned, genetic factors are probably operative in some children with GMBDS and this aspect of the inquiry may elucidate this etiological factor. It is also important to get information about the mother's school history, especially regarding learning disabilities and hyperactivity. The questions on maternal history of school learning problems, grade repeat, and behavior problems are designed to provide information in these areas.

Family History—Father

Sterility problems on the father's part may contribute to less than optimum sperm conditions for conception and a higher risk of embryonic abnormalities. One should give serious attention to the father's school history with regard to learning problems, grade repeat, and behavior problems, because present evidence suggests that the genetic factors appear more along the paternal than the maternal line. Although one should inquire into the father's medical problems, they are far less liklely to be of etiological significance for the MBD child. Again, one should inquire into the presence of the child's symptoms in the father's blood relatives to evaluate the presence of genetic factors.

Psychological Symptoms

Figures 5.10–5.13 present a list of a wide variety of psychological symptoms that are generally considered to be primarily, if not exclusively, psychogenic. Whereas most of the material in the questionnaire that has thus far been presented and discussed relates to

Figure 5.10

Most children exhibit, at one time or another, one or more of the symptoms listed below. Place a P next to those that your child has exhibited in the PAST and an N next to those that your child exhibits NOW. Only mark those symptoms that have been or are present to a significant degree over a period of time. Only check as problems behavior that you suspect is unusual or atypical when compared to what you consider to be the normal for your child's age. Then, on page 12, list the symptoms checked off on pages 9-12 and write a brief description including age of onset, duration, and any other pertinent information.

Thumb-sucking ____

Baby talk ____

Overly dependent for age ____

Frequent temper tantrums ____

Excessive silliness and clowning ____

Excessive demands for attention ____

Cries easily and frequently ____

Generally immature ____

Eats non-edible substances ____

Overeating with overweight ____

Eating binges with overweight ____

Undereating with underweight ____

Long periods of dieting and food abstinence with underweight ____

Preoccupied with food--what to eat and what not to eat ____

Preoccupation with bowel movements ____

Constipation ____

Encopresis (soiling) ____

Insomnia (difficulty sleeping) ____

Enuresis (bed wetting) ____

Frequent nightmares ____

Night terrors (terrifying night-time outbursts) ____

Sleepwalking ____

Excessive sexual interest and pre-occupation ____

Frequent sex play with other children ____

Excessive masturbation ____

Frequently likes to wear clothing of the opposite sex ____

Exhibits gestures and intonations of the opposite sex ____

Frequent headaches ____

Frequent stomach cramps ____

Frequent nausea and vomiting ____

Often complains of bodily aches and pains ____

Worries over bodily illness ____

Poor motivation ____

Apathy ____

Takes path of least resistance ____

Ever trying to avoid responsibility ____

190

Figure 5.11

Poor follow-through ___

Low Curiosity ___

Open defiance of authority ___

Blatantly uncooperative ___

Persistant lying ___

Frequent use of profanity to parents, teachers, and other authorities ___

Truancy from school ___

Runs away from home ___

Violent outbursts of rage ___

Stealing ___

Cruelty to animals, children, and others ___

Destruction of property ___

Criminal and/or dangerous acts ___

Trouble with the police ___

Violent assault ___

Fire setting ___

Little, if any, guilt over behavior that causes others pain and discomfort ___

Little, if any, response to punishment for anti-social behavior ___

Few, if any, friends ___

Doesn't seek friendships ___

Rarely sought by peers ___

Not accepted by peer group ___

Selfish ___

Doesn't respect the rights of others ___

Wants things own way with exaggerated reaction if thwarted ___

Trouble putting self in other person's position ___

Egocentric (self-centered) ___

Frequently hits other children ___

Argumentative ___

Excessively critical of others ___

Excessively taunts other children ___

Ever complaining

Is often picked on and easily bullied by other children ___

Suspicious, distrustful ___

Aloof ___

"Wise-guy" or smart aleck attitude ___

Brags or boasts ___

Bribes other children ___

Excessively competitive ___

Often cheats when playing games ___

"Sore loser" ___

"Doesn't know when to stop" ___

Poor common sense in social situations ___

Often feels cheated or gypped ___

Feels others are persecuting him when there is no evidence for such ___

Typically wants his or her own way ___

Very stubborn ___

Obstructionistic ___

Negativistic (does just the opposite of what is requested) ___

Figure 5.12

Quietly, or often
silently, de-
fiant of au-
thority ___

Feigns or verbalizes
compliance or
cooperation but
doesn't comply
with requests ___

Drug abuse ___

Alcohol abuse ___

Very tense ___

Nail biting ___

Chews on clothes,
blankets, etc. ___

Head banging ___

Hair pulling ___

Picks on skin ___

Speaks rapidly
and under
pressure ___

Irritability,
easily "flies off
the handle" ___

Fears
dark ___
new situations ___
strangers ___
being alone ___
death ___
separation from
parent ___
school ___
visiting other
children's homes ___
going away to
camp ___
animals ___
other fears
(name)

_____ ___

_____ ___

Anxiety attacks
with palpatations
(heart pounding),
shortness of breath,
sweating, etc. ___

Disorganized ___

Tics such as eye-
blinking, grimacing,
or other spasmodic
repetitive move-
ments ___

Involuntary grunts,
vocalizations
(understandable
or not) ___

Stuttering ___

Depression ___

Frequent crying
spells ___

Excessive worrying
over minor things ___

Suicidal preoccu-
pation, gestures,
or attempts ___

Excessive desire to
please authority ___

"Too good" ___

Often appears in-
sincere and/or
artificial ___

Too mature, fre-
quently acts older
than actual age ___

Excessive guilt over
minor indiscre-
tions ___

Asks to be
punished ___

Low self-esteem ___

Excessive self-
criticism ___

Very poor toleration
of criticism ___

Feelings easily
hurt ___

Dissatisfaction
with appearance
or body part(s) ___

Excessive modesty
over bodily
exposure ___

Perfectionistic,
rarely satisfied
with performance ___

Frequently blames
others as a cover-
up for own short-
comings ___

Little concern for
personal appear-
ance or hygiene ___

Little concern for
or pride in per-
sonal property ___

"Gets hooked" on
certain ideas
and remains pre-
occupied ___

Compulsive repe-
tition of seem-
ingly meaningless
physical acts ___

Shy ___

Inhibited self-
expression in
dancing, singing,
laughing, etc. ___

Recoils from affec-
tionate physical
contact ___

192

Figure 5.13

Withdrawn	___	Mute (refuses to speak) but can	___	Flat emotional tone	___
Fears asserting self	___	Gullible and/or naive	___	Speech non-communicative or poorly communicative	___
Inhibits open expression of anger	___	Passive and easily led	___	Hears voices	___
Allows self to be easily taken advantage of	___	Excessive fantasizing, "lives in his (her) own world"	___	Sees visions	___
Frequently pouts and/or sulks	___				

As requested above, please first list below symptoms marked with the letter P and next to each symptom give descriptive information such as age of onset, age of termination, and other important data. Then list symptoms marked with an N and provide similar information.

P or N   Symptom   Brief Description

___   _____   _____

___   _____   _____

___   _____   _____

___   _____   _____

___   _____   _____

___   _____   _____

___   _____   _____

___   _____   _____

___   _____   _____

___   _____   _____

___   _____   _____

___   _____   _____

___   _____   _____

___   _____   _____

___   _____   _____

___   _____   _____

193

neurophysiological dysfunction, the symptoms presented here are more likely to provide information about psychogenic disturbances. Some of the psychological disorders manifested by the symptoms are purely psychogenic in etiology; others are secondary to primary neurophysiologic disturbances, especially GMBDS.

Because most if not all children are likely to exhibit many of these symptoms at some time in their development, the parent is asked to check *only* those items that have exhibited themselves over a period. Without this instruction many parents would check most of the items. Furthermore, one wants to differentiate between those symptoms that existed in the past and those that are presently causing difficulty. Finally, in order to obtain further information about symptoms that have been checked in Figures 5.10–5.13, the parent is asked to provide further details about each symptom, for example, age of onset, age of termination, and other important data.

Siblings

In the questionnaire, Figure 5.14 provides only limited space for information about siblings. This is purposeful. The questionnaire is lengthy enough as it stands, and detailed information about siblings may not be warranted. However, some of the "key words" provided about the siblings may serve as a clue to the examiner that a more detailed inquiry during the interviews is justified. If a sibling, however, warrants treatment, then the examiner should ask the parent to fill out a separate questionnaire for that child.

Names and Addresses
of Other Professionals Consulted

Information from other professionals is most often useful. The questionnaire's face letter requests that parents bring copies of reports from previous examiners, and these can often provide valuable information. For the sake of completion, the questionnaire also asks for the names and addresses of previous examiners in order to insure that all reports will be received. Last, the parent is invited to record any additional comments. Although the questionnaire attempts to be thorough, there are often special issues relevant to the patient that may not have been focused upon.

Figure 5.14

SIBLINGS

	Name	Age	Medical, social, or academic problems
1.			
2.			
3.			
4.			
5.			

LIST NAMES AND ADDRESSES OF ANY OTHER PROFESSIONALS CONSULTED

1. _____

2. _____

3. _____

4. _____

ADDITIONAL REMARKS

Please use the remainder of this page to write any additional comments you wish to make regarding your child's difficulties.

INTERVIEWING THE CHILD AND PARENTS TOGETHER

Interviewing the parents and child together in the initial interview is not traditional. The traditional practice is for the therapist to invite the child alone into the consultation room while leaving the parent(s) in the waiting room. One of the main arguments given for utilizing this procedure is that separating the child from the parents at the outset communicates to the child that he or she is to have a special private relationship with the therapist—a relationship not shared with the parents. Proponents of this practice claim that this enhances the likelihood of a good therapist-patient relationship being established. As I will discuss in detail in Chapter Seven, I am dubious about this. In fact, I believe that the practice is more likely to work in just the opposite way, that is, having an exclusive relationship with the child—a relationship in which the parents are excluded—is more likely to interfere with the development of a good therapist-patient relationship in that it is likely to alienate the parents and thereby lessen their involvement with, respect for, and support of the therapist in his or her relationship with the child. Furthermore, pressuring the child to separate from the parents at that time may lessen the likelihood that a good relationship will be established. The tensions and anxieties that such separation engenders may produce untoward reactions to the therapist at the outset—reactions that will compromise the development of a good relationship.

Another reason often given for separating the child from the parents at the outset is that it allows the therapist to observe whether the child has "separation anxiety." It is difficult, however, to imagine any child not being anxious in circumstances where the therapy is an unknown, the therapist is a stranger, and the child has never before been in the clinic or office and has little appreciation of what is going on. It is likely that the youngster has been told something like, "You're going to see a nice lady," "We're taking you to see a nice man who'll be playing lots of games with you," or "We're taking you to see a teacher who will help you learn better." Because such explanations are cover-ups, they may not be believed and may therefore create tension. Or the child may be told that he or she is going to see someone who will help with the youngster's "problems." Although the child may not have the faintest idea what the parents mean by the word "problems," he or she is not likely to anticipate that the experience is going to be a pleasant one.

Thus, if a child exhibits anxiety when separating from the parents to go with the therapist, it is likely that this is a normal response. In fact, it is reasonable to say that not being anxious at that point would probably reflect significant psychopathology indicating that the child's capacity to form deep relationships is so impaired that it makes no difference whether he or she is with a parent or a stranger. Or it may reflect such a defect in the parent-child relationship that the child welcomes an opportunity to go off with a stranger. But these are unusual situations. Most often the child is anxious and does not want to be separated from the parents in strange surroundings. One of the worst experiences a child therapist can have is that of trying to force or cajole a screaming, panicky child into accompanying the examiner alone into a private office. As the child desperately implores the parents not to let the stranger take him or her off, the presence of others in the waiting room cannot but increase the child's humiliation. Once in the consultation room, the likelihood of gaining any meaningful information from the child is almost nil. The word *never* is not one that I like to use. However, I have no problem using it with regard to a therapist's forcibly carrying a panic-stricken child into his or her consultation room at the beginning of the initial interview. This should *never* be done. There is no situation in which it is warranted, and there is no question that it may compromise significantly the treatment—even to the point where it may not be possible, so great may be the initial psychological trauma caused by this injudicious (and even simple-minded) approach to the treatment of the child.

Many therapists argue that another reason for seeing the parents alone first is that the child's disruptions and interferences will inhibit the data-collection process. I disagree with this point. The disruptions and interferences can be an important source of information, especially with regard to the relationship that the child has with each of the parents. The ways in which the parents handle these disruptions can be a useful source of information. Another argument given for seeing the parents alone is that they may not be comfortable revealing certain information in front of the child and may even deprive the therapist of this vital data. My experience has been that many parents in this category are overprotective and their hesitation to provide information in the interview with the child is a clue to the presence of this symptom. (Their failure to provide this information does not deprive the therapist of the opportunity to obtain it, because time is still set aside for them to be seen alone during the course of the two-hour consultation.) Last, no matter how accurate the parents' description of the child is, it is very difficult, if not impossible, for the therapist to gain a reasonable appreciation of the kind of person the child is without actually seeing him or her. Although one could argue that asking to see pictures of the child might provide some information in this regard, it is clearly far less efficacious than the actual experience of interviewing the child him- or herself at the outset.

If the child absolutely refuses to come into the consultation room with the parents, the boy or girl should be allowed to sit outside. For example, if a boy obstinately refuses to leave the waiting room, the examiner might say something along these lines: "Your parents and I will be talking over there in my office. You're invited to come in and join us at any time. If you change your mind, we'll be happy to allow you to join us in the conversation, which, of course, will be about you anyway." If after ten or fifteen minutes he is still outside, the examiner might go out and try to draw the child into a general discussion in the hope of becoming a more familiar figure so that the child will become more receptive. For example, if the child is looking at baseball cards I might say, "You know, I'm not up with baseball these days. I used to be interested in it when I was a kid. I lived near the Yankee Stadium in the Bronx and the Yankees were my favorite team. Who are the big heroes now? Who's your favorite team?" In this way I try to establish some area of common interest with the child in the hope that it will catalyze and facilitate his involvement with me. Having similar interests can play a role in "breaking the ice." Or the therapist might send a parent out to the waiting room if that approach seems preferable. At the very worst, the child will never come into the examiner's office and will never become a patient. Under such circumstances, therapists should lose no sleep at night but should be satisfied with the knowledge that they have tried their best to engage the child and have therefore "done their duty."

Once the parents and child are in the room, I again depart from the traditional approach. In my own training in the 1950s, I was taught that the unstructured interview is best because it allows for free revelations from the universe of information that may come before the evaluator, and that specific questions are likely to be contaminating and restricting. Subsequent experience has led me to conclude that one need not lose the benefits of the open-ended inquiry if one asks specific questions. Both types of inquiry can provide useful information. Thus, during training, I was taught that the best question to begin with was something along the lines of: "Well, why have you come here?" or "So what's the problem?" The rationale for this approach is that since the question is an open one and does not draw the patient into specific areas, it therefore does not have any contaminants. Although this position is certainly valid, it does not give proper consideration to the fact that posing open-ended questions to a person who is tense or fearful will not yield helpful information. Accordingly, the initial interview is best begun with general questions that any human being would ask another in a new situation. One might ask whether the parents had trouble finding the office or whether they had difficulty because of the weather. These are innocuous enough questions and are not likely to contaminate anything. They do, however, serve to lessen anxiety and make the examiner (a total stranger) more familiar and "human."

The chairs have been previously arranged so that the four of us form a circle. Even at this point one is already gathering information. Who sits where? Are common courtesies observed? Is there jockeying or vying for a particular seat? Does the child sit in his own chair or does he cling to a parent? If so, which one and how is this responded to—with warm caresses, cold stiffness, rejection, and so on?

The child, at this point, may not wish to sit. If the activity engaged in appears to have possibilities for providing information that will be helpful, I may permit the "digression." For example, a child might attempt to reduce anxiety by trying to find similarity between the therapist's office and some other place that is familiar to him or her. Such a child might say: "I have a ball at home that's just like that." To such a comment I might reply: "Yes, you'll find that there are lots of things here that are just like those you've seen in other places." One adolescent, who had previously been in treatment with another therapist, on entering his first session, commented sneeringly: "You shrinks are all the same." He then glanced around the room and while pointing to different objects said: "The same stupid couches and those pictures of your crazy kids on the desk." Had I addressed myself to his hostility I would have missed the point entirely. I merely commented that he was perfectly right that Dr. X and I did have a number of things in common. He needed to see us as similar in order to be more relaxed and my response served to help him to be so.

Some parents, at this point, will make a humorous comment which may help to alleviate their anxiety. If they get a smile from the therapist, he or she becomes less menacing. It behooves the therapist, in this phase, to hear their message and comply with the parents' request for a friendly response. A poker face or austere, humorless mien will only increase anxiety and lessen the chances of obtaining accurate information. For example, as one family was taking seats, the father chose the larger, deeper chair and laughingly stated: "I hope I don't fall asleep in there. It looks so comfortable." The remark clearly revealed his desire to desensitize himself to his anxiety and avoid the anticipated threats of the interview. I smiled and replied: "I hope you don't. I usually find that I have a little more difficulty getting information from someone who is sleeping." The father laughed and seemed more relaxed. I did not go into the sources of his anxiety nor did I psychoanalyze the remark. I responded at the exact level at which he was functioning and directed my attention to his true request. A humorous response does more to reduce anxiety at such a time than direct statements about how the interview is really not so bad. With my response he had the *living experience* that I was benevolent.

Actually many things can happen at this point and the therapist must be alert to appreciate their meaning and sufficiently flexible to alter the interview in order to derive the maximum benefit from what may occur. Therapists do well to appreciate, however, that the most likely reason for atypical comments and responses during this very early phase relate to the need to reduce the anxiety associated with this first screening interview.

It is important to appreciate that most children under the age of ten or eleven are extremely uncomfortable about revealing deficiencies to a mental health examiner, even to the point of lying. This is not only true during the first session, but throughout the course of therapy and even at the time of termination. So common is this reluctance that I consider it normal and am often suspicious about the motivations of the child who openly admits deficiencies. This is another reason why examiners do well not to "push the point" regarding getting a child to admit inappropriate or maladaptive behavior. This phenomenon is one of the primary reasons why I have developed a variety of techniques, the purpose of which is to obtain information and provide input to a child who does not willingly discuss his or her problems.

The child is then asked a series of simple questions that will probably be easy to answer, questions about what the youngster's name is and how it is spelled and about his or her address, telephone number, age, school grade, teacher's name, the names and ages of the parents and siblings, and so forth. As the child gets "the right answers," fears are alleviated and the child is then in a better position to answer the more open-ended questions about why he or she is there. The specific questions only take a few minutes, do not contaminate, and will provide the examiner with a patient who will generally be in a good position to give accurate answers to the questions that will follow. What is even more important is that the examiner is much more likely to develop a good relationship with the child by starting in this way—with sensitivity to the child's fears—rather than by using an approach likely to produce more alienation and tension. Some insecure or dependent children will request, either by words or gesture, that a parent respond for them even though they know the correct answer, or they will look for reassurance that they have given the appropriate response.

Early in the discussion of the patient's problems, the therapist should try to learn about the type of preparation the child was given prior to the interview. Parents who use duplicity to "protect" their children from what they consider to be the detrimental effects of their knowing that they will be seeing a psychiatrist or other mental health professional will often tell their children absolutely nothing about the nature of the interview or will inform them that they are going to talk to a "nice man(woman)" or use some other euphemism or ruse. The parents may have been vague about the kind of doctor I am or may have tried to give their children the impression that I am a general physician, pediatrician, or tutor. In such cases I simply tell such children that I am a psychiatrist and ask them if they know what that is. If they do not, I tell them that I am the kind of doctor who tries to help people who have "troubles, worries, or problems." I specifically say "tries" in order to emphasize the point (elaborated upon in Chapter Three) that my job is to *try* to help people and that I cannot promise to do so. At that point, or subsequently, I will get across the idea that an important determinant as to whether or not I can be helpful is how much cooperation and involvement I have on the part of the child and both parents. Early in treatment I want to create an atmosphere of cooperative working together. If the mother and/or father appears upset by the disclosure that I am a psychiatrist, I usually tell the parent(s) that I appreciate that their withholding information was motivated by the desire to do what they thought was best for the child, but that it has been my experience that children are not so fragile as many adults think and that such concealment engenders distrust of the parents and unnecessary anxiety in the child. I tell them also that, all things considered, the arguments are overwhelmingly in favor of an open and honest discussion of just who I am and what my purpose is.

If the child becomes upset by the disclosure, I usually try to find out exactly what he or she considers to be the implications of going to a psychiatrist. Most often they involve fears that the child will be considered crazy or that people will laugh at him or her. If the child does not directly verbalize these fears, I will usually state: "Some kids think that only crazy people see psychiatrists. Do you think that?" If the answer is in the affirmative, I usually say, "Most of the people I see are not that sick that anyone would call them crazy. They just have some things wrong with *certain parts* of themselves which they want to change. I emphasize the words "certain parts" in order to get across the idea that I do not view the child to be suffering with all-pervasive psychopathology and is a total misfit, rather I consider the problems to be confined to certain specific areas. Such circumscribing of the deficits lessen the likelihood that the child will generalize from the isolated deficiencies and consider him- or herself totally loathsome. And for the nonpsychotic child, I will add, "Although I know you only a short time, I do have some information about you. I have spoken to your mother on the phone, and I have also had a chance to talk to you for a little while now. Although I don't know you very well, I can tell you already, from everything I do know about you, that there is nothing I have learned so far which would lead me to believe that you are crazy or insane." However, if the child appears to be psychotic, I will say, "That word *crazy* is a cruel word and sometimes people who have trouble like yours are laughed at and called crazy. I know that there are parts of you that you would like to change and that you would like to be more like other children. We psychiatrists think that it's sad to have such problems, and we do not laugh at people with them and call them names. People who do that often have something wrong with themselves."

Some children, in this early phase of the interview, may describe a few problems, but usually with some hesitation. A child might say, for example, "I don't get along with friends." To this response, I will ask, "In exactly what way?" Concrete examples serve well to clarify the exact nature of the problem. As mentioned in Chapter Three, generalizations are far less valuable in treatment than specific examples. If the child cannot describe the specifics, I will turn to the parents to provide them. In order to obtain such information, I usually look vaguely half-way between them so as not to focus on one, but rather to determine if either tends to be more active or to dominate. Throughout the interview my position is that of the *ignorant interrogator*. I use the word ignorant here in the true sense of the word, that is, as someone who is unknowing and that I am interrogating continually in order to lessen my ignorance.

I go back and forth, between child and parents, ever clarifying, ever adding to my knowledge. If there are contradictions between what the child says and what the parents say (a common occurrence), I might say to the child, "Now you say one thing and your parents say just the opposite. What about that? I don't understand. I'm confused." The question should be posed in the spirit of an honest, open desire to learn the truth and not with the implication that the therapist is trying to prove any particular person right or wrong. Such additional back-and-forth inquiry may result in agreement as to the presence or nature of a particular problem. If it does not, the particular line of inquiry should be abandoned for the time being, with a comment such as, "Well, it seems that you and your parents see it differently. Let's go on and talk about some of the other problems. Perhaps later I will be able to get a clearer picture about what's going on."

Although some children may suffer some embarrassment over their problems discussed so openly, there are compensatory therapeutic benefits to be derived from such confrontation. They clarify the reasons for the child's being in the therapist's office, and this serves to make them more ego-alien and more amenable to treatment. The therapist, a significant figure of authority, agrees that they are "problems" or "troubles" and by implication undesirable qualities without which the child would be better off. In addition, naming, labeling, and talking about unpleasant subjects reduces their anxiety-provoking potential. The child often anticipates that revealing defects will result in scorn, punishment, derogation, and/or other very unpleasant reactions from the therapist and/or parents. When the expected condemnation is not forthcoming, the child has what T. French and F. Alexander (1950) referred to as a "corrective emotional experience," and the feelings of self-loathing and anxiety that surround the symptoms may be reduced. Generally, the advantages of the open discussion more than compensate for the child's embarrassment. Those who avoid such confrontations deprive the child of these benefits.

It is important to concentrate on the child's assets, accomplishments, skills, and hobbies at this time. This serves to counterbalance the ego-debasing material that has been thus far focused upon. By necessity, therapy must concern itself, either directly or indirectly, with the problems that have brought the child to treatment. There is usually little in them that the child can be proud of and much that he or she is ashamed of. In the world beyond the consultation room, the problems may represent only a small percentage of the child's living experiences; in the consultation room, unfortunately, they represent a significant percentage if the therapy is to be meaningful. In order to counterbalance this unfortunate but necessary emphasis, therapists do well to take every opportunity to focus on ego-enhancing material. If warranted, the therapist should compliment the child on a *meaningful* accomplishment. There is no place for gratuitous or feigned praise in therapy. Interest (only if genuine) should be expressed in any activity that is a source of gratification for the child. This, too, can serve to enhance the relationship.

When the child has mentioned all the problems he or she can think of, I usually say: "Well, those are probably the worst things you can say about yourself. What are the best?" or "What are you good at?" The child must be given the opportunity to present assets in order to compensate for the probable embarrassment suffered while revealing the liabilities. An inquiry that concentrates only on defects can be ego-debasing and mortifying. If the child cannot think of any assets, I respond: "If you can't think of anything good about yourself, I'd say that that in itself is a problem." If the child still has trouble identifying admirable qualities, I enlist the aid of the parents. If they also cannot describe praiseworthy characteristics, it reflects deep inadequacy in their parental affection. I consider the healthy parent to distort *slightly* in the positive direction regarding a child's assets (Gardner, 1973c). The child who lacks such parental distortion is being deprived indeed. I am not referring to gross misrepresentations which are clearly not manifestations of healthy parental attitudes. For example, to consider the mediocre piano player to be "talented" is healthy; to consider him a "prodigy" is a delusion which can only create difficulty for the child in forming an accurate self-image. Probably more important than what the parents *say* regarding the child's laudable traits is their *feeling-tone* when presenting them. Is there the smile of pride and the warm glance, which are the hallmarks of the loving parent, or are the positive qualities described in a perfunctory way, as if they felt it behooved them to "dig up something" to bolster the child's ego? Such considerations are vital to the determination of the depth of parental affection.

The concentration on assets may also reveal the pathological do-gooder, the "Momma's boy," and others with hypertrophied super-egos. The list of their assets is long. They dote over mother when she is not feeling well; they are clean, neat, bathed, and make their beds without being asked; they rarely fight with siblings; they get straight As in conduct; they may be teacher's favorite, and so on. Other mothers say to their children: "Why can't you be like Tommy?" This constellation of symptoms is often difficult to treat because it does not produce pain or discomfort for the child or the parents, but is rather a source of pride and ego-gratification. Nevertheless, it can reflect significant difficulties.

The information obtained during this phase of the interview is the most important for making the decision as to whether treatment will be necessary. The decision should be made on the basis of *symptoms*, not on psychodynamics. The therapist must not only know the appropriate levels at which normal behavior ends and the pathological begins, but must also appreciate that everyone has psychodynamics and that having psychodynamics is not the same as having psychopathology. All children have nightmares on occasion. They are a pathological manifestation only when they are frequent.

All boys engage in hostile play. Such play is pathological when it's obsessive, dangerous, excessively morbid, or in some other way bears definite stigmata of neurosis. The projective material obtained when the child is seen alone in the next-described phase of the screening interview should be considered of secondary importance in deciding about treatment. The primary considerations are obtained in this phase when symptomatology and behavioral abnormalities are presented and described.

Conduct in the home is a poorer criterion of psychopathology than outside behavior. The home generally provides a more permissive atmosphere than the world at large. It does not assess well the child's ability to inhibit the more primitive impulses and adjust appropriately to the demands of reality. An old gym teacher of mine used to respond to the sassy or back-talking child with the invective: "Who the hell do you think you're talking to, your mother?" He knew well that mothers will often tolerate much more abuse than anyone else.

When the child has not acquired the skills and capacity to function properly in school or in relationships with friends, the presence of psychopathology is strongly implied. Good functioning in these two areas generally indicates that the child is not likely to be significantly disturbed. If not provided, I ask for information about these areas of functioning. (The questionnaire also provides information in these areas.) How does the child get along in school? What does the teacher say about his or her conduct? Does the child have a "best friend?" If so, how often do they see one another? Do children call on the child? If so, how often? Is the child invited to others' homes? Is the child in the "in-group," on the fringe, or is he or she a "loner"? Questions such as these are the most vital of the interview and provide the most meaningful data as to whether psychopathology is present.

One area of difficulty which I have not found helpful to dwell on at length is that of sibling rivalry. In my opinion, it is normally fierce, and to devote much time to its vicissitudes is wasteful because such inquiry adds little meaningful information. If the mother, for example, says that the child fights often with his brother, I'll ask her how often. If the frequency is less than ten-to-fifteen fights a day and if there is no history of dangerous trauma being inflicted then I usually say something like: "That sounds par for the course. What other problems are there?" Of course, if a sibling is having nightmares in which he screams out: "No, no, Jerry. Don't beat me!" then the rivalry is probably pathological. Also, the absence of overt manifestations of sibling rivalry suggests a family in which aggression is significantly inhibited.

At the same time that one is obtaining verbal accounts of the child's difficulties with the back-and-forth inquiry, one should also attempt to stimulate and catalyze interaction between the members of the family. It is hoped that the exact kind of interaction which takes place in the home will be reproduced. It is the unwise interviewer who attempts to squelch or circumvent arguments between family members and tries to "cool things" when an argument threatens to erupt because much of value can be learned from such encounters. Are feelings freely expressed or is the argument highly intellectualized? Who is dominant? Does the child side with any particular person? Are there tears? If so, what effect do they have? The healthy family will be somewhat embarrassed and restrained in its argument, whereas the sicker family will not be so self-conscious. The possible considerations are endless—it is a rich source of information indeed.

One thing that is important to look for in the context of the family discussion is the presence of laughter and humor. One or two humorous comments, mutually enjoyed by members of the family, speaks for a healthy element in their relationship regardless of what pathology may be present. The ability to laugh is a vital ingredient to health, whereas the humorless family is usually a very sick one. And the capacity to laugh at oneself indicates ego-strength, healthy insight, and makes one's foibles more bearable. Therapists who respond warmly, with a humorous comment at the right time, provide a setting that fosters these informative responses.

Of course, the therapist should not be party to pathological humor. The hail-fellow-well-met type, the back-slapping jokester whose humor is patently obsessive and defensive, should not be responded to in kind, for that would only encourage the utilization of this ploy to avoid honesty. The parent who uses wit in the service of expressing hostility should not be encouraged by the therapist's laughing at his or her jokes. Sarcasm, verbal scapegoatism, and laughing ridicule should be noted mentally but certainly not joined by the therapist.

If during the course of the parents' description of the presenting problems the child interrupts with comments such as, "Don't tell him that," or "I told you never to tell him that," or "You promised me you wouldn't talk about that," one might react with surprise and say something like "What! Keeping secrets from your own psychiatrist? Didn't you know that you're never supposed to keep secrets from a psychiatrist?" One might then reinforce this principle by asking the child to think about television programs he or she has seen in which this fact has been demonstrated.

During the discussion of the presenting complaints it is important to observe the various parties. One should especially observe the child's relationship with each of the parents. Glances and gestures, as well as vocal intonations, provide information about affection, respect, and other forms of involvement. Seat placement, physical contact, and direct statements to one another also give much information about the interpersonal relationships of the parties being interviewed. In fact, this aspect of the interview may be more important than the specific information about presenting problems that is ostensibly the focus.

At this point, one can proceed in a number of different ways. If the examiner suspects that there is much useful information that the parents can relate but have been hesitant to reveal in front of the child, the child might be told, "Now I'm going to speak with your parents alone, so I'd appreciate your having a seat in the waiting room. Then, I'll speak with you alone while they sit outside." To some children this might be followed by, "I'll be speaking with them about things that are personal for them. Then, when I'm with you, I'll be speaking about things that you may want to be kept personal." However, it is important for the reader to appreciate that the latter comment is not made very often. I much prefer that the atmosphere be one of an open pool of communication in which all things pertinent to the child are discussed freely with both parents and the child. The examiner may, however, see the child alone at that point, especially if the parents have stated that there is nothing additional that they wish to relate. Or, the interview with all three parties may be continued, if that appears to be the most judicious approach.

INTERVIEW WITH THE PARENTS ALONE

When the parents are seen alone, they should be asked about other problems that they have hesitated to discuss in front of the child. Often such reluctance is ill-advised, and the parents should be encouraged to discuss these issue(s) with the child (who is then brought back into the room). When this is not the case, and the parents are alone, one does well to get some information about the marital relationship. Time does not permit going into great detail at this point, but the therapist wants to get a general idea about its stability and whether significant problems are present. When making inquiries about the parental relationship, each side should be heard; but in the initial interview, it may not be possible to come to any conclusions regarding which party exhibits the greater degree of pathology. The examiner merely wants to obtain a list of the main problems; an in-depth inquiry goes beyond the scope of the initial consultation.

On occasion, both parents will claim that they have a good marriage and that they love one another. There are two possibilities here: One is that this is true and the other is, of course, that the parents are denying (either consciously or unconsciously) impairments in their relationship. When presented with the "happy marriage," the examiner might respond with a comment like, "Every marriage has some problems; no marriage is perfect. There are times, I am sure, when the two of you have differences of opinion. Every marriage has its fights from time to time. What are the areas of difference in *your* marriage?" When presented in this way, the parents are generally more comfortable about revealing areas of difficulty. Of course, there are marriages in which the partners never fight, but in such cases one or both generally suffers with a deep-seated anger-inhibition problem, and the "peace" they enjoy is paid for dearly with symptoms and/or character traits resulting from the pent-up hostility that inevitably arises in all human relationships. Sometimes parents who deny marital difficulties in the joint session will provide significant information about their marital problems in individual sessions. Of course, the therapist would then be negligent if he or she did not go into the reasons for the "cover-up" during the joint session.

It is desirable to get some idea about the depth and nature of psychopathology in each of the parents. The interviewer will usually already have some information along these lines from general observations. The level of tension in the initial interview is generally quite high from the outset. Strong emotions are evoked. In such an atmosphere it is likely that many forms of psychopathology will be revealed. This is especially so for such character traits as suspiciousness, dependency, volatility, low frustration tolerance, strong need to control and dominate, and seductivity. One of the easiest ways to obtain information about the parents' psychopathology is to ask whether either of them has ever been in treatment. If the answer is yes, the therapist should ask about the main problems for which the parent has been or is in therapy. A person who is in relatively good psychological health usually will not hesitate to discuss the major reasons for seeking treatment. Significant secretiveness may, in itself, represent a problem. One should not, however, expect a person in therapy to reveal every secret or personal problem in the presence of the spouse, although it is reasonable to expect that the major issues will be comfortably discussed. Time only permits an outlining of the major problems for which the parent sought therapy; more detailed information can be gained in subsequent interviews.

Before closing the part of the initial interview in which the parents are seen without the child, they should be invited to talk about anything else they consider important. If a presented issue appears to be significant, some time should be devoted to it—to a superficial degree—reserving detailed elaboration for subsequent sessions.

INTERVIEW WITH THE CHILD ALONE

The main object at this stage is to obtain as much information about the child in as short a period as possible, so that the interviewer can be in a better position to make definite statements about the presence of psychopathology and the necessity for treatment. Actually, the therapist should have a good idea already about these two issues, and this phase should serve to supplement what he has already learned. Although allowing the child to select the activity *he* or *she* wishes to engage in is my usual approach during at least some part of the *therapeutic* interview, in the *diagnostic* interview my inclination is to present the child with activities which are most highly calculated to provide me with meaningful psychodynamic information. If, however, the child shows a strong desire to engage in a particular activity (which is unusual), I do not stop him or her and I learn what I can from it. However, I might say: "Okay, we'll spend some of our time doing what you want, and then we'll spend the rest of the time with the games I'd like to play with you."

It is important to reiterate that at this point I am primarily concerned with symptoms and less with psychodynamics. My primary interest in this phase is to determine *if* psychopathology is present, not why or how it came about. In the context of the inquiry I observe for the presence of symptoms and am only secondarily interested in the psychodynamics which are revealed by what the child does. I look for manifestations of atypical and/or abnormal behavior, such as obstructionism, passive-aggressivity, attempts to destroy or lack of concern for my property, hyperactivity, poor concentration, speech impairment, being a "sore-loser," compulsive cleanliness, excessive questioning, inordinate need for reassurance, failure to understand directions, and so forth.

The Freely-Drawn Picture

A good way to start a meaningful interview when alone with a child is to ask the child to draw with crayons a picture of anything he or she wants. I will generally say something like, "I'd like to see how good you are at drawing a picture. Draw anything you want. After you've finished I want to see how good you are at making up a story about the picture that you've drawn. It has to be a completely made-up story, not something that really happened to you or anyone you know, not something that you saw on television or read in a book." By using the phrase "to see how good you are," I hope to enhance the child's motivation. Presumably, if the child draws a "good" picture, I will not only offer praise (which I will), but the child will feel good about him- or herself because of the accomplishment. And the same holds true with regard to the story I hope to elicit. If the child begins to draw something that looks like a design, I will ask what it is. If the child confirms my suspicions, I will say, "It's against the rules to draw a design. The rules of the game are that you have to draw something about which you can tell a story." Of course, the child is under no real compulsion to "follow the rules." Most children, however, will overcome the resistances that contributed to their drawing the design and provide a recognizable drawing.

It is important for the examiner to appreciate that only limited pressure, cajoling, and other forms of "encouragement" should be utilized in this phase of the evaluation. At worst, the child will refuse to draw. The only result of this will be that the examiner would be deprived of some information. In the extreme, the child will absolutely refuse to become involved in any of the diagnostic activities. If such is the case, the child will not become a patient. If the therapist considers this to represent a lack of professional ability, then it is likely that he or she will place undue pressures on the patient. As mentioned, the therapist should take the position that he or she did not cause the pathology—it is often generations in the making—and although it is important to *try* to help the patient, it does not behoove the therapist to bring about any kind of alleviation of the presenting problems. Psychopathology is most often complex and we are only at the most primitive levels of our understanding. Considering our ignorance, it is even a bit grandiose of therapists to take the position that help can be given to more than a small fraction of all those who come our way. With this more modest and realistic position, examiners are less likely to place undue pressures on themselves and their patients.

In Chapter Two I have commented on the analytic meaning of children's pictures. As is true of many aspects of psychodynamic theory, there is little that one can say with certainty. But even within the analytic framework, one must be aware that a psychological interpretation based on the picture itself is very risky business. For example, a boy may draw a picture of a happy scene: a house, a brightly shining sun, and beautiful flowers all around. From the appearance of the picture one is likely to conclude that the boy is a happy child who has an optimistic view of the world. However, one must consider the possibility that the picture represents a reaction formation against depression, hostility, pessimism, or various other unpleasant feelings. Accordingly, one is in no position to make any statements about a picture in isolation from the child who draws it. The more knowledge the therapist has about the child, the better able he or she is to understand the meaning of the picture. In addition, isolated interpretations are likely to be far less valid than persistent themes that exhibit themselves in many different ways. Thus, if the boy who drew the aforementioned scene was clinically depressed, had a generally "sourpuss" attitude, and had few friends, it is likely that the picture is reaction formation. And this would be supported if he exhibited both clinically and through projective material other manifestations of denial and reaction formation. This caveat about interpretating the child's projections cannot be emphasized too strongly.

The examiner should also appreciate that many age-appropriate, stereotyped pictures may appear to have complex psychodynamic significance when a simpler explanation will suffice and be far more accurate. For example, an eight-year-old boy who draws pictures depicting ships and airplanes in combat should not automatically be considered to have excessive hostility that is being released vicariously through the vehicle of the drawing and its associated war story. All individuals have pent-up anger that they cannot release directly. All of us must utilize various socially acceptable vehicles for vicarious release. Release through space-war fantasy is presently in vogue among children, and the child's utilization of it, to a reasonable degree, is normal and healthy. Accordingly, one should not impute too quickly pathological motives in this book, especially in Chapters Six, Eight, and Nine, I will dis- and story that should command our attention.

What has just been said regarding interpreting the meaning of a picture is also applicable to analyzing the self-created story for its psychodynamic significance. Some children will tell a relatively mundane story depicting events of the day. This is usually a resistance against the expression of more revealing material. Others will tell extremely elaborate stories, sometimes to the point where the examiner will have to interrupt because they appear to go on endlessly. These can also serve the purposes of resistance. However, the therapist may detect one or two themes that are repeated over and over. Such repeated themes may be significant. The repetition may serve the process of working through, in that reiteration and desensitization are central to that process. It is beyond the scope of this chapter to discuss in detail the wide variety of psychodynamic themes that may be revealed in children's stories. Elsewhere in this book, especially in Chapters Six, Eight, and Nine, I will discuss such analysis.

Draw-a-Person

During the initial interview many examiners ask the child simply to "draw a person." It is preferable to make this request after the child has drawn the free picture because asking the child to draw a person restricts fantasy significantly. From the universe of possible things a child can draw, selecting a person considerably narrows the child's options. However, there is still a universe of possible drawings and associations (a universe within a universe so to speak), and so the drawing is still fairly useful as a projective instrument. One should not ask the child to draw a person of a specific sex because that may further narrow the possibilities and restrict associations. *After* the child has drawn a figure of a particular sex, one can then ask for one of the opposite sex. Generally, the age and sex of the figure drawn is revealing. If a boy, for example, draws a picture of a girl and, in addition pays significant attention to such details as eyelashes, coiffure, fingernails, jewelry, and other attributes generally of great concern to females in our society, one should consider the possibility that this boy has a sexual identification problem. This would especially be the case if most observers, not knowing the sex of the child, would consider it to have been drawn by a girl. If, however, a boy draws a picture of an older woman, it is likely that the mother or her surrogate is being depicted.

By looking at the picture, the therapist can sometimes learn some important things about the child. However, the reader should be warned that such interpretations are highly speculative and interexaminer reliability is quite low. This drawback notwithstanding, useful information can still be obtained. This is especially the case if speculations from projective material are substantiated by clinical assessment. Placing the feet of a figure flush against the bottom of the paper may connote feelings of instability with a need to anchor or secure the body to a stable place. Children with marked feelings of inferiority are more likely to draw their picture in this way. Significant blackness, especially when drawn frenetically, sometimes symbolizes great anxiety and a view of people as threatening. This kind of picture is more frequently drawn by children who are clinically anxious. Large shoulders and other accentuations of traditionally "macho" features may represent a boy's attempt to compensate for feelings of weakness. This is especially likely in the adolescent with feelings of masculine inadequacy. The way in which the child deals with breast outline may provide information about the child's sexual feelings and attitudes. Family attitudes toward sexuality will often provide clues as to whether the examiner's interpretation in this area is valid. The way in which the child draws the eyes may provide information in a number of areas. Shy children and those prone to use denial mechanisms to a significant degree may draw a figure with the eyes averted. Staring eyes have generally been interpreted to connote suspiciousness and sometimes even paranoia. Again, the examiner does well to make such interpretations cautiously and to use clinical data for support or refutation of these speculations. Machover (1949, 1951, 1960) has written extensively on the psychological interpretation of children's drawings.

The examiner should try to get the child to tell a story about the picture. One can begin the process by asking for specific information about the person depicted. Some start with the general request that the child tell a story, and then only resort to specific questions if the request is not or cannot be complied with. What has been said about interpreting stories told in association with freely drawn pictures holds for the human-figure drawings as well. The therapist does well to differentiate between age-appropriate stereotyped stories (which are probably normal) and idiosyncratic ones. The latter provide the more meaningful information. But here again there is much speculation.

After drawing the first picture, the child should be asked to draw a picture of a person of the opposite sex. One should take care not to specify whether the picture should be of a child or an adult, lest the universe of possibilities be reduced. One might say, "Now that you've drawn a picture of a male, I want you to draw another picture. This time I want you to draw a female." Or, for the younger child, one might say, "Now that you've drawn a picture of a boy, I want you to draw a picture of either a girl or a woman." After as much information as possible has been extracted from the pictures, the examiner should ask the child to draw a picture of a family. Because of time limitations, it is prudent not to require the child to spend too much time on the details of the various family figures. Here, the therapist is primarily interested in the number and sexes of the figures chosen, their relationships with one another, and the story the child tells about the family. Stories elicited from the family picture are generally less revealing than those from the individual pictures. More frequently one obtains stereotyped stories about family excursions or day-to-day activities. These are usually resistance stories and provide little if any psychodynamic information. Of course, at times, one does obtain rich and meaningful stories. (The reader interested in further comments of mine on this instrument, should refer to Chapter Two.)

The Make-a-Picture Story Test

The Make-a-Picture Story test (MAPS) (Shneidman, 1947) is particularly useful for eliciting psychodynamic material from children, especially from those who may not be free enough to reveal themselves through the aforementioned less-structured methods for gaining psychodynamic material, namely, the freely drawn picture, the mutual storytelling technique, and the Draw-a-Person and Draw-a-Family tests. The equipment consists of a series of cards, each of which depicts a scene without human or animal figures, and the child is provided with a collection of figurines (cut from thin cardboard) representing a wide assortment of human and animal figures. The child is simply requested to select one of the cards and one or more of the figurines, put the figurines in the scene, and then make up a story.

Although there is a similarity between the Make-a-Picture Story test and the more commonly used Thematic Apperception Test (TAT) (Murray, 1936), there are definite differences—differences that, in my opinion, make the MAPS a superior diagnostic instrument. First, the scenes depicted in the TAT, although designed to be vague, are still definitely identifiable and have figures with recognizable sex and age. In the TAT these specific figures are placed in specific scenes. In the MAPS the child decides which figure(s) shall be in which scene, thereby increasing almost infinitely the number of possible stimuli for storytelling. In the MAPS the child is much more the creator of the facilitating stimulus. Furthermore, having more of a say in what the picture will be like and playing an active role in determining what picture to create, the child is generally more motivated to associate stories to it.

Another advantage that the MAPS has over the TAT is that the TAT cards are primarily designed for diagnostic work with adults. Although some of the TAT cards do depict children, most depict grown-ups. The adult scenes will certainly elicit fantasies around family life, especially the parents; however, the paucity of children is a definite detriment if one wishes to draw out stories from children. While some of the TAT cards are specifically designated as relevant to boys and girls, the author's experience has been that the child's opportunity to select the figures in the MAPS creates a situation in which more child-type fantasies are likely to be evoked.

Additional Diagnostic Instruments

The stories that the child tells in association with the freely drawn picture, the Draw-a-Person Test, and The Make-a-Picture Story cards, can sometimes be used as a point of departure for an informal introduction into the mutual storytelling technique (Chapters Eight, Nine, and Ten). I say *sometimes* because time limitations may not permit the examiner's responding with stories during the two-hour consultation. But more important, presenting responding stories during that early stage may be injudicious and even risky. The creation of a responding story is best done in circumstances in which one has extensive information about a child, especially after a thorough and intensive evaluation of the child and family members. However, there are times when the meaning of the child's story is so obvious, and the pathological adaptations contained therein so blatant, that the examiner may be in a good position to provide a reasonably accurate responding story. Under such circumstances, the examiner does well to respond with his or her story and take some time discussing it with the child.

There are other projective instruments that the examiner can utilize in the initial screening interview. Whether or not these are used depends primarily on the amount of time available. The three wishes question certainly does not take much time, unless elaborate discussions have been spun off from the child's responses. I generally try to get the child to tell me not only what he or she would wish for but *why*. However, I have not usually found this series of questions useful. Most often children provide relatively stereotyped and nonrevealing responses. A common response is, "All the money in the world" or some huge amount of money, like "a billion trillion dollars." When I then ask children who respond in this way what they would do with all the money, they generally provide a list of toys and other material possessions. (I have yet to interview a child who utilized the money philanthropically.) Another common response is, "My first wish would be that I could have as many wishes as I wanted." This response is usually provided as a "joke," but it is obviously also a resistance.

Another instrument that may be utilized in the initial interview for obtaining useful psychodynamic information is a series of questions described by N.I. Kritzberg (1966). The child is asked the question: "If you had to be turned into an animal, and could choose any animal in the whole world, what animal would you choose?" After the child responds, he or she is asked the reason for that choice. Following this, the child is asked for his or her second and third choices and the reasons why. Then the child is asked what three animals he or she would not want to be, and the reasons why. There are a series of similar type questions that I will describe in detail in the next chapter. Generally, time only permits the presentation of the aforementioned in the initial screening interview.

Generally, time does not permit my introducing The Talking, Feeling, and Doing Game (1973b) (Chapter Eleven) in the initial screening interview. However, there is occasionally a child who is so inhibited that no meaningful material has been obtained from the aforementioned projective instruments. Under such circumstances, I will devote some time to playing the game with the child. This not only may provide me with information that might not have otherwise been obtained, but gives me a hint as to whether the child is a possible candidate for therapeutic involvement. The inability to provide projective material certainly speaks poorly for therapeutic involvement, but *The Talking, Feeling, and Doing Game* may still be a viable instrument for utilization for such children.

The tests discussed are used with the child whom I suspect to be suffering with psychogenic difficulties. If, however, on the basis of information obtained from the parents and the questionnaire, I strongly suspect that a neurophysiological disturbance is present (GMBDS), I do not devote much time to projective instruments but rather administer some of the tests on my GMBDS screening battery (Figures 5.15–5.17). Obviously, in the 60–75 minutes during which time the child is seen alone, it is not possible to administer all of these instruments. Rather, I select a few that are most likely to assess functioning in areas in which clinical deficiencies are described. For example, if the parents describe hyperactivity, I will administer *The Steadiness Tester* (R.A. Gardner and A.K. Gardner, 1978; R.A. Gardner et al., 1979). If they describe "dyslexia" as manifested by a high frequency of letter and number reversals, I will administer the three sections of *The Reversals Frequency Test* (R.A. Gardner, 1978a, 1979c; R.A. Gardner and M. Broman, 1979). If an attentional impairment is described, I will administer the Digits Forward and Digits Backward sections of the *Digit Span* subtest of the *Wechsler Intelligence Scale for Children—Revised* (WISC-R) (D. Wechsler, 1974). If an eye-motor or visual-perceptual problem is described, I will administer the *Developmental Test of Visual-Motor Integration* (K.E. Beery and N.A. Buktenica, 1982).

Generally, it is in the intensive evaluation that I will have the opportunity to assess in depth the neuropsychological deficits of these children, not only with regard to the administration of my full screening battery but to the administration of other instruments that may be warranted for proper diagnosis. Because it is the primary purpose of this book to discuss the diagnosis and treatment of children with *psychogenic* disorders, I will not be devoting significant discussion to GMBDS childrens' diagnosis here. Elsewhere (Gardner, 1979c) I have presented in detail the instruments I utilize for the objective diagnosis of these childrens' difficulties.

Figure 5.15   The Group of Minimal Brain Dysfunction Syndromes

Screening Diagnostic Battery

Diagnostic Instrument	Primary Information Provided	Additional Information Provided	Age Range
			2 4 6 8 10 12 14 16 18 A
WISC-R: Information (Wechsler)	auditory linguistic reception long-term memory fund of inforation linguistic expression	intellectual curiosity	6-0 ———16-11
WISC-R: Similarities (Wechsler)	auditory analogous logic auditory conceptuali- zation abstraction	auditory linguistic reception linguistic expression long-term auditory memory	6-0 ———16-11
WISC-R: Arithmetic (Wechsler)	arithmetic logic auditory and visual conceptualization abstraction	auditory concentration short- and long-term auditory memory long-term visual memory	6-0 ———16-11
WISC-R: Vocabulary (Wechsler)	auditory linguistic reception linguistic expres- sion	long-term auditory memory intellectual curiosity	6-0 ———16-11
WISC-R: Comprehension (Wechsler)	social judgment common sense conscience		6-0 ———16-11
WISC-R: Digit Span, Digits Forward (Wechsler, Gardner)	short-term auditory sequential memory	auditory concentration	5-0 ———15-11
WISC-R: Digit Span, Digits Backward (Wechsler, Gardner)	short-term auditory sequential memory short-term visual sequential memory	auditory concentration visual concentration visual scanning	5-0 ———15-11

219

Figure 5.16

Diagnostic Instruments	Primary Information Provided	Additional Information Provided	Age Range
WISC-R: Picture Completion (Wechsler)	long-term visual memory	visual Gestalt	6-0 ——— 16-11
WISC-R: Picture Arrangement (Wechsler)	social judgment common sense visual organization visual Gestalt long-term visual sequential memory		6-0 ——— 16-11
WISC-R: Block Design (Wechsler)	visual analysis visual-motor synthesis visual-motor organization visual-motor Gestalt	dyspraxia	6-0 ——— 16-11
WISC-R: Object Assembly (Wechsler)	long-term visual memory visual-motor organization visual Gestalt visual conceptualization	visual concentration persistence	6-0 ——— 16-11
WISC-R: Coding (Digit Symbol) (Wechsler)	visual concentration visual-motor integration	short-term visual memory visual discrimination	6-0 ——— 16-11
WISC-R: Mazes (Wechsler)	impulsivity	visual concentration planning and foresight visual-motor coordination	6-0 ——— 16-11
Reversals Frequency Test: I, Execution (Gardner)	long-term visual memory		5-0 ——— 14-11
Reversals Frequency Test: II, Recognition (Gardner)	long-term visual memory		5-0 ——— 14-11

Figure 5.17

Diagnostic Instrument	Primary Information Provided	Additional Information Provided	Age Range
Reversals Frequency Test: III, Matching (Gardner)	visual discrimination	visual concentration	5-0——8-11
Purdue Pegboard (Gardner)	visual-motor coordination	fine motor coordination	5-0————15-11
Balls and Basket Test (Gardner)	gross motor coordination		5-0————15-11
Developmental Test of Visual-Motor Integration (Beery and Buktenica)	visual-motor coordination constructional dyspraxia visual Gestalt	visual discrimination	2————15
Steadiness Tester (Gardner)	hyperactivity concentration motor impersistence	tremors choreiform movements	5-0————15-9

221

Final Comments

At this point therapists should direct their attention to an issue that is second in importance only to the question of whether the child is in need of treatment. They should ask themselves the simple question whether or not they *like* the child being evaluated: "Can I relate well to him(her)? Does the child appear to be relating well to me? Have we established rapport? Is there some mutual emotional resonance?" If the answers to these questions are for the most part *no*, and it does not appear that there is a potential for improvement in the relationship, then the therapist should have serious reservations about treating the child. As stated already, *we cannot treat everyone.* We should not expect ourselves to establish a meaningful therapeutic relationship with all of those who seek our help. If this is truly to be a "screening interview" we must not indiscriminately try to treat all those who need it. We must try to treat all those whom we think might profit from working with us. There is a vast difference.

I cannot present specific criteria for making this discrimination, because the decision must be made primarily on the basis of the subjective feelings therapists have toward the patient and what they *surmise* the patient feels about them.

For example, I once saw an eight-year-old boy and his paternal grandmother with whom he was living (He had been abandoned by his parents). During the interview the grandmother showed me a bottle of pills which her pediatrician had prescribed. I considered them to be contraindicated for this boy's condition and suggested that she hold off giving him any further medication until I had had a chance to talk to the pediatrician. At this point, the child grabbed the bottle out of his grandmother's hands and quickly gobbled down two pills, looking at both of us with a victorious smile of defiance. Such blatant contempt in the first interview spoke quite poorly for his ability to establish a meaningful therapeutic relationship with me. But more important the act produced in me a strong feeling of aversion for this child and I suspected that I would probably be a poor choice of therapist for him. During the remainder of that interview and in two more he continued to exhibit passive-aggressive behavior, which frustrated my attempts to involve him in a friendlier relationship. I found myself becoming increasingly irritated with his obstructionism, to the point where I found him obnoxious, and so I recommended him to someone else. I must emphasize here that I appreciate that my anger might have been inappropriate. Whether appropriate or not is less important than the fact that after three sessions I was still unable to like this child. If the therapist, in the work with such a child, can express and/or otherwise utilize such resentful feelings—and thus successfully reduce them as well as the irritating behavior that provokes them—then treatment may still be salvaged. My attempts to do this with this child were unsuccessful.

In summary, what I am saying is: Don't treat a child you don't like. If you cannot bring about a change in such negative feelings then recommend someone else. Generally, during the first interview I am able to come to a decision regarding this issue. If not, I may suggest a second (and sometimes a third) session. If by then I feel there is hope for the formation of a good relationship with the child, I will suggest the full intensive work-up. If not, I save everyone time and trouble and either refer to someone else or, if the child has already been given up as untreatable by a few previous therapists, I suggest no treatment at that time and consider alternative recommendations.

CRITERIA FOR DECIDING
WHETHER TREATMENT IS WARRANTED

There are four areas of inquiry useful in helping the examiner decide whether a child needs treatment. Before elaborating on these, it is important to emphasize that transient symptomatic manifestations are extremely common in children. Practically every child exhibits occasional tics, short-term phobic reactions, temper tantrums, occasional stealing episodes, lying, bribing, sleep difficulties, and so on. An example of this kind of situation would be the child whose parents have recently announced that they are going to separate and then get a divorce. It is normal for such children to exhibit transient symptoms such as depression, impaired school curiosity and motivation, crying spells, psychosomatic complaints, withdrawal from friends, and antisocial behavior. The examiner should recognize this point and not quickly recommend therapy. It is only after these symptoms persist more than a few months that treatment is warranted.

Of course, some counseling with the parents may be useful during this period. It is often difficult to ascertain that level of symptomatology at which the normal frequency ends and the pathological begins. Also, it is only when atypical, inappropriate, or pathological behavior exhibits itself over time that one should consider therapy. Also, it is difficult, if not impossible, to provide a sharp cutoff point regarding how long symptoms should be present before treatment is warranted, but a few months is certainly reasonable. This important consideration is taken into account in the latest diagnostic and statistical manual—DSM-III (1980).

School

The school is the most important area of inquiry for determining whether or not a child requires therapy. The child is born a primitive infant. It is the role of parents, during the earliest years, to make every reasonable attempt to transform these primitive human beings into individuals capable of functioning in society. The school can be viewed as the first "testing grounds" as to whether they have been successful in achieving this goal—to the degree required for functioning in nursery or kindergarten. It is there that children must restrain their primitive impulses most consistently and predictably. The home is a much more relaxed atmosphere, and its toleration for atypical behavior much greater. In addition, parental denial of difficulties may also leave psychopathology undetected. It is in the school, however, that the teacher can compare more objectively the child with others his or her own age and ascertain whether atypical behavior is manifesting itself.

There are two areas of inquiry that most sensitively assess school adaptation, namely, academic performance and behavior. If the child is not reaching what the teacher reasonably considers to be his or her academic potential, then psychopathology may be present. In addition, one wants to know about the child's relationship to the teacher, especially with regard to cooperation, respect for the teacher's authority, and general willingness to comply reasonably with classroom routine. Inquiry into the child's relationship with classmates is also important. Children who are functioning well with regard to these classroom functions are not likely to have serious psychopathology.

However, there are occasional children with psychiatric difficulties who do well in school, both in the academic and behavioral areas. They may be over compliant and passive children who are quite fearful of any manifestations of defiance or failure to follow usual routines. They may be viewed by the teachers as "a joy" and may be an immense source of pride to their parents. Their "uptightness," however, will probably get them into trouble in some areas, especially when self-assertion is warranted. But these children represent a small minority and the basic principle still holds, namely, that the child who is doing well in school in both the academic and behavioral realms, in realtionships with teachers and peers, is not likely to be suffering with significant psychopathology.

Neighborhood

The second most important area to consider when deciding whether a child needs treatment is relationships with peers in the neighborhood. Whereas peers will tolerate more atypical behavior than teachers, they will not tolerate more than the child's parents. Accordingly, maintaining friendships does not require a degree of integration that successful school performance necessitates. In order to maintain good relationships with neighborhood friends, children must have learned to share, to consider the rights of others, to wait their turns, to adhere to the rules of games, and they must have developed a wide variety of other interpersonal accommodations that will enable them to maintain friendships. The therapist does well to inquire as to whether the child actively seeks friends and is sought by them. Does the child invite others to the home and do other children come around in order to play with the patient? One wants to know the kinds of children the patient plays with. Are they reasonably normal, healthy, and well integrated children or are they in the fringe groups, the atypical, the antisocial, or those who have such personality disturbances that most of the children do not want to involve themselves with them? If the latter is the case, then psychopathology may very well be present in the patient. But even this child may be healthier than those who have no friends at all.

Home

Home behavior is the least valuable area for ascertaining whether or not psychopathology is present. There, the consequences of atypical behavior are the least (when compared to school and neighborhood certainly), and the mechanism of parental denial may also operate to compromise the parents' capacity to ascertain whether or not behavior is atypical. Children normally do not behave as well in their homes as they do in the homes of their peers and in school. They often follow the rules applicable to each situation, and the rules at home are generally most lax and the consequences for breaking them most lenient. It is well to assume that children "get away with as much as they can" in each situation.

If a mother, for example, complains that her son fights frequently with his brother, I will often ask how many fights a day she observes. Often she will respond along these lines, "I really can't tell you, Doctor. There are so many, I can't keep count. Maybe it's 20 to 30 times a day." I will then ask her if the brother still has two eyes, two ears, one nose, one mouth, two arms, two legs, and whether other body parts are intact. She will most often respond affirmatively. I will then ask her if the brother wakes up in the middle of the night screaming, "No, no, Joey. Don't beat me!" If she responds that no such dreams have taken place, I will reassure her that the sibling fighting is probably within the normal range—so fierce is the usual degree of sibling rivalry. It is only when there is *no* fighting that one might consider there to be psychopathology in that one or both children are probably significantly inhibited in expressing the normal sibling rivalrous feelings.

It is reasonable to say that when the second child appears on the scene, the first child is going to often exhibit severe jealous reactions. After all, prior to the appearance of the second, the first child has been "king (queen) on the throne." Now, the newborn infant doesn't just take half of the parents' time, but maybe three-quarters or even more. One can compare the appearance of a new child in the family to the situation in which a husband, for example, comes home with another woman, introduces her to his wife, and says something along these lines: "Darling, I'd like you to meet Jane. She's going to be living with us from now on. She's a wonderful person, both in and out of bed, and I know you're going to like her. So give her a big kiss."

Parents will often complain that a child does not cooperate at home doing the usual chores and assisting in the household routine. For example, a mother may say that she has a hard time getting Billy to take out the garbage, and he always dawdles, finds excuses, or just flatly refuses to do it. My views on this are that there has probably been no child in the history of the world who ever wanted to take out the garbage. In fact, even garbage men generally don't like taking out garbage, although they are often paid quite well for these services (most often even more than the child's teachers)! It is the child who *wants* to take out the garbage who may be exhibiting difficulties. This is especially the case if the child wants to make sure that the garbage cans are completely clean, that there isn't a speck of dirt, and that every coffee grain is completely removed. Obviously, such a child is suffering with some moderately severe obsessive-compulsive symptomatology. I would go further and say that the child who does *not* occasionally exhibit uncooperative behavior probably has difficulties.

I recall, as a student at The Bronx High School of Science, a teacher named Mr. Levinson who was the school disciplinarian. If a child was sassy to him he would often respond, "Who do you think you're speaking to? Your mudda?" Mr. Levinson recognized well that children are likely to be more disrespectful of their parents (especially their "muddas") than their teachers. A child who exhibits similar disrespect to teachers has not "learned the rules" and is thereby atypical. Parents, like siblings, serve well as scapegoats, as targets for much of the pent-up hostilities of the day that cannot safely be released elsewhere.

The repercussions for "unloading" one's pent-up anger on one's family are far less than directing them toward their original sources. I am not stating that this is a "good" thing, nor am I recommending it. I am only stating that it is a widespread phenomenon and that examiners do well to appreciate it when assessing for the presence of psychopathology. It is extremely difficult, however, to differentiate between normal and pathological degrees of disrespectful and uncooperative behavior in the home. The level at which the normal ends and the pathological begins is very blurred. This is an extremely weak area of inquiry for determining whether or not a child needs treatment. However, it is not an area that should be ignored totally. If the child *rarely* cooperates, if sibling rivalry is so fierce that the fighting is almost incessant, if turmoil and conflict is the *modus vivendi* in the home, then psychopathology is probably present.

DSM–III

If a child exhibits no difficulties in the three areas, school, neighborhood, and home, it is unlikely that a DSM–III diagnosis will be applicable. However, on occasion, a child will exhibit such symptoms and still function well in the aforementioned areas. This would be the case for a child with obsessions and/or compulsions that do not interfere significantly in daily life. Or, other symptoms such as phobias, depression, and psychosomatic complaints may be present without significant compromises in these three areas of functioning. The main reason for this is that most children come to treatment with interpersonal, rather than intrapsychic, conflicts. The problems lie not so much *within* themselves but *between* themselves and significant figures in their environment, especially parents and teachers.

PRESENTING THE INITIAL RECOMMENDATIONS

By this time about one-and-a-half hours to one-and-three-quarter hours of interviewing have taken place, and the examiner should generally have enough information to decide whether or not treatment is warranted. Although little information may have been obtained about the underlying psychodynamic factors that have brought about the presenting symptoms, the *symptoms* are the important things to focus upon in deciding whether or not therapy is warranted. This is an important point. All behavioral manifestations have psychodynamics. And sometimes the psychodynamic patterns include pathological adaptations. Treatment should only be recommended if the symptomatic manifestations are interfering *significantly* in the major areas of functioning. I have emphasized the word *significantly* because all individuals exhibit, at times, transient pathological manifestations and even pathological manifestations that may be ongoing. Treatment should be recommended only when these are interfering in the patient's life to a significant degree. It is only then that the time, effort, and expense of involvement in treatment is warranted. At this point the parents should be brought back into the room and the examiner's findings and recommendations discussed with them.

Should the Child Be Present?

The question regarding whether the child should be present at the time of the presentation of the initial conclusions and recommendations is sometimes of significance. My general preference is that the child be present. As mentioned, children are not renowned for their insight into the fact that they have problems, and being witness to the presentation may contribute, admittedly in a small way, to the child's gaining some insight. Furthermore, not permitting the child to be party to the discussion may contribute to a compromise in the therapist-patient relationship because the child cannot but be aware of the fact that things are being spoken about him or her, "secrets" that the child is not being permitted to learn about. This engenders distrust in the therapist and the parents and thus compromises relationships with both.

There are situations, however, when it is probably judicious to have the child sit in the waiting room at this point. For example, if the parents have advised the therapist during their time alone with him or her that a separation is impending—but the child has not yet been told—the therapist should not be the one to divulge this to the child. Rather, I generally recommend that the parents be the first ones to tell the child. For the therapist to do this compromises the parents' capacity to deal with the residual reactions that inevitably will ensue. (This issue is discussed in greater detail in my *The Parents Book About Divorce* [1977b, 1979a].) Retarded children and those with borderline intelligence are probably best left outside the waiting room because of the likelihood that they will misinterpret significantly what is being said. A child with a severe physical disease such as leukemia might be psychologically traumatized by such a discussion, and so it is preferable that such a child remain in the waiting room at this point. There are other situations which would warrant a child's remaining in the waiting room, but these are relatively rare. My experience has been that, in the overwhelming majority of situations, I have the child present at the time of the presentation of my initial findings and recommendations.

When Therapy Is Not Warranted

On occasion, I have concluded that treatment is not warranted. Sometimes the parents have been overly concerned about the child and have not appreciated that the behavioral manifestations that have been a source of concern are within the normal limits. Sometimes these parents may need some counseling themselves; other times they just need some reassurance. This is more often the case with first-born children. With subsequently-born children the parents become more knowledgeable and less anxious and so are not as likely to seek unnecessary consultations. In some cases the child has been "cured" between the time that the appointment was made and the time of the consultation. Merely having been informed of the fact that an appointment has been made may result in a significant reduction and even complete alleviation of symptomatology. I refer to this as "threat therapy."

One could argue that treatment in such cases is still warranted because the underlying problems have not been resolved. Classical psychoanalysts, especially, would take this position. I generally do not embark on treatment or even continue therapy with anyone who is asymptomatic. The symptom gives me the "handle" for the therapeutic work. Our theories about psychodynamics are extremely theoretical and speculative. If the underlying processes that have originally caused the symptomatology are still present to a significant degree, they will erupt once again and bring about symptoms once more. Then, I will be in a better position to treat. I have even had situations in which a parent will call me a few days before the initial consultation and state that since the child was informed of the appointment, the presenting symptoms have disappeared. I will express my pleasure and advise such a parent not to hesitate to call me again if the situation has changed. Sometimes a new appointment is set up in the future and sometimes not.

I generally take a conservative approach with regard to recommending therapy. Recommending that the parents embark on the intensive evaluation (to be discussed in detail in Chapter Six) is an expensive and exhausting proposition. I do not recommend it lightly. Furthermore, therapy may be extremely expensive and extended—even more reason to be cautious about recommending it. In spite of what I have said, the vast majority of children who come for initial consultations do require therapy. One reason for this is that there may have been a long period of denial and refusal of treatment and, by the time the child does come, things have built up to the point where treatment is definitely warranted. This is especially the case when a school has recommended therapy. Schools will generally tolerate significant degrees of atypical behavior before recommending treatment. By the time they do so, it is likely that it is warranted.

When A Decision Regarding Therapy Has Not Yet Been Made

There are times when the two-hour consultation does not prove adequate to make a final recommendation. On those occasions I will recommend one or more further sessions for data collection. As mentioned in Chapter One, I will not allow myself to be pressured into coming to conclusions and making recommendations in a specific period. My experiences in the military taught me that such restraints are antitherapeutic. In the military, "orders is orders" and the psychiatrist may have little choice. Since that time (now 25 years) I have never permitted such constraints to be placed on me. When the parents are brought in I tell them in a matter-of-fact way, without any embarrassment or apology, that the situation is a complex one and that I have not been able to come to any definite conclusion at that point. I then advise them what further data collection will be necessary. Sometimes one or two sessions with child and/or parents is all I anticipate will be required. On some occasions I will need more information from the child's teacher, and this is preferably done by directly speaking with her. Sometimes the child has exhibited significant resistance during the initial session. Although psychiatric problems are present and warrant treatment, the child's resistance has been such that I cannot reasonably make a recommendation for therapy because there would be no patient to involve meaningfully in the process. I may recommend under these circumstances one or two more sessions with the child in the hope that I might then engage him or her. If this also proves unsuccessful, I discontinue my work with the child. I may provide some parental counseling, generally over a few sessions. On occasion, I might recommend that the child needs speech therapy, summer camp, organized recreational experiences, or treatment by a pediatrician or a neurologist. Under these circumstances, no further work with me is warranted.

When Psychotherapy Is Warranted

Most often, psychotherapy is indicated. I then outline to the parents what I consider to be the major problems, at the symptomalogical level as well as the family factors that may have contributed. I emphasize that these are my *initial* conclusions and that it is only with further experience with the family that I will be able to be more certain about the factors that are contributing to the child's difficulties. I advise them that it is going to be necessary for me to get to know each of them better if I am to work optimally with the child. In order to do this I will need to see each of the parents once or twice individually to get background information from them. Following the individual interviews with each of the parents I will want to see them together because I will often get conflicting information about what is going on between them. If there are older siblings I will often recommend a family interview. I also advise them that I will want to see the child two or three times more in order to collect more information from him or her. At times psychological tests will be indicated, and these will be administered concurrently with the intensive evaluation. I advise the parents that during the intensive evaluation I will be interviewing them as if they themselves were coming to me for a psychiatric evaluation. I then tell them that, when all the information is collected, I will review the material and present my findings and recommendations to them. I impress upon them the fact that I only recommend the intensive evaluation when treatment is warranted and that it serves as a foundation for my therapy.

It is important that the therapist invite the parents at this point to ask any questions they may have about the proposal. They have to appreciate (if they do not already) that, in the private practice setting, it is expensive and time consuming but that it is the optimum way to proceed. My experience has been that many parents do not "hear" me at this point. They may have come with the idea that I will give them a recommendation and send them on their way and that is all that treatment involves. Although there was nothing in the face letter to my questionnaire to suggest this, their wishes that this were the case or their misinformation about what treatment entails has led them to this conclusion. In such cases I try to impress upon the family the fact that the child's problems are complex and that they cannot be understood very easily.

Some parents at this point will ask my opinion regarding how long the treatment will take. As mentioned, I hesitate to use words like *always* and *never*. However, I have no hesitation in advising therapists that they should *never* speculate on how long treatment will take. This is one of the most foolish things a therapist can do. One cannot know how successful one will be in engaging the child, nor can one predict how successful one will be with regard to involving the parents. One cannot predict how slowly or rapidly the difficulties will be alleviated; in fact, one cannot even know whether or not one will be successful at all. Often significant social and cultural factors are operative in bringing about the problems and these are completely beyond the therapist's control. Accordingly, I firmly state to the parents that I cannot predict how long treatment will take and that it would be foolish on their part to put any circles on their calendars. I try to explain to them what I have just said about those factors that contribute to the unpredictability of the process. Such a statement also gets across the message that *their own participation* will play an important role in how rapidly or slowly therapy proceeds. I cannot emphasize this point strongly enough. If the parents view the treatment as a process involving their dropping the child off at the therapist's office, and then picking him or her up after a prescribed period of time, and then after X number of sessions, all will be well, they have a very misguided view of the process. This may work well for many forms of medical treatment, but it is completely ill-suited to the treatment of a child's psychiatric difficulties. The discussion at this point provides the therapist with an opportunity to get across this point.

I emphasize to the parents that I would not be making a recommendation for the extended evaluation if I were not certain that treatment was indicated. However, I may not be able at that point to be more specific about exactly how I am going to proceed. I may say that I would anticipate one or two sessions per week (my usual frequency), but that I cannot say at this point who will be involved. Perhaps it will be primarily the child, perhaps primarily the parents, perhaps a combination of both. It will only be after I have had the opportunity to collect more data that I will be in a better position to ascertain what the optimum therapeutic program will be. Here again, the examiner is foolish if he or she allows the parents to extract a specific statement at that point regarding exactly what the therapeutic program will be. Of course, there are times when one can state it with certainty at that time and, under such circumstances, there should be no problem in doing so. My own usual procedure at this point, however, is to inform the parents that even after the evaluation, my proposed therapeutic program will be the one that seems most propitious *at that time*. It may be that new situations will arise that will warrant an alteration of the therapeutic program. As mentioned, therapy is a slice of life. And like life, things are always happening that will warrant a change in one's plans.

Discussion of Fees

And now to the delicate subject of money. Although the face letter of my questionnaire indicates my fee policy, the subject may still come up. This is especially the case if the parents wish to discuss with me the question of whether they should be given a lower fee than my standard. Whereas Freud's patients in Victorian Vienna were inhibited in discussing sex, most adult patients today reveal freely their sexual activities to their therapists, but are quite restrained when discussing financial matters. Some therapists may, indeed, share their patient's inhibitions in this area. The problem is complicated for the child therapist because the person paying for the treatment is not the one receiving the treatment. The adult in therapy is available to discuss his or her reactions to the payment of fees; the parent of a child in treatment is often unavailable or unmotivated for such an inquiry. Accordingly, one cannot easily ask what the parents' income is. Even if one were to do so, and even if one were to obtain a figure, one is still not in a position to know exactly whether a fee reduction is warranted because gross income is only one part of the information one needs to assess properly a person's capacity to pay one's fee. One must also know about expenses, debts, and other financial obligations. In many situations one would have to have the expertise of an accountant to know whether or not a parent can afford the standard fee or whether a reduced fee is warranted. Even then, a question of family priorities must come into play, that is, what the parents want to spend their money on, and the examiner is in no position to make decisions in that realm.

What I do then is to proceed as if the standard fee will be paid and ask the parents if they are clear on my policy of payment, namely, that payment is due at the time of each session and that my secretary will be available to assist with insurance forms and payments from third parties. It is important for the reader to appreciate that my policy of requiring payment for each session is the one that I utilize for parents of children in treatment, but I do not use it for adults who are in therapy themselves. Asking a patient to pay for each session is essentially saying to the patient that there is no trust. Up until about five years ago I did indeed trust parents to pay each month for the treatment of their children. However, I believe that our society is becoming progressively more psychopathic and my former policy resulted in a significant percentage of defaulted payments. Accordingly, I have changed my policy and require parents to pay at the time of each session. This has not compromised my relationship with the child because he or she is generally oblivious to this aspect of the treatment. With adult patients, however, I have still maintained my original policy of their paying at the end of each month. To require the adult to pay at the time of each session is essentially extending the "no trust" communication to the patient him- or herself. And this cannot but compromise the therapeutic relationship. If, however, a patient does exhibit difficulties in paying promptly, then I may very well, after therapeutic discussion, institute a policy of more frequent payments after each session. Under these circumstances, the patient has so acted that my distrust is warranted, and to trust a patient under these circumstances is not only naive but antitherapeutic.

With regard to the question of a reduction to a lower level on my fee range (as originally described in the face letter of the questionnaire), I generally take a somewhat passive position when discussing this issue. It is preferable for the patient to step forth and make the request. And it also behooves the patient to present the information that supports his or her position. Otherwise, the examiner compromises him- or herself by becoming beholden to the parent to provide the information. In the context of such a discussion I might ask if the parents have insurance and exactly what coverage they have. If they cannot answer specifically these questions, then I reserve a decision until the information becomes available. If it is provided, and the examiner is still not in a position to ascertain whether a reduction is warranted, I might ask for other reasons why the parent feels a reduction is warranted. It is beyond the purposes of this book to go into details of such discussions. The examiner must be aware that there are some parents who pride themselves on their bargaining acumen, in the context of which guiltless duplicity is the rule. There are others who are ashamed to come forth with a statement of their difficulties in paying the higher fee. If the examiner suspects that such is the case, it behooves him or her to initiate the discussion of a lower fee. Some masochistic people may stay with the higher fee because of the self-destructive gratifications that it offers. Others may assess the value of the therapy with the level of the fee and would consider themselves to be getting less valuable treatment if they were to take a lower fee or even consider the therapist to be less adequate if he or she were to treat for less. Some parents feel a sense of superiority from paying the "top fee." Some may be too passive to request a lower figure or may feel that the reduced-fee patients get inferior treatment. A divorcée, whose former husband is paying for the treatment, may welcome a high fee as another weapon against her former spouse.

What I have said thus far regarding fees relates to the initial fee at the outset of treatment. A fee may be reduced (even below my minimum) when a patient, in treatment for a significant period and committed to the process, suffers financial reverses which are not related to the patient's psychopathological processes. (I use the term patient here to refer to an adult patient in treatment or the parents of a child in therapy.) Under such circumstances I will discuss a reduction, but never to the point where no fee at all is charged. It may even be a few dollars taken from a welfare check, but I do not give "free therapy." Patients who receive free therapy often get exactly the value of what they are paying for.

The Question of Payment for Missed Sessions

The question of charging for missed sessions is a difficult one. With adults, advance notice of cancellation varies from many months to no notice at all (the patient just doesn't show up). The reasons for missing can fluctuate from the most realistic (patient in the hospital) and appropriate (household emergency requiring the patient's presence) to the clearly psychopathological and/or acting out ("I forgot"—"I just didn't feel like coming"). The intermediate situations are probably the most common ("I had a bad cold"—"My bursitis acted up"). A physical illness may not be the patient's "fault," but psychological factors clearly play a role in the degree to which the patient is incapacitated.

Some therapists do not charge for missed sessions. Missing sessions and/or witholding fees may be among the most common ways in which patients act out with their therapists. Not charging for missed sessions may serve to encourage such behavior, and thereby entrench pathology. One approach is not to charge when the therapist is able to fill the session. Some charge if the session has not been filled *and* the absence was due to pathological behavior, e.g., "forgetting," or a voluntary decision that something else had priority, e.g., "an important business meeting." This approach has intrinsic defects which led me to abandon it after using it for a few years.

I prefer to charge my patients for *nonfilled* missed sessions *regardless* of the reason for the absence. Patients are informed that the time is reserved for them. They are told that if I am given advance notice I can usually fill the hour. In such cases there is no obligation to pay for the session.

In child practice, this approach is helpful. At one time I was proponent of the "no fee for illness policy." I would be called by a mother who would inform me that her child was sick and could not keep an appointment. In the next session the child would tell me about the wonderful time she had at a birthday party on the afternoon of the missed session. What does the therapist do in such a situation? Another mother is getting over "the grippe" and can't bring the child; another says that a sibling is sick and she can't get a babysitter. It was amazing how the frequency of such missed sessions diminished once I began charging. When describing my missed session policy, I inform the parents that I have found that when a child has to miss a session, seeing one or both parents instead has often been helpful.

When telling parents about my missed-session policy, I emphasize the fact that there is no *specific cutoff point* to determine whether or not they will be charged. I emphasize that the more advance notice I have, the greater will be the likelihood of my filling the appointment and, conversely, the shorter the notice the less the likelihood of the sessions's being filled. I strictly avoid mentioning any numbers, even in the negative sense. To do so is injudicious. For example, if I were to say, "I have *no* cut-off point, such as 24 hours. The determinant of whether you will be charged is purely whether or not I can fill the session." It is likely that that number 24 will be branded in that parent's brain as the cut-off figure. In fact, even though I studiously avoid mentioning numbers in presenting my policy, on a number of occasions, parents have quoted me as giving the 24-hour figure, and may even swear that they heard me say it.

In child practice, with many children going off to summer camp for two months and the therapist usually taking one, I inform patients that between July 1 and Labor Day there will be no charge for missed sessions for *pre-planned, out-of-town vacations* about which I am told in advance. I tell them the dates of my own vacation, and advise them that I will be available for treatment during the other weeks of the summer.

CONCLUDING COMMENTS

Before the family leaves, I generally give the child a complimentary copy of my book, *Stories About the Real World*, Volume I (1972a). I will often inscribe the book with a little message to the child such as "I hope you find this book useful" or "I hope you enjoy reading these stories." I also tell the child that he or she has to read the book as a homework assignment, and I'll be asking him or her about these stories during the next session. My purpose in giving the book is twofold. First, the present helps establish a good relationship, in that the overwhelming majority of children enjoy receiving presents. In addition, the material contained in the book is generally applicable to most if not all children's treatment. And, when the child returns for the intensive evaluation, I will often inquire whether the child read the stories and am particularly interested in knowing which ones produced special reactions.

If, at the time of the final discussion, the parents express ambivalence or hesitation, the examiner does well to invite them to discuss further their reactions. At times, it is judicious to suggest that the parents think over what has been said, rather than make a decision at that point. This is a most judicious policy. Sometimes, a parent will have deep reservations but will not express them at the time of the consultation. Such a parent might even then accept subsequent appointments, only to cancel them on short notice. It is very difficult to charge people who have indicated that they wish to discontinue treatment entirely. In fact, it might be unethical in spite of the aforementioned verbal agreement. Accordingly, for the sake of the parents as well as the therapist, it is wise to invite ambivalent parents to think about their decision before making appointments.

For those who say they wish to go ahead, I generally set up three appointments: one for the child, and one for each of the parents. Whereas my initial consultation is generally two hours, my subsequent sessions are generally 45 or 60 minutes, depending upon which appears to be most useful and judicious. Some patients (adults as well as children) use the full hour quite expeditiously; others find 45 minutes to be optimum. People who travel greater distances often prefer the full-hour session. One does well to clarify this issue before closing the initial session.

At this point, the reader may conclude that it is not likely I can accomplish all that has been covered in this chapter in a two-hour consultation. This conclusion is not completely unwarranted. Actually, I have tried to cover in this chapter many contingencies, all of which are not likely to come up with the same family. Accordingly, I generally am able to accomplish most of what has been presented in this chapter during the initial consultation. But, as mentioned, if I cannot, I have no hesitation requesting a third or even a fourth appointment.

SIX

The Intensive
Diagnostic Evaluation

Nam et ipsa scientia potestas est.
Indeed Knowledge itself is Power.

Francis Bacon

In the Greek language, the word *diagnosis* means *to know thoroughly* or *to know in depth*. Accordingly, when we use the term as a mere label we are not using it in the true spirit of its meaning. The initial two-hour consultation may enable us to provide a diagnosis in the superficial sense, but it does not enable us to provide a diagnosis in the true sense of the word. It is the purpose of this chapter to describe the techniques I utilize to provide me with a bona fide diagnosis, in accordance with the original meaning of the word.

This is being written at a time when shorter forms of treatment are increasingly in vogue. Many time-limited therapy programs provide a fixed number of sessions, ten or twelve not being uncommon. Considering the complexity of the problems with which we are dealing, it takes that number of sessions to understand what the basic problems are. The patients, therefore, are being discharged at just about the time when the therapist is beginning to understand what the fundamental problems are. To me such treatment can be compared to the surgeon who opens the abdomen, isolates the source of disease, and then, without doing any further operative procedure or closing the abdomen, discharges the patient from the hospital. I am not claiming that therapy cannot possibly take ten or twelve sessions; I am only claiming that one can generally not predict in advance how long it will take, and it usually takes longer than that. Time-limited therapy is generally appealing to those who want quick solutions to complex problems. It is particularly attractive to administrators and those who are supporting treatment for large numbers of patients. Accordingly, I consider it most often to be a rip-off of the poor; rich people (unless they are naive) generally do not have to accept time-limited therapy.

Here I present what I consider to be the judicious kind of evaluation, an evaluation that enables the examiner to learn in depth what the patient's basic problems are. The evaluation here serves as a foundation for subsequent treatment. The knowledge so gained puts the therapist in the best position to proceed most effectively with the therapeutic program.

THE EVALUATION OF THE MOTHER

I generally find it useful to begin with an interview with the mother alone. My experience has been that, of the three parties, she is the one who is most likely to give me important background information. Obviously the child is the least capable of the three because of his or her immaturity and ignorance of the processes that may be contributing to the difficulties. Fathers, unfortunately, are generally less receptive to "opening up." I believe this, in part, relates to the general pattern in our society that fathers are supposed to maintain a "macho" image and not admit weakness or deficiency. Discussing problems with a therapist is viewed by many fathers as being a sign of weakness. Another factor probably relates to the fact that, in the traditional home, the father is less likely to be knowledgeable about all the details involved in the child's life. He may also be more reluctant to admit difficulties in the marital relationship. Although these reasons are speculative, I am convinced that my generalization is a valid one, namely, that fathers are less likely to provide me with important background information than mothers. Accordingly, I find it judicious to interview the mothers first in the intensive evaluation. However, I am not rigid with regard to this and, if scheduling of the child or father first is more readily accomplished, I will certainly depart from this principle.

The Initial Inquiry

I generally begin the interview with the mother with an open-end question such as: "Is there anything special on your mind that you would like to say to me at this point, before I proceed with my questions?" The question is purposely vague and is designed to provide the mother with the greatest freedom to discuss any issue that she considers pertinent. I want to know here what is at the forefront of her mind, especially things that may be upsetting her, things that may be pressing for release. To ask a specific question at this point may deprive the examiner of this important information. Sometimes the mother's comments may suggest ambivalence for the intensive diagnostic program. It is important for the examiner to appreciate that bringing a child to treatment is generally viewed as an indication of the parents' failure to have raised a psychologically healthy child. The examiner's conclusion that treatment is warranted may then be viewed as confirmation that the parent is indeed deficient. In such cases I usually try to reassure the mother that I am convinced that she loves the child deeply and that, at every point, she did what she considered to be best for her child's healthy growth and development. I emphasize the point that the fact that she is coming for treatment for the child, and is willing to make the sacrifices of times, money, and energy for the child's welfare, is a statement of parental strength and commitment. Comments along these lines sometimes reduce the parental feelings of failure. Of course, it is not proper for the therapist to make such a statement if it is untrue, and there is severe maternal deficiency. However, mothers who are willing to bring their children for treatment do not generally fall in that category.

Some mothers will express guilt at this point. They may express the feeling that the child's illness was related to some minor indiscretion or lapse in parenting capacity. Many in the classical psychoanalytic school are quick to consider such guilt to be related to unconscious hostility toward the child and the parents' view that the child's illness represents the magic fulfillment of the parent's hostile wishes. I am dubious about this explanation. I believe that for most parents it represents a magic need to control, to undo, and/or to have prevented the illness. The element of control is intrinsic to the notion: "It's my fault." There is an element of validity in this guilt, because the child's pathology is often related to the parents' child-rearing practices; if the child had not been exposed to the parents' inappropriate behavior, he or she might not have developed the psychiatric difficulties. The issue of guilt in such parents is a complex one, and I have directed my attention to its psychodynamics in other publications (1969b, 1970b). To the mother who describes such guilt I will often make comments along the following lines:

> I'd like to say a few things to you about the guilt which most parents in your situation have. I recognize that it's a very painful thing to have to bring your child to a psychiatrist. Most parents look upon it as a grave sign of personal failure and wonder how and where they went wrong. I know enough about you already to know that, at each point, you did what you thought was best for your child and your bringing him(her) here today is just another example of this. I'm sure you basically love him(her) and want the best for him(her). However, it's clear to all of us that mistakes were made or else he(she) probably wouldn't be here today. So, in a sense, the illness is partially your responsibility. I say *partially* because we still don't know enough about all the factors that brought it about.
>
> Also, it's important that you distinguish, as the law does, between two kinds of guilt: guilt by commission and guilt by omission. Let me give you examples. Compare the man whose car runs over someone because of a factory defect in the brake system with the one who, in a calculating and premeditated manner, hits someone with his car. The first man is guilty by omission and is generally not punished. The second is guilty by commission and is usually punished. You people are certainly in the first category. You acted with the best of intentions, but because of your own blind spots—many of which you don't appreciate—you've contributed to the child's difficulties. Flagellating yourself over the past will accomplish nothing. Directing your efforts, as you are now doing, into learning about what went wrong and trying to change the situation is your best way of feeling less guilty. And I will be actively enlisting your assistance in the treatment. Now, is there anything you would like to ask me about this?

Generally, these comments are successful in alleviating some of the parent's guilt. One of the things I am doing here is to lessen the guilt by giving the parent a sense of control. Because an element in the formation of the guilt relates to the sense of impotence associated with the child's having developed the illness, my inviting the parent to participate actively in the treatment provides for the opportunity for gaining some control over what was previously considered to be an uncontrollable situation.

If the mother has not offered any responses to my initial open-ended question, I will ask, "I'd like to know what reactions you had to our meeting last time." Or, if she has given no response along the lines just discussed, I might ask, "Are there any other reactions you had to our meeting last time?" In both cases, I direct my attention specifically to the two-hour consultation. This question also enables me to learn about feelings about the treatment, both positive and negative. As I will discuss in detail in Chapter Seven, it is crucial for the therapist to have a good relationship with the parents if child therapy is to be successful. The answers to these questions at this point in the initial interview with the mother can provide information about the kind of relationship that is starting to develop between the mother and the therapist. It is the best opportunity for "nipping in the bud" difficulties that may already be starting to exhibit themselves.

I will then ask the mother what the child's reactions were to the interview. Here again there are a wide variety of responses. If the child's reactions have been negative, I will try to ascertain what the issues were that caused the reaction. If positive, I will want to learn what things attracted the child. If the mother states that she did not make inquiries in order to respect the child's "privacy," I will impress upon her the fact that my general therapeutic approach is to encourage all concerned parties to discuss the therapy as much as possible and she should err on the side of "invading the child's privacy." I do not recommend that she be intrusive here, only that she err on the side of being so and to let the child's own defenses and desire for privacy be the determinants of how much and how little the child will reveal. Such "respect" for the child's privacy often works against the aims of treatment in that it reduces the open communication that the therapist is trying to achieve in the family. Open communication among family members may be one of the most therapeutic experiences the therapist can provide. All too often psychological problems within families are the results of conspiracies of silence, suppressed and repressed thoughts and feelings, and other "skeletons in the closet." Therapy must open Pandora's boxes, and facilitating open communication is a step toward this goal.

The mother may, for example, say that the child told her something but made her promise not to divulge it to me. Here I will advise the mother that it was an error on her part to have agreed to keep a secret from me and that she would have done better to have said something like: "There must be no secrets from Dr. Gardner and I won't promise not to tell him." The mother may respond that if she were to say such a thing, the child might not give her the information. My response to this is that it is better that the child not provide the information than for her to be a participant in a conspiracy in which she and the child join forces to keep secrets from me. Also, I reassure her that important issues are likely to come out anyway and she need not fear that the nondivulged secret will compromise the treatment. (I will discuss this issue of confidentiality in more detail in Chapter Seven.)

I will then ask the mother what her husband's reactions were to the initial consultative interview. As mentioned, mothers are generally more candid to me than fathers, and so she might provide me with information about his reactions that the father himself might not so readily reveal. Often his comments relate to the financial aspects of the treatment, which may then open up a discussion again of the fee and the payment. If the husband has expressed negative reactions, I encourage the mother to tell her husband to express these directly to me. I use this as a point of departure to impress upon her that a common cause of disruption of treatment is parental discomfort regarding the expression of their grievances, disappointments, disagreements, and so on.

Inquiry into the Causes of the Child's Difficulties

At this point I will make the following statement to the mother: "I know that you're coming here to get my opinion about why your child has problems. However, it's important for you to appreciate that, at this point, you probably know more about the reasons why your child has to come to therapy than I do. After all, you've lived with the child all his(her) life. You have been observer to thousands of events that I have not witnessed. Accordingly, I'm sure that you can provide me with the very important information relevant to the question of why your child has difficulties." Most mothers will come up with some explanations at that point. And, interestingly, the issues they bring up are often extremely valuable and very much on point. Although not specifically trained in psychiatry or psychology, the mother's "guesses" are most often valid explanations and provide the examiner with extremely important information about the sources of the child's psychopathology.

I cannot emphasize this point strongly enough. Although the mother may never have gone to graduate school, she knows the child better than the examiner and her hunches regarding why the child has difficulties (her denial mechanisms notwithstanding) may be better than the examiner's. If the mother cannot come up with any explanations, I will often urge her to "guess" or "speculate." I encourage her to do so with the advice that her guesses may still provide me with valuable leads as to what is going on with the child. Again, these "wild" guesses are often valuable sources of information.

Inquiry Regarding Parental Dealings with the Child

My purpose here is to get more specific information about the way in which the parents have raised the child, with special focus on detrimental exposures and experiences. There are a number of ways of getting information in this area. I sometimes ask the mother to describe what she considers to be her strong points and weak points in the child-rearing realm. By presenting the question in this balanced way, one is likely to obtain information related to maternal weaknesses that the mother might otherwise have difficulty admitting. It is usually useful to ask questions in this area in such a way that guilt or embarrassment is reduced or obviated. For example, if the examiner were to ask: "Do you hit your child?" an accusatory finger is implied. But, if the examiner says: "All parents find, at times, that their backs are up against the wall and the child's behavior is so irritating that they feel that the only thing they can do is to give him(her) one. Then the child has a good cry, gets it out of his(her) system, and all is again well with the world. How often have you found this to be the case with your child?" Obviously, when the question is posed this way, the examiner is going to be in a better position to find out exactly how much (or how little) corporal punishment was utilized.

The same principle holds for questions in other areas. For example, if one says to a mother: "Did you like cuddling your child?" the answer is likely to be yes in that the mother generally recognizes that not to have done so represents a parental deficiency. One is more likely to find out what really went on with a question such as: "When they're born, some babies love cuddling and others do not. How was Billy when he was born?" Actually, there is a small element of duplicity in this question. The realities are that there are indeed some babies who do not like cuddling when they are born, but they are relatively rare. They are mainly children who are born with serious physical illness, congenital defects, mental retardation, autism, and other severe disorders that manifest themselves at birth. Children who are not in these categories not only love to be cuddled at birth, but the deprivation of such may ultimately prove lethal. Because I know that Billy is in none of the aforementioned categories, I know that he would have wanted cuddling at the time of his birth. If his mother responds that he was not that kind of a child, it generally suggests that she herself had some deficiency in providing cuddling and her motivation for doing so was impaired.

One could ask the question: "Did you like to have Janie cuddle with you in the morning when she was a toddler?" Again, most mothers will say yes, even though the response may not be an honest one. However, if one asks: "Some children, when they're toddlers, love to come into their parents' bed, especially on weekends. How was Mary when she was that age?" By presenting the question in such a way that there are two categories of children, some who like cuddling and some who don't, it becomes easier for the mother to state that Mary was not in the cuddling category. Again, the implication here is that the deficiency lies in the child and not in the parent.

Another useful question: "What are your husband's feelings about the way you've raised Bobby? What does he consider your strong points to be and what does he consider your weak points to be?" It is generally easier for the mother to talk about deficiencies about herself if they originate from someone else because she has the opportunity to present disagreements if she wishes to do so. The examiner does well to review the list of the father's reported descriptions, both positive and negative.

An important area of inquiry to ascertain maternal capacity is the mother's involvement in school activities. In fact, this may be the most important area of inquiry if one is looking for manifestations of parental deprivation of affection. I first begin with a general question about the mother's involvement in school activities and encourage her to provide me with a general description. Following that, I ask specific questions that give me information about the mother's participation in the PTA, attendance at conferences with teachers, and involvement in the child's extracurricular activities such as school plays, recitals, sporting events, et cetera. The latter area is extremely important. The healthy involved mother finds attendance at such performances extremely gratifying. It is a grand moment when little Susie comes out on the stage dressed as Cinderella. Tears well up in the mother's eyes and her heart swells with pride. The parent who knows no such joy is not only missing out on some of life's greater moments but, for the purposes of the interview, has provided the examiner with important information regarding maternal capacity. In the context of this discussion, I ask the mother about the father's participation in school activities. Does *he* attend teacher conferences? Does *he* attend the school performances and does he exhibit joy and pride at them?

One wants to know about who the child goes to in the middle of the night when he or she wakes up with nightmares, croup, or physical illness. One wants to find out about who takes the child to the pediatrician, especially during emergencies. Inquiry about what goes on during the evening, when both parents are home, is also important. One should inquire about homework and who helps the child with it. Does one parent do better than the other? One wants to know about parent's comfort with and patience with sitting on the floor playing childhood games. One should inquire into who puts the children to sleep at night, reads the bedtime stories, and has more patience for dawdling.

A concept that I have found useful in assessing parental capacity is what I refer to as "Grandma's criteria" (Gardner, 1986b). These are the criteria Grandma's ghost would use if she were to be roaming invisibly around the house collecting data about parental capacity. Because she doesn't have a Ph.D. in psychology she would be using more traditional criteria for assessing parental capacity, criteria related to the involvement of the parent in the everyday activities of the child-rearing process. Accordingly, the examiner does well to go through the course of a typical day with the mother, from the time the children wake up in the morning until the time they go to sleep at night, and find out exactly what each parent does with each of the children, especially the patient. One is especially interested in who takes on the more unpleasant tasks and who has the greatest willingness to make sacrifices. Because she knows nothing about unconscious processes, Grandma will be focusing on these more valid criteria for assessing parental capacity.

The reader who is interested in more information about assessment of parental capacity does well to read pertinent material in my *Family Evaluation in Child Custody Litigation* (1982). Because the assessment of parental capacity is so important to the custody evaluation, my discussion of this area is quite detailed in that volume.

Description of the Marriage

I will then ask the mother the general question: "Tell me about your marriage?" Of course, I may have gotten some information about this during the initial two-hour consultation; however, here I want to get more details, especially as they relate to the child's difficulties. This is an important area of inquiry. Children exposed to ongoing marital animosity are likely to be deprived, and such deprivations may contribute to the development of their symptomatology. And, if the children become actively embroiled in the parental conflict, there is even a greater likelihood that psychopathology will develop. It is reasonable to say that many (but certainly not all) children who develop psychological difficulties do so because of problems in their parents' marriages. If the mother describes difficulties, I will go into detail, especially with regard to those problems that the child is either aware of or exposed to. Some parents naively believe that children are in no way affected by parental problems that they are not directly exposed to or aware of. I attempt to impress upon such parents the fact that the effects of marital discord tend to filter down to children, even without the awareness of the concerned parties. I try to impress upon them that, if parents are depressed or otherwise unhappy over difficulties in the marital relationship, this is going to compromise the care of the children.

Some mothers routinely state that their marriages are good ones. This is their automatic response, and they may consider it the socially acceptable thing to say. Along with this, they will often say, "I love my husband." In some cases the marriages are quite poor, but denial mechanisms have resulted in both parents maintaining a façade that they have a "good marriage." In such cases, I might say, "You know, no marriage is perfect. Every marriage, like every human relationship, has strong points and weak points. In every relationship there are things that you like about the other person and things that you don't. There is no marriage in which there aren't occasional fights. What I want you to tell me now are what the strong points of your marriage are and what are the weak points. I'd like to hear about the things you agree on, and the things about which you don't agree." When the question is posed this way, it becomes more socially acceptable for the mother to reveal deficiencies in the relationship. When one begins with a discussion of the positive aspects of the marriage, it becomes easier to talk about the negatives. Because mothers are generally more comfortable talking about deficiencies in the marriage than fathers, the information obtained here will be useful to the examiner during the interview with the father.

Some mothers will describe the marital difficulties but state that their husbands have strictly warned them not to talk about them to me. There are many women who comply with this wish and I never learn about the marital difficulties. This, of course, compromises my evaluation. Other mothers tell me the problems, but request that I not tell their husbands that they revealed the information to me. Sometimes I am successful in my attempts to get such mothers to assert themselves and advise their husbands that they have provided me with this information. Others fear doing so and when I meet with the husband it becomes apparent that their wives have never revealed that they have disclosed the details of the marital problems to me. Sometimes I am successful in "smoking this information out" during the joint interview with the husband and the wife; and other times the mother is so frightened of "rocking the boat" that she continues to withhold the information. Such mothers are serving as models for passive submission to their husbands and this, of course, is likely to contribute to the child's difficulties. I believe that refusal to discuss marital difficulties is one of the most common reasons why parents do not agree to embark upon the intensive evaluation or, if they do so, it is one of the most common reasons why they interrupt it. Therapists who confine themselves to working exclusively with children, and do not delve deeply in the marital and/or family situation, are likely to attract such parents. However, I believe that the therapy is likely to prove useless.

Sometimes the marital conflict may center directly on the child. A mother may say, for example, "The only fights we have are over how to deal with Tom. I believe that if things went well with him, we wouldn't fight about anything." There are two possibilities here. One is that the statement is true, and the marriage is basically a good one with the child's problems the main source of parental friction. The other possibility is that the child is being used as a weapon or tool in the parental conflict and that differences over management are being utilized in the service of less noble goals. It behooves the examiner to inquire further into this issue in order to ascertain which of the two possibilities is the more likely one. When parents are involved in divorce, the second possibility is generally the more likely. Because divorced parents are living separately, they do not have direct access to one another to vent their rage. The children, who move back and forth freely between the two households, become good candidates to be used as weapons, spies, and tools in the parental conflict (Gardner, 1976a, 1977b, 1979a).

History of Psychiatric Treatment

I will then ask the mother whether she has ever been in treatment. If so, I want details about the phases of her life when she had therapy, the names of the therapists, the reasons for having entered into treatment, and what she recalls of the experience(s). This is a good way of getting into the question of the mother's own psychopathology. Simply to ask the question, "Do you have any psychiatric disturbances?" may produce defensiveness. However, a discussion of previous therapeutic experiences is more likely to provide useful data in this area. I am often amazed at how little people remember of their therapy. I am rarely surprised when an adolescent has little recollection of early childhood therapeutic experiences with me. But it does amaze me how little adults remember of treatment that took place 10 or 15 years previously, treatment that may have occurred while they were adults. They commonly do not even recall the name of the therapist. I am particularly interested in any marital counseling or conjoint therapy that the mother may have involved herself in with the father. This is another way of learning about marital problems. I often try to get information about what the therapist said, especially with regard to each party's contribution to the marital difficulties.

Background Information

Family Background   It may come as a surprise to some readers that my discussion of the acquisition of background information about the mother comes so late in this section. It is important for the reader to appreciate that we are not dealing here with the mother's psychoanalysis, but her involvement with her child—especially with regard to maternal capacity. Were we interested in psychoanalyzing the mother we might be much more interested in her early developmental life, her relationships with her parents, and the influences in her development that played an important role in shaping her present personality. Although I am interested in these subjects (and will discuss them in this section), I consider them to be less important than the areas of inquiry discussed thus far.

I begin with questions about the mother's date of birth, place of birth, and list of places where she has lived during her life. If the mother has moved frequently, especially during the child's own lifetime, then I may have a clue to a factor that may have contributed to the child's difficulties. Children who shift around from location to location during the formative years, especially if this involves frequent changes of schooling, may suffer psychologically from the disruptions. I then ask the mother about her own mother, whether she is living or dead, and where she lives at the present time. If dead, I want to find out about the cause of death. If the information hasn't been obtained already, I want to know about the ethnic and religious background of the maternal grandmother. Ethnic factors often play a role in the development of psychopathological processes. I want to know about the maternal grandmother's religion and how religious she was (or is). I am especially interested here in fanaticism or dogmatic religious beliefs that may contribute to the development of psychopathology. I ask the mother to describe the kind of person her mother was and the kind of relationship the mother had with the maternal grandmother during the mother's childhood. I am particularly interested in the kind of maternal care that the maternal grandmother provided the mother.

I also want to know whether the maternal grandmother worked or was a homemaker. If she worked, I want to know about her occupation and whether or not she was mainly out of the home or was actively involved in the mother's child rearing. This may provide informaton about the mother's own maternal capacity, in that if the model she had as a child was a good one, it is more likely that she is providing good maternal input into the patient. And the opposite is the case if the maternal grandmother was deficient in this regard.

I also want to know about the maternal grandmother's relationship with the mother's husband. If there is dissension between the maternal grandmother and the child's father, it may play a role in the child's difficulties. I am particularly interested in how much grandparental input the maternal grandmother has with her grandchildren, especially my patient. Good grandparenting can play an important positive role in a child's psychological development. The exaggerated high esteem that grandparents often have for their grandchildren can serve as a buffer for the criticism and the undeserved negative feedback that children (like the rest of us) often are subjected to in life. I also ask about the maternal grandmother's psychiatric status, whether she has ever been in psychiatric treatment or has suffered with unusual medical illnesses. I then ask the mother if there is anything else that she can mention about her mother that might be of importance to me.

Next, I ask the mother similar questions about her father. I ask about her father's occupation, especially with regard to how much time he had for input into the mother's own upbringing. Information about the mother's relationship with the father may provide useful data about the mother's relationship to her husband. The female-male relationship patterns laid down in childhood tend to repeat themselves in our subsequent lives. Here too I am particularly interested in the relationship between the maternal grandfather and the patient. This is especially important if there are deficiencies in the relationship between the mother's husband and her child.

I then ask the mother about the relationship between her parents. The model of the relationship between the parents that the mother observed during her formative years (whether good or bad) is often the model which is being repeated in the mother's present marital relationship. I am not saying that this is invariably so, only that it is quite a common phenomenon. If a mother, for example, frequently observed her father to be hitting her mother, it is more likely that she will marry a man who will treat her similarly—her vows never to marry such a man notwithstanding. If the mother's whole extended family operates in this way, it is even more likely that she will repeat the pattern in her own marriage. One could say that it is the only lifestyle she knows and that such a mother would be uncomfortable during the dating period with young men who treated her more benevolently. She would be like "a fish out of water" in such relationships and would find them strange and uncomfortable. She might even provoke men into maltreating her or always anticipate maltreatment—even though there is no evidence that it would be forthcoming. And this pattern is likely to transmit itself to a third generation and exhibit itself in the child, at a level commensurate with its level of development.

Sometimes, there may have been divorce in the mother's home during her childhood. In such cases I want to know about the reasons for the separation and whether or not there were remarriages.

If stepparents were involved in the mother's upbringing, I want to know about them and the nature of the relationships between the mother and stepparents.

I then ask the mother to list each of her siblings and get brief information about their age, occupation, and marital status. I am particularly interested in whether or not any of the siblings had serious psychological difficulties and, if so, the nature of them. Because genetic factors often play a role in various psychopathological processes, I want to know about the appearance of such difficulties in the child's aunts and uncles as well as the child's maternal grandparents.

The First Memory Question   I sometimes find the first memory question to be useful. I generally pose it in this way: "Go back as far as you can and tell me what the first memory of your life is. I'd like you to go further back than the begining of school if you can." Psychoanalysts, especially, are very interested in this question. Although it may not provide useful information, sometimes it serves as an epitomization of many factors that have played a role in the patient's lifetime. When it does, it can often provide valuable clues about central psychological themes in the mother's lifetime, themes that began in childhood and exist to the present time. Sometimes the actual memory is false and the incident never occurred. However, because the mother believes fully that it did, the response can still be a useful source of information. At this point I will present a few examples in order to impress upon the reader the value of this question.

One mother gave this response:

> I was about three years old. I remember my brother and my father urinating. I wanted to do what they did and I tried, but I couldn't.

This mother was an extremely domineering and aggressive individual. She was married to a man who was submissive and passive. This memory clearly reflects the desire to assume the masculine role, and it was certainly the case that she had done so in her marriage.

One mother responded:

> I was three years old and my mother and father and sister were fussing over me because of my dancing.

This woman was an extremely histrionic, hysterical individual. She was markedly exhibitionistic. As a child, she had been an actress and a model. But throughout her life she continued to exhibit her talents, which were probably much less than she professed. She was so self-centered that she gave little attention to her son, who was significantly deprived. It was this deprivation that played a role in the development of his symptomatology.

Another mother responded:

> I was two or three years old. I climbed out of my crib, fell, and broke my arm.

The memory reveals the mother's basic feelings that if she removes herself from a protected environment (a crib) she will be traumatized. The mother was basically an extremely dependent individual who did not view herself as capable of handling many of life's situations and anticipated that if she were unprotected by her husband and her parents, she would indeed meet with disaster. One could argue that the arm fracture incident was a psychological trauma which deserved to be remembered. My response is that this does not negate the aforementioned explanation. There were probably many other falls, accidents, and psychologically traumatic incidents in the mother's life. The fact that she remembered this one— after so many years—is a statement that it lent itself well to epitomizing themes in her life that were central to her personality.

One mother responded:

> After I was two years old, if I misbehaved, I would be tied to a table and spanked and kept there. These are the earliest memories of my childhood.

This mother was an extremely masochistic and martyristic individual. She constantly reminded her children about how much she sacrificed herself for their benefit. She stated that at times she did twenty hours of work a day in order to devote every spare moment to philanthropic work. She constantly reminded those she served (her children and others) how much they were in her debt for her benevolence. The seeds of her masochistic-martyristic tendencies are clearly present in this first memory. This mother worked on the principle that the only way she could get affection from others was to suffer pain. She also used her martyrdom as a mechanism for expressing hostility. She would get people to feel guilty over how ungrateful they were for not appreciating her suffering on their behalf.

Another mother's response:

> I was about three or four years old. We were taking family pictures and I was very shy. I didn't want my picture taken.

The memory reveals the mother's fear of exposing herself and her basic feelings that if she is "seen," the observer will be critical or rejecting of her. And she assumes that others share her own low opinion of herself. These personality qualities were playing a role in her son's difficulties in that he too was shy, submissive, and excessively dependent upon the opinions of others. These were qualities that he acquired by identification with his mother.

Another mother's response:

> I was about three years old. It was in Atlantic City. We had gone there on vacation. I was all sunburned and my mother made me put on a starched dress. It hurt my arms and I was crying.

This mother grew up in an upper-middle-class home where there was significant emphasis on propriety, attendance at the "proper schools," and appropriate manners and dress. Otherwise, her parents were not particularly interested in her, and her upbringing was given over to various housekeepers and maids. Although the memory suggests that the mother was resentful of this treatment by the maternal grandmother, she was actually reproducing the pattern in the upbringing of her own daughter. The mother worked full-time in order to send her child to the best private schools and gave little meaningful care and attention to them while she was at home.

One more example:

> Two memories come to mind. Both when I was about three or four years old. I remember being fed hot peppers by a little boy who lived next door. I thought he was giving me candy. In a second memory I remember being burned on the bottom as I backed into a gas heater.

This mother, although in analysis with another therapist, had never analyzed her earliest memories. I discussed with her their possible psychological significance and suggested that she try to analyze them. She responded:

> I come from a long line of masochists. In both of these memories I'm getting harmed. In the first I was tricked. It really wasn't candy but pepper. I still think men are untrustworthy. When they say they're gonna give you something sweet, it turns out that it isn't. The second one makes me think that I wasn't adequately protected by my parents. I feel they should have protected me.

This mother's analysis agreed with my own guesses as to the psychological significances of these first memories. In both she is harmed. In the first she is harmed by another's duplicity (being fed hot peppers) and in the second she brings about her own misfortune (backs into a gas heater). Both suggest the propensity to being hurt either by gravitating toward those who would maltreat her or by participating in behavior that would result in her being harmed. And these tendencies reflected themselves well in her life in that she married a man who, although superficially loving and benevolent, actually turned out to be an extremely hostile individual who subjected her to vicious litigation at the time of their divorce.

My presentation of these many clinical examples was done in the hope that it would impress upon the reader the great value of this question. Although I am often critical of psychoanalytic theory and technique, it would be a mistake for the reader to conclude that my criticism is so vast that I do not appreciate the benefits to be derived from certain aspects of classical psychoanalytic theory. In fact, I believe that much in this book is still very much within the psychoanalytic model, the alterations and modifications notwithstanding.

School Life I then ask the mother about her elementary school experiences, both in the academic and behavioral realms. I ask about friendships during this period as well as things that might have been going on in her home that might have affected her personality. Similar questions are asked about the junior high school and the high school periods. Just as information about school and neighborhood can provide vital data about the child, the same questions about the mother can be useful in determining whether or not she has psychopathology. With regard to high school, I am particularly interested in whether the mother dated and, if so, what kinds of experiences she had. I ask about academic and/or emotional problems.

Work History Next, I ask the mother what she did following graduation from high school. If she went to work, I get details of her work history, particularly with regard to how well she got along with colleagues and superiors. If she had numerous jobs, I want to know the reasons for the various changes, especially if she was repeatedly fired. If she is still working now, I want to know the nature of her job adjustment. I am particularly interested in her work history since the birth of my patient. I want to know how much time she spent out of the home and in it. If she gave the child's care over to housekeepers or other caretakers, I want to know who they were, how long they remained in the home, and the nature of their relationships with the child. This is an extremely important area of inquiry because it tells something about emotional deprivation, a common cause of psychopathology.

The Premarital Relationship with the Father I then ask the mother about the circumstances under which she met her husband and the qualities within him that attracted him to her. If there were previous marriages, I want to list each one and get information about them. I am particularly interested in any psychopathological trends that may have exhibited themselves in each of the previous marriages. Important questions in this area relate to who initiated the separation, what were the main problems in the marriage that resulted in the separation, and what criticisms former husbands had of the mother. Here again we see the question of criticisms other persons had of the interviewee. This can often be an important source of information about the interviewee's personality deficiencies, deficiencies that may not readily be revealed by the person him- or herself.

Projective Questions Projective questions are routinely used in interviews with children. They are not as frequently used in interviews with adults. I myself generally use them much more in interviews with children. However, I will occasionally present them in my interviews with adults as well, when I am having difficulty getting adequate information by direct questions. In this section I will describe some of the projective questions that I have found most useful.

Five wishes The traditional question is to ask the person what wishes they would make if three could be granted. However, it is nowhere written that one must limit oneself to three. I generally prefer to ask for five wishes because I am then less likely to get stereotyped responses. The first two or three may very well be routine, everyday answers. When one must "scratch one's brain" and provide one or two more, then one is more likely to tap unconscious sources that may provide more meaningful information.

One mother gave these responses:

1. Peace of mind.

2. Fulfillment. To do something more with myself.

3. Do a better job with Michael.

4. Take care of my husband. He has high blood pressure and he's high strung. I should try to handle situations better. When he gets very upset I should try to intercede and calm the situation down.

5. Achieve a better religious and spiritual outlook. I'm compromising with my religion. I should get back to believing.

This mother left high school after three years in order to get married and at 42 felt formidable frustration over not having a gratifying career or profession. She had three children who were then in their 20s and her six-year-old son, an unplanned pregnancy, was resented from the day she learned that she was pregnant. The boy's presenting symptoms (temper tantrums, antisocial behavior, and excessive dependency) reflected, in part, a response to his mother's rejection. Although her interest in self-fulfillment outside the home was reasonable and appropriate, it was also a reflection of her desire to flee from her obligations and involvements as a mother.

The first response reflects the mother's belief that there can exist a state in which one is free of conflict, frustration, and concerns about reality. It reflects her desires to flee from the predictable frustrations of reality.

The second response provides no new information. It is a statement of her conscious wishes to enter into a fulfilling career or profession.

The third response reflects some awareness on her part that she is not doing her best for her son, and the second response has given us one of the reasons why.

The fourth response is related in part to the first. Both suggest a deep need on her part to cover over, deny, smooth over, and otherwise obliterate unpleasantries. She would want to calm her husband down when he gets upset, to prevent emotional expression and to suppress feelings. The notion that such expression could be deleterious to this man with high blood pressure, although true, serves for her as an excuse to allow vicarious gratification (through her husband) of her own need to cover up emotional expression.

Interestingly, the fifth response had direct relevance to her feelings for her son. The mother was raised a rigid Catholic and in the few years previous to the evaluation had loosened up somewhat in her religious convictions. The two main areas in which she had changed her views were that she was now using contraception and she considered abortion to be appropriate and not sinful. It is of interest that both of these digressions from strict adherence to religious belief concerned childbirth. They relate to her desire to have avoided the pregnancy with her son, my patient, and the guilt that she felt over such transgressions from her earlier religious beliefs.

Another mother made these wishes:

1. Safety and good health for all of us.
2. Equanimity for myself in daily existence.
3. An ability to see further, to be less narrow, to comprehend more the meaning of the situation *while* it is happening.
4. An ability to make and keep decisions.
5. To be less self-absorbed—to be able to give of myself.

Superficially, the first wish appears to be normal in that most people will include good health for themselves and their family. However, the word *safety* does not usually appear. It suggests unconscious hostility toward her family and then, by a process of reaction formation, she protects them from trauma. One could, however, argue that wishing one's family good health also implies an initial thought of sickness and that response could also be considered a manifestation of hostility with compensatory reaction formation. Although this may be true, I can only say that *safety* is a rare wish whereas *good health* is an extremely common one. This lends support (but certainly does not prove) my belief that they have different psychodynamics. In this case this mother did indeed harbor formidable hostility toward her husband, a domineering and overbearing individual upon whom she was quite dependent.

The second wish reveals a wish for cessation of her chronic feelings of anxiety, depression, and inner agitation that was associated with her difficult relationship with her husband.

The third wish makes more specific reference to her inability to think for and assert herself, not only in her relationship with her husband but with others as well. Her statement, "to comprehend more the meaning of the situation *while* it is happening" makes reference to her problem in considering her own thoughts and feelings when they are contradicted by others. Subsequently, she sometimes realizes how submissive she has been. Her wish here is that she be more astute and less inhibited and denying when she is allowing herself to be suppressed.

The fourth wish also makes reference to her passivity and dependency on authorities, especially her husband. She cannot make a decision because she is too beholden to the opinions of others and to keep them against resistance is extremely difficult for her.

Last, the fifth wish refers to her self-absorbed state which was the result of the above-described pathology as well as her deep-seated inhibition in giving of herself meaningfully in an affectionate way. This mother significantly deprived her child, the patient, and described how when he was very young she refused to let him come into her bed in the mornings although he stood for hours scratching at the bedroom door.

Another mother gave these wishes:

1. Traveling. I'd like to do a lot of traveling. I'd love to go to Europe, to Germany, Denmark, and Spain.

2. I'd like to live very long.

3. I'd like to have a lot of money.

4. I'd like to eat more without gaining weight.

5. I'd like my children to succeed. I'd like them to be as happily married as I am, to enjoy the world, the blue sky and the grass. I don't want them to marry money. I want them to be basic individuals. I don't want them to be impressed by prestige.

These wishes reveal the mother's basic egocentricism. The first four are all concerned with herself, and no mention is made of her husband and children. They all reveal the desire for self-indulgence. The fifth, although possibly a normal response, is not so for this mother. She was an extremely hysterical and histrionic individual. The most mundane subjects were spoken about with extreme enthusiasm and exaggeration. The mechanism of denial was frequently utilized, and no matter how unfortunate or miserable the situation was she tended to see it in the best possible light. Her references to enjoying "the world, the blue sky, and the grass" are all part of the hysterical picture and cannot be considered bona fide desires for her children to enjoy these aspects of living. In addition, her wish that her children not "marry money" and not be concerned with prestige in their choice of a mate was in her case simple reaction formation to her basic desire that they be most concerned with these considerations. This mother was quite involved with social status, but she denied this through frequent utilization of the mechanism of "undoing," and spoke of her "tolerance" of social and ethnic groups which were usually discriminated against.

Last, one mother gave these wishes:

1. I wish I could be left alone. I always feel under pressure. I'd relax. I feel under pressure from my husband to be a perfect wife. He wants gourmet cooking. He wants me to be more aggressive and I am not. He wants me to friendly to people who might be important to him for business purposes. I just can't be that way.

2. I'd like to travel a lot. I've never been to Europe. But we can't go now because my husband would rather spend money on cars. He gets everything he wants. He's very selfish. He always does what he wants and never what I want. I feel helpless because he has control over all the money.

3. To be more self-assured.

4. I wish I was more tolerant of my parents. I don't know what it is, but whenever I'm with them I cringe. I know I'm their whole life. I can't forgive them for not being more affectionate to me when I was younger. They were always working.

5. I'd like to be completely independent so I won't have to rely on my husband for everything. If I wanted to do something I wouldn't have to ask my husband for everything. I'd like to be on my own and have my own money.

These wishes need little psychoanalysis. They described, quite succinctly, this woman's main psychological and marital difficulties. It was no surprise that near the end of the first interview she stated: "Although I came here for my child, I really think I have problems of my own and I guess I want treatment for myself as well."

Verbal projective questions   Although I routinely present children with verbal projective questions, I do not usually present them to adults. Again, when direct questions are not adequate to provide me with the information I desire, I may utilize verbal projective questions. Whereas with the child I generally ask questions about animals and objects, with the adult I generally ask about people. My usual question to the adult is this: "If you could not be yourself, but could live your life as any other person in history, living or dead, real or fictional, famous or not, whom would you choose?" Although this question may be immensely valuable for learning about adults, it is often of little value for children because of their limited repertoire of figures from which they can select. In addition, they will often choose superheroes or other age-appropriate figures. The stereotyped responses are not as revealing as the atypical. Accordingly, as will be seen below, the verbal projection question for people (as opposed to animals and objects) can be very useful for adults.

One mother gave these responses:

(+)1 Rita Hayworth. I try to copy her to a T. She led a very glamorous life. She was beautiful. She was sexy-looking.

(+)2 Maria Callas, of the Metropolitan Opera—she's not a dying thing. People adore her. People will worship her forever.

(+)3 Happy Rockefeller. She's a dream person. She's not cheap or rowdy. She's elegant. She's wealthy.

(−)1 a) A poor person. I'd never want to be poor.

b) My aunt. She was very promiscuous.

(−)2 My mother. She was very ignorant. She had a low IQ. She wasn't neat.

(−)3 The female murderer in the picture, *I Want to Live*. She kills other women. She was a murderer. She slept with men.

This mother was basically hysterical, exhibitionistic, deeply materialistic, and vain. Her vanity bordered on psychotic grandiosity. She looked upon those who did not profess adoration of her as being hostile. These cravings are well revealed in the verbal projective test. The (+)1, (+)2, and (+)3 responses all reveal her desire to be adored by large numbers of people, adored for beauty and wealth. The (−)1b and (−)3 responses reflect her guilt over sexual feelings, and (−)3 also reflects her guilt over hostile feelings toward other women.

Another mother gave this response:

> (+)1 Jacqueline Kennedy. She has glamor. She's respected and she's elegant. She has many intellectual interests. There is more for her in the future.
>
> (+)2 Picasso. He lives an isolated and contented life. He has inner contentment and satisfaction. He's not dependent on others. He's uninvolved with the rest of the world.
>
> (+)3 Jay. The man I'm now dating. He's serious-minded. He has a flair for enjoying life. He captures both worlds, the real and the unreal.
>
> (−)1 My ex-husband's brother's wife. She has no sense of morals. She has affairs with other men and she shows no reaction, no guilt. Otherwise, she's wonderful.
>
> (−)2 My mother. She's incapable of showing warmth. She always finds the bad side of things. She thrives on misery.
>
> (−)3 Candy, the heroine in a book. It's a sexual satire on a foolish young girl. She has sex with her father, with an uncle, with a resident doctor, with someone in a men's room, and a hunchback in the street.

This mother was an extremely infantile and self-indulgent woman. She was sexually promiscuous and neglected her children in order to go off evenings and weekends with a series of men. She was highly materialistic and extremely exhibitionistic. She was incapable of involving herself in a meaningful way with others. All these qualities are revealed in the verbal projective responses. Her choice of Jacqueline Kennedy for her "glamor" and elegance reveal her exhibitionistic and materialistic qualities. Her inability to involve herself meaningfully is suggested in the reason she gives for wishing to be Picasso, as well as the reasons she gives for not wishing to be her mother. Some guilt over her sexual promiscuity is revealed in (−)1 and (−)3 where she denigrates two other women who themselves were quite promiscuous.

Another mother stated:

> (+)1 Margaret Bourke-White. She was formerly a photographer. Now she's sick. She was well traveled and she led an exciting life.

She traveled all over the world. She was married to Erskine Caldwell but they were divorced. She was very creative. She was a very aggressive woman.

(+)2 E. Nesbitt. She wrote children's books. She wrote books on poetry, English, and wild life. She supported her husband and her husband's mistress in her own home. She entertained many interesting people. She was a very strong person. She was lively and full of energy.

(+)3 My Aunt Robb. She was always held up to me as a model. She was beautiful, charming, athletic, and always enjoyed life. She always lived in an academic world, but she was not an intellectual.

(−)1 My mother. She lead a hard life. She was always mixed up. I don't like her. She has no common sense. She's done all the wrong things. She favored my brother. She was unfair to me. She gave me no preparation for life. When I had to have my tonsils out, she didn't tell me in advance. I couldn't rely on her. I've never gotten any backing from her and now I can't depend on anyone.

(−)2 My father. He's lead a very unrealistic kind of life. He never found meaningful work. Although he graduated from Harvard, he always held menial jobs. I wouldn't want to be him because he married my mother. He was never happy with her.

(−)3 A man at my office. He's a no person. He's a zombie. He has no animation. He's just a dead pan.

This mother was a very intelligent, independent, self-assertive, and a fairly accomplished woman. She had been married to a very intellectualized man who was quite dependent on her. She was somewhat inhibited in the expression of her maternal feelings. In the (−)1 response, she reveals some of the sources of her exaggerated independence and self-assertion, namely, her own mother's neglect and disinterest in her. Not being able to depend on her mother she has never felt she could depend on anyone and had thereby become extremely independent and self-assertive. In (+)1 and (+)2 she selects women who have these qualities. The (+)2 choice exhibits this to an extreme degree where she selects a woman who supports not only her husband but her husband's mistress. The (+)3 response is not in itself pathological but tends to support the kind of independent life which this mother considers to be ideal. The (−)2 response again gives information about the reasons why this mother could have little respect for men and little belief that she could depend upon them, thereby having to depend only on her own resources. The (−)3 response also makes reference to her emotional inhibition and lack of spontaneity.

Draw-a-Person and Draw-a-Family I do not commonly ask parents to draw a person and then tell me a story about the person they have drawn. However, on occasion, I will do so. The Draw-a-Family test may not be particularly useful for children, because of the stereotyped responses they most often provide, but it can be much more useful for adults. My experience has been that adults are less prone to give me stereotyped stories. In this section I will not reproduce the pictures that the parents drew but will present verbatim the stories they provided and my analyses of them.

One mother drew a woman and told this story:

> She's a 25-year-old college girl. She lives alone is a small apartment in New York City. It's an East Side apartment. She works for a magazine as a news writer and editor. She's attractive. She has many boy friends. On her vacations she likes to go traveling. She lives frugally in order to have money to travel.
>
> She goes to England on a trip. She's in London and she meets an Indian—from India, not an American Indian. She's interested in him. They date a lot, and then he returns with her to the United States. He goes back to India, and they continue writing. They decide to marry. She goes to India for his parent's permission. His parents are very upset that he is marrying a nonHindu. He decides not to go against his parents' wishes.
>
> She then travels throughout India. She is depressed by the poverty there. She spends the rest of her life in India trying to convince people not to have children because of the population problem.

This mother was a highly intellectualized woman who married outside of her religion. I considered her clinically to be low in maternal expression, and the story reflects her deep-seated desires to be single and to proselytize nonconception as a way of life.

One mother told this story about the male figure, which was drawn first:

> It's a boy. He's warm, bright, and friendly. In school he gets into a fight with another little boy. He gets hurt and dies. His brother is not as attractive. His mother and father have always ignored the brother, who was not so attractive. He was neglected. The father is very similar to the brother who lives. But the father gives in to the domineering mother. The father tries to be kinder, but the mother browbeats and puts the father down. So the father joins the mother in saying "You should have died, and your brother should have lived. You're lazy and shiftless."

The brother then grows up and is in constant trouble. He gets into a lot of difficulty with the law. Then he married, but he can't keep a wife. He married four or five times. He never holds a job and never functions on his own. The father tries to help the boy without the mother knowing. The father sees himself in this boy. The father gets sick and he dies. As he is dying he wants the boy to be with him and not his wife.

The mother who told this story had a child with a severe school phobia. Her underlying hostility toward children is well revealed in this story. One of the mother's two children dies and the other is severely rejected. The story also reveals her feelings that it is the wife who not only controls her husband but is capable of turning him against his own child.

The same woman then drew a picture of a female and described the picture as follows:

She's a woman of about 38. She has a square jaw. She looks determined. She is lovable but neurotic. You can't see what's going on behind that face. I'm not sure about that smile.

The statement, "You can't see what's going on behind that face" reveals this mother's tendency to maintain a façade and not reveal her real inner feelings. She was an artificial person, vain, histrionic, materialistic, exhibitionistic, and false in many of her dealings with people.

This story was told about the male figure which another mother drew:

He has wide shoulders and a moustache. He is standing with his arms out. He's blond. He's not very happy. He has a sign. It says STOP. He's directing traffic. He's not well dressed. He's 40 years old and he's a traffic cop. He's standing on a corner. He's bored to death. He's in a rut. He doesn't know anything else. His family realizes that he's very tired, but he's good with the kids; involved with the Policemen's Benevolent Association. He dies and his wife collects PBA insurance but she's not happy either. He had a heart attack.

This story, of course, reveals this mother's hostility toward her husband whom she unconsciously wishes would die of a heart attack. He, in reality, was a psychopathic person who was constantly placing the family in great debt and she, for masochistic reasons of her own, suffered all the difficulties which this situation brought about. Her husband, depicted as a traffic cop with his hand saying STOP, reveals her view of him as an authority to be obeyed—especially when he directed her to refrain from expressing her resentment over his psychopathic behavior or her desire to flee the marital situation. Having him die appears to be one way out of this situation; but even then she would not be happy because her insurance benefits would not satisfy her needs.

Another mother told the following story about the male figure she had drawn:

> It's an astronaut who has landed on the moon, and he is surprised that the atmosphere is so suitable to man. He was able to remove his space suit. He was astounded that he could breathe. He was pleased about it and enjoyed it.

This story is most interesting in that it dovetails completely with a repetitious dream of the patient's husband (see page 294). He was the son of a rich man, and no matter how poorly he did in school, his father had always bought his way into another school. No matter how negligent he was in fulfilling his obligations, his father always assumed them. The husband had a repetitious dream in which he was drowning but, at the moment when he feared he would die, he suddenly realized that he could breathe underwater. The wife's story that she could miraculously breathe on the moon was similar to her husband's repetitious dream that he could miraculously breathe under water. These people were "made for each other" in that they were both extremely narcissistic and dependent on the husband's father, and my patient was following in his parents' footsteps in that he viewed the paternal grandfather to be the source of all support in the family, so much so that no one need do anything him- or herself to earn his or her way in the world.

Another mother told the following story about a female figure that she has drawn:

> She's all dressed up. She's ready to go on a trip. She's going to go on a holiday. She's waiting for someone to pick up her suitcases and bring her to the airport. She flies to a place where the climate is warm. She arrives at a tall, white shiny hotel. The ocean is all around. She's really been looking forward to this trip. She wants to swim. She surfs. She goes waterskiing.

While on the trip she sees a person coming down the road with bananas. She thinks this would be a good business. She goes back home and starts to import them to the United States. She starts a business in the United States importing and exporting bananas. She frequently visits the island to be sure that all is right at that end.

This mother suffered with an hysterical character disorder with much repressed sexuality and hostility. The story reveals a desire to be taken care of and indulged. The banana is most likely a phallic symbol. The importing and exporting probably reflects her ambivalence over receiving the penis or possibly whether or not she wants one herself.

The mother then told the following story about the male figure she had drawn:

He's warm, happy, and outgoing. He's the athletic type. He's a skin diver. He goes on trips that take him to all parts of the world in order to look for rare stones for museums. He's in Southern France and runs into difficulty with his scuba equipment. He has a fight with a large fish, but he comes up okay with his collection of stones.

My guess is that the stones represent the husband's testes or masculinity. She sees him as being essentially emasculated and searching the world in order to obtain his masculinity. However, when he does so they are only used for exhibitionistic purposes; that is, they are exhibited in museums. The story reflects the mother's feeling that her husband is emasculated and that if he were to achieve a greater degree of masculinity, she would use it only for exhibitionistic purposes and not take advantage of the increased sexual gratification and intimacy that such acquisition would allow.

Another mother told this story about the *family* she drew:

The mother and father are walking in Central Park with their little boy. It's a beautiful day. The birds are flying. They walk through the zoo and pass a lion in his cage. They go to a lake, get a boat, and row for a while in the sunshine. Everyone takes his turn at the oars.

Suddenly a frog jumps into the boat. The woman almost falls out of the boat because she is so frightened by the frog. She knows that it can't do her any harm, but she was shocked by its sudden arrival. She tips the boat. It overturns, but the woman can't swim. She flounders. She can't swim. The boy and the father can't swim either. In the confusion about who can save this woman she drowns.

Her obituary reads: "She drowned in confusion. Her husband and child could have helped her. She wasn't helping herself. She could have made it to the land. She slipped as the result of the mass confusion."

The mother was an extremely inhibited individual with massive repression of the extreme hostility she felt towards her only son. She had a strong need to present everything in terms of deep calmness and serenity in the service of repressing the rage within her. The caged lion reveals this tendency, especially as it appears in the setting of a pleasant walk on a lovely day. However, later in the story her unconscious reveals itself in the form of a frog which leaps out of the water into their boat, thereby upsetting the family's precarious serenity. The fact that this frog can throw this family into massive confusion, which ultimately results in the mother's drowning, reveals the great fear she has of dealing with that which is beneath the surface.

Another mother told this story about the *family* she drew:

The farmer and his wife are both 23. The children are 8 and 9. They live in the Arkansas dust bowl. They follow the crops. Then they go to Arizona. All the children are out in the field picking the crops. A reporter sees the family and details the story of their meager existence. He publishes it and it brings into national prominence their and the plight of other migrant workers. They keep working although they have trouble adjusting. They're still miserable trying to eke out a living. They do manage to save some money and their children get scholarships to college. This boy becomes a famous surgeon, but all this doesn't change their lives. The children get what the parents don't.

The mother sees herself as living in a dust bowl. She spends her life trying to squeeze nutriment out of the dry land. The work is hard and painstaking, but she manages to survive by "following the crops," that is, migrating to wherever there might be a little nutriment. Her whole life is spent in deprivation in the "dust bowl" but she manages to vicariously gratify her desires to leave it through her children's success in doing so.

Both this mother and her husband lived in an emotional vacuum. They were both severely inhibited in expressing tender and affectionate feelings and their primary mode of interaction was hostile. They bickered almost incessantly. She did indeed live in an emotional dust bowl and although she claimed gratifications of a more meaningful nature (as symbolized by food in the story), she only intermittently obtained them and was spending her life in the almost futile quest to get such satisfactions. The story was an accurate portrayal of her situation.

Dreams   I will most often ask a mother if she has had any dreams that have repeated themselves throughout the course of her life. I am in agreement with my colleagues in the field of psychoanalysis that this can be an important question. Repetitious dreams most often reflect an ongoing theme in the individual's life. If the mother has not had such experiences, then I ask her if she can recall *any* dream in her life. This, too, may be significant, especially if it is a dream that she had many years previously. The fact that she remembers it so many years later is a statement of its psychological importance. Another kind of dream that should be given serious consideration by the examiner is one that occurs before the first session. Often this may be a rich source of information about the patient's anticipations from treatment or about fundamental life problems. Unfortunately, the dream may be presented at a time when the therapist is least capable of analyzing it because of his or her unfamiliarity with the person. However, to the degree that one can analyze it, to that degree may one learn some useful information. On occasion, one files it away and may find it useful subsequently, when one is more familiar with the person.

One mother related this dream as having taken place just prior to the initial evaluation:

> I was in the waiting room of a dentist's office and there were three dogs there. They got into the garbage cans and the dentist was going to spray the dogs with MACE (that anti-riot stuff that makes you paralyzed).

The child's father was a physician who spent long hours in his office. The dream reveals the mother's feelings that the father (here depicted as a dentist) sees their three children as an unnecessary nuisance who have to be rejected and paralyzed if he is to be freed of the obligations of taking care of them. Their scrounging for food in a garbage can reveals her feeling that he has little to offer them. It is of interest, however, that she is passive to all of this and permits it to occur.

Another mother related this repetitious dream:

> I often dream that there is a fire in the house and I have to get the kids out.

The dream serves as an expression of the mother's hostility towards her children and her desire that she be free of the responsibilities and inconveniences associated with their upbringing. However, another part of her—a part which is genuinely concerned for their well being—salvages them in time. In summary then the dream reflects the mother's ambivalence toward her children.

Between her first and second evaluation sessions, a mother related this dream:

> A service man had to come to service the bidet. He didn't know what he was doing.

I understood this dream to mean that the serviceman was this examiner and it reflected the mother's feelings that I was incompetent. The mother had an hysterical character disorder with much repression of hostility and sexual feelings. I considered the bidet, as a cleanser of her genitalia, to reflect her desires that I might in some way alleviate her feelings that sexuality was dirty, or that I might in some way be involved in cleansing her sexuality. I did not attempt to analyze this dream in this case because I felt that she was not ready to deal with any of my surmised interpretations. Often a dream like this speaks poorly for the parents' commitment to the treatment process because of its implied distrust of the therapist. Fortunately, in this case, this did not turn out to be the case, and the child did well with full cooperation on the part of the parents. My guess is that the mother gradually became more confident in me, in spite of her initial hesitation.

One mother related this repetitious dream:

> I was at AB's house. She was having a birthday party for her daughter C. It really wasn't A's house but she was having a party there. She had an old-fashioned stove there, a pot bellied stove. It had a beautiful rare plant growing out of it. The plant had a beautiful

odor. I said, "Please tell me where you got this." A said, "Before you leave, I'll either tell you where I bought it or I'll give you a branch to plant yourself." It had pink and white pretty flowers. I kept asking her where she got it. Oh, yes, one other thing. The stove had originally been black, but it was painted white.

This mother had previously been in treatment for a short period, was intelligent, and was interested in analyzing this dream. As a result of her associations and my inquiries, we decided that the pot-bellied stove and plant represented the mother herself. She basically considered herself to be vulgar, inadequate (i.e., "black"), and she attempted to hide these deficiencies by presenting herself with a colorful façade. This was represented by the white paint and the beautiful flowers which everyone admired and which everyone enjoyed smelling. This may have reflected her way of dealing with her inner feeling that she "smells."

This mother was an extremely materialistic and exhibitionistic woman. She was quite wealthy and was obsessed with indulging herself with expensive clothing. She said, "I even dress up to go out for the mail." She was quite shocked after she understood what the dream meant. She subsequently went into therapy with me, and the dream served to catalyze her working on this problem.

Another mother told me she used to have this dream about once a week a few years prior to the evaluation:

> A very short, ugly man came up to me. He was exactly the opposite of the kind that I like. I asked him to make love to me. He was overjoyed at the idea. He couldn't believe his luck. He then made advances to me, and I told him that I changed my mind.

The dream reveals the mother's deep-seated hostility toward men. In the dream she selects an ugly man, that is, one who is most likely to respond with gratitude and enthusiasm to her suggestion of a sexual encounter and then thwarts him in the midst of his excitation. Her hostility toward men here is obvious.

During the evaluation this mother told the following dream:

> I was with a child. I was at Columbia Teacher's College. I went back and forth from making pottery to being in the apartment of a photographer. While I was making pottery, someone said that I should do it in a particular way but I insisted that I could do it better. Which was so.
>
> This photographer was trying to take a picture of a child and

he said that he was on the staff at the university. The child didn't want to let his picture be taken. I told the child that he should let the photographer take the picture. The child said that he would be nice to the photographer only until the picture was taken and then he wouldn't be nice any longer.

The child and I then went through many rooms and then we went out the back door and left.

The dream clearly reflects the mother's attitude toward the evaluation. The photographer is a common symbol for the therapist who "sees through," confronts, and accurately portrays the patient. The child is depicted in two ways: first as the pottery which the mother creates, and second in the form of a child. In the dream the mother reveals her feeling that she can do a better job in molding and forming her child's personality than I can and, therefore, insists upon doing it herself. In the dream she also has the child cooperate with me only until the picture is taken (that is, until the end of the evaluation) and then has him refuse to cooperate further.

The journey through many rooms signifies the complex inquiry of the evaluation and their leaving through the back door reveals their desire to remove themselves surreptitiously and prematurely, rather than through the front door which would reflect a desire to leave when treatment is completed.

The dream was a perfect statement of what ultimately happened and served as an accurate warning for the examiner. The child did cooperate until the end of the evaluation, and then both he and the parents decided not to pursue treatment. Although the dream was analyzed with the mother and she accepted its implications at the time, I was unable to alter the strong forces which compelled her to follow its dictates.

Another mother described having frequent fearful fantasies and an occasional nightmare that "my husband would lose both of his legs and I'll end up pushing him in a wheelchair."

This mother was extremely masochistic. Although she had a Ph.D. degree, she constantly berated herself intellectually and had always felt that she had to present herself as intellectually average or below average if she were to attract her husband. Her husband was a borderline psychotic who had little involvement with her and devoted himself to his academic pursuits (He was a professor at a university). He had her do most of the "dirty work," that is, boring research and typing, for his own doctoral thesis.

The fantasy reveals not only her unconscious hostility toward her husband, hostility which is expressed through the desire that he lose his legs, but also her feeling that the only way he could really need her was if he were to be helpless. When he was getting his doctorate degree he needed her. Following this he would no longer need her and the fantasy allowed her once again to play a meaningful role in his life. In addition, by straddling herself with a crippled man, she could gratify her masochistic desires.

The mother of an adolescent described this dream on the night before her first individual interview with me. (There had been a previous screening interview when I saw her in association with her son and husband):

> I was on one side of a sliding door. My husband was on the other side. I was trying to shut the sliding door and couldn't.

The dream, coming as it did on the night prior to her first interview with me alone, suggests that she would prefer to place a closed door between herself and her husband so that he would not see certain things which would be unpleasant for her to reveal to me. It suggested that she was not going to tell me freely very much about her real feelings about her husband. In the subsequent part of the interview this prediction turned out to be true. She described her relationship with him as a good one and had absolutely no complaints. Of him she could only say, "He's wonderful. He's good. Sometimes he talks a little too much, but that's nothing that concerns me. He talks a lot of common sense."

In reality, the husband was a person who was prone to make endless speeches over inanities. He would puff himself up and pontificate over the most simplistic issues as if he was spouting forth great wisdom. Only one of his four children was consciously irritated by these lectures. One of his sons (not my patient) identified with the father and at 21 was already filled with an air of self-importance.

The dream and the mother's subsequent comments revealed her fear of coming to terms directly with this quite alienating trait of her husband's.

I generally spend two or three interviews with the mothers, each one lasting 45 to 60 minutes. I hope the reader can appreciate that the information gained in the individual interviews provides me with a much greater knowledge of what is going on with her than is obtained in the initial two-hour consultation. In every sense of the word, the data collection in the initial interview is indeed superficial. The examiner who does not avail him- or herself of the more extensive interviews is being deprived of vital information—information that is crucial to have if one is to understand thoroughly what is going on with the patient.

Before closing the final interview with the mother, I may ask her how she views herself ten years from now. The answer provided can also be a useful source of information. The same question can be asked about her guesses about the child a decade from now. I am sure that the reader has a collection of his or her own questions that can also prove useful. In this section I have presented those that I personally have found most valuable.

THE EVALUATION OF THE FATHER

My discussion of the father's evaluation will be significantly shorter than that of the mother. This is primarily the result of the fact that many of the questions are the same and that there would be little point in my repeating the same questions in this section. However, another fact relates to my observation that fathers generally are less willing to reveal themselves than mothers and accordingly, their evaluations are often shorter. Whereas the mother's evaluation is generally two to three interviews, each of which is 45 to 60 minutes, fathers generally have nothing further to say to me after one to two interviews of the same duration. They often are much "tighter" when responding to the projective questions, as well.

The Initial Inquiry

As was true with the mother, I begin the interview with the father with an open-end question in which I ask him if there is anything special on his mind that he would like to speak with me about. He may or may not have something to discuss and, of course, I follow his lead. I then ask the father about reactions to the initial two-hour consultation. We then go on to questions in which I ask him his opinion regarding the causes of the child's difficulties. I inform him that I recognize that his main reason for consulting with me is that I should provide my opinion regarding the answers to this question. However, I advise him that his guesses and speculations can be an important source of information to me. I then proceed with the questions regarding his and his wife's dealing with the child, both assets and liabilities. I am particularly interested in whether the father involves himself in sports with the children, especially such activities as Little League, soccer, and so on. In investigating into this area, however, the examiner should find out whether the father is fanatical about it. If the father is having fist fights with the coaches at the Little League games, he is probably doing his children more harm than good. He is probably using the child for vicarious gratification to a degree beyond the normal.

Description of the Marriage

We then proceed to a discussion of the marriage. Here, especially, fathers may be particularly unreceptive to revealing difficulties in the marital relationship. A common situation is one in which a mother will claim that her husband had had an affair, and he has told her that he does not wish her to reveal this to me. In the session with me he will studiously avoid discussion of this issue, even though he knows that his wife is aware of the relationship. I ask the father the same questions about the marriage that I ask the mother, especially with regard to its strong points and weak points. If the father initially presents the marriage as "good," with no problems at all, I will state that all marriages have their areas of friction, and I encourage him to discuss those areas in which he and his wife have differences of opinion. Even with this sanction, the father may insist that there are no such difficulties in his marriage. If such a response is given by a father whom the examiner knows is having an affair (by some information provided by the wife), then there is little the examiner can do. It is hoped that she will bring the matter up during the joint session, but often she does not. As mentioned, in such situations, I often let the thing rest. To "rock the boat" may cause a disruption of the marital equilibrium, which may do the child more harm than good.

History of Psychiatric Treatment

I then ask the father whether he has ever been in treatment. Most child therapists will agree that boys are overrepresented in their patient population. In contrast, most adult therapists will agree that women are overrepresented in their patient population. I believe that this phenomenon relates to the fact that boys are generally more rambunctious, assertive, and "fighters." As every teacher and parent knows, boys are "tough customers" when compared to girls. Accordingly, they have greater difficulty complying with social constraints, especially in school. I suspect that there are probably genetic bases for these character traits in that they were probably more adaptive in evolutionary development. Hunters and fighters do better if they are more aggressive, and so men who possessed such qualities survived preferentially over men who did not. However, social and environmental factors have probably played a role as well in engendering these traits. At the adult level, however, men often feel the need to maintain their "macho image" and are less receptive to therapy—a process in which they are encouraged to reveal weaknesses and failings. If the father has been in therapy, I will ask the same questions that I have asked the mother regarding the nature of the problems for which he went into treatment and what benefits, if any, were derived from the therapy. I am especially interested in marital counseling and the marital problems that brought the parents into therapy.

Background Information

The questions to the father regarding background information are essentially the same as those posed to the mother. Specifically, I ask the father about his parents, their relationship with one another, and their relationships with him. I also inquire about his siblings, especially with regard to the presence of psychiatric difficulties. Here, I am particularly interested in the kind of parenting the father received in that his parents probably served as the model for his own parenting. I also want to know about the nature of the relationships between the paternal grandparents and my patient.

Military Service   One difference between the father's and the mother's inquiries relates to military service. If the father served in the military, one does well to find out about how he adjusted there and whether he received an honorable discharge. One should ascertain whether the father had difficulties adjusting in the service and whether he warranted disciplinary action and/or psychiatric treatment. The military generally requires a degree of integration similar to (if not more than) that which is required for adjustment in school. One must be willing to comply to a reasonable degree with authority and to exhibit self-restraint under stressful circumstances. If the father was in combat, one wants to find out whether he suffered with any psychiatric disorders commonly seen under such circumstances.

The First Memory Question   As was true for the mother, questions about the father's first memory can often provide useful information about underlying psychodynamics. I present here a few examples.

One father gave this memory:

> I was about four years old. I remember leaving my mother's and father's store. I climbed over a fence outside of the store and ripped my leg open. Then I ran back into the store.

This father, although 38 years old, was still working as an employee in his parents' store. He was extremely dependent on them and was quite passive in his relationship with them. Although he spoke on occasion of going out on his own, there was little evidence that he seriously intended to do this. Although he could not openly admit it to himself, it was clear that he was waiting for the day that they would die and then the business would become his. In his marriage, as well, he was quite dependent on his wife, who domineered him mercilessly. The memory reveals the father's basic feeling that were he to leave the domain of his parents he would be traumatized. The warning serves him well and he returns to the store where he feels comfortable and safe. This first memory epitomizes the basic theme of his life and his relationships both with his parents and with his wife.

Another father had this memory:

> I was about four years old. I was driving a little toy car and running over another kid's white shoes. He was a dandy. I was a dirty little kid. I liked to get dirty. He went crying to his mother. I don't know if after that I was chastised or what.

This father was a bright, somewhat cocky, and basically arrogant man. He was quick to anger and most of his comments about people were critical. He was in the plumbing supply business and psychologically he appeared to be "shitting" on the world. The memory reflects this life pattern. His greatest pleasure appeared to be dirtying those who were clean, that is, defecating on others. His relationship with me was in the same spirit. I felt that he saw me as a boy with white shoes and his primary mode of relating to me was hostile. He stated that in grade school his greatest pleasure came when he was head of the monitors, a position, no doubt that gave him further opportunity to be sadistic to others. After graduation from college the father was fired from his first job after six months of work. He considered his firing the result of his having been rebellious: "I didn't want to do what they wanted." He finally ended up working for his own father, with whom he described a very competitive and antagonistic relationship.

The father also stated that he feared women, stating: "I see them as aggressive birds who would want to scratch our eyes out." I considered this fantasy to be a reflection of his own hostility projected out onto women.

Another father's memory:

> I was in my crib. I must have been about two years old and I was picking the paint off the iron bars and eating it.

This father's parents were quite distant from him and he suffered definite emotional deprivation in his childhood. The recollection is symbolic of the deprivation he suffered in that he had to resort to the ingestion of inedible objects in his attempt to gain symbolic affection. The psychodynamics of his ingestion of inedible objects is similar to that of children with pica who ingest inedible objects because of neglect and a craving for oral-dependent gratifications.

Another father's first memory:

> I was two or three years old and playing in my backyard. My clothing got caught on a fence that I was climbing. A friend of mine came and had to lift me up and take me off.

This father had a schizoid character disorder and was severely dependent on his wife and parents. Although 31 and a law school graduate, he was still unable to function as an adult. He worked for his father, who was also a lawyer, and it was clear that he could not have been able to function independently in another law firm or in his own practice. The memory reveals his basic dependency problem. When he is confronted with an obstruction or some other difficulty in life, he is unable to get himself out of trouble and must depend on others to take care of him.

One father gave this response:

> I was about three years old and I remember trying to eat cement from a wall.

This man's father (that is the paternal grandfather of my patient) was a very intellectualized man who devoted himself to his scholarly interests instead of spending time with his children. The paternal grandmother had paranoid and depressive episodes for which she received ECT. At times she was suicidal. It is not hard to see how this father felt that the love and affection given to him was as digestible as concrete.

School Life   I ask the father about adjustment at the elementary school level. I am particularly interested in the father's comparison of himself with my patient during this period, especially if the patient is a boy. Many fathers will say that the patient is exhibiting behavior very similar to their own during this phase of their lives. One must consider the possibility that this reflects a genetic component. However, one also wants to ascertain whether the father is sanctioning atypical behavior (antisocial) or criticizing it. Possible genetic contributions notwithstanding, sanctioning may contribute to its perpetuation.

Although things are changing, women still have less necessity to dedicate themselves as assiduously as fathers to school and career planning. I am not claiming that this is a good thing; only that it is a reality of our world, recent changes notwithstanding. Accordingly, if a mother was insufficiently motivated during the high school period, it does not necessarily reflect as much pathology as a father who was similarly unmotivated. The pressures on the father to ultimately be a breadwinner are far greater than those placed on girls during the formative years. Accordingly, a girl's lack of school and work motivation during the high school period does not necessarily reflect as much pathology as in a father who is similarly unmotivated. I am also interested in the father's social relationships throughout his school career. These lay the foundation for adult relationships, including the relationship with his wife.

Work History   It is important to go into the father's work history. A long history of difficulty adjusting in jobs generally reflects psychiatric difficulties. And the father's commitment to work will generally affect the child's attitude toward school. If the child sees the father seriously involved in his work, it is likely that he will thereby serve as a good model for the child's involvement in school work. I cannot emphasize this point strongly enough. Many parents present with children who are unmotivated to do their school work. Yet the parents may provide an atmosphere in which work is viewed as odious and there is practically no intellectual curiosity. In such an environment the child is not likely to develop strong school interest unless exposed extensively to other models who demonstrate such commitments.

The Premarital Relationship with the Mother I want to find out the circumstances under which the father first met the mother and what his initial attractions were. The examiner does well to appreciate that most people do not provide what a judicious middle-aged person would consider reasonable reasons for marriage. So common are the frivolous criteria for marriage that one has to consider them to be in the normal range. For example, a father may claim that he "fell in love." When one asks what the particular qualities were that he fell in love with, he may be hard put to give other answers other than his wife was physically attractive and that she was "sweet." One should be particularly interested here in any atypical relationships that were established during this period.

Projective Questions Because fathers are generally more reticent to reveal themselves directly, one would think that projective questions might be useful. However, even in this area my experience has been that they are more reluctant to reveal themselves. This hesitation notwithstanding, one can sometimes still get useful information by the utilization of these questions.

Five wishes Some fathers can only go to three wishes. When they reach the fourth and fifth wishes, they become too anxious to continue because they run out of stereotyped responses. I present here some responses of fathers to the five wishes question.

One father gave these responses:

1. That Randy be okay.
2. That I have a happy marriage.
3. That I become independent and self-sufficient.
4. I can't think of anymore.

All three wishes relate to difficulties in the family. The third wish especially epitomized the father's main psychological problem, namely, that he was an extremely dependent individual. Although in his late 30s, he was very much under the thumb of his own father, whom he was working for, who was supporting him, and who controlled almost every aspect of his life.

Another father gave these responses:

1. Wisdom.
2. Patience.
3. Charity.
4. Free access to any library I wanted.
5. The writing style equivalent to George Travelli Macauley.

This father was a highly intellectualized man on the faculty of a major Eastern university. He was most fearful of intimate involvements with others and spent most of his time absorbed in his academic work. For years he had not slept in the same room as his wife and sexual contact was rare. Three of his five responses make direct reference to his intellectual and academic ambitions (#1, #4 and #5). In addition, this man flaunted his intellectual accomplishments in an attempt to bolster a very low self-esteem. This is well shown in wish #5 where he mentions the name of a person who was unknown to this examiner. When I asked him who Macauley was, he responded with condescending incredulity that I didn't know that Macauley was a famous historian. The implication of his facial expression was one of: "How stupid can you be, not ever to have heard of Macauley?"

Conspicuous by their absence is the fact that none of the responses refer to any human beings other than himself.

Another father gave these responses:

1. Good health and long life.
2. To be a contented, respected millionaire. To have enough material comfort to free me from worry.
3. To have stature and power. To be a better lawyer than anyone else and to be recognized as such. To be a member of the establishment.
4. For my children to have the same luck with their wives as I have with mine and to have as much money as I have.
5. The question I wonder about is whether it would be better for

my wife or for me to die first? It would be better for her if I went first, but you won't get me to say that I want her to die first. No, the best thing would be if there was an accident and we both died together.

This father was an extremely grandiose, self-centered, manipulative, and hostile individual. He actually considered himself to be uniformly admired, respected, and envied by all around him. In actual fact he had no real friends. His cruelty to his daughter (more verbal than physical) resulted in her being a very withdrawn and timid child.

Response #1 is within the normal range. Wishes #2, #3, and #4 reflect the already described grandiosity, materialism, and power fantasies. Wish #5 reveals his hostility toward his wife, which he then denied. Actually, this man's wife (my patient's mother) had significant personality problems, and the marriage was fraught with difficulties. However, he had to deny this in order to maintain the image of having a "perfect marriage." Under these circumstances there was formidable hostility toward his wife, reflected in his death wishes, but he could not allow these feelings entrance into conscious awareness.

Verbal projective questions Presented below are some verbal projective questions that provided important information in the fathers' evaluation.

One father gave these responses:

(+)1 Caruso or Lawrence Melchior. I can't sing very well, and I'd love to be a great singer, to be able to entertain people that way.

(+)2 Jacques Cousteau. He leads an active, interesting life. He's adventurous; he's in the outdoors; he does a lot of skin diving.

(+)3 "Dr. H. He's a very good surgeon. He does a lot of good for the people. His hours probably aren't too bad.

(−)1 Frank Sinatra or the Beatles, or others in the public eye. They have no private life. They're mobbed wherever they go.

(−)2 A politician. Most of them are phony phonies. They lie all the time. I couldn't keep track of all the lies.

(−)3 Just plain Joe. I want to get some recognition in life.

My full clinical evaluation of this man revealed him to be relatively stable and free from significant psychopathology. Although one might find evidences of psychopathology in the above responses, I considered them to be within the normal range. The (+)1 and (+)3 responses suggest that this father might have inordinate desires to be famous. However, his life situation was one in which he appeared to be very secure and adjusted in a fairly respectable but certainly not famous position. He was an engineer who was owner of a small manufacturing company. The (−)2 reply suggests the possiblity that the father himself engages in duplicity or would like to do so. However, this was not substantiated by the rest of my clinical evaluation. It is important for the reader to appreciate that repression of unacceptable material exists in all people, and projective tests reveal what is being repressed. In our culture there is probably a tendency in most people to lie at times and to crave fame. Lying and inordinate ambition are not acceptable traits and may very well be repressed. This does not mean that the person harboring such desires is suffering with psychopathology. It is only when there is acting out, obsessive preoccupation, or when these trends interfere significantly with one's life pattern that the term psychopathology can justifiably be applied.

Another father gave these responses:

(+)1 Elvis Presley. He's rich and famous. He's honest; he doesn't gamble. He's a good family man. I've always been a great fan of his.

(+)2 Mickey Mantle. I like to play ball. He's my idol. I adore his strength and skill as a ball player. He's also an upright family man. He doesn't have much of an education, just like me.

(+)3 John Kennedy. He had a close relationship with the common man, in spite of all his money. But he wasn't a big shot. He had compassion for the common man.

(−)1 Fidel Castro. He deceived people. He manhandled people. He caused a lot of pain and heartache.

(−)2 Hitler. He mistreated the Jewish people terribly. He rose to power by stepping over everybody.

(−)3 Jimmy Hoffa. He engaged in many underground activities. He's a vicious leader who robbed the union membership.

This 28-year-old father worked at the dairy counter at a supermarket. He graduated high school with mediocre grades and married at the age of 20. The paternal grandfather showed the father little warmth, and abandoned the home when the father was 18 years old.

The persons that this patient selected in both positive and negative categories could very well be within the normal range. However, the reasons he gives for choosing these people reflect certain manifestations of his personal psychopathology. In the (+)1 and (+)2 responses he introduces the "family man" theme, which are clearly personal associations to these figures, and certainly not typical. They suggest preoccupation with and cravings for a close-knit family in compensation for the deprivations he suffered as a child in this area. In the (+)3 response he chooses John Kennedy, in part because of his "compassion for the common man." His (−)1, (−)2, and (−)3 responses are all people who in one way or another have taken advantage of, deceived, and even killed the common man. These responses reveal this father's basic feelings of impotency in a world which he sees as malevolent and overpowering. He craves the protection of a benevolent authority symbolized by John Kennedy.

Another father gave this response:

(+)1 Paul Getty, for his business shrewdness. He got the oil reserve depreciation bill passed by Congress. He had no family life, so I wouldn't want to be like him for that.

(+)2 My old hometown doctor, Dr. O. He's someone who has done a lot for many people. He could talk to you about anything. He was a good family man.

(+)3 Supreme Court Justice White. He's an athlete. He's smart. He leads a well-rounded life.

(−)1 Adolph Hitler. He was a killer. His super-race idea was all wrong.

(−)2 Walter Reuther. He's a legalized crook. He warps our economy with the strength of his union.

(−)3 Malcolm X. He was trying to get a job done and wasn't doing it the right way. He was using violence rather than discussion.

This father had little interest in the patient, his adopted stepson, and spent 16 to 20 hours a day, six to seven days a week at work. He had strong psychopathic tendencies as well.

The (+)1 response reveals both his psychopathic tendencies as well as denial of his disinterest in family life. In the (+)2 reply we again see the denial of his disinterest in his family via his admiration for Dr. O, the "good family man." I considered the (+)3 and (−)1 responses to be within the normal range. The (−)2 response again relates to the father's psychopathy because I considered the father himself to be a "legalized crook." The (−)3 response as it stands cannot provide too much information. Had time been available to discuss the Malcolm X associations further, more revealing information might have been obtained.

One father gave these responses:

(+)1 Nathaniel Bowdich. He was a 19th century New Englander. He was a self-taught navigator and ship owner. He established many of the principles of navigation for whaling ships. Mariners still use Bowdich's book on navigation. He was very sharp and skilled. He taught mathematics at Harvard as well.

(+)2 Thomas Jefferson. He was a happy man. He had many interests. He enjoyed life.

(+)3 Jerry G., a colleague of mine. He's articulate, outgoing, and gets a bang out of life.

(−)1 Nat Turner. Although he was free, he was really still a slave. He had obsessions that he could not let go of. He was a double-dealing shackled madman.

(−)2 Nixon. He doesn't know what he wants. He doesn't know where he's going. He's not up to the responsibility. He has no convictions of his own.

(−)3 A psychiatrist. There's too much intimacy. They're bowed down with the inner world, which is a horrible one.

This father, although a successful professional man, was a borderline psychotic whose main symptoms were withdrawal and obsessive ruminations. He had little genuine interest in his family and only out of a sense of duty did he make attempts to involve himself with them. Consistent with this lack of involvement is the fact that in none of these responses is any mention made of family involvement. The (+)1 person, although admirable in many ways, appears to epitomize 19th century new England independence and self-assertion. He is the kind of a person who rises above hostile forces in nature and the hardships of life in a determined and single-minded manner. The choice of the navigator probably relates to the father's feelings that he himself needs some navigation and direction if he is to weather the storms of his life, especially those associated with the welling up of feelings (as represented by the ocean waves) which are so threatening to him. In the (+)2 and (+)3 responses the father reveals his desire to get some pleasure out of life, something he was not getting because of his psychiatric disturbances.

The (−)1 response reveals the father's basic feelings about

himself. He, like Nat Turner, is enslaved by his obsessions and his duplicity (which was associated with his contrived and artificial involvement in his family) and cause him to think of himself as "a double-dealing shackeled madman." In the (−)2 response reference is made to the father's indecisiveness related to his obsessive doubting and massive ambivalence. The (−)3 response again makes reference to the father's psychic conflicts and fears of relevation of his primitive eruptions from the unconscious.

One father was asked the animal questions in addition to the person questions. These are the responses he gave:

(+)1 A poodle dog. It gets good treatment.

(+)2 A black panther. It's shrewd and it's cunning. It's fast.

(+)3 A turtle. It goes on slowly but looks back to see if it's right or wrong.

(−)1 A cat. It's too self-reliant. It doesn't give. It just takes.

(−)2 A pig. It's only here to be eaten.

(−)3 A reptile or snake. It's misunderstood. People kill them and don't realize that they're just doing their own thing.

This father was an extremely psychopathic person. He had little interest in the patient, his adopted stepson, and spent most of his time away from the home at his job. He was a very conniving and materialistic individual who used people ruthlessly in order to obtain his own ends. His primary attaction to his wife, who was 10 years his senior, was that she was a good cook.

The (+)1 response reveals his strong impulses to passively lead a life of luxury. The (+)2 response reflects his admiration for psychopathic qualities. The (−)3 response suggests unconscious respect for the psychopathic personality type who is most circumspect, calculating, and reflective of his behavior.

In the (−)1 response the father's criticism of the cat who "doesn't give, just takes" is a clear statement of his denial of these qualities within himself, because he was a most taking person. The (−)2 response relates to the same attitude in that the father, seeing the world as a place where one is "eaten," chooses to be the "eater." The (−)3 response is a clear-cut rationalization for psychopathic behavior. The reptile and the snake are highly symbolic of the devious, the unacceptable, the cunning, and the surreptitious. The father cannot provide a logical justification for accepting such behavior but merely requests that these animals be accepted because they are "doing their own thing," and that in itself should be enough for people to accept them.

The verbal projective questions can also be used with adults to describe other family members. Just as the child is asked to select animals and objects that will suit his or her mother and father, the parent can be asked to present people, animals, and objects that will suit other family members, especially spouse and children. This father gave the following responses when asked to select animals that suited his wife's personality:

(+)1 A mynah bird. It's like a parrot. It's always jabbering.

(+)2 A rhinoceros. It goes where it wants. It doesn't have much of a brain. It tromps over everything in order to get what it wants.

(+)3 A Pekingese house dog. It has no worries. It's fed, then taken out to shit, and then put to bed.

(−)1 A mallard. It's graceful; she's not.

(−)2 A leopard. It's quiet and stealthy. She's loud. She has no tact. She's noisy.

(−)3 An alligator. He lives in the water and she's afraid of the water.

This father had very little respect for or involvement with his wife and the verbal projective associations clearly reflect this. The responses clearly reflect the massive feelings of disdain and disgust he had for her, and each response reveals a different type of deprecation. Here we see how all of these derogatory attitudes are on the conscious level.

Another father gave these responses when asked to select animals that suited his wife's personality:

(+)1 A lion. It's majestic. It's a leader. It's quiet and unassuming. It has perseverance. It likes to get things done in a quiet way. She's respected like the lion by the rest of the animal kingdom.

(+)2 A Mastiff dog. It protects the house. It's a strong animal yet it's gentle. It's respected by everyone.

(+)3 A deer because of its beauty and gracefulness. It's shy except when protecting its young and then it becomes very forceful. It's clear. It leads a quiet life. It's a choice food of carnivorous animals.

(−)1 A cat. They're nice until you go against them. Then they will turn against you. She won't do that.

(−)2 A snake. She's not repulsive. She doesn't instill fear in anyone.

(−)3 A bat because it's a spreader of disease. It's repulsive. It's a scavenger. It hides away from view.

This father was extremely passive and submissive in his relationship to a remarkedly domineering masochistic-martyristic wife. She was extremely controlling and coercive to all members of the family, but her manipulations were rarely overt. She played on their guilt through her martyristic self-sacrificing tendencies. Both the father and the children were very much in fear of her.

These qualities are reflected throughout the verbal projective responses. She, like the lion, is the "leader" and gets things done in a "quiet" and "unassuming" way. The "respect" that the lion enjoys from the "rest of the animal kingdom" is clearly the fearful subservience she has extracted from the members of her family.

The Mastiff dog, of course, exhibits qualities similar to the lion. The mother, like the Mastiff, is the "protector of the house" and is "respected" (= feared) by everyone. In the (+)3 response the statement that the deer is "the choice food for carnivorous animals" reflects the father's primitive and repressed hostility which he harbors toward the mother. By identifying himself with a carnivorous animal for whom the deer is "choice food," he can vent the rage he feels toward her. In addition, the fantasy probably represents a desire to acquire her strength through primitive incorporative, cannibalistic maneuvers.

The (−)1 response is denial pure and simple. The mother is a person who will turn against the father if he turns against her, and he lives in fear of her retribution. The (−)2 response reveals his true feelings towards the mother, namely, that she is repulsive and he lives in fear of her. The (−)3 response is again a clear statement of the real feelings the father feels about the mother. He sees her as "repulsive" and "a scavenger." The subtle and somewhat surreptitious coercive maneuvers that the mother utilizes are reflected in the comment that the bat "hides away from view."

Another father gave these responses:

(+)1 A tiger. She's ferocious at times. She yells and screams a lot.
(+)2 A horse. She likes horse races. She watches many on TV. She loves all sorts of gambling, but not to excess. She's a $2.00 better.
(+)3 Dogs, any kind of dog. She loves them and I despise them. She'd want to be a dog. (What kind?) A brown Scotch Terrier. I can just associate her with dogs. I don't know why.

(−)1 A cow. It's fat, cumbersome, and odd. She's not like that.

(−)2 A giraffe. It has a high neck and long strides. She doesn't have a high neck and she takes short strides.

(−)3 A snake. It's slimy. She's not.

The 12-year-old daughter of this man was constantly bickering with her mother, whereas he tended to indulge his wife. The mother was not a very strongly maternal person, and the patient turned to her father where she felt she could get greater affection. An hereditary loss of hair was a source of serious concern to the mother, although the father denied that it in any way lessened his attraction for her. When first seen, the family was going through what I would consider an "oedipal crisis," with the father and daughter strongly attracted to one another and denying their attraction with intermittent bickering. The mother was quite jealous over the relationship between the father and daughter and directed much of her jealous rage toward the daughter.

The (+)1 response refers not only to the father's awareness of the mother's overt hostility expressed toward the daughter but, in addition, probably reveals his sensitivity to some of the mother's additional hostilities as well. The (+)3 response reveals the father's inability to overtly express his anger and his lack of physical attraction to his wife. He could only go as far as saying that he "despises" dogs and he somehow associates his wife with a dog. Denial and reaction formation were strong defense mechanisms in this man. In the (−)1 response he reveals his basic feelings about her lack of attractiveness, and there is also suggested his awareness that she is not a very maternal person in that the cow lends itself well to being viewed as a powerful maternal symbol. Although the (−)2 and (−)3 responses could also reveal his lack of attraction to her, they also could be considered to be within the normal range of responses.

Draw-a-Person and Draw-a-Family One father presented this story about the person he drew:

> He is a man who is awakened in the middle of the night to find that his house has burned down, killing his wife and children. His feeling was one of bluntness and unfeeling. Sadness and loss and overwhelming numbness. There is nothing to do.
>
> He always sat after that. He goes back to his work as a blue-collar worker, as a machine operator. He works in a factory where they make furniture legs.

He doesn't think he's ever going to get back on his feet, but he is young and he eventually recovers.

The story reveals clearly the father's wish to remove himself completely from his wife and children, and to start life anew with others. In addition, the father, a successful professional man, depicts himself basically as a person much lower on the social scale.

It took another father ten minutes before he could begin drawing a picture. Each time he placed the pencil on the page he removed it anxiously with the excuse that he did not know what to draw, that he was sure it would not come out right, that he had never drawn pictures before, et cetera. The picture he finally did draw was very lightly and hesitatingly drawn. Although a head was present, facial features were completely absent. The picture reflected the father's basic lack of a sense of identity. The hands and feet had no definite shape and appeared to be evaporating into space. This reflected the father's lack of feeling that he had any capacity to handle his environment and his profound sense of instability. A large crotch defect was present, revealing his basic feelings of masculine inadequacy. The picture, in short, was one drawn by a man with severe feelings of impotency.

It was extremely difficult for this father to tell a story about the figure he had drawn. He stated, "He's just standing there. He's a farmer. He's just finished working. He's surveying everything that he has just accomplished, the work in the fields, he has harvested and reaped everything. He has sown the field and he has reaped the harvest."

This father was indeed a most impotent man, not only in the narrow sexual sense but in life in general. He worked for his own father and was completely under the latter's domination. His picture revealed his sense of impotency and the story he told was a feeble attempt at compensation.

One father drew a picture of a family and told this story:

> The family is on a hike. They pack their lunch. They are at Bear Mountain. Their son, Johnny, hears a yell and a crash. The father has lost his footing and slipped off the edge of the trail. He's lying fifty feet below the trail, holding onto a small tree, with several hundred feet of drop below him. The mother is hysterical.
>
> Little Johnny is very bright and has learned lessons in the Boy Scouts. He lets himself down to his father. He knows he doesn't have the strength to pull his father up. He ties the rope around the father.

He climbs up to the trail, takes the rope with him and ties it around a tree on the trail and then the father is able to climb back onto the trail. The family is overjoyed at the rescue. The parents are very proud of the boy.

The story reveals the father's feelings that his son will be his savior. This father did indeed place great pressures on his son to excel both in sports and in the academic area. He himself was poorly educated, although he did excel in sports. The family was constantly boasting about the child's unusually good performance in both of these areas. The story reveals the father's feelings that his well-being and possibly his very existence depends on the boy's performance.

This father of three boys drew a picture of a man, a woman, and a daughter. He told the following story:

> They are going for a walk in the park. The daughter is attached to the father. The father doesn't see her much, and so he wants her to be near him. The mother is resting because she has too much of the daughter every day so she wants some relief. They are a happy family and this is their time for relaxation. The man looks ugly, but the other two look cute.

The usual response is to draw one's own family. This drawing revealed clearly the father's desire to have a single daughter instead of three sons. This related to conscious feelings that the presence of his sons took away his wife's time from him. Somehow he saw a daughter as less of a threat. But the story also reveals that even if he were to have a daughter he would be neglectful of her, and he sees a wife as being neglectful of her as well. All this is denied at the end when he states that the family is happy. In addition, his basic feelings about himself is that he is ugly, as manifested in his final comment about the male figure.

Another father drew a picture of himself and his wife with one boy standing next to his wife and another boy standing next to him. He told the following story:

> The wife's hand is interlaced with her husband's. The children are side-by-side with the parents. They are happy children. The two people grew up together in life. The man achieved success with his wife growing up with him. They learned the importance of sharing. They learned to live with each other's idiosyncracies. They learned to live with one another.

After the husband graduated from graduate school, he met his wife and wanted to get married. The wife went to work. They struggled and worked together. Their children are happy.

This man's wife decided upon a divorce just prior to my first session with my patient, the older of their two sons. During our first interview he tried to get me to convince his wife not to go through with her divorce plans. The story is replete with references to a cohesiveness and sharing that never existed in the family. This is well confirmed by the fact that the father makes reference in the first sentence of his story to the interlacing of the hands of the two parents. In fact, in the picture he drew this was not the case. The parents were drawn entirely separate, without any hand contact. The mother had decided upon divorce because of the inability and disinclination to tolerate the father's idiosyncracies. The story reflects the father's desire that his wife be more tolerant of them. The happiness of their children is also in the service of denial, because their two sons were indeed most unhappy young boys.

This father drew a picture of a man, a woman, and a little girl. In actuality the family consisted of the parents, a 12-year-old boy (the patient), and two younger daughters. He then told the following story:

> A sociologist took a trip to England. He met a woman there who was a domestic. Although from totally different societies and social levels, and although mentally and emotionally they were far apart, they enjoyed one another.
> He knocked her up and rather than get an abortion, she decided to have the baby. Later they realized it was a mistake. They were delighted that they didn't get married. He earned enough money to care for the child. He left and returned to the United States, and she and the child managed quite well. She married a milkman, had two more kids, and they lived happily ever after.

The drawing itself reveals the father's wishes to remove himself and even abandon his wife and children. He was a cold and isolated man and could only involve himself to a minimal degree with his wife and three children.

This man left graduate school just prior to receiving his Ph.D. in engineering and married when his wife threatened to discontinue the relationship if he did not marry her. He never involved himself significantly in the marriage, and there were long periods during the patient's childhood when he worked seven days a week and came home late at night, resulting in his hardly ever seeing the patient.

This story reveals his basic feelings that he can only attract a woman far below him socially and intellectually. It also reveals his desire to involve himself in a most minimal and distant way. He does not marry the mother of his child, puts the Atlantic Ocean between himself and her, and abandons his child as well. He ends the story by assuaging some of his guilt over such rejection of his child and woman friend by having someone else assume the responsibilities.

Dreams The husband of the woman whose fantasy was described on page 267 reported this repetitious dream:

> I dream that I am submerged under water. I think that I can't breathe and that I'm trying to get to the surface. I then discover that I can breathe under water and I feel much better.

The father was completely dependent upon his own father who owned a large business. As he grew up he always knew that no matter how poorly he did in school he would ultimately end up owning the business. He never applied himself and each time he failed out of prep school or college, his father managed to buy him into another. He had many psychopathic qualities and felt no obligation to spend time with his children, be faithful to his wife, or commit himself in any way to anyone.

The dream reveals his basic life pattern—that he will be magically saved from catastrophe. Actually others would have suffered the consequences of such a life of self-indulgence, but he seems to feel that he has come away unscathed. Others get drowned; he can breathe under water. The dream epitomized his life pattern, especially his relationship to his overprotective father.

This father described the following repetitious dream:

> I was taking a test and I never had time to finish it. I felt pressured and pushed. I kept feeling that I wasn't going to finish.

This is a common repetitious dream of people from homes where the academic pressures have been great. In analyzing this dream with both parents and patients, I have most often found it to reflect a feeling that the people will not be able to live up to the standards of their parents, both in the academic as well as in the nonacademic areas of life. Because so much emotional investment has been directed to the academic realm, it serves as a general symbol for success in life. I have also found the dream to reflect ambivalence on the person's part toward successful achievements in life. Failing the test is not simply the academic test, but the test of life's success as well. Often the parents of such a patient have been ambivalent themselves with regard to their children's successful performance.

This father was a borderline psychotic who was a highly educated and moderately successful professional man. However, his extreme psychopathology prevented him from getting anything but the slightest gratification from his professional and nonprofessional life.

Another father related this dream:

> I was reading one of my competitor's private reports. He walked in and I was ashamed. I put the papers down.

Although this father did not exhibit specific psychopathic trends in the clinical interview, he was a fiercely competitive, materialistic, grandiose, and coercive individual. Although ostensibly ethical in his business dealings, the dream reflects an aspect of his personality that was not apparent in the clinical evaluation, but would certainly be consistent with his character structure. This dream demonstrates how a parent's dream may provide the examiner with added information about character structure—information that may be useful in understanding the child's psychopathology. In this case, some of the child's antisocial behavior could be considered the result of identification with his father's psychopathic traits and the desire to fulfill the unconscious wishes of the parent.

Throughout his life, one father had this repetitious dream:

> I had a gym all to myself. I spent a lot of time there with kids, teaching them to play basketball. I have no problems there when I am in the gym.

The father, although 38 years old, was still very much a child. He was still employed by his parents in their small store, and he was very much under the domination of his wife. He spent much time out of the house coaching young boys in various sports. This activity not only served as a way of removing himself from the domination of his wife, but also provided him with a feeling of authority and competence—which he lacked in his relationship with both his parents and his spouse. Furthermore, sports enabled him to express vicariously much of his pent-up hostility. Last, the dream enables him to engage in childish activities beyond the extent to which he involved himself in reality. It is a dream of an adolescent dreamed by a man who psychologically was still an adolescent.

Concluding Comments

My goal here is to show that the individual, whether mother or father, who is reluctant to give information directly may provide meaningful data with projective tests. However, analyzing such material can be risky. I am certain that many examiners may have come to different conclusions regarding the interpretations I have given to the material presented. In my defense, I might say my interpretations are made on the basis of my direct clinical experiences with the families. Analyzing this material in isolation from such clinical data is extremely risky and is generally a poor idea. But even when one does have clinical information, there is no question that there is still a certain amount of speculation. These drawbacks notwithstanding, I find such projective material useful, especially for the parent who is not comfortable revealing him- or herself in the direct clinical interview.

EVALUATION OF THE CHILD

Introduction

Pediatricians sometimes compare themselves to veterinarians in that both cannot rely on their patient's verbalizations to assist them in making their diagnoses. Carrying this analogy further, the child psychiatrist could be compared to the "veterinary psychiatrist," because neither can learn much by asking his or her patient: "Tell me about your problems." Both must rely on more indirect and nonverbal modalities of communication. This drawback of gaining information from children notwithstanding, there is still much that the therapist can learn.

When psychogenic problems are present, I generally devote

three sessions to the intensive evaluation of the child. And this is the kind of evaluation I will be describing here. If, on the basis of the information I obtain in the initial two-hour evaluation, I conclude that neurologically based difficulties are present, then a longer, extended evaluation is often warranted. I not only have to assess for the presence of the neurologically based problems, but for psychogenic problems as well. And the latter may fall into two categories. The first are those psychogenic problems that are secondary to the neurological impairment. They are derivatives of such impairment and would presumably not be present if the child did not have a basic organic disorder. The second are those that are independent of the neurological disturbance and often result from family problems and/or improper child-rearing practices. Of course, the two categories may overlap and each contribute to the intensification of the other. Obviously, the evaluation for these difficulties is much more complex and generally takes five to six meetings with the child.

It is important for the examiner not to pressure the child to participate in any particular part of the evaluation. The child's defenses *must* be respected. A severely disturbed child may become so upset by projective tests that he or she may close off any further revelations by this route for many months. The child who says that he or she cannot think of a story may be mildly encouraged, but certainly not shamed, cajoled, or otherwise forced into telling one. Children of low intellectual capacity, who mask their feelings of inadequacy, may become quite embarrassed over not being able to answer certain questions. The examiner does well to sense such reactions and not push the child further. It is generally preferable not to gain the information than to do so under duress, because data elicited under stress is not only of questionable validity, but worse, extracting information coercively interferes with the formation of a good therapist-patient relationship. The authors of the Group for the Advancement of Psychiatry report No. 38 aptly state (1957): "A test is never so important that a child should have to undergo severe anxiety or panic because of it."

On occasion, a child may be more comfortable with a mother or father present during the course of the interview. Many examiners object strongly to the parental presence and do everything possible to see the child alone. I, personally, do not have such strong feelings on this subject. If the parents' presence, especially at the beginning, makes a difference between the child's being cooperative and significantly uncooperative, I will generally allow the parent to be present. I cannot deny that I may be entrenching immaturity and dependency here, but I am willing to pay that price for the advantages of having a calmer and more cooperative child. Of course, as the child becomes more comfortable with me, it is generally possible to have the parent leave the room.

The presence of the parent has advantages in its own right. One may observe interactions between the child and the parent that would not otherwise have occurred. In addition, when the parent observes exactly what I am doing, the discussions during the final presentation become more meaningful. Having seen the instruments being administered and having observed the child's responses, the parent is more likely to have conviction for the examiner's conclusions. I am fully aware, however, that the parental presence may have a squelching effect, in that the child may not be as free to reveal certain material (both consciously and unconsciously) when the parent is there.

All these considerations result in my taking the flexible approach to the question of parental observation. In practice, most often children are comfortable enough to proceed without the parents being present. The reader who may be wondering at this point about how the child's confidentiality affects my decision as to whether or not the parents should be in the room, should appreciate that I have less respect for the role of confidentiality in child therapy than do most therapists. In Chapter Seven I will discuss this issue in much greater detail.

It is important for the examiner to appreciate that the purpose of the extended evaluation is more than simply data collection. An equally important, if not more important, goal is to lay the foundation for a good therapeutic relationship. This is not likely to be accomplished in one or two pressured interviews. The more relaxed the circumstances, the greater the likelihood the therapist will be able to engage the child meaningfully.

Direct Verbal Inquiry with the Child

When engaging children in direct verbal discussion, it is important for the examiner to appreciate certain basic facts about interviewing techniques with children. As mentioned already, children most often do not have insight into the fact that they have "problems" and the examiner is well advised not to attempt to get them to develop such insight. In fact, most children (especially younger ones) are not cognitively capable of making the kinds of linkages and associations that are necessary for an analytic type of inquiry (whether it be diagnostic or therapeutic). Accordingly, the examiner should not be looking for any kind of testimonial in this area. Furthermore, what we call "problems" are not generally viewed as such by children. To them the problem is often the people who are "on their backs" trying to get them to do things they don't want to. But even those children who clearly have differentiated the behavioral patterns which their parents consider pathological from those which their parents deem acceptable and desirable, are not likely to be motivated to direct themselves to alleviating the "unhealthy traits."

I will often start the interview with the traditional open-ended question: "So what's doing with you?" or "So what would you like to talk about?" On occasion (I would say about 5% of the time) the child will have something on his or her mind to discuss. But most often (whether it be in this evaluative session or in the therapeutic session), the child has nothing particular to tell me about. Examiners who feel frustrated about this might consider going into another field. This is the way our patients are, and it behooves us to work around this rather than to forcibly extract a conversation on the child's problems.

In Chapter Three I mentioned that abstractions and conceptualizations are of far less therapeutic value than concrete examples. This principle is especially important in the interview with the child. Questions beginning with "why" are far less valuable than questions beginning with "when, where, what, or how." Of course, as therapists we are interested in knowing *why*, but we are less likely to learn the reasons *why* from *why* questions than we are from questions utilizing other interrogatory words. For example, to ask a child why he or she misbehaves in school is waste of time and words. To ask the same child a series of questions about when, where, with whom, and under what circumstances there is trouble in school is more likely to provide useful data. Even here, because of the child's defensiveness, one may not get reasonable answers because the questions are related to the child's "problems"—a touchy subject if there ever was one. A preferable way to lead into a revelation about academic problems, for example, is to ask very specific concrete questions such as "What grade are you in?"

"What's your teacher's name?" "How many children in your class?" "How many boys, how many girls?" "Who is the smartest kid in the class?" "What do you like about him(her)?" "What don't you like about him(her)?" "Who is the dumbest student?" "Do you like him(her)?" These questions may then ultimately result in the child's talking about his or her own attitude toward academics, and this may be one of the presenting problems. Other questions that might lead into a discussion of the child's academic problems are: "What subject do you like most in school?" "What subject do you hate the most?" "What subjects are you best at?" "What subjects are you worst at?"

In order to discuss behavioral problems one might lead into the issue with questions such as: "Who are the kids in your class who get into trouble?" "What kinds of things do they do?" "What does the teacher do when they get into trouble?" The reader will note that I am talking here about *other* parties, not the patient. "Does the teacher yell at them?" "What does the teacher say to them when they get into trouble?" "What do the other kids feel about those troublemakers?" "What kinds of punishment do they get?" "Who's the best person in the class in conduct?" "Do you like him(her)?" From this point one might say, "*All* kids get into trouble once in a while in class, what kinds of things do *you* do that get *you* into trouble?" By stating first that "all" children get into trouble, at times, it becomes easier for the child to describe the situations when he or she has behavioral difficulties. The reader will note also that I do not ask yes-no questions. These are most often of little value because, after one has received an answer, one does not know if it is really valid. Questions requiring specific answers are much more likely to be useful.

In order to learn more about peer difficulties, one again might start off with specific, nonthreatening questions, for example: "Tell me the names of some of the kids who live in your neighborhood?" "Who are the ones you spend the most time with?" "Who is your best friend?" "What is it about that person that makes you like him(her) so much?" "What kinds of things do you like doing most with him(her)?" "What kinds of things do you *not* like doing with him(her)?" "Of all the kids in the neighborhood which one do you dislike or hate the most?" "What is there about that person that makes you dislike or hate him(her) so much?" "What do you think are the things that a child can do that will turn off other kids?" For the child who is teased and/or scapegoated, one might ask what are the specific things other children say to him or her when taunting is occurring. These children might also be asked what things their parents and siblings tell them they do that get them into trouble. One might also talk here about the various activities the child involves him- or herself in and, if there are difficulties, the details regarding why.

With regard to pathological behavior in the home, again, the examiner does well to follow the aforementioned principles. Some good lead-in questions: "What do you like doing most with your mother(father)?" "Of all things you like doing in the house, what things are the most fun?" "What are the things you don't like doing with your mother(father), the things that are no fun at all?" "All kids get scolded sometimes. What kinds of things do your parents scold you over?" "All kids get punished sometimes. What kinds of things are you punished for?" "Who punishes you?" "What kinds of punishments does your mother(father) give you?" "How long do they last?" "Are these fair punishments?" "I want you to tell me the best things you can about your mother?" "Now tell me the worst things about your mother?" "Now I want you to tell me the best things you can about your father?" "Now tell me the worst things about your father?" "What's the best thing that ever happened to you in your whole life?" "What's the worst thing that ever happened to you in your whole life?"

In my discussion of the interview with the mother, I mentioned "grandma's criteria" for assessing maternal and paternal capacity. One can question the child, as well, to get information about parental capacity. This can be done by going through the events of the day, from the time the child gets up in the morning until the time he or she goes to sleep at night. In association with each event, one tries to find about which parent is involved and the nature of the involvement. For example, one might ask which parent gets the child up in the morning and whether there are difficulties, and continue with such questioning about the whole course of the day. Particular emphasis should be given to those times when both parents are available. Most often, this is during the evening. In the discussion one could ask about homework—who helps with the homework, who has the most patience, and whether there is any conflict and fighting over it. The bedtime scene, also, can provide useful informaton about parenting capacity. One should find out about who reads the child bedtime stories and how much patience each parent has regarding reading to the children. Also, one can learn about cuddling. Rather than saying, "Does your mother(father) like to cuddle?" one does better to ask, "Is your mother(father) the kind of person who likes to cuddle?" By using the latter form, there is the implication that there are two kinds of mothers(fathers): cuddlers and noncuddlers, that neither is better than the other, and that the examiner is just trying to find out in which category the child's mother(father) is. When questions are posed in a way that there is minimal disparagement implied of any of the involved parties, the examiner is more likely to get an honest answer.

The examiner must be aware that children generally have weak egos and will utilize a variety of maneuvers to avoid direct confrontation with their deficits. They commonly utilize such phrases as "I don't know." Accordingly, the examiner should pose questions that circumvent embarrassing confrontations. To say to a child, "Tell me about the things you're scared of?" or "What are the things that frighten you?" is an injudicious way of finding out about a child's fears. A preferable way of getting information in this area is to say: "Most children have some things that scare them once in a while. What things scare *you*?" By presenting fears as a normal response, the child is more likely to divulge what his(hers) are. Also, by starting off with the positive, easily admitted aspects of an issue, it is often easier to get into the embarrassing opposite. For example, one might ask, "What are the things about yourself that you are most proud of?" I will then go into a detailed inquiry of the sources of the child's pride. With ego enhancement, then, as a buffer one is in a better position to ask the question: "Everybody has times when they do, say, or think things they're ashamed of. I'd like to hear one thing that you're ashamed of." Again, the question is so posed that shame is presented as a normal phenomenon and all I'm asking of the child is to mention one thing that has caused him or her shame.

Some children in treatment are particularly fearful of expressing their feelings. On occasion, feelings are relegated to the unconscious, and questions about them prove futile. However, there are some children who can verbalize their feelings but are uncomfortable doing so. The worst way to elicit his or her feelings from a repressed child is to ask the question: "How do you feel about that?" or "How does that make you feel?" One could ask the question, but should not be surprised if the repressed child does not answer. In such cases, the examiner might say, "You must have felt really sad when your parents told you they were going to split up." "You must have *really* felt lonely when the children didn't want to play with you." Even then one might get the answer: "It doesn't bother me!" One might respond then with, "Well, I find that hard to believe. I believe that you *do* have feelings about it but that you're not comfortable talking about it now. I hope the time will come soon when you'll feel more comfortable talking about these things."

There are occasions, however, when the aforementioned kinds of catalytic questions do serve well to precipitate an emotional response on the part of the child. They serve to fan and enlarge sparks of feelings that were only dimly appreciated by the child. Another way of facilitating the expression of such feelings is to precede them with comments that make them socially acceptable: "Most kids get very upset when they learn that their parents are going to get a divorce. What were the kinds of feelings *you* had?"

A discussion of the child's interests and hobbies can be very useful. Sometimes, the examiner does best to start the interview with this topic, because it is the least threatening. At other times, it may be useful as a way of decompressing a situation and diverting a child from a particularly difficult area of inquiry. One might ask very simply: "What are your hobbies?" or "What are your favorite games?" or "What do you like doing after school?" "What's your favorite sport?" These can serve as a point of departure for a discussion in which the therapist discusses his or her own knowledge of this area. Such discussion can serve to entrench the therapist-patient relationship. Sometimes the discussion may reveal pathological trends. One boy may say that his hobby is dinosaurs. However, the discussion of dinosaurs reveals that he has such a massive preoccupation with the subject that he spends little time on anything else. When asked about his favorite TV program, one child responded, "Divorce Court." A psychotic child's favorite hobby may be watching the phonograph player's turntable revolve.

I have already mentioned that I routinely give every child at the time of the first session, whether it be for a consultation or treatment, a copy of my *Stories About the Real World*, Volume I (1972a). As mentioned, the issues raised in this book are likely to be pertinent to most children's therapy. Sometime during the first evaluative session I will ask the child if he or she has read the book. If the answer is affirmative (the case for most children), I will inquire about which stories the child liked the most and which the least. I attempt to use the book as a point of departure for further inquiry. If the child is vague or nonrevealing, I may ask about a particular story that I suspect is likely to be most relevant to the child. For example, I might ask the child to tell me what he or she remembers of *Jerry and the Bullies*, a story that deals with self-assertion, the use of profanity, and fighting back. I might ask a shy child about *Helen, The Girl Who Wouldn't Try*, or the child who lies might be asked about the story, *The Hundred-Dollar Lie.*

Three Wishes

Whereas I generally ask adults for five wishes, I usually ask children for only three. My main reason for this is that I have found this question to be less useful for children than for adults. More often, children provide somewhat stereotyped responses that are age appropriate and not particularly valuable sources of information. The unusual or idiosyncratic response may, however, provide useful information. A common response a child gives is "a million dollars" or "all the money in the world." Generally, a list of toys and other material objects is provided, a response that I consider to be in the normal range. Another normal response, that also serves the purposes of resistance, is "all the wishes I wanted." In response I will generally advise the child that this answer is not acceptable and that the child must select specific things that he or she would want to happen or have.

Fred, an eight-year-old boy, gave as his first wish, "Love from everybody." The response implies that the patient felt deprived of affection and wished that everyone in the world would give him love in order to compensate for the deprivations that he suffered at home. His second response was, "Peace all over the world." I considered this response to reflect Fred's desire that there be no anger, either within himself or within everybody else. The response served to squelch or repress all the resentment that existed both within Fred and his parents. His third response: "Respect to everybody." This was clearly a unique response. It again related to his desire to suppress the hostility he felt toward his parents.

Sally, a nine-year-old girl, presented with symptoms of immaturity and dependency. Her mother worked full-time and left her to the care of a succession of maids. The patient was very involved with her pets with which she spent significant time when she was alone. Her first wish: "Pets, all the different kinds of pets in the world, except insects." Her second wish: "Money to buy things for the pets, birdfeed, peanuts for the elephants, bananas for the monkeys." I considered the first and second responses to represent the patient's strong identification with lower animals. By gratifying their needs, she was vicariously gratifying her own. By projecting herself into the animals she fed, she could gratify vicariously her own dependency needs. She was also demonstrating at the same time how inferiors and underlings should be treated. Her third response: "A bird, because it can fly anywhere it wants." I considered this response to reflect her desire to remove herself from her home environment because it was not particularly gratifying.

A ten-year-old girl presented with symptoms of depression, stuttering, poor relationships with peers and generalized tension. Her mother was extremely punitive and her father passively permitted the mother's sadistic behavior. Her first wish: "To have magical powers to make someone exactly like me. We'd then go and live in a big mansion in Florida." I considered the first wish to reveal her desire to have a "clone," someone just like herself. She would then have a playmate to compensate for the deprivation she suffered in her household. The playmate, of course, would be kind to her, unlike her mother. She would also remove herself from the home and go to Florida which represented, I believe, a climate of emotional warmth, ease, and relaxation. Her second wish: "I'd have a farm of horses." Although this might be a normal response, in this girl's situation I suspected that it related to her desire to be in the company of animals because her experiences with human beings had been so difficult. Her third wish: "To grow up fast and get married to a man who would love me a lot and take good care of me." Considering this child's background, the meaning of the wish is obvious. It is another reflection of the patient's general unhappiness in her home situation. Although ten, she was preoccupied with sexual fantasies involving teenage dating, seductivity, and kissing. This was partially derived from her mother who, in addition to her hostility, was a seductive woman, preoccupied with sex, but was basically a sexually inhibited person.

The mother of a nine-year-old boy had a schizoid personality and was not able to give him very much affection and attention. His father, a businessman, was extremely materialistic and was constantly boasting about the monetary values of his cars, boat, homes, et cetera. The patient's presenting symptoms were antisocial acting out in the classroom and temper tantrums at home. His first wish: "Never break anything like I do when I have a temper tantrum." I considered this wish to reveal some guilt and remorse over the anger he was exhibiting. In a sense, it was a good therapeutic sign in that the child wanted to do something to reduce this symptom. His second wish: "Every year I'd buy all the cars I like and I'd have enough money to do it." This wish, although it might be age appropriate in our society, had heavy loading from the family because of his father's exhibitionistic consumption of material things. He was clearly modeling himself after his father. His third wish: "Be a teacher at the Abraham Lincoln School because they give good lunches there." I considered this response to reflect this boy's emotional deprivation. Although the family was quite wealthy, he was significantly deprived of affection. Although I did not ask him for a fourth wish, the patient spontaneously gave me one: "Have a gigantic garage for thousands and thousands of cars." Although his second wish revealed some cravings for consumption and exhibition of material goods, the fourth wish carries this to an absurd extreme—not surprising for a child with such a father. (And his mother had no complaints about the father's materialism. In fact, she enjoyed the same indulgences.)

First Memory

A child's first memory is generally a less valuable source of information than that of adults. One might argue that the child's first memory is more likely to be a useful source of information because the time gap between the event and the time the question is posed is much shorter than the time lag for the adults. When adults are asked this question, they are reaching back into the distant past and are selecting the event from a much larger storehouse of recollections, and thus it usually has a much greater psychological significance. One cannot label a child immature or regressed if he or she remembers being in a crib, being fed a meal, or being taken care of in bed when sick. As is true in all projective information, one must take care to differentiate the age-appropriate from the idiosyncratic and atypical.

A very bright 11-year-old boy had great difficulties in his relationships with his parents. His mother was an extremely cold, critical, coercive, and controlling individual. His father did not protect the boy adequately from his mother's maltreatment of him. When asked for his first memory, the patient responded: "I was being put into a crib a few minutes after I was born." I believe that the patient was being honest with me; however, I also believe that the fantasy had a reality for him because it was so deeply entrenched in his psychic structure and so well lent itself to symbolizing his life situation with his mother. It reflected well his feelings of having been separated from his mother a few minutes after he was born and placed where he could not enjoy any contact with her.

A ten-year-old girl's mother was self-centered, materialistic, and exhibitionistic. Her father was quite rich and prided himself in how much he could indulge his wife. This child was essentially raised by a series of caretakers. The parents traveled extensively, to various parts of the world, and on occasion, brought the patient with them. At such times, her care was entrusted to nursemaids and other caretakers. This was the response she gave to the first memory question: "I was 14 months old. It was London. I didn't want to take naps. I stayed in my crib. I screamed. The maid said, 'Let her cry.' I tried to climb out of the crib, but I didn't make it. Somebody came and took me out. I was mad at my mother for making me take a nap. I ran and I jumped up and down on her bed. She wasn't there." The response reveals the patient's feelings of having been abandoned by her mother. Her cries for contact with her remain unanswered. Even the maid, under whose care the rejecting mother left her, does not respond to her cries for warmth and affection. "Someone" (not her mother) does finally remove her from her imprisonment. She then runs to her mother's empty bed. The implication of this is that she hopes to gain some affection from her mother there. However, her mother is not there and she responds angrily by jumping up and down on her mother's bed. Not being able to express her hostility to her mother directly, she vents it on her mother's bed.

A nine-year-old girl was brought to treatment because of poor motivation in school and difficulty in her relationships with friends. Her mother was rejecting of the patient and left her care to a housekeeper, Anna. The mother also treated Anna somewhat shabbily. This was the response she gave to the first memory question: "I was three years old. We had a Portuguese maid. Her name was Anna. She's still with us. I hate hot dogs and I've always hated hot dogs. Anna made them when my mother didn't want them. My mother didn't speak up to Anna and tell her not to make them. So Anna gave me the hot dogs and I didn't like eating them." First, the realities were that Anna would not have defied the mother, so hostile and strong was the mother and so weak and passive was

Anna. The memory, probably a distortion, served to split the patient's mother into a "good mother" and a "bad mother." Anna, here, is made the "bad mother." She forcefeeds the patient hot dogs (a food the patient doesn't like) in spite of the mother's objections. Implied in the mother's objections is the notion that her mother did not want to give her the undesirable food. The patient thereby suppresses hostility felt toward the mother for her rejection and coercion of her and puts the blame on Anna. It is safer to blame Anna because Anna is not as likely to retaliate.

An eight-year-old boy suffered with a neurologically based learning disability, associated with gross and fine motor coordination problems. He was a disappointment to his mother who had high academic aspirations for him. And he was a disappointment to his father who had hoped that his only son would be more outgoing and athletic. One of the ways he handled the home difficulties was to regress. This is the response he gave to the first memory question: "I was a little boy. I was in the bathtub. I was taking a bath. Someone was cleaning me with soap." Although one might argue that the memory has regressive, "return-to-the-womb" fantasies, as symbolized by emerging in water (possibly symbolic of amniotic fluid), I am dubious about this explanation. More important, I believe is the emphasis on the cleansing process. I believe that the fantasy revealed the patient's view of himself as dirty and as being cleaned symbolized his desire to cleanse himself of the dirty feelings about himself derived from his parents' frequent criticism of him.

This 12-year-old boy's parents both had minimal involvement with him. His father was a hard-driving businessman, a workaholic, who was often absent from the home because of long business trips. His mother was a frustrated, angry, embittered woman who ranged from tolerance of the patient to utilization of him as a scapegoat. This was the first memory he provided: "I was in kindergarten. The school nun was there. The milk she gave me was frozen and I was scared to tell her that the milk was no good. The other kids told her for me. I was afraid that if I bothered her, she would yell at me." The fantasy needs little analysis. The frozen milk is a clear statement of the patient's view of his mother as unmaternal. In addition, he fears complaining about her lack of affection because he might then be traumatized in retaliation and thereby add to the difficulties he was already suffering in association with his emotional deprivation.

A 14-year-old girl was referred because of severe outbursts of rage. She described this event occurring when she was five:

> My mother went down a one-way street in a car. She went the wrong way. A policeman stopped her. I didn't like police at that time. I thought they were mean. I was scared of them. I cried a lot and said, "Don't hurt my mother." I was screaming and crying and yelling. It got him so frustrated that he said, "The heck with it," and he got rid of us. And he didn't give us a ticket.

The patient's mother was a woman who felt overwhelmed by the world and was often confused about where she was heading and what her future would be. One manifestation of this was her poor sense of direction, which prevented her from adequately driving distances more than a few miles from her home. The patient's recalling of her mother going down a one-way street is a statement of her view of her mother as a woman who doesn't know which way she is going in life. The patient's recollection of avoiding the consequences of her behavior by having a violent outburst of rage epitomizes her life pattern. The patient's temper outbursts did indeed enable her to avoid the consequences of her unacceptable behavior. Early in life she had learned that if she were to rant and rave long enough, she would get her way. In this case the policeman, the symbol of the punitive authority, is dissuaded by her tantrums from administering appropriate punishment.

Free Picture

As mentioned in the initial two-hour evaluation, I generally provide the patient with a blank piece of drawing paper and crayons and request that he or she draw a picture and then tell me a story about it. In the intensive evaluation, as well, I will often utilize this technique once or twice more. It is one of the standards in child therapy that deserves its good reputation. Drawing is something that most children enjoy and telling a story about a picture is a common childhood activity. Again, one must differentiate between age-appropriate, stereotyped pictures and stories and those that are atypical. As mentioned, I do not accept designs, which often are used as a way of resisting revelation of unconscious fantasies. In addition, if a boy draws a picture of rockets, airplanes, spaceships, and tanks in battle, one learns very little. It is difficult, if not impossible, to differentiate between the normal utilization of such fantasies for socially acceptable release of hostility and the pathological use of these vehicles for such release. I do not "reject" such stories but merely recognize that they are of little psychological significance in most cases and then go on to other instruments. I present here some examples of the way in which these pictures and their attendant stories provide valuable information about a child's underlying psychodynamics.

This ten-year-old boy's parents were involved in vicious custody litigation. He was continually being used as a weapon and spy by each of his parents, especially his father. Furthermore, he recognized that his mother was being seriously traumatized by his father. The boy drew a bird whom he described as "a blue and red-footed flying dragonbird." This is the story he told about the bird he drew:

> He became famous because he saved tons of birds from being shot by arrows and being eaten at the king's banquet. He flew where the bow and arrows were being made and the trees were chopped down for firewood for roasting the birds. He grabbed the trees and logs with his claws and went into a dive and dropped them (the trees) on the men and their tools. He dropped the logs in a circle and set fire to them. He broke the arrows with his claws and burned the bows and arrows up. He then became king of the birds.

I considered the king in the story to represent the boy's father and the flock of birds his mother. Birds are a common symbol for females because of their beauty and grace. The hero of the story, the "blue and red-footed flying dragonbird," represents the patient himself. He prevents the king's men from making weapons to kill the "tons of birds." By destroying the arrows and bows and burning up the king's men, he puts a cessation to all hostilities, especially the ability of his father to traumatize his mother. In addition, he protects himself from the traumatization that he himself suffered as a bystander and intermediary in the parental warfare.

This eight-year-old girl was the oldest of three children. The parents were highly intellectualized professional people whose involvement in their academic pursuits was so extensive that the children were significantly neglected. The father, especially, was away from the home for long periods in association with his professional lectures and academic pursuits. The mother, although more involved with the children, was quite ambivalent in her relationship with them. At times she would reach out and at other times she would withdraw. The patient dealt with this situation by passive-aggressive maneuvers. She was obstructionistic and at times tantalizing. When her mother would reach out to her, she would gain sadistic gratification from rejecting her.

The patient drew a picture of a boat in the ocean. Above the boat is a bright yellow sun and beneath the boat are three fishes. A clown is in the boat, reaching toward the fishes below the surface. When asked to tell a story about the picture, she related the following: "The clown is trying to catch the fishes with his hands. But he can't. The sun is shining." When I asked her to relate more, she stated that that was the whole story.

I considered the three fish to symbolize the patient and her siblings. I considered the boat to represent her mother. The boat, like the womb, holds within it human life and lends itself well, therefore, to symbolizing the mother. She views her mother as enjoying the sunshine, warmth, and affection. However, she views herself and her siblings as being below the surface of the water, under the boat, where the sunshine does not reach. Because fishes cannot generally get into boats, the picture further reflects her feelings of separation from her mother. The story about the clown reaching out for the fish, but their eluding him, is a reenactment of what actually went on in her relationship with her mother (the clown being depicted as a male notwithstanding). She did make a fool out of her mother by her elusive behavior, thus the symbolization of her mother as a clown. This game with the mother provided the patient with an outlet for the hostility she felt toward her because of the mother's ambivalence and frequent rejection.

A six-year-old boy was referred because of disruptive behavior in the classroom and hostile acting out. He stole, lied, and did dangerous things to his classmates such as throwing scissors and knives at them. His mother was an extremely petulant, irritable, fault-finding individual. Both he, his sister, and his father could do no right. She was basically a miserable, bitter, unhappy woman, who made the lives of those around her equally unhappy. The boy drew a picture of a whale and then told the following story about it:

> The whale is swimming under the water. He's trying to catch a school of fish. He eats all of them. There was a boat above him, and it was connected to the bottom of the ocean to a plug on a long chain. He electrocuted himself because of the plug under the water. He put his mouth on it, and he got electrocuted, and he got pulled into the

fishing boat. They cut him up, cleaned him out, put him in a package, and sent the pieces to the market. Then people bought him and ate him.

I considered the whale to represent the patient himself and his swimming under water, his feelings of being submerged and overwhelmed by the environment. As was true of the previous example, the boat symbolizes the patient's mother and the long chain, her umbilical cord. Because of his significant deprivation of affection, he has an inordinate appetite and eats up a whole school of fish. Then he attempts to form contact with his mother by eating the end of her umbilical cord (the plug at the bottom of the ocean). When he bites it, in order to form a bond between himself and his mother, he is electrocuted. This is a dramatic statement of his feelings that attempts to gain dependent gratification from his mother can be lethal. He is not only electrocuted when he tries to reestablish a bond between his mother and himself but is also cut up into little pieces and eaten by others. This represents his view of his mother as being murderous and may also be a statement of his feelings that he might ultimately prove of some value to someone, that is, others might gain nourishment from his dead body.

Another patient's father had an inordinate need to be loved by the world and devoted just about every waking minute to that end. He was a lawyer by profession but spent practically every evening furthering his political career. On weekends, as well, he was most often away from the home. And even when at home, he was ever available to friends and neighbors to help them do repairs on their houses, take their children to emergency rooms, listen for hours to their problems, and so on. He failed to appreciate, however, that his family was paying a heavy price for his ostensibly benevolent ego trips. The patient's mother was extremely angry over these difficulties in her marital relationship. Rather than express resentment to her husband, she directed her hostility to her daughter, whom she used as a scapegoat. When the patient was asked to draw a picture, she drew a house. On the window sill was a flower box in which there were yellow flowers. Overhead was a bright blue sky with the sun and clouds. The grass was green and the house quite pretty, with colored curtains. This is the story she told.

They're flowers on a lady's window sill. They're all yellow. They're fake. They couldn't stay yellow that long because the woman forgot to water them. They say goodbye and they jump out of the window and they crack their heads. The lady says goodbye to the house and she jumps out of the window and lands on the flowers and smells like flowers. The lady gets married because someone liked the smell of her flowers.

If one were to look at the picture, it would appear to be a normal, healthy one for a seven-and-a-half-year-old girl. The sun is shining, the grass is growing, the sky is blue, the house is pretty, and all appears right with the world. However, the story reveals something quite different. I considered the flowers to represent the patient. Their being fake reveals her basic feelings of lifelessness and her need to present a façade of happiness. The flowers are deprived of life-giving qualities by the woman who does not water them, that is, her mother is not providing her with enough affection, and therefore she feels somewhat dead. She then abandons this rejecting home (the flowers say good-bye and jump out of the window), but sees herself as being traumatized upon leaving her house (they crack their heads). However, her mother joins her and the fragrance that the mother thereby derives from the flowers serves to attract a suitable husband.

Although the story involves a girl and her mother, no mention is made of the father which, of course, is an accurate reflection of the fatherless home she was basically growing up in. The story reflects her desire that her mother attract another man and the patient plays an active role in the luring process. The picture itself (as is often the case) does not enable one to come to specific conclusions about the child's psychodynamics. It is only when one hears the related story that one is able to appreciate the picture's true significance. When one looks at the picture then, one is likely to conclude that it is a statement of reaction formation and denial by this depressed, unhappy girl.

This ten-year-old boy entered treatment because of academic underachievement, poor peer relationships, and behavior problems in school. He was taunted by other children because of his oddball behavior: silliness, inappropriate laughter, and "saying the wrong thing at the wrong time." His father, a car salesman, was very involved in his business and gave little time to the boy. He therefore had little, if any, paternal model. His mother was a self-centered woman whose primary sources of gratification were shopping, playing golf, and spending time at her hairdresser. The free picture he drew was one of a fairly ugly looking creature standing in the middle of a blank page. This is the story he told:

> It's Frankenstein. He's lonely and he hardly does anything but just stands there. He has no friends. He just stays at home. Everything he tries to do would just scare people, so he never had any friends. He looked like he was going to hurt people, but he really didn't want to. He didn't care and so he stayed at home.

The description reflects clearly the patient's feelings about himself. He considered himself ugly. He was teased by friends and handled their taunts by withdrawal. The patient tended to deny his own participation in his alienation, especially his hostility toward others. The statement, "He looked like he was going to hurt people, but he really didn't want to" reflects the basic anger he felt and his inability to express it directly. And the statement: "He didn't care" is a reflection of the denial mechanisms which the patient utilized extensively.

Draw-a-Person and Draw-a-Family

I generally confine the Draw-a-Person and Draw-a-Family tests to the initial two-hour evaluation. On occasion, I will administer the instruments again during the course of the extended evaluation. The examples presented here were derived from that phase.

This seven-year-old boy's mother was extremely rejecting. She openly admitted that she harbored hostility toward all men, including her husband and two sons. She related this to the maltreatment she had received from her father during her childhood. Her son entered treatment because of hostility toward her and acting out in school. The boy drew a picture of a little girl picking flowers. When asked to tell a story, he stated, "She's picking flowers. She's smiling. She wants to find a butterfly." The butterfly, like the bird, lends itself well to symbolizing a female. It is pretty and graceful. In the picture there is no butterfly. The little girl wants to find a butterfly. There is nothing more to say about this picture and the story. The patient's few words say it all.

This nine-year-old girl came to treatment because of low academic curiosity and motivation in spite of high intelligence. She was the youngest of three children, having two teenage brothers. The older siblings were excellent students whom the mother referred to as "superstars." The patient felt that she could never live up to her parents' expectations of her and psychologically had "dropped out" of the academic race. This is the story she told about the person she drew:

> This little girl lived with her mother and father. She had two brothers and two sisters. One day she went out for a walk. She saw a hurt baby rabbit. She bought it to a vet. It had a broken leg and he fixed it, and she brought it back home, and she let it go where she had found it.

On occasion the story in the Draw-a-Person test provides information about the patient's relationship with the therapist and his or her expectations from treatment. In this story the patient revealed her basic feeling of being traumatized and she looks upon the therapist (the vet) to cure her. However, he does so in such a way that her only participation is that of passive compliance. She does not actively participate in her own cure. In addition, the story reveals her basic feeling that she is not a member of the household and that even after therapy she would still be an outsider.

On occasion, during the course of the evaluation, I will provide the patient with a responding story if I am clear about the meaning of the patient's story and if I believe that a responding story might be useful at that point. I am especially likely to do this if the story reveals the patient's unrealistic expectations from treatment, as was the case here. This is one of the ways in which I introduce children to the mutual storytelling technique, which I will discuss in Chapter Eight. In this case I told a story about a sick rabbit who was required to do various exercises and take a variety of medicines in order to assist the vet in the healing of his broken leg. When he was lax in his following through the doctor's recommendations, the leg did not heal well; when he was assiduous in his application of the treatment, the leg healed more rapidly.

This eight-and-a-half-year-old boy entered treatment because of timidity, exaggerated response to the teasing of his classmates, excessive weight, and frequent utilization of psychosomatic complaints to avoid stressful situations. This is the story he told about the person he had drawn:

> He's a 12-year-old boy. He's working with his chemistry set. He wants to make a smoke bomb with his friend. He's going to throw

the smoke bomb up in the air in front of somebody and then run away. He's going to blindfold the person he threw the smoke bomb at. He's a man and he's 20 years old. Then he's going to take the man to his own house and hypnotize him and make him tell him what the secrets are that he knows. He then is going to let the man go away. (Therapist: "What secrets is he going to learn from the man?") That the man is going to go to the 12-year-old boy's house and try to find out information from the boy—information about his club and what he's going to do the next day. And if the 12-year-old boy is going to do something to the man.

The story reveals clearly the patient's marked fear of the therapeutic inquiry. The 20-year-old boy represents the therapist and, of course, the 12-year-old boy, the patient himself. In order to avoid the therapeutic inquiry, he is going to throw smoke screens around the therapist, blindfold him, then hypnotize him, and do to the therapist what he anticipates the therapist is going to do to him, namely, force him to reveal his inner secrets. The patient's response to the therapist's question regarding what secrets the boy will learn lends confirmation to this explanation: he anticipates that the therapist will come into the boy's house, that is, enter into his psyche and find out information about his clubs, his movements, and his whereabouts. The patient was indeed a timid and inhibited boy who was extremely fearful of revealing himself. The story confirmed well the clinical situation.

An 11-and-a-half-year-old girl came to treatment because of antisocial behavior both at home and at school. She was very resistant to the idea of coming for treatment, told this to her family, but not to the therapist. This is the story that she told about the family she drew:

> This family was very happy. They had one dog, but he didn't get his picture taken. He wanted to be in the picture, but the family wouldn't let him be in it.
> The next-door neighbors, they were snooping around trying to find out why the family wouldn't let the dog have his picture taken. They found out that the dog kept jumping on the cameraman all the time. They had to shut the dog up in a closet so that he couldn't get on the cameraman.
> The reason the dog was always jumping on the cameraman is because the dog thinks that every time the cameraman would take a picture, a gun would come out of the camera and kill the family.

Finally one day the neighbors told the family why the dog was doing that—because he thought the cameraman had a gun. The family laughed and said, "There's nothing. There is no gun."

But then the cameraman did shoot the family. He was a robber and he wanted jewelry. Then the neighbors called the police and the police put him in jail and gave the dog a medal for capturing the cameraman.

The dog, of course, represents the patient. In the beginning of the story the dog's failure to get his picture taken reflects early treatment anxieties in which the patient does not want to be seen by the eye of the camera, that is, by the therapist. Depicting herself as a dog also reflects her feelings of low self-esteem. She sees herself as being rejected by the family and "locked in a closet." The cameraman's murder of the family represents her own hostility toward her family members and the cameraman is used as the perpetrator of the crime, thereby assuaging her own guilt over the act. The dog has little remorse over their demise. By having the camerman jailed she further assuages the guilt she feels over her hostility. Providing the dog with a prize serves further to reinforce suppression of hostilities.

This seven-year-old boy's mother was an extremely harsh and critical individual. She utilized biting sarcasm as a primary mode of interacting, expecially with men. She was a highly intelligent woman, but was clearly envious of male prerogatives in society. The patient's younger brother reacted to the mother's anger by withdrawal and inhibition in the expression of his anger. My patient reacted with antisocial behavior, directed both at his mother, father, and teachers. The picture he drew consisted of a father and two sons. This is the story he told:

> The mother lived and died. The stepmother loved the children dearly and very well. And they lived happily ever after. The end.

The meaning of the story is clear. The mother is removed as a statement of the patient's desire to obliterate her from his life. The story reflects his wish that she be replaced by a loving and more benevolent stepmother.

This nine-year-old boy's mother was an extremely angry, rigid, condescending, and arrogant individual. She was mercilessly critical of the patient who, although very bright, entered treatment because of academic underachievement. He was an only child. The family of three that he drew was clearly grotesque. All of the heads seemed to be off-center and the eyes were odd-shaped, as were many of the other bodily features. This is the story the patient told:

> The kid has a funny neck. It's off-center (laughter). They all look funny and messy. All of their necks are in the wrong place. Their necks come off their shoulders.
> This is the Kook family. The little boy is Johnny Kook. The mother is Lady Kook. The father is Chris Kook; no, him name is Bill Kook. (The patient's father's name was Chris.)
> Lady Kook is making breakfast for her son. He trampled down the stairs. He broke his skull and had a concussion. That puts him out of the story. Lady Kook fainted and went to the hospital 'till the end of the story. Bill Kook worried. He went to the hospital and stayed with them 'till they both came out of the hospital.

The story reveals the patient's concept of his family as "kooky" or atypical and disturbed. The off-center heads and necks also reveal this. He sees himself as damaged in the head and his mother as one who psychologically removes herself by the loss of conscious awareness of her environment. He sees his father as the only stable person in the family, who comes to the rescue of both himself and his mother.

Verbal Projective Questions

The verbal projective questions described in the initial two-hour evaluation can be elaborated upon to their full degree in the extended evaluation. Generally, time does not permit the presentation of all questions in the initial evaluation. The basic questions that I have found most useful are, for younger children, the animals and objects that they would like to be if they had to be so transformed (positive and negative, first, second, and third choices) and the animals and objects that would suit each of their parents (first, second, and third choices, positive and negative). As mentioned, the person transformation question is not generally useful for younger children because of their limited repertoire.

This 11-year-old boy came to treatment because of severe conflicts with his father. His father was a shrewd businessman who prided himself on his business acumen. However, he was insensitive to others, to the point of being psychopathic. The mother was passively submissive in her relationship with her husband, thereby abandoning the boy to her husband's maltreatment of him. These are the responses he gave to the question regarding which persons he would choose to be changed into had he to be so transformed:

(+)1 The actor who played "Oliver." He was an orphan boy. He lived in an orphanage. He had very little food. He unknowingly meets his grandfather, and then he lives happily ever after with his grandfather.

(+)2 Mr. Robinson. He's the father in the TV program "Lost in Space." It's a space family and they go around exploring space. In one program the father was drifting from the ship into space, and they catch him just in time. They catch him just in time to get away from monsters. He's the pilot. He's the leader of the family.

(+)3 President Johnson. He signs civil rights bills, making sure that all races have equal rights.

(−)1 Mary Martin. I saw her in that play, *The Sound of Music*. She makes this mean father into a nice man. He was very strict to his kids and she changes him so he isn't strict. I would not want to be there in the beginning of the picture when she was married to the mean father.

(−)2 My sister Ruth (age 14). She's a real kook. She thinks of love all the time. If the house was on fire and she was talking to her boyfriends, she wouldn't make an attempt to get out.

(−)3 My sister Jane (age 16). She's a big shot. She thinks she's real great. She bosses everybody around all the time. She snitches on me to my parents.

Response (+)1 reveals the patient's feelings of having been abandoned and rejected by his father and his desire to be protected by him. The (+)2 response reflects the patient's ambivalence toward his father. On the one hand, he would want him separated and removed (drifting into space) and exposed to the dangers of monsters. On the other hand, he would want him retrieved. In the (+)3 response, his desire to be President Johnson stems here from the wish to be assured equal rights, that is, to be given humane treatment from his parents.

The (−)1 response reflects the patient's desire that someone come into his home and transform his father into a benevolent and loving person. The (−)2 and (−)3 responses are, in part, normal responses for a 12-year-old boy and reflect usual sibling rivalry problems. However, in (−)2 the introduction of the house burning down theme reflects the patient's hostility toward his family. There is possibly a sexual element here as well: the fire representing his sexual desires which he harbors toward his sister and the devastating results should he express such.

Both of this 14-year-old girl's parents were extremely rejecting and angry people. The patient herself harbored deep-seated retaliative hostility toward her parents which she was unable to express. I considered such feelings to be playing a role in the anxiety attacks with which she presented for treatment.

> (+)1 A bird, a small one, a bluejay. It's sweet. It can sing and fly. They care for their children even though they are animals.
> (+)2 A deer. It's gentle, sweet and pretty. Deers care for their children.
> (+)3 An otter. It's playful. Their main objective is not to kill.
> (−)1 A lion. All animals are scared of you. Lions kill, and I wouldn't want to do that.
> (−)2 A snake. They're mean and ugly and horrible.
> (−)3 A bug or spider. They're horrible. They're so horrible and creepy, but I couldn't kill it. I can't kill any insect.

In (+)1 and (+)2, the patient admires birds and deer because they "care for their children," a quality which she does not enjoy from her parents. The (+)3 choice, the otter, whose main objective is "not to kill," reveals the patient's desire to repress her own murderous rage.

The same holds true regarding her desire not to be a lion (−)1 because a lion kills, that is, she wishes to disown her own hostility. The (−)3 response clearly reveals her basic feelings that she is like a bug or spider, prone to be obliterated by overwhelming forces. In addition, her inability to kill small insects reveals her great conflict about the expression of hostility.

This seven-year-old boy came to treatment because of social difficulties associated with his neurologically based learning disability. I considered his parents, especially his mother, to have dedicated themselves in an unusually healthy way to his education and treatment. These are the responses he gave to the animal questions:

> (+)1 A horse. It's fun to go on a horse. Cowboys go on horses.
> (+)2 A cow because I like to pet a cow and get milk.
> (+)3 A skunk. It smells. It's fun to make smells to people.
> (+)4 A pig. They can go oink-oink.

(−)1 A lamb. I can't say the sound of a lamb.
(−)2 A llama. It has a bad smell.
(−)3 I don't know no other animals.

The (+)1 response is normal. The (+)2 response relates to the patient's affection for his mother and his dependence on her. It speaks well for their relationship which, clinically, was an excellent one in that she was warm and tender and was unusually patient with him. The (+)3 answer reveals the so-called "sweet-lemon" way of dealing with a defect. In this process, which is the opposite of "sour grapes," the person lessens the psychic pain he or she would experience regarding a deficiency by turning it into an asset. The patient basically considers himself to smell like a skunk, and this attitude toward himself is related to his awareness of his deficits. This self-loathing contributed to an actual symptom in which he considered himself to smell. By using the odor in the service of expressing hostility—and rationalizing then its usefulness—he thereby reduces his feeling of self-deprecation. In (+)4 he again reveals his low self-esteem and again claims to enjoy those qualities within himself which he inwardly despises.

The (−)1 response suggests something about feelings of performance impairment but little else can be said about this answer. In (−)2 the bad smell theme appears again, but this time he more overtly wishes to reject those qualities within himself which have become epitomized in the "bad smell symptom."

This 11-year-old boy entered treatment because of a difficult relationship with a very competitive father, who not only competed with colleagues but with his own children. This sequence is presented because it demonstrates how, on occasion, the three questions can bring about responses that go progressively deeper into the unconscious. In this case, the boy's third response made reference to a symptom of his mother's (compulsive laughing) that he denied being consciously aware of.

(+)1 A beautiful butterfly. When she's dressed up in formal clothes, she's really beautiful.
(+)2 A colorful bird. She's nice. She's so busy she needs a natural way of transportation, like flying.
(+)3 A mocking bird. She talks a lot.

The (+)1 response is a socially acceptable comment reflecting the patient's conscious admiration of his mother's appearance, and could be considered a normal response. However, response (+)2, although initially complimentary, introduces critical elements: "She's so busy. . . ." In (+)3 he expresses overtly a critical response: "She talks a lot." However, the response is most interesting for another reason. As mentioned, this patient's mother suffered with a compulsive laughing problem. She could not control herself from laughing loudly in situations where the appropriate response was sadness, depression, contrition, etc. For example, when told of the death of people she considered herself close with, she would compulsively laugh, much to her own and her husband's embarrassment. The patient denied any awareness of this problem, and yet the response "mocking bird" clearly reveals that at some level he appreciated its presence. The use of the mocking bird also reveals his appreciation of the hostile element in his mother's symptom.

The next series of responses to the animal question is presented because it basically provides normal responses. The patient entered treatment because of excessive sibling rivalry with an older brother who was doing far better than he academically. In addition, he would often use somatic complaints in order to avoid going to school. His relationship with his mother was essentially a good one and his responses to the questions related to animals that would suit his mother's personality did not reveal significant difficulties in his relationship with her.

> (+)1 A soft kitten. She's playful, helpful, happy, fun to be with.
> (+)2 A butterfly. They go places. They're fast. They never touch the ground. My mother's always doing something.
> (+)3 A deer. She likes to investigate and find new things.
> (−)1 A bear. She's not grouchy.
> (−)2 A beaver. She doesn't like to destroy things. A beaver will cut down a tree.
> (−)3 An ant. My mother wouldn't like to be small. She wants important things. She works for the PTA and in the community.

These are examples of normal responses. There is nothing here that is significantly pathological. In (+)2 the mother's going fast from place to place is not a reflection of actual rejection on her part or such active interest in other things that the patient is neglected. Knowing the clinical situation here helps in making the decision as to whether the response is normal or pathological. In (−)2 we see some evidence of ambivalence in that the child is sensitive to certain hostile elements in the mother but the degree here is not pathological. One expects ambivalence and a certain amount of repression of unacceptable ideas about a parent. These are considered pathological when they deal with morbid themes or are excessive.

This eight-year-old girl was brought for psychiatric consultation because of power struggles with her parents, especially her mother. She thwarted her mother in practically every household activity and chore. From the moment she got up in the morning she balked at dressing, eating breakfast, and going to school. On the weekends she refused to cooperate in family activities and household chores. Even getting her to go to sleep resulted in frequent power struggles with her mother. In school she was not concentrating and showed little inclination to complete her school work. Rather, she enjoyed talking with the other children and defied the teacher's reprimands and disciplinary actions.

The patient's maternal grandmother was a woman with very little interest in her daughter, the patient's mother. The mother, too, exhibited little maternal involvement in her own daughter, the patient. She much preferred to spend time with her friends or in her small, part-time business. Although well meaning, the mother could not devote herself with conviction to child rearing for a significant period.

During her second session of consultation the patient gave these responses to the question regarding which animal would most suit her mother's personality if she had to be transformed:

(+)1 Wild horses. She'd like to be one. She could run free and do what she wants and wouldn't have to do things for children. If a child says, "Take me out for candy," the child has to keep begging her and she won't do it.

(+)2 A puppy. They're cute and she is.

(+)3 A lion. She lays around a lot. When I come home from school at 3:15 she's still in her nightgown and sleeping.

(−)1 A pig. She doesn't eat like one.

(−)2 A German Shepherd. When someone comes in she doesn't just jump up and bite them.

(−)3 A kangaroo. She doesn't have a pocket to carry her baby in. She doesn't jump up and down like one.

The (+)1, (+)3, and (−)3 responses all reveal well the patient's view that her mother is deficient in her maternal capacities. Like a wild horse, she would prefer to run free and remove herself completely from all maternal obligations. And like the lion (as the patient views it) she would prefer to remain lying around than getting up and fulfilling her maternal obligations. Of course, the most poignant symbol of her mother's impairment in maternal involvement is the comparison between her mother and the kangaroo. Whereas the kangaroo lends itself well as a powerful maternal symbol with its womb in a sense being external, the patient's mother is just the opposite. She doesn't have a pouch to carry her baby in, that is, she doesn't have the capacity to hold a child.

This 11-year-old boy came to treatment because of severe passive-aggressivity in the home and at school. His obstructionism was a constant source of irritation to his teachers and school personnel. The patient's father was an extremely insecure and inadequate man who compensated with a pathetic pseudo-intellectuality. He fancied himself an arm-chair philosopher and as a man who was exquisitely sensitive to the deeper processes and workings of the human mind. His seemingly erudite pontifications were most often fatuous. When frustrated, he exhibited severe rage outbursts. These are the responses the patient provided to the question regarding which animals would most suit his father if his father had to be so transformed:

> (+)1 Half-gorilla and half-lamb, because sometimes he yells and sometimes he's nice.
> (+)2 Half-cat and half-lion, because sometimes he yells and sometimes he's nice.
> (+)3 Half-tiger and half-playful dog, for the same reason. Sometimes he screams a lot and other times he's nice.
> (−)1 A gorilla. He doesn't always yell.
> (−)2 A tiger, because he doesn't always yell.
> (−)3 A lion, because he doesn't always yell.

When providing answers to these questions, it was clear that the patient was not going to exert himself or in any way inconvenience himself to think of elaborate answers. The easiest thing for him to do was to perseverate the same reasons for his choices. However, his resistance notwithstanding, he provided meaningful material. The perfunctory way in which he gave his responses, as well as their repetitive similarity, revealed his basic passive-aggressivity. His (+)1, (+)2, and (+)3 responses all indicate that the patient appreciated his father's dual personality. On the other hand, the father is "half-gorilla," a reflection of the patient's appreciation of his father's rage outburst problem. On the other hand, his father is "half-lamb," a reflection of the patient's appreciation that his father is basically a weak person. The gorilla is also a façade and serves to compensate for the basic feelings that his father is a lamb. The (−)1, (−)2, and (−)3 answers are basically repetitions of the gorilla, tiger, and lion themes, given without much thought and deliberation. Nevertheless, they reveal his appreciation of the compensatory personality traits of his father.

At this point, I present in detail (with many verbatim vignettes) a child's responses to the verbal projective questions. I will demonstrate here not only the use of the child's responses as a source of information about underlying psychodynamics, but as a point of departure for the acquisition of additional information and therapeutic interchange. Charles was brought to treatment at age 13 because of destructive behavior in the classroom, poor academic performance in spite of high intelligence, defiance of his parents at home (especially his mother), and alienating behavior toward peers. He was fiercely rivalrous with his nine-year-old brother who was more successful in the classroom, in the neighborhood, and in his relationship with their parents.

During the initial consultative session I was not able to determine the sources of Charles' difficulty in the family. Charles' mother was a housewife and, to the best of my knowledge, was dedicated to his upbringing and showed no manifestations of significant psychopathology. His father, however, was a somewhat "uptight" individual who was inhibited in expressing his feelings. In spite of this he did devote significant time to both boys, especially on weekends, and involved himself extensively in their recreational activities where he served as a coach for a variety of sports.

Charles' problems are said to have started when he was three-and-a-half years old, following the birth of his younger brother. By the end of my two-hour consultation I concluded that fierce sibling rivalry was probably playing an important role in Charles' difficulties, and I could not ascertain any other significant family problems that might have contributed to his antisocial behavior. In addition, Charles had a weight problem from excessive eating—a problem for which he was frequently criticized by his parents (especially his father).

In the second session, the first of my extended evaluation, I asked Charles the first animal question. His response: "A tiger because I would be able to defend myself from other animals. Also, they're very fast."

Charles' second choice: "A bird." Consistent with the principle that one does well to ask for species in that there are a wide variety of birds that can symbolize many different things, I asked Charles what bird he would like to be. He responded, "A robin because they can fly wherever they want." I then asked Charles where he would fly to if he were a robin. He responded, "To Florida. I've never been there. I want to go there with my family."

Charles' third choice: "A seal because everyone likes them. They can swim wherever they want."

Before we had the opportunity to go on to the animals Charles would *not* want to be, he asked me if it was all right to change his first choice from a tiger to a chimpanzee. I told him there would be no problem there, but asked him why he wanted to be a chimpanzee. He responded, "Because they're smart and intelligent. They're active and people love them because they're cute." He then told me he would like to leave the tiger answer as his fourth choice. Again, I told him there would be no problem with that.

We then went on to the animals he would not want to be. His first choice: "A rhinoceros because everyone hates them because they're strong and they kill other animals. People are afraid of them because of the way they look with their big horns."

His second choice: "A hippopotamus because they're big and ugly. People are scared of them because of their looks."

His third choice: "A shark because everyone is scared of them. No one wants to be near them. They're killers."

I believe that Charles' request to substitute the chimpanzee for the tiger was a reflection of his strong desire for the chimpanzee response to take priority over the other three. His reasons for selecting the chimpanzee related to the problems for which he entered treatment. He described the chimpanzee as smart, intelligent, active, and "people love them because they're cute." Doing poorly in school, Charles did not consider himself smart or intelligent. Both he and the chimpanzee are "active." Charles' "activity" was associated with antisocial behavior and resulted in his being alienated from others. The chimpanzee's activity, however, does not result in such alienation; rather, "people love them because they're cute." The response reveals Charles' desire to be loved in spite of his alienating behavior. The robin and the seal responses share in common the desire to be free from constraints. At times this is a normal response, given by many children who view school and home restrictions to be constraints from which they wish to free themselves. Last, Charles' original first choice, the tiger, was chosen because of its capacity to defend itself from other animals. The response suggests that Charles sees himself as vulnerable to attacks by outsiders and would like to be strong enough to defend himself.

The three animals that Charles chose not to be share in common the hostility element. The rhinoceros "kills animals." People are "scared of" the hippopotamus. And sharks are "killers." In addition to the hostility there is the appearance element that is described in the rhinoceros and hippopotamus responses. Of the rhinoceros Charles stated: "People are afraid of them because of the way they look with their big horns." And with regard to the hippopotamus: "People are scared of them because of their looks." The hostile elements in the undesired animals may very well be in the normal range. However, they may also reflect inordinate hostility which Charles wished to disown. One cannot justifiably come to this conclusion from these three responses taken in isolation from other data, especially because they were given in response to the question regarding what animals he would *not* want to be. Not wanting to be an animal that is ferocious is within the normal range. Bringing in the element of appearance, however, is definitely idiosyncratic and suggests that Charles has special feelings about how he looks. This may have related to his mild obesity problem in that Charles was frequently criticized by both of this parents (especially his father) for being overweight.

Charles was then asked what objects he would want to be changed into, if he had to be so transformed. His first response: "I'd want to be a computer. It knows a lot of stuff. It knows more than a man. It's smart and intelligent. People like to use them." We begin to see here a theme emerging on the issue of intelligence. The responses suggest that Charles has feelings of intellectual inadequacy associated with his academic underachievement. His revised first choice on the animal question was the "smart and intelligent" chimpanzee and now his first choice on the object question again relates to intelligence.

Charles' second choice of object: "A pen because people would use me a lot and I'd have a lot of people around me." Charles was then asked what was the particular value of that and he replied, "People *need* them. People need them to write and writing is important." The response here not only reflects Charles' need for others to respect him for his abilities, but the particular quality for which he wants respect is that of writing. And writing, of course, is best done by those who are "smart and intelligent."

Charles' third object: "A stereo. People love to listen to music. I'd be used a lot." The response reflects Charles' desire that he be liked and be needed by other people, probably a reaction to the alienation he suffered from parents and peers because of his psychological problems.

The first object Charles would not want to be: "A box for corn flakes because once people are through with it they throw you away." Again we see the theme of being needed and the fear of being viewed as useless.

His second choice: "A baseball bat. You're always getting hit with a ball and someone can break you. People don't treat you well. You're just a piece of wood to them. They just throw you around." The response again reveals Charles' feelings of being rejected by others and being viewed as subhuman, as someone whose feelings are not considered. In addition, there is the element here of maltreatment from others, and this response is similar to one of the reasons why he did not wish to be a tiger, namely, because it is unable to defend itself from other animals.

The last object he would not want to be: "A gun because I wouldn't want to be used to hurt anyone else." Although one might ascribe hostility here, it is also possible that the response reflects a humane attitude toward others. Of course, both needs would be gratified by this response.

Charles was then asked what animals would suit his mother if she had to be so transformed. His first response: "A chimpanzee. They're nice, but when you get on their bad side they won't be nice to you." I then asked Charles how he gets on his mother's bad side. He replied, "If I don't listen to her she gets mad." I then asked him what he could do about this and he responded, "By stopping myself from being on her bad side." I next asked him why he was still continuing to be on her bad side and why he couldn't stop doing so. His reply: "I know I shouldn't. If I get into my moods I just think 'Who does she think she is bossing me around like that?' " I finally tried to elicit from Charles information about what factors contributed to his getting into one of his "moods." He was unable to provide me with any meaningful response and so we proceeded.

Charles' second choice of animal that would suit his mother: "A bird." Again, I generally do not accept readily such a response and asked him what specific *kind* of bird would most suit his mother's personality. He replied, "A bluejay because she is a nice person. Bluejays keep on coming back if you are nice to them and give them food. If you are nice to them, they'll be nice to you, and it's like that with my mother. I've got to stop being on her bad side." I asked Charles if he thought he could do so and he replied, "Yeah, I've got to try harder. If I put my mind to it. The problem is, I've got to put my mind to it." When asked why he had not done so in the past, he replied, "I don't know. I just get into one of my moods." Again, Charles was asked what situations get him into one of his moods. He replied that when he has trouble with other children, he gets moody. Although I was able to get him to see that his difficulties with peers related to provocative behavior on his own part, I did not feel at that point that my message was sinking in. And so we proceeded.

The third animal that Charles considered to suit his mother's personality: "An owl because they're smart. She's smart. She knows a lot of things I don't know. She knows a lot of math and she can help me with my math." Again, the issue of intelligence emerges and Charles is stating here that he views his mother to be a smart woman, as someone who could help him with his studies. Children generally view their parents as smarter because that is the reality of the situation. Parents do help children with homework and generally have a much vaster fund of knowledge. I suspect, however, that Charles' response here is not simply related to this reality. Rather, it probably relates to feelings of intellectual inadequacy resulting from his academic underachievement.

Charles was then asked what animals would not suit his mother's personality. His first response: "A shark because she isn't a mean person. A shark is." His second animal: "A pig, she's a neat person and she's smart. A pig isn't." His third animal: "A gorilla, because she's not like a savage." The first and third responses could very well be considered to be within the normal range. The pig, however, again reveals the theme of intelligence, lending weight to the conclusion that this issue is very much on Charles' mind.

I then proceeded to ask Charles what animal would suit his

father if he had to be so transformed. His first response: "An owl, just like my mother. I have the same answers for my father as I do for my mother." At this point I urged Charles to come up with different responses for his father in that his father and mother were two different people and I was sure that he could think of animals that indicated these differences. Giving the same answers is a common avoidance maneuver, and the examiner should encourage children to ponder the question a little longer before taking the easy route of giving identical responses for both parents. In response Charles replied, "Okay then, a cheetah. He's fast and he can defend himself."

At that point, Charles interrupted and asked me if he could give me another animal that would suit his mother because one had just come to mind. Of course, I agreed and he responded: "A dog and a cat." I suggested that we start with the dog and that he name a specific kind of dog. I cannot emphasize this point strongly enough to the reader. There are a wide variety of dogs, each species of which lends itself well to symbolizing a different personality characteristic. And, as the reader will see in just a few seconds, my asking Charles to select a specific kind of dog provided useful information. His response: "A Saint Bernard, because you can depend on them. If you have a problem, you can tell them and they'll help you. They're famous for rescuing people in the snow." The response reveals Charles' view of his mother as nurturing and protective. However, it also suggests that he feels himself in a situation of emotional deprivation (lost in the snow). Perhaps this relates to his father's problems in expressing feelings and his mother's capacity to provide him with the affection that his father cannot.

Because Charles had stated that his mother resembles a "dog and a cat," I asked him then why he had chosen a cat. He responded: "You can also depend upon them. If you need a friend it's always there, and they're always by your side." The response again is a statement of Charles' view of his mother as warm, nurturing, and reliable. It is important to appreciate that this response, coming as it did as an interruption, must be given extra attention and credibility when assessing a child's responses. Just as the chimpanzee interruption provided useful information earlier in the inquiry, this interruption did so as well. The examiner does well to view these interruptions as reflecting significant pressure by unconscious processes to express important issues. The comments about Charles' mother's warmth, protectiveness, and affection came in the midst of descriptions of his father. They suggest that his descriptions of his father's coldness was anxiety provoking and that he needed his mother's warmth and protection as an antidote.

We then continued and Charles gave as the second choice of animal that would suit his father: "A dog, a Saint Bernard." Again, I asked Charles if he could give me a different animal because I considered the Saint Bernard response to be a manifestation of resistance in that he had just given that animal as one that would suit his mother. Without much delay he stated, "A Dalmation, because you can depend on them for help." It is difficult to assess his answer, coming as it did immediately after one that described Charles' mother as being someone on whom he could depend. I believe that Charles' father *was* dependable in certain areas such as involvement with Charles in sports. What he could *not* depend upon from his father was open displays of emotion, intimacy, and warm tender feelings. His father could, however, *do* those things that were necessary for adequate child rearing.

The third animal that would suit Charles' father: "A beaver because it works hard." Charles' father's work occupied him for long hours during weekdays; however, he was available to a significant degree on weekends to devote himself to his sons. From the ensuing discussion I could not be certain whether or not Charles felt any deprivation in association with his father's midweek work obligations. He denied such feelings. I suspect that the reality was that Charles did not consciously experience his father as depriving because he was there to a significant degree on weekends. The deprivation that he was not consciously aware of was the emotional deprivation which is more subtle—but deprivation nevertheless.

In answer to the question which animals are not similar to his father, Charles replied: "A lion because he is not mean or savage." The second animal unlike his father: "A fox because he is not a con artist." And the third animal: "A snake because he is not a slippery snake that goes around biting people." I considered the first and third responses (the lion and the snake) to be within the normal range, not only with regard to the animals chosen but the reasons why. However, the second response is, in my experience, atypical. And atypicality is one of the criteria for ascertaining psychopathology. It certainly is an unusual response and suggests that the patient, at some level, may consider his father to be duplicitous. It may be of interest to the reader to learn that on the day following this interview I did have an individual interview with the father.

There was no question that he was not candid with me. He described the marriage as always having been a good one and denied that there were any problems. Charles' mother, however, during the interview prior to the one with Charles in which the verbal projective test was administered, described a number of serious marital problems, among which were infidelity on her husband's part. Although Charles' response here created only a mild suspicion that his father was duplicitous, and although such a view was not supported by subsequent responses on the test, there was indeed "fire beneath the smoke," and the initial suspicions engendered in me by this response proved to be verified in the next interview with his father.

Charles was then asked questions regarding the objects that would suit his mother's personality. His first response: "A bandaid because she helps me heal." His second response: "A chair because she is comfortable." And his third response: "A computer because she is smart and so intelligent." The first two responses, of course, make direct reference to his mother's nurturing and protecting roles. The third again is another example of the theme related to intellectual functioning which, as we know, was an area of difficulty for Charles.

When asked what objects would not suit his mother's personality, his first response was, "A knife because she's not a dangerous person." His second response: "A machine gun because she doesn't go around hurting people." And his third response: "A camera because she doesn't spy on people." As is usually the case, it is more difficult to make firm statements about the meaning of the negative responses than the positive. Negative responses do not necessarily indicate unconscious material that the patient is guilty and/or anxious about and must thereby relegate impulses to unconscious awareness. They can also be explained simply as age-appropriate negative attitudes that the child has derived from the environment. Here again, one looks for atypicality for leads to psychopathology. The knife and machine gun are, in my experience, normal responses, although the machine gun may be a little strong in that a simple gun is more often chosen. The camera serving as a vehicle for spying, however, is a more atypical response and suggested feelings that the patient has that his mother spies on him. However, most children have these feelings, and so I cannot consider this response to be significantly representative of psychopathology, especially because there was no repetition or pattern of such imagery throughout the assessment.

Charles was then asked what objects would suit his father's personality. His first response: "A computer because they're smart." Once again, we see the concern with intellectual capacity, clearly a problem for Charles.

His second response: "A thermostat because it keeps you warm and cool." This was an unusual and somewhat confusing response and so I questioned Charles for further details. Accordingly, Charles was then asked to elaborate on the point that his father, like the thermostat, keeps one "warm." In response he stated, "If I have a problem, he'll say don't worry about it and that makes me feel better." When asked to elaborate on the association between his father and the thermostat helping someone become "cool," he replied, "He's comforting and he helps you." When I tried to understand better what Charles was referring to here, the best I could determine was that he was using the word *cool* in the sense that many adolescents use it, that is, to refer to one's being unemotional and not taking upsetting experiences seriously. To the degree that this response implies improper suppression and repression of feelings, to that degree it is pathological. In my subsequent interview with Charles' father, I found him to be quite inhibited in expressing his feelings and suspected that Charles' response here related to this aspect of his father's personality.

Charles' third response: "A car." Again, just as I asked Charles to tell me the specific *kind* of dog and bird he had selected, I asked him to tell me the specific *kind* of car that would suit his father's personality. There are many different kinds of cars and they lend themselves to different kinds of symbolization. In response, he stated, "A Ferrari, because he has one and he's interested in cars." The response suggests that Charles' father may be swept up in the common materialism of our society. This is not to say that every person who buys a Ferrari is necessarily exhibitionistic; only that there are many purchasers of this car who certainly are so, and the response should alert the therapist to look into this issue.

Charles was then asked to name those objects that would not suit his father's personality. His first response: "A hand grenade because he doesn't kill people." His second response: "A knife because he doesn't stab people." His third response: "A match because he doesn't burn people." Although the level at which normality ends and pathology begins may be difficult to ascertain with the negative questions of the verbal projective test, I believe that the responses here go beyond the normal frequency of dangerous implements that one gets in response to these questions. They suggest Charles' view of his father as inordinately hostile—hostility that Charles is trying to suppress and repress. Considering the fact that Charles had an acting-out problem, the responses here suggest that a contributing factor to this symptom related to Charles' relationship with his father, especially with regard to hostile elements that often contribute to such difficulties.

As mentioned, the interchanges derived from my administration of the verbal projective test with Charles are presented in detail in order to familiarize the reader with the administration of the test and its utilization not only for learning about psychodynamics but for providing material that may serve as a point of departure for further inquiry, both diagnostic and therapeutic.

Dreams

Children are less capable of analyzing their dreams than adults, but the dream may nevertheless be a rich source of information about a child's underlying psychodynamics. The ability to utilize the dream metaphor probably exists at about the age of two or three in most children. However, the ability to appreciate the process, that is to separate cognitively the symbol from the entity that it denotes, is a later phenomenon and for the average child does not take place until the age of 10 or 11, the age at which the child reaches what Piaget refers to as the stage of *formal operations*. Accordingly, I will often be interested in a child's dreams, especially during the extended evaluation. However, I do not generally spend much time attempting to help the child gain insight into the dream's meaning. Rather, I use the information in the course of the treatment. In Chapter Thirteen I will discuss dream analysis for the rare child who can be involved meaningfully in this procedure.

I ask the child to tell me any dreams he or she can remember, and that I am particularly interested in repetitious dreams. As mentioned, these often provide valuable information about basic themes that pervade the patient's personality structure. Here I will describe and analyze some dreams that children presented me during the intensive evaluation. I will present my understanding of the dream's meaning. I will not go into detail about any discussions I may have had about the dream's meaning. (In Chapter Thirteen I will discuss dream analysis in greater detail.) My primary purpose here is to demonstrate how a child's dream can often be a rich source of information about underlying psychodynamics. Even when the child is not capable of analyzing the dream, the examiner's hunches and speculations about the dream's meaning can often be useful in the child's treatment.

This ten-year-old boy presented with complaints of severe difficulties in his relationships with peers, both in the classroom and in his neighborhood. He was extremely bright and did well academically. However, he would flaunt his academic successes to his peers and this, of course, was alienating. He would not share and had a low frustration tolerance in play with other children. When he won a game, he would also flaunt his success to his opponent. He was an only child and had severe power struggles at home with his mother who was an extremely cold, aloof, and condescending woman. Throughout my total experiences with her, she was continually critical. As will be discussed in Chapter Seven, I most often work closely with parents—to the point where they actively work with me in the session. This mother was so condescending and hostile, that I considered it best for the boy's treatment that she sit in the waiting room throughout most of the session. She was not the kind of a person whom I could confront with these difficulties and who would be receptive to my suggestion that she give some thought to her attitude. I viewed her as a fixed negative constant in the family and the child's treatment. The patient's father was totally blind to his wife's alienating personality traits. He too was an unemotional individual who, like his wife, had little capacity to extend warm, tender feelings to the child. The patient told me this dream during the extended evaluation:

> I was in clockland. Everyone there turned into a clock and I turned into a clock. I had a hard time getting out of there and turning human. I was an alarm clock and I rang my bell in the guard clock's ear. He was guarding the gate and so he popped and broke and so I was able to get out of the gate and turn human again.

I considered the clock, as the central figure in the dream, to represent the patient. The guard clock probably represented his mother. Depicting himself and his mother as clocks is a statement of his view of himself and her as mechanical devices, that is, not human. In addition, his viewing himself as an alarm clock may represent some desire to communicate to the world (especially this examiner) the terrible conditions under which he was living. It may also represent the threatened eruption into conscious awareness of profound hostility that had to be repressed and suppressed if he were to protect himself from even further rejection from his parents (especially his mother). His ringing his bell in the guard clock's ear is therefore a hostile manifestation as well as a plea for help. The only way he can escape is to destroy the guard clock. However, it is not he himself who destroys the guard clock; rather, the guard clock spontaneously "popped and broke," and so he was able to escape (without guilt over having killed the guard) and "turn human again." The dream is a clear statement of this boy's view of his family as one in which he is living amongst mechanical devices, is a mechanical device himself, and the only way he can become a human being is to escape.

This ten-year-old boy came to treatment because of impaired motivation in the classroom. He had little academic curiosity or motivation and did not seem to be bothered by the fact that he was getting low grades and was on the verge of being asked to repeat the fifth grade. The patient's paternal grandfather was a self-made multimillionaire who owned factories in various parts of the world. The patient's father (see page 294) was basically a ne'er-do-well. He too had little interest in schooling and had flunked out of a series of private schools over the course of his education. Each time, however, the paternal grandfather used his money and influence to gain his son admission to another preparatory school. In high school the patient's father began drinking heavily and his four years in college were basically spent womanizing and imbibing alcohol. Then, he went into the paternal grandfather's business where he automatically rose up the ladder, without any particular competence or skill. He was basically disrespected by the people with whom he worked, but he had to be tolerated because of the fact that he was the owner's son. The patient's mother (see page 267) had been a model and had little interest in being a homemaker or mother. Both she and the father had had affairs during the marriage. With regard to his school problems the patient openly stated that there was no point in his studying very hard because he would ultimately go into his grandfather's business. During the initial two-hour consultation and during the extended evaluation, the patient reported this dream, which was essentially the same on both occasions:

I was looking out the tower window at my grandfather's farm. My grandfather's car was coming down the road. He parks the car in a parking lot and he opens the tailgate door. My sister and I come out of the house to meet him. He takes out everything with a white sheet over it. He puts it on the ground. He takes out some other stuff and lifts off the white sheet. Then I saw an electric minibike. I asked whose it was and he said it was for me. I say, "Can I ride it now? How can I start it?" And then I awoke.

The dream reveals the patient's view of his paternal grandfather as the provider of material things. He provides the patient with a minibike, that is the vehicle for moving along life's course. The paternal grandfather, not surprisingly, was the one who provided the patient's father with a new automobile every year. The minibike, like the automobile, lends itself well to symbolizing an individual's view of him- or herself with regard to the capacity to move independently along life's path. Here, it is the paternal grandfather who provides the minibike, that is, who provides the vehicle which the patient will use to move along life's course. And this, of course, was the case with the patient's father as well. But the patient does not know how to ride the minibike and asks the grandfather to teach him. This fantasy is a reflection of the patient's insecurities about his own capacity to move along life's course and his viewing his grandfather as the person who can teach him how. The complete absence of the father, and the view of the grandfather as the provider and teacher, was certainly a reflection of the reality of this boy's situation.

This eight-year-old boy was referred for treatment because of timidity, depression, somatic complaints, impaired motivation in school, and passivity in his relationships with friends. His mother was a homemaker and his father a businessman. However, his father had a moderately severe drinking problem and, when inebriated, would on occasion beat the patient's mother. She passively accepted this situation as a necessary concomitant of the marriage. During the extended evaluation, the patient described this repetitious dream:

I saw this old-fashioned train. It was very dirty. It needed to be washed. Some people were trying to clean it, but it was very dirty.

I considered the train to represent the patient's father. From a child's point of view, a parent can readily be considered "old-fashioned." The train needs to be washed. This I believe represents the patient's view of his father as "dirty" and in need of cleansing. Certainly, when the father was inebriated, he presented a most unsavory appearance and his personality qualities, especially those associated with his beating the patient's mother, were characteristics that the patient justifiably considered to warrant cleansing.

This eight-year-old boy entered treatment because of depression, excessive worrying, and poor school performance in spite of high intelligence. He was the proverbial "worrywart." He had little capacity to enjoy himself and took the weight of the world on his shoulders. He would see the worst in most situations, and his pessimism compromised his capacity for enjoyment. The patient's father was an extremely successful lawyer who spent little time at home, so involved was he in his practice. Even on weekends, he spent little time with his family. His mother was also a pessimistic, depressed, worrysome individual whose capacity for pleasure was compromised significantly. During the first session of the extended evaluation, the patient told me about the dream he had had the previous night: "My parents are run over and I become an orphan." I considered the dream to provide a vehicle for the expression of the considerable hostility this boy felt toward his parents because of the deprivations he suffered in his relationships with them. However, he recognizes that if these hostile wishes were to be fulfilled, he would be left an orphan.

During the second evaluative session, the patient brought in another dream: "My brother and I were sitting alone in the back seat of our car. No one was in the front seat. The car was rolling. I was scared." The dream is a poignant statement of the patient's feelings that neither of his parents are in the driver's seat, that is, available to provide him with guidance, support, and direction in life. He and his brother feel alone, abandoned, and fearful of the consequences of being so rejected.

This 11-year-old girl presented with psychosomatic complaints, especially headaches, nausea, vomiting, and occasional diarrhea. She had a variety of allergies as well. Her mother, who was an extremely tense and angry woman, had little meaningful capacity for child rearing. The mother openly stated that she should have never become a parent. Her relationship with her husband was a difficult one because he too felt frustrated over his wife's tension and rejection of him. When either he or the children (the patient had a 14-year-old sister) would express any anger toward the mother, she would have violent rages which were extremely frightening to both the children and their father. The patient related this dream during the extended evaluation:

> I was at the beach with my friend at Atlantic City. I was in the water. A giant wave came. I had to duck under. Another big wave came and it drowned me.

This is a common dream. I consider the most likely explanation for a dream in which a patient is being drowned or submerged by waves to reflect the feeling that suppressed or repressed emotions are going to break out of the unconscious into conscious awareness. The emotions, however, are viewed as dangerous and even lethal. Often patients will wake up from the dream relieved that they have not been drowned. And I believe that this explanation was applicable to this girl. The feelings here represent the massive hostility she felt toward her mother—hostility that could not be expressed overtly lest she suffer even further rejection and retaliation. Her feelings overwhelm her and she will drown in them. I considered many of her symptoms to be manifestations of the tension she felt in association with her attempts, both conscious and unconscious, to suppress and repress her anger toward her mother. Her dream confirmed my clinical speculations.

This 14-year-old boy asked his parents to bring him to therapy because of strong homosexual fantasies. His father was an extremely domineering, controlling individual who always presented with a façade of reasonableness. However, in any discussion in which differences of opinion were expressed, he maintained a rock-like rigidity. The patient's mother was passive and submissive in her relationship with the father. Neither parent had much capacity to involve themselves emotionally with the patient and his older sister, then 17. During the extended evaluation, he described this repetitious dream:

> My family and I were in a car going up the driveway to my school. It was a school day. There was a little shack next to the school. I went into the shack. There was a hand there in a white glove. It was a mechanical hand. I had to be very quiet. It was very dangerous, so I couldn't make any noise. Once I sneezed and the hand went over my mouth.

I considered the little shack, next to the school, to symbolize the patient's view of himself as isolated from the mainstream of his peers and possibly his family as well. I considered the mechanical hand, covered by a white glove, to represent his father who did not allow the patient to express his genuine thoughts and feelings. Even the sneeze, which the patient could not control, is suppressed by the white-gloved hand. It is a statement of his great pressure for expression of the patient's repressed thoughts and feelings. Viewing his father as a mechanical hand in a white glove is a statement of his belief that his father is machine-like rather than human. The white glove implies sterility and cover-up of "blackness" and other undesirable personality qualities. It also symbolizes the father's veneer of reasonableness to disguise inhumane (mechanical) qualities.

Concluding Comments

The kinds of inquiries and assessment instruments described above are the primary ones that I utilize in the extended evaluation of the child. They generally provide me with a wealth of information. However, on occasion, I will utilize other instruments. Younger children (ages four to six, the youngest I treat directly) may engage in doll play. The fantasies that I elicit in association with such play are sometimes useful. I say *sometimes* because they are often merely normal age-appropriate and stereotyped fantasies. One less often elicits the kind of idiosyncratic material that is the richest source of information. Also, during the extended evaluation, I will spend some time (generally 15 or 20 minutes in each of two sessions) playing *The Talking, Feeling, and Doing Game* (to be discussed in detail in Chapter Eleven). My purpose here is not simply to gain some data. Rather, I am interested in ascertaining how successful I will be in engaging the child. Of course, I am assessing this with other modalities such as straight discussion, mutual storytelling, and the ability to gain insight (as mentioned, not a promising area). But *The Talking, Feeling, and Doing Game* involvement will enable me to learn about just how formidable resistances are in that only the most severely resistant children will not play the game. Last, I will sometimes refer children for psychological tests. I feel comfortable doing the WISC-R and the WIPPSI but I do not consider myself trained to do the Rorschach Test and I will occasionally refer a child for this assessment.

JOINT INTERVIEW
WITH THE PARENTS

Following the individual interviews with each of the parents alone, I will conduct a joint interview with both parents together. It is extremely important that the examiner conduct this interview as part of the extended evaluation. At times, parents may object to this because they will claim that each parent has already provided information. Sometimes, they will even claim that the information has already been given twice, in that mother has related it during her individual interview and the father during his. When I explain to them that I often get different renditions of what is happening in the home, they will become more receptive to the joint interview because they recognize that it is important that any distortions which have been introduced into the evaluation should be corrected. Besides utilizing this interview to gain the most accurate data, the interview enables the examiner to observe interactions between the parents. This is truly a situation in which the whole is greater than the sum of the parts. It is a rare situation in which I do not learn new things from the joint interview. This relates both to the acquisition of new information as well as the things I learn from the interactions. During the initial two-hour consultation, only a limited time is spent in the joint interview so that the opportunity for observation of interactions is small.

The Correction of Distortions
and Other Kinds of False Data

It is extremely important for the reader to appreciate that all human beings distort their perceptions in situations of stress. At the Columbia University School of Law, it is not uncommon for a professor to stage a totally unanticipated interruption in the class. Specifically, a group of young men and women may suddenly charge into the classroom. There is screaming, a scuffle, shouts, shrieks, and angry words. Feigned gun shots, knife stabbings, and other forms of violence are likely to ensue. Then, as quickly as it began, the group suddenly leaves the room. The professor then asks each member of the class to write exactly what he or she observed. He advises them that they have been witness to a crime and that they will be asked to testify under oath regarding what they have seen and heard. The class is generally around 300 young people, just about all of whom have been extremely high in their college classes and have performed extraordinarily well on the Law School Aptitude Test. Presumably, then, we are dealing here with a very bright group of young men and women. The professor generally receives 300 different renditions of what occurred. And each of these young people is being honest. Such is the nature of the human mind. So great is the capacity to distort under situations of stress.

Another example of this phenomenon. As the reader may know, I lecture extensively throughout the United States and occasionally abroad. Most often, I give a full-day of presentations, generally three or four lectures. The most common format is four one-and-a-half hour presentations, two in the morning and two in the afternoon. Frequently, a person will ask me a question in which there is a misquotation and/or a misunderstanding of what I had previously said. When I inform the person that I have been completely misunderstood and that I said exactly the opposite of what he or she is attributing to me, the individual often responds with incredulity. I have often had the thought that a wonderful experiment would be to make a videotape of the first presentation. Then, I would hand out an objective test (such as one with multiple-choice questions) that would be based *entirely* on the material just presented during the previous hour and a half. I am convinced that most people in the audience would give some incorrect answers and would, in addition, swear that their recollection of what I said was accurate. Then, we would get the videotape's opinion regarding what I said. These individuals would react with amazement that they could have so misunderstood me.

Our memories play tricks on us, especially if the topic is one that is emotionally charged. And when one lectures in the field of psychiatry, one is likely to touch on emotionally charged situations. If I am lecturing on the subject of divorce, there are likely to be many individuals in the audience who have been or are going through the process of divorce, and this is likely to be a charged subject for them. Under such circumstances, distortion is almost inevitable. I am not being critical of these individuals who distort or misinterpret what I say. I myself would be likely to make such errors occasionally were I in their situation. And when one is interviewing parents about their marriage and the ways in which they deal with their children, especially in a psychiatric interview, it is inevitable that distortions will arise. The joint interview can serve to correct these for both the parents and the examiner.

It is extremely important for the examiner to appreciate that one's interpretation of any situation is determined by two factors. One is the actual facts, the actual reality, and the other is what one brings to it, what one interprets it to mean, what one *wants* to understand about the significance of the events. As mentioned earlier, I often say that life is like a Rorschach test. In fact, one could view this as a fundamental dictum of human experience. All phenomena can be divided into two factors: the reality and what the human being brings to the reality. The viewer's hopes, anticipations, denial mechanisms, et cetera, are all going to play a role in determining what the individual sees and how he or she reacts. Both the external entity and the viewer's thoughts and feelings about it are realities in their own right, and both play an important part in determining how one will react in a particular situation. There is a glass with water in it. One person sees it as half full, another sees it as half empty. And when parents are talking about their marriage and their children, the likelihood of these superimposed attitudes playing an important role in their discussions is very high. In fact, it is so great that I consider it to be universal. Accordingly, distortions, misrepresentations, and exaggerations are inevitably going to be present, and it is in the joint interview, especially, that the examiner is in the best position to determine what these are.

In Chapter Three I gave as examples of this phenomenon the split-screen sequence from Woody Allen's movie *Annie Hall*. Both Woody Allen and Diane Keaton complain bitterly about the other with regard to sexual interests. Woody complains about Diane's unreceptivity and frigidity; Diane complains about Woody's voracious sexual appetite. Both agree on the two-to-three times a week frequency, but their attitudes about this frequency result in extreme pain and discomfort for both of them. Similarly, the reader may recall the anecdote in Chapter Three about the old rabbi who didn't know whether he was in heaven or hell. Again, his wishes regarding the interpretation of the relationship between his old mentor and his beautiful young companion played an important, if not crucial, determinant in his conclusions regarding whether he was in heaven or hell.

Accordingly, the examiner must recognize that the information gathering process in this interview occurs at two levels. One must attempt to ascertain, to the degree that one can, exactly what is happening. Sometimes this is possible if the two individuals come to some kind of a compromise or when one's credibility is clearly greater than the other's. At other times it may not be possible and the examiner does well to go on to the next issue. In such cases, I might say, "Well, you say one thing and your husband(wife) says just the opposite. We've gone back and forth a few times and you each stick to your own positions. I suggest we go on to another issue. Perhaps in the future, I'll learn what's really going on."

The other level, and possibly the more important, is the attitudinal. It relates to the thoughts and feelings of the individual about the particular event. Shakespeare's Hamlet said it well: "There's nothing either good or bad, but thinking makes it so." A father, for example, may put his three-year-old son on his lap while driving the car, and while both of their hands are on the steering wheel, the father gives the child the impression that he is helping drive the car. Early in the marriage, when there was a loving relationship between the parents, the mother may have considered the father's act to be a benevolent one, one designed to help the child feel like "a big man." In contrast, at a time when the marriage has deteriorated, she may complain vehemently to the examiner about the kinds of dangerous things her husband used to do with the boy, and she may give this as an example.

In the individual interviews, one may get diametrically opposed stories resulting in a complete inability to find out what has really gone on. In the joint interview, one can sometimes "smoke out the truth." For example, in the individual interviews, each parent might describe attendance at all school functions to which parents are invited, both curricular and extracurricular. However, during the joint interview the mother may say, with regard to the father, "Yeah, he came, but I always had to pull him. It was a big struggle. And when he finally got there, he used to fall asleep during the plays and recitals." The father may then sheepishly admit that he "sometimes" did fall asleep for short periods of time, but that his wife is exaggerating the frequency and the duration of the time spent sleeping. In the subsequent discussion, the father may admit reluctance and occasional sleeping. Although the two may differ regarding the degree of reluctance and the frequency in duration of sleeping episodes, the examiner has still learned about the father's lack of enthusiasm for these events. And this I would consider to be a parental deficiency.

"The Whole May Be Greater Than the Sum of Its Parts"

The joint interview with the parents is one of those situations in which the whole may be greater than the sum of its parts. In fact, in most of the interviews, I find that the whole proves to be greater than the sum of its parts, because information is derived which was not or could not have been obtained in the individual interviews. This phenomenon is the result of the interaction between the parents. Because of the shortness of the joint interview during the initial two-hour evaluative session, time often does not allow for the emergence of this additional information. It is only under more relaxed circumstances, during the extended evaluation, that there is a greater likelihood that this additional data will become available.

Let us take the example of a passive and somewhat quiet man who is married to an assertive and more talkative woman. In the short joint interview, during the two-hour screening evalation, one may sense that this is the nature of the relationship, but questions are still being directed toward both parties. In the individual interview(s) with the father, the examiner is spending most of the time posing questions (as described in detail in the above section on the interview with the father). More than 95% of the time is spent with the father's talking. He is a "captive audience." The individual interview should not be conducted like a classical psychoanalytic session in which the examiner sits back silently and waits for the patient to talk. (This does not preclude, however, an occasional open-ended question.) Rather, the examiner is generally concerned with obtaining answers to a whole series of questions. In the joint interview, however, one may observe directly how the mother may actually consume 99% of the time, while the father sits silently, allowing her to "roll." Now that he is no longer captive audience, now that the examiner is not posing one question after the other, now that he is being permitted to either talk or remain silent as he chooses, his severe problem in verbal inhibition becomes apparent. In addition, his passivity problem also manifests itself, especially when he remains silent on issues of disagreement with his wife. The father may say, "I was never one who had much to say in social situations. I never had the 'gift of gab.' I guess one of the reasons why I was attracted to my wife was because she always had something to say at all times." And, with this lead, the examiner may also learn about the father's passivity in his relationship with the mother and his fears of asserting himself. A derivative of this would be a discussion of the patient's identifications in these areas, with the father and/or the mother.

A father may claim in the individual interview(s) that the marriage is a good one, that there were never any difficulties, and that there was never any talk of separation. In her individual interview(s), however, the mother may claim that on two occasions during the course of the marriage, she found love letters from other women. She suspects that there were probably other infidelities that she cannot be certain of. She claims also that when her husband was confronted with these letters he admitted to her that he had been unfaithful and that he would discontinue the affairs. In some circumstances I will recommend that the mother bring up the issue of infidelity in the joint meetings with her husband, and on other occasions I will not. On the one hand, I may consider it important for the child's treatment to do so, especially if the mother has good reason to believe that there is an ongoing affair taking place during the time of the evaluation. On the other hand, I may consider it antitherapeutic to do so in that it might cause additional marital discord which I suspect both parents would rather avoid. One just doesn't go after the truth, no matter what the consequences. One goes after the truth in the service of doing what is best for the child's treatment. In order to determine whether or not this issue should be brought up, I will ask the mother her opinion on the subject, and her input here will be very important. Of course, I too will have input into the decision. All marriages involve a certain amount of acceptance and resignation of qualities in the other party that one would prefer did not exist. The examiner must respect such equilibria and not attempt to change every single source of marital difficulty. If one is going to "rock the boat," then one should be sure that one is in a position to deal completely with the repercussions of such a disruption of the marital equilibrium.

Let us say that both the mother and I decide that it would serve the best interests of the marriage and the patient for her to bring up the affair in the joint session. In the joint meeting, the mother confronts the father with her suspicions about ongoing infidelity. She expresses incredulity that his "business meetings" so frequently go on until two in the morning. She also expresses her disbelief that they always take place at places where he cannot be reached and cannot call her either and tell her that he has been detained. She expresses her conclusion that she believes that he is with another woman (or with other women) and that he is either at their homes or in hotels. In response the father somewhat sheepishly and unconvincingly gives various explanations. At this point the mother may say, "Doctor, I've been living with this man for 15 years. I know him inside out. Right now he's lying. Look at that shit-eating grin on his face. That's how he looks when he's lying." The father might still hold to his original story and claim that his wife has a vivid imagination and that she has delusions of jealousy. On occasion, under such circumstances, the mother may turn to me and ask my opinion on the subject. My response, under these circumstances, has been along these lines: "Well, I can't be 100% certain. Your wife, however, is certainly giving some very convincing reasons why she suspects infidelity, and your responses don't seem to carry much credibility. Although I'm not sure at this point—pending more convincing information from you—I'm inclined to believe that your wife has good reasons to be very suspicious."

However, I do not stop there. I will then say something along these lines: "Regardless of whose version is valid here, there is no question that you and your wife have some serious marital difficulties. However, you are not candidates for marital counseling at this point, at least on this issue. Either she is delusional and believes her delusions or you are lying. In either case, people like yourselves, with this kind of a conflict, are not candidates for marital counseling." I then proceed with other issues. My point here is that the joint interview enables the examiner to learn better about a parent's personality characteristics. In the example cited above, I learned about the father's probable duplicity. On other occasions, under the same circumstances, I have learned something about the mother's delusional system. In both situations, the confrontation by the spouse provided important input in my determining what was most likely the situation.

Many other forms of interaction can be observed in the joint interview. For example, sado-masochistic tendencies that may not have been apparent in the initial screening interview may manifest themselves. As the joint interview progresses, a father may become increasingly hostile toward the mother, speak in a condescending way to her, and denigrate her. Rather than asserting herself and expressing her resentment that her husband is treating her so shabbily, she may passively sit and accept his deprecations. These personality traits on the parts of the parents are likely to be playing a role in the child's difficulties. Or, a mother may continually interrupt her husband with nitpicking and hairsplitting corrections. Rather than tell her how offended he is by her behavior, he passively explains himself repeatedly, continually trying to justify himself. Again, these patterns are not likely to have manifested themselves in the individual interviews.

The Marriage

It is in the joint interview, with both parents together, that one is likely to learn much more about the marriage than in the individual interviews. Confrontations between the parents not only enable the examiner to correct distortions but to make observations in which the interactions often provide more information than actual statements. Because marital difficulties are such an important factor in bringing about psychogenic pathology in children, I will often devote a significant portion of the joint interview to the details of the marital relationship. Although some parents who bring children to treatment will not have any difficulties in this area, my experience has been that this is uncommon. Accordingly, I most often have little trouble getting parents to discuss the marital problems; often, each has discussed them at some length during the individual interviews.

On occasion, a parent who has discussed the marital problems in individual interview will show hesitancy in discussing them in the joint interview. Most often, I consider such discussion warranted. Therefore, in order to catalyze the discussion I may make a comment such as: "Each of you has told me at length what you consider to be both the assets and the liabilities, the strengths and weaknesses, of your marriage. I would now like to discuss them here with the two of you together. Why don't we start off with the strong points." At this point, I do not specify which parent I would like to start; rather, I leave it open because I would like to ascertain which parent is going to be the more assertive and forthright with regard to the marriage, both its assets and liabilities. Suggesting that they talk about the assets first generally "breaks the ice" and makes it easier to discuss the liabilities thereafter.

On occasion, one or both parents will be reluctant to discuss the marriage and say that they don't understand how their marital difficulties have anything to do with their child's problems. Others will go further and state that my delving into the marriage is improper and that if they wanted marital counseling, they would have asked for it. I try to explain to such parents that their view of child therapy as a process which is focused on the child primarily, if not exclusively, is improper and injudicious. I explain to them that I cannot separate their child's difficulties from their own, that there are therapists who would be willing to treat their child without any contact with them, but I am not that kind of therapist. I try to explain to them that children exposed to and/or embroiled in marital problems are likely to develop psychological difficulties themselves. The parents may respond that they have been completely successful in protecting their children from any knowledge of their marital difficulties. In such cases I try to explain to the parents that this is practically impossible. I try to get across the point that if the parents are unhappy this is going to compromise their parenting, even if the children don't know exactly what the parents are unhappy about.

I also advise them that my view of therapy involves my counseling parents on how to take care of the children and deal with their problems, and I hope that they will be receptive to this part of the therapeutic program. It is the rare parent who is unreceptive to this; in fact, I cannot recall a parent saying that he or she did not want my advice regarding how to handle the children's problems. I also advise them that treatment for their own problems is an overlapping but separate issue. If they *wanted* treatment for their problems, I would be happy to discuss with them the question of whether I should do such counseling or someone else should. In such discussions I point out the advantages of my doing it, but try to avoid giving the impression that "I am looking for extra business." Rather, I impress upon them the fact that by having one therapist treat the whole family, I will be more in touch with those issues that are affecting the child than I would be if another therapist were to do the marital counseling.

On occasion, it will become apparent that the child's problems are a small and incidental spinoff of the parents' difficulties and that the main thrust of the therapeutic approach will have to be with the parents if there is to be any hope of alleviation of the child's problems. (I will discuss this issue in the section devoted to the final presentation of my findings.) On occasion, it has become apparent that one of the parents is basically using the child's symp-

toms as an "admission ticket" for marital treatment. At some level
the parent recognizes that the major problems lie within the marriage, and the hope was that by bringing the child, the parental
difficulties would surface and perhaps a reluctant parent would be
more motivated for therapy. My experience has been that this is a
common situation and that the mother, much more than the father,
is likely to have been the initiator in such a process.

On a number of occasions, it has become more apparent during this joint interview that the marital problem must be considered
a fixed constant in the child's treatment. Sometimes one of the parents is adamantly against any kind of counseling. My experience
has been that the person who is most often resistant to the counseling is the father. On other occasions, a parent may recognize that
there are serious problems in the marriage but may be afraid to
"rock the boat." My experience here has been that it is the mother,
more than the father, who is often in this position. One has to respect defenses in a marriage. One has to respect the equilibria and
the benefits of maintaining the status quo, the drawbacks of such
silence notwithstanding. All marriages involve a delicate balance
between healthy and pathological forces, and the examiner must
respect these balances and not bulldoze the parent into "putting
everything out on the table." The likelihood of people gaining anything from such tactics is small, and the therapist, under such circumstances, may do the family much more harm than good.

Dealing with the Children

The second important area that I generally focus on in the joint
interviews is the parental dealings with the children. Generally, I
have asked each of the parents in the individual interviews to describe him- or herself and the other parent with regard to this area.
Here I want to get feedback that each parent has about the other.
I generally encounter far less reluctance and resistance in the discussion of child-rearing practices than I do in the discussion of the
marriage. I usually start with a general question such as: "Now let's
talk about the children and how each of you handles the various
problems that have arisen." This is generally enough to get things
moving. Sometimes I will have to be more specific with questions

such as: "Although we've covered child-rearing practices to some degree in the individual sessions, I'd like to go into further detail here, especially with regard to how you see each other in this area. So why don't we talk first about what you see as your own strong points and the other party's strong points with regard to dealing with the children." Again, I do not ask a particular parent to start speaking. Rather, I want to see who initiates the discussion.

Following a discussion of the strong points and assets, I then shift to the more difficult subject of liabilities. Again, I want a statement by each person regarding how he or she sees his or her own weaknesses and how the other party sees them. Sometimes I will divide the liabilities issue into specific areas of inquiry. For example, I may ask a mother what she suspects her husband's criticisms of her have been with regard to punishment techniques and/or what she recalls him to have said in this area. Then, I will turn to the husband and ask him directly what his criticisms are. I will then repeat the procedure with the father's stating first what his recollections are of the mother's criticisms of his disciplinary techniques and then ask the mother directly to state them.

In the course of the discussion on child-rearing practices, I may give advice. Although my primary goal in the extended evaluation is to collect as much data as possible, this does not preclude my spending time providing recommendations. I am not referring here to the kinds of recommendations that can only emerge from extended experience; rather, I am referring to those that are simple, short, and do not detract significantly from the time spent in the data-collection process. But such *en passant* recommendations can also serve the purpose of data collection in that parents' reactions to my suggestions often provide additional information that may be useful. I am particularly interested in the parents' degree of receptivity to my advice. And there is a whole range here from the parent who passively and gullibly accepts every bit of advice to those who are completely resistant and antagonistic to it. The ideal is that they be at some point close to the receptive end of the continuum, but not to the point of blind acceptance of everything I say. I would like them to have conviction for my recommendations because when they do, it is far more likely that they will implement them effectively. In addition, parents who are too passive in their relationship with me serve as poor models for their children. The children should not view me as their parent's "boss"; rather, they should view their parents as receptive to my advice but retaining the final decision-making power.

Concluding Comments

The joint interview with the parents not only serves the goal of data collection but, if successful, can help entrench the parents' relationship with the therapist. As will be discussed in greater detail in Chapter Seven, the establishment of a good relationship with parents is one of the cornerstones of effective therapy with the child. It is here, more than in the other interviews, that one may learn about criticisms each has about the therapist, criticisms that may not have been revealed in the individual interviews. Here, one parent may bring these criticisms up in the presence of the other. And it is crucial that they be discussed. Otherwise, the parents may harbor their resentments silently, and this can compromise the treatment and even bring about its cessation—without the therapist's knowing exactly what has gone on to compromise the treatment.

Before closing the joint interview with the parents, I discuss the family interview. Generally, I want teenagers present and those younger children who can be relied upon to contribute significantly. My experience has been that a good cutoff age is five or six. Although one may learn from the observations of interactions between the parents and the preschool nonpatient sibling, the disruptions of their presence throughout the course of the interview may outweigh the advantages of such observations. Furthermore, even children of five to eight may not be valuable contributors and may just sit there quite bored during the course of the family interview. After eight or nine, the older the youngster, the greater the likelihood of meaningful input. (The reader should not view these ages as fixed guidelines; rather, they are approximate.)

Once the decision has been made regarding which children shall participate, we discuss the issue of what to tell the siblings regarding the purpose of the family meeting. I generally advise the parents to tell the siblings that it will be helpful to me in my work with their brother or sister to get information from them about what is happening in the family. I advise the parents to reassure the siblings that they want them to be open and honest and that there will be no repercussions for their divulgences. On occasion, parents are reluctant to tell the siblings about the patient's treatment because they fear that the siblings might taunt the patient, tell others, or involve themselves in other inappropriate reactions to the disclosure. Most often, I advise the parents to tell the siblings about the treatment and to deal with any inappropriate reactions if and when they arise. I impress upon them the fact that keeping the patient's treatment a secret is likely to contribute to and even intensify the patient's feelings of low self-worth, because such withholding implies that the patient is suffering with a disorder that he or she should be ashamed about. There are occasions when a sibling is so sadistic and disturbed that the divulgence might indeed work against the patient, but this has been a rare situation in my experience.

THE FAMILY INTERVIEW

In Chapter Fourteen I will discuss in detail the family interview techniques that I utilize. Here I discuss only some basic principles of the family interview in the extended evaluation. It is important for the examiner to appreciate that both the patient and the siblings may be quite tense at the beginning of the family interview. The patient is likely to be uncomfortable over the fact that his or her siblings are now going to discuss embarrassing issues. And the siblings may be fearful of criticizing their parents or may be appreciative of the fact that what they say may be upsetting to the patient. Accordingly, I generally do not sit silently at the outset of this session and wait for someone to open up. Rather, I myself begin with some reassuring statement to the various parties. I will turn to the siblings and say something along these lines: "I appreciate your coming here today. I want you to know that my experience has been that brothers and sisters can often provide me with very valuable information that helps me in the treatment of their brother or sister. I know that this is probably uncomfortable for you. But I know that I speak for your parents when I say to you that they want you to be open and honest to me and that you shouldn't be afraid that there'll be any terrible consequences afterwards if you say critical things about them." At this point, I may actually ask the parents to make some statements along these lines. I will also say to the siblings: "I want you to know, also, that I appreciate that I am placing you in a difficult position with regard to the things that you're going to say about your brother or sister. However, I hope you'll appreciate that it's important for me to have this information and that you, probably more than anybody else, can provide it to me."

I will then turn to the patient: "I know that this is difficult for you, as well. I appreciate that I'm asking your brother and/or sister (or whatever the number and sexes are) to say things about you that may be upsetting and embarrassing. I hope, however, that you are big and strong enough to appreciate that it is important for me to get this information if I'm to help you." When I make this statement, I generally do not expect the child to agree with me that such divulgences are likely to be in his or her best interests; I make the statement, however, in the hope that some of it does get through, and the child does appreciate my sensitivity to his or her situation.

I will then ask the siblings why they think their brother(sister) is coming to see me. This is an important base from which to operate. The derivative questions make more sense if this issue is brought out first. On occasion, the siblings do not know of the basic problems, but most often they do. In addition, their opinions regarding the problems may be at variance with the parents and this can also be useful as clarifying data. Furthermore, their confrontations may help the patient gain some insight into the fact that he or she has problems although, as mentioned so many times previously, I don't push for this.

At this point I may ask the siblings to talk about the parents. I may ask them to say good things about their parents and things about their parents that they do not like. I start with the parents here because I want to take the focus off the patient and discuss criticisms of the parties who have "thicker skins," namely, the parents. Often, the information about the parents that the children provide me at this point proves quite useful. They may come up with parental characteristics that were not previously brought to my attention. I may then go on to the subject of exactly how they see their parent's personality problems and difficulties to have contributed to the patient's. Sometimes siblings will give me very insightful information about this relationship. For example, a teenage sister might say, "I think Billy's main problem is my mother. She spoils him sick. He's the big baby of the family. She doesn't know how to say no to him like she used to say to me and my brother." Although I may recognize that an element in such criticism may be jealousy, there also may be significant truth to the allegations. I will then use this as a point of departure for family discussion. For such a criticism, I may turn my attention to the mother and ask her for her response. I may ask Billy himself what he thinks about this criticism. The likelihood is that Billy (age eight) does not consider himself to be too indulged; in fact, he may believe that his mother is too withholding from him and indulging of his sister.

The general principle I follow when conducting family interviews is that I use each issue as a point of departure for further back and forth confrontations and discussion. Usually I ask each party what he or she thinks about what the other party has just said. Sometimes I will ask an individual what he or she thinks about what has been said previously by a few members on a particular point. I try not to let things become chaotic; rather I try to come to some tentative conclusions on each issue raised. Getting input from the other family members serves to clarify as well as generate family discussion, interaction, and information about their various relationships. Last, the family interview may have direct therapeutic benefits in that it may open up, sometimes for the first time, the kinds of discussion that have never taken place previously—and this cannot but be therapeutic for the patient. I cannot emphasize this point strongly enough. The data collection interviews are often stressful to the patient and other family members. To the degree that one can help the family derive therapeutic benefits during the course of these interviews, to that degree will the therapist be compensating the family for these negative elements in the extended evaluation.

I generally do not set aside a standard 45-minute interview for the family. Rather, I will set aside an hour to an hour and a half, depending upon how much information I suspect will be emerging. It is not my intention during this time to follow up every issue to its limit. Rather, I want to focus on major problems and collect some information about each of them. I am not conducting family therapy here; rather, I am collecting data about the family, my patient, and the various interactions of the family members. On occasion, a second family interview may be warranted. Also, on occasion, the initial family interview may have served as a breakthrough for the family, and ongoing family therapy may be agreed upon. What was originated, then, as a diagnostic data-gathering procedure, ends up being an important therapeutic experience.

PREPARATION
OF THE PRESENTATION

I recognize that the extended evaluation that I conduct is probably more time-consuming and involved than that conducted by most examiners. In fact, I myself do not *routinely* conduct such extended evaluations. On occasion, on the basis of the two-hour initial consultation, I sense that all the aforementioned interviews may not be necessary. For the purposes of this book, however, I have described in detail the full evaluation and recognize that the reader (like myself) will also find situations in which it is not warranted. Similarly, the preparation of the final presentation may not necessarily be as intensive as that which I describe here. Again, for the sake of this book, I present the full preparation procedure.

The ideal way of organizing the formidable data that the examiner may have accumulated is with the use of a word processor. The examiner who has one available will save much time. Those who do not have one available must utilize the more primitive procedure that I used prior to my acquisition of this valuable instrument. Accordingly, I will first describe the method I use with the word processor and then describe the more painstaking method that I utilized previously. In addition, if the examiner enjoys the indulgence of a secretary, this can obviously save time. If not, then the examiner must perform these procedures him- or herself. Fortunately, I have both a word processor and a secretary and can indulge myself these shorter and more efficient procedures.

I begin the dictation by instructing my secretary to set up on the word processor a series of basic topics. Then, I will go through my material—from beginning to end—and dictate comments and quotations within each of these categories. The secretary scrolls up and down the screen inserting the material within each of the topics. The topics are: Basic Data, Presenting Problems, Mother's Assets, Mother's Liabilities, Father's Assets, Father's Liabilities, Patient's Psychodynamics Derived from Patient Interviews, Patient's Psychodynamics Derived from Parents and Family Interviews, Conclusions and Recommendations. When dictating the material, I do not concern myself with organization of the material *within* each of the categories. Rather, it serves the purpose of the final presentation to the parents to have just the aforementioned degree of organization. If I want to use this material in the preparation of a written report, then I will reorganize (again by word processor) the material *within* each category, but utilize the aforementioned outline as my starting point. On occasion, when the question of the child's having a neurologically based learning disability has also been raised, I will include a section in which the results of special tests in this area are also presented. I include this immediately after the section on the child's presenting complaints. I generally entitle it: Evaluation for the Presence of the *Group of Minimal Brain Dysfunction Syndromes* (GMBDS).

The basic data material is often taken directly from the face sheet of the parents' questionnaire. It generally includes the patient's name, age, date of birth, grade, and whether in a regular or special class. It also includes the names and ages of the parents and their occupations. In addition, I include the names and ages of the siblings and what grades they are in. Stepparents, also, are included.

With regard to the chief complaints, I generally start with those that have been presented by the parents (and sometimes the child) at the beginning of the two-hour consultation. I select here only those problems I consider to be psychological difficulties and not those mentioned by the parents which I have decided are not. I include here, as well, those problems described on page 2 of the questionnaire where I request the parents provide me with a three line summary of the main difficulties. I will then scan pages 9 through 12 of the questionnaire and select those symptoms that I consider worthy of therapeutic focus. I do not generally include here every single item checked off by the parents because some parents will list as a symptom atypical behavior of normal frequency, my warning to this effect in the introduction on page 9 notwithstanding.

In the section on parental assets and liabilities, one does well to include quotations. The quotations here enhance the accuracy of the presentation and may also prevent inappropriate antagonism toward the therapist. If one takes care to quote criticisms from the opposite parent, one is likely to prevent such occurrences. Such quotations are especially important if a written report is to be prepared. In these days of burgeoning malpractice, one wants to be certain that one's written report is not used to one's disadvantage in any possible subsequent litigation. And accurate recording of quotations can serve this end in that it is not the therapist who is making the critical allegation but one of the family members. (It is a sad commentary on our times that his must be mentioned here, but not to do so would be a disservice to the reader.)

When dictating the section on the child's psychodynamics, I not only describe each observation, but the meaning that I ascribe to it. This might include a behavioral manifestation and then an interpretation, or it might refer to some verbal projection and my interpretation. For example, I might quote certain key statements from the story that the child told in association with a human figure that was drawn, and then I will dictate my understanding of the meaning of the child's story. The same is done with the verbal projective animal and object questions. With regard to the verbal projective questions about those animals and objects that would suit the parents, I make sure to state that this is how I interpret how *the child* sees the parent(s) and emphasize to the parents that this may not necessarily be the way they are, but the way the child sees them. This is not only a more accurate way of stating things, but also can assuage the pains and discomforts of more defensive and/or insecure parents.

In the conclusions and recommendations section I will summarize the major themes in the family that are contributing to the child's difficulties. This generally ranges from two or three to about ten or twelve elements. It may include genetic predisposing factors and psychodynamic issues, both interpersonal and intrapsychic. This summary statement can also be useful in the course of therapy in that I may refer to it from time to time to refresh my memory about the variety of problems for which the child has presented as well as to assess progress. I then state the recommended treatment program with regard to the number of sessions per week (generally one or two) as well as who shall be involved in the treatment. If the reader does not have a secretary and word processor, then the aforementioned must be done by hand. One generally writes the titles on separate sheets of paper and then skips back and forth from page to page inserting the proper information under each category.

PRESENTATION OF THE FINDINGS
TO THE PARENTS

I generally set aside an open-ended session for this presentation. It generally takes about two hours, sometimes longer. I make it open-ended in order to insure that we are not rushed. Sometimes I invite the child to join us and sometimes not. The older the child the greater the likelihood he or she will be invited. The primary criterion that I utilize, however, is not the child's age but how much therapeutic benefit I think the child will derive from attendance. Younger children are more likely to squirm during the course of the presentation and not attend for long on the information that I present. In addition, younger children are not likely to appreciate my discussion of underlying psychodynamics as well as family factors that may be contributing to their difficulties. Generally, I will invite children from ages nine or ten and upward, although the reader should not view this age level as a sharp cut-off point.

I usually begin the interview by telling the parents how I prepared the presentation. I directly show them the computer print-outs and enumerate the various categories within which I have placed the information as it has been dictated. I then go step by step, from one section to the next, reading and commenting on what has been written therein. I advise the parents to interrupt me at any point if they have any questions or wish further discussion. I prefer that the issues raised serve as points of departure for limited discussion, but not the kind of extended discussion that might be more appropriate during therapeutic interviews. Sometimes, I may have been in error with regard to a particular point or quotation and I invite the parents' correction. I inform the parents that my goal here is not to be "right" but to be "accurate." Unless there are a formidable number of such errors, the parents will generally appreciate my receptivity to corrections. If the child is present, I will invite his or her participation as well.

On occasion, I will have ordered psychological tests. I generally make a photostatic copy of the psychological report, give the parents one copy, and we read them over together in detail. This report is their property and they take it with them at the end of the meeting (regardless of whether or not they have chosen to have a full written report prepared by me). Examiners who do not give the parents a copy of this psychological report are asking for trouble. The parents are entitled to it and not to give it to them exposes one to criticism. They are also entitled to discuss the report in detail with the examiner, especially because such reports are often confusing and anxiety provoking to parents. Obviously, when such a report is discussed in the final presentation, it is going to add to the meeting's length.

The discussion of the final treatment program is quite important. Because it comes last, I want to be sure that we have the time to discuss this in depth. And this is one of the main reasons why my final presentation is open-ended. Parents will often ask how long the treatment will take. I generally advise them that I cannot know in advance and that the most important determinants relate to how successful I will be in engaging their child and how receptive they will be to involvement in the therapy. Of course, by this time I have definite information in this area and will make comments on it. It is a serious error for the therapist to even proffer a guess with regard to the number of weeks, months, or years treatment will take. No matter how many qualifications he or she may give, the parents are still likely to put a circle on their mental calendar (if not their real calendar). Only the number becomes branded in the parent's brains; the qualifications never seem to have reached their ears. Even if accused of being vague, obstructionistic, or hostile, the therapist should not speculate about how long the treatment will take. It would be a rare situation in which he or she would not regret having made such a speculation.

I also discuss with the parents the nature and degree of their participation. Most often the parent who brings the child will be invited in at the beginning of the session and then remain to varying degrees depending upon the situation. Often this involves the parent's remaining throughout the course of the whole session. I will generally invite the parent who will not be bringing the child most often to feel comfortable to join us without necessarily providing advance notice. If greater family involvement is warranted, I will discuss this issue.

I will also talk about the difference between counseling the parents on dealing with the child vs. treating the parents for marital difficulties which they may have. It is important that the examiner not coerce the parents into treatment regardless of how formidable the marital problems are. Rather, the examiner does well to ask questions like: "Do you consider yourself to have marital problems?" "Have you ever given thought to having therapy for such problems?" and "What do you think about obtaining therapy for these problems?" It is crucial that the examiner take a passive attitude here and merely sound the parents out on their receptivity. To use coercive or guilt-evoking tactics is contraindicated, for example: "If you want to salvage your marriage, you're going to have to go into treatment. I can't imagine the marriage surviving without it" or "For the sake of your child, it's important that you people have treatment for your marriage. If you don't, it's going to be extremely difficult, if not impossible, for me to help your child."

People who enter treatment in response to such threats are not likely to be helped. If the parents decide that they want therapy for the marital problems, then the therapist does well to make a statement along these lines: "Well, as I see it, you have two choices here. One is to work with me and the other to work with someone else. As you know, I do treat parents of my child patients and have often found the combination useful, but recognize that some parents feel more comfortable working with someone else on their marital problems, while being counseled by me regarding how to deal with their child. I am interested in your thoughts and feelings on this; however, it's important that you be direct and honest with me and not hold back your true feelings from fear that I might be offended. Many parents have chosen to see others and I respect that choice." This approach, I believe, protects the therapist from the parental reaction that "he(she) is looking for business." It does, however, provide the parents with an option that they may not have appreciated they had and helps them appreciate both the pros and cons of each alternative—information they are entitled to have.

If medication is warranted, I will discuss this with the parents at this point. Here again, one must leave ample time for such discussion in order to assuage unnecessary or irrational fears that the parents may have. It is likely that they have some unrealistic ideas about what medication can do and cannot do, and the therapist must give them the opportunity to express their ideas if he or she is to correct distortions (very likely). For parents who are very reluctant for medication, I will emphasize that I am only suggesting a *trial* on medication and that they not commit themselves to a full course of treatment before knowing about the drug and ascertaining empirically whether or not it will prove helpful to their child. Often, by reassuring them that a few pills are not likely to produce lifelong damage to the child's body, they will be more receptive to the trial.

Before closing this meeting, the therapist should invite the parents to ask any further questions. Often they may have heard of quicky-type treatments that promise results in a shorter period of time. I will generally ask them about the particular form of treatment and present them my views on it. When contrasting psychotherapy with these other forms of therapy, the examiner should be cautious with regard to making any claims about the efficacy of psychotherapy. The examiner does well to emphasize to the parents that there is no "proof" that psychotherapy works but that the examiner has definite convictions that it can be useful for certain children and their families, especially those who involve themselves with commitment to the process.

Finally, before closing the session, I ask the parents if they would like a full written report prepared. Examiners who charge for the extra work involved in the preparation of such a report should have told the parents about this much earlier. I make mention of it in the face sheet to my questionnaire (Figure 15.1) so that the parents know about it even prior to the first meeting. Examiners who do not use such a document do well to mention this charge during the initial consultation. Otherwise, I believe parents have a justifiable complaint when they are advised of this new extra expense at such a late point. Even here many parents have "forgotten" about this charge and will express surprise (and even resentment) that it will cost them more money for me to prepare this report. If the parents choose to have a written report, I prepare a copy for them, give it to them directly, and let *them* decide whom they wish to give it to. This is an important point; in fact, it may be the most important point I make in this book. In these days of burgeoning malpractice litigation, the safest course is to give the parents the report themselves and let them decide whom they wish to give copies to, whether it is the school, the child's pediatrician, or anyone else. In this way, the examiner cannot be accused of having sent out critical and/or personal information to parties to whom the parents did not wish to have this information available.

Sometimes parents will ask me to prepare a modified report for certain parties, such as a school. I generally refuse to do this. I say to them, however, that if they wish to delete certain parts of the report before turning it over to the school, that is their privilege. However, I strongly urge them to make a copy of the report, cut out the deleted paragraphs, and advise the school of such deletions. Some may do this, some may not. I tell them about the injudiciousness of not telling the school that the report has been altered. But, if they do not follow my advice, I cannot be considered to have been at fault. The therapist does well to appreciate that we are living in a time when there is approximately one lawyer for every 850 individuals in the population. With such a ratio, there are many hungry lawyers who view malpractice litigation to be a very promising livelihood. (Remember the bumper sticker: "Become a Doctor, Support a Lawyer.") Giving parents the report and letting them make copies for distribution to others is an excellent way of protecting oneself in this unfortunate atmosphere.

SEVEN

Parental Involvement in the Child's Treatment

Considering the primitive state of the art/science we call psychotherapy, therapists need all the help they can get.

R.A. Gardner

For many years I practiced in the traditional manner and saw my child patients alone. Usually the mother rather than the father was available to bring the child. My procedure was to have the mother bring the child and then sit in the waiting room. However, I did not strictly refrain from involving her in the treatment. I would intermittently bring her in to discuss certain issues with the child, and also had occasional separate sessions with her and/or the father. In my initial evaluation, I would see the mother and father, both individually and together. In addition, during the initial evaluation, I would also have a session or two with the child and the parents together, and even occasionally bring in one or more siblings. However, the basic therapeutic program after the initial evaluation was that the child and I were alone in the room. As is true of most trainees, I automatically accepted as optimum the methods of treatment used by my teachers and supervisors. I believed that being with the child alone was crucial to the development of a good therapist-patient relationship, and that to the degree that I brought third parties into the room, to that degree I would compromise our relationship. In addition, I believed that it was very important to have a confidential relationship with the child, a relationship in which he or she would have the security of knowing that I would not reveal to the parents anything he or she told me.

Over the years I became increasingly dissatisfied with this procedure. When something would come up in a session that I thought would be important for the mother to know about (nothing particularly confidential), I would bring her in and, in the last few minutes of the session, quickly give her a run-down of what had happened and then would make some recommendations. Most often this was done hurriedly; however, on occasion we would run overtime because I considered it important that she fully understand what had happened in the session and what my recommendations were. My usual experience was that the mother had little conviction for the recommendations, primarily because she had not been witness to the situation that brought them about. When I started keeping the mothers in the room for longer periods, I found that the children generally did not object and, in addition, the mothers had greater conviction for my recommendations because they had been witness to the situations that had brought them about. They not only had the opportunity to observe directly the events that resulted in my suggestions, but they had ample time to discuss them with me in detail. This resulted in their much more frequently and effectively carrying out my recommendations. To my surprise, the children did not express any objections. They had not read the books that I had read—books that had emphasized the importance of my seeing the child alone and the crucial role of the confidential relationship.

In this chapter, I discuss in detail the ways in which I utilize parents in the treatment of children. I generally refer to my approach as *individual child psychotherapy with parental observation and intermittent participation*. Although this title may appear cumbersome, it states exactly what I do. In addition, I will often indicate to the parents that they are my *assistant therapists*. This designation communicates the point that their active participation in the therapeutic process will be utilized.

Before discussing the ways in which I use parents in the child's therapy, it is important for the reader to learn about my views on confidentiality in treatment, especially in the treatment of children. I will describe my position on confidentiality, therefore, before I present descriptions of the ways in which I enlist the aid of parents in the child's treatment.

THE ISSUE OF CONFIDENTIALITY AS IT RELATES TO THE PARENTS' INVOLVEMENT IN THE CHILD'S TREATMENT

Many therapists believe that the active involvement by a parent(s) would significantly compromise the child's confidentiality, and this they believe is crucial if there is to be meaningful therapy. I believe that such therapists are placing too much weight on confidentiality. The patient is coming primarily for treatment, whether the patient is a child or an adult. The patient is not coming primarily for the preservation of confidentiality. I believe that to the degree that the preservation of the confidential relationship serves the ends of treatment, to that degree it should be respected. If it is a choice between confidentiality and doing what is in the best interests of the patient therapeutically, then, I believe, the therapeutic indications should be given priority over the confidences. One must not lose sight of the primary aim of therapy: to do what is in the best interests of the patient. In order to describe my position more specifically, I will consider the confidentiality issue as it pertains to the treatment of the adult, the adolescent, and the child. Although there are differences with regard to confidentiality in these three areas, there are basic similarities that hold for all three categories.

Confidentiality in Adult Therapy

If the adult is to have a successful therapeutic experience, he or she must have the feeling that the therapist will not disclose to others what is revealed during the course of treatment. Otherwise, the freedom to reveal will be significantly compromised—to the point where therapy may become meaningless. Most therapists would agree, however, that there are certain situations in which strict adherence to the confidentiality may be antitherapeutic. Such is the case when there is a strong suicidal or homicidal risk. Basically, when a human life is at stake, concerns about confidentiality are reduced to the point of being trivial. If the patient is suicidal, it behooves the therapist to enlist the aid of family members and close friends to do everything possible to protect the patient. This usually involves their active participation in hospitalizing the suicidal patient. It would be unconscionable, in my opinion, to "respect" such a patient's request that the suicidal danger not be divulged to the nearest of kin. Similarly, when there is a homicidal risk, the therapist should do everything possible to warn the potential victim.

When a patient in treatment raises the issue of confidentiality, I will openly state that he or she can feel secure that I will not reveal what is divulged—with the exception of situations in which there is a homicidal or suicidal danger. In most cases, the patient is thereby reassured that confidences will not be divulged because neither of these eventualities seems likely. On occasion, however, a depressed patient will be told that I might divulge the suicidal danger. In such cases I will reassure the patient that everything will be done to avoid such disclosure. However, I inform the patient that there might be an occasion in which I might divulge the suicidal risk, if such divulgence might prove lifesaving. Interestingly, most patients are not upset by this. Some healthy part of them appreciates that they could conceivably "go crazy," and that at such a time they might impulsively commit a self-destructive act that could cause irreparable damage and even death. My position provides reassurance that should such a situation occur some healthy and stabilizing intervention will take place. My experience has been that this is usually reassuring.

In recent years there have been a number of cases in which the litigation has centered on this issue. Psychiatrists were sued for malpractice because they preserved patients' confidences, and there was a resultant suicide or homicide that could conceivably have been prevented. The usual defense was that the therapist was respecting the patient's confidentiality and acting in the highest ethical traditions of the medical profession. Even in former years, I did not subscribe to this view. It is not in the highest ethical tradition of the medical profession to sit by and do nothing when there might be a suicide or homicide taking place. It is in the highest interests of the medical profession to protect human life. Fortunately, the courts and ethical committees in medical societies are shifting in the direction of supporting divulgences in such cases. This is a good trend.

Confidentiality in Adolescent Therapy

It is not uncommon for me to have the following conversation with an adolescent:

> *Patient:* Everything I say to you is just between me and you. Right? You'll never tell my parents anything I tell you. Right?
>
> *Therapist:* Not right.
>
> *Patient:* You mean you're going to tell my parents everything I tell you?
>
> *Therapist:* No, I didn't say that either.
>
> *Patient:* But my friend goes to a shrink, and his shrink told him that everything they speak about is strictly confidential, and his shrink says that he'll never tell my friend's parents anything about what goes on in a session.
>
> *Therapist:* Yes, many psychiatrists work that way. But I don't. Let me tell you how I work. As long as you don't do anything dangerous, to either yourself or others, you can be quite sure that what we speak about here will be held strictly confidential. I'm in full appreciation of the fact that it's important that you have the feeling that what we talk about is strictly confidential. However, there are certain exceptions. And these exceptions hold for anyone, regardless of age. My policy is the same for all. It's not just for teen-agers. It's the same whether you're 5 years old or 85 years old. The basic policy is this: As long as you're not doing anything dangerous, you can be sure that I won't reveal what you tell me. However, if you're doing something that's dangerous, I reserve the right, at my discretion, to reveal to your family whatever I consider important to reveal to help stop you from doing the dangerous thing. I may need their help. What do you think about what I've said?

At that point the patient may ask me to tell him or her what things I would reveal. I will not then provide "food for thought." I do not wish to give the youngster suggestions for various forms of antisocial and/or self-destructive behavior that may not have entered his or her head. Rather, I ask the adolescent to tell me what things he or she might do that might warrant such divulgence. I may then use this as a point of departure for a therapeutic inquiry. However, I do have a "list." It includes: heavy use of drugs (not occasional use of marijuana), heavy use of alcohol, dangerous driving (especially when under the influence of drugs or alcohol), criminal behavior, and for girls, a desire to have an out-of-wedlock child (occasional sexual intercourse is not a reportable item). I also impress upon the adolescent the fact that should one of these dangerous situations be arising, I will not automatically discuss the problem with the parent. Rather, I will exhaust all possibilities of discussion with the patient and the adolescent group before divulging the risk. Usually, such discussions are enough. However, when they are not, the youngster usually knows beforehand that I am going to divulge the information.

There is another aspect of the confidentiality issue in adolescence which warrants comment. The parents have a reasonable right to know whether there is a significant risk of dangerous behavior. When this issue is broached, generally in the initial evaluation, I will tell them that they should know that "no news is good news," that is, that I will divulge dangers to them, and if there are no such divulgences, they can feel assured that no great risks are imminent.

I am fully appreciative of the fact that the adolescent needs a special, separate relationship with the therapist. This is part of his or her developmental need to establish a separate identity from that of the parents. This autonomy is necessary if the adolescent is to grow into an independent, self-sufficient adult. Active participation of the parents in the adolescent's therapy can compromise this goal. However, the goal can still be achieved by some participation on the part of the parents. Occasional joint sessions in which the youngster is seen along with the parents need not interfere with this goal. There can still be a significant percentage of sessions devoted to the adolescent, him- or herself, and the confidential relationship can also serve the purpose of enhancing separation and autonomy. The potential divulgence of a dangerous situation also need not interfere with this sense of autonomy so important to the adolescent's development.

Confidentiality in Child Psychotherapy

By child psychotherapy I am referring to the treatment of children between the ages of about four and ten. In my opinion, the confidentiality issue has little if any place in the treatment of most of these children. There are many therapists who will say to such children something along these lines: "Whatever you tell me here in this room is just between you and me. I promise I'll never tell your mother or father what you tell me. You can trust me on that." Many children might wonder exactly what the therapist is referring to.

They know of no great secrets that they have from their parents. And this is especially the case for younger children. The parents know quite well that the child is soiling, stealing, lying, truant, and so on. They more than the child are aware of these problems, and it is they who initiated the treatment. So the statement must be confusing and even irrelevant to many children.

In addition, the statement sets up a structure in which there are "we" (the therapist and the patient) and "they" (the parents). "We" and "they" can easily become "we" versus "they." And this concept can introduce schisms in the family. The family has enough trouble already; it does not need an additional problem brought about by the therapeutic program. The system also impedes open communication. Generally, communication impairments contribute to the development of and perpetuation of psychopathology. The confidential relationship with the child is likely to increase the communication problems of the family. The thrust of the therapy should be to encourage open expression of the issues that are causing people difficulty. A conspiracy of silence usually serves only to reduce communication and defeats thereby an important therapeutic goal.

The therapist should attempt to create an atmosphere in which there is an open pool of communication—an atmosphere in which all things pertinent to the child's treatment are discussed openly with the parents. I do not make any statements about this; I do it as a matter of course. I make no mention of the confidentiality. If the child says to me that he or she does not wish me to tell his parents something, I will get very specific about what it is he or she wishes me not to divulge. Almost invariably it is an issue worthy of being discussed with the parents. Usually, the child fears repercussions that are unreal and exaggerated. Encouraging the child to express to the parent(s) the forbidden material, either in my presence or at home, is usually therapeutic. It can teach all concerned that the repression (unconscious) and suppression (conscious) of thoughts and feelings is likely to perpetuate problems; whereas civilized discussion is the best way to resolve family problems.

A boy, for example, will say to me that he doesn't want me to tell his parents something. On further inquiry the issue almost invariably is one that should be discussed with the parents, and the child's fears of what will happen if such information is disclosed are unrealistic. Encouraging the child to express the forbidden material to the parents can teach him that the hidden thoughts and feelings are not as terrible as he considered them to be and the anticipated consequences are not forthcoming. The therapist can serve as a catalyst for such expression, and his or her presence can make the atmosphere a safer one for the child to first make such revelations.

There is an aspect of S. Freud's famous Little Hans case (1909) that is pertinent to my discussion here. During the one joint session that Freud held with Little Hans and his father, Hans expressed some hostility toward his father that he had not previously revealed. I believe that it is unfortunate that Freud did not direct his attention to this in his report of the case. I would speculate that the reason why Hans had not expressed the hostility previously was that he was afraid to do so because of fears of his father's retaliation. However, in the presence of "Professor Sigmund Freud," a man of whom both the patient and his father were in awe, Hans could safely reveal his anger because of his awareness that his father was not likely to react with severe punitive measures in Freud's presence. I suspect that Hans' having had the living experience that his father would react to his hostility in a civilized manner made it easier for him to express his resentments elsewhere. And this, I believe, was a contributing factor to the alleviation of his symptoms. Later in this chapter I will discuss in greater detail this and other aspects of the Little Hans case.

Classical psychoanalysts, in particular, are strict adherents to the confidentiality principle. It is they, more than other therapists, who make it a point at the outset to emphasize to the child that they will respect confidences. It is of interest that Freud did not consider confidentiality to be an important issue in his treatment of Little Hans. Hans' father was the therapist and Freud was the supervisor. When reading the transcript of the treatment, one observes that Hans revealed just about every intimacy one can imagine a child might have: bowel movements, urination, masturbation, interest in observing his mother's toilet functioning, sexual fantasies toward his mother, and so forth. If he were indeed hiding material that a child might be ashamed to reveal, I would find it hard to imagine what such material might be. Little Hans knew that his father was revealing their discussions to Freud. In the one joint session that Freud had with Hans and his father, there was open discussion of these intimacies. Classical analysts often point to the case of Little Hans as the proof that Freud's theories of infantile sexuality, the Oedipus complex, and castration anxiety are valid.

Libraries have been written on these theories—which are supposedly proven by the Little Hans case. However, the structure of Freud's therapeutic program is often ignored by the same psychoanalysts. They do not utilize the parents as assistant therapists (as did Freud), and they enter into a strictly confidential relationship with the child (which Freud did not do). In both cases, I believe, they do the child and the family a disservice.

REASONS FOR PARENTAL AMBIVALENCE REGARDING A CHILD'S TREATMENT

Parental involvement in a child's treatment is at best tenuous. Although parents may profess commitment to the therapeutic process, there are many reasons why they are generally quite ambivalent and their mixed feelings about the treatment may interfere significantly with its progress and even result in their prematurely terminating therapy. In this section I discuss some of the more common reasons for impaired parental commitment to the therapeutic process. An understanding of these factors can be useful in increasing the likelihood that the therapist will be able to engage the parents more successfully and thereby increase the likelihood of the child's involvement in treatment. Some of the more common ways in which parental resistance exhibits itself: lateness to the sessions, canceling sessions for frivolous or weak reasons, forgetting to follow through with the therapist's recommendations, complaining to the child about treatment (its cost, time consumption, et cetera), and withholding payment (one of the most predictable ways to ultimately bring about a cessation of treatment).

One of the most important reasons for compromised parental commitment to therapy is the financial privation that it often involves. This is especially the case when the child is in private treatment. Whereas the parents may agree initially to commit themselves to the cost of the treatment, when the bills start coming they often have a change of heart and remove the child prematurely from treatment or support the child's resistances, which are inevitably present. There is also a time commitment in that the parent who brings the child (more often the mother) will generally think of better ways of spending her time than bringing the child to a therapist. If she has other children and cannot afford housekeepers, then bringing the child to treatment may become an additional burden.

Here again, these extra pressures compromise her commitment to the therapeutic process.

Most parents experience guilt when the therapist advises them that their child needs treatment. They consider it proof that they somehow failed in the child's upbringing (H.S. Lippman, 1962). A common way that parents use to assuage such guilt is to rationalize withdrawal of the child from treatment. This is done either overtly or covertly. After all, if they can justify removing the child from treatment, especially if they can believe that he or she does not need it, they thereby absolve and even obviate their guilt. Therapists should tell such parents that they appreciate that at every point in the child's development the parents did what they considered to be in the child's best interests (usually the case) and that through misguidance and/or unfortunate circumstances, and/or the unavoidable effects of their own difficulties, their child developed psychiatric problems. Furthermore, the therapist does well to advise such parents that, at the present state of our knowledge, we do not understand all the factors that contribute to a child's psychiatric difficulties. Thus, even if they themselves had no psychiatric problems, and even if there had been no detrimental circumstances, and even if they had assiduously followed the best available advice, their child might still have developed difficulties (J.W. Kessler, 1966). Moreover, they must be helped to appreciate that innate temperamental factors may be contributing significantly to the child's problems (A. Thomas, S. Chess et al., 1963). My experience has been that a discussion of these factors can often be useful in reducing parental guilt and thereby increasing the likelihood that they will support the child's therapy.

Many parents become jealous of the child's intimate relationship with the therapist and may act out such feelings by undermining the treatment. They may consider themselves to have been the ones to have done all the "dirty work": changed the diapers, taken the child to pediatricians at all hours of the night, and made the hundreds of other sacrifices necessary for successful child rearing. Yet the therapist is "the good guy" who is viewed by the child as benevolent, kind, and sympathetic. Often the parents are threatened by the anxiety-provoking revelations about themselves that inevitably emerge in the child's treatment, and the desire to avoid these can contribute to their impaired commitment to the process.

One of the most effective ways of reducing parental guilt and the resistances that emerge from it is to have the parents participate actively in the child's treatment. Parents who believe that they are somehow at fault in bringing about the child's disorder can assuage their guilt by actively contributing to the therapeutic process. They are thereby helping "undo" what they have "done." By working closely with the parents, the therapist is more likely to develop a good relationship with them. The child will sense the parents' feelings about the therapist and will then be more likely to develop such involvement him- or herself. When parents have a good relationship with the therapist, they are more comfortable expressing resentments and disagreements. The failure to express such differences and complaints is one of the most common sources of parental resistance to the child's treatment and removal of the child from it.

Therapists who believe that it is their role to protect child patients from the indignities suffered at the hands of their parents are likely to alienate parents. The preferable position should be one of impartiality. The therapist should be viewed by all family members as someone who criticizes the parents when such criticism is warranted and, similarly, criticizes the child, again when such criticism is warranted. His or her criticisms, however, should be benevolent and he or she should not "keep score" regarding who is getting more or less. The therapist neither takes the side of parent or child; rather, he or she supports the side of healthy behavior regardless of who exhibits it.

Another common source of parental resistance to treatment derives from the situation in which the parent may not genuinely want the child to be relieved of his or her presenting symptoms, despite protestations to the contrary. The child's problems may play an important role in the family equilibrium. (This will be discussed in greater detail in Chapter Fourteen.) For example, the overprotective mother may want her child with separation anxiety disorder to stay at home and may undermine the therapist's efforts to get the child back to school (R.A. Gardner, 1984). Parents of delinquent youngsters often gain vicarious gratification from their children's antisocial acting out (A.M. Johnson, 1949, 1959; R.L. Stubblefield, 1967). Parents may ostensibly want their child to do better academically but, unconsciously, may undermine the treatment because they fear that the child will surpass them educationally and socioeconomically.

It behooves therapists to appreciate these and the multiplicity of other factors that may contribute to parental undercommitment to the therapeutic process and even removal of a child from treatment. The therapist should try to detect these compromising factors during the initial evaluation and deal with them at the outset. Otherwise, they may cause a compromise and even a cessation of the therapy. In this chapter I discuss the ways in which parents can be utilized in the child's treatment. Such utilization has many benefits for the child's treatment and is one of the predictable ways to obviate, circumvent, and avoid the aforementioned potential compromises in the child's therapy.

WAYS IN WHICH PARENTS [USUALLY THE MOTHER] CAN BE USEFUL IN A CHILD'S THERAPY

Gradually my procedure evolved to the position of informing the parents that they would be my therapeutic assistants in the child's treatment. Recognizing that it would most often be the mother who would be bringing the child, I invited the father to feel free to attend, without any prior notification, any session when he was available. My experience has been that this occurs from 5 to 10% of the time. For ease of presentation I utilize the term *mother* when I refer to my therapeutic assistant. However, it should be understood that fathers are available on occasion to serve in this role. My usual procedure is to have the mother come into the session with the child at the outset, and then to keep her in the room as long as I consider it warranted. This ranges from five to ten minutes to the full session.

The mother can be useful in a number of ways. The younger the child, the less likely that he or she is going to be able to recall many of the important events that occurred since the last session. This is especially the case if the child is seen only once a week. My usual experience is that when I ask a child at the outset what has gone on since I saw him or her last, there is no response. It is almost as if the child were frozen in ice or transfixed in space since the previous session. Knowledge of these events is often vital for the understanding of many of the child's therapeutic productions. The mother, almost invariably, is a ready source of this important information. I have mentioned that the more knowledge the therapist has about the child, the greater will be his or her capacity to respond with a meaningful story utilizing the mutual storytelling technique (Chapters Eight and Nine). These stories, like dreams, often relate to important events that have occurred in the day or two prior to their creation. The child is often not in touch with these events, nor will he or she readily provide them. Many mothers, when hearing the child's story, offer these vital data. It is important for the therapist to appreciate that the mother knows the child far better than he or she. Although not trained as a therapist, her hunches about the meaning of a story may be better than the therapist's—regardless of the number of years of psychoanalytic training the therapist has had. In the post-story discussion period, as well, the mother's input can prove most valuable.

In analyzing the dream the mother's assistance can also be invaluable. The child may include in the dream a figure who is entirely unknown to the therapist. The therapist certainly should obtain as many associations as possible from the child. This, of course, is the best way of ascertaining exactly what the dream figure symbolizes for the child. However, most children provide only a paucity of associations to their dream symbols, and the mother's input can be extremely valuable. She can ask the child leading questions about the figure, and she can often be a better interrogator than the therapist because she has some hunches about what may be important. And, when this fails, her specific and direct comments about the dream figure can often provide the therapist with useful information for understanding the dream.

The presence of the mother in the room enables the therapist to observe mother-child interactions that would not have otherwise be seen. The mother's observations of the ways in which I handle the child, especially when he or she is being difficult, can be useful to her in that it provides her with a model for handling these situations herself. (I am not claiming that I always handle every situation in the most judicious fashion. However, I believe that I do so more frequently than most of my patient's parents.)

The effects of parental participation on the treatment are important and may be even more important than the specific way in which a parent can be useful to treatment. Whereas originally I was taught that such participation would compromise my relationship with the child, my experience has been just the opposite. It is hard to have a good relationship with someone who is a stranger, and whose only or primary contact is the monthly bill. Not only is such a situation likely to produce some alienation, but the paucity of contact increases the likelihood that negative distortions and misinterpretations about the therapist will not be corrected. Having the mother in the room provides her with the opportunity to air her grievances, express her resentments and disappointments, ask questions, and so on. This is the best way to prevent or resolve such problems. Both parents' feelings toward the therapist are extremely important in determining what the child's feelings will be. A parent's animosity toward the therapist frequently, if not invariably, will be picked up by the child. If there is a dispute between the therapist and the parents, the child will have a loyalty conflict. Most often he or she will side with the parent. After all, the parents are providing the food, clothing, and shelter; they are the ones who are with the child the remaining hours of the week. The child knows where his or her "bread is buttered," and it is extremely unlikely that the child will, over a period of time, basically support the therapist's position when it is in conflict with the parents'. Accordingly, anything that can improve the relationship between the therapist and the parents is likely to strengthen the tie between the therapist and the patient.

Parental participation can strengthen the therapist's relationship with the parents in other ways. Seeing the therapist "in action" enables the parents to know firsthand exactly what is going on in the sessions. They are not left in the dark about the therapeutic procedure. In the traditional method, parents are ignorant of what is going on, and this can be a source of irritation and alienation. This is especially the case when the parents are paying for the treatment. When they know what they are spending their money for, they are less likely to harbor negative distortions and criticisms. Of course, if the therapist is spending significant amounts of time with traditional play therapy—which is much more play than therapy—then the parents may have a justifiable criticism and may reasonably consider themselves to be wasting their money. The play techniques that I describe in this book (Chapters Eight–Eleven) are, I believe, much more *therapy* than play. I believe that one of the main reasons child therapists often hesitate to allow parents to observe them is that they are basically ashamed of what they are doing.

Parents most often feel ashamed of the fact that they are bringing their child for treatment. No matter how much the therapist may try to assuage their guilt, they generally feel that they were at fault. And even though the therapist may initially say to the parents that they did their best and that they should not feel guilty, he or she then proceeds to ask questions that are basically designed to elicit information about what the parents did wrong. And the acquisition of this vital information cannot but entrench and enhance guilty feelings. The facts of the matter are that the parents did make mistakes, or else the child would not have developed psychogenic difficulties. As benevolent as were their motivations, as dedicated as they may have been to the child-rearing process, they were indeed deficient in certain areas and that is why the child is coming for treatment. Platitudes and gratuitous reassurances regarding the inappropriateness of such guilt are not likely to work. One way of genuinely reducing such guilt is to invite the parents to be active participants in the therapeutic process. In this way they become directly engaged in reducing and alleviating the very problems that have brought about their guilt. And the working-together process produces a sense of camaraderie with the therapist which also entrenches the relationship with him or her.

In the field of psychiatry, people like to give labels and names. I am often asked what I call this therapeutic approach. It is not family therapy because it is rare for all family members to be present. In addition, when I do have family sessions, they are primarily during the diagnostic phase. While I do practice family therapy in certain situations, that is not what I am describing here. It is more than parental counseling, which is also part of my therapeutic process, because the parent is actively involved in the child's treatment. The name that I use for the method is *individual child psychotherapy with parental observation and intermittent participation*. Although this name is somewhat cumbersome, it describes accurately what I do. It focuses primarily on the child and the techniques that I utilize are primarily designed for child therapy. Accordingly, it is a form of individual child psychotherapy. However, there is parental observation in that the parent (usually the mother) observes directly the therapeutic process. In addition, she actively participates to the degree that it is warranted during the session. To date I have not come up with a better name for this procedure.

I wish to emphasize again that the presence and participation of the parents do not usually compromise the therapist-patient relationship with the child—although this is what I had been taught, and this is what many still believe. The basic determinant of the relationship between the therapist and the child is their own personalities. A healthy mother does not believe that her relationship with her first child will be significantly compromised by the appearance of the second or third. No competent therapist would advise a parent to have only one child, lest the relationship with the first be compromised by the appearance of a second. No healthy mother strictly excludes the father's presence on those occasions when she is with her child, with the argument that it will compromise her relationship with her son or daughter. It is not the presence of one or a few others in the room that is the primary determinant of the relationship between two people. The relationship depends more on qualities that exist within and between the two of them. Therapists who strictly adhere to the traditional view may be providing the child with an antitherapeutic experience. This view expresses, both explicitly and implicitly, the notion that exclusivity is crucial for a good relationship. This can only engender possessiveness, egocentricity, intolerance for sharing, excessive dependency, and other untoward reactions.

SITUATIONS IN WHICH THE PARENTAL PRESENCE IS CONTRAINDICATED

It would be an error *always* to involve a parent throughout all of the sessions. In my view, this would be substituting one inappropriate therapeutic procedure for another. Those who strictly refrain from parental involvement are providing their patients with what I consider to be a significantly compromised form of treatment. Similarly, those who would strictly adhere to the opposite, that is, insist that a parent be present in every session—throughout the session—are imposing an equally rigid and, on occasion, antitherapeutic treatment procedure. What I am suggesting is that the therapist have the flexibility to tailor each therapeutic program to the particular needs of the patient. Most, but not all, patients do best with active parental participation. However, there are some children for whom the active parental participation is contraindicated. And it is these situations that I discuss here.

First, there is the issue of the child's age. I generally do not treat children below the age of about four. There is no strict cutoff point at the fourth birthday. There are children who are younger than four who are psychologically older than four, and these may be good candidates for treatment. And there are children who are older who still might not be candidates for direct therapy. But generally, it is around the age of four that the average child becomes a potential candidate for a meaningful therapeutic endeavor. Prior to that age my therapeutic focus is primarily on work with the parents, with intermittent interviews with the child, both alone and with the parents. I want to establish familiarity and groom the child for treatment if the counseling does not prove to be adequate to relieve the problem(s).

At about the age of 11, children may start revealing confidences that should not justifiably be communicated to the parents. (As I will discuss later, below that age I do not believe that most children have a significant amount of material that warrants the special confidential relationship so frequently utilized by many therapists.) Also at about the age of 11, many children begin to appreciate that their projected fantasies are revealing of their own problems, and they may become defensive about utilizing such techniques. In fact, children at this age generally consider traditional play therapy approaches to be beneath them. Accordingly, after the age of 11 or thereabout a high degree of parental involvement in the treatment may be contraindicated. Again, there should be no sharp cutoff points here. It depends upon the child's maturity and the nature of the information being discussed.

When an overdependent child is in a symbiotic relationship with an overprotective mother, the therapist would not want to utilize the mother to a significant degree in the therapeutic process. To do so might only entrench the pathology. Such a child needs "breathing space" and the freedom to develop a separate relationship—separate from that which he or she has with the mother. To actively involve the mother in the treatment may defeat this goal. However, this does not mean that the mothers of such children should be strictly excluded from all aspects of the child's treatment. No harm is done, in my opinion, by having the mother come in during the first few minutes of the session in order to apprise the therapist of the events that have occurred since the previous session. In addition, she can be kept in the waiting room to be "on call" should her further participation be warranted. (This is standard procedure for me. I do not support a mother's going shopping or attending to other activities while the child is being seen. I emphasize to her the importance of her being available, at a moment's notice, during the session. And this can only be accomplished by her remaining in the waiting room.) Even when a child is suffering with separation anxiety disorder, some active participation with the mother can be useful. Here again one would not want to keep her in the room for significant amounts of time.

There are some parents who are so psychologically fragile that they cannot tolerate the criticisms and other forms of negative feedback that would come their way during the therapeutic session. This is especially the case for parents who are psychotic or borderline. Such a parent may be so defensive that he or she would not be able to handle many of the therapeutic revelations, even though expressed symbolically. Were the parent to sense the underlying meaning of a hostile symbol, it could be ego-debasing and precipitate psychological deterioration. Exposure of such a parent to the child's therapy could be considered cruel and would be likely to alienate significantly both the parent and the child. Any benefits that the child might derive from the parent's presence might be more than offset by the compromise of the therapist-patient relationship that such exposure might result in. In addition, such benefits might also be obviated by the parental psychiatric deterioration and its resultant compromise of parenting capacity. This is not a common situation, but I mention it because it does occur.

There are parents who are extremely hostile, and such hostility might be exhibited toward the therapist. No matter how hard the therapist tries, such parents never seem to be satisfied. No amount of explanation or discussion seems to reduce the hostility. Yet, such parents may bring their children. When they are invited to participate actively in the child's treatment, they may use the opportunity for the collection of ammunition, for example, "Is this what I'm spending all my money on?—to hear you tell those stupid stories?" "How is answering questions about whether or not he touches his penis going to help him obey me at home?" and "My husband is right: psychiatry is just a lot of bullshit!" Such parents tend to "cramp my style" when I am working under their observation and scrutiny. I have the feeling that everything I am doing is going to be used as ammunition against me. Attempts to discuss their negative attitudes have often proved futile. Accordingly, I have found it in the child's best interests to have such parents sit in the waiting room. Although I am deprived of their input, such loss is more than counterbalanced by the enhanced efficiency of the individual therapeutic process with the child. It is the lesser of the two detrimental alternatives. Therapy, like life, often boils down to such a choice. If there were a better option, I would utilize it. So I work under these compromised circumstances.

One might ask the question: "What about the overbearing mother who is always intruding in the child's therapy? Shouldn't she be kept out of the room?" My answer to this question is: "Not so quickly." Let us take, for example, the following situation. I am in session with Jimmy and his mother. I ask Jimmy a question. His mother answers. At that point I consider myself to have a golden opportunity for a meaningful therapeutic interchange—an opportunity that would have not been possible had the mother been out of the room. At that point I will say to Jimmy, "Jimmy, what just happened?" Jimmy may respond, "You asked me a question." And I will respond, "And what happened then?" Hopefully, Jimmy will respond, "My mother answered you." To which I will respond, "Right! And what did you do?" Jimmy may answer, "I didn't do anything." To this I will respond, "Yes, Jimmy, that's right. You didn't do anything. But I believe that you had certain thoughts and feelings when your mother answered my question and didn't give you a chance to answer it yourself. What exactly did you think at the very moment she answered? Exactly what were you feeling at that time?" Here, of course, I will try to get the child to express the thoughts and feelings that he must have had about his mother's intrusiveness. It is generally easier for the child in the therapist's presence. The child recognizes that the therapeutic situation reduces the likelihood that the mother will react with severe punitive measures in the therapist's presence. The child may fear that there will be "hell to pay" when he or she gets home, but the child also knows that there will be at least some protection in the consultation room. If the therapist can encourage such expression during the session and use it as a point of departure for a therapeutic approach to the mother's intrusiveness, it will have served a very useful purpose in the child's treatment.

As mentioned, the richest therapy is that which provides experiences. When the parent is in the room, there is a much greater likelihood that significant experiences will take place. The therapist should view such experiences as golden opportunities, to be grabbed onto and milked to their utmost. They are the most meaningful aspects of the therapeutic process, and they should be cherished. Accordingly, I do not quickly remove intrusive parents from the room. I can conceive of the possibility of a parent being so compulsively intrusive that I would not have the opportunity for such interchanges, and that no living space would be provided the child. However, this has not yet occurred, and I have been successful in utilizing the situations in which the intrusiveness was exhibited as a step toward a reduction of the problem.

This same principle is operative in the more common situation where the child is fearful of expressing hostility toward a parent, hostility engendered by a wide variety of parental deprivations and maltreatment. In a session in which there is the implied therapist's protection the child can be most comfortable in first expressing his or her resentment. Having done so under protected conditions, the child will generally feel more comfortable doing so outside of the session.

I had an experience a number of years ago that demonstrates this point quite well. A boy repeatedly complained to me in sessions that his father insisted that he finish every morsel of food at every meal. His father would be extremely angry at him if he did not eat every speck of food. I asked him if he had expressed to his father the resentment he felt over this. The patient stated that he was afraid to do so. I knew the child's father in that I had interviewed him on a couple of occasions during the evaluative process and, in addition, had seen him on two occasions in joint session with the mother and the child. I knew that he was not as punitive as the patient viewed him to be, and that although he was indeed insisting that the child finish all the food on the plate, he would not have reacted anywhere nearly as violently as the patient anticipated. Accordingly, I felt comfortable encouraging the child to express his resentment. I would not have done so had the father been more punitive. In that case, I would have tried to work more directly with the father himself.

Each week I encouraged the child to express his resentment and told him that I would be asking him in the next session what had happened. Each week he returned with some excuse: "Oh, I forgot to tell him this week." "I was very busy this week." "I had a lot of homework to do this week." I knew that this could go on for months and contribute to the perpetuation of the symptomatology that was a derivative of the pent-up hostility the child was feeling. Accordingly, I had a family session during which I encouraged the child to express his feelings about the mealtime situation. He hesitantly did so and had the *living experience* (again that important concept) that his father did not react as punitively as he had anticipated. We all recognized that he was expressing his anger in a safe situation, with the implied protection of the therapist. However, it was following that session that he became freer to express resentments in other areas and to assert himself more generally. Had I not brought the father into the room, it might have taken a much longer time to achieve this result.

A rarer, but nevertheless very important situation in which the parent's presence is generally contraindicated, is the one in which the parent is suffering with an incurable disease. If the parent is openly discussing the disease, then the parental involvement can be salutary for both the child and the parent. However, if the parent is using denial and other related defense mechanisms as a way of dealing with his or her reactions to the illness, then participation in the child's therapy can be detrimental to the parent. One would not want to have such a parent exposed to the child's working through his or her reactions to the inevitable death of the parent. Such exposure can be cruel and inhumane. Having the parent there will probably lessen the likelihood that the child will reveal his or her true feelings because of the appreciation (depending upon the child's age, sophistication, and intelligence) that his or her revelations may be detrimental to the parent.

CLINICAL EXAMPLES

Freud's Case of Little Hans [The Boy Who Feared Horses]

Here, I will present as my first clinical example Freud's case of Little Hans. Although all the other case examples in this book are derived directly from my own clinical experience, I have chosen to discuss Freud's case of Little Hans here because it lends itself well to demonstrating some important points made in this chapter as well as other sections of this book. However, I will only focus on certain aspects of the case that pertain to issues focused on in this chapter: confidentiality and the utilization of the parent (in this case the father) in the child's treatment. For those readers who may not be familiar with the details of the case and for those who may wish to refresh their memories, I present this brief summary:

> At the age of four-and-three-quarters Hans developed the fear that if he went out into the street, a horse might bite him. Accordingly, he dreaded leaving his house and preferred staying at home with his parents and sister Hanna, who was born when he was three-and-a-half. He was especially fearful of a horse's falling down, "making a row" with its feet, and possibly dying. Large dray horses, especially those pulling heavy wagons, were particularly frightening, as were

horses with black muzzles around their mouths and flaps around their eyes.

Freud did not conduct the analysis; rather, he instructed the father in the analytic method. The latter conducted the treatment and brought back to Freud detailed notes of his interchanges with his son, and these are recorded verbatim in the article. Freud saw the boy only once during the four months of therapy. The interview with the child and father together took place a little less than three months after the onset of the phobia.

Freud considered Hans' symptoms to be manifestations of oedipal difficulties. The horse symbolized his father, who he feared would castrate him (bite off his penis) in retaliation for his incestuous wishes toward his mother. Horses with black muzzles and flaps around their eyes were particularly reminiscent of his father, who had a black mustache and wore glasses. His fear that the horse might fall down and die was a reaction formation to his wish that his father would die—thereby leaving him the uncontested possessor of his mother.

Freud was presented with a child who exhibited neurotic symptoms. There were many ways in which Freud could have involved himself with his little patient. As mentioned, he had no guidelines. From all the possible alternative methods, he chose to have the father serve as therapist. It would have been more consistent with his previous pattern for Freud himself to have seen the child. Freud gives us his reason for this dramatic departure (p. 149):

> No one else, in my opinion, could possibly have prevailed on the child to make any such avowals; the special knowledge by means of which he was able to interpret the remarks made by his five-year-old son was indispensable, and without it the technical difficulties in the way of conducting a psycho-analysis upon so young a child would have been insuperable.

It is of interest that Melanie Klein, Anna Freud, and the child psychoanalysts who followed them—although basically accepting the Freudian theory (the differences between them notwithstanding)—did not generally utilize the parents in the treatment process. In fact, at the present time most classical child analysts, although they may get a history from the parents, confine their treatment exclusively to the child. They recognize that involvement with the parents may have therapeutic benefit; but the greater such involvement, the less they consider the treatment to be justifiably called psychoanalysis—which they consider to be the most definitive, reconstructive, and therapeutic form of therapy for those patients for whom it is the indicated treatment. Yet there is no question that Freud considered Hans to have been psychoanalyzed. A strange paradox.

Many therapists (not only classical child analysts) do not involve the parents directly in a child's treatment because they believe that disclosure of the child's revelations to the parents would compromise the therapy. Many hold that having the parents present in the session would restrict the child from freely expressing important material. Many believe that it is important to establish a special relationship with the child which is "all his(her) own." The preservation of the child's confidentiality is looked upon as an important prerequisite to effective treatment. From the outset this is communicated to the child. At the first meeting he or she alone is brought into the therapist's office (most often with tremendous anxiety and resistance) while the parent or parents are left in the waiting room. One purpose of this separation is to communicate this special relationship at the onset. In addition, the child is often told, quite early in treatment, that what is said to the therapist will not be revealed to the parents.

Although Freud was a strong proponent of confidentiality for his adult patients, there were no such considerations for Little Hans. His deepest and most humiliating secrets were to be directly revealed to his father, the person with whom one would think he would be most hesitant to discuss them. There is little evidence that Hans felt the need for confidentiality or that the therapy was an "invasion of his privacy." There is little reason to believe that Hans' treatment was in any way compromised or otherwise interfered with by his being asked to reveal himself to his father. Even in Freud's one interview with Hans, the father was present. Yet, the more ardently and strictly the classical child analyst adheres to the Freudian theories, the less the likelihood he or she would have such an interview.

Most therapists, regardless of their therapeutic orientation, would not instruct a parent in the therapy of his or her own child. First, to be a therapist requires many years of exacting training and experience. Because parents (with rare exception) have not had such training, they are ill-equipped to conduct such therapy, and to teach them to treat their own children would be a disservice to the patients. In addition, the child's parent cannot have the objectivity which the therapist must have toward the patient if the therapy is to be successful. Yet Freud seems to have ignored these considerations. I. Stone, in his novel on Freud (1971), states that Hans' father was one Max Graf, a graduate in jurisprudence, a doctorate in music, and an editor. He was one of the members of Freud's weekly discussion group and therefore had some familiarity with psychoanalytic theory. Neither Freud nor Stone described him to have had any previous experience as a therapist. But even if he did, Freud did not believe that he would be impaired enough by lack of objectivity to disqualify him as an effective therapist (which he apparently proved to be).

Whereas the theoretical conclusions that Freud came to in his work with Little Hans have often been too literally and even rigidly adhered to, the implications of Freud's mode of conducting the analysis have been largely ignored by the classical analysts. And this, I believe, has been most unfortunate.

Had Little Hans been working with Freud alone (with Freud having no therapeutic contact with the parents, and his "respecting" Hans' right to confidentiality) and had Freud encouraged him to discuss his sexual and hostile feelings with his parents, I believe it would have taken Hans far longer to do so. In the single interview with Freud Hans was encouraged to talk about these matters, and there was, I believe, the implied protection of a man who had already achieved formidable stature in Hans' eyes. Even prior to this interview, Hans knew that everything he said could be brought back for Freud's consideration, and in this way too Hans was reassured (from what had been communicated to him about Freud) that he would get Freud's benevolent protection. Further, I believe that the repeated discussions of the anxiety-provoking material with the father served to desensitize Hans to them in a way that would not have been accomplished as quickly had Freud himself seen the boy alone. Hans repeatedly had the *living experience* that the terrible retaliations he anticipated from his father did not occur.

Four months is a very short time for an analysis. One of the reasons for its short duration was, I believe, the intensive experience which Freud provided the child with his father; the father was the person for whom the horse stood in the first place—the person to whom Hans had to learn to desensitize himself, as well as the person with whom he had to work out the other problems he had in his relationship with him. This experience was a significant (and largely unappreciated) element in Hans' cure. *Hans was afraid of horses, and Freud had Hans work with the "horse."* Whether Freud did this by choice, hunch, intuition, or chance, we will probably never know. It is indeed unfortunate that Freud did not tell us more of the reasons for his decision (if there were any). If his followers had heeded this aspect of the case as diligently as the more theoretical, the whole course of child psychoanalysis might have taken a different path.

What factors, then, were instrumental in bringing about Hans' cure? The most important, I believe, was the improvement in Hans' relationship with his father. To conduct the analysis, the father assiduously noted all of Hans' comments which he considered relevant. This new attention and interest was a potent antidote to his previous deprivations and traumas. The analysis provided Hans with the opportunity to have the *living experience* that his father was more benevolent than he had believed and that his father did not, in fact, retaliate for Hans' hostility in the way that he had feared. This was most rapidly and conveniently accomplished via Freud's choice of the father as the child's therapist. To go further with this, I believe that the psychoanalytic experience—working together in it—provided the father and son with a new intimacy that they probably did not previously enjoy. Mutual revelation of inner feelings, in a benevolent setting, invariably brings people closer together. For a boy who was suffering some deprivation of affection in his relationships with his parents, this experience was clearly therapeutic. I do not think that *what* was said (in fact, the father made some hostile comments and a number of analytic blunders) was nearly as important as the experience of spending time alone together in a mutually enjoyable and productive endeavor. Regarding this issue, Freud stated (p. 285): "the only results of the analysis were that Hans recovered, that he ceased to be afraid of horses, and that he got on to rather familiar terms with his father as the latter reported with some amusement." Freud described Hans' improved relationship with his father as a fringe benefit of the treatment; I consider it a crucial contributing factor to the cure.

Another critical factor in Hans' cure relates to his relationship with Freud. The parents' admiration of Freud, which must have been formidable, could not but have been transmitted to Hans. He was repeatedly told that Freud was going to cure his phobia; therefore, the suggestive element, I believe, was strongly operative (although Freud denied this). In addition, the single interview with Freud must have had a powerful influence on the boy, observing as he had the awe and respect his parents had for "the Professor." It is reasonable to assume that everything that happened during this interview (pp. 184–185) must have considerably affected Hans. These suppositions are well substantiated by Hans' comment to his father upon returning home (p. 185): "Does the Professor talk to God?" Hans' fantasies of Freud's omnipotence and omniscience were reinforced during the interview by Freud's statement to him (p. 185):

> Long before he was in the world, I went on, I had known that a little Hans would come who would be so fond of his mother that he would be bound to feel afraid of his father because of it; and I told his father this.

Following the interview Hans expressed to his father his amazement that (p. 185) "he can tell all that beforehand." It is reasonable to assume that all that Freud told Hans, either directly or through his father (but especially directly), was received with greater receptivity and was held onto more tenaciously than if he had been in treatment with a more mortal and fallible therapist.

Also, there was uniform agreement between the father and Freud. At no point did Freud describe any differences of opinion between himself and the father. Only on the question of whether Hans should be told about vaginas and sexual intercourse was there the faintest possibility raised of the father's not following through with Freud's suggestions. Other than this possible exception, the father dutifully followed all of Freud's advice. Few therapists enjoy such cooperation on the part of a parent. More often than not parental jealousies, resentments, and other neurotic problems interfere with our work and place the child in the position of being torn between us and the parents—no matter how hard we try to establish a good working relationship with them. Hans had no such conflicts—and this, I am sure, was one of the reasons why his therapy proceeded so rapidly. However, such cooperation on the father's part was not without its drawbacks and dangers. His credulous attitudes caused him to transmit many communications which were not valid or relevant to Hans (Gardner, 1972b). Hans, however, got better in spite of this misinformation. In addition, the father did not serve for Hans as a good model for independent thinking and healthy self-assertion, so slavishly dependent was he on every one of Freud's words.

I think that the most important thing that happened in the interview was Freud's making it easier for Hans to express his angry feelings toward his father. Freud stated (pp. 184–185):

> I then disclosed to him that he was afraid of his father, precisely because he was so fond of his mother. It must be, I told him, that he thought his father was angry with him on that account; but this was not so, his father was fond of him in spite of it, and he might admit everything to him without fear.

Soon after this comment Hans reported that his father had hit him. Hans had unexpectedly butted his head into his father's stomach, and the latter had responded with a "reflex blow with his hand" (p. 185). Hans had not previously mentioned this incident, and the father then "recognized it as an expression of the little boy's hostile disposition towards him" (p. 185). It is reasonable that Freud's comments not only made it easier for Hans to express his hostility toward his father but made him feel less guilty about his anger. He was able to test his father's reaction in Freud's presence and gain thereby Freud's implied protection from any retaliation on his father's part. Such an experience, I believe, made it easier for Hans to express his hostility in subsequent situations when Freud was not present—contributing thereby to Hans' cure. Three days after the interview Freud described the (p. 186) *"first real improvement"* in Hans' phobia.

I do not believe it an oversimplification to state that all psychogenic symptoms are, in part, the result of a lowering of one's self-esteem and that, in a misguided and often self-defeating way, they attempt to enhance compensatorily one's feelings of self-worth. Therefore, helping a patient improve self-esteem is one of the most predictable ways to alleviate psychopathological symptomatology. There were a number of things which happened to Hans that enhanced his feelings of self-worth and in this way contributed to his cure. The improved relationship with his father (especially the greater attention he was receiving) must have made him feel better about himself. There is a self-deprecatory element in guilt ("How terrible I am for these thoughts, deeds, etc."). With an alleviation of the guilt Hans felt over his hostility toward his parents came a corresponding enhancement of his self-worth. Lastly, the attention that Hans was getting from the famous Professor must have also made him feel very important. The reader who is interested in reading further my comments on the case of Little Hans might wish to refer to my article on the subject (1972b). Therein I discuss other aspects of the case, aspects that go beyond those discussed in this chapter, namely, confidentiality and the use of the father in the child's treatment.

The Case of Jack
["Daddy, please take me fishing"]

The way in which a mother served well as an assistant therapist is well demonstrated by the case of a boy whom I will call Jack. He was six when he entered treatment. The chief complaint was stuttering. I consider stuttering to have a strong neurophysiological basis; however, I also believe that psychogenic factors can affect the stuttering in that in tense situations the stuttering is more likely to be worse. Accordingly, my psychotherapeutic approach with such patients is to make every attempt to reduce their tensions in the hope that the benefits to be derived from such reduction will ameliorate the stuttering symptomatology as well. I therefore explore other areas of difficulty, especially those that may produce tension and anxiety. In Jack's case, such difficulties were not hard to find. He was significantly inhibited in asserting himself, especially with his father. He was particularly fearful of expressing resentment toward his father and expected dire repercussions for such expression. His father, unfortunately, was very insensitive to Jack. However, he would not have responded with the terrible punishments Jack anticipated. In those situations in which Jack squelched his anger, his stuttering would predictably increase. Jack's anger-inhibition problem was so profound that he was generally viewed as a "model child" by his teacher, parents, and the parents of his friends.

One Monday afternoon (the day is pertinent) Jack began the session with his mother (whom I had learned could be an extremely valuable "assistant therapist"). He said that he had nothing much to talk about and asked if he could draw something with crayons. Suspecting that he had something important to "say" with this medium, I readily agreed. First he drew a blue pond. Then he drew grass and trees around the pond. Lastly, he drew some fishes in the pond and then put down the crayon. When I asked him if the picture was finished, he replied that it was. I then asked him to tell a story, and he stated, "A boy went fishing there, and he caught a few fish." When I attempted to get him to elaborate upon the story, he flatly denied that there was anything more to the story. I told him that I considered him an excellent storyteller, and that I was sure that he could do better. Again, he stated that there was nothing more to the story. When I asked him if there was anything else he could add to the picture, he again stated that the picture was completed. I noted that there were no figures in the picture, either human or animal, and suspected strongly that this had some significance. However, it would have been antitherapeutic to suggest that he place figures in the picture, in that this would have been a significant contaminant to the purity of his fantasy.

I turned to Jack's mother and asked her if she had any ideas regarding the meaning of Jack's picture and "story." She responded strongly in the affirmative, and then turned to Jack and began an inquiry. She first asked him if he recalled what he had asked her on arising the previous morning, which was a Sunday. Jack had no recollection. Upon further urging he did recall that he had asked her to ask his father to take him fishing. She then asked him what her response was, and Jack replied, "You said that Dr. Gardner said that it's a bad idea for you to be my messenger boy, and that if I wanted to ask Daddy something, I should ask him myself." The mother agreed that that was what happened, and then asked him to continue telling what had happened. Jack replied, "I asked Daddy if he would take me fishing, and he said that he wouldn't take me now, but that the would take me later." In the subsequent inquiry by the mother it was revealed that for the next five hours Jack repeatedly asked his father to take him fishing, and the father repeatedly said that he would do so, not then but later. Finally, by midafternoon, Jack's father told him that it was too late to go fishing.

The mother then described how Jack's stuttering immediately became severer. Whereas earlier in the day the stuttering had been relatively mild, it became so bad following this final rejection that Jack was practically unintelligible. And the increased severity was still present when I saw him the following day. The picture and its associated story now became completely understandable. It clearly represented the fantasy that had existed in Jack's mind throughout the previous day. There was a pond that he hoped to visit. The story about the boy who went fishing represented his wish that he were indeed to have gone, but he never did. In the egocentricity of the six year old, if he is not there fishing, then no one is there—thus the conspicuous absence of human figures. In this situation, I decided not to tell a responding story but to use the picture and the associated inquiry with his mother as the point of departure for further discussion.

I then asked Jack what his thoughts and feelings were after what had happened with his father the previous day. Jack denied any resentment at all over the rejection. He reiterated his father's statement that it was really too late, in such a way that it was clear that he considered his father's excuse to be justified. I responded incredulously that I could not believe that there wasn't even a little bit of anger over what had happened. In the ensuing discussion Jack did admit to some anger and then we went on to discuss what he feared would happen if he were to express his resentment. I reassured him that his father, although insensitive at times, was not the kind of person who would be as punitive as Jack anticipated. I then suggested a joint session with the father in which the whole issue could be discussed.

In the following session Jack hesitantly and with some fear did express his disappointment over his father's rejection the previous Sunday. The session proved to be a meaningful one, and was the first of a series in which Jack *had the experience* (that word again) that expressing resentment did not result in the terrible consequences he had anticipated. If Jack's mother had not been present in the session, I would not have known what the picture meant, and we would not have then gone on to the series of meaningful and therapeutically useful discussions that focused on issues that were at the core of Jack's anger-inhibition problem.

The Case of Howie
[Nude Bathing in New Zealand]

Howie came to treatment at the age of eight with chief complaints of severe tics of the face and occasionally of the shoulders. No verbal tics were ever present, and I did not consider him to be suffering with Gille de la Tourette's syndrome. In addition, there was a stuttering problem. He was an extremely tense boy and the combination of tics, stuttering, and tension was interfering with his properly attending to his school work. He could not state exactly what distracted him while in the classroom but he found it extremely difficult to concentrate there. At home, as well, he was always "on edge," and would "fly off the handle" at the slightest frustration or provocation.

By the time five minutes had passed during my initial interview with Howie and his parents I had a fairly good idea about an important contributing factor to Howie's symptoms. His mother was the most sexually seductive woman I have ever encountered off the movie screen. Not only did her perfume proceed her into the room but her breasts were so propped up that they might more probably be referred to as torpedoes. So prominent were they that the rest of her body appeared almost as an afterthought that trailed after them as they entered the room. They seemed to me to defy the laws of gravity. Just about every movement, every gesture, and every vocal intonation oozed sexual seductivity. In accordance with the important therapeutic principle that the therapist should attend to distracting stimuli that appear to be interfering with what are ostensibly the issues under consideration in the interview, I recognized immediately that a likely cause of Howie's symptoms was the anxiety he was suffering over the sexual excitation he was constantly exposed to in the presence of his mother. His tics and other tension manifestations related to his fears of expressing directly his sexual thoughts and feelings. (I did not know at that time about how great these fears were and what the special situations were in the household that made these formidable.) Were I to have had a deeper therapeutic relationship with the family, I would have brought the mother's sexual seductivity up at that point. However, I considered it more judicious to suppress my distraction and proceed with the interview (as best I could).

In the course of my evaluation I learned that Howie's mother considered herself to be "liberal and modern" with regard to the undressing situation in the home. Specifically, she considered it unnatural to do anything but undress in front of her children and husband. She also considered it "natural" to take baths and showers with Howie and/or his sister. When I suggested to her that this might be sexually titillating to Howie, she scoffed and accused me of being old-fashioned.

Howie's parents both complained about the fact that Howie's mother was frequently propositioned by men. Typically, she would report the experience to her husband who invariably would go into a raging fit with threats such as, "I'll kill the bastard," "Just wait till I lay my hands on that son of a bitch," "I'll cut off his balls," and "There ought to be laws that can get guys like that thrown in jail." The parents had described how on a number of occasions they had been invited to dinner parties where a man would make sexual advances toward the mother. Typically, Howie's mother would respond with a loud shriek: "How dare you make sexual advances to me. Imagine, a married man and your wife is only standing a few feet away!" Needless to say, the room was generally completely silent by the time she reached the end of this little speech. Invariably, Howie's father would go into one of his fits and on a few such occasions physically assaulted the man who had made passes at his wife. As might be expected, Howie heard about what had happened and on many occasions was witness to his father's rage outbursts and threats.

I mentioned elsewhere (Gardner, 1968a, 1983a) my belief that when children exhibit oedipal symptomatology there are most often specific family influences that are likely to produce the oedipal constellation of symptoms, specifically sexual titillation by the mother and/or castration threats by the father. Howie had an extremely seductive mother. He had a father who literally threatened to kill those who had illicit sexual designs on his wife and to "cut off their balls." Howie could not but place himself in the category of those who were not only titillated but who risked being castrated and/or murdered for their sexual excitation. It was no surprise that Howie was an extremely tense boy who stuttered and ticked. His situation and symptoms certainly warrant being viewed as oedipal.

Early in therapy I recommended that Howie's mother discontinue the practice of undressing in front of and bathing with him. She was most unreceptive to my recommendation, claiming that I was "old-fashioned." However, she finally agreed to follow my recommendation with the response, "Well, you're the doctor." My experience has been that this comment invariably reveals lack of conviction for compliance. In the following session Howie's mother described how she had "really" followed my advice. She had gone to the bathroom to take a shower and made sure to tell Howie that he was not permitted to come into the bathroom. However, when she got out of the shower she realized that she had "forgotten" to bring in a towel. Accordingly, she called to Howie and asked him to bring a towel into the bathroom; but warned him that he should cover his eyes with his hand and be very sure not to look through the slits between his fingers. Unfortunately, I was totally unsuccessful in my attempts to get his mother to appreciate the seductivity of what had gone on. She merely accused me of "having sex on the mind all the time, just like all men." She also told me that she had heard about psychiatrists who find a sexual interpretation to everything and she was beginning to suspect that I was like the rest of them.

One day, early in treatment, Howie came into the waiting room and his ticking was significantly bad. When I asked what had happened the mother replied, "I can't understand it Doctor, he was perfectly fine until he came to this office." It is not uncommon for therapists to be accused of making symptoms worse. I replied by asking the mother exactly *when* things got worse.

She replied, "I don't know Doctor, he was fine while we were riding over here in the car. And he was fine when we got into your waiting room. It happened while we were sitting down there waiting for you." I then asked her what she and Howie were doing while waiting.

She responded, "We weren't doing anything Doctor. We were only reading a magazine together. It was Time Magazine." I asked her to bring the magazine up and I sat the two of them down on the couch and requested that they try to reconstruct the situation as carefully as they could. I asked them to try to recall the exact page where they had started reading the magazine together, to go through the pages one at a time, and try to recall the discussion that ensued. The magazine was brought up; they sat down together and began perusing the magazine.

Finally, after four or five minutes, Howie said, "Mommy, I think you said something funny when we were looking at this picture." He pointed to a *Qantas Airlines* advertisement in which was depicted a beach scene. The advertisement read: "It is not generally known that Australia and New Zealand have among the most beautiful beaches in the world. Call you travel agent. *Fly Qantas.* Come and see for yourself." I then asked exactly what the conversation was around this advertisement.

The mother responded, "I don't think anything happened, Doctor. All I said to Howie was 'I wonder whether they have nude bathing there in Australia and in New Zealand?'" Again, my attempts to get Howie's mother to appreciate that she was introducing sex into a situation where others would not have had a sexual association proved futile. She again accused me of being a sex maniac.

As the reader might expect, my efforts to help Howie failed completely. Both the mother and the father had too great an investment in the mother's seductivity to give it up so quickly or easily. It was the mother's primary source of attention and ego enhancement. Over many years this woman had devoted significant time and energy to perfecting her seductive skills and talents. In addition to providing her with an inordinate amount of attention, her seductivity served as a hostile outlet. She tantalized men and not only rejected them herself but could rely upon her husband to attack them as well. For her husband, having such an attractive wife was a source of ego enhancement. In addition, having a wife whom other men appeared to prefer in preference to their own wives was also a source of pride. And his wife's complaints about those who propositioned her provided him with an outlet for his own pent-up hostility. After a few months' treatment the family discontinued therapy and informed me that they were going to find another psychiatrist—one who "didn't have so much sex on his mind." I wished them luck in their quest for such a psychiatrist.

The Case of Walter
("Stop touching the walls")

Walter was referred to treatment at the age of ten because of a touching compulsion. Specifically, he felt compelled to run his hands along walls as he walked past them. The movements were executed with his finger tips in the vertical direction. Not only was he compelled to perform these motions indoors, but outdoors as well. Accordingly, his finger tips would often become irritated to the point of bleeding and in recent months many had become callused. In the classroom, as well, Walter was compelled to touch the walls. The compulsion was so strong there that he could not restrain himself from getting up out of his seat during lessons and going over to the side of the room to touch the walls. And this of course interfered with his learning in school. He was getting poor grades in spite of high intelligence. He was also the subject of ridicule in the classroom because of this symptom, so much so that at times he would resist going to school entirely. I had never before encountered this particular symptom (and I never have since, for that matter).

By the time we reached the end of my two-hour consultation with Walter and his parents, I still did not have the faintest idea why Walter had this unusual compulsion. As we stood near the door making the next appointment, wherein I was going to explore the matter further, the reason for the compulsion immediately became apparent. As the four of us stood talking, Walter was stroking his mother's breasts with both hands. The movements were identical to those used when he executed his compulsive ritual. The parents appeared to be completely oblivious to what was going on and carried on the conversation as if nothing unusual was happening.

In accordance with my belief that it is very important to give serious consideration to certain therapeutic "distractions," I interrupted the conversation and asked the parents if they had noticed anything unusual going on while we were talking. They both replied in the negative—even though Walter was still stroking his mother's breasts. I then directed their attention to what was happening and the mother laughed and said, "Oh he does that all the time. It doesn't mean a thing." The father agreed that this was a common occurrence but considered it harmless.

As is clear, Walter's symptom certainly could be explained along oedipal lines. As is clear, as well, there was obvious maternal seductivity that was a primary contributing factor. In Walter's case, the therapy proceeded well. I did not have too much difficulty impressing upon the parents the relationship between Walter's symptoms and the mother's titillating him. The mother did not have difficulty complying with my suggestion that she no longer permit Walter to caress her breasts. Within a week there was a marked reduction in the symptomatology. The parents had some sexual problems (as the reader might have guessed), and I was successful in effecting some improvement in that area. And this, of course, lessened the mother's need to gain her gratifications from her son. Walter had other problems as well and these were dealt with successfully so that by the end of the five months of treatment he was asymptomatic.

The Case of Tara
[Your Brother's in Heaven]

The way in which the educational element and parental involvement can combine to effect dramatic improvement in a child's symptoms is well demonstrated by the case of four-year-old Tara, who was referred because of phobic symptoms of about six months' duration. When Tara was two, her brother Kevin (then 16) was found to be leukemic. During the next one-and-a-half years, Tara's mother was swept up in the care of her oldest child. Her mother's involvement in the care of Kevin was so extensive that little time was left for Tara. Tara was never told that her brother's illness would be fatal; at the time of his death she was simply told that he had gone to heaven, where he was very happy. The family was European, and the father had been temporarily assigned to his organization's office in the United States. At the time of Kevin's death, the family returned to their native country for the burial. Unknown to Tara, her brother's body was in the cargo compartment of the airplane. When they arrived in their native country, Tara was quickly sent to stay with friends while her brother was buried.

Upon returning to the United States, Tara began exhibiting the symptoms that ultimately brought her for treatment. Whereas previously she had attended nursery school without difficulty, she now refused. When the doorbell rang, she panicked and would hide under the bed. Whereas previously she enjoyed visits at the homes of friends, she now refused. She seemed comfortable only when she was close to both of her parents and would scream hysterically if they left. Although her parents had told her that Kevin was in heaven, she repeatedly asked questions about her brother. Apparently she was not satisfied with the answer her parents had given her. Observing Tara to be so upset by her brother's absence, the parents decided to destroy most of his personal possessions and stored away the remainder.

My inquiry with the patient confirmed my initial speculation that Tara's symptoms were the direct result of the way in which the parents had handled Kevin's death with regard to Tara. From Tara's viewpoint, people, without explanation, could suddenly disappear from the surface of the earth. Accordingly, there was no safety because one never knew why such disappearances occurred. It might be that someone came to the door and took children away; or perhaps it occurred at nursery school; or maybe one was abducted from the homes of friends and relatives. No place was really safe. In addition, there was no point in trying to get explanations from one's parents as to how such disappearances occur, because their answers would also prove unsatisfactory.

With this speculation regarding the origin of Tara's symptoms, I asked the parents what their genuine beliefs were regarding the brother's whereabouts. Both claimed that they had no conviction for any type of existence in the hereafter and their religious convictions were not particularly deep. They said it was their view that telling Tara that her brother was buried in the ground would be psychologically deleterious. I told the parents what I considered to be the source of their child's problems. I explained to them that although their explanation was benevolently motivated, I considered it to be doing her more harm than good. I suggested that they return home and tell Tara exactly what they believed happened to their son—as simply and as accurately as possible. I suggested that they give her one of her brother's few remaining mementos and tell her that it would always be hers. Although initially reluctant, they finally gained some conviction for my suggestion and decided to follow my recommendations.

I then explained to them the psychological importance of mourning and described how Tara had been deprived of this important salutary experience. I suggested that they encourage Tara to ask the same questions that she had asked in the past and to recognize that the repetition of these conversations was an important part of the mourning and working-through process. Further, I suggested that they slowly urge her to face once again the various phobic situations and to reassure her each time that she, unlike Kevin, would not be taken away. I suggested that they impress upon her the fact that Kevin was sick and that he died of physical illness. She, however, was well, and there was no reason to believe that her death was anything but remote.

Within one week, there was a dramatic improvement in Tara's condition. After having been told about the true circumstances of her brother's death, Tara cried bitterly. As I had suspected, Tara repeatedly questioned her parents during the next few days, and this time the parents responded in detail and with patience. She was given a picture of her brother, which she carried around at all times and proudly showed to friends and relatives. With such presentations, she would once again discuss in detail her brother's death. Concomitantly, there was a marked diminution in all of her fears. Within a week she was again attending nursery school without difficulty. She no longer cowered at the ringing of the doorbell and once again began visiting friends. Moreover, she experienced only mild fear when her parents went out at night. No further sessions were scheduled, and the parents were advised to contact me again only if there was a need for further consultation. Six months later, I learned through the referring colleague that Tara had remained asymptomatic.

This case demonstrates well the value of education in treatment and how active participation by parents can be extremely useful in child therapy. Although seeing Tara alone might have ultimately brought about the same alleviation of her symptoms, I believe that active work with the parents and my "educating" them caused the therapy to proceed much more rapidly than it would have had I seen the child alone.

The Case of Mack
[The Baseball Hall of Fame]

Mack entered treatment at nine and a half because of disruptive behavior at school and home. There was a basic organic deficit characterized by hyperactivity and impulsivity. His father had left the home about one year previously and was most unreliable regarding his visits. When he was home he was frequently condescending toward Mack. And the anger Mack felt in response to these indignities was being displaced onto siblings, peers, his mother, and his teacher.

Near the middle of his eighth month in treatment, Mack spoke about his father's visit to the home that previous weekend. Although he tried to speak enthusiastically, it was quite clear that he was forcing the impression that the experience was pleasurable. Mack's mother, however, related how he had followed his father around all weekend "like a puppy dog." She stated that it was pathetic to see how Mack would not resign himself to his father's lack of interest. She described how whenever Mack would try to elicit his father's attention or interest he would be responded to with a "shut up" or "don't bother me." Mack became upset by what his mother said and denied that there was any validity to it.

He then described two dreams. In the first he was in a hotel in Cooperstown, New York, the site of the National Baseball Museum. (Mack was an avid baseball fan.) There he was trying to get onto a cable car of the kind seen in San Francisco. The patient could not figure out the meaning of the dream. He did describe, however, a pleasurable experience at Cooperstown with his mother and teenage siblings a week previously but could provide no further associations. Mack's mother then offered further information. She described how the whole family had gone to San Francisco when Mack was about five and this had been one of the high points of his life. This occurred long before his father had left the home and Mack often referred to the experience with great pleasure. The meaning of the dream then became clear: In response to the frustrations that he had experienced with his father the previous weekend Mack was dreaming of a return to happier days with his father in San Francisco. The more recent experience with his mother in Cooperstown was marred by his longing to regain the joys of the San Francisco trip with his father (as symbolized by his trying to get on the cable car). However, he is not successful in getting onto the cable car. This reflected his appreciation, at some level, that his father could no longer provide him with the kind of gratifications he had given him in the past.

Had the mother not been in the room I would not have understood the meaning of this dream. Its analysis is a good example of the vital role that a parent can play when actively participating in the child's therapy. Both the mother and I agreed that the aforementioned interpretation was valid. When it was presented to Mack he admitted that it might be possible, but I did not get the feeling that he accepted our explanation with much conviction.

Mack then went on to relate his second dream. In it he was walking to school with a classmate and they were going to be late. There was a bus ahead and Mack wanted to run ahead and catch the bus. His friend, however, was resistive to the idea. The dream ended with neither boy reaching the bus. Rather, there was a confused discussion regarding whether they should have boarded it. Again, Mack was unable to ascertain the meaning of the dream and I, myself, could offer no specific suggestions. Mack's mother, however, stated, that in her opinion, buses appeared to be the symbol of Mack's father. When he lived at home, Mack's father commuted into New York City and returned each day in a bus to the suburban New Jersey home where the mother and children lived. Especially when he was younger, Mack would often ask if his father was on a passing bus. With this new information the dream became clear. It reflected Mack's ambivalence about joining his father. On the other hand, he desperately wants to catch up to the bus (as symbolized by Mack's pursuing it); on the other hand, he does not anticipate acceptance by his father or gratifying experiences with him so lags behind (as symbolized by his friend's [Mack's alter ego] resistance to such pursuit).

Again, when Mack was offered this explanation for the dream he passively accepted its interpretation, but I did not feel that I was "hitting home." However I did have the feeling that there was some receptivity, that some seeds were planted, and subsequent experience bore this out. Had Mack's mother not been present these advances would have been much more slowly achieved.

CONCLUDING COMMENTS

I believe that the traditional practice of seeing children alone while mothers are in the waiting room compromises seriously therapeutic efficacy. My experience has been that children's treatment proceeds much more rapidly when there is active participation by parents. I believe that thousands (and possibly even millions) of hours have been wasted by having mothers sit in waiting rooms reading magazines while their children are being seen alone by their therapists. In many cases such therapy is basically a waste of time. I am referring here to therapy that is primarily play. If the parents are paying for this, they are paying for a very expensive playmate. But even when the therapy is providing the child with a richer experience, it is still not as efficient nor as effective as it might have been if there were more active parental involvement. Throughout the rest of this book, I will be describing the techniques I believe can be useful in the treatment of children. Throughout I will be describing also the ways in which parental participation has been useful in their treatment.

EIGHT

The Mutual
Storytelling Technique

Originality is a return to the origin.

Antonio Gaudi

HISTORICAL BACKGROUND

The use of children's stories as a source of psychodynamic information is well known to child psychotherapists. To the best of my knowledge, this was first described in the literature (in German) by Hug-Hellmuth in 1913. (The first English Translation appeared in 1921.) A fundamental problem for the child therapist has been that of how to take the information that one can derive from such stories and bring about psychotherapeutic change. Children's stories are generally easier to analyze than the dreams, free associations, and other verbal productions of adults. Often, the child's fundamental problems are exhibited clearly to the therapist, without the obscurity, distortion, and misrepresentation characteristic of the adult's fantasies and dreams.

A wide variety of psychotherapeutic techniques have been devised to use therapeutically the insights that the therapist can gain

404

from children's stories. Some are based on the assumption, borrowed from the adult classical psychoanalytic model, that bringing into conscious awareness that which has been unconscious can in itself be therapeutic. The literature is replete with articles in which symptomatic alleviation and even cure quickly follows the patient's gaining insight into the underlying psychodynamic patterns. My own experience has been that very few children are interested in gaining conscious awareness of their unconscious processes in the hope that they can use such insight to alleviate their symptoms and improve their life situation. I believe that one of the reasons for this is that the average child of average intelligence is not cognitively capable of taking an analytic stance and engaging in a meaningful psychoanalytic inquiry until about the age of ten. This corresponds to Piaget's level of formal operations, the age at which the child can consciously differentiate between a symbol and the entity which it symbolizes.

Of course, brighter children are capable of doing this at early ages. But even those children are generally not interested in assuming the analytic stance and delving into the unconscious roots of their problems—unless there are significant environmentally stimulating factors. The child who grows up in a home in which both parents are introspective and analytic is more likely to think along these lines as well. Accordingly, it is only on rare occasions that I do direct analytic work with children under the age of 10 or 11. And when this occurs, it is usually a patient who, 1) is extremely bright, and 2) comes from a home in which the parents have been or are in psychoanalytic treatment themselves, and who in addition, are deeply committed to introspective approaches to dealing with life's problems. But even in adult therapy, professions of commitment to analysis notwithstanding, most of my patients are not deeply committed to psychoanalytic inquiry. And they are generally even more resistant to analyzing their resistances to such inquiry. Hence, I attempt to employ a psychoanalytic approach to the therapeutic utilization of children's stories very infrequently.

In the 1920s Anna Freud and Melanie Klein—both influenced deeply by Hug-Hellmuth's observation—attempted to work analytically with children, and the analysis of their stories was essential to their therapeutic approaches. Although they differed significantly regarding the interpretations they gave to children's stories, they agreed that the gaining of insight into the story's underlying psychodynamic meaning was crucial to meaningful therapeutic change. Beginning in the 1930s Conn (1939, 1941a, 1941b, 1948, 1954) and Solomon (1938, 1940, 1951, 1955) described the same frustrations this examiner experienced with regard to getting children to analyze meaningfully their self-created stories. They were quite happy to analyze those children who were receptive to such inquiries. But for those who were not, they were equally satisfied discussing the child's story at the symbolic level. They believed that therapeutic changes could be brought about by communicating with the child at the symbolic level. For example, if a child told a story about a dog biting a cat and was unreceptive to analyzing it, they found that discussions about why the dog bit the cat and what better ways there were to handle the situation could get across important messages without producing the anxiety of analytic inquiry.

During my residency training in the late 1950s I first began to suffer the frustration of children's unreceptivity to analysis. I was much more comfortable with the work of Conn and Solomon. It was from these experiences that I derived in the early 1960s the technique that I subsequently called *the mutual storytelling technique.* Basically, it is another way of utilizing therapeutically children's self-created stories. It stems from the observation that children enjoy not only telling stories but listening to them as well. The efficacy of the storytelling approach for imparting and transmitting important values is ancient. In fact, the transmission of such values was and still is crucial to the survival of a civilized society. Every culture has its own heritage of such stories that have been instrumental in transmitting down the generations these important messages.

It is reasonable to speculate that in the early days of civilized society attempts were made to impart directly important messages necessary for people to learn if they were to cooperate meaningfully in the social group. It was probably learned quite early that such direct confrontations, especially in the presence of others, might not be the most effective way to teach individuals in the hope that they would incorporate these messages into their psychic structures. It is reasonable to speculate that a subsequent development involved the recognition that storytelling might be a useful vehicle for incorporating such messages in a disguised and therefore less threatening way. After all, storytelling is an ancient tradition and, up to the twentieth century, it was probably one of the most popular forms of evening entertainment.

It was in such storytelling sessions that people would relate the events of the day and, considering the fact that external sources of entertainment were limited and infrequent, a certain amount of elaboration of events was probably welcomed. Furthermore, it is reasonable to speculate that a certain amount of "expansion of the truth" was not seriously criticized because of the extra entertainment value that such elaboration provided. It is reasonable to assume further that the popularity of this form of entertainment made it an attractive vehicle for the incorporation of messages that were important to impart to individuals for immediate purposes as well as for perpetuation down the generations. It was probably appreciated that one could circumvent listeners' defensiveness regarding being told about their wrongdoings by describing the transgressions of *others* and the lessons *they* learned from their departures from acceptable patterns of behavior. The basic principle was: "Of course, none of us here would ever do such terrible things, and most of us probably wouldn't even think of such terrible things. However, it's interesting to hear about others who did these things and what they learned from them." Adding violence and sex (traditionally attractive modalities in any story) enhanced their attractiveness to listeners. Ultimately, these stories became the primary vehicle for transmitting down the generations important messages necessary for the survival of the group. In fact, I would go further and state that societies that did *not* have such a heritage did not survive because they did not have this important vehicle for transmitting their values to subsequent generations.

Much more recently, with the development of the written language, these stories achieved a new permanence. Our Bible is one example of such a document. The Old Testament is basically a collection of those stories that were prevalent from the period around 750 BC to 250 BC. Most consider these stories to be combinations of fact and fantasy. Each individual, of course, must make a decision regarding how much of these two elements are present. There are some who claim that everything in the Bible is completely true and others who go to the other extreme and claim that it is complete fantasy. Although people may differ regarding what they consider the fact/fantasy ratio to be, most will agree that these stories have had a profound influence on mankind and have contributed significantly to moral development and the perpetuation and survival of civilized society.

The mutual storytelling technique is in this tradition. It attempts to rectify one of the fundamental problems of storytelling as a vehicle for transmitting important messages, namely, that any story, no matter how well tailored to the needs of a particular audience, is likely to be relevant to only a small fraction of those who listen to it. After all, an audience generally consists of men and women of varying ages from childhood through old age. It is unreasonable to expect any particular story to "turn on" more than a small fraction of such a heterogeneous group. The mutual storytelling technique attempts to circumvent this drawback by using a story that is designed to be specifically relevant to a particular person at that particular time. The stories are tailor-made to the individual and therefore, they are more likely to be attended to with receptivity and incorporated into the listener's psychic structure.

THE BASIC TECHNIQUE

In this method the therapist elicits a self-created story from the child. The therapist then surmises its psychodynamic meaning and then tells a responding story of his or her own. The therapist's story utilizes the same characters in a similar setting, but introduces healthier resolutions and adaptations of the conflicts present in the child's story. Because the therapist is speaking in the child's own language—the language of allegory—he or she has a better chance of "being heard" than if the messages were transmitted directly. The direct, confrontational mode of transmission is generally much more anxiety provoking than the symbolic. One could almost say that with this method the therapist's messages bypass the conscious and are received directly by the unconscious. The child is not burdened with psychoanalytic interpretations that are generally alien and incomprehensible to him. With this technique, one avoids direct, anxiety-provoking confrontations so reminiscent of the child's experiences with parents and teachers.

The technique is useful for children who will tell stories, but who have little interest in analyzing them (the vast majority, in my experience). It is not a therapy per se, but one technique in the therapist's armamentarium. Empirically, I have found the method to be most useful for children between the ages of five and eleven. I generally do not treat children under the age of four (I find it more efficient to counsel their parents). In addition, children under the age of five are not generally capable of formulating organized stories. In the four- to five-year age bracket, one can elicit a series of story fragments from which one might surmise an underlying psychodynamic theme which can serve as a source of information for the therapist's responding story. The upper age level at which the technique is useful is approximately eleven. At that time, children generally become appreciative of the fact that they are revealing themselves. They may rationalize noninvolvement with the technique with such justifications as, "This is baby stuff," and "I don't feel like telling stories." Lastly, the technique is contraindicated for children who are psychotic and/or who fantasize excessively. One wants more reality-oriented therapeutic approaches such as *The Talking, Feeling,* and *Doing Game* (to be discussed in Chapter Eleven) or else one may entrench their pathology.

Dolls, drawings, and other toys are the modalities around which stories are traditionally elicited in child psychotherapy. Unfortunately, when these facilitating stimuli are used, the child's story may be channeled in highly specific directions. They have specific forms that serve as stimuli that are contaminating to the self-created story. Although the pressure of the unconscious to create a story that serves a specific psychological purpose for the child is greater than the power of the facilitating external stimulus to contaminate the story, there is still some contamination when one uses these common vehicles for story elicitation. The tape recorder does not have these disadvantages; with it, the visual field remains free from distracting and contaminating stimuli. The tape recorder almost asks to be spoken into. Eliciting a story with it is like obtaining a dream on demand. Although there are differences between dreams and self-created stories, the story that is elicited by a tape recorder is far closer to the dream than that which is elicited by play material.

In earlier years I used an audio tape recorder. In more recent years I have used a video tape recorder. For the therapist who has this instrument available, it can enhance significantly the child's motivation to play the game. Although hearing one's story on the audio tape recorder can serve to facilitate the child's involvement in the game, watching oneself on television afterwards is a much greater motivating force. But the examiner should not conclude that these instruments are crucial. They are merely devices. Long before they were invented children enjoyed relating self-created stories, and the therapist should be able to elicit them from most children without these contrivances. They should be viewed as additional motivating facilitators and, of course, they have the additional benefit of the playback which provides reiteration of the therapeutic messages. In earlier years many children would bring their own tape recorder and simultaneously tape the stories with me, and then listen to them at home for further therapeutic exposure. Recently, I added a second video cassette recorder to my office closed-circuit television system. A child can now bring his or her own video cassette (to be found with increasing frequency in homes these days), tape the story sequences along with me, and then watch him- or herself at home.

SPECIFIC TECHNIQUE FOR ELICITING SELF-CREATED STORIES

I begin by telling the child that we are now going to play a game in which he or she will be guest of honor on a make-believe television program. In earlier years I would ask the child if he or she would like to be the guest of honor on the program; in more recent years I seduce him or her into the game without the formal invitation. Of course, if the child strongly resists, I will not pressure or coerce. We then sit across the room from the mounted camera, and the video cassette recorder, lights, and camera are turned on. I then begin:

> *Therapist:* Good morning, boys and girls. I would like to welcome you once again to "Dr. Gardner's Make-Up-a-Story Television Program." We invite boys and girls to this program to see how good they are at making up stories. The story must be completely made up from your own imagination. It's against the rules to tell stories about anything that really happened to you or anyone you know. It's against the rules to tell a story about things you've read about, or heard about, or seen in the movies or on television. Of course, the more adventure or excitement the story has, the more fun it will be to watch on television later.
>
> Like all stories, your story should have a beginning, a middle, and an end. And after you've made up your story, you'll tell us the lesson or the moral of your story. We all know that every good story has a lesson or a moral. Then, after you've told your story, Dr. Gardner will make up a story also. He'll try to tell one that's interesting and unusual, and then we'll talk about the lesson or the moral of his story.
>
> And now, without further delay, let me introduce to you a boy(girl)

who is with us for the first time. Tell us your name young man(woman).

I then ask the child a series of questions that can be answered by single words or brief phrases. I will ask his or her age, grade, address, name of school, and teacher. These "easy" questions reduce the child's anxiety about the more unstructured themes involved in "making up a story." I then continue:

> *Therapist:* Now that we've heard a few things about you, we're all interested in hearing the story you've made up for us today.

Most children at this point begin with their story, although some may ask for "time out to think." Of course this request is granted. There are some children, however, for whom this pause is not enough, but will still want to try. In such instances the child is told:

> *Therapist:* Some children, especially when it's their first time on this program, have a little trouble thinking of a story. However, I know a way to help such children think of a story. Most people don't realize that there are *millions* of stories in everyone's head. Did you know that there are millions of stories in your head? (Child usually responds negatively.) Yes, right here between the top of your head and your chin (I touch the top of the child's head with one finger, and the bottom of his or her chin with another finger), right between your ears (I then touch the child's two ears), inside your brain which is in the center of your head are millions of stories. And I know a way how to get out one of them.
>
> The way to do this is that we'll tell the story together. And this way, you won't have to do all the work yourself. The way it works is that I start the story and, when I point my finger at you, you say exactly what comes into your mind at the time that I point to you. You'll see then that your part of the story will start coming into your brain. Then after you've told the part of the story that comes into your mind, I'll tell another part, and then I'll point to you. Then we'll go back and forth until the story is over. Okay, here we go. (The reader will note that I again did not ask the child if he or she wished to proceed, rather I just "rolled on.")
>
> Okay, here we go (I now speak *very slowly*). Once upon a time . . . a long, long time ago . . . in a distant land . . . far, far away . . . far beyond the mountains . . . far beyond the deserts . . . far beyond the oceans . . . there lived a. . . .

I then quickly point my finger at the child (jolting the child out of the semi-hypnotic state that I have tried to induce by this "introduction" which basically says nothing). It is a rare child who does not offer some associative word at that point. For example, if the word is "cat," I will then say, "And *that* cat. . . . " and once again point firmly to the child, indicating that it is his or her turn to tell more of the story. I follow the next statement provided by the child with, "And then. . . . " or "The next thing that happened was. . . . " Or, I will repeat the last few words of the patient's last sentence, with such intonations that continuation by him or her is implied. Every statement the child makes is followed by some connective term supplied by me and indicates to the child that he or she should supply the next statement. At no point do I introduce any specific material into the story. The introduction of such specific phrases or words would defeat the purpose of catalyzing the child's production of his or her *own* created material and of sustaining, as needed, its continuity.

This approach is successful in eliciting stories from the vast majority of children. However, if it is unsuccessful, it is best to drop the activity in a completely casual and nonreproachful manner, such as: "Well, today doesn't seem to be your good day for storytelling. Perhaps we'll try again some other time."

While the child is telling his or her story, I jot down notes. These help me analyze the story and serve as a basis of my own. When the child completes the story, I then elicit its lesson or moral. In addition, I may ask questions about specific items in the story. My purpose here is to obtain additional details which are often helpful in understanding the story. Typical questions might be: "Is the dog in your story a boy or a girl, a man or a woman?" "Why did the horse do that?" or, "Why was the cat so angry at the squirrel?" If the child hesitates to provide a lesson or a moral, or states that there is none, I will usually reply: "What, a story without a lesson? Every good story has some lesson or moral! Every good story has something we can learn from it."

Usually, after completing my story, I will ask the child to try to figure out the moral or the lesson of my story. This helps me ascertain whether my message has been truly understood by the child. If the child is unsuccessful in coming forth with an appropriate lesson or moral to my story, I will provide it. Following the completion of my story, I generally engage the child in a discussion of its meaning to the degree that he or she is capable of gaining insight and/or referring the story's message to him- or herself. Many children, however, have little interest in such insights, and I do not press for them. I feel no pressure to do so because I believe that the important therapeutic task is to get across a principle, and that if this principle is incorporated into the psychic structure (even unconsciously), then therapeutic change can be brought about.

FUNDAMENTALS
OF STORY ANALYSIS

Obviously, the therapist is in no position to create a story of his or her own unless there is some understanding of the basic meaning of the child's story. The greater the familiarity with the child, the greater the likelihood the therapist will be in the position to do this. Also, the more analytic training and experience a therapist has, the more likely he or she will be able to ascertain correctly the meaning of the child's story. I first try to ascertain which figure(s) in the child's story represent the child him- or herself and which symbolize significant individuals in the child's milieu. Two or more figures may represent various aspects of the *same* person's personality. There may, for example, be a "good dog" and a "bad dog" in the same story, which are best understood as conflicting forces within the same child. A horde of figures, all similar, may symbolize powerful elements in a single person. A hostile father, for example, may be symbolized by a stampede of bulls. Malevolent figures can represent the child's own repressed anger projected outward, or they may be a symbolic statement of the hostility of a significant figure. Sometimes both of these mechanisms operate simultaneously. A threatening tiger in one boy's story represented his hostile father, and the father was made more frightening by the child's own hostility, repressed and projected onto the tiger. This is one of the reasons why many children view their parents as being more malevolent than they actually are.

Besides clarifying the particular symbolic significance of each figure, it is also important for the therapist to get a general overall "feel" for the atmosphere of the story. Is the ambiance pleasant, neutral, or horrifying? Stories that take place in frozen wastelands or on isolated space stations suggest something very different from those that occur in the child's own home. The child's emotional reactions when telling the story are of great significance in understanding its meaning. An 11-year-old boy who tells me, in an emotionless tone, about the death fall of a mountain climber reveals not only his anger but also the repression of his feelings. The atypical must be separated from the stereotyped, age-appropriate elements in the story. The former may be very revealing, whereas the latter rarely are. Battles between cowboys and Indians rarely give meaningful data, but when the chief sacrifices his son to Indian gods in a prayer for victory over the white man, something has been learned about the boy's relationship with his father.

The story may lend itself to a number of different psychodynamic interpretations. It is part of the creativity of the unconscious, even in the child, that these can be fused together in the same symbols. The themes may exist simultaneously or in tandem. In selecting the theme that will be most pertinent for the child at that particular time, I am greatly assisted by the child's own lesson or moral. It will generally tell me which of the various themes is most important for the storyteller him- or herself. At times, however, the child may not be able to formulate a relevant moral or lesson. This is especially the case for younger children and/or older ones with cognitive or intellectual impairment. In such cases the therapist is deprived of a valuable source of information.

I then ask myself: "What is the main pathological manifestation in this story?" or, "What is the primary inappropriate or maladaptive resolution of the conflicts presented?" Having identified this, I then ask myself: "What would be a more mature or a healthier mode of adaptation than the one utilized by the child?" I then create a story of my own. My story generally involves the same characters, setting, and initial situation as the child's story. However, very quickly my story evolves in a different direction. The pathological modes are not utilized although they may be considered by various figures in the story. Invariably, a more appropriate or salutary resolution of the most important conflict(s) is achieved.

In my story I attempt to provide the child with more *alternatives*. The communication that the child not be enslaved by his or her psychopathological behavior patterns is crucial. As mentioned in Chapter Three, therapy, if it is to be successful, must open new avenues not previously considered by the patient. It must help the patient become aware of the multiplicity of options that are available to replace the narrow, self-defeating ones that have been selected. After I have completed my story, I attempt to get the patient to try to figure out its lesson(s) or moral(s). It is preferable that the child do this, but if the child cannot, then I present it for them. (It is nowhere written that a story must have only one lesson or moral.) My lesson(s) attempts to emphasize further the healthier adaptations I have included in my story. If, while telling my story, the child exhibits deep interest or reveals marked anxiety, then I know that my story is "hitting home." I know then that I am on the right track, and that I have ascertained correctly the meaning of the story and have devised a responding story that is relevant. The anxiety may manifest itself by jitteriness or increased activity level. If the child is bored, it may mean that I am off point. However, it may also be a manifestation of anxiety, and the therapist may not know which explanation is most relevant.

Following the completion of my story and its moral, I usually try to engage the child in a discussion of our stories. For the rare child who is interested in gaining insight, we will try to analyze our stories. For the majority there may be a discussion along other lines, and these are usually at the symbolic level. In earlier years, when I used the audio tape recorder, children were sometimes interested in listening to the tape. In more recent years, since I have been utilizing the video cassette recorder, the interest in watching the program has been much greater. Playing the program makes possible a second exposure to the messages I wish to impart. And, as mentioned, I have recently purchased a second video cassette recorder—which enables the child to bring his or her own tape and replay it at home. This not only provides the opportunity for reiteration of the therapeutic messages, but also serves to entrench the therapist-patient relationship.

CLINICAL EXAMPLES

The Case of Martin
(The Bear and the Bees)

Martin, a seven-year-old boy, was referred because of generalized apathy, lack of involvement with peers, and disinterest in school in spite of high intelligence. His mother was an extremely angry woman who stated during the first session: "Doctor, my father died when I was two and I have no memory of him. I grew up with my mother and two older sisters. I don't know anything about men and boys. To me they're like strangers from another planet. I can't relate to them. My daughter I can relate to. We're on the same wavelength. I can understand her. Although I know nothing about men, I do know one thing about them and that is that I *hate them all.*" Very early I found the mother to be a bitter, self-indulgent woman who used biting sarcasm as a primary mode of relating to men. She told me about a series of male therapists she had seen herself and who had seen her son, and she had only critical things to say about each of them. I could not help thinking while she was talking that my name might soon be added to the list and be mentioned with an equal degree of denigration to the next therapist. (This prophesy soon proved to be true.) The patient's father was obsessively involved in his work, was away for weeks at a time on business trips, and when home had practically no interest in his son. He had a passive-dependent relationship with his wife and served as a scapegoat for her.

In his first session, Martin told this story:

> Once upon a time there was a bear. He was trying to get some honey from a beehive. He got it from the beehive. He went home with it. The bear ate the honey.

I considered the beehive in the story to represent Martin's mother. She is the source of honey, that is, love; but this love is covered with stinging, poison-injecting, potentially painful contaminants. Seeking affection from her inevitably exposes one to her venom. In the story the bear easily acquires honey from the beehive without any interference at all by the bees. This is an atypical element in the story that is our best clue to its meaning. Typically, bees do not sit silently by while bears put their paws in their beehives and gobble up their honey. Rather, they usually sting the bear in the obvious hope that it might retreat. The absence of this reaction on the part of the bees in Martin's story is a statement of his wish that his mother's hostility not manifest itself when he attempts to obtain love and affection from her. In short, the story reveals his wish to gain her love without being traumatized by her malevolence.

The story epitomizes well, in a few words, the mother's basic personality pattern and her relationship with the patient. It is an excellent example of how a child's first story may reveal core problems. Because the mother's psychopathology was deep-seated and because she had absolutely no interest in entering into treatment herself, I considered her prognosis for change to be extremely poor.

However, even if she exhibited motivation for treatment, under the best of circumstances it would have taken many years to bring about reasonable changes. By that time Martin might be an adolescent or even an adult. I considered it antitherapeutic to tell a responding story that would provide Martin with any hope for a dramatic change in his mother's personality, either in the present or the future. Accordingly, I told Martin this story:

> Once upon a time there was a bear. This bear loved honey very much. There was a beehive nearby, but he knew that the bees were not always willing to let him have some. Sometimes they were friendly, and then they would give him a little bit. Other times they were not, and he knew then that it was wise to stay away from them or else he would get stung. When the bees were unfriendly, he would go to another part of the forest where there were maple trees which dripped sweet maple syrup. When the bees were friendly, he would go to them for honey.

In my story I attempted to accomplish two things. First, I tried to help Martin accept his mother as she really was at that time—someone who could, on occasion, provide him with some affection but who, at other times, could be punitive and denigrating of him. In my story I advise him to resign himself to the situation and to take her affection when it becomes available, but not to seek it otherwise. Second, I attempted to provide Martin with alternative sources of gratification by suggesting that there are others in the world who can compensate him somewhat for his mother's deficiency. This is an important therapeutic point. It is unrealistic to expect patients to resign themselves to giving up an important source of gratification if one does not, at the same time, offer some kind of compensatory satisfactions. Martin might not be able to have the bees' honey at times, but he certainly could have sweet maple syrup as a reasonable substitute.

The Case of Mark
[The Farmer and the Stone]

Mark, a nine-and-a-half-year-old boy, was referred for treatment because of disruptive and hyperactive behavior in the classroom. At home he was difficult to manage and frequently uncooperative. Particular problems existed with regard to Mark's doing his homework. He frequently refused to do it, and his parents' warnings and threats regarding the consequences of his not doing homework proved futile. He generally subscribed to the life philosophy: "I'll worry today about today and I'll worry tomorrow about tomorrow." Another dictum by which Mark lived was: "I'll cross that bridge when I come to it." His parents' concerns and warnings about the future repercussions of his inattentiveness to his school work were continually of no avail.

Investigation into the background of Mark's difficulties, did not reveal factors that I were certain were playing a role in his difficulties. The one factor that I considered possibly operative was the fact that his father had made significant contributions in his field, and Mark probably had the feeling that he could never reach his father's level of competence and renown. He didn't want to confront the fact that he might not achieve his father's levels of competence. This reaction, however, is inappropriate because if it were indeed justified, then all the children of distinguished contributors would end up academic failures. There are still many things to be done in this world and many ways of achieving a sense of competence. Furthermore, one need not be a super-achiever or well known to lead a gratifying life.

During his second month of treatment Mark told a story which lends itself well to being divided into three parts. Accordingly, I will present each of the parts separately and describe what I considered to be its meaning.

> *Patient:* Well, once there was this farmer and he liked to plant all kinds of crops, and he raised chickens and cows and horses. He liked to work out in the garden. He liked to feed the chickens and get their eggs.
>
> One day he took an egg out of underneath a chicken and the chicken bit him. And he didn't know what to do because the chicken never bit him before. So he sold the chicken to a man and this man got mad and he sold the chicken to another man. And this person that he sold the chicken to got mad and said he didn't want it. So he gave it back to him and that man gave it back to the farmer. And then that chicken died so he was kind of glad.

Generally, the protagonist of a story represents the patient. In this case, the patient depicts himself as a farmer. The other "protagonist" of the first part of the story is the chicken. The chicken lends itself well to representing a female in that it is the layer of eggs—the origin of life and a source of food. In this case, I considered the chicken to represent Mark's mother. This speculation is further supported by the fact that the chicken bites the farmer. I considered the biting to symbolize the mother's harping on Mark to do his homework. Mark would like to get rid of the chicken, that is, "get his mother off his back." But Mark, like all other human beings, is ambivalent in his relationship with his mother. A part of him would like to get rid of her, and yet another part of him recognizes that to do so would be a devastating trauma. The chicken, then, goes back and forth between Mark and two prospective purchasers. Selling the chicken involves some comfort with duplicity on Mark's part in that the farmer does not inform the buyer of the chicken's alienating defect (biting) which caused him to sell it. The buyer, presumably after being bitten himself, similarly exposes the bird to a third person. The latter, equally dissatisfied, returns the chicken to the second who, in turn, gives the unwanted creature back to the original owner.

Having learned that one cannot so easily rid oneself of people who irritate us, the farmer utilizes a more expedient solution: the chicken conveniently dies. This solution, often resorted to in inferior novels, provides a quick solution to a complex problem and is generally not particularly adaptive in reality because those who hound, persecute, and otherwise make our lives miserable generally do not die so conveniently. In fact, they often appear to live longer than those who treat us benevolently.

In addition, we are not told why the chicken suddenly decides to bite the farmer. All the farmer had done was to take an egg (equals love). The farmer is portrayed as innocent without having done anything to provoke this hostile act on the chicken's part. There is no consideration of the possibility that the farmer may have contributed to the chicken's behavior by some provocation or negligence, as is so often the case in reality. This segment of the story is also a statement of Mark's desire to solve the problem with the biting chicken (equals mother) by hostile acting out rather than civilized discussion. And now to return to the second part of Mark's story.

> So he went along with his farming and when he was planting his crops—you know corn—in his cornfields, he found like a little, whatever you want to call it, stone. And he kept it because it was kind of pretty. So when he was keeping it, he kept it in his dresser, you know.

And every time when he went out to work in his crops he had the stone with him. He would put it in his pocket and every year he held that in his pocket the crops would come up just the way he wanted them to, and when he didn't have it with him something went wrong. So he always had the stone with him. And then he thought that it was a magic stone.

Here, the farmer finds a magic stone which brings him good fortune as long as he keeps it in his pocket. He need only keep the stone in his pocket and his crops will flourish; failure to do so causes them to "grow wrong." I considered this part of the story to be a manifestation of Mark's life philosophy that he need not exert any effort; things will somehow work out. He need not show any forethought or planning; somehow all will go well. He need not put in any effort to accomplish things in life, especially learning in school. He utilizes the magic stone to counteract the insecurity engendered in him by parental threats and suggests that at some level he is fearful that things will not work out. The magic stone provides him with the power to bring about a favorable outcome without any effort on his part. Again, this is a maladaptive response to his school difficulties. And now to the third and last part of Mark's story. I include here the post-story discussion which is also important if the examiner is to be certain about the meaning of a child's story:

> And then one day when he was riding along in his wagon pulled by a horse, it went across the bridge and the wheel came off, you know. And the bridge started to crack. So he grabbed the stone and put it in his pocket and then just got up and walked across to the other side. And then he took the horse to the other side with him and the bridge fell out, you know. As soon as he took it [the stone] out of his pocket the bridge fell into the river. So he had to go and tell the people about it so they could put up a sign so nobody else could run into it. They put up a sign that said, "Bridge Out." And the townspeople paid to put up a new bridge.
>
> And when the man found out that he lost the stone he was very unhappy and like he didn't tell anybody ever that he had the stone. So one time he was walking along in the same spot that he found the crop, he found the stone again. And he always had good luck forever on.
>
> *Therapist:* Tell me something. Is it true that it was because the man had taken the stone out of his pocket that the bridge fell down?

Patient: Yes.

Therapist: And that if he had kept the stone in his pocket the bridge would not have fallen down.

Patient: Right.

Therapist: What about the wheel of his wagon? Would that have broken had he kept—

Patient (interrupting): Well, the wheel broke and the weight of it pushed and cracked the bridge.

Therapist: I see, but it was because he didn't have the stone that the bridge fell down?

Patient: Right.

Therapist: And what's the lesson of that story?

Patient: If you've got something you believe in, you should try to hold on to it, like you know, not try to lose it. If you really believe in it don't you know, fool around with it.

Therapist: Okay.

Here, the farmer is riding a wagon. The wagon lends itself well to symbolizing an individual's feelings about his or her ability to move along life's course. It is analogous to the automobile in this regard. A man, for example, has a repetitious dream in which his automobile is just sitting there with all four tires deflated. The dream is a statement of his sense of impotency with regard to his capacity to move along life's course. A neurologically impaired girl has a dream that she is driving her father's car and each time she puts her foot on the brake, the car doesn't stop. The dream reveals her feeling that she cannot "put the brakes on" her thoughts, feelings and actions. In Mark's fantasy the wheel of the wagon "came off." This is a statement of Mark's sense of instability. It probably reflects his awareness, at some level, that his failure to work in school is compromising his capacity to move along life's course. Furthermore, it may relate to his parents' warnings that if he does not "shape up" his future will be a bleak one.

But it is not only the wheel that comes off, the bridge itself "started to crack." This is a statement of an even more profound sense of insecurity in Mark. The supporting structure under the wagon is also weak. The wagon on the bridge symbolizes Mark's view of his capacity to move along life's course. After all, the bridge connects one point to another and facilitates such progress. If the bridge breaks, one is stopped (at least temporarily) from moving along life's path. In short, the breaking of the wagon's wheel and the falling of the bridge depict Mark's belief that his world is falling away under him. His difficulties at school and at home were interfering with his gaining a sense of competence in coping with life. In both the academic and behavioral realms he was not acquiring the talents and skills which are necessary if one is to feel confident about coping with reality. In compensation for his feelings of inadequacy in these areas, he provides himself with a magic stone which protects him from the dangerous results of his incompetence. Furthermore, the magic stone fantasy is consistent with his life philosophy that somehow things will work out.

In the post-story discussion, I questioned Mark in order to be certain that I understood completely the facts of his story. If the therapist is not completely clear about the incidents in the story, he or she is ill-equipped to analyze it. And, of course, any stories that the therapist creates that derive from an incorrect rendition of the child's story are likely to be completely off point and of little or no therapeutic value. Just as Mark's story lent itself well to being divided into three segments, I divided my responding story into three segments, each of which corresponded to one of the patient's. This was the first of the three segments of my responding story:

> *Therapist:* Now I'll tell my story. The title of my story is "The Chicken and the Stone."
>
> Once upon a time there was a farmer and this farmer had a chicken and this chicken would lay eggs. And one day he went over to the chicken to get an egg, and the chicken bit him. He got very angry and he thought, "I know what I'll do. I'll get rid of this chicken. I'll sell this chicken to someone else." He also thought, "Maybe it will die. Then I won't have any problems with it."
>
> So another man came along and he said, "Would you like to buy a chicken?"
>
> And the man said, "Well, tell me about this chicken. Is he a good chicken? Is he kind? Does he bite?"
>
> The farmer said, "Well, he may bite."
>
> "Look," the man said, "I don't want a biting chicken."
>
> And the farmer didn't know what to do because there he was stuck with this chicken. He said, "Gee, I wish this chicken were dead."
>
> The second man said, "Look, here you have a chicken that's biting. You want to get rid of him. You want him to die. Is that the only way you know how to solve a problem with a biting chicken? You know, you can't solve life's problems by killing off or selling off the people who are bothering you. You've got to work it out with them. You can't get rid of people so easily and you can't even get rid of

biting chickens so easily. So I suggest that you try to figure out some way of solving this problem with the chicken."

Well, he talked to the chicken. (In my story this chicken talks.) And he found out that there were things which he was doing which were bothering that chicken and that's why the chicken bit him. And when they were able to settle that problem and he stopped doing the things which bothered the chicken, the chicken stopped biting him and then the chicken continued to lay many more eggs and he then no longer wished to get rid of the chicken to sell him and he no longer wished that the chicken were dead.

Whereas the first buyer in Mark's story gullibly buys the chicken without asking questions, in my story he inquires about the chicken's habits—especially whether he bites. I attempted thereby to communicate that buyers in reality may not easily be taken in by the seller's duplicity. I hoped to let Mark know that one doesn't easily get away with lying and in this way lessen his tendency to lie in order to achieve his ends. The farmer then tells the truth and hopefully serves as a model of honesty for the patient. Thwarted in his attempts to get rid of the malevolent chicken, the farmer expresses the wish that it die. Again, reality considerations reign and the chicken remains very much alive. At this point the buyer becomes more directly the transmitter of my healthier communications and adaptations. He advises direct inquiry into the difficulties in the farmer-chicken relationship in the service of resolving them in ways more civilized (discussion rather than hostile acting out) than those already attempted by the farmer.

Accordingly, the farmer invites the chicken to express his grievances ("In my story this chicken talks.") rather than act them out with biting. The chicken does so and the problems are resolved. Because the patient's story did not specify the nature of the chicken's source(s) of irritation, I made only general reference to them. Had I wished to get more specific I would have first asked Mark why the chicken bit the farmer. The information so gained could have served to provide me with specifics for my story. But I already had so much information to work with by the time Mark finished his complete story that I decided not to add any more material. Overloading can reduce the child's receptivity to the therapist's stories. My main message then was that if someone is hostile toward you, rather than trying to get rid of him or her by separation or death, try to work out the problem through civilized inquiry and nonviolent action.

Whereas in Mark's story the potential purchaser refuses to buy a biting chicken, and then goes his way, my purchaser conducts an inquiry and provides advice. This is a common maneuver that I utilize in the mutual storytelling technique. It is one of the ways in which I provide my therapeutic messages. I wear many guises. Sometimes a passerby stops to watch the action and then, without any invitation on the part of the protagonists, enters into a discussion with them in the course of which he dispenses advice. Sometimes, unbeknownst to the participants, a "wise old owl" has been sitting on a bough of a tree watching the activities below. Then, at some judicious point, he or she interrupts the proceedings and starts pontificating. Again, there is full attention and receptivity to everything the owl says. The protagonists "hang on every word." Sometimes I use a teenager for this purpose. The reader will do well to recognize the value of the teenager in the treatment of latency-aged children. There is no one in the world who possesses more omniscience than the teenager. He knows everything and is in no way modest about his vast knowledge of the world. The reader might be interested to learn that in the 25 years or so that I have been utilizing this technique, not once (I repeat *not once*) has the recipient of such gratuitous advice ever responded with a comment such as: "Listen, Buster, I would appreciate your not butting into our business. If I wanted your advice, I would have asked for it. And until that time comes, I'd appreciate your keeping your trap shut."

Now onward to the second part of my responding story which, as mentioned, directs its attention to the second segment of the child's.

Now, one day this farmer was working in his cornfields and he found a very pretty stone. It was very shiny and very pretty. And he said, "I wonder if this is a magic stone. I'd sure like to have a magic stone. My crops haven't been doing too well lately. So he rubbed the stone and he hoped that the crops would do better. But nothing happened. The crops still were poor.

But one day he was in town and he was in a general store buying provisions and the owner of the store noticed that the farmer was rubbing the stone and holding it in his pocket. And he said, "What are you doing there?"

The farmer said, "Oh, that's my magic stone. That gives me luck."

He said, "Has it ever given you luck?"

The farmer replied, "Well, no, but I'm hoping it will make my crops better."

And the man in the store said to him, "Well, I never heard of a magic stone." He said, "What are you doing with your crops? Are you using any fertilizers and things like that?"

The farmer said, "Well, not really. I really don't believe too much in them. It's a lot of extra work putting in those fertilizers and it costs money."

And the man said, "Well, I think that the reason why your crops aren't doing well is that you're not taking care of them well enough. You're not putting in fertilizers." And he asked the farmer some other questions about what he was doing and it was clear that the farmer was not doing everything that he could. And the man in the store said, "Instead of rubbing a magic stone I suggest you get to work on your farm and start taking good care of your crops. I think there's a better likelihood that they'll do well than if you rub a magic stone."

And the farmer thought about what the man had said and he decided to try him out. So he got the fertilizer and he started to work harder on his crops, and sure enough that year he had a better crop than he had ever had before. Well, although the farmer was impressed with what the storekeeper had said, he wasn't fully sure that the stone still wasn't magic.

In my responding story, the magic stone is not effective in improving the farmer's crops. No matter how much he rubs it, the crops remain weak and malnourished. My advice to utilize more realistic and predictably effective methods is transmitted through the owner of the general store. As I am sure is obvious to the reader, this is another one of the disguises that I utilize in my responding stories. The farmer is receptive to this advice and, although it works, he still does not give up hope that his stone will perform magic. We are generally more attracted to easy and quick solutions than to difficult and complex problems, and the farmer is not immune to this human frailty. It will take a more dramatic proof of the impotency of his stone to convince him of its worthlessness in controlling natural events. (See part three of my story below.)

The above transcript does not provide the reader with information about the boy's facial expressions and gestures while I told my story. While relating the second phase of my story, the patient began to blink his eyes. I considered this to be a manifestation of the tension I was arousing in him with my statement that his fantasies of a magic solution to his problems were not going to be realized. Furthermore, he placed his right hand in a seemingly strange position, namely, as if he were holding a stone in it. His arm was flexed at the elbow and his fingers so positioned in cup-like fashion that he could very well have been holding a stone. I believe that this gesture was unconscious, and it reflected his need to "hang on" to the stone that I was symbolically taking away from him. It certainly provided me with confirmation that my story was indeed "hitting home" and touching on important issues.

I then continued and related the third part of my story:

> And on his farm there was a bridge which was somewhat old and weak, and he used to look at it and say, "I wonder if I should fix it up one of these days. Na, I'll rub my stone. It will keep it going." So he used to rub his stone every time he'd pass that bridge in order to keep the bridge solid. But one day as he was riding his wagon across the bridge a wheel broke and his wagon fell down and sure enough the bridge broke as well, even though he had had his magic stone in this pocket. And there he was in the water—his horse jumping around very scared, the wagon broken even more than it had been, the farmer sitting in the water all wet, and his wagon broken even more, and the bridge completely crushed. And there he was with the magic stone in his pocket! And as he sat there, he realized that this stone really wasn't magic. Finally it took *that* to make him realize and after that he decided to build a new bridge. He threw away the stone and he built a new strong bridge and that was the end of his belief in a magic stone. And do you know what the lesson of that story is?

I interrupt the transcript here before the post-story discussion which begins with the patient's response to my request that he provide the moral of my story. As is obvious, in my story, I again attempt to drive home the point that the magic stone will not work. Just as the patient's third segment is basically a restatement of his second, in that in both the magic stone is used to assuage tension (induced by his parents' threats) and perpetuate his life philosophy that all will go well even if he doesn't put in effort, my third segment is basically a restatement of my second. Here, while I related my story, the patient involved himself in even more dramatic gesturing. Specifically, at the point where I described the farmer sitting in the water, after the bridge had broken through, the patient spontaneously began to rub "water" off his thighs. He then resumed the gesture of holding the stone. However, at the point where I described the farmer's throwing the stone, the patient, without any prompting on my part, engaged in a stone-throwing maneuver. I wish to emphasize to the reader that there was no suggestion, either overt or covert, by me that the patient dramatize or in any way gesticulate the elements in my story. His spontaneous involvement in this way was confirmation that he was swept up in my story and that my message was being incorporated into his psychic structure.

As is my usual practice, rather than tell the moral myself, I generally ask the patient what he or she understands to be the lesson of my story. In this way I can often determine whether my messages have been truly understood because a correct statement of the moral requires a deep appreciation, at some level, of the story's fundamental meaning.

This is the interchange that followed my question:

Patient: Don't count on something else to do your work for you.

Therapist: Right! That's one lesson. That's the lesson with the magic stone. What's the lesson of the part with the chicken and the egg and the biting?

Patient: You should fix your own problems now if you can, or else somebody else will fix them for you.

Therapist: Well, *that* and if you have a problem with someone it's not so easy to get rid of them.

Patient: Try to figure it out.

Therapist: Try to figure it out with them. You can't kill them off, you can't sell them generally. Human beings are not like chickens. You can't just sell them or kill them so easily. If you try to, you know, you'll get into a lot of trouble. So the best thing is to try to work the problem out with the person. The end. Wait a minute. I want to ask you something. Do you want to say anything about this story?

Patient: No.

Therapist: Did you like it?

Patient: Yeah.

Therapist: Any particular part?

Patient: The part where he found the stone and it was pretty and shiny.

Therapist: Uh huh. Any other part?

Patient: No.

Therapist: Did you learn anything from this story? Did this story teach you anything?

Patient: No.

Therapist: Not at all?

Patient: Well, yeah.

Therapist: What does it teach you?

Patient: Well, you should kind of figure out your own problems and don't count on other people to do stuff for you.

Therapist: Okay. What about magic? What does it say about magic?

Patient: Magic—well, if you've got a magic stone make sure it's *really* a magic stone and then go counting on it. (laughs)

Therapist: Do you think there are such things as magic stones?

Patient: No. (laughs)

Therapist: I don't believe so either.

Patient: You can keep them as a good luck charm—as a pretty piece, but not as a magic stone.

Therapist: Do you think a good luck charm *really* brings good luck?

Patient: Hhmmm, not really.

Therapist: I don't think so either. No. Okay. So that's the end of the program today. Good-bye, boys and girls.

It is unrealistic for the therapist to expect that a single confrontation or story, or any other single experience in therapy, is going to bring about permanent change. Those who have conviction for time-limited therapy believe that this is possible, and they will attract patients who are gullible enough to believe this as well. If such rapid changes could indeed take place, Mark might very well say to me something along these lines: "Dr. Gardner, you're right. There's no such thing as magic. You've convinced me of that today. I can promise you that I will never again believe in magic. Now let's go on and talk about my next problem."

There are, of course, patients who say things along these lines. It is one of the more common forms of resistance and/or ingratiating oneself to the therapist. In the real world, the world in which there is no magic, the best one can hope for is to introduce an element of ambivalence regarding the patient's belief in magic. And this is what I believe occurred here. The post-story discussion reveals some discomfort on Mark's part with my message, but also some receptivity to it. In ensuing stories there were statements of negation of magic ("There's no such thing as a magic stone") which is certainly not a manifestation of "cure" of the problem. True "cure" comes when there is no mention of magic at all. Doing and undoing is not the same as never having done at all. Mark did reach the point, however, about three or four months later, in which magic did not appear in any form whatsoever in his stories. It was then, I believe, that he reached a healthier level with regard to this problem.

The Case of Evan
[The Killed Guide
and the Grilled-Cheese Sandwiches]

Evan, an eleven-and-one-half-year-old boy, was referred because of generalized inhibition and withdrawal from peers. His personality structure was schizoid, but he was not schizophrenic. He had trouble asserting himself, and showed little enthusiasm in school. His grades were quite poor although his intelligence was above average. This was the first story Evan told in treatment:

> One day I went up with a group of people and a guide to go mountain climbing in Colorado. It was a big mountain and we were all very tired, but the view was fine. At about 1000 feet I picked up a rock and threw it down. It bounced off the stones and went all the way down. It was a dangerous climb, but we had ropes and a guide and waist chains. He would go up ahead of us on to a ledge. It was a very steep mountain. There were very few grips for our hands and feet. Then we got to the top of one of the ledges, but the guide fell off and he got killed. Then we built a fire and had grilled-cheese sandwiches.
>
> After that it was easier to climb because the mountain wasn't so steep. However, we couldn't get to the top, so we went all the way down and went around to the other side of the mountain. We found a spot that looked good. We got another guide, but he got killed also on the way up. We got to the top and there was a pretty view. It was 5000 feet high and it took us six hours to climb it. We could see a hundred miles in every direction. We stayed up there awhile, enjoyed the view, and then we went down. It was much easier to get down.
>
> *Therapist:* What's the moral of that story?
> *Patient:* I can't think of any moral.

The most striking thing in this story was Evan's total lack of feeling for the guides who fell and were killed. He spoke of their falls with the same emotionless tone used when he described the rock that he had thrown down the mountain. The sentence describing the death of the first one is immediately followed by: "Then we built a fire and had grilled-cheese sandwiches." And the death of the second causes not a moment's hesitation or interference in the journey's progress. The story reveals severe superego deficiencies: an utter lack of sensitivity to the pains of others and an inability to place oneself in the position of someone who suffers.

This is the story I told in response:

One day a group of friends of mine and I decided to go mountain climbing. We were in Colorado and we were in the Rockies. We had a guide who was a very fine person and we all liked him very much. He had many years of experience and we felt very secure with him. He went ahead of us and we all had ropes and waist chains for protection. When we were about half-way up the mountain, he was on a ledge ahead of us and suddenly the rocks slipped from under him and, although he tried to catch on to the ledge, he slipped off and his body plummeted at least 1000 feet to the bottom of the mountain. It was a horrifying experience and we all felt completely helpless. We knew that it was sure death for him.

We were so upset that there was no question in our minds that we could not continue the trip. We were grief-stricken over this man's death, especially since he had died in the process of trying to be helpful to us in climbing this mountain. Well, we all slowly went down the mountain along the path that we had originally taken and when we got to the bottom, there we saw what we all feared and knew to be the case. There was his mangled body on the ground and it was a horrible sight. It was clear that he had probably died in the fall or died at the moment he struck the ground. Most of us cried bitterly. We then went back to the main cabin and notified the authorities. His wife was brought over and it was most painful when we had to tell her the very tragic news. The man had three children who were now left without a father as well. It was, without question, one of the most terrible experiences I have ever had.

In my story I included every ramification of the guide's death that might elicit emotional reactions. The written transcript can only convey a suggestion of the emotionalism which I tried to convey while telling my story. My hope here was to impart to Evan some sensitivity to the agony and torment which others might suffer. It would have been unreasonable to expect that this self-involved boy would, in his first session, respond significantly to an emotion-engendering story, and his overt reaction was minimal. My hope was that Evan might ultimately be reached, and this story was a step in that direction.

The Case of Todd
[The Club of Mean Tigers]

Todd entered treatment at the age of nine-and-a-half because of withdrawal, apathy, and shyness. His parents described him as rarely smiling and "a very unhappy boy." He never reached out for friendships, and few children found him to be a desirable or interesting playmate. He was easily scapegoated because of his fear of fighting back. With regard to this he stated, "I'm afraid I might hurt somebody real badly, so they might die." Although he is described as having been somewhat depressed since he started kindergarten, his depression increased three months prior to referral when he moved into a new neighborhood. At times he spoke of committing suicide, but there was no history of suicidal gestures or attempts.

Todd was the oldest of two sons and was an extremely over-protected boy. Both of his parents pampered him significantly. Although in the fourth grade, and although his school was only six blocks away from his home, he was routinely driven back and forth from school four times a day. Although the vast majority of children remained in school during the lunch break, Todd refused to do so. He wouldn't wait on line at the lunch counter, for fear he might get involved in the usual shoving, name calling, and horse play that typically takes place in that situation. Furthermore, he feared the inevitable teasing and rambunctiousness that took place in the schoolyard when children played there after eating their lunch. His mother would drop him off at school in the morning, pick him up at the beginning of lunch break, serve him his lunch at home, return him to school at the end of lunch break, and then bring him home at the end of the day. Todd had never gone to day camp (not to mention sleep-away camp) because he had initially reacted negatively when his parents proposed the idea a few years previously. In fact there had not been one day in his life that he had been away from his parents.

Todd's father was an extremely domineering man, and his mother was passively dependent on her husband. Her overprotectiveness stemmed primarily from her submission to her husband's dictates regarding indulging Todd. (She was so passive that it would have been difficult to predict how she would have been with another husband, other than that she would have been passive to him.) I believed that an element in Todd's anger was related to the resentment he felt over his father's overbearing manner. However, he was so dependent on both of his parents that he could not dare express his hostility. I considered his pent-up hostility to be a factor in his depression. His inhibition in asserting himself served to protect him from the consequences of hostile expression that would inevitably arise were he to have been more outgoing.

During his second session, Todd drew a picture of a tiger and then told a story that I believe epitomized some of his central problems. I recognized the story as one that would lend itself well to the mutual storytelling game, and so I suggested that he show the picture on television and tell his story again on my "Dr. Gardner's Make-Up-a-Story Television Program." The patient readily agreed:

Therapist: Now our guest has just drawn a picture and he's told me a story and I thought it was such a good story that I suggested that we play the storytelling game. So first he's going to show you the picture. Put it up and show it. Okay. Now what do you want to do, what is that a picture of?

Patient: A picture of a tiger.

Therapist: Okay, now what we want you to do is tell a story about your tiger and then I'll tell a story about a tiger, too.

Patient: Okay. This tiger wants to join this club, but the club has new members.

Therapist: It has what?

Patient: It has people—the tigers are bad in the club.

Therapist: The tigers in the club are bad, yeah.

Patient: And this tiger wants to join, but he's not mean so he's thinking about it in the picture if he should join and then he says, "I'll join the club if I don't have to be mean."

And then he talks to the club leader of the club and he says, "You gotta be mean to join our club."

And then he says, "No, I cannot. I should be myself."

Therapist: I should be myself, yeah.

Patient: And that's all.

Therapist: And so what happens?

Patient: Everybody should be theirself.

Therapist: Okay. So does he get into the club?

Patient: No.

Therapist: Okay. And so the lesson of that story is what? Is that the end of the story? He just doesn't get into the club?

Patient: Yeah.

Therapist: Okay. And the lesson of that story is?

Patient: That you should be yourself.

Therapist: Hmm. Be yourself. You don't want to be mean. Is that it?

Patient: Yeah.

Therapist: What should you do?

Patient: Be yourself.

Therapist: Be yourself. In his case this tiger didn't want to be a member of the club unless they did what?

Patient: Unless he was mean.

Therapist: Oh, they said he couldn't be a member of the club unless he was mean?

Patient: Yes.

Therapist: And what did he say to them?

Patient: He said, "No."

Therapist: Did you say—I remember when you told a story before—did you say something about he told them that they should not be mean?

Patient: No.

Therapist: When you told the story before didn't you say, "I'll only join the club unless you people promise not to be mean?" Didn't you say that?

Patient: He said that if he could be nice. . .

Therapist: If you people in the club.

Patient: No, I said if *he* could be nice then he would join.

Therapist: Oh, you said, "I'll join your club if you let me be nice and let me not bother people." Oh, if you let him not bother people, but the others could bother people. Is that it?

Patient: Yes.

Therapist: I see. He just didn't want—he didn't want to be the one to bother people.

Patient: Yeah.

Therapist: I see. Okay. And the leader said, "You can't join the club because to join our club everybody has to bother people." Is that it?

Patient: Yeah.

I considered the club of tigers who always bother other people to symbolize Todd's view of his peers, namely, a pack of ferocious animals who were ever scapegoating and teasing him. The only way he can gain membership into their club is to become mean himself. This is something Todd is frightened of doing and so he refuses to comply with this provision of admission with the statement, "I should be myself." For Todd to be himself is to be inhibited in asserting himself. His view of his peers as mean tigers stems from Todd's timidity and fear of self-assertion and hostile expression. From his vantage point they appear ferocious. In addition, I believed that the mean tigers were made even more threatening by the projection onto them of Todd's own unconscious anger. He thereby distances himself from his anger by refusing to join the club that requires its expression as a provision for membership. His statement, "I should be myself" makes reference to his determination not to express resentment. With this understanding of Todd's story, I related mine.

Therapist: Okay, I get the idea. Okay. Now, as I've said before, the way it works on this program is that first the guest tells a story and then Dr. Gardner tells a story. And my story may start like yours, but different things happen in my story. Okay?

Patient: Okay.

Therapist: Okay, here we go. Once upon a time there was a tiger, and this tiger wanted to join a club and in this club—this was the mean club. Everybody in the club was mean. And he said, "I want to join your club, but I don't want to be mean. I don't want to bother people ever, and will you let me join your club if I don't bother people?"

And they said, "No, no, no. You can't join this club because here we bother people." So he couldn't join the club.

Anyway, he decided that he would find another club, a club where nobody bothers people. So he looked around and people said, "Well, there are other clubs that don't bother people. In fact, there are two other kinds of clubs. There's one other kind of club where everybody agrees *never* to bother people at all, and then there's another club where the people agree that *sometimes* they will bother people and *sometimes* they won't bother people."

So really there were three clubs. There was the original club where all the tigers always bothered people. There was a club in the middle where sometimes they would bother and sometimes they wouldn't. And then there was the other club where nobody ever bothered people. So which one of the other two clubs do you think this tiger in my story wanted to join?

Patient: He wanted to join the one where he was always nice.

Therapist: Yeah, he said, "That's the club for me, always nice." Nobody ever bothers people. He said, "That's the club for me." So he went to that club and he says, "Can I join your club?"

And they said, "Remember the rule of our club. You must *never* bother anybody. You must *never* get angry at anybody, you must never hit anybody, you must never bite anybody, and you remember that."

He said, "That's the club for me." So he joined that club and he took an oath that he would not bother people. And he said, "I swear that I will never bother people. I'll never bite people, no matter what."

Anyway, that club, the one that never bothered anyone, used to have its meetings, and one day a tiger came along while the club was having its meeting—a lion, excuse me—this is a tiger's club. It was a lion, and an elephant. And the lion and the elephant started coming around and growling and bothering the tigers in the club. And the tigers said, "Oh, please don't bother us. We mean you no harm. We're very nice. We don't bother people. Please don't bite us. Please don't bother us."

Well, that elephant and that lion weren't listening, and they started to make trouble and these tigers all ran way. They didn't want to fight. And then what happened was that the elephant and the lion got a lot of the food that the tigers had collected and a lot of their possessions and stuff. And the tigers felt very sad and depressed about it. And that used to happen from time to time because they made a promise that they would never fight, they would never bother people, they would never bite, even if people started with them. Then they used to be taken advantage of, and that made them feel very bad about themselves.

And finally the tiger decided that maybe he ought to try the second club, the club in the middle. And he went there and said, "What are your rules?"

And the club in the middle said, "Well, our rules are these. Our rules are that we're not going to start fights with other people, but if other people, if other animals start with us, we're going to fight back. So it's not that we never fight. It's not that we always fight. We're in the middle."

And this tiger said, "Maybe I'll try this club and see what happens." So he joined that club of tigers. And one day, as the middle tiger club was meeting, a couple of lions and some elephants came along and some other animals, and they started to make trouble. And the tigers in the middle club said, "Listen, we're warning you. Stay away. We didn't bother you. Don't bother us. But we can tell you this: If you bother us, you're going to be sorry."

Well, the lions and the elephants didn't listen and they started to snarl and bite, and they started to go where the middle club's food was and they started to make trouble. And these tigers in the middle club got together and they started to fight and growl and hiss and jump and claw and there was a fight. Soon the lions and the elephants who came along realized that they were going to get into a lot of trouble. They'd get bitten up and they'd get hurt and so gradually they pulled back and they ran away. And then the tigers in this middle club began talking about the importance of . . . what did they talk about?

Patient: Hm.

Therapist: What did they decide after everybody left, after the lions and the elephants left? What did they decide?

Patient: I don't know.

Therapist: Well, did they think that their plan was a good one?

Patient: Yeah.

Therapist: What was their plan in this club? How did they work things?

Patient: They didn't want to start trouble, but if some other animal started trouble, they would fight back.

Therapist: Right! That was their rule. That was the middle club.

And so after that the animals that came around to bother them, like other tigers and elephants and other animals, realized that these guys wouldn't start up, but that they would protect their rights. They would protect themselves when there was trouble. And gradually other animals realized that that was the best of the three clubs. That was the best thing to do with animals who were always bothering people. Don't start, but if others start up, fight back. Now what about the club of the animals that never bothered people? What was the drawback of that? What was the disadvantage? What kinds of trouble did they get when they never bothered people?

Patient: And then other people would pick on them.

Therapist: Right.

Patient: And they wouldn't fight back.

Therapist: Hh hmm. So which do you think is the best of the three clubs, in your opinion?

Patient: The middle club.

Therapist: Because?

Patient: Because if they starting picking on you, you can pick on them.

Therapist: Right. Right. You defend yourself. You protect your rights. Okay, how did you like this program?

Patient: I liked it.

Therapist: Do you want to see yourself on television?

Patient: Okay.

Therapist: Do you want your parents to come up and watch?

Patient: No.

Therapist: You don't want them to. Why not?

Patient: I'm shy.

Therapist: You're shy.

Patient: Uh hmm.

Therapist: I think it would be a good idea. It's good practice for shyness to do things that you're shy about, and then you find out that it's not so terrible. That's the way to conquer shyness. Do you want to try it?

Patient: Okay.

Therapist: All right, let's call them and have them watch and you'll see that for the person who is shy, each time you do the thing that bothers you, you become less scared of that thing. Okay?

One of the purposes of therapy is to introduce options to the patient that may not have been considered or, if they have, have not been incorporated into the patient's psychic structure. In therapy one helps the patient consider the advantages and disadvantages of the various options, the pathological as well as the healthy ones. *The mutual storytelling technique* provides opportunities for such introductions and comparisons, and this is what I have done here. The story demonstrates symbolically the discomforts and indignities one suffers when one lives by the principle that anger expression under any circumstances is undesirable. It also demonstrates the benefits accrued to those who have a more flexible attitude about anger and use it appropriately.

The patient was deeply involved in my story and readily understood its significance. Although he expressed some hesitation about his parents' viewing the videotape, his enthusiasm more than counterbalanced this negative reaction. I believe this interchange served to catalyze his involvement in treatment.

The Case of David
[The Family with Sixteen Children]

David was referred at the age of nine-and-a-half by his pediatrician. Three months prior to referral, he began suffering with abdominal pains. These began about one month after starting the fourth grade and were so severe that he had not attended school during the six weeks prior to my initial consultation with him. Thorough medical evaluations by three pediatricians revealed no organic cause for his difficulties, and he was therefore referred for consultation.

David was the youngest of six children, the older siblings ranging in age from 23 to 16. Accordingly, there was a 6½-year hiatus between David and his next oldest sibling. During the five years prior to the initial consultation, the older siblings began to leave the household, one at a time. The oldest three had already left the home and the fourth, an 18-year-old sister, was starting to apply to college. In addition, his 16-year-old brother (the fifth of the siblings) had already left the home three years previously for six months as an exchange student in Europe. The family was a tight-knit one, and these losses were painful for David.

Of pertinence to David's disorder was the fact that there was a strong history of appendicitis in the family. Four of his five older siblings had had their appendices removed and appendicitis was under serious consideration during David's hospitalization. However, absolutely no evidence for appendicitis was found. David's father was a highly successful businessman who enjoyed significant prestige in his community. The family members considered themselves paragons of what a family should be. In such an atmosphere the expression of deficiency was strongly discouraged as were crying, depressed feelings, profanity, and any other manifestations that were considered to be deviant. Lastly, David's new teacher had the reputation of being unusually strict and David found this particularly difficult to handle.

During the initial interview I concluded that David was suffering with a separation anxiety disorder. In his case it was not so much separation from his mother that was painful, but the progressive and predictable loss of his older siblings who were serving as parental surrogates. It was as if David had seven parents: mother, father, and five significantly older siblings. As they progressively left the home, he felt increasingly alone and fearful about the loss of his various protectors. The closeness of his family intensified the problem. Had there been a looser family involvement he might not have been so anxious. Furthermore, the family pattern in which everyone was required to present a facade of perfection and imperturbability made it extremely difficult for David to express the anxieties, anger, and depression he felt over these losses. Lastly, the family history of appendicitis provided a model for excused withdrawal. Others were seen to get extra attention and affection in association with this illness, and that probably served to give David the idea that he could enjoy such extra protection by the utilization of the symptom. Of course, the abdominal complaints themselves might also have been a manifestation of his tension and anxiety. During his third session, while playing the mutual storytelling game, the following interchange took place.

Therapist: Good afternoon, boys and girls, ladies and gentlemen. Welcome to "Dr. Gardner's Make-Up-a-Story Television Program." We have a new guest on our program today. Tell me how old are you?
Patient: Nine.
Therapist: Nine years old. What grade are you in?
Patient: Fourth.
Therapist: Fourth grade. Okay, now, let me tell you how it works. On this program we invite boys and girls down to see how good they are in making up stories. Now it's against the rules to tell a story about anything that really happened to you or anyone you know. The story must be completely made up from your imagination. It can't be about anything you've seen on television or read in books. Then, when you've finished telling the story, you tell the lesson or moral of the story—what we learn from the story. As you know, every good

story has a lesson or a moral. And, of course, the more exciting the story is the more fun it will be to watch on television afterwards. Now, when you've finished telling the story, you tell the lesson or moral of your story. Then I'll tell a story and we'll talk about the lesson or moral of my story. Okay, you're on the air.

Patient: It can't be from a book?

Therapist: No, it can't be a story from a book. It has to be completely made up in your own imagination.

Patient: There's this man and a woman, and they lived on top of a huge rock. And they had 16 children and they couldn't find another room. They only had one room.

Therapist: Okay, so there's one room for 16 children. Uh huh.

Patient: And they were all running around and making so much noise that they didn't know what to do. So they called their friend who was really smart. . .

Therapist: So they couldn't handle all the kids? Is that it?

Patient: So the man said if they had any lobster pots. And they said "yes, 16." And he asked them to get the lobster pots. . . .

Therapist: This is the friend?

Patient: Yeah. So he took the lobster pots on his bicycle.

Therapist: He took the 16 lobster pots on his bicycle?

Patient: Yeah, to his home and then at home he got some candy and rope and then he rode back and climbed up to the house, and then when he got up to the house, he said, "Hello . . . " So he tied the lobster pots outside the windows. He had 16 pieces of candy and he put all the candy he had in them.

Therapist: In the lobster pots?

Patient: Yeah, and then the children ran to get their candy . . . and then they jumped into the lobster pots and ate the candy. And the children stayed in the lobster pots.

Therapist: The children stayed there?

Patient: These were big lobster pots. They even had dinner there.

Therapist: They even had dinner there? Who served them?

Patient: The mother and father.

Therapist: So they had more room . . . is that it?

Patient: Yeah.

Therapist: Uh huh. Okay. Is that the end?

Patient: That's the end.

Therapist: Lesson?

Patient: Some people will do anything just to have some privacy.

Therapist: Who's having the privacy there?

Patient: The mother and the father . . . they would do anything just to have some privacy.

Therapist: And what did they do to the children?

Patient: They just lived with them.

I considered this story to represent well the patient's situation with his family. Although his family consisted of six children, he symbolizes it with a family of 16 children. In either case the number is large and both figures share the numeral 6. The story enabled David to gratify his fantasy of entrapping his siblings in such a way that they could not leave the house. Each window contains a lobster pot into which a sibling can be lured with candy. There the child is trapped and cannot flee or leave. Ostensibly, the parents do this in order to provide themselves with some privacy. If that were indeed their motive, they could have allowed all the children to leave the house in such a way that there was little if any link or tie to the home. Accordingly, I considered this reason to be a rationalization. It is the opposite of what the parents *really* want: entrapment of the children in the home. Of course, it is not the parents who want this; it is David who attributes this desire to the parents to serve his own purposes. The story also reflects some ambivalence about closeness with his siblings. On the one hand, he wants them close enough to be seen and ever present (thus he traps them in lobster pots). On the other hand, he puts them outside the window, thereby providing him with a little distance and breathing space (a little privacy after all). With this understanding of David's story, I related mine.

> *Therapist:* I see. Okay, now as I said, when you finish telling your story, I'll tell a story and we'll talk about the lesson and moral of my story. Now, my story will start off like your story, but different things happen in my story. Okay?
>
> Once upon a time there was a family and this family consisted of a mother and a father and 16 children . . . a big family . . . and they lived in one room. Now everyone was getting kind of edgy . . . living on top of one another and things like that.
>
> And finally they decided to consult a friend of theirs who was very wise. And they said to him, "What do you think we can do about this?"
>
> And the father said, "I have an idea. I think maybe I ought to get lobster pots . . . and put candy in them and put them outside the windows and then they'll go into the lobster pots and then there will be less people around the house and I'll have more room."
>
> And the wise friend said, "Well, look, how old are some of your children? What are their age ranges?"
>
> He said, "Well, they range from very little ones to very big ones."
>
> And the friend said, "Well, aren't the big ones getting ready to leave soon? . . . go off on their own and become adults?"

And the father said, "Well, I think that the problem will solve itself as the older ones grow up and leave the house. I think that you want to hold onto these kids too long. If you're going to put them in lobster pots and have them hanging around the house, that tells me that you want to hold them back and keep them in the house forever and not let them grow up and become independent, self-sufficient adults."

And the man of the house realized that the wise man made sense. And he said, the man of the house said, "However, the young ones are going to miss the older ones terribly and maybe we ought to try to keep those older ones there for the young ones' sakes."

The wise friend said, "It isn't fair to the older ones. The younger ones have to accept the fact that the older ones are going to be going. They may feel lonely but you know, they have one another. And they also have other friends they can make."

And the father said, "What about the youngest one? When the other 15 leave, what's going to happen to him?"

The wise man said, "Well, he'll be old enough by then to have his own friends. He'll still have time with the older ones. He'll go and visit them and they'll come to visit him. It's not like they're lost forever. He'll still have some time with them. He'll speak to them on the phone. And then he can make his own friends. He can still be with you people, his mother and father. So it's not the end of his world that he doesn't have that many people around. So. . .

Patient: So they just let them grow up?

Therapist: They let them grow up and then what happened to the younger ones?

Patient: Then they. . .

Therapist: Are they sad?

Patient: I guess so.

Therapist: Uh huh. What happened to them? Anything happen to them?

Patient: I don't know.

It is a well-known principle in treatment that if the therapist is going to attempt to take something away from a person, he or she does well to try to find some reasonable substitute at that point. Even the suggestion that the substitutes be provided at some time in the future is generally not as effective as recommending substitutes in the present. Accordingly, although I recommended in my story that the younger ones resign themselves to the fact that the older ones inevitably are going to leave, I provide definite substitutive gratifications. I recommend that the younger ones involve themselves with one another. The patient still had one younger sibling in the home and so this recommendation was applicable. I also suggested intensified relationships with peers as another way of obtaining compensatory gratification. Last, I reminded David that one can still have frequent and meaningful contacts with older siblings even though they are living outside the home. Telephone conversations and visits are still possible and the awareness of this can help assuage the sense of loneliness one might feel after one's older siblings leave the home. At that point I attempted to engage David in a conversation to ascertain whether he appreciated on a conscious level any relationship between my story and his own situation. As mentioned, I do not consider it crucial for the treatment of the patient to have such awareness. What is important is that the message "gets through" and I am not too concerned whether it is received on the conscious or unconscious level, on the direct or the symbolic level. This is the conversation that ensued.

> *Therapist:* Well, do you think this story I told you has anything to do with you? Has anything to do with your situation?
> *Patient:* Ah, yes.
> *Therapist:* In what way? How?
> *Patient:* My brothers and sisters have gone away.
> *Therapist:* How many brothers and sisters did you have?
> *Patient:* Six . . . five.
> *Therapist:* Five besides yourself. And what are their ages? How old is the oldest? What are their ages?
> *Patient:* Sixteen, 19, 20, 22, and 24.
> *Therapist:* Uh huh. How many live in the house now?
> *Patient:* Not counting when they go to college?
> *Therapist:* Right. If they're off at college, let's consider them out of the house.
> *Patient:* Two.
> *Therapist:* Two. You and. . .
> *Patient:* My brother, Bart.
> *Therapist:* Who is 16? And what year in high school is he?
> *Patient:* Sophomore.
> *Therapist:* Sophomore? So he still has a couple more years at home?
> *Patient:* Uh huh.
> *Therapist:* Uh huh. Now, how does the story I just told relate to yours?
> *Patient:* It's like me. My brothers and sisters are going away.
> *Therapist:* Uh huh. And how do you feel about accepting that fact?
> *Patient:* I think I can.
> *Therapist:* You think you can?
> *Patient:* Yeah.

Therapist: Does it upset you a lot?

Patient: Not a lot.

Therapist: Do you think being upset about them has anything to do with your stomach? With your cramps and your going to the hospital?

Patient: No. I don't think so.

Therapist: Do you think your story has anything to do with your problems or the situation with your brothers and sisters?

Patient: No.

Therapist: I do. I think it has something to do with it. In your story, you put them in cages and keep them around the house. Isn't that right? In your story the mother and father's friend put the boys and girls in cages . . . lobster pots . . . they're kind of cages, aren't they?

Patient: Yeah.

Therapist: And they keep them around the house. They don't go anywhere. They're kind of trapped into staying around the house. I think your story says that you would like to have your brothers and sisters trapped around the house.

Patient (appearing incredulous): Not really.

Therapist: You don't think so. Do you think your story has anything to do with you?

Patient: No.

Therapist: Do you think *my* story has anything to do with you?

Patient: Just a little.

Therapist: Just a little. Okay, Well, anyway, the important thing is that if brothers and sisters stay around the house too long, they don't grow up.

Patient: Yes.

Therapist: And they have to grow up and they have to leave and the other kids left behind have to make friends with others, and it isn't the end of the world.

Patient: Yeah.

Therapist: That's the main message. It's not the end of the world when your brothers and sisters leave. You still have other people . . . other friends. And you can still get in touch with your brothers and sisters too, and still see them. Okay, do you want to watch this for a little while?

Patient: Okay.

Therapist: Do you want to have your mother come up and see it?

Patient: Okay.

As can be seen, the patient did not gain too much insight into the relationship between his story and mine. Nor did he have much insight into the relationship between his story and his situation.

There was some appreciation of some superficial similarity but basically he was unappreciative of the various relationships. He did, however, listen with interest to my story, and I believe that the message got through.

The Case of Harry [Valentine Day's Candy from a Loving Mother]

Harry entered treatment at the age of ten because of acting-out behavior in the classroom. Although very bright, he was doing poorly academically. He did not do his homework and would lie to his parents about his school assignments. He did not pay attention in the classroom; rather, he would whisper, hum, shout out, and disrupt the classroom in a variety of ways. He did not exhibit proper respect for his teachers and his principal. At home, as well, he was a severe behavior problem. He was openly defiant of his mother's and stepfather's authority and did not respond to punishment. In spite of this, Harry had an engaging quality to him. Adults, especially, found him "a pleasure to talk to." The parents of the few friends he had also found him a very likable and charming boy, and they often could not believe that he involved himself in antisocial behavior. Harry's mother was married three times. He was the product of her second marriage. He had an older sister who was born during his mother's first marriage. His father was a sales representative for a large corporation and had frequently been away from the home during the first two years of Harry's life, when his parents had still been living together. When the father was with the infant, he tended to be cool, aloof, and disinterested. Harry's mother was a secretary who began working fulltime when Harry was two months of age. He was then left to the care of a series of babysitters, most of whom were unreliable and some of whom were punitive. Unfortunately, both parents tended to ignore the signs of the babysitters' maltreatment.

When Harry was two years old, his parents separated. During the next year he and his sister lived alone with his mother. Following the separation of Harry's parents, there was a custody dispute. Both parents wanted custody, and each claimed to be the superior parent. Harry's father claimed that his wife was promiscuous and, therefore, unfit to take care of the children because she had had a transient affair during the marriage. The trial took place in a rural area in the Midwest, and the judge supported the father's position. After three months with his father, the latter returned the children to the mother with whom they were still living at the time of treatment.

When he was three, his mother's second husband moved into the home and they were married when Harry was four. This was a very stormy relationship, and Harry witnessed many violent battles between his mother and her third husband. In addition, her second husband used corporal punishment in order to discipline Harry. About two years after he moved into the house, Harry's mother's second husband deserted, and neither the mother nor Harry heard from him subsequently.

When Harry was nine, his mother's new husband moved into the house, and he was the stepfather who was involved at the time Harry began treatment. Like his predecessor, Harry's new stepfather was also extremely punitive. He used the strap primarily with the argument, "It was good enough for my father, and it's good enough for me." Harry's mother basically encouraged her husband to use the strap on Harry. When I expressed my opinion that, at ten, Harry was much too old for physical punishment and that I did not believe that corporal punishment was serving any purpose for Harry, both parents disagreed. I emphasized to them that it was my belief that they were making Harry worse, not better, and that there was no evidence that such beatings were reducing his antisocial behavior. In fact, I expressed to them my opinion that it was increasing the frequency and severity of his acting out. Again, they would not listen.

During his second month in treatment, the following interchanges took place while playing the mutual storytelling game:

Therapist: Okay. And now ladies and gentlemen our guest is going to tell us his own original made up story. You're on the air!

Patient: A man was riding his motorcycle on the street and he crashed and eventually he went to the hospital, and when he was in the hospital, his wife came to visit him. While his wife was visiting him the next day would be Valentine's Day. So she brought him on Valentine's Day lots of candy and sweets and the nurse said no candy and sweets for the patient but she did not listen. And so she gave him the candy and sweets he got even sicker.

So then he had to go for an operation. The operation was successful, but the wife was not allowed in the hospital. So eventually she called the police and she told the police what happened. And she wanted to speak to her husband and she broke into the window that he was in—the room window and she took him out of the hospital and he couldn't survive on his own and she didn't get him back to the hospital on time almost. So then he had another operation that was not successful and she was not happy because he died.

Therapist: Okay, now were you going to say something else?

Patient: No, that is it.

Therapist: Okay, the lesson?

Patient: Lesson?

Therapist: Yeah. Every story has a lesson or a moral.

Patient: To tell you when something is told to you, to go by it. To go by the rules.

Therapist: To go by the rules! And how did this wife break the rules?

Patient: She kept on giving him things that he was not supposed to have.

Therapist: Like?

Patient: Candy and taking him out of the hospital.

Therapist: Okay, so she broke two rules?

Patient: Right!

Therapist: Why did she break those rules?

Patient: Because she wanted her husband.

Therapist: She wanted her husband. . .

Patient (interrupts): to be with her.

Therapist: She wanted him to be with her even though the doctors had said it was a bad idea?

Patient: Right, he could not handle it.

Therapist: When you say he could not handle it, what do you mean?

Patient: Like he would not even do anything else.

Therapist: You mean he did just what his wife said?

Patient: Yeah.

Therapist: I see. That is when she gave him the candy?

Patient: No, before the candy when he got even sicker.

Therapist: I see, and what was he like when she took him out of the hospital?

Patient: He was really sick, he was coughing and he was weak.

Therapist: What was the nature of his illness? What was wrong with him?

Patient: He didn't have the right type of medicine. Like he was supposed to have every so often, so he could not survive.

Therapist: I see.

I believed that the man, the protagonist of the story, represented Harry and the man's wife, Harry's mother (the only female in Harry's life). Under the guise of being benevolent she is quite malevolent. She does what she considers to be in Harry's best interests, even if what she does is directly opposed to the doctor's orders. Harry is too weak and passive to say no and suffers the consequences of her "benevolence." He eats the candy and knows that it will make him sicker—and this is exactly what happens. He allows himself to be taken out of the hospital—seemingly because of his mother's love and her desire not to be separated from him— and he gets sicker, and ultimately dies.

The story demonstrates well what Harry Stack Sullivan referred to as the "malevolent transformation." This phenomenon is seen in individuals who grow up in homes where a parent professes love and affection; however, whenever such love is dispensed, it most frequently results in pain to the child. Somehow the affectionate maneuver results in a painful experience—always under the guise that love is still being provided. For example, a mother while professing strongly her love and affection will so vigorously hug the child that significant pain is produced. Under such circumstances the child comes to associate professions of love with physical and/or psychological pain. This produces a fear of those who display affection because there is ever the anticipation that the pain will be soon forthcoming. Here, Harry's mother expresses her affection by giving a box of Valentine's Day candy. A more direct and undisguised symbol of love would be hard to find. However, for Harry it is poison because his physical condition is such that sweets are specifically detrimental. Then his mother takes him out of the hospital against the doctor's advice—again because of her love and her strong desire to be close with him. And he almost dies because of her "affection."

This story also had implications for Harry's therapy. The doctors might very well represent this examiner. Harry's mother and stepfather were both beating him with a strap under the guise of affection. It is another example of the malevolent transformation in that Harry could not but experience pain in association with their allegedly well-meaning attempts to help him become a law-abiding citizen. The story also has some prophetic elements in that it implies that if Harry continues to get such "love," it may kill him.

With this understanding of Harry's story, I continued.

> *Therapist:* Okay, now it's my turn to tell a story. Remember I said that I would tell a story? My story may start like your story but different things happen very quickly. Okay, here we go.

Once upon a time there was a man, and he was sick in the hospital and the doctor said to him that he was absolutely not to have sweet things like candy and things like that.

Patient: Oh, too bad, I like that . . . (mumbles) . . .

Therapist: Now, what did you say? Too bad what?

Patient: Too bad. I'm glad I'm not him because I like candy.

Therapist: Well anyway, this man knew that it was important to obey the doctor's orders. Anyway, one day his wife came in, and it was Valentine's Day, and she said "I love you very much dear. Oh my dear husband, I love you very much. You are really my love, and I brought you this big box of Valentine's chocolates."

And he said, "Well, they sure look good, but the doctor said no sweets, no way." And she said, "Just go ahead and eat them."

And he said, "No, no. It's a bad idea. If I eat those sweets I may get even sicker." And he just absolutely refused to eat them, and she realized that he meant what he said and in no way would he eat those candies.

He also said, "If you want to get me something else as a present, something that would not harm me, I would be very happy."

Patient: How about some ice cream?

Therapist: No ice cream! The same thing. It's also sweet. What do you think she came up with?

Patient: A Valentine's card.

Therapist: A Valentine's card, right. Anything else?

Patient: A new car.

Therapist: Well, that is some Valentine's present! How about something more reasonable? Something that costs more than a Valentine's card and less than a car?

Patient: A kiss.

Therapist: A kiss is good. She gave him a big kiss! And he *really* liked that. He said, "That's very nice."

Patient: Did she get him candy then?

Therapist: No, no. She realized that he was right and that he shouldn't eat the candy. Anyway, the next day she said, "I don't like that hospital. I don't like my husband in that hospital because they don't let me do the things that I want, and I'm going to get him out of the hospital." So she came and tried to get him out. She wanted him to get signed out against doctor's advice, and he absolutely refused. So she said, "I love you very much, and I want you at home."

And he said, "If you love me very much, you'll listen to the things that *I* want. Right now I want to be with you, but I must stay at this hospital and get better. If you really loved me as much as you say, you would *listen* to what I want and would also do many of the things I want. If you want to spend sometime at home, okay. But if you want to spend sometime at the hospital with me, okay. *But I will not go home now.*

Well, after he said that she started to raise a real fuss. She had a tantrum and a fit. And she started screaming, "But I love you so much I want you home!"

Then the doctors and the nurses said, "If you don't cut out that screaming, we'll call the police. You can't have him home and you can't steal him out of the hospital."

And the man didn't want to go with her, and he said, "Right, I have to be in this hospital 'til I'm better." Well, she realized that once again he wasn't going to do what she said just because she said it, and then he said, "If you really love me, you'll listen to the things I want and try to do some of those things, not just the things you want." So she realized that maybe he had a point. So what do you think happened then?

Patient: You said, "They called the police when she set foot in the door."

Therapist: No, no, they didn't have to. They threatened her. They said, "If you don't stop these fits and all this screaming and everything, we will call the police." But you see they didn't have to because she listened to reason.

Patient: I see, and she stopped screaming.

Therapist: Yes, well now what was happening was she was sad about it, but she realized that what her husband said made sense, that it was certainly true that he had to stay in the hospital. (Patient making sounds.) What's the matter?

Patient: Nothing.

Therapist: What were those noises?

Patient: My stomach.

Therapist: Your stomach. Okay. Do you want to settle down? Do you want to hear the rest of the story?

Patient: Yeah.

Therapist: Anyway, she realized that what he said made sense. She realized that he needed to be in the hospital and that getting him out of the hospital early, before the doctors said his time was up, was a bad idea. So what do you think then happened?

Patient: Was his time up?

Therapist: In the hospital?

Patient: Yes.

Therapist: Well, not at the time she wanted him out. But what happened after that?

Patient: He stayed there and he got lonely.

Therapist: And then what happened?

Patient: Then he signed out.

Therapist: No, no. He did *not* sign out. He did *not* break the rules. He listened to the doctors, and he finally got better, went home, and then he and his wife had much more time with one another. And do you think she changed after that?

Patient: Yes.

Therapist: She began to realize that he had a point. And what was the big problem his wife had in my story?

Patient: Not listening.

Therapist: Not listening to what?

Patient: The rules, just like mine.

Therapist: The rules, but something else she did not listen to.

Patient: The rules, just like mine.

Therapist: The rules, but something else she did not listen to.

Patient: Her husband. She wanted her own way.

Therapist: Right, and not listening to what her husband wanted to do. And what should you do with other people?

Patient: Take their thoughts into consideration.

Therapist: Right, take their thoughts and feelings into consideration. You have to compromise. Anyway, that is what happened. They went home. What do you think the lessons of my stories are? Try to figure them out.

Patient: To tell you to listen and you've got to take other people's thoughts into consideration.

Therapist: Right!

Patient: And you have to go by the rules.

Therapist: Very good. You got the lessons. Take into consideration other people's feelings and then compromise. Sometimes you do what they want, sometimes they do what you want. Right?

Patient: Right.

Therapist: And then follow the rules if you think they are important ones and good ones like the rules the doctor makes about getting better. Okay, well, ladies and gentlemen, this is the end of our program today. Do you want to watch this?

Patient: Yeah.

Therapist: Okay, let's turn this off now.

On a few occasions I interrupted my story to ask for the patient's input. The patient's suggestions regarding presents that would be preferable to Valentine chocolates were for the most part reasonable (with the exception of the car). In addition, I periodically interrupted my story to be sure that the patient understood my main points.

Whereas in the patient's story the man is passive (and conspicuously so), in my story he takes an active role in protecting himself from his wife's (symbolizing mother) misguided and coercive benevolence. It is a statement to the patient that, even though he was ten, he was not completely helpless to protect himself from some (but certainly not all) of the indignities he suffers in his home. My story also attempted to help Harry appreciate the basic malevolence behind some of his mother's professions of benevolence. Such clarification can lessen the likelihood that the patient will become involved in pathological interactions. His stomach churning noises were, I believe, a concomitant of the anxiety my message was creating. It is a statement also of the fact that my story was "hitting home."

The Case of Frank
[The Nutcracker and the Three Peanuts]

The last patient I will present exhibited typical manifestations of the Oedipus complex. In order for the reader to appreciate better the way in which I dealt with this boy's oedipal story, I will present first my views of the Oedipus complex.

Freud's Theory of the Oedipus Complex Freud described the Oedipus complex as a normal childhood psychological phenomenon in which the boy or girl, between the ages of three and five, exhibits sexual-possessive fantasies toward the opposite-sexed parent and simultaneously views the same-sexed parent as a rival. The boy anticipates that his father will castrate him for his incestuous designs on his mother and the girl is said to fantasize that she once did indeed have a penis but lost it or it was cut off. Freud's theory of the Oedipus complex was derived from the analysis of adults— most of whom Freud considered neurotic and some of whom we would today consider psychotic. To the best of my knowledge, Freud only published one article on the treatment of a child, the case of Little Hans (1909), and, as mentioned previously, even here Freud was not the therapist. Rather, the boy's father treated him with Freud serving as the supervisor. In the three-and-a-half month course of treatment, Freud saw the boy only once. Freud believed that Hans' treatment confirmed his theories of infantile sexuality and the Oedipus and castration complexes. Furthermore, Freud believed that sexual attraction toward the opposite-sexed parent and jealous rivalry against the same-sexed parent universally appeared in children between the ages of about three and five.

Freud's Theory of the Resolution of the Oedipus Complex   Freud believed that the healthy child resolves the Oedipus complex at about five years of age and then enters into a six-year period of relative sexual quiescence—the latency period. According to Freud, the resolution of the Oedipus complex comes about partly via natural developmental processes. He compared oedipal resolution to the loss of the milk teeth and the growth of the permanent teeth. In addition, he believed that natural psychobiological processes also contributed to the resolution, specifically that the boy's fear that his father would castrate him contributed to the development of his superego and subsequent suppression and repression of sexual fantasies toward the mother (S. Freud 1924). Freud held that the therapist's role in helping children alleviate oedipal problems was to foster resignation that the boy cannot gratify his sexual-possessive cravings toward his mother. However, he is consoled with the hope that someday he will get a suitable substitute, someone "as wonderful, beautiful, etc." as his mother. In short, the boy is asked to forestall gratification in this area for many years. Last, Freud believed that the failure to resolve the Oepidus complex successfully was a central contributing factor in *all* neuroses.

The Author's View of the Oedipus Complex   My own experience over the 28 years that I have worked intensively with children is that only a small fraction, less than two percent, exhibit oedipal problems. The remainder have difficulties that are unrelated (or only remotely related) to oedipal difficulties. And when oedipal problems are present, there are usually specific factors in the family constellation that are directly contributing to the development of such. They do not arise naturally, as Freud would have us believe, but are the result of very specific family patterns that are conducive to the development of such symptomatology.

To elaborate, I believe there is a biological sexual instinct that attracts every human being to members of the opposite sex. From birth to puberty this drive is not particularly strong. Although weak and poorly formulated during the prepubertal period, it nevertheless exhibits itself through behavior that I consider manifestations of *oedipal interest*. A normal boy may speak on occasion of wishing to marry his mother and get rid of his father. These comments may even have a mildly sexual component such as "and then Mommy and I will sleep in bed together." I believe that the possessive, more than the genital-sexual, interest predominates here. The child is primarily interested in a little more affection and attention undiluted by the rival.

In a setting where the child is not receiving the affection, nurture, support, interest, guidance, protection, and generalized physical gratifications (such as stroking, warmth, and rocking) necessary for healthy growth and development, he or she may become obsessed with obtaining such satisfactions and develop one or more of a wide variety of symptoms that are attempts to deal with such frustrations. One possible constellation of symptoms are the kinds of sexual urges, preoccupations, and fantasies that Freud referred to as oedipal. The instinctive sexual urges, which are normally mild and relatively dormant, have the *potential* for intensive expression even as early as birth. Getting little gratification from the parents, the child may develop a host of fantasies in which frustrated love is requited and the rival is removed. Such fantasies follow the principle that the more one is deprived, the more one craves and the more jealous one becomes of those who have what one desires. Such manifestations can appropriately be called oedipal problems in the classical sense. The foundation for the development of neurosis is formed not, as Freud would say, through the failure to resolve successfully one's sexual frustrations regarding the parent of the opposite sex but through the failure to come to terms with the more basic deprivations from which the child is suffering.

Furthermore, I believe other specific factors must also be operative in order that oedipal paradigm symptomatology be selected. It is not simply the aforementioned deprivations. There must be other factors that channel the adaptation in the oedipal direction. I believe that the most common of these for the boy are sexual seductivity by the mother and/or castration threats (or the equivalent) by the father. It is important for the reader to note that the oedipal paradigm includes two phenomena: 1) sexual attraction toward the opposite-sexed parent, and 2) fear of retaliation by the same-sexed parent. Although the latter is considered to be caused by the former, this is not necessarily the case. A boy, for example, might be threatened with castration without there necessarily being any kind of sexual seductivity on his mother's part. A boy, for example, might be threatened that his penis will be cut off if he plays with it, and this threat might be made in a situation where there is no seductivity on the mother's part (this is what I believe took place in little Hans' case [Gardner 1972b]). Or there might be maternal seductivity without any retaliatory threats by the father. When either one or both of these processes are operative—on a preexisting foundation of parental deprivation—then, I believe, there is the greatest likelihood that symptoms will arise that can justifiably be referred to as oedipal. Of course, one might ascribe "unconscious" oedipal factors to a wide variety of other symptoms, but I am confining myself here to the phenomenological definition, one based on observable or accurately reported symptoms.

My discussion focuses here primarily on boys. I do not believe that this reflects any bias on my part; rather, it reflects the fact that Freud himself elaborated much more on oedipal manifestations in the boy and had great difficulty applying oedipal theory to girls. (It is beyond the purpose of this book to speculate on the reasons for this.) It is also important to differentiate between *sexual seductivity* and *sex abuse.* Oedipal problems may arise when there is sexual seductivity, but not when there has been sex abuse. When there is sexual titillation, the child develops cravings that cannot be gratified, and symptoms may then emerge which are designed to deal with these frustrations and deprivations. In sex abuse, there is no sexual frustration and an entirely different constellation of symptoms may emerge, such as symptoms related to distrust, fear of disclosure of the sexual activity, and generalized fear of involvement with adults who are of the same sex as the abusing parent.

The Author's Approach to the Alleviation of Oedipal Problems   Freud used the term "resolution" to refer to the passing of the Oedipus complex between the ages of five-and-a-half and six. I prefer to use the term *alleviation* because I do not believe that oedipal involvements and interests are ever completely resolved. At best, oedipal problems can be alleviated. In fact, I generally go further and use the term alleviation to refer to the therapeutic aim of just about all psychogenic symptomatology. Considering the present state of our knowledge (perhaps the word ignorance would be preferable here), it is premature to use such strong words such as *resolution* and *cure.*

My therapeutic approach to the alleviation of oedipal problems reflects my concept of the Oedipus complex itself. The problems to be alleviated relate to the general problem of emotional deprivation and, if present, parental seduction and/or threats of castration. I attempt to ascertain whether there has been parental seduction. If so, I inform the parents of my opinion that their behavior is seductive and strongly recommend that they refrain from such activities. At times they are consciously aware of the process and, at other times, they are not. In the latter situation, it may be very difficult to impress upon them the seductive elements in their behavior. (The Cases of Howie and Walter discussed in Chapter Seven are excellent examples of this principle.) I also try to learn whether there have been castration threats, overt or covert. Again, if present, I do everything to discourage them. (The case of Howie in Chapter Seven and Frank [below] are good examples of this aspect of the treatment of oedipal problems.)

When addressing myself to the deprivational element I consider the improvement in the parent-child relationship crucial to the alleviation of oedipal problems in children. An attempt is made to improve the boy's relationship with his mother so that he will obtain the gratifications that are due in childhood and will be less obsessed with gaining them in neurotic ways. A similar approach is used with girls exhibiting oedipal problems in their relationships with their fathers. In addition, such children are helped to accept the fact that they cannot completely possess either of their parents and that the affection and attention of each of them must be *shared* with other members of the family. This sharing concept is an important one to impart. The child must be helped to appreciate that no one can possess another person completely: The father shares the mother with the children; the mother shares the father with the children; and the child has no choice but to share the mother and father with the siblings. In the context of such sharing, children must be reassured that, although they may not get as much as they might want, they will still get something. In addition, they must be helped to gain gratifications from others during the present time. Whatever deficiencies may exist in the parent–child relationship can be compensated for to some degree by satisfactions in other relationships. It is a well-known therapeutic principle that if one is going to take something away from a patient, one does well to provide substitute gratifications at that time, that is, gratifications which are healthier and more adaptive. My approach does not involve suggesting to the child that he wait. To wait for his possessive gratifications may appear to consume an endless number of years. Rather, he has the potential to gain some of these satisfactions in the present and he is given the hope that as he grows older he will have greater autonomy to acquire the more exclusive type of possessive relationship enjoyed by his father. The clinical example I will now present demonstrates how I utilize these principles in treatment.

The Case of Frank   Frank, a seven-and-a-half-year-old boy, was referred for psychotherapy because of generalized immature behavior and poor school performance. Both his teacher and his parents described him as being silly to the point where he rarely took things seriously. He was ever trying to avoid responsibility and typically took the path of least resistance. Most often he would deny responsibility for any unacceptable behavior and was always blaming others. Not taking school work seriously and rarely doing homework, his grades were suffering. He played well with younger children but did not get along with children his own age because of his low frustration tolerance, impulsivity, and inability to place himself in other children's situations to the degree appropriate for his age.

Although there was nothing in the presenting symptoms to suggest that Frank was suffering with oedipal problems, many of the stories he told centered on the theme of rivalry with the father figure for possessive control of the mother figure. In addition, castration anticipations and fears, symbolically presented, were common. As mentioned, when I do see oedipal problems, there are generally specific factors in the family situation that are conducive to the development of this typical reaction pattern. Frank's family situation is an excellent example. His father, an obstetrician, was away for significant periods from the time of his birth right up until Frank began treatment. In the early years this was associated with his residency training and in later years with the building of his practice. Frank and his two younger brothers were left alone with his mother. Although she was by no means seductive, the long periods of being alone with his mother provided Frank with opportunities for intimacy (physical and social, but not sexual) that other boys do not usually have. His father exhibited slightly effeminate gestures, but there were no signs of homosexuality.

Frank was born with undescended testicles which required frequent examination. Often, it was his father who conducted the examinations and reported his findings to the consulting urologist. In addition, at the age of three, an inguinal hernia was found and this, too, was periodically examined by Frank's father. Frank's appreciation that his father's work as an obstetrician and gynecologist involved extensive manipulation of the genital region of people who lacked external genitalia was conducive, I believe, to Frank's viewing his father as a "castrator." Frank's father did, indeed, operate on women in the genital region and it is easy to see how Frank could have viewed his father as having castration potential.

We see, then, three factors in Frank's family situation that were conducive to the development of oedipal problems:

1. The long absences of Frank's father from the home allowed Frank an unusual degree of intimacy with and possessive gratification from his mother.

2. The father's occupation as an obstetrician and gynecologist—an occupation in which the father literally performed operations on the genitalia of people who already lacked a penis and testes—contributed to the father being viewed as a potential castrator.

3. The frequent examination by his father of Frank's own genitalia also could have induced castration anxieties in that such examination was indeed performed to assess Frank's readiness for surgery in that area.

On the Rorschach test, Frank often saw as female those blots traditionally seen by boys as male. In addition, there was some evidence for identification with the stereotyped passive female. This, I believe, was the result of the long contact alone with his mother, depriving Frank of opportunities for more masculine identification models. In addition, the somewhat definite, albeit slight, effeminate gestures of his father probably played some role in this feminine identification problem. However, the Rorschach and TAT did not reveal a complete absence of masculine identification. Rather, a sex-role confusion was evident. Oedipal themes were also apparent. On one TAT card, Frank related this story:

Now his father dies . . . .He and his mother went to the funeral and after to the Greek hall to eat something. He got shrimp cocktail and she ate the same. Then they went home and got into bed and thought about their husband and father. His mother had him before she married his father and so he loves his mother more than his father.

This was the story Frank told during the third month of treatment:

Patient: Once there was three little peanuts and a nutcracker lived down the block. And every day when they went outside, the nutcracker would try to crack them open. So they said they'd have to move from their mother's house because the nutcracker lived right down the block. So they moved. So they found a house that was sold to them and they had a new house. They had a mansion. But the nutcracker moved right across the street from them.

Therapist: Wow.

Patient: And every time they went out in the street to play again, the nutcracker would come out and try to crack them open. So one day the nutcracker came to the door and looked in the window and saw them playing cards. So he shut the window real fast. And then right there was a metal monster eater and he just loved nutcrackers. He gobbled the nutcracker up and there was never a nutcracker again. The end.

Therapist: What did he do?

Patient: He liked metal and especially nutcrackers. He ate the nutcracker whole and there was a happy ending and they never were aware of the nutcracker again. So that's the end of the story. The end. Good-bye.

Therapist: Okay. And the lesson of that story?

Patient: Ah, think smart and you'll be smart.

Therapist: And what was the smart thinking here?

Patient: Uh, they put a metal monster eater right underneath the window.

The three peanuts, as the protagonists of the story, symbolize the patient and his two younger brothers. The nutcracker, who lives down the block, represents Frank's father. He is already out of the home and Frank has gratified his oedipal wishes to possess his mother completely. However, the nutcracker, castrator that he is, is obsessed with the notion of cracking the three peanuts. Their attempts to elude him prove unsuccessful as he pursues them to their new home. Interestingly, it is a mansion—implying that Frank has the wherewithal to live with his mother in "high style." The problem of the nutcracker's relentless pursuit is solved by the peanuts' engaging the services of a "metal monster eater" who "just loved nutcrackers." The story ends with his gobbling up the nutcracker and "there was never a nutcracker again. The End." Finally, "there was a happy ending and they never were aware of the nutcracker again." Now all is well with the world. Frank gains complete possession of his mother and his father is not only removed from the house but is completely obliterated assuaging, thereby, Frank's castration fears.

It was with this understanding of Frank's story that I told mine:

> *Therapist:* Okay. Now it's time for me to tell my story. Now my story may start like your story, but different things happen very quickly. Once upon a time there were three peanuts. And these peanuts lived in a neighborhood where they lived with their mother.

Patient: Yeah.

Therapist: They also lived with their father.

Patient: Yeah, uh huh.

Therapist (looking at patient): In my story, the father is a nut-cracker! (At this point, the patient looks up toward the therapist, somewhat incredulously.)

Therapist: That's my story.

Patient: Uh, huh.

Therapist: And the three peanuts are very upset because they think that their father wants to crack them. So they said to him one day, "Are you going to try to crack us? Are you going to try to crack us open?" (Patient now rolling his kneesocks down.) And the father said, "No, but at times you boys get me angry and I sometimes feel mad at you. But I don't have any desire to crack you or crumble you up or get rid of you that way." (Patient now rolling his kneesocks up.)

Patient: Or throw you out of the window or throw you on the concrete floor or make you smashed. (Patient now laughs nervously.)

Therapist: "No, I'm not going to do that."

Patient (in a reassured tone): Uh, huh.

Therapist: He said, "However, you boys sometimes get me angry." They said, "Yeah, we know that we sometimes get you angry." And (turning toward the patient) do you know when the boys would sometimes get the father angry?

Patient: When?

Therapist: What kinds of things do you think they did that would get the father angry?

Patient (now bends over, puts his elbows on his knees, and supports his chin in his cupped hands): Let's see now. They would do things that the father didn't tell them to do? (Patient now resumes his original position of facing the examiner.)

Therapist: Like what?

Patient: Like, when he wanted them to clean his car and they wouldn't do it.

Therapist: Yeah, that would be the kind of thing that would get him angry. One of the things that would get him angry was when they would want the mother all to themselves, and they wouldn't want him to spend any time with the mother. You know, that would get him angry sometimes, when they would say, "We don't want you around. We don't want you to be with Mommy all the time. We don't want you to be with her. Things like that." He said, "That's the kind of thing that gets me angry." (Patient now tying his shoelaces.) And they said, "Well, that's the kind of thing that makes us think you want to get rid of us. That you want to kill us. That you want to get rid of us. That you want to crack us up and get rid of us, and then have Mommy all to yourself." You see the father and the three boys were kind of rivals. (Therapist now turns to patient.) Do you know what *rival* means?

Patient: Uh, huh.

Therapist: What does rival mean?

Patient: I don't know.

Therapist: They were kind of fighting for the mother to have time with her. Each wanted the mother all to themselves. The father wanted the mother a lot of times and the boys wanted her. The boys wanted to have her to take care of them, to teach them things, and to read books with them, and things. (Patient now stops tying his shoelaces and interlocks the fingers of one hand with the other.) And the father said, "I get angry at you when you want her all to yourself." And they said, "And we get angry at you, because we don't want you around. We want her all to ourselves." They were kind of fighting for her. So what do you think happened?

Patient (now resting hands in his lap): I think the father got so mad that he cracked them open.

Therapist (shaking his head negatively): No way! No. What they decided to do was . . . they realized that the father shouldn't have the mother all to himself, because the boys were still part of the family. And that the boys shouldn't have the mother all to themselves because the father was still part of the family. So they decided to compromise. And they decided that they will *share* the mother. That sometimes the boys will have time with the mother (patient now takes his hand out of his lap and slaps his thighs) and sometimes with the father. (Patient now puts his hands on his thighs.) Now this still made the boys feel a little bit sad, because they didn't have their mother all they wanted to. (Patient now whistling and flapping the palms of his hands on his thighs.) So what did they do then?

Patient: They had a whole day with the mother and didn't let the father have . . . no . . . they had a whole week with the father. (Patient now moving his hands toward his groin area.) No (patient now rubbing his penis), and had a whole week with the mother (still rubbing his penis) and then the father had a whole week with the mother.

Therapist: That was one way. Sharing. That's one thing they can do. (Patient still rubbing himself.) And another thing that made the boys feel better was to spend time with their friends. When they weren't with their. . .

Patient: . . . mother. . .

Therapist: mother, they could spend time with their friends. And also, another thing (patient still rubbing his penis), was they knew that when they grew up they would have (patient now grasps his penis with his left hand and pulls up his shirt with his right hand) a lady. Each one would get married. Or live with somebody, or have a girlfriend. Something like that. (Patient now pulls his pants forward, at the belt level, with his left hand and puts his right hand inside and starts stroking his penis.) And then they would not feel so jealous of the father, you know. (Patient now pulls his right hand out of his pants and strokes his penis from the outside.) Because they would have. . . .

Patient (slapping his both hands now on his thighs with an air of certainty): . . . a lady of their own.

Therapist: . . . a lady of their own. (Both the patient and the therapist's statement, "a lady of their own" was said simultaneously. It was clear that the patient knew exactly what words the therapist was going to say and so they both made the exact statement simultaneously.) Right!

Patient (laughing with a sigh of relief): Uh, huh. (Patient again moves both hands toward the groin and rubs the penis area.)

Therapist: And that's exactly what happened. (Patient still rubbing penis.) And what do you think the lessons of that story are?

Patient: Uh. (Patient still holding penis and laughing nervously.)

Therapist: What are the lessons?

Patient: Let me see. (Patient now removes hands from groin and puts them on top of his head.) Share.

Therapist: Share.

Patient: Share with other people.

Therapist: Right. And is there any other lesson?

Patient (hands now clasped behind his head): . . . and you'll get along together.

Therapist: Share, and you'll get along together. Any other lesson?

Patient (hands on top of head, nodding negatively): No.

Therapist: There's another lesson. What you can't have in one place, you can have in another. Like they couldn't have the mother all the time, but they could have friends: boys and girls that they played with in the street or in the home. . .

Patient (interrupting): Did they have a busy street?

Therapist: Yeah. There were a lot of kids around.

Patient: Were there a lot of cars? (The patient then removes his hands from his head and imitates moving cars with buzzing sounds.)

Therapist: Yeah. But they had quiet streets too in that area. If there weren't friends in their neighborhood, they would go elsewhere. And also, if you can't have something now there's always the hope that you can get it in the future. You know?

Patient: Yeah. (Patient now playing with his wristwatch.)

Therapist: And then they could have a girl all their own. Anything you want to say?

Patient: No.

Therapist: Do you like this game?

Patient (while clasping his hands): Yeah.

Therapist: Do you want to watch this?

Patient (with an excited expression on his face, while still clapping his hands): Yeah!

Therapist: Okay. Let's watch this. Do you want to have your mother come in and see it?

Patient (still excited): Yeah.

Therapist: Let's do that. (Both arise.)

When creating responding stories, the therapist often has a conflict. If the therapist retains the original symbol used by the child, pathological elements may have to be retained. For example, if the child uses a worm or pig to symbolize him- or herself, the utilization of these in the therapist's story implies agreement that the child warrants being symbolized by such loathesome animals. In contrast, to dispense with such symbols entirely may rob the therapist of rich symbolism that significantly enhances the impact of the therapeutic communications. I generally will retain the symbol and make sure, in the course of my responding story, to emphasize the healthy element associated with it and to deemphasize, ignore, or directly negate the unhealthy aspects of the symbol. In my responding story here I purposely retained the nutcracker symbol because I considered the advantages to far outweigh the disadvantages. However, after informing the patient that the father was a nutcracker, I quickly emphasized the point that he has the *potential* for castration but that he does not use his power. Rather, I focused on behavior manifested by the peanuts that might cause the father to be angry and studiously avoided any possibility that the anger could reach such proportions that castration, symbolic or otherwise, could possibly occur.

In addition, at the beginning of my story, I make it quite clear that *the father lives with the peanuts.* This is in contradistinction to the father in Frank's story who has already been ejected from the household. In my story the problem with the father is worked out through discussion rather than acting out. In Frank's story the father is already removed and the father is a castrator. In mine, the father is present, is not a castrator, and engages in meaningful communication to discuss problems with his peanut sons.

The main point that I make in my responding story is that it is not a question of *either* the father or the peanuts having full possession of the mother. Rather, they can *share*. Sometimes the peanuts spend time with the mother, sometimes the father spends time with the mother, and sometimes all of them spend time with her. And, when the father is with the mother, the peanuts can still spend time with others in their neighborhood to compensate for their loss. In addition, they are provided with the hope that when they get older they will have more opportunity for greater possession of an appropriate female peanut.

According to Freud, the Oedipus complex naturally passes like the milk teeth that give way to the permanent teeth. In addition, fears of the father castrating the child contribute to the development of the superego which suppresses and represses the boy's possessive, sexual longings for the mother. Lastly, the boy is consoled with the fact that someday he will have a female of his own. Most therapists agree that it is very difficult to take something away from patients without offering something in return. In Freud's formulation, the boy is consoled with the knowledge that someday he will have a female of his own. For the child of five, this future is like a million years away and is not likely to serve well as a meaningful consolation.

In the kind of oedipal resolution I propose, the boy is not asked to give up entirely his *present* desires for possessive involvement with his mother. Rather, he is advised to share her with his father. It is certainly easier to share a prized possession than to give it up entirely. In addition, the boy is given the consolation that there are opportunities with others at the present time. Last, he is also told about future possibilities.

In the course of telling my responding story, the patient continuously rubbed his genital area and pulled his pants tightly against his penis. It became apparent that he had an erection and that the prospect of possessive opportunities with a female were sexually titillating. Frank's response was clear evidence that my story was indeed dealing with issues that were most important for him and that my message was a most meaningful one. The vignette is an excellent demonstration of a situation in which the therapist knows that his responding story is indeed being received with interest and receptivity and that it is touching on important psychological issues.

The reader who is interested in more detailed discussions of my views on the etiology and treatment of oedipal problems may wish to refer to other publications of mine in this area (Gardner, 1968a, 1973c, 1983a).

CONCLUDING COMMENTS

I have described the basic rationale of the mutual storytelling technique. I do not claim to have invented a new method of treatment. The principle is an ancient one, and many therapists have no doubt utilized the method. I believe that my main contribution lies in having written articles on the subject and having formulated more specific criteria for analyzing and creating stories. The utilization of the method in the treatment of a wide variety of psychiatric disorders of childhood is discussed in a number of other publications of mine (Gardner, 1968a; 1969c; 1970c,d; 1971c; 1972d,e; 1973f; 1974b,c,d; 1975a,b; 1976a; 1979d,e; 1980a; 1981a; 1983a). A comprehensive description of the details of utilizing the technique (with regard to story analysis and the therapist's story creations) is provided in my full-length text on the subject (Gardner, 1971a).

Nine

Dramatized Storytelling

Give a man a mask and he'll tell you the truth.

Ancient Greek aphorism

All the world's a stage
And all the men and women merely players.
They have their exits and their entrances
And each man in his time plays many parts.

William Shakespeare

INTRODUCTION

Children call us "talking doctors." Many of us do not fully appreciate the significance of this epithet, especially with regard to its implication that our therapeutic approach is a relatively narrow one. Let us compare, for example, the following experiences with respect to our involvement in a play. First, we can read the play. Such an experience is purely visual with regard to the reading as well as the visual fantasies that the reading material may engender within us. Compare this to attending a theatrical performance of the play. Here, in addition to seeing the performance, we hear it as well. Auditory stimuli have been added to the visual. With two sensory modalities of communication, acting simultaneously, there is a greater likelihood that the play will affect us. Imagine, then being an actual participant in the play as an actor or actress. Now, added to the visual and auditory sensory modalities are the kinesthetic, tactile, and possibly even the gustatory and olfactory. With these additional modalities of sensory input, it is even more likely that the play will have an impact. However, no matter how skilled and experienced the actor may be, his or her emotions are feigned. No matter how much both the actor and the audience may be swept up by the part, all recognize that everything is basically being dictated by the script: it is "not real," it's "only a play." Compare now play-acting in which there is an actual living experience in which emotional reactions are elicited by real events. Here the linkage between the emotions and the aforementioned sensory modalities is deep and genuine. Nothing is play-acted. Rather, the individual is having an *experience*. And it is the experience that has the greatest affect on us. To the degree that we provide our patients with experiences—as opposed to relatively sterile insights—to that degree we improve our chances of helping them.

Because the therapeutic situation may not allow us to provide our patients with as many natural and uncontrived experiences as we would like, we do best to provide them with every possible encounter that comes as close to them as we can. Although play-acting does not have as much "clout" as an actual experience, it may be a superior form of interaction and communication than merely talking—and this is especially true for the child. Just as the mutual storytelling technique was developed from the observation that children naturally enjoy both telling and listening to stories, the idea of dramatizing them arose from the observation that children would often automatically (and at times without conscious awareness) gesticulate, impersonate, intone, and enact in other ways while telling their stories. I found that when I introduced such theatrics myself the child became more involved in my stories and receptive to their messages.

Whereas originally I introduced the dramatic elements *en passant*, that is, in the process of telling my story (just as the children tended to do), I subsequently formalized the process by inviting the child to reenact our stories as plays following our telling them: "I've got a great idea! Let's make up plays about our stories. Who do you want to be? The wolf or the fox?" At times I would invite the mother and even siblings to join us. (We often face the problem of having a shortage of available actors.) We see here another way in which mothers can be useful in the child's treatment. (A little encouragement may be necessary at times to help some mothers overcome their "stage fright.") Of course therapists themselves must be free enough to involve themselves in the various antics that are required for a successful "performance." They must have the freedom to roll on the floor, imitate various animals, "ham it up," etc. They have to be able to be director, choreographer, writer, and actor—practically all at the same time. They may have to assume a number of different roles in the same play, and quickly shift from part to part. Such role shifts do not seem to bother most children nor reduce their involvement or enjoyment. Nor do they seem to be bothered by the therapist's "stage whispers," so often necessary to keep the play running smoothly.

Younger children, especially those in the four- to six-year age group, who may not be inclined to tell well-organized stories, will often improve in their ability to relate them when the dramatic element is introduced. Others, who may have been initially unreceptive to or too inhibited to freely tell stories, may do so after the enjoyable dramatic elements are utilized. The experience becomes more fun and the child tends to forget his or her reservations. In this younger group, as well, the strict adherence to the pattern of the child's first telling a story and then the therapist's telling his or hers may not be possible or disirable. A looser arrangement of interweaving stories and plays back and forth may be more practical and effective.

Children generally enjoy television (a statement which I'm sure comes as no surprise to the reader). Even more, children enjoy seeing themselves on television (something a child rarely has the opportunity to do). Therapists who have available a camera and video cassette recorder can provide children with an immensely beneficial therapeutic modality. Making a video cassette recording of a therapeutic experience increases significantly the likelihood that children will expose themselves to reiteration of the therapeutic communications. In the 1960s, when I first developed the mutual storytelling technique, the child and I would often listen to the audio tape recording of the mutually told stories. In the late 1960s,

I began encouraging children to bring to the sessions their own audio cassette recorders (a practice initiated by a child) and to listen to these stories at home afterwards.

Around 1970 I purchased a closed-circuit television system and began making videotapes of our stories, both the standard interchanges as well as those that were dramatized. Around 1980 I purchased a standard home video cassette system and camera. This enabled me to lend the videotape to those children who had such an instrument at home. In the last few years, I have added a second video cassette recorder and invite the child to bring his or her tape to the office. This enables the child to watch at home the various therapeutic interchanges that we tape. Of these, probably the most valuable are those in which dramatizations occur because this insures even more that the child will listen to the tape and profit from what is contained therein.

CLINICAL EXAMPLES

The Case of Adam
["Can a Dead Frog Be Brought
Back to Life?"]

Adam, an eight-year-old boy with a neurologically based learning disability, exhibited significant social difficulties. It was very difficult for him to place himself in another person's position and this caused him much pain and rejection in social situations. Intellectual impairment (his IQ was about 85) and difficulty in conceptualizing and abstracting resulted in his failing to appreciate and learn many of the subtleties of social interaction. Many of these appear to be learned almost automatically by normal children. Children with minimal brain dysfunction may find this their most crippling problem and it behooves the therapist to appreciate this when working with such children. In Adam's case it was the primary focus of his treatment.

In session one day his mother reported that on the previous day Adam had pulled off the leg of a frog that he had caught in his backyard. I immediately responded with disgust: "Ych, that sounds terrible!" Although I knew that my response was going to lower Adam's self-respect at that point, I felt it was the price that had to be paid for a little superego development. I then asked Adam if he would like to play a game in which I am a frog and he is a boy who wants to pull off my leg. He hesitantly agreed. I lay on the floor and invited him to try to pull off my leg. My moans were immediate: "Ooooh, that hurts! Please stop. Please, my leg is going to come off. Ahhhh—." I asked the patient what the boy then did. He replied that he stopped because he didn't want to hurt the frog any longer. "That's right," I replied. "When the boy realized how much he was hurting the frog, he stopped pulling its leg." I then asked Adam if he would like to play a game in which the boy doesn't stop after the frog screams out and he pulls off the leg and the frog dies. He agreed. This time, in spite of my bloodcurdling cries, the boy pulled off the frog's leg. "Now my leg is off and I'm dead," I mumbled as I lay stiffly on the floor. "Try to bring me back to life," I whispered to the patient as if giving stage directions (a maneuver commonly required in such plays). In spite of the patient's attempts to revive me (these included poking, pulling, artificial respiration, and a little feigned mouth-to-mouth resuscitation), I remained stiff and prostrate, all the while mumbling, "Even that doesn't help. When you're dead, you can never be brought back to life." The game ended (as such games usually do) with questions: "How does a frog feel when someone tries to pull off its leg?" "What can happen to a frog if someone pulls off its leg?" "Can a dead frog be brought back to life?"

One might argue that the above approach is a little too strong and that it might create intense feelings of self-loathing in the child. I can only reply that I do not believe that this has been my experience. Whatever transient lowering of self-esteem the child may suffer in such a game (and I grant that he or she certainly may) is more than compensated for by the ultimate enhancement of self-worth that results from heightened sensitivity to the pains of others and his or her ceasing to inflict unnecessary and wanton pain on others. Last, if such a game is indeed too ego-debasing to the child, he or she can usually be relied upon to refuse to play it or to discontinue it if it gets too "hot." It is grandiose of the therapist to consider to know beforehand whether a healthy communication is going to be devastating to a patient. I tend to try it out and respect the patient's defenses when they exhibit themselves.

The reader should appreciate that I am fully aware that this child's cruel act related to hostility that was being redirected from other sources onto the frog. One cannot focus simultaneously on many of the multiple factors which usually contribute to a pathological act. Here I chose to direct my attention to the egocentricism issue (the child's inability to project himself into the situation of another living thing) and his ignorance of certain aspects of social reality.

The Case of Frank
(Gonga Wants Too Much More)

Frank's situation demonstrates how a child's feelings about a competent sibling can contribute to the development of an antisocial behavior disorder that interferes with academic functioning. Frank was 11 when I first saw him. He had been referred by his school psychologist because of antisocial behavior. The parents claimed that Frank's antisocial behavior began when he was three years old, about the time of the birth of his only brother. He became restless, distractible, and exhibited frequent temper tantrums. He was evaluated by a child neurologist who diagnosed him as "hyperactive" and, at the age of four, he was placed on methylphenidate—on which medication he remained for over six years.

When he began the first grade, things deteriorated significantly. He would not concentrate on his school work. Rather, he would engage in various types of horseplay in the classroom, tell jokes, laugh at the teacher, make faces, thump on his desk, and disrupt the class in a variety of ways. Frank was considered to be very bright but, not surprisingly, received very low grades and did not learn very much. He was always trying to avoid school responsibilities and rarely did meaningful homework. This behavior continued and he was finally placed in a special educational class in the third grade, where he still was when I first saw him when he was at the fifth grade level.

Peer difficulties were also described. He sought friendships but was not sought by peers. He insisted upon having his own way and had temper tantrums when thwarted by friends. He did not respect the rights of others and exhibited little ability to put himself in other children's situations. He taunted other children and became excessively argumentative. He would cheat while playing games and generally "didn't know when to stop." He often felt cheated or gypped and tended to blame others when there were difficulties.

At home, as well, Frank had many problems. He did not respect parental authority, exhibited impulsivity and low frustration tolerance. He had temper outbursts and, on occasion, would physically abuse his younger brother. He did not seem to learn from punishments that were dispensed in the attempt to control Frank's antisocial behavior.

Frank's parents were very proper, well-to-do, upper-middle-class people for whom everything seemed to be going smoothly. The father, an attorney, was in a law firm that had been started by his grandfather. I viewed them as somewhat "uptight" people but did not consider this enough to explain Frank's severe antisocial behavior. His younger brother was getting along quite well and was viewed by the family as being a "wonderful boy" who excelled in academics, sports, and social relationships. The fact that he was so stable suggested that Frank's parents could not have been significantly deficient in their parenting role—even considering the fact that Frank was their first-born and they might have been more tense with him than his younger brother.

During the first three months of Frank's treatment I really could not say why he was so angry. At the beginning of the session when his mother and/or father was present he would be obstructionistic, used profanities toward them, and at times made himself thoroughly obnoxious. However, although initially resistant to involve himself in the therapeutic activities, I was able to engage him in a meaningful way. The vignette presented here demonstrates how dramatizations enhanced the therapeutic efficacy of doll play. Among the dolls and puppets I have in my office is a small gorilla whose name is *Gonga*. In the show he used this doll as well as a monkey doll that he called *Chip*. He then drew an announcement sign for the program: *Gonga Never Listens*. Prior to the program he requested that I sit on the sidelines and not be within the view of the camera. The dolls were placed on a bridge table and, during most of the performance, the patient hid himself either behind or under the bridge table so that only the puppets were in direct view of the camera.

> *Therapist:* Good afternoon, boys and girls, ladies and gentlemen. Today is Saturday, the 27th of February, 1982, and I'm happy to welcome you once again to Dr. Gardner's program. Our guest today is going to present a show. Now will you please tell us the name of the show?
> *Patient:* Gonga Never Listens. (Holds up sign: GONGA NEVER LISTENS.)

Therapist: Okay, before I turn this off and get ready for the show, is there anything else you want to say?

Patient: This cartoon show is animated.

Therapist: This animated cartoon will be shown in just one minute. We'll be right back.

And now ladies and gentlemen, we are back with you with our show. Our guest has requested that I not be in the picture at this point so I will sit on the sidelines. Okay? You're on the air!

Patient: Hello, my name is Gonga. (Patient holds up gorilla doll named *Gonga.*) And here is my friend, Chip Monkey. (Patient holds up monkey doll.) The show is named *Gonga Never Listens* because that's exactly what I do. I never listen. So here's one of my stories of what I have done. Okay.

Patient (as Gonga): (Patient turns on tape recorder he has brought to the session and plays loud rock music.) I really love that tape recorder. I want to buy it from the store. I'm going to go in there and ask that guy how much it is.

Patient (as man): Yes, what do you want?

Patient (as Gonga): I want to know how much that tape recorder is.

Patient (as man): $97.

Patient (as Gonga): And how much is the tape above?

Patient (as man): $9.50

Patient (as Gonga): Boy, how am I going to get that much money?

Patient (as man): I hope you do because that's a very fine model. I only have three of them left.

Patient (as Chip Monkey): How are you going to get that money?

Patient (as Gonga): I'll find a way.

Patient: (Whispers in therapist's ear.)

Therapist: Now our guest has asked me to play the part of the mother. I'll be the mother's voice and he's told me what lines I say. Okay.

Patient (as Gonga): Mommy, at the record shop today I saw a very neat tape recorder. It's really neat and it's only $97.50.

Therapist (as mother): $97.50!!!!!!! Are you asking *me* for the money?

Patient (as Gonga): Yes, I am but I'll help out with $7.00 of it.

Therapist (as mother): No, you can't have it. If you want to get one of those, you've got to earn the money yourself. You've got to save up from your allowance and you've got to do work.

Patient (as Gonga): But how can I earn enough money for that?

Therapist (as mother): It'll take a long time, but there are things you can do.

Patient (as Gonga): But they only have three of the tape recorders left!!! (Gonga waves hands during conversation.)

Therapist (as mother): Well, you know it's never the case that there are no more. The store may only have three left, but the person who manufactures that tape recorder has thousands that they send all over, and I'm sure that that store can get you more. And when you earn enough money, then you can buy it.

I'll tell you what I will do, though. If you earn $87.50, I'll give you $10 as a present. Because if you earn the $87.50, that shows me that you have worked very hard and then I'll give you the extra $10.

Patient (as Gonga): Gee, that's great. Thanks, mom.

Therapist (as mother): Well, I'm very happy to do that in order to help you work harder and you'll really feel good after you've earned that $87.50, and then you'll get that tape recorder. You'll see.

Patient (as Gonga): Okay, goodbye. I'm going up to my room.

Therapist (as mother): Okay.

Patient (as Gonga): With Chip Monkey. I'm taking him up to my room too.

Therapist: Okay. Now what happens?

As can be seen, I drive a somewhat hard bargain with Gonga regarding the purchase of the coveted tape recorder. I will give him $10, but he must earn the remaining $87.50. Again, I introduce the old work ethic. Although Gonga seems highly committed to the proposition (talk is cheap and it is only a story) it would have been nice if the patient were a fraction as committed as he professed. We then continued.

Patient: The next day, they were playing *The Talking, Feeling, and Doing Game*. (Sets up *The Talking, Feeling, and Doing Game* on the table.)

Patient (as Gonga): Boy, I really like this *Talking, Feeling, and Doing Game*. I'm glad that Dr. Gardner let me use it.

Patient (as Chip Monkey): I like it too. Considering I'm losing, it's still a pretty funny game.

Patient (as Gonga): Well, I'm going to win this game because I'm ahead of everybody . . . naturally. . . .

Patient (as Turtle): Don't brag, Gonga.

Patient (as Gonga): Don't tell me what to do. It's my turn.

Therapist: Do you think Turtle sort of likes Gonga when he brags or is he sort of turned off by Gonga?

Patient: Yeah, turned off.

Therapist: But not enough to stop playing the game. He just thinks he's a drag to play with.

Patient (as Gonga): (Continues to play *The Talking, Feeling, and Doing Game*.) Boy, let me check this card!

Therapist: What does Gonga's card say?

Patient (as Gonga): "Scratch your backside" . . . that's something I'm really good at doing . . . (Gonga scratches backside.)

Therapist: Okay.

Patient (as Turtle): It's disgusting, Gonga.

Patient (as Gonga): But that's what the card told me to do.

Therapist: Yes, but you don't do that in front of other people.

Patient (as Gonga): I know that. Well, I'll move my piece. (Moves piece and purposely knocks Chip Monkey's piece off the table.) Your piece (speaking to Chip Monkey) is always in the way.

Patient (as Chip Monkey): Don't knock my piece on the floor, Gonga.

Patient (as Gonga): Chip Monkey, you can get it yourself.

Patient (as Chip Monkey): Boy, Gonga has been really mean today. (Begins to have a side conversation with Turtle.)

Patient (as Turtle): I'm not playing everything down here. I know.

Patient (as Chip Monkey): Do you want to go home?

Patient (as Turtle): No, I still like this game.

Patient (as Chip Monkey): Well, if he bothers me one more time, I think I'll leave.

Patient (as Turtle): Well, maybe me too.

Patient (as Gonga): So I go 12 spaces, 1-2-3-4-5-6-7-8-9-10-11-12. I landed on "Go back one." No! (Patient slams down hard on the table.) A stupid game! I'm going to my room.

Therapist: Why'd he get so angry? What happened?

Patient: Because he had to go back one.

Therapist: Boy, he really has a temper! So what did the turtle think of that when Gonga messed up the whole game just because he had to go backward one space?

Patient (as Turtle): Let's go home, Chippy.

Patient (as Chippy): Yeah.

Therapist: The turtle didn't want to play with him any more?

Patient: No.

Therapist: I don't blame him.

Patient: Cut.

Therapist: Okay. Cut. (Patient puts away *The Talking, Feeling, and Doing Game.*)

Patient: Later, after Gonga has gotten over his tantrum, "Boy, was I a dum-dum! Well, I don't care about him. Well, I'm going to call Chippy and see if he still wants to play. (Dials phone.) 652-1301. (Bring-g-g-, B-r-rring . . .)

Patient (as Gonga): Hello, may I speak to Chippy?

Patient (as Chippy): This is Chippy.

Patient (as Gonga): Oh, hi, Chippy. This is Gonga, do you want to play? (Sound of phone hanging up and dial tone.)

Patient (as Gonga): I wonder why he hung up on me?

Therapist: Why do you think he hung up?

Patient: Because he was mad at Gonga.

Therapist: Mad at him for what?

Patient: Getting sore, having a tantrum, and knocking his piece on the floor.

Therapist: So what did Gonga do then?

Patient: She went to her room.

Therapist: *She* went to her room? Is Gonga a *he* or a *she*?

Patient: A he.

Therapist: So he went to his room and did what?

Patient: Sulked.

Therapist: And then what happened?

Patient: He decided to come back down and call Chippy again.

Therapist: Call Chippy again. Okay. So go ahead and call Chip Monkey.

Patient (as Gonga): I can't because Chippy just hung up.

Therapist: That was the first time. Try a second time and see what happens. Maybe if Gonga says that he's *really* sorry and he *means* it, maybe Chippy will listen to him.

Patient (as Gonga): I'll try one more time. (Dials) 652-0210. (Ring-ring.) Hello. Can I speak to Chippy? Okay. Hello, Chippy?

Patient (as Chip Monkey): What do you want, Gonga?

Patient (as Gonga): I'm really sorry about when I threw a temper tantrum.

Patient (as Chip Monkey): I'll bet you are.

Patient (as Gonga): Wait. Don't hang up. I'm sorry. You can come back and play with me if you want to.

Patient (as Chippy): Well, if you won't get so mad over things.

Patient (as Gonga): Okay. Good-bye. (Hangs up.) I want to play more of the *Talking, Feeling, and Doing Game.* I'm going to call Turtle.

Therapist: Okay, he calls Turtle.

Patient (as Gonga): 652-0352. (Ring-ring, ring.) Hello. Hello, Turtle? Can you play?

Patient (as Turtle): Who is this?

Patient (as Gonga): It's Gonga.

Patient (as Turtle): Gonga, why did you get so mad?

Patient (as Gonga): Well, I get mad at things like that. You know I can never listen.

Patient (as Turtle): Well, only if you aren't so mean to me and Chippy. Okay, I'll call Chippy.

Patient (as Gonga): I've already done that.

Patient (as Turtle): He came?

Patient (as Gonga): Yes.

Patient (as Turtle): Okay, I'll be right over. Goodbye.

Patient: I've got to put this telephone away.

Therapist: Mmm. Okay, so they forgave him?

Patient: Yup.

Therapist: So what happened then?

Patient: I can't . . . they're coming.

Patient (as Turtle): I want to play some more of that game?

Therapist: Okay. Why don't you set it up again on the TV and start playing it. Shall I help you?

Patient: Cut it so they can't see you.

Therapist: You don't want me in it, huh?

Patient: So they can't see me either.

Therapist: I'll cut it.

Patient (as Gonga): Boy, oh boy, let me get my dice. Boy, am I doing good at this game! Let's see my card. (Picks card.) That card's no good.

Therapist: What does it say?

Patient (as Gonga): (Puts "bad" card back and takes another.) That's not . . . that's good. "Good Luck! You get an extra turn."

Therapist: No, no, he's not playing fair.

Patient (as Chip Monkey): Wait, Gonga, you can't do that.

Patient (as Gonga): Why not?

Patient (as Chippy): Because you're cheating!!

Patient (as Gonga): I can do what I want to!

Patient (as Chippy): Gonga, you never listen!

Patient (as Gonga): Well, I'll do what I want to.

Patient (as Turtle): Well, you're not going to do what you did last time.

Patient (as Gonga): Okay, jerks. (Picks previously discarded "best" card.) "Jump up and down three times."

Therapist: So Gonga decided to follow the rules now. Huh?

Patient: Uh-huh.

Therapist: What would the guys have done?

Patient: They would have left him.

Therapist: Do you think they would have played with him again this time?

Patient: No.

Therapist: Yeah, he probably realized that.

Patient (as Gonga): Well, I did that. I jumped. Now it's your turn, Chippy.

Using the puppets as players of *The Talking, Feeling, and Doing Game* (a play within a play), Frank exhibits some working through here. A part of him, as represented by Gonga, is the primitive, impulsive individual who acts out his anger. The other part, as played by Turtle and Chip Monkey, represent the civilized superego aspects of his personality. In the end of this segment Gonga becomes somewhat civilized and suppresses his infantile behavior so as not to alienate his friends.

The question must be considered here as to what the therapeutic significance of all this is. It is clear that Frank knows the "right answers." Gonga knows well what is the "wrong" thing to do and his friends know well what is the "right" thing to do. This knowledge is really Frank's. If Frank knows what's right, why is he still doing what's wrong? The answer relates to the fact that without resolution of the fundamental problems that are generating the anger in the first place, it is likely that there will be some acting out or, at least, anger expression in some other way. Here Frank is attempting consciously to suppress the angry impulses in order to protect himself from the alienation of his friends. He is gratifying this desire via his play fantasy.

I believe that something else is being accomplished here as well. The reiterative process serves to entrench the dictates in the superego. Each time the principle or caveat is repeated, it becomes incorporated into the psychic structure. The hope is that such incorporation will ultimately be strong enough to modify behavior even though the fundamental problems have not been dealt with. The superficiality of this process notwithstanding, it is still contributory to therapeutic change. At this point, the play turns back to an as yet incompleted theme: the purchase of the tape recorder.

> *Patient* (as Chip Monkey): Gonga, remember when you wanted to get that tape recorder?
> *Patient* (as Gonga): Yeah.
> *Patient* (as Chip Monkey): Well, they only have one left.
> *Patient* (as Gonga): They do?
> *Patient* (as Chip Monkey): Yeah.
> *Patient* (as Gonga): Well, I'm going to get that.
> *Therapist:* How's he going to get that?
> *Patient:* He's going to get it any way he can.
> *Therapist:* And what way is that?
> *Patient:* He'll do anything he can to get it.
> *Therapist:* Like what, for instance?
> *Patient:* Work as hard as he could. Steal it.
> *Therapist:* Steal it?
> *Patient:* He's crazy. Gonga doesn't listen.

Therapist: Oh, I see. He's going to steal it. . . .

Patient (as Gonga): I might steal it.

Patient (as Chip Monkey): You're crazy, Gonga!!

Patient (as Gonga): Well, who cares. I'm not going to get into trouble.

Patient (as Chip Monkey): You'll get caught and you'll be in the pen. You'll get sent to jail.

Patient (as Gonga): Well, I don't care. It's getting late. You guys ought to go home.

Patient (as Turtle and Chip Monkey): Well, thanks for inviting us. Bye!

Therapist: Well, what happened now with the tape recorder?

Patient: We'll see.

Therapist: We'll see what happened!!

The interchange between Chippy and Gonga is somewhat reminiscent of Jiminy Cricket and Pinocchio. Pinocchio, the "bad boy," is in perpetual conflict with Jiminy Cricket who clearly serves as his conscience. In this part of the story the primitive impulses win out over social dictates.

Patient: (Holds Gonga in the center of the camera field.) "Gonga's Dream." Where am I? (Sounds of "alien" people coming on stage with Gonga.) Who are you people?

Patient (as People): You are in the land of "Don't Listen". . . .

Patient (as Gonga): "Don't Listen???" What is this some kind of joke. Where am I? You move out of the way. (Pushes "alien.")

Patient (as Alien): Gonga, don't touch me or I'll zap you.

Patient (as Gonga): Don't touch me. I'll punch you across the room.

Patient (as Alien): Boy, some specimen this is!

Patient (as Gonga): What are you calling me a specimen for?

Therapist: They're calling Gonga a specimen?

Patient: Yeah.

Therapist: Okay, go ahead.

Patient (as Gonga): I wouldn't talk so much about you guys either. . . .

Therapist: Why are they calling him a specimen?

Patient: These guys are from another planet. . . .

Therapist: Yeah, listen, we have to stop very soon so get to the end of the story.

Patient (as Gonga): Well, what are you people?

Patient (as People): We're moon people. . . .

Patient (as Gonga): Moon people . . . what's that? I'm not going to listen to anything you say.

Therapist: So what do they say when he says that?

Patient (as Moon people): Strange specimen!

Patient (as Gonga): I'm not listening . . . (Tries to put fingers in ears.) Hey, my hands won't go into my ears. . . .

Patient (as Moon people): That's right. We have secret powers.

Patient (as Gonga): Well, I don't know, but I'm getting out of here. I can't move either. . . .

Patient (as Moon people): Yeah, that's why. Well, we are here to talk to you about the tape recorder.

Patient (as Gonga): Tape recorder . . . Oh, rats, well I'm going to get that any way I can . . . I may have to steal it.

Patient (as Moon people): Steal it????

Patient (as Gonga): Oh yeah. You guys haven't been listening to anything I said. . . .

Patient (as Moon people): Yeah. . . .

Patient (as Gonga): Well, I don't care what *you* think. . . . I think you're crazy.

Patient (as Moon people): Well, we don't think you're crazy. We think you never listen. We're trying to teach you a lesson.

Patient (as Gonga): How?

Patient (as Moon people): By getting you with all our creepers.

Therapist: They're going to teach Gonga a lesson for not listening. What are they going to do to him?

Patient: You'll see.

Patient (as Gonga): Hey, where'd you guys go? Hey, you look scary. . . . (Gonga attacked repeatedly by creepy crawlers, little monsters, and a variety of weird creatures.)

Therapist: What are they doing to Gonga?

Patient: Trying to scare him.

Therapist: Why are they trying to scare him?

Patient: So they can teach him a lesson.

Therapist: What's the lesson they're trying to teach?

Patient: To listen.

Patient (as Gonga): Help! Get that spider off me!!! Help me! I'll listen all the time. (Screams as creatures attack him.) And then Gonga woke up from the dream screaming.

Therapist: So did Gonga learn a lesson?

Patient: Yeah.

Psychodynamically, the same process is occurring here as described previously with the rejection of Gonga by his two friends. We see here an excellent demonstration of intrapsychic conflict. There is a conflict between the patient's superego (as represented by the punitive creatures) and his primitive impulses (as represented by Gonga who is the one who threatens to steal the tape recorder). By this process the patient is attempting to entrench and strengthen his superego dictates.

> *Therapist:* I have one question. Why did Gonga not listen in the first place?
> *Patient:* Because he wanted everything his way.
> *Therapist:* Why was that?
> *Patient:* Because he was a snob.
> *Therapist:* Because he was a snob? How did he get to be a snob?
> *Patient:* Well, he just wants everything in the world.
> *Therapist:* He just wants everything in the world.
> *Patient:* It's a she.
> *Therapist:* Okay, I've been a little confused on that point. Okay. How'd she get to be that way? How'd it happen that she wants everything in the world? Why is she so different from others who do listen?
> *Patient:* She wanted everybody to do what she wanted them to do.
> *Therapist:* Yeah, but how did she get that way? How did it happen?

I decided not to analyze the reasons why the patient was switching Gonga's sex. Rather, I decided to persist with the inquiry regarding how Gonga got to be so selfish and why she wouldn't listen. One answer had been provided: "Well, he just wants everything in the world." Although this is not a deeply significant comment, it does provide some insight into the feelings of deprivation with which the patient was suffering. I suspected that the change in sex at this point related to Frank's desire to provide further disguise. I say this because of the very important information that was soon to follow. Now, to return to the transcript at the point where the patient is responding to my question: "Yeah, but how did she get that way? How did it happen?"

> *Patient:* Well, a long time ago when she was really young, she had this little brother, and he was getting so much attention that Gonga went crazy. She wanted everything. She wanted all the attention.

I hope the reader shares the excitement I felt at this point. I considered this last statement to represent a real "breakthrough" in Frank's treatment. For the first time, I learned about an important psychodynamic factor in Frank's antisocial behavior. Using

Gonga as the vehicle for expressing his thoughts, Frank is essentially telling us that his anger began a long time ago at the time of the birth of his brother. At that time he suffered a loss of attention that was so painful that he "went crazy." In addition, it tells us something about his insatiable demand to have his own way: "She wanted everything." The revelation demonstrated well the old Greek aphorism: *Give a man a mask and he'll tell you the truth.*

In the ensuing interchange I made an attempt to get Frank to consider an alternative to dealing with the problem of lost attention following the birth of a younger brother. His way of dealing with this situation involved antisocial acting out, insatiable demands for attention, and indulgence of his whims.

> *Therapist:* So what finally happened to her?
> *Patient:* She turned into wanting everybody to do everything for her. When they did something for her, she would give them a lot of grief.
> *Therapist:* Okay, so how'd it finally end up for her?
> *Patient:* The dream taught her a lesson.
> *Therapist:* Oh . . . well, what would have been a better thing for Gonga to do after the birth of her brother?
> *Patient:* Try to help.
> *Therapist:* How? In what way?
> *Patient:* Like feeding it . . . by looking after the baby.
> *Therapist:* Well, what about the fact that the baby got so much attention. What would have been a better thing for Gonga to do about that? Rather than wanting everything her own way, what would have been a better thing? Instead of wanting everything her own way and getting very angry and not listening, what would have been a better way once the baby's there and the mother and father are giving the baby attention, what should you [sic] have done? To get away from what she did?
> *Patient:* Not ignore it.
> *Therapist:* The thing is what would have been a better way for Gonga to have dealt with the new baby rather than want everything to herself and never listen?
> *Patient:* To help.
> *Therapist:* To help is one thing but there's another thing I'm thinking of.
> *Patient:* To stay out of the baby's way.
> *Therapist:* Well, I would say another thing. To *share* the parents' attention. Can you elaborate on that? What does that mean to *share* the parents' attention?

Patient: To let the baby have someone and Gonga have someone. Not let Gonga have it all.

Therapist: Right! That's the key thing . . . to *share!* So that Gonga would have some attention and the baby would have some attention. Because when Gonga was being so selfish and mean and wanting everything himself, what happened to him? Did he get attention from the parents?

Patient: No.

Therapist: He got a kind of attention, but

Patient (interrupts): Bad attention.

Therapist: Bad attention rather than good attention. So he was worse off. So what did he finally decide to do?

Patient: Stop after the dream.

Therapist: And what did he do?

Patient: He became better.

Therapist: And what kind of attention did he then get from his parents?

Patient: Good attention. He worked really hard and got the $80 . . . $87. . . .

Therapist: $87 . . . and the mother kept her promise and gave him the $10. Okay. Do you want the actors to introduce themselves now that the show is over? (Patient stands, bows.)

Shall I come over and I'll be the person who was the voice. I'll take a bow, okay. So long everybody. Okay, do you want to watch this? Okay, but we don't have enough time to watch it all. We'll watch a little of this now.

Frank's first solutions were not, in my opinion, likely to be efficacious. He suggested trying to help take care of the baby by feeding it. One could argue that via this mechanism he would gratify vicariously his own desires to be an infant and thereby regain in fantasy some of his parents' lost attention. It also might have provided some compensatory enhancement as he assumed the position of the adult who feeds the child. Perhaps, there is an "identification with the aggressor" element here in that feeding the baby is clearly a parental function. Although this mechanism may have provided some compensation, I did not consider it a high priority solution. In addition, I did not consider it warranted to attempt to help Frank analyze this suggestion. I do not think that he was capable of doing so, and I felt that our time would be better spent continuing along other lines.

His next suggestion was that the baby be ignored entirely. Basically, this suggestion involved the utilization of denial mechanisms. These are rarely judicious and are just the opposite of what one attempts to do in the treatment of most people.

His next solution was to "stay out of the baby's way." I believe that this is another statement of the denial mechanism and avoids dealing directly with the problem.

I believed that at that point the patient exhausted all possible solutions that he could think of. Therefore, I introduced mine: for Gonga to *share* his parents' affection with his brother. This is an important point in the treatment of such problems. The patient has to be helped to appreciate that getting parental attention is not an all-or-none situation. He may not be able to get all the attention he wants, but he does not have to settle for no attention at all either. I utilize a similar approach in the treatment of oedipal problems (discussed in Chapters Seven and Eight). The boy is helped to appreciate that although he cannot get all of mother's affection, it does not mean that he will end up with none of it. He can share her with father in certain areas.

The reader may have noted that at one point I used the word "you" when I was referring to Gonga. This often happens in discussions in which the symbolic material is being used as a thin disguise for the patient's own behavior. Sometimes the patient may interrupt and remind me that we are not talking about him- or herself. At other times, the patient may actually switch into a discussion of the issues in such a way that he or she is aware that the conversation is self-directed. Here, Frank made no mention of the slip and might have missed it entirely.

The story ends with the patient's appreciation of the difference between "bad attention" and "good attention." Lastly, Gonga decides to earn the $87 rather than steal it. Again, a healthy resolution. One cannot expect dramatic behavioral change following such an interchange, but my experience has been that sessions such as this do contribute to a reduction of antisocial behavior and other psychogenic problems.

Five days later we once again played *The Talking, Feeling, and Doing Game*. Prior to the program he drew a sign for the announcement: "Gonga wants too much." This was held close enough to the camera to serve as a general title of the program.

> *Therapist:* Our guest today is going to put on another show called, as you can see on the screen, "Gonga Wants Too Much." We'll be back with you in just a minute. Do you want to say anything at this point?

Patient: No thank you.

Therapist: Before our program starts, I'd like to introduce our guest. Here he is. (Patient waves.) Do you want to introduce Gonga to us also?

Patient: Here's Gonga.

Therapist: Put him on the screen. Here he is. (Patient holds up Gonga.) Hi, Gonga. Okay let's turn this off and we'll be right back with you. (At the patient's request, the therapist and patient set up a table with Gonga, Chippy, Turtle and *The Talking, Feeling, and Doing Game.*)

Patient: Hi, and here are Gonga's friends, Chippy. (Holds up Chip Monkey.)

Therapist: Hi, Chippy.

Patient (Holds up Turtle.): The Turtle.

Therapist: Hi, Turtle. That's it? Just those two friends? Okay.

Patient: And now we must start the show.

Patient (as Gonga): (Patient now under the table.) Hello. My name is Gonga, and this is another one of my great stories. This is Chippy. (Holds Chip Monkey above table and says "Hi" in a high voice, as if speaking for Chip Monkey.) And this is Turtle. (Holds Turtle above table and says, "Hi, there" in high voice, as if speaking for Turtle.) As you all know, this is my best show yet . . . We're really working on this one. This one is called "Gonga Never Listens." Okay.

Therapist: Our guest has asked me to play *The Talking, Feeling, and Doing Game* with Gonga. Okay? So how do you want to proceed now? What should we do? Shall I roll the dice for Gonga or do you want to roll the dice for Gonga?

Patient (as Gonga): Um . . . you can do it.

Therapist: I'll roll the dice for Gonga. Okay, Gonga got a seven 1-2-3-4-5-6-7. Do you want to read Gonga's card or should I?

Patient (as Gonga): I'll read it.

Therapist: You'll read it. Here's Gonga's card. What's it say?

Patient (as Gonga): "What is the worst problem a person can have?"

Therapist: Okay, Gonga, what is the worst problem a person can have, Gonga?

Patient (as Gonga): Ummm, let's see. I'd say that the worst problem a person can have is probably a bad handicap.

Therapist: A bad handicap. For example, what kind of handicap, Gonga?

Patient (as Gonga): No legs.

Therapist: No legs.

Patient (as Gonga): No arms, or deaf, or blind, or dumb.

Therapist: I see, those are pretty bad handicaps. Which of all those would you say is the worst?

Patient (as Gonga): No legs.

Therapist: No legs. Why would you say that?

Patient (as Gonga): Or blindness.

Therapist: Or blindness. Why would you say that?

Patient (as Gonga): Because you need your eyes for a lot of things. Or no hands, because you need your hands for a lot of things, too. And your eyes you need . . . you can't do many things without your eyes.

Therapist: Uh huh. You know there are some people, Gonga, who have eyes that are good . . . You test their eyes with an eye chart, and they're fine. However, they don't want to see things that they do that are causing all kinds of trouble. And that's a kind of trouble. And that's a kind of blindness, also. Did you ever hear about that?

Patient (as Gonga): No.

Therapist: Never heard about that?

Patient (as Gonga): No.

Therapist: Are you serious?

Patient (as Gonga): Yeah.

Therapist: That's called psychological blindness. Do you understand what I'm talking about?

Patient (as Gonga): No, not really.

Therapist: You don't really . . . try to figure out what I'm. . . .

Patient (as Gonga): They don't see because they don't want to?

Therapist: Right! They don't want to. Why? Why don't they want to?

Patient (as Gonga): They're afraid of what they might see.

Therapist: Right! And what do you think would happen if they were to look at the thing?

Patient (as Gonga): They would get scared.

Therapist: Yeah, but do you think it would be better or worse for them to look at it and not be psychologically blind?

Patient (as Gonga): Better.

Therapist: Why do you say that?

Patient (as Gonga): Well, because then you can do more things.

Therapist: Right! If you make believe there's no problem, then you can't solve it. Did you ever read that book, *Stories About the Real World*?

Patient (as Gonga): Ummmmm. *Stories About the Real World* . . . which one is that? Is that the one with Mack and the Beanstalk?

Therapist: No, that's a different book. That's a book of fairy tales, called *Modern Fairy Tales*. *Stories About the Real World* has one story in it called "Oliver and the Ostrich." Remember that one?

Patient (as Gonga): The ones I read were *Dorothy and the Lizard of Oz* and "Mack and the Beanstalk" and yeah, the one with "Oliver and the Ostrich" and "The Million Dollar Lie."

Therapist: Right. What did we learn from "Oliver and the Os-trich?" What did we learn from that?

Patient (as Gonga): He didn't want to hear. He made believe there was nothing wrong, but there really was something wrong.

Therapist: Right! What was the trouble?

Patient (as Gonga): He was failing in school.

Therapist: Right! Now how does the ostrich fit into that?

Patient (as Gonga): Well, he thought that the ostrich would poke his head underneath the sand and make believe nothing was there. But really the ostrich would fight as hard as he could . . .

Therapist: The ostrich does what?

Patient (as Gonga): He'd fight as hard as he could.

Therapist: Fight . . . but if the animal who attacked him was too big, what would he do?

Patient (as Gonga): He would run.

Therapist: Yeah, but does he ever hide his head in the sand?

Patient (as Gonga): No.

Therapist: Do human beings do that?

Patient (as Gonga): Well, maybe.

Therapist: Really, or do they act as if their heads are in the . . .

Patient (as Gonga, interrupts): They act. They never really hide in the sand.

Therapist: Right! That's called psychological blindness. Tell me something. Do you do anything . . .

Patient (as Gonga, interrupts): What you can't see can't hurt you.

Therapist: Yeah, but what you can't see *can* hurt you. If the ostrich has his head in the sand, he can't see anything, but can he get hurt?

Patient (as Gonga): Yes.

Therapist: So, is it true that what you can't see, can't hurt you?

Patient (as Gonga): No.

Therapist: It's not true. Tell me something, do you do anything that's like that . . . when you make believe that there's no problem when there really is?

Patient (as Gonga): Oh, yeah.

Therapist: Yeah? How do you do it?

Patient (as Gonga): At school.

Therapist: How do you do it at school?

Patient (as Gonga): Well, I don't listen too much.

Therapist: Uh huh. You don't listen.

Patient (as Gonga): Especially in social studies.

Therapist: Why especially in social studies?

Patient (as Gonga): Because social studies is so boring.

Therapist: So what do you do in social studies?

Patient (as Gonga): Talk about the great explorers.

Therapist: Yeah, but what do *you* do when everybody's talking about the great explorers.

Patient (as Gonga): Play with my fingers . . . (mumbles).

Therapist: Pardon me?

Patient (as Gonga): Play with my fingers sometimes.

Therapist: Uh huh. Why do you do that?

Patient (as Gonga): Because there's nothing else to do.

Therapist: Uh huh. Anything else?

Patient (as Gonga): No.

Therapist: Any other reasons why?

Patient (as Gonga): No, not really.

Therapist: Do you make believe that there's no problem for you there?

Patient (as Gonga): Sort of.

Therapist: Do you think there's a problem that you play with your fingers?

Patient (as Gonga): Yes.

Therapist: Why do you think you do that?

Patient (as Gonga): Because I don't want to listen.

Therapist: How come?

Patient (as Gonga): Because it's sort of boring to listen.

Therapist: Well, so okay. Let's say it is a little boring. What's so terrible about a little boredom . . . hmmm?

Patient (as Gonga): Yeah, well, nothing's so terrible about a little boredom.

Therapist: There's nothing wrong with a little bit of boredom?

Patient (as Gonga): No.

Therapist: You say it's boring; therefore, you're not going to listen. It sounds to me like you have the idea that anything that's unpleasant you shouldn't do. Is that right?

Patient (as Gonga): Well, sort of.

Therapist: But, you know, do you think there's any problem with that way of handling things—that if it's unpleasant you're not going to do it.

Patient (as Gonga): No.

Therapist: There's nothing wrong with that?

Patient (as Gonga): No.

Therapist: I see. I disagree. I think that there are times in life you have to do things that are unpleasant because if you don't, you get into even worse trouble. What do you think about that?

Patient (as Gonga): Well, it's sort of true.

Therapist: I mean everybody can't like every subject in school, and if you decide if you don't like one subject, you're not going to do it or you're not going to push through a little boredom, then you're going to get into a lot of trouble. You fail. So, at times, you have to do things you don't like. What do you think about that?

Patient (as Gonga): Well, that's okay.

Therapist: That's okay? Have I changed your mind on the subject?

Patient (as Gonga): Yeah.

Therapist: Are you sure?

Patient (as Gonga): Yeah.

Therapist: Okay, but what are you going to do now when you go to school.

Patient (as Gonga): I'm going to listen.

Therapist: Well, people don't usually change that fast—I hope you're right—I hope you will listen, but I hope that you'll someday appreciate what I'm saying. Maybe you will now, but people usually take some time to change, and just saying that you're going to listen isn't enough.

By this point, the reader has probably forgotten that this discussion began with the patient's card regarding what is the worst thing that can happen to someone. I used his response about going blind as one of the worst things to embark on a discussion of "psychological blindness," utilization of the denial mechanism. There was some receptivity on Frank's part to accepting the fact that he utilizes denial and "makes believe" that there is no problem when there really is. I also used the opportunity to make reference to my story, "Oliver and the Ostrich" from my book *Stories About the Real World* (1972a) which deals with the same issue via a discussion of the ostrich. Basically, in the story the child learns that ostriches do not stick their heads in the sand when there is trouble ("they would never do such a stupid thing"). Rather, they scrutinize the danger and decide whether to fight or flee (like all the other animals, except the human being).

In the ensuing discussion we touched upon the patient's failure to take seriously his school assignments and other obligations. I believed that Frank, like many children who feel deprived, subscribed strongly to the pleasure principle. Specifically, he had the feeling that he had gotten very little pleasure in life, and he therefore was not going to tolerate any discomforts or frustrations: In Frank's case, the deprivation related to the birth of his brother and the attendant attention that the latter received. In this vignette he appeared to be resolving to tolerate the discomfort of occasional classroom boredom in order to avoid the discomforts of failure, which he agreed is worse than boredom. However, the facility with which he promised to reform was unconvincing and I described my incredulity. At this point, I resumed my conversation with Gonga. The reader should recall that the patient was still under the table during the course of this conversation and that I was continuously speaking with "Gonga," the doll that he was holding above the table in my view.

Therapist: Let me ask you one other question.
Patient (as Gonga): Yeah?
Therapist: Why do you think, Gonga, you don't want to accept anything that's unpleasant. Why do you go around just doing just what you like? Why do you say, "I don't like to do it, I'm not going to do it . . . I'm not going to do what I don't like," when most other people mix it. You know, they have some things they like, some things they don't like and they accept the fact that there are times they have to do things they don't like?
Patient (as Gonga): I give up!
Therapist: You give up? You haven't any idea why you do it?
Patient (as Gonga): No.
Therapist: Just try to guess. Why do you do that?
Patient (as Gonga): Can you say it again?
Therapist: Okay. You go around with the idea that if it's unpleasant you say: "I don't like it, I'm not going to do it."? Do you do that, Gonga?
Patient: Yeah, sometimes.
Therapist: Give me an example of how you do that. When you don't like something, you just don't do it.
Patient (as Gonga): When Chippy and I play *The Talking, Feeling, and Doing Game* at home, when I cheat, he tells me, "Don't cheat or else I'm going to go home." Then I do what I want.
Therapist: You play *The Talking, Feeling, and Doing Game* at home?
Patient (as Gonga): You let me borrow it.
Therapist: I didn't let you borrow it. I don't lend the game to kids to play at home. Is Gonga making that up? Is that it? No, say it, it's all right.
Patient (Gonga): You really did . . . let's say you really did let Gonga borrow it. . . .
Therapist: Oh, you're making believe that I let Gonga borrow it. Because I usually don't let people borrow that game. It's not a game for home. Oh, so you're saying that Gonga is saying I lent it. But I'd like you to make up something that's real . . . that really happened

. . . that Gonga . . . that really happened to Gonga . . . not a made-up thing.

Patient: We play a regular game.

Therapist: You play a regular game . . . then what does Gonga do?

Patient (as Gonga): And I cheat, and Chippy says he'll go home and he won't play with me.

Therapist: So you cheat.

Patient (as Gonga): I don't listen to him.

Therapist: You don't listen to him . . . you just cheat. Why do you cheat?

Patient (as Gonga): Because I want to win all the time.

Therapist: Uh huh, you want to feel good all the time.

Patient (as Gonga): Because I want too much.

Therapist: You want too much . . . uh huh . . . you don't want to hear "no" for an answer, huh?

Patient (as Gonga): That's right.

Therapist: Uh huh. How come? How come you don't want to hear "no" for an answer?

Patient (as Gonga): Because I just like to have a lot of stuff.

Therapist: You just like to have a lot of stuff. And you just want to feel good all the time, huh?

Patient (as Gonga): Yeah.

Therapist: And you never want to feel bad?

Patient (as Gonga): Yeah.

Therapist: Why is that?

Patient (as Gonga): Because I don't like feeling bad.

Therapist: Okay, and what did I say before about bad feelings in life?

Patient (as Gonga): That you have to face them.

Therapist: Yeah, at times you have to have bad feelings. Besides, you have to do things you don't like. What do you think about that?

Patient (as Gonga): I think it's true.

Therapist: And if you don't, what will happen?

Patient (as Gonga): You'll get in trouble.

Therapist: Yeah. You'll feel even worse than you did if you just had a few sad feelings.

Patient (as Gonga): Yeah.

Therapist: Now, why haven't you learned that lesson? Most kids, Gonga, learn that lesson. They know that they've got to do things at times they don't want to do, because they know that if they don't, they'll feel even worse and they'll get left back, or they'll be punished, or they'll be sent to the principal's office, or they'll be grounded, or things like that. Why haven't you learned that lesson yet, Gonga? Why do you think that is?

Patient (as Gonga): I give up.

Therapist: Do you want my guess?

Patient (as Gonga): Yeah.

Therapist: My guess is . . .

Patient (as Gonga): That I don't want to . . .

Therapist: But why don't you want to.

Patient (as Gonga): I don't know.

Therapist: There are many reasons, but I have a guess about one of the reasons.

Patient (as Gonga): What?

Therapist: My guess is that a long time ago . . . like you said at the end of the last program . . . when you were very little, and your brother was born, and before that time, you were like "king of the world." You were the only kid. You were the first grandchild. Everybody doted over you; everybody thought how great you were; and you were really sitting there on the throne. And then, boom, whammo, along came your brother.

Patient (no longer as Gonga): My dumb old [mumbles] brother. . .

Therapist: What did you say? Your dumb little brother?

Patient: Dumb.

Therapist: Dumb, okay. So I say this: You got so mad that you said, "I'm very angry at everybody, because they give him all that attention." That's one thing. And another thing you said was, "I'm not going to suffer any more pain. I'm going to do what I want, when I want, and I've got enough pain with everybody giving him attention. No more pain for me." You see, you say two things: "No more pain for me; I'm just going to get pleasure," and "I'm going to get attention by being bad." What do you think about that?

Patient: That's being greedy.

Therapist: That's being greedy? What did I say? Tell me the two things I said that happened to you when your brother was born.

Patient: When my brother was born, I didn't like it. After my brother was born, everybody paid attention to him and not to me. Then I wanted it all so I took over . . .

Therapist: You wanted what?

Patient: All the attention.

Therapist: So how do you get the attention now?

Patient: By being bad.

Therapist: That's one thing you do. And what else are you doing since your brother was born? You get the attention by being bad and what else did I say you do?

Patient: I don't listen.

Therapist: Yeah, but what happens when you don't listen?

Patient: Well . . .

Therapist: I said that not listening was the same as being bad. I said something else about pleasure. What did I say about that?

Patient: I wanted it all.

Therapist: You wanted it all—why?

Patient: Because I was greedy.

Therapist: Uh huh. And why do you say that you were greedy?

Patient: Because my little brother was born.

Therapist: And . . .

Patient: And I wanted all the good things.

Patient: Yeah.

Therapist: You wanted only pleasure, no pain.

Patient: Yeah.

Therapist: Now, what's this got to do with playing with your fingers in social studies class? Can you link that up?

Patient: No.

Therapist: In social studies, it's boring, right?

Patient: Right.

Therapist: So, that's pain, right? So what do you do? What's the pleasure?

Patient: Playing with my fingers.

Therapist: Right. Do you think that's true?

Patient: Yes.

Therapist: Do you think it has something to do with your brother being born?

Patient: Yeah.

Therapist: How would you link it up?—just so I'm sure you understand.

Patient: I get all pleasure. When my brother was born, I wanted all pleasure and no pain and in social studies I wanted all pleasure and no pain.

Therapist: Right! But what'll happen to you if you live a life in which you only get pleasure and avoid pain.

Patient: You'll be a snob.

Therapist: Anything else? Snob doesn't tell me much . . .

Patient: Be greedy.

Therapist: Yeah. Any other thing that'll happen?

Patient: When you want something and you get it, you'll get a lot of grief.

Therapist: You'll get a lot of grief?

Patient: Yeah.

Therapist: Why will you get a lot of grief?

Patient: Ummmmm. Because . . . well, I don't know!

Therapist: Well, if you don't do your social studies and you just sit there avoiding the pain and the boredom of social studies and just getting the pleasure of playing with your fingers, what's going to happen?

Patient: You can do that all the time.

Therapist: And what'll happen with your social studies?

Patient: You won't learn.

Therapist: And what'll the teacher do?

Patient: Get you in trouble.

Therapist: Yeah, you won't learn anything, so you'll be kind of dumb or ignorant, right? And you'll also get in trouble. So, in my opinion, it's probably worth it to push through the boredom and learn what you have to from the teacher, and then enjoy some of the other subjects more.

Patient: Okay.

Therapist: What was the last thing I said, just so I'm sure you understand it, Gonga?

Patient (as Gonga): I would get in trouble and I would be in trouble instead of learning.

Therapist: Yeah. And what causes more trouble? Which is more painful? The boredom of school or the trouble of failing and getting in trouble with the teacher and not learning and being ignorant, being dumb.

Patient (as Gonga): The second.

Therapist: You say it so I'm sure you understand it. Which is more trouble? Say it, I want to make sure you understand.

Patient (as Gonga): Getting in trouble with the teacher and failing in school and not being able to learn . . .

Therapist: . . . is more trouble than . . .

Patient (as Gonga): boredom.

Therapist: Right, right. By the way, you get a chip for that. That was your question.

I attempted here to help the patient gain some insight into the relationship between his antisocial behavior and the birth of his brother. I had the feeling that some inroads were made here, but I certainly can't say that he responded with the kind of strong emotional response one sees in patients (especially adults) when the therapist has "hit home." Although the insight was at a minimal level, I believe it was nevertheless there.

The reader may have noticed that at the point where I began speaking about the birth of the brother the patient dropped the Gonga disguise and began talking about himself. Near the end of the interchange, I purposely returned him to the Gonga role in order to "preserve anonymity" and thereby assure a freer flow of revelation.

After being awarded the chip the patient requested that Gonga and I discontinue playing *The Talking, Feeling, and Doing Game* and go on to another activity. The reader may note that only one card had been drawn between the outset and the time we went on to another activity.

> *Therapist:* Our guest now has decided that we stop *The Talking, Feeling, and Doing Game* and now he's going to put on a little play about Gonga and his friends and the fire truck. Okay, you're on the air!
>
> *Patient* (as Chip Monkey and Turtle): Boy, look at that. That's really neat. I love that. Hey, wow, look at that neat thing with the little sprays.
>
> *Therapist:* What are they looking at?
>
> *Patient:* The fire engine.
>
> *Patient* (as Gonga): Hi, guys. (Gonga knocks Chip Monkey.) Oops, sorry, Chippy.
>
> *Therapist:* So Chippy and Turtle are looking at that fire engine and think it's really neat. Okay, go ahead.
>
> *Patient* (as Gonga): Boy, that's really . . . Neato . . . Boy, it's neat.
>
> *Therapist:* Gonga thinks it's neat, too, huh?
>
> *Patient* (as store manager): Hey, kid, don't touch.
>
> *Patient* (as Gonga): Shut up. Boy, wow. I really want this . . . look at those pieces . . .
>
> *Therapist:* He really wants it.
>
> *Patient:* Those little pieces, those little sprays on the fire engine, everything its got . . .
>
> *Patient* (as store manager): Kid, you're not supposed to touch it.
>
> *Patient* (as Gonga): Shut up, mister.
>
> *Patient* (as store manager): Okay, out of my store.
>
> *Patient* (as Chip Monkey): Gonga!!
>
> *Patient* (as Gonga): Who cares about that dumb old guy anyway!!
>
> *Therapist:* The guy kicked Gonga out of the store because he touched the fire engine?
>
> *Patient:* Yeah.
>
> *Therapist:* Okay, and then what did Gonga say?
>
> *Patient:* Shut up.
>
> *Therapist:* Who'd he say shut up to?
>
> *Patient:* The guy.
>
> *Therapist:* The owner of the store?
>
> *Patient:* Yeah.
>
> *Therapist:* And then what happened?

Patient: He left.

Therapist: Gonga left. Okay, now what happens?

Patient: (Whispers to therapist.)

Therapist: You want a cut, okay. Gonga is now home and our guest wants me to play the role of Gonga's father and has told me what to say. Okay, go ahead, you begin.

Patient (as Gonga): Daddy . . .

Therapist (as Gonga's father): Yes, Gonga, what is it?

Patient (as Gonga): There's this fire engine at the store, and I want it very bad. Can I have it?

Therapist (as Gonga's father): Well, how much does it cost?

Patient (as Gonga): $36.00.

Therapist (as Gonga's father): $36.00?

Patient (as Gonga): Well, it's because it's remote control.

Therapist (as Gonga's father): Well, that's a very expensive toy, Gonga, and that's a lot of money for a toy. I'll tell you what I'll do. I'll be happy to give you part of the money, but you're going to have to save up from your allowance and your earnings in order to pay for most of it. I'll pay for $10.00 of it, and you've got to pay the other $26.00.

Patient (as Gonga): No, I want the whole thing!! (Gonga jumping up and down, imitating a temper tantrum.)

Therapist (as Gonga's father): I'm sorry, Gonga . . . I'm sorry you just can't have everything you want when you want it, and you just can't have every toy you want and that's the answer.

Patient (as Gonga): Get you . . . (mumbles) . . .

Therapist (as Gonga's father): What was that?

Patient (as Gonga): No, I want it now. (Gonga has another temper tantrum.)

Therapist (as Gonga's father): Now look, Gonga. If you're going to continue with those tantrums, I'm going to have to send you to your room because I just don't like the noise of those tantrums. So either you're going to stop the tantrums or off to your room.

Patient (as Gonga): If I'm good, can I have it tomorrow?

Therapist (as Gonga's father): Well, I'll tell you . . .

Patient (as Gonga): And then pay you back . . .

Therapist (as Gonga's father): You want to borrow the money?

Patient (as Gonga): Yeah.

Therapist (as Gonga's father): Well, I won't lend you all the money. I'll lend you part of the money, but you'll have a debt. The total amount that you owe for that is $26.00. Now, how much money do you have right now in your bank?

Patient (as Gonga): $11.00.

Therapist (as Gonga's father): $11.00. Okay, so how much do you want me to lend you?

Patient (as Gonga): Could you lend me. . .

Therapist (as Gonga's father): Well, we're running out of time, so I'll lend you $15.00. Fifteen dollars and $11.00 is $26.00, and I'll give you $10.00 toward it. That's $36.00. But remember you owe me $15.00 that you have to earn, right?

Patient (as Gonga): Yeah.

Therapist (as Gonga's father): Okay, so here's the $15.00 and you can buy it.

Patient (as Gonga): Okay. (Patient whispers in therapist's ear.)

Therapist (as Gonga's father): Our guest now has asked me to play the part of the storekeeper. Okay?

Therapist: I'm going to play the part of the storekeeper. Okay. Hiya, Gonga.

Patient (as Gonga): I want that. (Gonga points to fire engine.)

Therapist (as storekeeper): Okay. You got $36?

Patient (as Gonga): Yeah, right here.

Therapist (as storekeeper): Okay. Give me the money. Ten, 20, 30, 35, 36 dollars. Here you are, my good friend.

Patient (as Gonga): Thanks.

Therapist (as storekeeper): Now you have a remote control fire engine. Tell me, how did you get this money?

Patient (as Gonga): My father lent it to me but I had $11.

Therapist (as storekeeper): Uh huh. So your father lent you some money.

Patient (as Gonga): Yeah.

Therapist (as storekeeper): Okay. He lent you money. How much did he lend you?

Patient (as Gonga): Ummmm. Fifteen dollars.

Therapist (as storekeeper): Okay. And that makes $26. Where'd you get the other $10?

Patient (as Gonga): Ummm. He gave it to me.

Therapist (as storekeeper): That was pretty nice of him. I guess you're going to have to work now to earn the $15 to give him back the money, right?

Patient (as Gonga): Yeah.

Therapist (as storekeeper): Good for you. That'll give you a really good feeling when you work off that debt. And then you'll have that all yourself when you know that you worked for it.

Patient (as Gonga): Okay, thanks.

Therapist (as storekeeper): Okay. I hope you enjoy that fire engine.

Patient (as Gonga): Okay. Bye.

Therapist (as storekeeper): Bye. Okay. Now we're coming to the very last part of the show. Go ahead.

Patient (as Gonga): Boy, am I sure glad I earned all that money, and I paid back my debt and I got that money from my father by doing the paper route, mowing lawns, and raking leaves.

Therapist (as storekeeper): Uh huh.

Patient (as Gonga): Boy, do I feel good about myself.

Therapist (as storekeeper): Uh huh. You really feel good about yourself?

Patient (as Gonga): Yeah.

Therapist (as storekeeper): Uh huh. Okay. Now how's it working out with that remote fire engine?

Patient (as Gonga): Great!

Therapist (as storekeeper): Are you really enjoying it?

Patient (as Gonga): Yeah, watch this. You just press the button and it goes.

Therapist: Okay, before we close, I'd like to hear from you, Gonga, what are the lessons of this story? All the different lessons we can learn from this story, which is quite a long one. See if you can figure them out.

Patient (as Gonga): Umm. Don't be greedy . . .

Therapist: Because . . .

Patient (as Gonga): It will never bring you good.

Therapist: Why will it never bring you good?

Patient (as Gonga): Because it's not good to be greedy and nobody will pay attention to you.

Therapist: Well, yeah, they won't like you if you're greedy. They may pay attention if you make yourself a nuisance, you know?

Patient (as Gonga): Yeah.

Therapist: Okay. Go on, why isn't it good?

Patient (as Gonga): Ummm. Because it's not good for you.

Therapist: How come?

Patient (as Gonga): Well, when you grow up, you'll keep wanting stuff.

Therapist: And . . .

Patient (as Gonga): You'll turn into a snob.

Therapist: What is a snob as you see it? What do you mean by snob?

Patient (as Gonga): A jerk.

Therapist: Be more specific.

Patient (as Gonga): You want too much.

Therapist: And then what'll happen if you want too much.

Patient (as Gonga): When you get it, you'll get grief.

Therapist: Why will you get grief?

Patient (as Gonga): You'll give grief.

Therapist: Why will you give grief?

Patient (as Gonga): Because once you get your way. . .

Therapist: How do you give grief when you get your way?

Patient (as Gonga): You misbehave.

Therapist: Uh huh. Okay. And any other lessons?

Patient (as Gonga): Things aren't always as bad as they really are.

Therapist: Say that again.

Patient (as Gonga): Well, we were playing *The Talking, Feeling, and Doing Game.*

Therapist: What did you learn from that?

Patient (as Gonga): Let's see. Ummm. I think . . .

Therapist: What did we learn in that game?

Patient (as Gonga): We learned that . . . umm . . . that getting in trouble and pain is much worse than boredom pain.

Therapist: Right, right! And what did we learn about how sometimes you have to take a little pain. Huh?

Patient (as Gonga): Yeah.

Therapist: To avoid bigger pain.

Patient (as Gonga): Yeah.

Therapist: Uh huh. And that's part of life, right? And what'd we learn about you and your brother? That's the last thing before we close. What did we learn about you and your brother?

Patient (as Gonga): Ummm. We learned that . . . you can't . . . you mean about me and my brother?

Therapist: Yeah, what did we learn about you and your brother?

Patient (as Gonga): (Patient crawling on floor around table.) We learned that you can't have all the attention all the time.

Therapist: Right. That we share.

Patient (as Gonga): Yeah.

Therapist: And what did we learn about what you're doing? After your brother was born, to get attention, what do you do?

Patient (as Gonga): Get into trouble.

Therapist: And that gives you attention. What did we learn about your feelings about pleasure and pain after your brother was born?

Patient (as Gonga): That I wanted bad pain.

Therapist: You wanted what?

Patient (as Gonga): Umm . . . I don't know.

Therapist: You wanted . . . how did you feel about getting pleasure and pain after your brother was born? What did you want?

Patient (as Gonga): Just pleasure.

Therapist: Right, right. Okay, do you want to come up and say good-bye to everybody, to show your face now? Okay. This is our guest. (Patient stands up and bows.) He's been the guy . . . he's been the voice that you've been hearing. Okay. So long everybody. And now, ladies and gentlemen, we just want to announce that this is *The*

End. (Patient holds up sign which says *The End.*) We hope you enjoyed this show. Good-bye, everybody. Do you want to say good-bye?

Patient: So long.

Therapist: So long. Bye.

Within the few weeks following this session there was a definite reduction in Frank's antisocial behavior. He was much more compliant in school and cooperative at home. I believe that these sessions played a role in the behavioral change. I do not believe that this was simply related to the insight he gained about the relationship between his antisocial behavior and the birth of his brother. I believe that he gained some appreciation of the fact that his antisocial behavior caused him more pain than the discomforts associated with doing what is socially acceptable and desirable. In addition, I believe he gained some solace from the concept of sharing. He could not have his parents as much as he wanted, but he could have them to some degree. Unfortunately, this patient's therapy had to be interrupted because his father was required to relocate for business purposes. Arrangements were made for him to continue therapy with a psychiatrist near his new home. A follow-up conversation six months later revealed that Frank continued to improve.

The Case of George ["This Damn Magic Wand Is No Good"]

This eight-year-old boy suffered with a neurologically based learning disability. He was quite immature in many ways and was overprotected by his mother. His view of the world of magic was very much like that of the five year old and his magic-cure expectations were strong. Near the end of his second month in treatment he told this story.

Patient: The name that I'm gonna have—I'm gonna have two names of the story each.

Therapist: Go ahead.

Patient: One name is gonna be "Little Ducklings" and the second name is gonna be "One of the Ducklings Turns into a Grown Man." There's only gonna be one duckling.

Therapist: Okay.

Patient: There's the mother, the father, the brother.

Therapist: Okay. Now do you want to start the first story? Go ahead.

Patient: I said there's going to be two names and that's the story.

Therapist: Oh, just one story with two names?

Patient: Yeah.

Therapist: Okay. Start the story.

Patient: And two lessons.

Therapist: And two lessons. Okay. This is a story, one story with two names and two lessons. Go ahead. Let's hear.

Patient: Once there's a duckling. He said, "Ooh, how did I get changed into a duckling? I was a person all my life. How—how could this happen? How did this happen? I must even act like a duck now so a fairy godmother will come and save me. Quack, quack, quack, quack." But no fairy godmother came. So he said, "Quack, quack, quack, quack, quack" and he was begging for his fairy godmother.

Therapist: Okay, then what happened?

Patient: Then he said, "Quack, quack. Oh, I wish a fairy godmother would come. Quack, quack, quack, quack." And he was quacking so hard that he flew over to the water and fell in.

Therapist: Okay. Then what happened? This is a very good story.

Patient: Then he said, "Caw, caw, quack, quack, coo, coo, quack, quack," and he was . . . (mumbles) . . . up.

Therapist: And he was what?

Patient: Burning up.

Therapist: He was burning up. Why was he burning up?

Patient: Because he said, "Quack, quack, quack, quack, quack!" Like that.

Therapist: Okay. Then what happened?

Patient: Then he said, "Quack, quack, quack." (Patient speaking in singsong manner.) "Oh, I wish a fairy godmother, a fairy godmother." That's a little song the duckling made up.

Therapist: Okay. Go ahead.

Patient (sings again): "Oh, I wish a fairy godmother would come and get me out, would come and get me out, would come and get me out." And he was going, "Quack, quack, quack, quack, quack!" And then he turned into a horse!

Therapist: He turned into a horse! Yeah. Go ahead.

Patient: Then he said, "Boy, what happened with me? I was a duckling before. I used to go heeee, heeee. I hope a fairy godmother comes this time. Heeeeewwwwww, quack, quack." And then he changed back into a duck because he went "quack, quack" by accident.

Therapist: Uh huh. Then what happened?

Patient: And then the fairy godmother *really* came and said, "Huh!

What, what. I thought I heard somebody calling me. I don't see any-body. Hhmm. Must be my magic wand . . . (mumbles) . . . by accident.

Therapist: Wait a minute. The fairy godmother said, "What, I thought I heard somebody calling me," and then she said what about a wand?

Patient: And then she said, "Hhhmmm! My magic wand probably made him disappear." But the duck was really in the pond under the water.

Therapist (interrupts): She thought that her magic wand made the duck disappear. That's why she didn't see him in the pond. Go ahead.

Patient: "Ooh, oh, oh, oh, I tricked her."

Therapist: Wait a minute. I don't understand that. Who's talking now?

Patient: The duck.

Therapist: And what did he say?

Patient: "Ooh, I tricked that fairy godmother by accident. I'll go get her. Fairy godmother, quack, quack. I'm a duckling. Change me back into a person." But the fairy godmother was in the clouds.

Therapist: So what happened then?

Patient: Then he was there again and when the fairy godmother came again she saw him turned into a horse. And she said, "Hey, what happened, horse? You were quacking before. Don't you know how to make a horse sound? A horse goes, 'Heeehawww, heee-hawww.' You went 'quack, quack, quack' and clapping your hands. I'm not gonna help you. Keep this magic wand and try yourself." And then the fairy godmother went away.

Therapist: And then what happened? (Pause) So the fairy god-mother went away and wouldn't change him into a person?

Patient: No, because she was so mad at him. He didn't know how to make a horse sound. He changed before the fairy godmother came there.

Therapist: Oh, the fairy godmother was mad because he changed from a duck into a horse?

Patient: Yeah, and she heard him quacking.

Therapist: Oh, she heard him quacking and then he turned into a horse. Okay, and then what finally happened? So the fairy godmother got angry at him and went away. Then what finally happened?

Patient: Then the magic wand worked on him and that's the end.

Therapist: It worked on him. And what happened when the magic wand worked on him?

Patient: It flew back—it was um—it flew back to the fairy god-mother.

Therapist: What happened to the duck or horse?

Patient: He turned back into a boy before it went. . . .

Therapist (interrupts): Oh, he turned back into a boy. Oh, I see. Okay. And the lesson of that story?

Patient: Two lessons, remember?

Therapist: What are the two lessons?

Patient: Never (long pause).

Therapist: Never what?

Patient: Never be mad at a duck!

Therapist: Never be mad at a duck? And the other lesson?

Patient: Don't think there's no such thing as fairy godmothers. There's, there's a lesson that goes with that also. And the third lesson is: Don't believe in fairy godmothers because there's no such thing and if you heard a duck quacking and it changed into a horse it was really the duck and don't be mad at it.

Therapist: I see.

Patient: That's the lessons.

Therapist: Okay. Now it's my chance to tell a story.

This story is typical of that told by many children with neurologically based learning disabilities. It is somewhat disorganized and the patient does not concern himself with whether his listener understands what is going on in it. Frequent questioning is required if the therapist is to surmise the story's psychodynamic meaning. In analyzing such a story it is best to think about main issues and general trends and not get bogged down in minutiae. The main event in this story is that a boy is turned into a duck and in that state he has the power to change himself into a horse. Finally, after a few somewhat confusing experiences with the fairy godmother, he is turned back into a boy. George had a speech defect for which he had received some therapy. In addition, his lower lip protruded somewhat and occasionally saliva dripped from it. (Characteristically, his mother was ever at hand to catch the saliva and it was not until I recommended it that she taught George how to use a handkerchief and to think about his tendency to salivate.) His depicting himself as a duck related, I believe, to his speech deficit as well as to his protruding lip. The horse, with his odd vocalization, also lends itself well to symbolizing the patient and his speech defect.

The story also depicts some hostile interchanges between the duck-horse and the fairy godmother: the duck tricks the fairy godmother by making a quacking sound and then changing into a horse; the duck hides from the fairy godmother so that she cannot find him; and the fairy godmother throws her wand at the horse.

To play a trick on someone is a common childhood way of expressing hostility. In this case, the tricks involve hiding from the fairy godmother and fooling her by back-and-forth transformations between a horse and a duck. I suspected that the fairy godmother might have symbolized me (the magic curer) and that the hostility might have related to anger over my not having provided George with a magic cure—but I was not certain.

The story, then, contains two themes: a desire for magic transformation from infrahuman to human status and the expression of hostility (probably toward the therapist). His first lesson: "Don't think there's no such thing as fairy godmothers. There's, there's a lesson that goes with that also." This lesson makes reference to a previous story in which I promulgated the notion that there is no such thing as a fairy godmother. This idea apparently produced such anxiety that he had to negate it with a lesson in this subsequent story. He then continued. "And the third lesson is: Don't believe in fairy godmothers because there's no such thing and if you heard a duck quacking and it changed into a horse it was really a duck and don't be mad at it." Here we see apparent acceptance of my message that there is no such thing as a fairy godmother. Clearly the patient is ambivalent regarding this idea. However, one can't expect immediate receptivity regarding a patient's giving up such an attractive symptom and a phase of ambivalence is a step toward its elimination. Furthermore, the third lesson also makes reference to the hostility issue by advising the listener (? me) not to be mad at a quacking duck that changes into a horse. The request suggests that the patient anticipates that I will be angry at him for his tricks.

I decided not to attempt to create a story that would simultaneously incorporate both the hostility and magic themes. It is generally judicious of the therapist to select *one* of the themes from the patient's story and use only that for his or her responding story. To try to do more may not only be too much for the child to handle, but the therapist's ability to create a unified story with more than one theme is not as great as the capacity of the child's unconscious to do this. I decided to choose the magic transformation theme rather than the anger. First, I was more certain of its meaning. Second, I reasoned that if I could help the patient reduce his dependency on magic he would rely more on realistic solutions to his problems. Because that goal had a greater likelihood of success, he would then be less likely to be angry at me.

Another problem that I faced in formulating a responding story was that of what to do with the duck. As described, the duck lent itself well as a symbol of the patient because of his speech problem and his salivating, protruding lip. To portray the patient as a duck in my story might entrench this pathological personification and might thereby be antitherapeutic. However, to depict the patient as a boy would then rob me of the opportunity to deal with the magic transformation issue in a manner that was close to the patient's representation of the problem. If the therapist's story gets too remote from the patient's it becomes less therapeutically effective.

In addition, the child's ability to create a fantasy that most efficiently and effectively synthesizes the symbols is far greater than that of the therapist. I believe that we lack the ingenuity not only of our child-patient's unconscious, but of our own unconscious as well. We ourselves cannot consciously create a dream as rich and as efficient as that which can be created by our own unconscious. The efficiency and ingenuity of our unconscious processes to utilize simile, metaphor, allegory, and efficient and innovative symbol fusion far surpasses that of our conscious mind. Therefore, I do not try to reconcile all elements of my story nor do I strive for one-hundred percent consistency. In this case I chose to be a little inconsistent (and even possibly a little antitherapeutic) in order to preserve the duck symbol for the larger purposes of my story, that is, to present a story which focused on the patient's magic cure delusion.

Also, using another symbol would remove us from the scene of the patient's metaphor. This shift would lessen the likelihood of the patient and I then moving along the same psychological track and would lessen thereby his receptivity to my story. However, when I retain the undesirable symbol I am quick to modify it or introduce qualifications that reduce its psychologically detrimental import. When introducing the duck I was quick to point out that the duck was a regular, "plain," and "nice" duck and that his only defect was that he had a speech problem. As will be seen in the transcript, the patient was relieved by this circumscription of his deficits. It wasn't that the duck was totally loathesome; rather he suffered only with an isolated defect. In short, I considered the advantages of retaining the duck symbol to far outweigh the disadvantages and told this story in response.

> *Therapist:* Once upon a time there was a duck and he was just a duck. He was a real duck. He never was a person.
> *Patient:* What's the name of the story?

Therapist: The name of my story is: "The Duck and the Fairy God-mother." Okay? No, excuse me. I'm going to change the name: "The Duck and the Old Lady." Okay?

Patient: (laughs)

Therapist: "The Duck and the Old Lady" is the name of my story. Once upon a time there was a duck. And he was just a duck, a plain duck. He was a very nice duck but he thought it would be better not to be a duck. He thought it would be best to be a person. So he used to go around saying, "Quack, quack, quack, quack, quack quack," hoping he would find a fairy godmother. And he would sing a song and the song would go. How did the song go?

Patient (in singsong manner): "Quack, quack, quack, quack, quack, quack."

Therapist: He'd go, "Quack, quack. I wish I saw a fairy god-mother." He'd go, "Quack, quack, quack, quack, quack, quack, quack. Fairy godmother! Where's the fairy godmother?" No fairy godmother came.

Patient: Talk slow. The duck talks so fast, I can't hear you.

Therapist: He would say, "Quack, quack, quack."

Patient (joins in): "Where's my fairy godmother?"

Therapist: "Where's my fairy godmother?"

Patient: And he was shaking his hands . . . (mumbles) . . .

Therapist: But he couldn't find any fairy godmother. Then one day he saw an old lady. She was walking by the river.

Patient: Did that old lady—was that old lady really a wicked witch?

Therapist: No.

Patient: Or a good witch?

Therapist: No, she was just an old lady, but this old lady . . .

Patient (interrupts): Did she have a wand?

Therapist: This old lady used to think that she was a fairy god-mother. She thought that maybe there was such a thing as a fairy godmother and she thought . . .

Patient (interrupts): You told—you told this the other day except it didn't have a duck in it.

Therapist: No. This is a different story. Do you want to hear my story?

Patient: Yes, but the other day you told it about the old woman.

Therapist: Yeah, but this is a different story about an old woman. Okay? Do you want to hear this one?

Patient: Yes.

Therapist: So the duck went over to her and he said, "Quack, quack, quack, quack. Fairy godmother, will you change me into a person?"

And she thought that she had magic powers so she said, "Okay." (Therapist waving imaginary stick over patient's head.) And she had a wand—she had a stick and she said to the duck, "Magic . . . magic . . . duck . . . duck, quack three times and I'll change you into a person. Quack three times." Okay, you make believe you're the duck.

Patient (while therapist rotates imaginary stick over his head): "Quack, quack, quack."

Therapist: And she waved it around and do you know what happened?

Patient: What?

Therapist: The duck still remained a duck!

Patient: (laughs)

Therapist: And she said, "Say quack again. Say quack harder."

Patient (yells): Quack!

Therapist: Harder!

Patient (yells louder): Quack!

Therapist: Harder!

Patient (yells again): Quack!

Therapist: Harder!

Patient (screams): Quack!

Therapist: And he still stayed a duck. And she got very angry . . . "Ooh, this magic wand! (striking the imaginary wand against a table) I'm hitting this magic wand. This magic wand (makes angry sounds) is no good! We'll try it again! Now you say quack again three times. Go ahead. Magic wand. . . .

Patient (while therapist is waving wand again over patient's head): "Quack, quack, quack."

Therapist: And he still remained a duck. And she got very . . . "This damn magic wand!" (Therapist angrily breaks the imaginary wand over his knee.) And she took it and threw it away. (flings the wand away): She said, "Wait, I'll get another magic wand." She came back with another one and she said, "I'm going to say a new thing (waving wand over patient's head). Abracadabra, hokus, pokus, turn this boy (sic, therapist's error) into a person. He's a duck!" What happened?

Patient: He still remained a duck?

Therapist: Right! And she said, "I can't stand these magic wands. Umph!" And she took it and she broke it on her knee (breaks wand on knee) and she threw it away (throws wand away)! She was very mad.

As she was standing there, a man came along and he saw her.

Patient: Who was that man?

Therapist (jumping up and down): And she was jumping up and down screaming and crying, and this man said to her—who was this man? He was just a man walking by, an old man. And he said, "What are you so mad about old lady?"

She said, "My magic wands don't work. I want to turn this duck into a boy, into a person."

And the man said, "There's no such thing as a magic wand."

And she said, "You know, I'm beginning to see that."

Patient (interrupts): In the other story there was a woman with a magic wand like that, but there was no man; there was an owl. There was no duck.

Therapist: Right. In the other story there was a wise old owl. Right.

Patient: And the boy.

Therapist: What's that?

Patient: And in the other story there was a boy who wanted to be turned into a duck, I think.

Therapist: Well, it was a different story, but let's talk about this one. Anyway, so this man said, "There's no such thing as magic wands."

And the old lady said, "You know, I'm beginning to see that. I thought that I would like to be a fairy godmother and do this duck a favor and turn him into a boy."

And the man said, "Well, why would you want to turn him into a boy? He's a perfectly fine duck!"

And the duck said, "No, I'm not! No, I'm not!"

And the man said, "Why? What's wrong with you?"

He said, "I don't speak too well."

Patient (with sigh of relief): He doesn't speak too well.

Therapist: Yeah. And he said, "That's the reason why you want to turn into a person? You can *learn* to speak well."

And the duck said, "No, I can't! No, I can't!"

What did the man say?

Patient: "Yep, you could."

Therapist: And what did the man say as to how he could learn to speak well?

Patient: By going to a speech teacher.

Therapist: Right! So what do you think the duck did?

Patient: Go to a duck speech teacher.

Therapist: He went to a duck speech teacher. He left the old lady who he realized could not really change him into a person. He was a duck. And he went to the speech teacher and then after that, it was very hard and it took a long time, but after that what happened?

Patient: He, he, he—oy, yoy yoy—he . . . (mumbles) . . .

Therapist: He what?

Patient: He, he . . .

Therapist: What happened after that?

Patient: He . . .

Therapist (interrupts): Forget something?

Patient: He . . . uh . . .

Therapist: What happened after he went to the speech teacher?

Patient: He (long pause) . . .

Therapist: Come on, you can . . .

Patient (interrupts): He could talk well.

Therapist: Right! Very good! He could talk well. He practiced very hard and then after that did he keep wishing then he would be a person?

Patient: No.

Therapist: He was happy he was a duck. And the lesson of that story is what? What are the lessons of that story? Can you figure them out?

Patient: How many . . . (mumbles) . . .

Therapist: The first lesson. What's the first lesson?

Patient: Uno (Spanish: *one*) lesson is . . .

Therapist (interrupts): Uno lesson.

Patient: Never think you can change your magic wand into a person or a duck.

Therapist: Right. There's no such thing as magic. There's no such thing as a magic wand. Okay. Come over here. What's the second lesson?

Patient: Number dos (Spanish: *two*) lesson is never cry—eey, yie, yie.

Therapist: Never cry. That's not a lesson. Sometimes people cry. That's perfectly all right. All right. Let me tell you the second lesson. The second lesson of that story is: If you are a duck and you have some trouble speaking, the best thing you can do is to what?

Patient: Is to go to a duck speech teacher or a regular speech teacher.

Therapist: Right. And practice hard and after that you'll be able to speak well.

Patient: The end.

Therapist: The end.

Patient: Could we stay here all day until I want to go home, until I get tired?

Therapist: Well, we'll stay a little while longer.

Patient: Goody!

Therapist: Right. Do you want to watch this program?

Patient (running to turn on TV monitor): Good-bye!

Therapist: Good-bye, everybody.

The purpose of my story is obvious. I attempted to impart the notion that there are no such things as magic cures and that a more practical and predictably effective course toward overcoming one's handicaps is through constructive action. The written transcript

cannot completely convey all the theatrical elements that I introduced in order to enhance the patient's interest in my story and
encourage receptivity to my therapeutic messages. The therapist
who is able to "ham it up" in this manner provides the patient with
a valuable therapeutic adjunct. The child was swept up by my wild
gestures and readily participated in the little play. His statement at
the end: "Could we stay here all day until I want to go home, until
I get tired?" confirms quite well the kind of enthusiasm that such
dramatizations can evoke.

When I started my story I was not completely clear about exactly how I was going to develop it. I did know, however, that it
was going to center on a denial of the efficacy of magic. When a
child asks me to tell the title of a story I generally provide one that
epitomizes the story's primary theme or message. In this case, the
patient's question caught me a little bit off guard because I had not
yet precisely formulated my story. Accordingly, I gave the title "The
Duck and the Fairy Godmother." I immediately recognized that this
title implied that there would actually be a fairy godmother in the
story. Accordingly, I quickly retracted the title and substituted "The
Duck and the Old Lady." Therapists should not hesitate to change
their minds in the course of storytelling if they suddenly realize that
they can do better for the patient by doing so. It is unrealistic to require of ourselves that we create, on the spur of the moment, pol-
ished theatrical performances or cohesively written stories. In the
split second between my stating the first title and then retracting it,
I decided that my story would include an old lady who aspired to be
a fairy godmother but who was unsuccessful. Hence, when I presented the second title I specifically omitted any reference to magic.

In the early part of my story the patient interrupted to point
out that there were similarities between the story I was telling and
a story I had told during a previous session. He was referring to a
story in which a wise old owl was the conveyor of my therapeutic
messages and that story as well dealt with the magic cure theme.
His recognition of the similarities well demonstrates that the messages I communicate in my stories do sink in and are remembered.

This principle is again demonstrated by the sequence presented below which took place nine days later. On this day, instead
of only the patient and his mother appearing for the session, his
father and two younger siblings (his six-year-old brother and four-
year-old sister) also appeared in the waiting room. The father was
about to take the younger siblings out for a walk while the patient
and his mother were in session with me. I invited the father to bring

the children in because of my previous experience that their participation might be useful. The children were quite enthusiastic about the idea because they had heard from their brother such wonderful tales about the exciting things that go on in my office. Also, they had listened to some of the audiotapes that were made during their brother's sessions and had enjoyed what they had heard. George's father, however, was somewhat hesitant to come in because he feared the younger children would be disruptive. Accordingly, I told the younger children that they could come into the room as long as they behaved themselves and that if they did so, they might be allowed to participate in some of the games that George and I played, but I could not promise for certain that they would be invited to join us. The children were quite cooperative and did not interrupt George when he told this story on the television program.

> *Therapist:* Good morning, boys and girls, ladies and gentlemen. Today is Friday, the 20th of April, 1973, and I am happy to welcome you all once again to "Dr. Gardner's Make-Up-a-Story Television Program." Our quest today is now going to tell us another one of his own original made-up stories. You're on the air.
>
> *Patient:* The name of the story is: "Animals Who Can't Talk and Animals Who Can Talk."
>
> *Therapist:* "Animals Who Can't Talk and Animals Who Can Talk." Okay. This sounds like a very good title for a story. Go ahead.
>
> *Patient:* Once there were two animals and they couldn't talk and on the farm and on that farm there were cows who couldn't talk and all animals who couldn't talk. And there was another farm far, far away—there was another farm—and on that farm animals could talk and those animals said to the other animals, "Buh, buh, buh, buh," and the other animals didn't understand those animals.
>
> *Therapist* (interrupts): Excuse me, the animals who could talk or the animals who couldn't talk said, "Buh, buh, buh?"
>
> *Patient:* The animals who could talk.
>
> *Therapist:* Who could talk said, "Buh, buh, buh." Go ahead.
>
> *Patient:* And the—what am I up to?
>
> *Therapist:* You're up to—there were two farms. One farm had animals who couldn't talk and one farm had animals who could talk. And the animals who could talk said, "Buh, buh, buh," to the animals who couldn't talk. That's where you're at. Right?
>
> *Patient:* (nods affirmatively)
>
> *Therapist:* Now go ahead.
>
> *Patient:* Then the animals who couldn't talk said (scratches ear)—

didn't say anything, just went like this. (Patient's arms outstretched, shrugs shoulders, palms up, and has wistful expression on face.) That's all. And they—the animals who could talk—didn't know what that meant. And then finally the animals who could talk thought that they were saying it wrong. Instead of saying, "Buh, buh, buh," they said, "How come you can't talk?"

Therapist: Go ahead.

Patient: And then the animals who couldn't talk said (moves lips), just opened their mouths.

Patient's mother: (Gestures that therapist look at patient.)

Therapist: Do that again. I wasn't looking. Your mother said I missed something. What about the animals who couldn't talk? What did they do?

Patient: (Moves lips and mouth without sound coming forth.)

Therapist: Okay. Then what happened?

Patient: And then the animals who could talk said, "Ha! You still can't talk and I was trying to make you talk. I'm going to get a fairy godmother." And he just sat there and he didn't call for a fairy godmother. He didn't wish for a fairy godmother.

Therapist: Who didn't wish for a fairy godmother?

Patient: The animals.

Therapist: Which ones?

Patient: The ones who could talk, to make the ones who couldn't talk, talk.

Therapist: Oh, the ones who could talk wanted to get a fairy godmother in order to make the ones who couldn't talk be able to talk. Is that it?

Patient: (nods affirmatively)

Therapist: Okay, then what happened?

Patient: When he was just standing—sitting on the porch waiting for a fairy godmother . . .

Therapist (interrupts): Who was standing waiting for a fairy godmother?

Patient: Uh (pauses).

Therapist: Who was waiting for the fairy godmother?

Patient: . . . (mumbles) . . .

Therapist: Who?

Patient: The . . . (mumbles) . . . peeg . . . or the giraffe.

Therapist: A peeg?

Patient: A pig!

Therapist: A pig! Was this one of the pigs who could or couldn't talk?

Patient: Who could.

Therapist: Who could talk.

Patient: Or it could be a giraffe.

Therapist: A giraffe who could talk. So a pig or a giraffe was waiting for the fairy godmother. Okay.

Patient: And they just sat there doing nothing. They were looking up in the sky saying, "What happened to my fairy godmother? I probably didn't wish for one or say it out loud." And then he began to scream, "Fairy godmother" so loud that all the animals who could talk and couldn't talk ran away.

Therapist: Why did they run away?

Patient: Because he screamed so loud.

Therapist: Then what happened?

Patient: And then he said . . .

Therapist (interrupts): Who's he?

Patient: And then the pig said, "Oh, wow, I really screamed loud that time. I scared all the animals who couldn't talk away. That's the name of the animals.

Therapist: What?

Patient: Couldn't Talk and Could Talk.

Therapist: Okay. His screams scared away all the animals who couldn't talk. Then what happened?

Patient: Then he said (in singsong manner), "Oh, I wish for a fairy godmother, a fairy godmother," and he sang and sang until he believed, until somebody, until he realized there's no such thing as a fairy godmother.

Therapist: Okay. You mean she never came?

Patient: No.

Therapist: Then what happened?

Patient: The end.

Therapist: Well, I have a question. What happened to the animals who couldn't talk? What happened to them?

Patient: They had to go to a teacher.

Therapist: Hh hmm.

Patient: They went like this (makes grimacing facial expressions) and the teacher couldn't understand what the animals were saying.

Therapist: So what happened then?

Patient: I'm all done.

Therapist: Well, did they learn to talk?

Patient: Yes. They said—they tried hard like this (makes facial contortions) and they made a couple of sounds: "Buh, buh, buh, yup, yup, yup," and then they started talking loud (voice gets louder): "Yup, yup, yup, yup, yup." And they talked so loud that they grew up to be a giant.

Therapist: Uh huh. I see. Okay. Is that the end of the story?

Patient: Yes.

Therapist: And what's the lesson of that story?

Patient: There are two lessons.

Therapist: What are the two lessons?

Patient: Never sit there but if you want a real fairy godmother don't believe in fairy godmothers. My third lesson is: *There's no such thing as fairy godmothers.*

The story demonstrates well how my messages from the sequence of nine days previously had been remembered by the patient and were retold in his story. One could argue that such repeating is not specifically therapeutic and that the child might be doing it merely to ingratiate himself with me. There is no question that this was probably going on. However, there is also no question that such repetition for the purpose of ingratiating the therapist is part of every patient's cure, regardless of age. It is hoped that the patient will reach the point at which new ways of thinking and doing things will be done for their own sake, rather than merely for the therapist's. In addition, I believe that George repeated my story because of his appreciation, at some level, that it had validity and that it offered him more promise for improvement than fairy godmothers.

Because the story had so many healthy elements, I decided not to alter it in my responding story. Rather, I decided to entrench the message by its repetition in the dramatic mode. The presence of George's younger siblings provided me with a source of willing recruits for participation in my planned theatrical performance.

Therapist: Okay. Now I'll tell you what. I think that was such a good story that instead of my making up a story, what I think we ought to do is let's make up a play. Okay? Do you want to make up a play in which we'll make up a play about your story? Do you want to do that?

Patient: What does that mean?

Therapist: Well, what we'll do is we'll act it out. We'll tell your story and we'll play the parts of different animals—you and me. Okay? Do you want to do that?

Patient: (nods affirmatively)

Therapist (points to sister and brother sitting in another part of room): Do you want your brother and sister to be in the play?

Patient: (nods affirmatively)

Therapist (speaking to brother and sister): Would you like to be in a play?

Voice heard from out of camera range: Yes.

Therapist: Okay, come on over here. We'll make a play now. I'll show you how we'll do it. (Sister Sue and brother Bob walk over to where patient and therapist are sitting. Therapist starts moving furniture around.) Let's make a play in which we have two farms. Come over here (motions to Sue and Bob to come closer). These are our two guests on our program today (has Sue and Bob face camera). These two guests are going to be in the play (moves microphone to side).

Patient: But how are you going to be by the microphone?

Therapist: The microphone will pick up our voices. Now here's what we're going to do. We're making believe that there are two farms. Okay?

Patient: (nods affirmatively)

Therapist: On one farm the animals can't talk and on the other farm the animals can talk. Now, let's make believe, first of all, the animals who can talk. Let's make some animal sounds (points to patient). What kind of animal sound do you want to make? What kind of animal sound?

Patient: (just stares in space)

Therapist (to patient while Sue and Bob just remain standing motionless): What animal sound do you want to make?

Patient: What kind of a sound . . .

Therapist (interrupts): Any sound.

Patient: does a giraffe make?

Therapist: I don't know. What kind of sound could a giraffe make?

Patient: (still pondering, while other children are still standing motionless)

Therapist: I don't really know. What's your guess? (after a pause) Well, Pick an animal whose sound you know.

Patient: A pig.

Therapist: Well, how does a pig go?

Patient: Oink, oink, oink, oink.

Therapist: Okay, so you'll be the pig. (turns to Bob) Now what animal do you want to be?

Bob: Dog.

Therapist: You'll be the dog. What sound does the dog make?

Bob: Ruff, ruff!

Therapist (turns to Sue): What animal do you want to be?

Sue (in low voice): A dog.

Therapist: A dog. What sound does a dog make?

Sue: Ruff, Ruff!

Therapist (to all three children): Okay, now, now all the animals make sounds. Let's make believe first we're the animals on the farm making the sounds. Okay, every animal make his own sound! Go ahead. Let's do it, (joins in with them) oink, oink, ruff, ruff.

Patient: Oink, Oink.

Sue: Ruff, ruff.

Bob: Ruff, ruff.

All: Oink, oink, ruff, ruff, oink, ruff, oink, ruff, etc.

Therapist (to Sue): Okay, let's hear you.

Sue: Ruff, ruff, ruff, ruff.

Therapist: Okay, Now those are all the talking animals. Now—turn around (twists Bob around toward camera) so everybody can see you on television. All right? Now (places Sue in one spot) you stand over here. Okay. Now you (places Bob on his left side) stand over here so you'll be seen on television. Now, so those are the animals who *can* talk.

Now, then, there are other animals who can't talk. They just go like (makes strained facial expression), "Mmmmmmmmmmm." Okay (points to Bob), you do that. (Bob tries to imitate therapist.)

Patient (to therapist): I hear noise out of you.

Therapist: Yeah, but I'm not saying (points to Sue). Go ahead, you try words to do it.

Sue: (just stares at therapist)

Therapist (grimaces and strains face again, trying to evoke some kind of sound): Go ahead (pointing to patient), you try to do it.

Patient: (makes contorted and strained facial expression)

Therapist (joins patient and makes straining expression and sounds again): Now (placing right hand on Sue's shoulder and looking directly at her), you do that.

Patient (interrupts): They should be . . .

Therapist (interrupts while still looking at Sue): Go ahead.

Patient: . . . like this (strains face and clenches hands).

Therapist (again has strained facial expression as he joins in with patient): "Mmmmmmmmm," and they just can't talk. Then the animals — now the other animals come along and say, "Let's get a fairy godmother to help those animals talk." So let's call out for the fairy godmother. (shouts) "Fairy godmother."

Bob (joins in with therapist): " . . . godmother."

Therapist: Go ahead. Call out for her.

All children: "Fairy godmother."

Therapist (joins in): "Fairy godmother. Would you help those animals talk? (looks around at all the children) Go ahead, do it (points to patient). Yell out for the fairy godmother.

Patient (shouts): "Fairy godmother. Will you help those animals talk?"

Therapist (pointing to Sue): You say it.

Sue (in rushed, garbled voice): "Fairy godmother. Will you make those animals talk?"

Therapist (pointing to Bob): What about you?

Bob (shouts): "Fairy godmother. Will you make those animals talk?"

Therapist: All right. Let's look up there. (They all look up at ceiling.) Do you see any fairy godmothers up there?

Patient: No.

Bob: (points toward window): Look up there — nothing!

Therapist: Let's yell louder. Maybe she'll come.

All shouting together: Fairy godmother!

Therapist: Yell louder. Maybe she'll —

All (shouting even louder together): Fairy godmother!

Therapist (showing increasing anguish): Fairy godmother, fairy godmother. (looks all around) Do you see any fairy godmother?

Bob (turning around toward window and holding curtain open in one hand): No, she might be coming.

Patient: Just lights.

Therapist (talking to Bob and then turning toward window and puts hand on curtain): Do you think she may be out the window here? Let's look out.

Bob (as he separates curtain and looks out): She may be coming.

Therapist (to Bob): Well, look out here. Do you see any fairy godmothers out there?

Bob (looking out of window): No.

Patient and Sue: (looking out window from where they are standing)

Therapist (to patient and Sue): Do you see any fairy godmothers?

Sue: (nods head negatively)

Patient: I only see the light but no fairy godmother.

Therapist: Let's try once more. Maybe she'll come.

All (shouting loudly together): Fairy godmother! Fairy godmother. (all look around and up at ceiling)

Therapist: Will you come down and make the animals talk? (with dismayed expression on face) I don't see her. Do you see her?

Children: (seem completely absorbed and interested in what therapist is saying)

Therapist: Now what's going to happen? Now here are all the animals—let's make believe that we're all the animals who can't talk. Okay? (makes strained facial expression)

Children: (imitate facial expression)

Bob: (bends down for a second and pretends he's a dog)

Therapist: "We can't talk." Then what are those animals going to do? (directs attention toward patient) What's going to happen now? What are they going to do?

Patient: I think the other animals will tell where they know a good speech teacher.

Therapist: Right! So all the animals who can't talk go to a speech teacher. (looking at all three children) Who wants to make believe that they're the speech teacher? Who wants to be the speech teacher.

Patient: (raises hand)

Therapist (pointing to patient): You be the speech teacher. Okay, we three are animals. (begins strained facial expression and makes garbling sounds again, and points to Bob) You do it.

Bob: (makes garbling sounds)

Therapist (points to Sue): Okay, you do it.

Sue: (nods head up and down, smiling, tries to imitate garbling sounds)

Patient (looking apprehensive): What should I do?

Therapist: Well, what does a speech teacher do?

Patient: Help people?

Therapist: All right. So what are you going to do?

Patient: Help.

Therapist: Okay, How are you going to help us speak?

Patient: By teaching you how to.

Therapist: Okay, make believe that you're the speech teacher teaching us how to.

Patient: Now say "Moo."

Therapist (pointing to Bob): You try it first. You try to say "moo."

Bob: Moo.

Therapist (all excited): Hey, he said "Moo!" (pointing to Sue) Now you try it. (talking to patient) Teach her to say something.

Sue: Moo.

Patient: Say "Good."

Sue: Good.

Therapist: Okay, now tell me to say something.

Patient: Good, bad, and hat.

Therapist: What is that again?

Patient: Good, bad, and hat.

Therapist: Good, bad, and hat. Okay. (with strained facial expression) G...g...g It's very hard—you see, it's very hard to learn how to speak. It isn't easy. G...g...goo...goo...good. Hey, I said it. Hey, I can start to speak! (talking directly to patient) Now you say to the children, "It takes a lot of practice and you've got to work very hard.

Patient: It takes a lot of practice and you got to work very hard.

Therapist (looking around at all three children): So, all of us, let's say we work very hard for a long time and we're all learning, and we can speak now. Okay?

Patient: (nods affirmatively)

Therapist: Okay. So everybody speak. Speak! Moo, moo.

Bob: Oink, Oink.
Therapist: Oink, moo, meow, oink.
Bob: Ruff, ruff.
Therapist: Ruff, ruff, ruff, meow.
Sue: (seems to be too entranced to join in making animal sounds)
Therapist: Hey, we're all speaking! Thank you very much, speech teacher (shakes patient's hand) for teaching us how to speak. (shakes hand again) Thank you very much. Let's shake this speech teacher's hand.
Bob: (shakes patient's hand)
Sue: (shakes patient's hand)
Therapist: Okay. And that's the end of the program. Let's say good-bye. The end.
Bob and Sue: (wave good-bye)
Patient: So short?
Therapist: So short?
Patient: Yes.
Therapist: Do you want to make it longer?
Patient: No.
Therapist: Do you want to add a part?
Patient: Noooooo!
Therapist: Okay. Do you want to watch this?
All: Yes.
Therapist: Raise your hand if you want to watch this. (patient and Bob raise hands)
Sue: (just looks amused and pensive)
Therapist: Okay, we'll watch.

Again, the written transcript cannot fully convey the children's involvement in the play. They were all genuinely swept up in it and found it exciting and absorbing. The patient's comment at the end, "So short," was only final confirmation that he was having a good time and that the experience was a meaningful one for him. I added nothing new in the way of content; rather, I attempted to entrench the healthy message from his story in a powerful and absorbing manner. This experience marked a turning point in his therapy; following it there was very little talk of magic. This is not to say that there was absolutely no talk about magic; it is unrealistic to expect to remove such an attractive adaptation entirely. In fact, it is probable that none of us give up such hopes completely no matter how old we get. The important thing was that it was no longer a primary mode of adaptation for George.

TEN

Mutual Storytelling Derivative Games

When they're offered to the world in merry guise,
Unpleasant truths are swallowed with a will —
For he who'd make his fellow, fellow, fellow creatures wise
Should always gild the philosophic pill!

William S. Gilbert
Yeoman of the Guard

INTRODUCTION

During the first few years of utilization of the mutual storytelling technique, I found some children to be inhibited with regard to their freedom to create and verbalize stories. Accordingly, I began to think of other ways that could be useful in facilitating children's providing me with such material. Recognizing that children enjoy immensely playing board-type games, especially those in which there is a competitive element, a series of games was devised. These games involve traditional board-game materials such as dice, reward chips, and playing pawns. The introduction of the reward chips serves to enhance children's motivation to provide projective material. Whereas in the mutual storytelling technique no rewards are provided, in these games token chips are given, and the winner (the person who has accumulated the most reward chips) receives a prize.

Although reward chips are given, it would be an error for the reader to conclude that these games represent a kind of "behavior therapy." These games share with behavior therapy the use of reward chips, but the similarity ends there. In behavior therapy one uses rewards in order to change behavior at the manifest level. Behavior therapists differ with regard to their views about the presence or absence of unconscious processes and whether, if present, they play a role in symptom formation. But they are in agreement in not generally giving significant attention to unconscious processes in the therapeutic process. Many take the position that the symptom is basically the disease and its removal represents a cure.

My use of chips here serves an entirely different purpose. I am using them to reward the child for providing self-created free associations and stories, for psychotherapeutic use. My utilization of reward chips is based on the belief that unconscious processes do exist and that the understanding of them (especially by the therapist) plays an important role in the therapeutic process. In short, I am using reward chips for the elicitation of psychodynamically meaningful material, material derived often from unconscious processes. Behavior therapists, in contrast, use the reward chips to change behavior at the manifest level. We share in common the use of reward chips, but we use them for entirely different purposes.

It would be an error, also, if the reader were to conclude that I have absolutely no conviction for behavior therapy. This is not the case. One cannot deny the importance of positive and negative reinforcement in human development. One of the primary reasons why children are "good" is that they hope to gain the affection and love of their child rearers; and one of the main reasons why they inhibit themselves from being "bad" is their fear of loss of such affection. When two-year-old Johnny decides not to run into the street, it is not because he is aware of the fact that he may be endangering his life; rather, he restricts himself from doing so because of his anticipation that significant caretaking individuals will react with strongly negative feedback and even painful physical responses (a slap on the backside or a not so gentle wrenching of his arm) if he does so. The experimental rat presses the bar in order to obtain food pellets and will drop down to the random level of bar pressing frequency if the pellets are permanently withdrawn.

So ubiquitous is this pleasure-pain principle that one could argue that behavior therapy is basically nature's form of treatment. In part, I agree that it is. However, the human brain is so complex and sophisticated that other mechanisms, beyond pain and pleasure, are operative, and so more sophisticated methods of psychotherapy are warranted when psychological disorders are present. This does not mean that we must select between the two. Rather, we can combine both approaches.

Furthermore, I generally prefer to utilize behavioral therapy techniques in the context of my psychotherapeutic program. I consider their isolated utilization to be somewhat artificial and sterile. For example, one could help an agoraphobic woman desensitize herself to her fear of open places by suggesting that she force herself to tolerate increasingly the fears that she experiences when she sets forth from her home. This would basically be the traditional behavior therapy approach. One might even try to quantify the times of exposure on a chart while pointing out to the patient her progressive improvement. My own approach would be to focus on what I consider to be the primary factors that are contributing to the agoraphobia, factors such as excessive dependency on the people with whom she lives and fears of asserting herself as an adult in a world of adults. This would not preclude, however, my encouraging desensitization and some kind of more informal assessment of her progress. Even the most staunch subscribers to the psychoanalytic theory would not dispute the value of desensitization. The crucial question is whether one believes that one can get a significant degree of symptomatic alleviation over a long period by merely focusing on the removal of the agoraphobic symptom. I believe that one is not likely to achieve long-term improvement by the behavior therapeutic technique alone. Even if one does, I would still consider the therapeutic work to have been only partially completed because the underlying factors that have contributed to the formation of the symptom have not been dealt with.

These games also make use of the competitive element. Basically I am using competition to enhance the child's motivation to acquire chips. There are some readers who probably would take issue with me on this point because of their belief that competition is basically a dehumanizing experience that we would do best to dispense with entirely. Obviously, I do not share this view. I think that one must differentiate between healthy and unhealthy competition, between competition that is humane and competition that is inhumane. In healthy competition one strives to win, but one still has respect for one's opponent. In unhealthy competition, the primary purpose is to degrade and destroy for a variety of pathological purposes such as hostility release, compensation for feelings of inadequacy, and self-aggrandizement. At any particular time there are thousands of people working in laboratories hoping someday to win a Nobel prize. Although only an extremely small fraction of these individuals will attain their goal, most would agree that society is a better place for the existence of the prize. And one could say the same thing about a wide variety of other awards in the arts, sciences, and other fields of endeavor—awards that have served to enhance human motivation and striving toward excellence. If not for healthy competition, we might still be living in caves. If not for unhealthy competition, many people who reached premature death might have lived longer lives.

When using the games described in this chapter, the therapist should keep in mind these differentiations and do everything possible to keep the competition at a healthy level. Ideally, the patient and therapist will be so swept up in the game that both will forget whose chance it was and who is to get the reward chip. But even when this ideal is not reached, the therapist should strive to make the game so exciting that the child will frequently forget that it was his or her turn. When the child does appear to be more interested in acquiring chips than providing psychodynamically meaningful material, the therapist does well to discourage such preoccupations with comments such as: "Wait a minute. Don't throw the dice yet. I haven't finished giving my answer." "Hold on, I'd like to ask you a question about what you've just said." and "That's a very good beginning for your story. Now let's hear the middle and the end of your story. Every story has a beginning, a middle, and an end."

The general principle I follow when playing these games is that the child receives one chip for making a statement and two for telling a story. The statement option is introduced for children who are so restricted that they cannot relate a self-created story. As mentioned, the material so elicited should be used as a point of departure for various kinds of psychotherapeutic interchange. Often, the therapist may wish to respond with a story that is created to address itself to pathological manifestations in the child's story. For some children one might want to discuss the child's story at the symbolic level with comments such as: "Why did the cat run away from the rabbit?" and "Was there something else the cat could have done, something better than running away?" The rare child who is interested in an introspective inquiry, might be asked: "Is there anything in your story about the three squirrels that is like what's happening in *your* house?"

THE BOARD OF OBJECTS GAME

In The Board of Objects Game, designed with N. I. Kritzberg, a board of sixty-four squares (a standard checker board serves well) or a larger board of one hundred squares is used. In each square is placed a small figurine of the type readily purchased in most stores selling children's games and equipment (Figure 10.1). The figurines include family members, zoo animals, farm animals, small vehicles (police car, fire engine, ambulance, etc.), members of various occupations (doctor, nurse, policeman, etc.), and a wide assortment of other common objects (baby bottle, knife, gun, lipstick, trophy, lump of brown clay, etc.). A pair of dice is used with one face of each die colored red. Last, there is a treasure chest filled with token reward chips.

The game begins with the child's throwing the dice. If a red side lands face up (and this should occur once every three throws of the dice) the child can select any object from the board. If the child can say anything at all about the object, he or she gets *one* reward chip. If the child can tell a story about the object, he or she gets *two* reward chips. The therapist plays similarly and the winner is the one who has accumulated the most chips when the alloted time is over. If a person is "lucky" and both red sides land face up, the player can select two objects and gets double rewards. The player may tell one story in which both objects are included or two separate stories. When commenting on, or telling a story about, an object it is preferable for the player to hold it and sometimes even move it about in accordance with what is going on in the story. The child will often do this spontaneously and the therapist should do so as well in appreciation of the enhanced efficacy of the dramatized communication. The therapist's various gestures, animal sounds, vocal imitations, accents, etc. can further involve the child and enhance receptivity to the therapeutic messages. After being used, the figurine can either be replaced on the board or placed on the side, depending upon the preference of the players.

Although the figurines are selected so as to elicit fantasies cov-

Figure 10.1

ering a wide range of issues usually encountered in most children's therapy, their exact nature, form, and variety is not crucial. The pressure of unconscious material to be released in a form specifically meaningful for the child is far greater than the power of the facilitating stimulus to distort the projected material. Accordingly, the therapist need not be too concerned about the selection of objects if he or she wishes to put together such a game. The usual variety of such figurines found in most toy stores will serve well.

Again, the therapist should try to create an atmosphere in which conversations may take place about the comments made or stories told; rather than one in which there is fierce competition for the accumulation of chips. The therapist plays in accordance with the same rules to create stories of his or her own that are either specifically related to the comments or stories just related by the child or else relevant in other ways to the child's life and problems.

The game is a very attractive one and it is a rare child who does not respond in the affirmative when shown it and asked: "Would you like to play this game with me?" Children below five or six, who have not yet reached the point where they can appreciate meaningfully the rules and organization of standard board games, will still usually want to "play." Some will enjoy throwing the dice until they get a red and will then choose an object. Such younger children may not be able to tell well-organized stories but may still provide meaningful, although fragmented, fantasies—especially because there is a reward chip that can be obtained for such revelations. The therapist must try to select from the disorganized fantasies those threads or patterns that are atypical, idiosyncratic, or pathological, and then use these as foci for his or her own responding comments. Often such younger children will be content to just play, fantasize, and collect chips without giving the therapist his or her turn. Generally, in such situations, I allow the child to tell a few "stories"—by which time I have gotten enough material to create one of my own. I then invoke my right to take my turn to tell stories and use the opportunity to relate my responding messages, either in story or nonstory allegory.

When the allotted time is up, the person with the most chips takes a prize from the box of *Valuable Prizes* (Figure 10.2).

The aforementioned "rules" are those that I have found most useful. However, the therapist may wish to utilize his or her own variations and I, too, at times have modified the game (as in the aforementioned description of its use with younger children). I have

Figure 10.2

found the game particularly useful with children at the kindergarten to second-grade level. At that age their reading ability is usually not great enough for them to play some of the more sophisticated games I describe in this chapter. Yet they do appreciate game structure and so generally become absorbed. At about the age of nine or ten, most children consider the game "babyish" and prefer the more advanced games described herein.

Clinical Example

The Case of Norman (The Cowboy Whose Gun Was Missing)
Norman, a five-and-a-half-year-old boy, presented with a history of lag in his developmental milestones and coordination deficits. He had a tendency to withdraw and to "tune out," especially when an activity might expose his deficits. At such times he seemed to be in another world. A problem that was particularly apparent at the time the interchange below took place was inhibition of self-assertion. He could not fight back when teased by other children; accordingly he was being scapegoated.

The patient often spontaneously told stories about the various figurines on the *Board of Objects* without formally playing the game. The cowboy, which he chose to talk about in the interchange below, had a removable holster belt attached to which were two holsters with guns inside. In order to remove the belt, however, one had to pull the top half of the figurine away from the bottom half, to which it was attached by a small plug. If the holster belt were so removed and then the two halves of the body replaced, a waistline defect was still present where the holster belt had been. This is the interchange that occurred regarding the cowboy.

> *Therapist:* Hello, today is Monday, August 28th, 1972, and I'm here with Norman and he and I are going to play a game with these objects. Norman, can you pick one? The storytelling game. Okay. What is that?
> *Patient:* A cowboy.
> *Therapist:* Okay, that's a cowboy. What are you going to tell me about the cowboy?
> *Patient:* Cowboys have guns.
> *Therapist:* They have guns. Yeah.
> *Patient:* And they shoot.
> *Therapist:* Yeah. Go ahead.

Patient: Make believe he took his pants off.

Therapist: Okay.

Patient: He took his pants off.

Therapist: Yeah.

Patient: If he take his holsters with it only would that be as far as it would be?

Therapist: If you take his holster off what? I'm not clear what you're saying.

Patient: I think I'll try taking. . . .

Therapist: Go ahead. Now what? You took off his holsters. Right?

Patient: Right.

Therapist: Now what did you ask me about that, about taking off his holster? I didn't understand your question. What was your question?

Patient: Is this as far as it goes when you keep the gun on but you take the holsters off?

Therapist: Yep. Right. You mean does the body go together with the feet after you take the holsters away?

Patient: Yeah.

Therapist: No, it doesn't. There's still a space there. What do you think about that?

Patient: Why is there still a space?

Therapist: Because that cowboy was made so he should have guns and when he doesn't have his guns his body and his feet don't go together. That's the way they made him. Do you know why they made him that way?

Patient: Why?

Therapist: What do you think? Why do you think they made him so that the gun should be there? Hh hmm?

Patient: Mmm.

Therapist: Why do you think they made him that way?

Patient: I don't know.

Therapist: Hh hmm?

Patient: I don't know!

Therapist: Does a cowboy need guns?

Patient: Yeah.

Therapist: What does he need them for?

Patient: Shooting.

Therapist: Now do you know why they made him with guns? Why do you think?

Patient: I don't know.

Therapist: What are the guns for?

Patient: Shooting.

Therapist: And why does he do that?

Patient: In case someone starts to bother him.

Therapist: Right, in case someone starts to bother him. Right. So what can he do in case. . . .

Patient (interrupting): Some Indians have bow and arrows.

Therapist: Right. Hh hmm. That's right.

Patient: Did you ever see a bow and arrow?

Therapist: Of an Indian? Sure. What would happen to that cowboy if he didn't have his guns?

Patient: I don't know.

Therapist: What would happen now? You say the guns are good because if someone starts to bother him then he could use them. Right?

Patient: Right.

Therapist: Now what would happen to him if he didn't have his guns?

Patient: If he had a bow and arrow (pauses) . . .

Therapist: Yeah and then what?

Patient: If someone comes along . . . (pauses) . . .

Therapist: Yeah.

Patient: . . . and bothers an Eskimo.

Therapist: If someone comes along and bothers an Eskimo? Is that what you said?

Patient: He said, "If you don't go away, I'll kill you with this spear!"

Therapist: All right. Who says that? Who said that?

Patient: The Eskimo.

Therapist: Is the Eskimo the same as the Indian or is he somebody different?

Patient: He's somebody different.

Therapist: Okay. So what good is the spear then? How does the spear help the Eskimo?

Patient: He hunts with the spear.

Therapist: Right. What else does it do for him? How else does it help him?

Patient: I don't know.

Therapist: What did you say before about what the Eskimo does with his spear?

Patient: Hunts.

Therapist: Anything else?

Patient: Yes.

Therapist: What?

Patient: "If you don't go away I'll kill you with this spear."

Therapist: Right. And what is the person trying to do who the Eskimo says that to—the person to whom the Eskimo says, "If you don't go away I'll kill you with this spear"? What is that person trying to do to the Eskimo? Huh?

Patient: Trying to shoot him.

Therapist: All right. Now what about the cowboy and his gun? What is the good of the guns? What would happen to the cowboy if he didn't have his guns?

Patient (accidentally drops the holster belt on the rug and can't find it): The guns disappear into the rug.

Therapist: Oh my, we can't find it.

Patient: I got a G.I. Joe at home.

Therapist: I want to ask you a question that you're not answering.

Patient: But he's a bigger G.I. Joe. These are smaller G.I. Joes.

Therapist: All right. I want to ask you one question now. What happens to the cowboy if he doesn't have his guns?

Patient: If he doesn't have—if he left his guns at his ranch . . .

Therapist (interrupting): What would happen to him?

Patient: He would have to go back to his ranch.

Therapist: Why would he have to go back?

Patient: To get his guns.

Therapist: What does he need them for?

Patient: He says, "If you don't go away I'll shoot you."

Therapist: Right, if people bother him. Right? Is that right? Huh? Oh, here's the gun. Is that right that if people bother him he'll have the gun?

Patient: Hh hmm.

Therapist: Now why did they make this cowboy with guns then? Why did they make him with guns?

Patient: And then another boy comes along.

Therapist: Yeah and then.

Patient: "Then if you don't go away I'll jump on you." (hums to self) (puts down the cowboy and picks up an airplane)

Therapist: What happened there?

Patient: New airplane and then he flew . . . (makes airplane sounds) . . .

Therapist: Then what happened?

Patient: And then the propeller breaks off.

Therapist: Then what happens?

Patient: And then the propeller broke my—and then his fa-ther . . .

Therapist: His father what?

Patient: Glues it back on.

Therapist: Hh hmm. And then what happens?

Patient: So it can never grow, so it cannot, so it can never, so it can't . . .

Therapist: Can't what?

Patient: So it can never—so the propeller can never come off again.

Therapist: Uh huh. Did he watch it himself to make sure that it didn't come off?

Patient: Yeah.

In this interchange I did not directly tell a story; rather, I tried to introduce my therapeutic communications in the context of the discussion about the cowboy and, subsequently, the Indians and Eskimo. I tried to communicate the importance of weapons in defending oneself. It was hoped that Norman would utilize this information in more effectively asserting himself. And this is what ultimately happened. Sequences such as these were contributory toward the patient's ultimately asserting himself more effectively with peers.

Some readers may have wondered why I did not make any comments about the use of guns as lethal weapons and their inappropriateness as a first line of defense (if not a last line of defense). At the time of this interchange (1972), I was not as appreciative as I am now of the insidious influence of gunplay in childhood. Had this interchange occurred at the time of this writing (1985), I would have emphasized that guns are just about the worst way of defending oneself and that they should only be used as a last resort and only then under extreme circumstances. I have come to appreciate that their utilization by children in "war games" contributes to the frivolous attitude that many individuals in our society have toward murder. It would be an error for the reader to conclude that I consider toy guns to play a central role in adult homicide. People who are homicidal generally are so because of severe psychiatric disturbance that has its roots in formidable family difficulties during childhood. Although the influence of childhood war games is small, it is nevertheless operative.

The interchange demonstrates well how many children of this age (including those without neurological impairment) will introduce new figures into the conversation without informing the listener of their appearance in his or her mind. This is what happened here with the sudden introduction of the Eskimo about whom I had heard nothing previously. However, the Eskimo and his spear certainly served as well as the Indian with his bow and arrow and the cowboy with his guns to not only manifest the patient's inhibition in expressing hostility but served as well as excellent objects for my own communications.

At the end of the interchange the patient suddenly put down the cowboy and picked up a toy airplane. While flying it in the air he spoke about how the propeller had broken off and then how his father fixed it so it would never come off again. Classical psychoanalysts might consider this aspect of the child's story to represent a reaction formation or an "undoing" of castration anxiety. Breaking off of the propeller, according to this theory, would symbolize castration and the father's repairing it would represent the boy's fantasy that his father would undo the trauma.

I am dubious about this possible explanation. I think a more reasonable explanation is that it represents the boy's view that his father can correct and/or repair any injuries that may befall him. Another possible explanation is that the boy's father represents the therapist whose story had just served to help him feel more intact and helped him compensate for the feelings of impotence he felt prior to our interchange. Because of my uncertainty regarding the meaning of the story, I chose not to respond to it. Because I had already provided what I considered to be meaningful therapeutic communications, I had no trouble not doing so. Also, I have found that "overloading" can dilute and undermine previous messages that may have been effective.

THE THREE GRAB-BAG GAMES

The Bag of Toys Game

The games described in this section are attractive in that they appeal to the child's traditional enjoyment of the grab-bag game in which the child closes his or her eyes and pulls out an unknown object from a bag. In each, one reward chip is given for a simple response and/or two if the player can tell a story about the object that has been taken from the bag. The therapist enhances the child's curiosity and enthusiasm by occasional warnings not to peek and by exhibiting excitement him- or herself when it is the therapist's own turn. The reward chips are contained in a treasure chest, which serves to further enhance their value. Again, the winner is the player who has accumulated the most chips at the end of the allotted time and he or she selects a prize from the same box of prizes (Figure 10.2) described for previous games.

The *Bag of Toys Game* (Figure 10.3) requires a bag clearly labeled BAG OF TOYS containing about forty to fifty figurines of the kind used in *The Board of Objects Game* (Figure 10.1). When putting his or her hand into the bag, the child is warned against peeking ("Keep your eyes closed. Remember, it's against the rules of the game to peek."), and spending time feeling the objects is also discouraged ("No fair feeling. Just pick out one of the objects."). After the object has been selected and used as a focus for comment and/ or story, it is laid aside rather than returned to the bag. Again, the child will often add dramatic elements to the story and it behooves the therapist to do so as well. As is true for the other grab-bag games, the child's comments are used as a point of departure for psychotherapeutic interchanges.

Clinical Example: The Case of Bernard (Let Sleeping Dogs Lie, But Give Them a Bone)   Bernard entered treatment at the age of seven and a half because of significant classroom difficulties. He was disruptive in the classroom, fought frequently with his classmates, was not attentive to his studies, and concentrated poorly. Although very bright, he was not doing well academically. At home he was frequently argumentative and often entered into power struggles with his parents. The parents often used him as a focus for their own marital conflict.

During his third session, the following interchange occurred while Bernard and I were playing *The Bag of Toys Game*.

> *Therapist:* Okay, ladies and gentleman. This is Bernard and the date is April 19, 1974. Okay, you go first. No looking. Close your eyes. You can only open your eyes after you take the thing out of the bag.
> *Patient:* (reaches into bag and pulls out a dog figurine)
> *Therapist:* What's that?
> *Patient:* A dog.
> *Therapist:* A dog. Okay. Now if you can say anything at all about that dog you get one chip. But if you want to tell a story about that dog, a completely made-up story, you get two chips.
> *Patient:* Once upon a time there was this dog. So this dog went away with his master. He was looking for hunting and they were hunting for ducks.
> *Therapist:* Go ahead.
> *Patient:* And when they came back he went to sleep.
> *Therapist:* Hh hmm.
> *Patient:* And after he woke up he got a bone and then he went back to sleep again.

Figure 10.3

Therapist: Excuse me. I'm a little confused. He went hunting with his master for ducks and then he went to sleep and when he got up there was a bone there for him?

Patient: Yeah.

Therapist: What about the—is that the whole story?

Patient: No.

Therapist: Okay. Go ahead.

Patient: And then he went back to sleep.

Therapist: Hh hmm.

Patient: Then he woke up and he went around with a boy.

Therapist: Hh hmm.

Patient: And he was walking him with the leash.

Therapist: The boy was walking this dog. Yeah. Go ahead.

Patient: And the boy hurt the dog.

Therapist: Go ahead.

Patient: He had to go to the, the—he had to go where? Where's the place that dogs have to go to when they're sick?

Therapist: Oh, a veterinarian?

Patient: Yeah.

Therapist: Well, how did the boy hurt the dog? What happened?

Patient: He was pulling on the leash too hard and his neck started to hurt.

Therapist: Go ahead. And they went to the vet.

Patient: And he fixed his neck up. And it took two days.

Therapist: Uh huh.

Patient: And then he went back and he had a bone, another bone.

Therapist: Uh huh.

Patient: And that's the end.

Therapist: Okay. Good.

Patient: I get two chips.

Therapist: Two chips. Right. Now it's my chance.

Patient: I'm winning.

Therapist: What? You're winning. All right. But I go now (reaches into Bag of Toys). Whoops. What do I have here? (picks out a boy figurine) I've got a . . .

Patient (interrupts): It's a boy. Are you going to tell a story?

Therapist: Yeah. Right. I don't have to, but I want to. The same rules hold for me. It's a game. If I can say anything about the boy I get one chip, but if I can tell a story about the boy I get two.

Patient: If it's a tie then you mean we . . .

Therapist (interrupts): Then we both get prizes. Right, if it's a tie. Okay.

The patient's story presents two themes, both of which were relevant to Bernard's difficulties. The dog's main activity appears to be sleeping. Although there is some mention of his going with his master and hunting for ducks, the emphasis is on his sleeping and on his acquiring a bone. The issue of his working for his reward is deemphasized. This quality reflected well Bernard's attitude toward his schoolwork and complying with his parents' requests that he perform chores around the home. He much preferred to shirk responsibilities.

In addition the story exhibits the magic cure fantasy so frequently seen in children during the early phases of treatment. It is especially common among children, like Bernard, who do not wish to apply themselves. The dog is injured, goes to a vet, and is cured in two days. Little is said about any efforts on the dog's part to cooperate or inconvenience himself during the course of his treatment. The way in which the dog got sick is also of psychodynamic interest. We are told that the boy was pulling on the dog's leash too hard and this hurt the dog's neck. I believe that this image symbolized Bernard's relationship with his mother, who was somewhat rigid in her handling of him. Although she nagged, in part, in order to get him to do his homework and household chores, there was no question that her standards were high and she would have been "on his back" even if he were more receptive to her requests. She would insist, for instance, that he finish every bit of food on his plate and was rigid with regard to his bedtime. It was not surprising then that Bernard exhibited this fantasy. Depicting himself as a dog might also have been a reflection of his feelings of low self-worth.

It was with this understanding of Bernard's story that I told mine.

> *Therapist:* Once upon a time there was a boy and he had a dog and this dog went out with him hunting, but instead of—they were going to go duck hunting—and when they got to the place where they were to hunt ducks, this dog suddenly decided to go to sleep. And the boy said, "Hey, come on. I brought you out here to hunt ducks, to help me hunt ducks. You're not doing anything."
>
> And the dog just ignored him completely and went to sleep. And as the dog was sleeping he was dreaming that when he woke up there would be a big nice juicy bone there as a kind of surprise. And when he woke up, he looked around and he smelled around and there was no bone, and he was kind of disappointed. And the dog said to the boy, "Do you have a bone?"
>
> And the boy said, "I would have given you a very nice juicy bone

had you helped me with the hunting for ducks, but you didn't want to do that. Instead you just went to sleep. I'm not going to give you a reward." Do you know what a reward is? What's a reward?

Patient: It's something that you do very good on and you get something.

Therapist: Right. It's kind of a prize or present for doing something. He said, "I'm not going to give you a bone. You didn't help me hunt ducks. You just went to sleep."

Well, anyway, as they were walking home the leash that the boy had the dog on got caught in a bush. It stretched and it injured the dog's neck. The boy didn't want to injure the dog. It was one of these accidents that sometimes happen. Anyway, they had to go to a vet. The vet said to the boy and the dog, "Now look I'm going to give you some medicine. You have to take this three times a day." And also he said to the dog, "You have to do certain exercises with your neck in order to help the muscles get better and the tissues get better."

So they took the bottle of pills and when the boy gave the dog the first pill, the dog didn't want to take it. And the boy said, "Listen, if you want to get better, you'd better take these pills."

The dog said, "Nah, I don't have to take those pills.

Patient: Dogs can talk?

Therapist: Well, you know, in my story a dog can talk. It's a make-believe story. And the boy said, "What about those exercises that the doctor said you should do, you know, stretch your neck and move it in different directions so that the muscles will get strong?"

He said, "I don't have to do that."

Well, a week later the dog had not taken any of the medicine and the dog had not done any of the exercises, and they went back to the vet and the vet said, "It doesn't look very good here. It doesn't look very good at all. Have you been taking your medicine?"

And the dog said, "Ah, I don't need that medicine."

And the vet said, "Have you been doing the exercises?"

And the dog said, "Well, I'm kind of busy."

He said, "Well, it's up to you. If you take the medicine and do the exercises your neck will get better. It's not going to get better on its own. It just doesn't happen like that, by sitting there and doing nothing. The only way that neck is going to get better is if you do the exercises and take the medicine." So what do you think happened?

Patient: He took the medicine.

Therapist: Well, he didn't like it. He didn't like it because he had to think about it three times a day, but he realized that the vet was right. And what do you think he did about the exercises?

Patient: He did them.

Therapist: Yeah. He found that the more he did the exercises, the faster his neck got better. And the lesson of that story is—well, actually there are two lessons to that story. One has to do with the duck hunting. What do you think the lesson of that part of the story is?

Patient: That if your neck gets hurt . . .

Therapist (interrupts): No, the duck hunting part. The story has two lessons. What do you think the lesson is about the duck hunting?

Patient: Hmm. I don't know.

Therapist: Well, what did we learn from that about—remember the boy and the dog and the hunting?

Patient: Oh, yeah, I remember.

Therapist: Okay. Go ahead.

Patient: The boy went duck hunting with his dog and the dog didn't want to go duck hunting, and he fell asleep. He wanted a bone, but in the morning when he woke up the dog found that there was no bone.

Therapist: So what did he learn from that?

Patient: He learned that if you do something the other person will get a bone.

Therapist: Put that in other words. I'm not sure I understand you.

Patient: If you help another person with hunting then you will get something.

Therapist: Right! You don't get something for nothing. If you're just going to sleep you're not going to get any of the rewards or prizes or things that come to those who work at it. That's the first lesson. So if you're going duck hunting, and if you're a dog, and you're helping a boy hunt ducks, he's going to be very unhappy with you if you don't work and he won't give you any presents, prizes, or rewards.

The second lesson is that if you are sick, if you have some problem like your neck is injured, you just can't sit around and wait for it to get better; you have to do the things the doctor says if you really want to get better. Usually things don't get better just by doing nothing. You have to do something about them. The end. Okay. I get two chips. Huh?

Patient: (nods affirmatively)

In my responding story I communicated two messages to alter the unrealistic views of the world that Bernard held. I have found that such communications can be quite helpful in reducing such magical views of the world. I did not deal extensively with the issue of Bernard's mother's nagging him, as symbolized by the boy's pulling the dog's leash too hard. In my story the neck is injured by accident. I attempted here to convey to Bernard a feeling of his mother's psychological blindness with regard to this trait. More importantly, however, I was dealing with this directly with her and she was quite capable of reducing some of her pressures on him. Accordingly, I did not introduce anything into the story encouraging Bernard to handle this problem. In addition, it is unwise to try to introduce simultaneously too many themes into one's story. The child can just absorb so much at a time. When I have tried to introduce too many messages into my story, I have found the child to be overwhelmed and then he or she becomes bored and disinterested and tunes out from the multiple stimuli.

Clinical Example: The Case of Tom (The Bed That Dumped Its Occupants) Tom, seven years old, was referred because of significant disinterest in his schoolwork. Although he was very bright, he would spend hours in the classroom dawdling and preoccupying himself with nonacademic activities. Even when given individual attention by both his teacher and special tutors, he would not concentrate and would refuse to apply himself to his tasks.

An older brother, seventeen, had a neurologically based learning disability and was a significant disappointment to Tom's father. Over the years Tom had observed frequent fighting between his father and older brother and this exposure was, without doubt, contributing to Tom's difficulties. In addition, his father was a somewhat aloof man who could not involve himself meaningfully with his children.

During his second month in treatment, the following interchange occurred while we were playing *The Bag of Toys Game*.

> *Patient* (selects bed object): A bed.
> *Therapist:* A bed. What are you going to say about a bed?
> *Patient:* (mumbles)
> *Therapist:* What's that?
> *Patient:* This bed is plastic.
> *Therapist:* The bed is plastic. Okay, you get one chip for that.
> *Patient:* (mumbles)
> *Therapist:* Pardon me.
> *Patient:* I think we're going to have a tie today.
> *Therapist:* We're going to have a tie? Well, maybe.
> *Patient:* Yeah.
> *Therapist:* Hmmm. Who can tell?
> *Patient:* Once there was a bed and it was a very hard bed and it was very mean.

Therapist: It was very mean?

Patient: Yeah, it was a very mean bed.

Therapist: How was it mean?

Patient: If someone laid on it, it would dump—it would tilt itself—and it would dump everybody off and the lady liked it until one day she died. And that's the end. It's short. It's like yours, a little short one.

Therapist: Uh huh. I see. Let me understand something. This bed was mean and it dumped everybody off it who would want to lie on it. Is that it?

Patient: Yeah.

Therapist: And the lady who owned the bed died?

Patient: No, the bed died.

Therapist: The bed died.

Patient: Make believe.

Therapist: Yeah. How did the bed die?

Patient: By doing that when everybody, when . . . when . . . when he tilted himself always he was getting weaker and weaker 'till he died.

Therapist: I see. Okay. You get two chips for that story. Now it's my chance.

I considered the bed to represent the patient's father. In his comment about the bed he stated that it was plastic. And this was reminiscent of his father's personality—especially his lack of feeling. But more important, the bed's practice of dumping everyone who tried to use it is a good representation of his father's rejecting attitudes. Those who would try to get close to his father, as symbolized by getting into the bed, would be rejected. Finally the bed dies. This, I believe, represents Tom's hostility toward his father being released in symbolic fashion. The lady, who owned the bed, represents his mother. Although not stated, the story suggests that even she was dumped from the bed and this too is a good representation of the parental relationship.

With this understanding of Tom's story, I related mine.

Therapist: Now it's my chance. All right. Let's see what I have. (reaches into the Bag of Toys and pulls out a table) A table!

Patient: That's a table?

Therapist: Yeah, what do you think it is?

Patient: Yeah, oh yeah. (patient throws bed onto nearby chair)

Therapist: What are you doing? Do you want to keep your things over there?

Patient: Yes.

Therapist: Okay, Now we'll keep things over there. This table. The table didn't like people to sit next to it. I get one chip. Now for my story.

Once upon a time there was a table and this table, when people would put food on it, it would wobble. It would go (imitates by sound wobbly table) . . . let's say this was food here . . . somebody put a plate on it or something (puts reward chip on table to simulate a plate of food). It would go (imitates wobbly sound while shaking table) and it would knock it off. They'd put it back on and (imitates wobbly sound again and puts back chip) it would knock it off. It just didn't like to have food on it. Once in a while it did. Once in a while you'd put food, you'd put a plate on it and it would let the plate stay. But other times it just didn't want the plates and it would go "ooooooohhhhh" and the plates would go off.

So the people in the family decided that the best thing that they could do was to see what the table's mood was. If they saw the table was going to shake they'd put a little something on it. If the table would shake they'd just take it off and then they'd say, "Okay, we'll just use another table. That's all." But if they put something on it and the table let it stay, then they'd all sit around and they would then use it. Now sometimes they would get angry at the table . . .

Patient (interrupts): They should—you know what they should do? Cut it if it shakes all the plates out. Cut it in half.

Therapist: Cut it in half?

Patient: Yeah.

Therapist: Why do that?

Patient: Just do it.

Therapist: Why? Are you saying that—why should they cut it in half if it—you mean when it shook the plate?

Patient: Yeah.

Therapist: Why cut it in half? What would that do?

Patient: They should.

Therapist: But why? What would that accomplish? What would that do if they cut it in half?

Patient: Nothing. It would just, you know, then it would be no good and then they'd be sad about it.

Therapist: It would be no good?

Patient: Yeah, then it wouldn't have—it wouldn't be—then he wouldn't have a lot of fun or anything.

Therapist: Who's that, the table?

Patient: Yeah.

Therapist: Oh, in other words . . .

Patient (interrupts): They would shake it and shake it and everything.

Therapist: You mean they would punish him that way? Is that what you are saying?

Patient: Yeah.

Therapist: I see. Would he still shake things off the table if they cut him in half?

Patient: No.

Therapist: Why not?

Patient: He wouldn't have two legs to do it.

Therapist: I see. Well, now one of the kids in the family thought that would be a good idea to cut the table up in half and to hurt it that way. But one of the teenagers, an older kid, said, "No, that's foolish because that table is still good. Sometimes it stays still and sometimes it lets us put plates on it. We might as well use it when we can and when we can't we'll just use another table and this way we can get some use of the table because it's a very fine table. It's a very good table." So they said it was a good table and there's no reason ruining it or cutting it up. So what do you think finally happened? Hmm?

Patient: Uh, they didn't . . . (pauses) . . .

Therapist: They didn't what?

Patient: They didn't ruin it.

Therapist: They didn't ruin it. What did they do?

Patient: They just left it alone and they wouldn't use it anymore.

Therapist: At all?

Patient: Yeah.

Therapist: Or did they use it when it wasn't rocking around?

Patient: No, they didn't use it at all.

Therapist: No, that's not how my story ends. In my story they use it when it's not rocking around and when it is rocking around they don't use it. That's how my story ends. So I get two chips for that.

Patient: That was a long one.

Therapist: Okay, let's put this table over there. Okay, you go now.

In situations in which a child's mother and/or father have significant inhibitions in involving themselves with a child, one should not encourage the child to attempt to establish a deep involvement with such parents. In fact, it would be cruel to do so because it would only increase the child's frustration and resentment and this could only intensify his or her difficulties. Accordingly, in such situations, I generally try to help the child appreciate that the parent has deficiencies with regard to providing affection, but I try to help the child recognize that such a parent can still provide affection at times. It behooves such children to develop realistic views of their parents and to involve themselves when such involvement is rewarding and to remove themselves and seek gratifications elsewhere when the parent is not inclined to provide it.

In my story I make this recommendation symbolically. The table in my story (like the bed in Tom's story) represents the father. Just as the bed dumps those who would try to sleep in it, my table wobbles and shakes off any food that would be set on it. However, my table is not uniformly rejecting. There are times when it will allow the food to remain. Those who use the table learn to test it first to determine whether the food will be allowed to stay. In this way I encouraged Tom to approach his father and involve himself with him when the latter was receptive and to remove himself when his father was not.

During the telling of my story Tom suggested that the people cut the table in half as a punitive action, as well as a way of preventing it from shaking off the food. Again, he was not only expressing his hostility in an extreme way but also trying to find a method of stopping the rejection. Neither of these represented reasonable adaptations. He could not kill his father nor could he prevent his father from rejecting him. Accordingly, I rejected these alternatives for incorporation into my story in order to maintain what I considered to be the healthier adaptations.

The transcript does not fully communicate the various movements of the table and plates that were utilized to enhance Tom's interest. Although he stated in the end that it was a long story, he did appear to be involved significantly throughout most of it.

The Bag of Things Game

The Bag of Things Game requires a bag clearly labeled BAG OF THINGS, in which are forty to fifty objects that are far less recognizable than those in the BAG OF TOYS (Figure 10.3). Whereas in *The Bag of Toys Game* the objects are readily identified (soldier, car, boy, fire truck, etc.), in *The Bag of Things Game* objects have been specifically selected because they are not clearly recognizable. Accordingly, the bag contains various kinds of creatures, monsters, wiggly things, a lump of clay, a few blocks, a plastic ring, an odd-looking seashell, some strange-looking robots, and assorted figurines that vaguely resemble people or animals. Because they are not clearly recognizable they tend to be less contaminating of the child's fantasies than toys in *The Bag of Toys Game*. Often the child tends to anthropomorphize the objects; but their amorphous quality allows their utilization for a wide variety of fantasies. In the course of play, used objects are laid aside and dramatizations are encouraged.

Although *The Bag of Things Game* was designed to circumvent the problem of contamination of projected fantasies, my experience with the game did not prove the instrument to be significantly superior to *The Bag of Toys Game* or *The Board of Objects Game*. In all of these games (and the other projective games described in this chapter), the external facilitating stimuli do not appear to differ with regard to their capacity to elicit meaningful material. I believe that the reason for this is simply (as mentioned before) that the pressure of unconscious processes to express relevant psychodynamic material is far greater than the capacity of the external eliciting stimulus to contaminate such fantasies. Although the objects in this game are more amorphous and less recognizable than those in the other games described thus far, they do not appear to affect significantly the nature of the fantasies that they evoke. However, it would be an error for the reader to conclude that this game should therefore be dispensed with. It is another variation which can serve to facilitate the child's telling self-created stories when other games are losing their novelty.

Clinical Example: The Case of Betty ("Get Off My Back")   Betty came to treatment at the age of eight because of shyness, generalized tension, and poor peer relationships. She was quite tight, restricted, and inhibited in expressing emotions. She feared asserting herself and was easily scapegoated. Her parents were highly intellectualized professional people who were similarly fearful of expressing feelings. During her second month of treatment the following interchange took place while playing *The Bag of Things Game*.

> *Patient* (picking from the bag): I hope I get something good.
> *Therapist:* I hope so too.
> *Patient* (holding up an amorphous creature with a similar smaller creature sitting on its head): What's this?
> *Therapist:* What does it look like to you?
> *Patient:* I don't know what it is.
> *Therapist:* Well, make it into anything you want. People see it differently. Call it whatever you want, what it looks like to you.
> *Patient:* It looks like some kind of monster or something like that.
> *Therapist:* Okay, do you want to call it a monster?

Patient: Okay.

Therapist: Now, if you can say something about that monster you get one chip.

Patient: The monster had a little monster sitting on the top of his head and he was green.

Therapist: Very good. You get one reward chip. Now you can get two more if you can tell a completely made-up story about that monster, one completely made up from your imagination.

Patient: Once upon a time there was this monster. And he had this little monster sitting on the top of his head. And he [the big monster] wanted the little monster to get off because he was heavy and he was bothering him.

Therapist: You mean the little monster was bothering the big monster?

Patient: Yeah.

Therapist: What was the little monster doing?

Patient: He was poking him and he was very heavy.

Therapist: So then what happened.

Patient: So the big monster was walking along one day and the little monster fell off his head, landed on the sidewalk, and he died. The end.

Therapist: Is that the whole story?

Patient: Yes.

Therapist: Okay.

The story is a clear statement of the patient's feeling of impotence regarding effective self-assertion. Just as she cannot effectively defend herself against those who tease her (many of whom were smaller than herself), the monster (who symbolizes Betty) is unable to assert himself and use his own powers to rid himself of the little fellow who is bothering him and is a heavy weight on his head. The problem is solved by the little monster's conveniently falling off and dying. No effort is required of the big monster, no self-assertion, no struggle, no anxiety.

The game continued.

Therapist: Okay. Now it's my turn. I wonder what I'm going to get. I hope it's something good. Let me see. (Pulls out a red creature with large lobsterlike claws. On its head is a little yellow creature with similar, but much smaller, claws.) Wow, look what I've got. What do you think that is?

Patient: It looks like some kind of a lobster or something like that.

Therapist: Okay. We'll call it a lobster. Once upon a time there was this lobster. And on his head sat this obnoxious little lobster. And the little lobster was always poking the big lobster. And he would take his little claws . . . do you see his little claws here?

Patient: Yes.

Therapist: Well, he'd take his little claws and he'd sometimes pinch the big lobster on the ears. And he'd poke him with his claws too. So what do you think the big lobster did?

Patient: I don't know.

Therapist: Well, try to guess.

Patient: The little lobster fell off?

Therapist: Well, that's how it happened in your story but it didn't happen in mine. First, the big lobster kept hoping that the little lobster would fall off and hit his head and even die, but as much as he wished that that would happen, it didn't. He wished it very hard. He would go, "Oooh, oooh, I wish so hard that he falls off." But the little lobster just kept sitting there and poking the big lobster, and biting him with his claws.

And sometimes the big lobster used to cry because it hurt him so when he was poked and bitten. And he'd cry, "Oooh, ooh, you're hurting me." But because he didn't *do* anything the little lobster just kept on bothering him and biting him.

Patient: Did he bleed?

Therapist: Yes, a little bit. In fact, it was the day that he began to bleed when the lobster's teenage brother was passing by and he saw what was happening. And he said to the lobster, "Why are you letting him do all those terrible things to you? You have very big claws and you could easily get him off your head. Look how tightly closed you keep your claws." (Therapist now talking to patient and pointing to tightly closed claws.) Do you see how tightly shut he keeps his claws?

Patient: Yes.

Therapist: Why do you think his claws are shut so tight?

Patient: Because he's scared?

Therapist: Right! Because he's scared. So what do you think happened then?

Patient: He opened them up?

Therapist: Right! He was very scared to do it and his knees were knocking and his claws were chattering like this (therapist chatters his teeth) and he was scared all over. And the teenager said, "Go ahead, snap at him. You'll see how fast he'll jump off your head." So the big lobster snapped, but it was a very soft and low snap, and so nothing happened. "That's no snap," said the teenager. "Do it harder," the teenager said. Well, the big lobster was even more scared, but he did it.

What do you think happened then?

Patient: The little lobster still stayed?

Therapist: No! The little lobster began crying, "Ooooh, oooh, you've hurt me. Look what you've done to me. I'm bleeding. Mommy, mommy, I'm bleeding." And he jumped off the big lobster's back and went crying to his mother.

And the teenager said, "You see. That wasn't so bad. I knew you could do it."

And how do you think the lobster felt then?

Patient: He felt very good.

Therapist: Right! He felt wonderful. And after that, whenever the little lobster wanted to get on his head to poke him, he would just snap his claws and the little fellow would run away. But at other times, when the little lobster wanted to be friendly and play, they had a good time together.

And do you know what the lesson of that story is? What we can learn from that story?

Patient: If someone bothers you, don't let him do it?

Therapist: Right! If someone bothers you, don't let him do it. It may be scary at first, but if you still fight—even though you're scared—you'll get people to stop bothering you. The end.

The message of my story is obvious. The patient's solution to the problem of dealing with those who bothered her was totally maladaptive. Mine served, I believe, to encourage greater self-assertion, and this is what ultimately happened in the patient's treatment. Stories such as this played, I believe, a role in bringing about such changes.

When rereading this transcript for publication, I realized that I made a therapeutic error in my responding story. The big lobster hopes that the little lobster will get off his head and then wishes very hard that he do so. After that he cries when the little lobster maltreats him. Then, at the advice of the teenager, he asserts himself by using physical force. It would have been better had I had the big lobster *ask* the little lobster to stop maltreating him and then to make various threats before resorting to physical action. The reader does well to note my utilization of the teenager in this story. I often have found teenagers useful as the supreme authorities in my stories. As all the world knows, teenagers are omniscient and omnipotent and are viewed as such, not only by themselves but by younger children. They serve well, therefore, as high authorities in children's stories, and therapists who are not utilizing their services are depriving themselves of valuable sources of wisdom.

Clinical Example: The Case of Ronald (The Robot Baby Who Receives Unconditional Positive Regard)   Ronald, age seven, exhibited many social perceptual difficulties as a manifestation of his neurologically based learning disability. He was of at least average intelligence and did not have significant visual-perceptual or auditory-perceptual problems. However, he did behave differently from other children, mainly because of his impulsivity, angry outbursts, and insensitivity to the nuances of appropriate social interaction.

While playing *The Bag of Things Game* he drew an object that closely resembled a robot. There was a slot in the back enabling one to use the figurine as a bank. This is the interchange that took place.

Therapist: Just stick your hand in and take whatever one you want. One thing, please.
Patient (taking figurine out of bag): Ooh, what's that?
Therapist: I don't know. What does it look like to you?
Patient: Bank.
Therapist: A bank? I guess it can be used as a bank.
Patient: But how would you get the money out of it?
Therapist: I think it's more than a bank—well, what does it look like?
Patient: A bank because of that (points to a slot in the back).
Therapist: Right. You can put money in it. But what is the bank? I mean there are things like piggy banks. What is that? What kind of a bank is that? This is a treasure chest bank here we're keeping the reward chips in. What kind of a bank would you call that? What does that look like?
Patient: Maybe a robot bank.
Therapist: Now if you want to say something about the robot you get one chip and if you can tell a story about it you get two.
Patient: Once upon a time there was a robot and it had one little baby and everybody loved that little baby. Everybody came to visit him. And they loved that little baby so much. The end.
Therapist: I have a question about that. What was there about that baby that they loved so much?
Patient: Uh, his eyes. They liked to play with that baby.
Therapist: Hh hmm. What else made them like the baby?
Patient: Everything.
Therapist: Is that it?
Patient (whispers): Yeah.
Therapist: Okay. You get two.

The story is typical of those told by many children with minimal brain dysfunction. Having few assets that they consider worthy of gaining them the affection of others, they hope to be loved for innate qualities. In this case the baby is liked because of his eyes. In addition, we are told that people like to play with the baby; but again, no specific ingratiating qualities on the baby's part are described. Last, when I specifically asked the patient, "What else made them like the baby?" he replied, "Everything." Again, this is an avoidance answer and does not provide specifics.

With this understanding of Ronald's story, I related mine after choosing a somewhat nebulous little wiggly creature from the bag.

> *Therapist:* Now it's my chance. (holds up figurine) What does this look like?
> *Patient:* I don't know.
> *Therapist:* Okay, let's just call him a baby. Okay?
> *Patient:* Okay.
> *Therapist:* Once upon a time there was this baby and everybody looked at this baby and everybody said, "Ooh, what a cute little baby. Isn't that a nice little cute baby? Ooh, how cute." (pretends he's kissing baby while making kissing sounds) They used to coo with him and they would hold him and hug him. "Ooh, what a cute little baby."
> This little baby, as he grew up, he found that people weren't cuddling him so much and weren't saying, "Ooh, what a cute little baby." And he thought that just by sitting there and doing nothing that people would continue to love him. Well, that's how it is with babies. Babies can sit and do nothing and everybody will love them, or most people will love them. But as you get older, if you want to get people to like you, you have to be doing things. You have to be nice to them or make things that they may like or do things for people and you just can't sit there and smile and expect everybody to love you.
> But he didn't know this, so when he became five, six, seven years old and he would just sit there and do nothing he found out that people weren't going over and saying, "Ooh, how lovable you are. Ooh, we like you so much." And he got kind of lonely because they weren't loving him like they used to when he was a baby. But then when he started doing things—when he started being nice to people, being friendly, and he started learning a lot of things that made him interesting to talk to—then people started liking him more and he wasn't so lonely.
> And do you know what the lesson of that story is?
> *Patient:* No.
> *Therapist:* Try to figure it out. What do you think the lesson is?

Patient: (silent)

Therapist: Well, do people like you for sitting there and doing nothing?

Patient: No.

Therapist: Do they like little babies when they sit there and do nothing?

Patient: Yeah.

Therapist: Yeah, but when you get older what happens?

Patient: They don't like you anymore.

Therapist: Right. And what do you have to do when you are older in order for people to like you?

Patient: Be nice to them, make things that will make a person happy.

Therapist: Right. Right. And that's how you will get friends when you're older. The end. Okay. I get two chips for that. Right?

Patient: Right.

Therapist: Okay. Your chance.

The purpose of my story is obvious. I attempted to help the patient appreciate that one is loved for assets and qualities which attract people, and that if he is to be liked by others he must apply himself. Children with neurologically based learning disabilities must be strong adherents to the work ethic if they are to overcome their deficits. And it is the purpose of therapy to help bring about such commitment. Elsewhere (Gardner, 1973c) I discuss in detail this important aspect of self-esteem development.

The Bag of Words Game

The Bag of Words Game requires a bag labeled BAG OF WORDS. In it are approximately four hundred words, each of which is printed with thick ink (a "Magic Marker" or "Flair" pen will serve well) on a 2"x3" card (Figure 10.3). Different colored cards and inks can be used to make the game more attractive. Words have been chosen that are most likely to elicit comments and stories relevant to issues commonly focused on in therapy, e.g., *breast, anger, mother, father, boy, girl, foolish, doctor, love,* and *hate.* A full list of the words I have found most useful is shown in Tables 10.1–10.3; however, readers are likely to think of a number of words on their own and may find some of my words less useful than I have found them. In accordance with the aforementioned principle of the pressure of unconscious material being more powerful than the con-

Table 10.1

accident	bird	Christmas	dollar
adult	birthday	cigarettes	draw
afraid	birthday party	circus	dream
airplane	black	clay	dumb
allowance	blame	clean	early
alone	blood	climb	egg
ambulance	boast	clothing	enemy
anger	boat	clown	escape
animal	body	club	eyeglasses
annoy	book	cockroach	fail
ant	bottle	compliment	fall
ape	bowel movement	conduct	famous
apple	boy	cookie	fat
ashamed	boy friend	cop	father
automobile	Boy Scout	counselor	fear
ax	brag	cow	feeling
baby	brat	cowboy	fight
baby-sitter	brave	cripple	finger
backside	bread	crook	fire
bad	breast	cruel	fire engine
bad habit	bug	cry	fireman
bad luck	build	crybaby	fish
bad thoughts	bully	cuddle	fix
ball	calf	curse	flour
balloon	cake	dad	food
bang	camera	danger	fool
bare	camp	daughter	foolish
bath	camp director	dentist	forget
bathroom	candy	die	fox
bathtub	car	dinosaur	freak
beat	care	dirty	friend
beautiful	cat	dirty trick	frog
beaver	catch	dirty words	fun
behavior	cheat	discover	funny
belly button	chewing gum	disgusting	game
best	chicken	doctor	garbage
bicycle	child	dog	garbageman
big	children	doll	gift

Table 10.2

girl	invisible	mean	peacock
girl friend	jail	medal	penis
Girl Scout	jerk	medicine	pet
God	job	mess	phony
good	joke	message	pick on
grab	joy	milk	picture
grade	judge	mirror	pig
grandfather	kangaroo	mistake	piggy bank
grandmother	kill	model	pill
grown-up	kind	mom	plan
gun	king	money	play
hamster	kiss	monkey	playground
happy	knife	monster	please
harm	lady	mother	poison
hate	lamb	mouse	poke
healthy	large	mouth	police car
hear	late	mucus	policeman
heaven	laugh	mud	polite
hell	lazy	nag	pony
hen	leave	naked	poor
hide	letter	nasty	praise
hit	lie	naughty	pray
hole	like	new	present
holiday	lion	nice	president
homework	lipstick	nightmare	pretty
honest	little	nipple	prince
hope	lollipop	note	princess
horrible	lonely	nurse	principal
horse	lose	old	prize
hospital	love	operation	proud
house	lucky	ostrich	psychiatrist
hug	mad	owl	psychologist
hungry	make	paint	punish
hurt	make believe	parent	pupil
ice cream	magic	parrot	queen
ill	man	party	quiet
Indian	manners	pass	rat
insult	matches	pay	refrigerator

Table 10.3

respect	sleep	stone	train
reward	slob	story	treat
rich	sloppy	strong	tree
right	sly	student	trick
robber	small	stupid	tricycle
rotten	smart	suck	trip
sad	smell	surprise	truck
scaredy-cat	snail	sword	try
scary	snake	talk	turtle
school	sneak	teacher	ugly
scold	soap	teacher's pet	upset
scoutmaster	soldier	tease	vagina
scream	son	teenager	vomit
secret	song	telephone	water
secret plan	sore loser	television	weak
see	sorry	temper tantrum	weep
selfish	spanking	thank	whip
share	spear	therapist	whisper
sheep	spend	thief	win
shoot	spider	threaten	wish
shout	spit	thumb	wipe
shy	spoil	tickle	wolf
sick	sport	tiger	worm
silly	steal	toilet	worry
sissy	stick	tooth	worst
sister	stingy	touch	young
skunk	stink	toy	zoo

taminating effect of the eliciting stimulus, the specific choice of words is not vital. Occasional cards provide the child with extra reward chips ("You get two extra reward chips"), and these increase the child's excitement while playing the game. Used cards are laid aside and dramatizations are encouraged. Again, the child's responses are used as points of departure for therapeutic interchanges.

Clinical Example: The Case of Marc (The Man Who Picked the Big Coconuts Off the Palm Tree)   Marc came to treatment at the age of seven because of tics, excessive tension, and agitated behavior in the classroom. His mother, a very buxom woman, was quite seductive with him. Near the end of his first month in treatment the following interchange took place while playing *The Bag of Words Game.*

> *Patient:* I've got the word *tree.* Once there was a tree and it was a talking palm tree.
> *Therapist:* A talking palm tree. Go ahead.
> *Patient:* It was so full of coconuts that he couldn't even move or talk. He was too heavy. So one day it decided that it would quit and just try and make all the coconuts come off, but they wouldn't come off. So he looked around until he found somebody with a gun shooting birds, and he asked him if he would . . .
> *Therapist* (interrupts): Who is *he* now?
> *Patient:* He was just looking—the palm tree was looking around and he just found someone.
> *Therapist:* Oh, the palm tree wanted to get his own coconuts off?
> *Patient:* Yeah.
> *Therapist:* Okay. It was a *he* palm tree?
> *Patient:* Yeah.
> *Therapist:* And then he finally found someone with a gun.
> *Patient:* Yeah.
> *Therapist:* Okay.
> *Patient:* Who was shooting birds with a shotgun. But it wasn't easy because he just had to look around because he couldn't move. So he called him and he asked him if he would shoot them off. And he [the man] said, "I won't shoot them off, but I'll pick them off. I love coconuts." The end.
> *Therapist:* So what happened?
> *Patient:* And the lesson was if you're a palm tree and you have coconuts on you, you shouldn't just try and take them off, but if you're a palm tree there's nothing you can do.
> *Therapist:* Wait a minute. The lesson is if you're a palm tree, what?
> *Patient:* There's nothing to do except stay where you are just like other trees.
> *Therapist:* And don't do what?
> *Patient:* Don't try to take your coconuts off.
> *Therapist:* Why not?
> *Patient:* Because they're supposed to come off theirselves.
> *Therapist:* I see. So what was the trouble? Did this palm tree get into any kind of trouble by having this man shoot the coconuts off?
> *Patient:* The man said that "I wouldn't, um, I won't shoot them off but I'll pick them off because I love coconuts."
> *Therapist:* So he picked them off.
> *Patient:* Yeah.

Therapist: The man picked off the coconuts. I'm not clear what the lesson is.

Patient: The lesson is that if you are a palm tree you shouldn't want to make your coconuts come off because they'll come off themselves and all that you should do is stay where you are just like other trees.

Therapist: Hh hmm.

Patient: They don't move.

Therapist: Okay. Now it's my chance.

Although Marc represented the tree as male, I considered it to represent his mother. The coconuts, being round and filled with milk, well serve as a breast symbol. They are high up on the tree and inaccessible. The central theme of the story is whether or not the coconuts will be made available to those on the ground. We are told that the tree was so full of coconuts "that he couldn't even move or talk." This, I believe, represented Marc's view of his mother as being buxom and that her breasts were the most prominent part of her anatomy. Marc's mother was well-endowed in this area and was a very seductive woman, as well.

The man with the gun, I believe, represents Marc's father. He has a powerful phallus which somehow enables him to gain access to the coconuts, that is, the mother's breasts. There is some ambivalence on Marc's part regarding whether or not the coconuts should come off the tree. The tree asks the man to take the coconuts off (with the help of his powerful weapon), but the man refuses to shoot them off. Rather, he decides to pick them off stating, "I love coconuts." Although Marc's presentation is somewhat confusing, the main element that comes through is that the tree is advised not to encourage premature removal of the coconuts; rather, it should wait until they come off naturally.

In essence, I considered this story to reflect Marc's wish that his father not have such ready access to his mother's coconuts, that is, her breasts. He would prefer that she withhold them from access to him as long as possible. However, he sees his father as having the power to get them at his will; but he gets his father to take them by hand, rather than with a gun. Possibly, this represents Marc's fear that his father might destroy the coconuts and then they would be completely unavailable to him. If his father has to get the coconuts he might as well preserve them. However, Marc would much prefer the tree to be less receptive to the father's ready access to them. The story reveals, as well, his appreciation that his mother wishes to provide the father access, and this is symbolized by the tree's wishing that the coconuts would come off. It was with this understanding of Marc's story that I related mine.

Therapist: Okay. Now it's my chance. (picks card from bag) I've got the word *boy.*

Once upon a time there was a palm tree and this palm tree had many coconuts on it, and there was a boy who lived next door to the property where this palm tree was. He used to look up at that palm tree and he would say, "Boy, those would be great coconuts to have. That would be terrific if I could have those coconuts. I'd like to get them off that tree. I'd like to split a couple open and eat the coconut and drink the milk that's in the inside and . . . "

Patient: (gestures to speak)

Therapist: Do you want to say something about that?

Patient: I just wanted to say that I hate coconut trees.

Therapist: You hate coconut trees. Anyway . . .

Patient (interrupts): Coconut juice!

Therapist: Anyway, in my story this boy liked coconut juice and he liked those coconuts, and he used to eye those coconuts every day. And one day he thought, "Gee, it would be great to get those coconuts." But he knew they belonged to the man next door.

So one day—he knew that if he went on the property there or tried to climb the tree to pull down those coconuts the man would get very angry. So one day he thought he would get a gun, and probably shoot down some of those coconuts. Anyway, as he was taking aim to shoot down a coconut, just at that moment, the owner of the house—the owner of the coconut tree—came out and he saw the boy and he said, "What are you doing, Sonny?"

He said, "Oh . . . I . . . uh." He was really trying to think of some kind of a lie but he really couldn't because it was obvious what he was really doing and he sort of had to confess that he was going to try to shoot down the coconuts.

Patient (interrupts): I know what he could say.

Therapist: What could he have said?

Patient: He could have said that he was trying to shoot down birds.

Therapist: Well, the man could see that he was aiming directly at the coconuts and he wouldn't have gotten away with that story. So he had to kind of confess that he was trying to shoot down the coconuts.

And the man said to him, "I'm very sorry. Those coconuts are mine. I'm not letting you shoot them down. But there are two things that we can do. One, I'll give you one of the coconuts because there are lots of coconuts on my tree. However, my suggestion to you is that you plant your own coconut tree or save up some money and buy some coconuts from a store or buy some coconuts from someone else because I'm not selling any." What do you think the boy did?

Patient: He did what the man told him to.

Therapist: What did he decide to do?

Patient: He decided to save up his money and buy more coconuts or buy it from somebody else.

Therapist: Right. He got a job as a newspaper delivery boy and saved up some money and bought some coconuts. In addition, every once in a while the man let him have some of his coconuts and let him know that those were really his and he couldn't have them, but that he could have a little bit. But the main thing was that the boy learned that he couldn't get them from the man so he had to get them elsewhere.

And the lesson of that story is: If you like coconuts and the coconuts you like are owned by another person, ask him. Perhaps he'll give you some or a little bit. But if he won't give you all, which is usually the case, because nobody is going to give you all the coconuts he owns, then try to get them elsewhere, like earning some money and buying some, or planting your own coconut tree. That's the lesson of that story. Anything you want to say about that story?

Patient: (nods negatively)

Therapist: Did you like that story?

Patient: (nods affirmatively)

Therapist: Good. What was it about the story that you liked?

Patient: Well, the coconuts.

Therapist: What was the main thing about it that you liked?

Patient: When he was trying to shoot down the coconuts.

Therapist: Hh hmm. Okay. When he was trying to get down the coconuts. Okay.

In my story I tried to communicate to Marc the fact that his mother's breasts were his father's possession. However, he could have some physical gratifications with her, but only to a limited extent. The father, however, does not react punitively. Rather, he is willing to allow Marc some of these physical gratifications, but encourages him to seek them elsewhere through his own efforts, both in the present and in the future. This is typical of the kinds of story I utilize in helping youngsters resolve oedipal problems.

In Chapter Eight I discussed my views on the Oedipus complex. I stated that, when I do see oedipal problems in boys, they are generally the result of maternal seductivity, with or without paternal castration threats (overt or covert). In Marc's case, his mother was extremely seductive. She wore low-cut blouses, tight fitting clothing, invariably used perfume, and spent significant time at beauty parlors. In addition, she undressed in front of Marc up to the time he began treatment. In my responding story, I introduced the element of sharing. As mentioned, this is a central factor in the resolution of oedipal problems. My telling Marc that the man (equals father) will occasionally allow him to have *some* coconuts, but he must get most of those he wants elsewhere through his own efforts, is a way of giving Marc some oedipal gratifications, but to a limited degree. It was not that I was going to actually encourage Marc to caress (pick) his mother's breasts; rather, I was only suggesting with symbolism that he could get some kind of physical and possessive gratifications in his relationship with her. I do not recommend, however, that Marc wait until he is an adult; rather, I suggest that he obtain at that time substitute gratifications elsewhere. And these are important elements in my helping boys deal with oedipal problems.

SCRABBLE FOR JUNIORS

Whereas in the standard game of adult *Scrabble** the players form their words with letter tiles on a blank playing board, in the child's version, *Scrabble for Juniors,*† simple words are already printed on the board and the child attempts to cover the board letters with his or her own letter chips (Figure 10.4). In the modification of the *Scrabble for Juniors* game devised by N.I. Kritzberg and myself, all the letter tiles are first placed face down along the side of the playing board. The patient and the therapist then select seven letter tiles each and place them face up in front. The game proceeds with each player in turn placing two letters over those on the board. The patient is advised to try to so place the letters that he or she will be working toward the completion of a word. The player who places the last letter necessary to finish a word (this need not be the final letter of the word, it can be anywhere in the word) receives a reward chip. If the player can say anything at all about the word, he

*Manufactured by Selchow & Richter Co., Bay Shore, New York.
†*Ibid.*

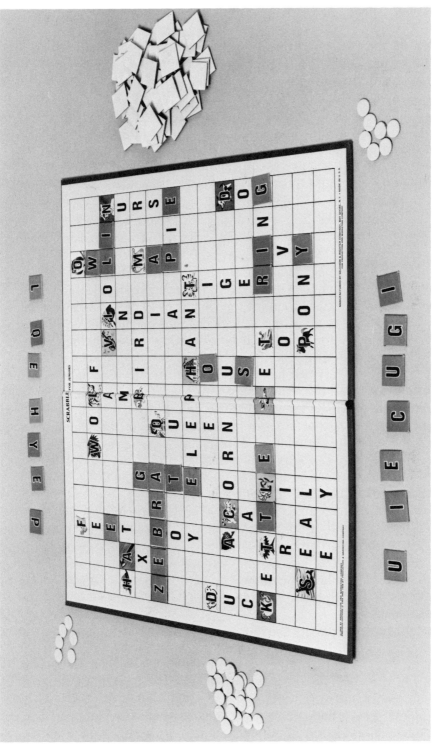

Figure 10.4

559

or she gets a second reward chip. And if the child can tell an original story about the word, he or she gets two extra reward chips. (Accordingly, the maximum number of chips obtainable for completing a word is four.)

Generally, I try to let the patient be the first to complete a word in order to learn those issues that are uppermost in the child's mind at that time. This information enables me to relate more meaningful communications when my turn comes to comment on or tell a story about a word that I have completed. Because the players' letter tiles are placed face up, I can see what letters I can place on the board that would make it most likely for the patient to complete his or her word first. In addition, I may fail to complete a word that I am capable of and "by mistake" use the letter elsewhere. Although I, like most therapists, am a firm believer in being totally honest with my patients, there are times in child therapy when a little duplicity is justified because it serves the purposes of the child's treatment.

Sometimes children will focus on a particular word on the board and try to complete it because they are especially eager to tell a story about it. In such situations the therapist can be fairly certain that the word has triggered significant associations. More often, however, the child's choice of a word is dependent upon the letters he or she happens to choose. In addition, most children tend to favor words that are closest to their side of the playing board. In spite of the drawbacks implicit in these determinants of the words chosen, my experience has been that the completed word will generally be used in the service of expressing those issues most pertinent to the child at that time.

Again, the winner is the player who has accumulated the most chips at the end of the allotted time. A slow pace is encouraged so that the words, comments, and stories can serve as points of departure for discussion. Dramatizations are also encouraged during the course of play. The game is useful from the late first-grade to about the fourth-to-fifth-grade level. Older children find the words too "easy."

My attempts to use the standard adult *Scrabble* game with older children have not worked out well. They tend to get much too involved in the point values of the various letters and so swept up in the strongly competitive elements in the adult version that comments and storytelling tend to take a secondary role. Accordingly, I do not have adult *Scrabble* available in the office as one of the games the child can choose to play. Also, the child is no match for the adult because of the latter's larger repertory of words. If the therapist then plays with full conviction and honesty, the child will be demeaned. If the therapist feigns ignorance to equalize the game, the strongly competitive factors intrinsic to the game will still serve to contaminate it for therapeutic purposes.

Clinical Examples

The Case of Cary (The Frog and the Seal)   Cary entered treatment at the age of ten because of a number of difficulties—mainly interpersonal. He refused to fight back when teased or picked upon and so was easily scapegoated, even by younger children. The only way he was able to attract friends was to beg them to come to his house where his parents had always made sure there was a plethora of toys and attractive games. He was very fearful of new situations and would often be unable to fall asleep for two or three nights prior to an anticipated event.

During his third session we played *Scrabble for Juniors*.

Therapist: Now Cary has finished the word *lily* for which he gets a chip. Now, wait a minute, hold it; don't go on yet. If you can say anything at all about the word *lily*, you get a second chip—anything at all.

Patient: What do you mean?

Therapist: Just say anything at all about a lily, any sentence which includes the word *lily*.

Patient: A lily grows on a pond.

Therapist: A lily grows on a pond. Okay, so you get a second chip. Now, if you can make up a story about the word *lily*, any story at all, but it must be completely made up from your own imagination, then you get two more.

Patient: Once a frog sat on a lily in the swamp and then the frog jumped off onto another lily.

Therapist: All right, that's a good beginning of a story, but that's not a whole story. A story has a beginning, a middle, and an end.

Patient: Hhmmm. I can't think of one.

Therapist: Well, try. See, if I can tell a story about a lily I can get two as well, although you end up with four, I can end up with two. So, you know, the person who has the most chips wins, so if I can tell a story about a lily I can get two and then we'd be even.

Patient: What I said was a beginning. Right?

Therapist: Okay, well, say it again. The frog jumped . . .

> *Patient:* A frog jumped on a lily in the swamp and then it jumped off to another lily.
> *Therapist:* Okay.
> *Patient:* And then—and then the lily started floating down the pond.
> *Therapist:* Okay.
> *Patient:* Then there was this waterfall and the lily fell right into the waterfall.
> *Therapist:* The lily fell into the waterfall?
> *Patient:* Hh hmm.
> *Therapist:* And the frog was on it?
> *Patient:* (nods affirmatively)
> *Therapist:* Then what happens?
> *Patient:* The frog died.
> *Therapist:* Okay, you get two for that. Now . . .
> *Patient* (interrupts): I still have one more letter to go.
> *Therapist:* Okay, yeah, but now it's my chance to tell a story. You put it down later. I can get two for telling a story about a lily.

I considered the frog to symbolize Cary. His being on a lily pad is a reflection of Cary's feeling that his situation is an unstable one and that he could easily "sink." Worse, he could meet his doom and be helpless to prevent his demise. Floating down the river and being killed by being thrown over the waterfall is a poignant statement of his feelings of impotence with regard to the destructive forces of the world.

It was with this understanding of Cary's story that I related mine.

> *Therapist:* Once there was a frog and he jumped on a lily pad and he noticed that the water was kind of moving, that it wasn't just a stagnant pond. The water was kind of moving and he saw that the water was moving kind of rapidly. It became more and more rapid and then he heard some noise and it sounded like a waterfall, and he realized that the lily was moving toward a waterfall. So he leaped off onto another pad and then leaped to another one, and leaped from pad to pad until finally he got to shore. He went along the shore and there he saw that there really was a waterfall and he was glad that he had looked around and was careful and had avoided the catastrophe of going over the waterfall.
>
> And the lesson of that story is: Look around you and listen. It may help you avoid trouble.

In my story I tried to impress upon Cary the fact that he has the capability to protect himself against the dangers of the world; that if he uses his senses and utilizes foresight he can prevent many of the calamities that may befall him. Cary was clearly not trying very hard to deal with his difficulties and my hope was that my story might contribute to his taking a more active role in solving his problems.

The game continued.

> *Therapist:* You got the word *seal.* You get one chip for the word *seal* and another one if you can tell something about the word *seal.*
> *Patient:* I once saw a seal.
> *Therapist:* Okay. Two more for a story.
> *Patient:* There were two seals swimming in the Atlantic Ocean and they were swimming really far out and they would have fun. They were playing around and one time the seal—there was this big fish and the seal saw it and started to swim away and the big fish saw it and went and tried to eat it.
> *Therapist:* Tried to eat one of the seals? Yeah, go ahead.
> *Patient:* And then they went over a rock and then the fish hit a rock and the seal got away.
> *Therapist:* Wait a minute, now. Thre were two seals. Right?
> *Patient:* Right.
> *Therapist:* And were any of them hurt by the big fish or what?
> *Patient:* No, the big fish was hurt.
> *Therapist:* Oh, the big fish hit a rock and that's why the seals got away?
> *Patient:* Right.
> *Therapist:* And they weren't hurt at all?
> *Patient:* Right.
> *Therapist:* I see. Okay. Now it's time for me. Did you take your two chips?
> *Patient:* No.
> *Therapist:* Take two chips for that.

In this story the seals, who represent Cary, are confronted with a big fish who tries to eat them. The latter represents, I believe, Cary's tormenting peers and all others who may be hostile to him. The problem of their attacking him is readily solved without any effort on Cary's part. The pursuing fish conveniently hits a rock and the seals get away. The story reflects Cary's wish that his problems will be neatly solved by external events favorable to him, with no effort on his part necessary to bring about the desired changes in his situation.

With this understanding of Cary's story, I responded.

Therapist: Once upon a time there were two seals. They were out in the ocean there swimming and all of a sudden this big fish came along and the fish started to attack them. Now that was kind of foolish of that fish because these were two seals against one fish, and they were very good friends and they started to fight this big fish. And the first seal was really happy that he had such a good friend because this good friend helped him fight the big fish. In addition, all of a sudden they saw a rock near the shore and they took this rock and they threw it right at the big fish—they threw it right at the big fish. And this hit the big fish right on the head and that big fish then swam away and they got rid of that guy, and they were glad that they had fought him.

One of the fish would have hoped that the big fish might swim into a rock or something like that and in this way they would be able to avoid a fight, but the second one said, "Listen, that's not going to happen. Those big fish don't swim into rocks. He has eyes and he has fins and that's not going to happen to him. If we want to get rid of him we've got to hide and throw some rocks at him." And that's exactly what happened.

And the lesson of that story is: If you are a seal and if a big fish is trying to bite you, there are two things you can do, among other things. You can have a friend and the two of you can fight the big fish or you can do some things, like throw rocks at that fish. But don't just sit back and hope that the big fish will swim into a rock and hurt himself and then go away. Things like that just don't happen. The end.

Okay, I get two chips for that.

In my story I attempted to impress upon Cary the fact that his somewhat magical solution to his problem of being scapegoated was unrealistic. The seal who hopes that the fish will hit a rock and thereby cease his pursuit is dissuaded from this passive and dangerous way of handling the situation. Rather the seals fight, and are successful in driving away their tormentor. In addition, they make use of the strength they have in numbers. In this way I hoped to provide Cary with the motivation to make friends, in part, that they might serve as his allies against those who bullied him.

The Case of Timothy (The Seal and the Cat)   Timothy entered treatment at the age of nine and a half because of severe behavior problems in school. He was disruptive in the classroom and irritated both his teacher and other children with his antics. A mild neurologically based learning disability was present; however, this was only a small contribution to his academic difficulties. In addition, his parents had been separated but did not get divorced and had been living apart for two years. His father, although consistent in providing for his family's financial needs, was erratic with regard to his visits. When he did come to the home, his relationship with Timothy was poor in that he had little interest in those things that involved Timothy.

After about a year and a half of therapy Timothy exhibited significant improvement in his classroom behavior and, in addition, was able to handle better the angry feelings he felt toward his father. Specifically there was far less displacement of such anger toward classmates and a healthier adjustment to the reality of his relationship with him. It was during this period that the following interchange took place while playing the *Scrabble for Juniors* game.

> *Therapist:* Okay, you finished the word *seal* for which you get one reward chip. If you can say anything at all about the word *seal* you get a second chip.
>
> *Patient:* Once upon a time there was a seal . . .
>
> *Therapist (interrupts):* No, no, no. That's a story. First, just say anything at all about the word *seal*—just a statement about the word *seal*.
>
> *Patient:* The seal is an animal that lives in the cold.
>
> *Therapist:* Okay, you get one for that. Now, you can tell a story about the word *seal*.
>
> *Patient:* Once upon a time there was an Eskimo hunter who was going to catch a seal and there was a couple of the seals. This one seal said, "I'm too smart for that guy." And like he, um, uh—so he put some bait, you know, kind of like fishing, you know, fish and he got the bait and he caught the seal, and the seal was, you know, he killed the seal or put him in a zoo, more or less, put him in the zoo.
>
> And in the zoo he didn't have as much fun. He was in the zoo, you know, bored.
>
> *Therapist:* Hh hmm.
>
> *Patient:* He couldn't catch his own fish and stuff so he was bored. That's where I quit. That's my story.

Therapist: That's the whole story. Lesson?

Patient: That don't think you're so smart on catching in traps.

Therapist: Don't think you're so smart . . . ?

Patient: Don't think—don't be so sure in traps.

Therapist: Can you be a little bit more specific?

Patient: Like, um, don't . . . that's what I really mean . . . don't, uh . . .

Therapist: Don't what?

Patient: Just because you see a little piece of bait lying out you don't just get it.

Therapist: Hh hmm.

Patient: Because it might be led to a trap.

Therapist: Hh hmm. Okay, you take two chips.

Patient: I got two chips already.

Therapist: You got one for completing the word *seal* and saying seals live in the cold. Take two more for the story. Okay.

I considered the seal to represent the patient and the Eskimo trapper those around him whom he considers to be malevolent. There is a healthy element in the story in that the seal's wise-guy attitude is being criticized. However, the seal does get caught and this, I believe, is a statement of the patient's feeling that he is somewhat helpless to protect himself from those who would be malevolent to him. Being put in the zoo symbolizes, I believe, the patient's feeling that he is entrapped by overwhelming forces.

With this understanding of the patient's story, I related mine.

Therapist: Now wait a minute. It's my chance to tell a story now. Okay, you want to wait.

Patient (proceeding with the game): Yeah.

Therapist: Just hold up. Now I tell a story about the word *seal* and I can get two chips for it. Once upon a time . . . actually you get one for getting the word, one for saying something about it, and two for the story. Okay?

Patient: (nods affirmatively).

Therapist: Now I go. I get two if I can tell a story.

Once upon a time there was a seal and this seal lived up north where it was cold and there were Eskimos who were constantly trying to capture seals. So this seal's mother and father said to him, "Now listen, you know the Eskimos are out to catch us and we have to be very careful. We have to watch out for their traps and watch out for their bait."

Well, this seal was kind of a wise guy and he said, "Ahh, I don't have to watch out for their bait. I don't have to watch out for their traps. I don't have to watch out. Nothing is going to happen to me."

So whereas the other seals listened very carefully to their teachers and their mothers and fathers regarding the kinds of traps the Eskimos used and the kinds of bait that they used, this seal didn't. And sure enough, one day he got caught in a trap, but fortunately only his fin got caught. He was able to pull himself out of it and he got away. And he had his fin, his little paw—I don't know what they call them—the seals have little flappers. His flapper was . . . (to patient's mother) what do they call it?

Patient's mother: Flipper.

Therapist: Flipper. His flipper had a little piece of flesh nipped off, but otherwise he was all right. And he came back to his parents and he was bleeding, leaving a kind of trail of blood, but they managed to fix him up.

And for the rest of his life he remembered that little experience and every time he looked at his flipper and saw the scars there it reminded him to be careful. And, of course, after that he learned very much about the kinds of traps that Eskimos have and how to avoid them.

And what do you think the lesson of that story is?

Patient: It's your story, not mine.

Therapist: Okay, the lesson of that story is that often it pays to learn about the things that can be useful to you in life and that can often save you a lot of trouble. The end.

Patient: You can see the scar on his flipper. Nothing was . . . nothing was . . . he didn't have anything cut off.

Therapist: No, no. Just a . . .

Patient (interrupts): . . . scar.

Therapist: A scar and a little piece of tissue was taken out, but the scar filled that up. Okay, I get two chips.

In my story, I confirmed the healthy element in Timothy's story by reiterating the inappropriateness of the wise-guy attitude. However, in my story the seal, although scarred, learns that one can avoid certain dangers by considering their possibility in advance. The scar serves as an ever-present reminder of his trauma and helps him remember to avoid difficulties throughout the rest of his life. My main message here, of course, was that one need not be helpless with regard to dangers that may be present; one has the power to avoid them if one wishes to attend to them. I was referring here not only to the patient's classroom difficulties but to his problems with his father as well.

Subsequently, the following interchange took place.

Therapist: Okay, you completed the word *cat*. Wait, you get one chip for the word *cat*.

Patient: A cat is an animal. It's a smaller animal related to the lion.

Therapist: Okay, now you get. . . .

Patient (interrupts): Then there's tigers; zee, um, chet . . . cheetahs and jaguars are all cats.

Therapist: All right, now if you can tell a story about the word *cat* you get two more.

Patient: Once upon a time there was a cat and the cat really liked these people, you know. They didn't think—they didn't like him, you know. They. . . .

Therapist (interrupts): Wait. The cat liked the people, these people?

Patient: Yeah.

Therapist: Go ahead.

Patient: And it kept on . . . (mumbles) . . .

Therapist: What?

Patient: And the cat didn't like the people . . . the cat liked the people, you know. The people didn't like the cat and the cat's an old bugger.

Therapist: Wait. The cat liked the people, but the people didn't like the cat.

Patient: Yeah.

Therapist: Okay.

Patient: And, um, they'd tell the cat, "Get lost, you old cat." The cat came back the very next day. The cat would not stay away. Hey, that rhymes!

Therapist: Okay, go ahead.

Patient: And they did it again. They kept on doing it and doing it because the cat like was abandoned and he wanted someone to own him, you know, love him.

Therapist: Hh hmm.

Patient: And the cat . . . they'd kick it out and it kept on doing it and this cat came back (sings) the very next day. The cat would not stay away.

Therapist: Okay.

Patient: And, um, so the cat . . . so the cat foretold them, "Don't think that . . . " the cat . . . well, they looked around the place where there were rats, you know, rats and mice.

Therapist: Yeah, I'm not clear. What's that about rats and mice?

Patient: Well, the people lived around a place where there were rats and mice and stuff.

Therapist: Yeah.

Patient: And the cat killed them all, you know.

Therapist: Yeah.

Patient: The cat was hanging around and when the cat was hanging around there weren't any mice, so they decided, "Hey, that cat's really helpful. He gets rid of the rodents and stuff." So they got the cat and the moral of the story is like you don't just kick around someone because you don't like them, like they might be very useful and they like you. That's the moral of the story.

Therapist: Hh hmm. Okay. Okay. You get two for that. That was a very good story.

I considered the cat to represent the patient himself and the owner, his father. At first, Timothy is abandoned; however, when he proves that he has a worthwhile skill he is then reaccepted into the household. The story reveals the patient's lingering feelings of rejection; however, it also reveals his appreciation that one way that one can counteract rejection is to exhibit useful and ingratiating qualities. The fantasy, therefore, is a reflection of a healthy adaptation. However, it does reveal the fact that Timothy has not given up completely his hope to regain his father's affection. With this understanding of the patient's story, I related mine.

Therapist: Okay, now it's time for me to tell my story. Once upon a time there was a cat and he lived with this man and this man decided that he didn't like this cat too much. The cat was all right in some ways, but he decided that he didn't want him. So he told the cat to leave. And the cat went out and he was very unhappy. He said, "Aw, come on, let me come back and live with you."

The man said, "Ah, you're no use."

And the cat said, "I'll show you. I'll show you that I can be useful. You don't like me anymore and you won't let me live with you anymore. Okay, we'll see."

Anyway, the cat went to a nearby house and there were some people there who were really having a lot of trouble with mice and rats and things like that. And he said to them, "You know, I can be very helpful to you in killing off these mice and rats."

And they said, "You can? Would you come to live with us?"

And he said, "You people look like you'll appreciate me." So he went to live with these other people and he was very useful, and they gave him a good home, they gave him good food, and they gave him a good place to sleep.

And then the other man that he had left realized that he had made a mistake in sending this cat off, but it was too late. The cat had already lived with these other people, but he saw his first owner once in a while. He would see the old owner once in a while and the old owner realized that he had made a big mistake in sending this cat off, but it was too late. The cat had another home. And the cat realized a very important lesson, which was what?

Patient: It's your story!

Therapist: Okay, the lesson is that if someone doesn't like you or, you know, may like you very little, it doesn't mean that no one else in the whole world will like you. There are always other people in the world who can appreciate the good things in you. The end.

Anything you want to say about that story?

Patient: (nods negatively)

Therapist: Okay.

Whereas in Timothy's story, his father's appreciation of him and reconciliation with his father are accomplished, in my story there is no reconciliation. To foster such reconciliation would have been unrealistic because of the long period that the patient had been separated from his father and the fact that there was absolutely no reason to believe that the father was going to return to the home. However, I did emphasize the ingratiating qualities that the patient possessed so as to reinforce this element from his story.

More significantly, however, in my story the cat finds love and affection in another home but still maintains some relationship with the previous owner. My attempt here was to help Timothy appreciate that others can show him affection in compensation for the deprivations he suffers in his relationship with his father. This need not mean, however, that he has to break completely his relationship with his father; rather, he can maintain gratifying relationships with a number of individuals.

THE FEEL AND TELL GAME

In the three grab-bag games, the bags are open at the top and the child merely retrieves an item from the bag. In *The Feel and Tell Game* (Figure 10.5) objects are placed in a double canvas bag bound at the top. On the outside of the bag are written the words FEEL

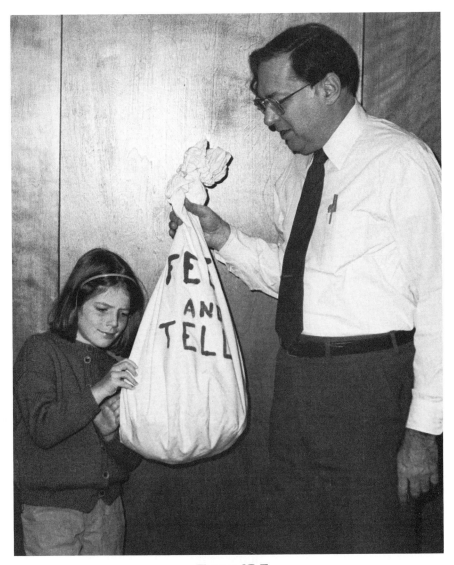

Figure 10.5

AND TELL. The child is merely asked to feel an object through the double canvas bag and state what he or she believes the object to be. Because the bags are bound at the top, the child cannot stick his or her hand inside the bag in order to identify the object. A chip is given for merely stating what the child guesses the object to be. It is not necessary for the child to identify accurately the object; it is only necessary for the child to make a guess regarding what the object *might* be. Because the objects have been selected for their amorphous shape or unusual configuration, it is not likely that the child will identify most of them correctly.

The child obtains one chip for making a guess (any guess will do), a second for making a statement about the object, and a third for telling a story about the object. The game, in a sense, can be considered a "tactile projective game." The more successful the examiner is in utilizing objects that are amorphous, the greater the likelihood the child's projections will be the primary determinant of what he or she considers the object to be. Accordingly, the examiner does well to select objects that are not easily identifiable while being felt through a double canvas bag. Often, junk items that should have been thrown out long ago serve well for this purpose. In Figure 10.6 the reader is shown those objects that I utilize in my *Feel and Tell Game.* I am sure that most people have similar collections of junk objects that can now be put to good use.

Clinical Example

The Case of Mary (The Kangaroo in the Mother's Pouch)   Mary was referred for treatment at the age of nine because of fear of going to school. She was significantly dependent on her overprotective mother and presented with a typical picture of separation anxiety disorder. As is often the case in such families, her father was passive in his relationship with her mother and viewed the mother's overprotectiveness to be a manifestation of superior maternal capacity. Each morning, when Mary's mother would prepare her to go to school, she would complain of a variety of somatic difficulties: headache, stomach ache, nausea, fever, pain in the joints, and so forth. Typically her mother would indulge these complaints and often kept her home from school, even though there was rarely evidence for bona fide illness. During her second session, the following interchange took place:

> *Therapist:* Okay, Mary, here's how this game is played. I'll hold up this bag. What does it say on this bag?
> *Patient* (looking at the bag): Feel and Tell.
> *Therapist:* That's right. Now the way this game is played is that you have to try to figure out what's in the bag by just feeling it. Actually, it's a double bag and there's a string on the top so that you

Figure 10.6

can't put your hand inside. And you can't look inside either. You have to try to guess what's in the bag, or the two bags, by feeling through them. Okay, let's see you do it.

Patient (feeling the bag): I don't know what this is. What is it?

Therapist: As I told you, you're supposed to try to guess what *you* think is in there. There's no right answer. Just saying what you *think* is in there will get you a chip. Then you'll get another chip if you can say something about that thing. And then you'll get two more chips if you can tell a story about that thing. Okay, let's see you make a guess.

Patient (feeling different objects in the bag): I don't know what these things are. This one feels like a kangaroo. Yes, I think it's a kangaroo.

Therapist: That's a very good answer. You get a chip for that. (therapist gives the patient a chip) Now you can get another chip if you can say something, anything at all, about the kangaroo. Let's see you do it.

Patient: The kangaroo was in his mother's pouch.

Therapist: That's a very good answer. The kangaroo was in his mother's pouch. You get a chip for that. (therapist gives the patient another chip) Now let's see you tell a story about a kangaroo. It must be a completely made-up story. It can't be about anything that really happened to you or to anyone you know. It can't be from television or books. It has to be completely made up. Okay, let's see how good you are at making up a story about a kangaroo. If you can, you get two more chips.

Patient: Well, once there was this baby kangaroo. And he was in his mommy's pouch. He liked it there. The end.

Therapist: What you've said so far is a very good *beginning* for a story. But every story has a beginning, a middle, and an end. Now tell us the *middle* of your story. Go ahead.

Patient: I can't think of anything else. That's all I can think of.

Therapist: You know, if you want to get two chips, you have to tell a whole story.

Patient: That's all I can think of.

Therapist: Okay, you get one chip for that story, because it's only a part of a story. I hope that you'll be able to tell longer stories next time and then you'll get more chips.

Patient: Okay.

The fact that the patient envisioned a kangaroo is in itself of significance. The object she was feeling (a small, somewhat round teddy bear) in no way had the configuration of a kangaroo. The fact that she felt it to be a kangaroo is a statement of the power of the projective process. And this is an important principle for the therapist to appreciate when utilizing this game. The greater the disparity between the objects and the child's fantasy regarding its identity, the greater the likelihood that powerful forces are distorting the item for the purposes of satisfying unconscious needs. A kangaroo, of course, lends itself well to symbolizing a maternal figure. I consider it to be equal (if not superior) to the cow in this regard. The baby in the pouch (of course) symbolizes the patient and the kangaroo her mother. Although the story is a short one, it is, in essence, a complete story. The little baby kangaroo wants to stay in the pouch and remain indefinitely in a dependent state. That is essentially the whole story and when the patient initially said that it was the end of the story, I was basically in agreement with her. However, in the hope that I might get more material and elaborations, I encouraged her to add more to the story—but I was unsuccessful. With this understanding of the patient's story, I told mine:

> *Therapist:* Okay, now I'll tell my story. Once upon a time there was a kangaroo. And this kangaroo liked to stay in his mother's pouch. It was nice and warm in there and the nipples of her breasts were always next to him. Whenever he wanted to suck on the warm milk, he could do so. And his mother didn't mind his staying there, even though other kangaroos his age were already outside and not spending so much time in their mothers' pouches.
>
> Well, one day, while this kangaroo was resting comfortably in his mother's pouch, he suddenly heard some noises outside. They got louder and louder and he began wondering what they were. He stuck out his ear, above the edge of his mother's pouch, and he could hear other children kangaroos laughing, singing, and dancing, and having a lot of fun. Then he pulled himself up above the edge of the pouch and looked down to see what was happening down there. Then he saw all the kangaroo kids having a good time. The children kangaroos were jumping up and down and they were having a grand time, laughing, singing, and dancing, and things like that.
>
> Well, he wanted to join in the fun but he was scared to leave his mother's pouch. He was frightened that something terrible would happen to him out there. His mother was always telling him to play near her or to stay inside because there were rough kangaroos outside who might hit him. Also, she had warned him a lot about getting hit by cars, getting drowned, getting taken away by strangers, and even such things as getting stabbed and shot. And so, when he was thinking about leaving the pouch, he began to think about all these things his mother said could happen, all these terrible things that he didn't want to happen to him.
>
> Well, as he was thinking about these things, the other kangaroos

outside started calling up to him and asked him to come out of his pouch and play with them. The kangaroo told them that he was very busy and that he would come out some other time. But they could see, by the look on his face, that he was frightened. And so they started calling him "scaredy cat" and other names like that. They started yelling up, "Hah, hah, hah, the baby's afraid to go out and play" and other things like that. This made the kangaroo feel very embarrassed. He also felt very sad. He really wanted to go out and play and he really wanted the other kids to stop calling him names like that. (therapist now turning toward patient) So what do you think he did?

Patient: He just stayed in the pouch and didn't listen to the other children.

Therapist: Well, a part of him wanted to do that because he was scared to go out, and he wanted to remain in a safe place in his mother's pouch. However, another part of him wanted to go out and play with the other kids and join in the fun. Also, he didn't want the kids to be teasing him that way and calling him all those terrible names. So, he decided that he was going to try to go out of the pouch, even though he was very scared. And so, little by little, he pulled himself out of the pouch and little by little, more and more of him came out. As he was doing that, the little kangaroos outside were all cheering him for trying. And this gave him more confidence that he could do it. But, the more he was outside the pouch, the more scared he became. A few times he went back in, and then the other kangaroo children started laughing at him and calling him names. But, when he pulled himself out, they cheered him and that made him feel better. (therapist again turning to patient) So what do you think finally happened?

Patient: Well, I think that he was still too scared to get out.

Therapist: Do you think that's a good thing?

Patient: I don't know.

Therapist: Well, would you like to hear my opinion about that?

Patient: Yes.

Therapist: Well, in my opinion, it would have been better for the kangaroo to go out, even though he was scared at first. And that's exactly what happened. He finally got out. It took some time, but he finally did it. He was scared at first, but, after a while, he got used to being outside and he found that it was a lot of fun to play with the other kangaroos. And each time he did it, it was easier and easier, and that's how he got over being scared to play with the others and being scared of being out of his mother's pouch.

My story obviously needs no explanation. It encourages desensitization to a fearful situation and is part of the treatment of any child with fears.

THE ALPHABET SOUP GAME

The Campbell's Alphabet Soup Game* is packaged in a container that closely resembles a very large can of Campbell's tomato soup (Figure 10.7). The container is quite attractive and therefore readily appeals to the child who is looking over the toy shelves for a game to play. The equipment consists of a plastic bowl filled with plastic letters and two spoons. The modification that I have found most useful therapeutically is for both the patient and therapist to each scoop a spoonful of letters from the bowl and form a word with them. The patient (whom I generally allow to go first) gets a reward chip for having been able to form a word. If the child can say anything at all about the word, he or she gets a second reward chip. And if the child can tell a story about the word, he or she gets two extra reward chips. I then similarly respond to my word. The responses, of course, are used as points of departure for psychotherapeutic interchanges.

The game can then proceed in a number of ways. One variation is for the players to attempt to form other words from the same batch of letters in order to obtain more reward chips. When the player is no longer able to, he or she can take a second scoop by "paying" two chips to the bank. These can be added to the original group of letters (the preferable alternative because there are then more letters with which to form words), or serve as a replacement for them. Sometimes trading letters with one another adds to the enjoyment of the game. Or the two players can decide to trade their whole batch of letters with one another to see if they can form other words, not previously used. Whatever the variations utilized (and I am sure the reader can devise his own) the basic principle holds that a player gets one reward chip for the word, a second for a comment, and two more for a story. Again, the winner is the player who has received the most reward chips at the end of the allotted

---

*This game is no longer being manufactured. The interested reader, however, should be able to put together a reasonable facsimile. All that is necessary are two spoons, a soup bowl, 1″ plastic letters available in most toy stores, and a treasure chest of reward chips.

Figure 10.7

time. He or she, of course, receives one of the *Valuable Prizes* from the previously described box of prizes.

Clinical Example

The Case of Larry (The Boy Who Felt His Mother's Breasts)
Larry entered treatment at the age of seven and a half because of compulsive touching of walls and furniture. He was a very tense boy and intermittently exhibited tics of the neck and shoulders. On occasion his tics took the form of yawning and throat-clearing sounds. However, the verbal tics were not that prominent that one could justifiably consider him to have a Gille de la Tourette's syndrome. Excessive masturbation was also described by the parents. At the end of the initial interview, while I was standing and talking with the parents and Larry, he began to caress his mother's breasts. She continued to talk to me as if nothing were happening. When I brought this to the family's attention the father stated that he had not noticed that anything was happening and the mother said that Larry caressed her breasts on occasion, that it was an innocuous practice not associated with sexual excitation by either of them, and that she did nothing in response.

In my subsequent evaluation I found the father to be a man who compulsively spoke about sexual matters—especially in a humorous way. The mother was coquettish and undressed frequently in front of Larry. On one occasion, early in treatment, Larry wrote the following note to his mother: 'Fuck shiter old god damn mommy. Happiness is watching mommy pull her god damn fuckin pants down."

I considered Larry's tensions to be related to pent-up sexual excitation which could not be released directly. As expected, many of his stories revealed sexual and oedipal themes. My responding communications attempted to help him resolve his oedipal conflicts. During the second month of treatment the following interchange took place while playing *The Alphabet Soup Game.*

> *Therapist:* What word do you have?
> *Patient:* Jug.
> *Therapist:* Okay. Now you get one chip for completing the word jug. Now if you can say something about *jug* you can get another chip, and if you can tell a story about *jug* you can get two more chips.
> *Patient:* Don't you get—um, oh yeah.

Therapist: Go ahead.

Patient: Okay. I'm going to tell a story and. . . .

Therapist (interrupts): . . . and say something. Go ahead.

Patient: Okay. A jug could hold flowers.

Therapist: Okay, that gets another chip. A jug could hold flowers. All right. Now a story can get you two more chips.

Patient: Okay. Once there was a girl and she was picking flowers. She was cutting off flowers on one of her trees and . . . (pauses) . . .

Therapist: Yeah. Go ahead. And . . .

Patient: And she was putting it in her mother's jug. So . . . (pauses) . . .

Therapist: Go ahead.

Patient: And so when she was putting it in she brought the jug over so she could put in all the flowers that she got and it broke because she dropped it.

Therapist: What broke?

Patient: The jug.

Therapist: Okay. She dropped the jug, yeah, as she was putting the flowers in?

Patient: Yeah.

Therapist: Yeah. Go ahead. You don't have to wait for me. Go ahead. You tell your story.

Patient: And . . . (pauses) . . . she—so she—so she stopped to think and her friend and her friend's mother were going out to the flower shop and she—and that was the same flower shop where her mother bought the jug so the girl asked her friend's mother if she could go. And she said, "Why?" And she told her the story and then she went to buy her a new one. And so when they got back her mother was just coming back and then she put the same kind of flowers—she just—since she broke that one she cleaned it out and then the flowers that she picked out of the dirt she put in so that . . .

Therapist (interrupts): Oh, did they bring her another jug—this friend and the mother?

Patient: Yeah, but she went.

Therapist: She went with them. And she got another jug.

Patient: Yeah.

Therapist: Go ahead. And then what happened?

Patient: That's the end.

Therapist: And she put the flowers in?

Patient: Yeah.

Therapist: Okay. And the lesson of that story? What do we learn from that story?

Patient: That you should tell your mother if you do something or something bad happens. Or you shouldn't take a jug or a vase and, um, and bring it in the front but in the back you could just take another vase or make your own. You don't have to take your mother's vase or jug.

Therapist: You don't have to take your mother's vase or jug, or, or—

Patient: jug.

Therapist: —or jug. You can get another one. Is that it? I'm not clear what that last part is.

Patient: You can make one of your own or you can buy one, or if you have your own you should use your own.

Therapist: Hh hmm.

Patient: You shouldn't use your mother's.

Therapist: Hh hmm. You should use your own.

Patient: Yeah.

Therapist: Okay. Very good.

I understood the jug to represent Larry's mother's vagina. The flowers, which were taken from a tree, in this case I felt were phallic symbols. Although flowers are traditionally a female symbol, in this situation I considered them more likely to represent male genitalia in that they were inserted into a jug. In addition, their being taken off a tree suggests that Larry is acquiring his father's genitalia for his own purposes.

Although Larry represented himself as a girl in this story, I did not consider him to have a sexual orientation problem. Children will often represent themselves as a person of the opposite sex to disguise the figure and prevent realization that they are talking about themselves. As the girl consummates the sexual act, that is, as she inserts the flowers into the jug, it drops and breaks. I felt that this represented Larry's basic feeling that his mother's genitalia were "too hot to handle." By dropping the jug he avoids getting "burned," that is, suffering various anticipated repercussions for this "transgression." In addition, the jug's dropping represents his ambivalence about consummating the sexual act. Dropping the jug prevents the flowers from remaining in it.

He then acquires a jug on his own. I considered this to be a healthy step in the alleviation of his oedipal problems. By getting his own jug he gives up the quest for his mother's. I believe that this story revealed, in symbolic form, an appreciation of messages that I had communicated in previous sessions in which I advised Larry to consider alternative sources of gratification, both in the present and in the future. This, of course, is an intrinsic part of helping a child resolve oedipal difficulties.

With this understanding of the patient's story, I attempted to form a word from my own letters that would enable me to respond appropriately. This is the interchange that followed.

Therapist: Now it's my chance. Okay?

Patient: (nods affirmatively)

Therapist: Now I've got the word *box*, (spells) b-o-x. Now I get a chip for the word *box*. All right?

Patient: (nods affirmatively)

Therapist: And, let's see now, if I can tell something about the word *box* I can get a second chip. I'll say that a box—there are some boxes that are very pretty, very fine boxes. So I get a chip for that. Okay?

Patient: (nods affirmatively)

Therapist: Now if I can tell a story about the word *box* I get a third one. Right?

Patient: (trying to form new word with his letters)

Therapist: Listen, do you want to hear my story or do you want to try to make your word now? What do you want to do?

Patient: Hear your story.

Therapist: Okay, then leave this and then you'll try to make another word from your letters after I finish. Okay?

Patient: (nods affirmatively)

Therapist: Okay. Once there was a girl and she wanted to take some flowers off a tree and her mother had a very beautiful box— and this box had been given to the mother by the father—and the father told the girl that she could look at the box once in a while and she could use it once in a while, but that she couldn't have it for herself. It wasn't hers, that it was the mother's. It was a very fine, beautiful box.

Now one day the girl wanted to put the flowers in that box—the flowers that she had picked—and she was kind of scared about that. She was afraid that if she put the flowers in that box, that her father would really get very very angry at her and he might beat her, hit her, or punish her very severely. And so as she was putting the flowers in the box—and her hands were shaking—in fact, it was so much so that she almost dropped it, her hands were shaking so.

Her father came in and he said, "What are you doing?"

And she said, "I'm oh, I'm just using this box for some flowers." She had to tell him what she was doing. It was clear what she was doing.

And the father said, "You know what I told you about that box. That's not your box. That box belongs to your mother. You can use it a little while, but if you want to really keep those flowers, you'd better get your own. And you can use that box for a while to keep those flowers in, but I want you to go to a store with your own allowance and buy your own box and then you can transfer the flowers to that box from the one I gave your mother."

The girl wasn't too happy about it because she thought the box was quite beautiful and she said, "Gee, I wish I had a box like that someday."

And the father said, "Well, someday you may. There's no reason why you shouldn't and when you're older you may get one like that. At any rate now you can't have it. You can only use it a little bit once in a while."

And so she put her flowers in the box and then she went to the store. She took some of her allowance and some money she had saved and bought herself a box, and then put the flowers in that.

And do you know what the lesson of that story is?

Patient: (nods affirmatively)

Therapist: What is the lesson?

Patient: If somebody has something and you want it, you can't have it.

Therapist: Or they may let you use it a little bit, but you can go out and get your own. Do you know what the other thing is called when you get your own?

Patient: No.

Therapist: It's called a substitute. Do you know what the word *substitute* means? What does *substitute* mean?

Patient: Well, is it the kind of person who like when the teacher is absent a substitute comes in?

Therapist: Right! You get a substitute teacher. Right. Okay. So I get two chips for that one. Right?

Patient: Right.

Therapist: Okay.

Patient: I get 50¢ allowance.

Therapist: Who gets 50¢?

Patient: Me, and my brother.

Therapist: Yeah. What do you spend it on?

Patient: . . . (mumbles) . . .

Therapist: What?

Patient: I save it.

Therapist: Uh huh. Are you saving up for something?

Patient: Yes.

Therapist: What?

> *Patient:* At Woolworth's they have a motor that I want to get.
> *Therapist:* Hhmmm. Good. Okay. Let's turn this off.

In my story the box is very much the mother's. However, the girl (again representing Larry) was permitted to use it once in a while, that is, share mother's affection with father. I emphasized the fact in my story that the box is the mother's and that it was given to her by the father. In my story I introduced the element of Larry's fear of paternal retaliation if he were to take his mother's box and use it for himself. Although this issue did not come up specifically in Larry's story about the jug, I knew it to be one of his problems and a significant element in his tension. Because his story contained what I considered to be part of a healthy resolution of the oedipal conflict (namely, acquiring a substitute gratification), I decided to focus on what I considered a still-to-be-resolved element in Larry's oedipal difficulties.

In my story the father does not react punitively to Larry's "transgression." He does allow him to use the box once in a while. He encourages Larry, however, to purchase his own box with money saved from his own allowance. Here, I introduced the notion that Larry will have to apply himself if he wishes to get the same kinds of gratification from a woman that his father enjoys.

In helping a boy resolve oedipal difficulties I try to help him appreciate that his mother's affection must be shared with the father. He can get some physical contact with his mother but cannot enjoy the intense degree of intimacy that his father does. The younger the child, the less likely he is to appreciate that such intimacy involves sexual intercourse. However, the young child is generally not particularly interested in that kind of experience; rather, he is more interested in generalized physical contact, sole possession, and occasional physical pleasure.

We continued to play the game and it was now Larry's chance to form a word.

> *Therapist:* Okay. Now what word did you make?
> *Patient:* Gun.
> *Therapist:* Okay. You get a chip for the word *gun*. Now you can get a second one if you can tell a story with the word *gun*.
> *Patient:* Okay.
> *Therapist:* Or you can say something about the word *gun*. Do you want to say something about. . . .

Patient (interrupts): You need a license to have a gun.

Therapist: Okay. You need a license to have a gun. That gets a chip. Now a story.

Patient: Um. Once there was a man who had a gun and he found a spaceship—part of a —when he was in the ocean on a boat by himself 'cause he was fifteen years old. So. . . .

Therapist (interrupts): Did you say he was on a spaceship or he found a spaceship?

Patient: He found part of a spaceship in the ocean when he was on a boat because he's old enough to have his own boat.

Therapist: He found a spaceship in the ocean?

Patient: Part of it.

Therapist: It was floating in the ocean or it was underneath the ocean?

Patient: Floating.

Therapist: Okay.

Patient: Do you know, when a rocket blasts off if it has three stages the stages fall off them?

Therapist: Oh, so he found one of the stages.

Patient: You don't have a capsule, just a stage.

Therapist: Okay. So he found one of the stages floating in the ocean. Go ahead. Then what?

Patient: And he wanted it so he had a rope. So he took the rope and he tied it onto the boat and he tied it on to that part and he got on and he took the motor off of his motorboat and put it on the rocket ship, the stage of the rocket ship.

Therapist: Oh, he took the motor off his boat and he put it on the rocket ship.

Patient: Yeah.

Therapist: Okay.

Patient: So that would move and pull the boat. So when he was moving along he found he went deep, deep, deep into the ocean, all the way in. Out there there were sharks and whales and it was very rough. It was so rough that he fell off the rocket ship. So there was a shark in the water coming toward him; so there was only one thing that he could do. There was an island and the only problem was that it was full of snakes. So the rocket ship went down. So quickly he took the motor off and put it back on his boat. He started it up and he went past it, but he just got a little bite in his foot, and he went back home and he didn't want to go back in the ocean again. That's the end.

Therapist: Okay. And the lesson of that story?

Patient: If you have your own boat or if you're in the ocean and see something that you want, like something big, you can't have it unless it's like a toy gun or something. You can't take something big.

> *Therapist:* Oh, you can have a toy gun, but you can't have a big rocket stage. Is that it?
> *Patient:* Yeah.
> *Therapist:* Because? Hhmm? Because?
> *Patient:* Because it's too big and anyway there's nothing more you could do with it and there's no room for it.
> *Therapist:* Uh huh. Okay. Very good. You get two chips for that. Okay. Let's turn the tape recorder off while I try to get a word, and then I'll tell a story about my word.
> *Patient:* Turn it off.

In this story we again see strong oedipal themes. The patient wishes to hook his boat up to a rocket ship stage that is floating in the ocean and to be pulled around by it. He would take the motor off his own boat and attach it to the rocket ship stage. I believe that the rocket ship capsule probably represents Larry's father and that the stage that fell off it, Larry's mother. In essence, he has his father discard his mother and she is then available to him as she floats in the ocean. Larry's motor, as a symbol of his genitalia, is hooked up to his mother. However, it is she who pulls him around, and this, I believe, symbolizes his dependency rather than his sexual ties to her. However, the father once again appears—this time as a school of sharks and whales. He immediately "fell off the rocket ship" and tries to find safety on a nearby island. However, "the only problem was that it [the island] was full of snakes." Again, the punitive retaliating paternal figure appears to be ubiquitous. Accordingly, he flees from the scene suffering only a "little bite" in his foot. The story ends with his not returning to the ocean again.

This story is a dramatic statement of Larry's oedipal fears. The retaliating father is ever-present. However, his "bark seems worse that his bite" in that Larry suffers only a "little bite" in his foot. I believe that this represented an appreciation of my message given in the previous story that father will not be as punitive as Larry anticipates. In addition, in the "lesson" Larry sets his sights on smaller prey, namely, a toy gun—in other words, something closer to Larry's size and his ability to handle. One could argue that the rocket ship stage represents Larry's father's penis and that the story reveals Larry's desire to acquire his father's penis and his fear that such acquisition will be met by powerful and dangerous retaliation. This interpretation does not preclude my original. Rather, it is probable that both are operating simultaneously here. And, they are not inconsistent with one another in that they both serve the purpose of Larry's desire for a more intimate involvement with his mother. In short, if the rocket ship represents Larry's mother, the story reveals his attempt to "hook on" to her. If the rocket ship represents Larry's father's penis, the story reveals Larry's desire to acquire this large penis for the purposes of becoming more attractive to his mother so that he can "latch on" to her.

It was with this understanding of Larry's story that I responded as follows.

> *Therapist:* Now I've got the word *pet.* Okay?
>
> *Patient:* (nods affirmatively)
>
> *Therapist:* Now I get a chip for the word *pet.* I can get a second chip if I can tell a story about pets. Okay? Or a second chip if I can say something about pets. People like their pets and sometimes they don't want to share their pets, or they don't want to share their pets all the time. And now if I can tell a story about the word *pet,* I'll get two more chips.
>
> Once upon a time there was a man and he had a boat and he was riding his boat in the ocean—it was a motorboat—and he saw a stage of a rocket that was floating in the ocean. And he said, "Boy, it would be great to have that great rocket and then I could really zoom around the ocean here, zoom around the water, zoom around the island, and everything else."
>
> Well, he didn't know that the sharks who lived in that water and the snakes who lived on the islands had kind of adopted that stage—that rocket stage—as a pet. They liked it and they would swim around it. They would play in it and they would go inside it. The sharks would swim through it; the snakes would swim through it. And when this man put his motor on that stage, they got very upset and they said to him, "Listen, that's ours, that rocket stage. You can't have it. We'll let you play in it a little while, but you're going to have to get your own."
>
> Well, he said, "No, I want it all my own."
>
> And they said, "Listen, you can't have it all your own. It's ours. You can play with it a little bit." And he realized that the sharks meant business and the sharks and snakes were really kind of powerful.
>
> But he said, "Well, what can I do?"
>
> And they said, "Well, look at this ocean—we're near Cape Canaveral here and they fire off these rockets every once in a while and there are other stages here which fall into the ocean. Now we suggest you go over there and find out when they're going to shoot off the

next rocket and then you just take your boat out into the ocean along the path of the rocket, and I'm sure you'll be able to get a stage.''

So what do you think happened?

Patient: He got one.

Therapist: He got one! How did he get it?

Patient: He found out when the next rocket was going off and then one that fell.

Therapist: Right! That's exactly what happened.

Patient: Are you finished?

Therapist: Did you think I was finished?

Patient: Yeah.

Therapist: Yeah, I was finished, but I was just trying to talk about the lesson of it. That's what I was trying to do. What do you think the lesson of that story is?

Patient: Same as mine.

Therapist: What's the lesson?

Patient: In my story it was that if you want something, you can't have it if it's too big or something, like if it's very big and you just want it, like the rocket stages there's no use for it. You take it out of the water or something and there's no place to keep it.

Therapist: Hh hmm.

Patient: Or back in the water if you have a dock.

Therapist: Hh hmm. Well, in my story what does the man do when he finds out that the sharks and the snakes won't let him have that rocket, except that they'll let him play with it for a little while?

Patient: He has to get his own.

Therapist: Right, so that if you want a rocket stage and it's already adopted as a pet by sharks and snakes, then go and get another one. There are usually others around. The end.

Okay. Now I get two chips for that story. Look, I'll tell you. Would you like to watch some of this now?

Patient: Yeah.

Therapist: Okay, let's watch some of it now.

Patient (counting the reward chips): It's even.

Therapist: It's even. Right. So we both get prizes.

In my story the sharks and snakes do permit Larry to spend some time with their rocket ship stage. However, they are firm in not permitting him full ownership of it. However, they suggest that he acquire his own and inform him that there are many other rocket ship stages that fall into the waters because they are quite close to Cape Canaveral.

The post-story discussion revealed that Larry did appreciate my message. On the clinical level Larry did subsequently enjoy an alleviation of his tics and touching compulsion. I believe that interchanges such as those presented here played a significant role in the alleviation of his difficulties.

As mentioned earlier in this book, I consider less than one percent of all the patients I have seen to be suffering with what could justifiably be referred to as oedipal problems. All of the rest have problems which are better explained by other mechanisms. However, when I do see oedipal problems, very specific family problems are operative. As discussed in Chapter Eight, I consider oedipal difficulties to rest on a foundation of parental deprivation of affection. The child's preoccupation with possession of the opposite-sexed parent is related to the desire to compensate for the frustrations felt over not being given the affection, love, attention, guidance, and protection that it wants. Furthermore, there is usually some seductivity by the opposite-sexed parent but no sexual fulfillment. The child is titillated but not given sexual gratification. Accordingly, we are not dealing with sexually abused children; rather, we are dealing here with children who have parents who are sexually seductive, but not to the point of providing gratification. When the seductive parent is a mother, there may be castration threats (overt or covert) by the father. These are not necessarily present and are not, as Freud believed, an intrinsic part of the paradigm.

Larry's mother was very seductive with him. She allowed him to play with her breasts (through clothing) but denied that there was any sexual excitation for either her or him. Larry's father was observer to this practice and considered it innocuous. I believe the excitation so produced contributed to his tics and generalized tension. His father's compulsive talk about sexual matters also contributed to Larry's excitation, but I could not find therein specific evidence for castration threats. I did not consider Larry's problems to be the result of normal sexual cravings; rather, I considered them to be the result of specific family factors that engendered the development of the oedipal paradigm.

THE PICK-A-FACE GAME

Creative Playthings manufactured wooden plaques depicting various facial expressions (Figure 10.8). Although not designed specifically to be utilized as a therapeutic game, they lend themselves well to this purpose. Unfortunately, Creative Playthings is no longer

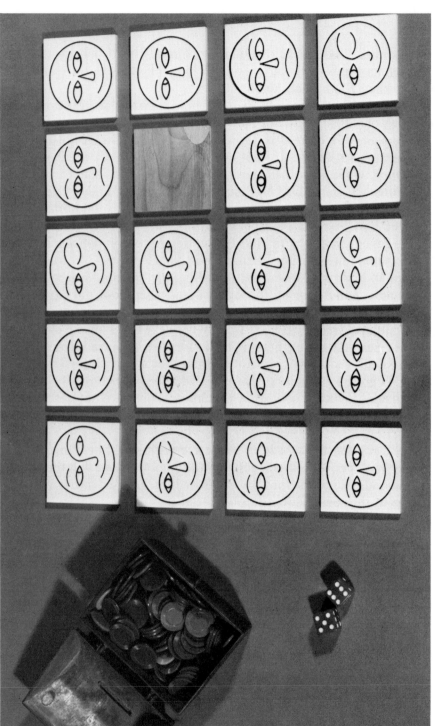

Figure 10.8

590

in business. The same game can be devised by mounting pictures of various facial expressions on small wooden plaques.

I have used these faces primarily as a mutual storytelling derivative game, which I call *The Pick-a-Face Game*. For this purpose, I use the plaques, a pair of dice (one side of which is covered), and a treasure chest of reward chips. The tiles are placed on the table face up (Figure 10.8). Each player in turn throws the dice and if a die lands with a covered facet up, that player is permitted to select any face. One point reward chip is then given. If the player can make a statement about the face, he or she receives another chip. And, if the player can tell a story about the face, he or she receives two more reward chips. Again, the material so elicited is used as a point of departure for a wide variety of therapeutic interchanges. Although these specific facial expressions might be restricting of free fantasy, my experience has been that they are not. A child will generally ascribe to them a wide variety of emotions that are likely to be present in most self-created stories. After a face is used, it is turned over. The person who has the most chips at the end of the allotted time receives one of the prizes.

Clinical Example

The Case of Gloria (Make Believe There's No Trouble, and You Won't Be Bothered By Things)   Gloria was eight years old when her parents brought her for treatment. The main problem was poor performance at school in spite of high intelligence. She spent most of the day in class involved in her own fantasy world. She was oblivious to her poor report cards, notes of complaint sent home by her teacher, and threats of parental punishment for her lack of commitment to her education. Gloria's father had his first heart attack at the age of 38 and his second at 44. Two years prior to the beginning of treatment, he had undergone a bypass operation. Both parents had made every attempt to cover up the import of the father's illness and had used a wide variety of ploys to protect her from the knowledge of his condition. In the first few months of treatment, I impressed upon them the importance of giving her accurate information. Although they complied with my request in this area, they did so without full conviction. The result was that Gloria continued to utilize the denial mechanisms she had learned from her parents. I believed that if they had had greater conviction for my recommendation, Gloria would not have been so denying.

In her fifth month of treatment, while playing *The Pick-a-Face Game*, the following interchange took place:

Therapist: Okay, the dice say you can pick a face. Which face are you going to pick?

Patient: I'm going to pick this one here. It's a smiling face.

Therapist: Okay. You get one chip for picking that face. (therapist gives patient a chip) Now you can get another chip if you can say something about that face.

Patient: He's smiling.

Therapist: What's he smiling about?

Patient: He's smiling because he's happy.

Therapist: What's he happy about?

Patient: He's just happy. He's not happy about anything. He's just happy.

Therapist: You can't just be happy about nothing unless you're a retard or something like that. You have to be happy about something.

Patient: Okay, he's happy because his mother bought him some ice cream.

Therapist: Okay, you get a chip for that. (therapist gives patient a reward chip) Now you can get two more chips if you can tell a story about that boy and his smiling, happy face.

Patient: Okay, let me think. . . . Once upon a time there was a boy. And he was a happy boy. He was a very happy boy. He was the happiest boy in the whole world. He got good grades in school. He got all As. He got As in conduct. The teacher said that he was a "pleasure to have in the class." And he was happy at home. Everything was good at home and he was happy there. And he had lots of friends who liked him very much. One day the family went on a picnic and they had a good time. They went home and the children watched television and then they went to sleep. The End.

Therapist: That was a fairly good story, but I've heard better ones. It didn't seem to have very many exciting things happen in it. Can you jazz it up a bit? Can you add things to make it more exciting?

Patient: I can't think of anything else.

Therapist: You know, in every family, both good things and bad things happen. What about this family? Did only good things happen to them? Or were there some bad things that happened also?

Patient: Only good things.

Therapist: Only good things? Nothing bad at all? Never at all?

Patient: Never at all.

Therapist: You know, in any family, things can happen like people getting sick or things like that. Didn't that ever happen in their family?

Patient: Well, once one of the children got the flu and had to stay home from school for a few days. But the parents were always okay.
Therapist: Anything else you want to say about that story?
Patient: No, I'm finished.

I considered the story to represent Gloria's significant utilization of denial mechanisms. The child in her story is doing well in school; Gloria was doing abominably. The family of the child in Gloria's story are all happy; all is going well with them; and neither of the parents is sick. This, of course, is opposite to what was the situation in reality for Gloria. With this understanding of Gloria's story, I proceeded as follows:

Therapist: Okay, it's my turn. The dice show that I can pick a face now. I'm going to pick this one. (therapist selects a face with a smile) Once upon there was a boy, named Jack, and he was always smiling. I didn't say that he was always happy; I only said that he was always smiling. In fact, he was the kind of a person who would smile even when he was sad, even when he was unhappy, even when he was *very* unhappy, even when he was *very*, *very* unhappy. In fact, Jack thought that the best thing to do about bad news was to make believe that it didn't exist, to make believe that it just wasn't there. Of course, that doesn't help anything because when you make believe that a problem isn't there—when it really is—then you don't do anything about the problem. Did you ever read any stories of mine that tell about people who do that kind of thing, people who don't talk about problems when they really have them?
Patient: No.
Therapist: Try to think hard. Don't you remember the stories I gave you?
Patient: No.
Therapit: Think again. When you first came here, I gave you a book and I told you to read the stories either by yourself or with your parents. Do you remember that book?
Patient: . . . Oh, yes.
Therapist: You remember the name of that book or what it was about?
Patient: There was some stories in it, but I don't remember.
Therapist: Do you remember one about an ostrich?
Patient: Oh, yeah, it was about an ostrich who put his head in the sand.
Therapist: No, it was just the opposite. Do you remember what it said about the ostrich and whether or not it put its head in the sand?

Patient: I don't remember. I thought he did when there was trouble.

Therapist: No, he does just the opposite. He wouldn't do such a stupid thing. When there's danger, the ostrich either looks at it and thinks what to do or runs away, but never makes believe that there's no danger. Only people think that way. And they think that ostriches do it that way also, but they don't. They're wrong. Do you remember that now?

Patient: Yes.

Therapist: Do you do that?

Patient: No.

Therapist: What about in school?

Patient: I don't think so.

Therapist: Well, I think you do. I think you make believe that there's no trouble in school, when there really is. What do you think about that?

Patient: Well, maybe I do it a little bit.

Therapist: Well, give me an example of a time when you do it, a time when you say you do it a little bit.

Patient: I don't remember now.

Therapist: Okay, I'll continue with my story about the boy Jack who was always smiling. One day Jack learned that his mother was sick and that she would have to go to the hospital. She was very sick and they thought she might die but they didn't know for sure. When Jack first heard the news, he was sad for a short time. Then, he pushed the whole thing out of his mind and began smiling. He just smiled and made believe that there was no trouble. His teenage brother, Fred, however, came up to him one day and asked him what he was smiling about. Jack said that he was very happy. His brother Fred said, "I don't know what you're so happy about, Mom's very sick."

Jack answered, "I don't want to talk about it. I don't want to think about it."

The big teenage brother Fred then said, "Well, I think you'd better think about it, because it's really going to be terrible around here if something bad happens to her, like if she dies."

Jack then began to scream and shout and said, "I told you, I don't want to talk about it."

Again, Fred told him that it was important to talk about it. Jack then ran off into his room and began to cry. As he lay in bed, he thought of himself out in the cold snow, starving and freezing, and that made him even more upset. Finally, his older brother Fred came into the room and heard him mumbling, "I'll freeze to death. I'll starve to death. No one will take care of me."

Fred then said, "I see now why you didn't want to talk about things. You think that if something happens to Mom that you'll freeze to death or starve to death, and there'll be no one to take care of you. But you've forgotten one important thing.

And Jack said, "What's that?"

And Fred said, "We still have a father. If something happens to Mom, we still have Dad."

As soon as Jack heard that, he felt better. He realized then that he had forgotten that his father would still be around and could be a *substitute* if anything happened to his mother. Do you know what a *substitute* is?

Patient: Yes, like a teacher, a substitute teacher.

Therapist: That's right, when your teacher is sick, you get a substitute teacher who takes over for her. And a father can be a substitute for a mother if the mother gets sick. Well, anyway, when the boy heard that, he realized that he had been stupid for not talking more about it and making believe that there was no trouble. And his teenage brother too helped him realize that it is important to talk about problems and that if you do, you can often do something about them and that if you don't, then they often get worse. Do you know what the lesson of my story is?

Patient: Talk about things.

Therapist: Right!

I cannot say that this was one of the most successful interchanges I've ever had with a child who exhibits denial mechanisms. However, a little progress was made. It takes many bricks to build a house and every brick contributes.

THE MAKE-A-PICTURE STORY CARDS

The Make-a-Picture Story Cards (MAPS) (Schneidman, 1947) is a valuable instrument. In fact, I consider it to be one of the most useful diagnostic and therapeutic instruments in the child therapist's armamentarium. First, I will discuss its standard use as a diagnostic instrument and then the modifications that I utilize for therapeutic purposes.

Diagnostic Utilization

The instrument consists of 22 cards (Figure 10.9) on each of which is depicted a scene, e.g. a doctor's examining room, the attic of a house, an empty street, a stage, an empty raft floating on the ocean,

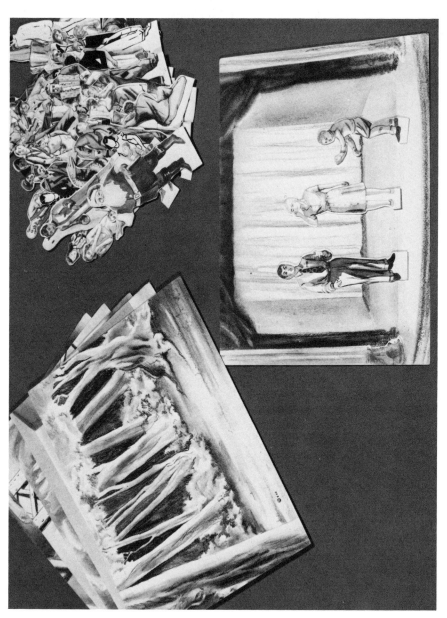

Figure 10.9

a forest, and so forth. In addition, there is a blank card. No figures, either animal or human, are present in any of the scenes. In addition, there is a collection of figurines, both human and animal. Some of the human figures appear to be typical family members, but others are readily identified as a pirate, clergyman, soldier, doctor, nurse, Santa Claus, superhero, and maid. A few animals are also included, such as a snake and a dog. The patient is asked simply to look through the pictures and select one. Next, the patient is asked to review the figurines, select one or more, place them on the selected scene, and then create a story. I consider the stories to be valuable sources of information about underlying psychodynamics.

As a diagnostic instrument, I consider *The Make-a-Picture Story Cards* (MAPS) to be superior to *The Thematic Apperception Test* (TAT) (H. Murray, 1936) and the *Children's Apperception Test* (CAT) (L. Bellak and S.S. Bellak, 1949), which it resembles. In the TAT and CAT the scenes, although designed to be somewhat vague, still include figures that are definitely recognizable. In the TAT one can state easily whether the depicted people are male or female, young, middle-aged, or elderly. In the CAT there is even greater specificity with regard to the activities of the various figurines (invariably animals). Accordingly, although there is a universe of possible responses to the TAT and CAT cards, there is still a certain amount of contamination of the child's fantasies by the eliciting stimuli. The MAPS pictures, however, are created by the child. Thus, there is less contamination than one has with the CAT or TAT instruments, and so there is a larger universe of responses that may be elicited. For this reason I consider the MAPS instrument to be superior to the TAT and CAT.

However, there is one major drawback to the utilization of the MAPS cards. Specifically, the facial expressions on all of the figures appear to this examiner to be somewhat grotesque, macabre, and hostile. At best, they are poorly drawn; at worst, they are morbid. My experience has been that one gets more hostile and morbid fantasies than would be obtained from more neutral and/or benevolent figurines. Accordingly, in order to offset the contaminating effect of this drawback of the instrument, I generally present the child with both the figurines provided by the manufacturer and my own set of small play dolls that I traditionally use in my work with children. When the instrument is used in this way, I have found that I get a better balance of fantasies.

Therapeutic Utilization

The MAPS cards lend themselves well to therapeutic utilization (Figure 10.10). All one needs to do is add the treasure chest of reward chips to the aforementioned equipment and one has what I consider to be an extremely valuable therapeutic game. The game begins with the child's being told that he or she will receive one chip for creating a picture by placing one or more figurines on the selected card. An additional chip is given for a statement about the picture and two more for a self-created story. Again, the therapist plays similarly and the material so elicited is used as a point of departure for a wide variety of psychotherapeutic interchanges. The winner is the person who has accumulated the most chips at the end of the allotted time.

Of the various mutual storytelling derivative games described in this chapter, I consider this one to be the most valuable. One of the problems with the other games is that the unconscious well appears to run dry quickly after four or five stories, and the material then elicited tends to be more stereotyped and less idiosyncratic. Somehow, the MAPS cards and figurines appear to give the unconscious "new ideas." However, with the MAPS these are less likely to be contaminations than with the other instruments; they are more likely to be catalysts for the expression of important psychodynamic themes.

Clinical Example: The Case of Ruth (The Army of Babysitters) Ruth entered treatment at the age of six, when she was in kindergarten, because of "hyperactivity and poor attention span." Because of these symptoms the school considered her to be suffering with a neurologically based learning disability. Although the school authorities were aware that both of her parents were suffering with serious physical illnesses, they still considered Ruth to be neurologically impaired, and the question was raised about her repeating kindergarten and possibly entering a class for learning-disabled children. In addition, Ruth exhibited manifestations of depression, withdrawal, apathy, disinterest in play, and generalized sad affect.

My own evaluation revealed absolutely no evidence for the presence of neurologically based deficits. There were, however, definite family problems that provided a much more likely explanation for Ruth's difficulties. When Ruth was three her father de-

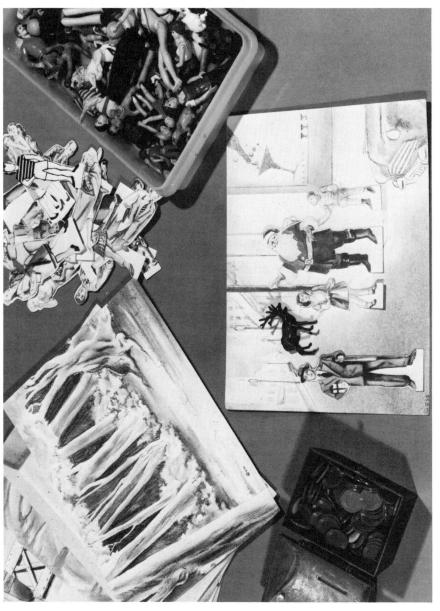

Figure 10.10

veloped signs and symptoms of a brain tumor. This was diagnosed and removed; however, his prognosis was considered guarded. When I saw her at six, her father exhibited mild neurologically based sensorial deficits—deficits that were probably not apparent to the unsophisticated observer. However, because he was bald and did not wear a hair piece, his operative scars were readily apparent. He was back at work and, I suspected, was not functioning at the same level of performance that he was at prior to his illness.

About one year prior to her initial visit, when Ruth was five, her mother exhibited various sensory and ocular changes that were ultimately diagnosed as multiple sclerosis. During the subsequent year she suffered with a number of significantly severe exacerbations, some associated with sight loss (bordering on bilateral blindness) and intermittent weakness in both lower extremities (that required the assistance of crutches or a cane).

In her projective play Ruth routinely cluttered every scene with as many humans and animals as were available. When administered the MAPS cards, Ruth covered every card with as many figurines as she could find. I considered such utilization of the play dolls to be a manifestation of her separation anxiety and the desire to compensate for the potential loss of one or even both of her parents. By cluttering the scene with as many human and animal figures as possible, she reassured herself that there would be substitutes for these potential losses. In line with this, I considered her symptoms of hyperactivity and attentional deficit to be concomitants of the fear that she felt in relation to her parents' illnesses. Furthermore, I considered her depression the predictable result of the spectre that hung over her household. Her depression served as a confirmation of my view that when someone is depressed, there is either something in the patient's reality that justifies a depressed reaction or he or she views the situation in such a way that depression is a predictable effect.

During her third month of treatment the following interchange took place while using *The Make-a-Picture Story* cards as a point of departure for mutual storytelling.

> *Therapist:* Good afternoon, boys and girls, ladies and gentlemen. Today is Monday, the 28th of December, 1931—I mean 1981—and my guest and I are playing games. Now what we have here are these cards and our guest selects one card and then we have all these dolls here. We have these regular kinds of colored dolls like this, and we

have these black and white flat dolls like this—and you pick whichever ones you want—and you put them on whatever scene you want and then you tell a story about it. Okay?

Patient: Okay. All right. (Patient creates a picture.)

Therapist: Let's see the card you have here. Now what is this card of? What does that show?

Patient: The baby of the house.

Therapist: The baby of the house.

Patient: It's a picture with the mother, and the father, and the baby.

Therapist: Okay, the mother, father, and the baby. Go ahead.

Patient: Okay. I'll set this up.

Therapist: Set it up.

Patient: One day the mother and the father with their little baby went into the mother's and father's bedroom. The baby was bouncing and bouncing and bouncing and bouncing on the bed. "It's time for bed, Junior," said mother. Junior fell asleep right away.

Therapist: It's time for bed and then Junior fell asleep right away. Okay, then what happened?

Patient: Then the mother and father climbed into bed. Junior was their *only* child.

Therapist: Junior was their only child and they climbed into bed with Junior.

Patient: And that night they had a real big dream.

Therapist: They had a dream. Yeah.

Patient: About them having a family to. . . .

Therapist: A dream that what?

Patient: About a family babysitting Junior.

Therapist: Oh, a family was babysitting Junior.

Patient: And they were out shopping for the night.

Therapist: The family was outside for the night? The babysitting family?

Patient: No, the regular family. The mother and the father had gone out for the night and this other family was babysitting little Junior.

Therapist: Oh, in other words when the mother and father were out this *whole* family was babysitting Junior. Is that right?

Patient: Hmm. (Patient adds family of five to the scene.)

Therapist: Okay, this *whole* family was babysitting Junior. Then what happened? Where are they out? Now they're in bed there with Junior?

Patient: Yeah, but they're dreaming.

Therapist: Oh, they're dreaming that they went out. They really weren't out. They were just dreaming that they were out and they were dreaming that this whole family was babysitting.

Patient: Yeah.

Therapist: Okay, then what happened?

Patient: Then when they woke up in the morning the baby started to . . .

Therapist: When they woke up in the morning, they what?

Patient: When they woke up in the morning the mother said to Junior, "We'll have a family babysit you today."

Therapist: The mother told Junior they're going to have the whole family babysit. Okay.

Patient: Junior soon got down behind mother. He didn't want mother to go to work. "I'm sorry, Junior, but I can't take care of you, but . . . (mumbles) . . . "

Therapist (interrupts): Wait a minute. Junior didn't want Mommy to leave for work and Mommy said what?

Patient: "I'm not going to work, Junior. I . . . (mumbles) . . . "

Therapist: I'm not going to what?

Patient: "I'm not going to work yet."

Therapist: "I'm not going to work yet?"

Patient: "Because you're going to have a new baby sister. Besides, you're already very little. I know that. You'll have to do with your new friend in the house."

Therapist: Wait a minute. You'll have to what with your new friend in the house?

Patient: "You'll have to do good with your *new* little kid in the house."

Therapist: "You'll have to do good with the new little kid in the house?" You mean the brother or the sister?

Patient: Yeah.

Therapist: Uh huh.

Patient: One day mother and father came home with twins!

Therapist: Wow! They came home with twins. Oh, twins. Instead of coming home with one, they came home with two. Then what happened?

Patient: Mother said, "Meet . . . " I mean mother said to Junior, "Meet Peter and your sister Ann."

Therapist: "Meet Peter and your sister Ann?"

Patient: Yeah.

Therapist: Oh, okay. So there was a Peter and Ann. Then what happened?

Patient: Peter's nickname is *clean.*

Therapist: Peter's nickname is what?

Patient: Is *clean.*

Therapist: Is *clean?*

Patient: Yes.

Therapist: Clean is his nickname and Ann's nickname is what?

Patient: Is *dirty.*

Therapist: Peter's nickname is *clean* and Ann's nickname is *dirty.* Okay. Then what happens?

Patient: That night the mother and father slept in the bed with Peter on the floor and the two twins at the foot of the bed.

Therapist: Okay. Okay, Peter on the floor and the two twins on the bed.

Patient: And they woke up in the morning and they had no more troubles with babysitting, because the whole family was babysitting! (Patient now takes out the remaining dolls [about 15] and fills up all the remaining spaces.)

Therapist: They had no more troubles because the whole family— you mean, this wasn't a dream. They really were there?

Patient: Hh hmm.

Therapist: Is that the end of the story?

Patient: Yes.

Therapist: Okay. Now it's my chance to tell a story. Okay?

Patient: Oh, brother!

Therapist: Brother. You don't want me to tell a story?

Patient: Well, you can, but you can't use some of these characters.

Therapist: Okay. Which characters can I use and which characters can I not use?

Patient: Well, one thing. I just don't think you should use just those four. (Patient sets aside four adult dolls, two males and two females.) You can use any of the others.

Therapist: I can't use these four?

Patient: Yeah.

Therapist: I can't use these four over here, but I can use any of the others?

Patient: Yes.

Therapist: Okay, I can use any of the others. Why can't I use these four over here?

Patient: Because I'm going to need them for my next one and I think I might want them. I know what they might do.

Therapist: Okay. I will not use them. I will use these others. Okay?

Patient: Okay.

My slip at the beginning of this interchange, in which I gave the date as 1931, rather than 1981, like the overwhelming majority of slips, is not without psychological significance. The year of my birth is 1931. I suspect that I too was anxious about Ruth's parents dying ("Send out not for whom the bell tolls, it tolls for thee.") and probably unconsciously wished to regress back to a point where I could start all over again as a way of forestalling the inevitable. Had Ruth been old enough to understand the significance of this slip I would have certainly discussed it with her. It probably would have provided her some psychological benefit. Knowing that others have similar concerns can in itself be therapeutic. I suspect, as well, that other therapeutic benefits might have been derived from such a discussion.

This story is typical of those Ruth told in the early phases of her treatment. Rather than simply have a single babysitter she has a whole family babysitting. She starts off as an only child and when mother is expected to come home with one new baby, she comes home with two. By the end the babysitting family expanded to include just about every doll in sight, resulting in a total coverage of the card that she had chosen. Her final request that I not use the four adult dolls in my story was, I believe a reflection of her separation anxiety. She wanted to save them for herself, a symbolic reassurance that she would not be separated from them. I then told my story.

> *Therapist:* Once upon a time there was a family and in this family was a Mommy and a Daddy. There was a baby and there was a girl. Okay? They lived together. Now this girl's father got sick one day, and he had to go to the hospital. But he came back! While he was away she was scared that he might not come back, but he came back and then her fears were over. But while he was there the mother said to the girl, "Are you scared that Daddy may not come back?"
>
> And she said, "Yes, I am scared."
>
> The mother said, "Well, it would be sad if he didn't come back. However, there are many other people in the world. There's this man over here. (Therapist picks up male doll.) There's an uncle. (Therapist displays another doll.) There's a grandpa. (Therapist picks up a third.) There's a grandma (and a fourth). There are lots of other people. In fact, while Daddy was in the hospital Grandpa came to the house to stay. Now when Daddy came back the Grandpa went home and lived with Grandma."
>
> One day Mommy had to go to the hospital and the little girl got very sad, and she was worried that her mother might not come back. But the Daddy said, "Do you remember what your mother said when I was in the hospital?"
>
> And the little girl said, "Yes."
>
> And what had the Mommy said to the little girl when the Daddy was in the hospital?

Patient: I want to . . . (mumbles). . .

Therapist: What?

Patient: Let me think.

Therapist: Okay, you think.

Patient: That it would be sad if he didn't come back.

Therapist: That he would be dead?

Patient: It would be said if he didn't come back.

Therapist: It would be sad . . .

Patient (interrupting): Because there are lots of other people in the world.

Therapist: Right! If he didn't it would be very sad, but there are lots of other people in the world. Right. And then what happened was that the Mommy had to go to the hospital. And what did the Daddy say to the girl?

Patient: Probably the same thing.

Therapist: Which was?

Patient: It would be sad, but there are lots of other people in the world.

Therapist: Right. And he said, "There's Grandma." And Grandma came to the house and Grandma stayed at the house to help take care of the little girl and the baby while Mommy was in the hospital. Did the Mommy come back from the hospital? (All this is done with appropriate doll transfers.)

Patient: I don't know.

Therapist: Yes, she did. She came back and the little girl hugged her and kissed her, and her Daddy hugged her and kissed her, and the baby hugged her and kissed her, and everybody was glad she was back. And the Grandma said, "Okay, I don't have to stay here any more now, because your Mommy is back." And Grandma went home and stayed with Grandpa.

And then what happened was when the weekend came they had dinner guests. There was an uncle who came and there were friends. (Again appropriate dolls are introduced and removed.) There was a cousin—a teen-age cousin. Here is a teen-age cousin. And there was a boy. He was 12. He came. And there was another girl. And there was another uncle. And there was an aunt. And there were lots of friends and relatives that came. And so this made the girl feel very good, because she knew there were a lot of people in the world and that if ever anything were to happen to anybody in her family, like her mother or her father—if they were to get sick—she knew that there would be other people who could help take care of her.

And although she thought it would be very sad if something were to happen to one of her parents, she knew that there were a lot of other people. And do you know what the lesson of that story is?

Patient: No.

Therapist: What do we learn from that story?

Patient: Let me try and remember now. I don't know.

Therapist: We learn that if something happens to your mother or your father. . . .

Patient: Don't worry—that there are lots of others in the world.

Therapist: Right. Although it's very sad, there are lots of other people in the world. Okay? Now would you like to watch this television program?

Patient: Of course. . . .

Therapist: Okay, let's watch it.

Whereas in the patient's story the scene is cluttered with a multiplicity of figures simultaneously, in mine a more realistic approach to the parental substitute problem is provided. Specific individuals are defined and they are placed on the scene one or two at a time. At no time is the scene cluttered with a host of figures. I provided reassurance about the presence of substitutes, but introduced a healthier utilization of such surrogates, namely, one or two at a time rather than a horde. This is certainly more consistent with what would be her situation if her parents were indeed to die.

Ruth's therapy was conducted at what I considered to be a low level of efficiency. Had her parents not been sick, she probably would not have needed treatment. The most therapeutic experience that Ruth could have would be the total and complete cure of both of her parents. Because no one could honestly reassure Ruth that her parents would completely recover, it is not likely that her therapy could be completely successful.

At the time of this writing, she has completed three years of treatment. Fortunately, her mother is enjoying a prolonged period of remission from her multiple sclerosis and her father's condition still remains stable. There is no question that these are important factors in her improvement, although I would like to think that her therapeutic experiences have played some part. However, she still exhibits significant insecurity about her situation. In the middle of her second year of treatment she saw the movie *Annie* and became preoccupied with children who live in orphanages. This was primarily reflected in her therapeutic play. Clearly, she identified with the children whose parents had died and envisioned herself being placed elsewhere if this calamity were to befall her. Even though I had early in treatment advised the parents to discuss with Ruth who she would be living with if they were to both die, she still persisted in believing that she would somehow be cast out into an orphanage. Reassurances such as those provided in the aforementioned story played some role in reducing this fear.

CONCLUDING COMMENTS

I consider the mutual storytelling derivative games to be valuable therapeutic instruments. Although they are basically quite similar to one another with regard to the "rules," they are generally not considered so by most children (especially younger ones). The situation here is similar to that which is found in children's game in general. Many board games are basically identical with regard to the fundamental rules of play; the differences are the figures and equipment that are utilized when playing the seemingly different games. Accordingly, children are used to this sort of thing and generally do not object to these similarities in the derivative games. They are generally less valuable than pure mutual storytelling because the fantasy created with "Dr. Gardner's Make-Up-a-Story Television Program" is essentially completely free of external contaminations. These games should then be viewed as instruments of second choice. It is preferable for the therapist to be presented with a free self-created fantasy that is told into the atmosphere. Although the external facilitating stimuli here do provide some contamination, my experience has been that the pressure of the unconscious to project fantasies relevant to issues meaningful to the child at that particular time are far more powerful than the capacity of the external facilitating stimulus to provide significant contamination.

The mutual storytelling derivative games are generally useful for children from about the age of four (the earliest age at which I treat) to about eleven. At that age, children begin to appreciate that their stories are revealing of underlying psychodynamic processes over which they are likely to feel anxiety and/or guilt. Accordingly, most will then refuse to play the game with rationalizations such as: "This is a baby game" and "I'm not in the mood to play those kinds of games." This is one of the reasons why I devised *The Talking, Feeling, and Doing Game*, which I will be discussing in detail in the next chapter. Another reason for the game's development was that there were some children who were still not providing me with psychologically meaningful material, even though I presented them with one or more of the games described in this chapter. *The Talking, Feeling, and Doing Game* proved useful not only in eliciting material from these more resistant children but by extending, as well, the upper age limit for obtaining useful projective material that could readily be utilized in therapy. I found that I could engage most children up to the age of 14 or even 15 with *The Talking, Feeling, and Doing Game*, five or six years after the mutual storytelling technique and its derivative games were no longer therapeutically useful.

ELEVEN

The Talking, Feeling, and Doing Game

When the One Great Scorer comes to
  write against your name—
He marks—not that you won or lost—
  but how you played the game.

Grantland Rice

The mutual storytelling technique (Chapters Eight and Nine) proved useful in facilitating children's telling self-created stories and providing other fantasy material that was of value in therapy. There were, however, children who were not free enough to tell stories using the relatively unstructured format of "Dr. Gardner's Make-up-a-Story Television Program." It was for these children that the derivative games (Chapter Ten) were devised. However, there were still some children who were so inhibited, constrained, or resistive that even these more attractive modalities did not prove successful in getting them to reveal themselves. It was for these children that *The Talking, Feeling, and Doing Game* (Gardner, 1973b) was devised. This game proved useful in engaging the vast majority of such children. In addition, for children who were free enough to reveal their fantasies, it proved useful an *another* therapeutic modality.

THE BASIC FORMAT OF THE TALKING, FEELING, AND DOING GAME

The game is similar in appearance to the typical board games with which most children are familiar (Figure 11.1). It includes a playing board, dice, playing pawns, a spinner, a path along which the pawns are moved, reward chips, and cards that are drawn from the center of the game board. This familiarity, as well as the fact that it is a *game*, reduces initial anxieties and attracts the child to the therapeutic instrument.

To begin the game both the therapist and the child place their colored pawns at the START position. Alternatively, they throw the dice and move their pawns along a curved path of squares which ultimately end at the FINISH position. For younger children, one die can be used. A pawn can land on one of a number of squares: white, red, yellow, SPIN, GO FORWARD (a specific number of squares), and GO BACKWARD (again, a specific number of squares). If the pawn lands on a white square, the player takes a Talking Card; on a yellow square, a Feeling Card; and on a red square, a Doing Card. If the pawn lands on SPIN, the player spins the spinner and follows the directions. Generally, these provide gain and loss of chips, or forward and backward movement of the playing pawn. Similarly, landing on GO FORWARD or GO BACKWARD squares results in movement of the pawn. The spinner and movement squares are of little, if any, psychological significance. They are included to insure the child's fun and relieve some of the pressure associated with a high frequency of drawing only the aforementioned three types of cards.

Of course the core of the game is the directions and questions on each of the cards. As their titles imply, the Talking Cards instruct the player to make comments that are primarily in the intellectual and cognitive area. The Feeling Cards focus primarily on affective issues. The Doing Cards usually involve play acting and/or some kind of physical activity. The child is given a reward chip for responding to each of the cards. Although a token reinforcement is provided, the game is by no means a form of behavior therapy. Positive reinforcement is not being given for behavioral change

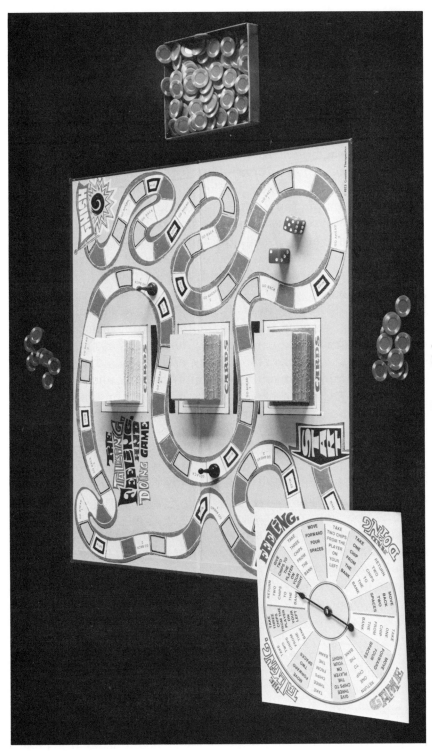

Figure 11.1

at the manifest level. Rather, the child is being reinforced for providing psychodynamically meaningful material for psychotherapeutic utilization. The child's and the therapist's responses are used as points of departure for psychotherapeutic interchanges.

There is no actual time limit for the game. Both the therapist and the patient play similiarly, and each responds to the cards. The first player to reach the FINISH position receives five extra reward chips. The second player continues to play until he or she also reaches the FINISH position. If the game is interrupted prior to one player's reaching the FINISH position, the player who is closest to that position receives three extra reward chips. The therapist should discourage active competition on the child's part for the acquisition of chips. The game should be played at a slow pace, and each response should serve as a point of departure for psychotherapeutic interchange.

There are 104 cards in each stack. I always randomize them and have never "stacked the deck" with specific cards that I hope the child will draw. The cards are so designed that any card will be relevant to any player. About five percent of the cards in each stack are so simple and nonthreatening that just about any child will respond. These are basically placed there for the extremely fragile child who would be threatened by the cards that will touch on basic problems of living. These simpler cards insure that the child will get chips and thereby remain motivated to participate in the game. The most liberal criteria are used when deciding whether or not a child should be given a chip for responding. Again, the therapist wants to do everything possible to draw the child in and maintain his or her interest. Some typical low-anxiety cards: "How old is your father?"; "What's your lucky number? Why?"; "What is your telephone number?"; "What is your address?"; "What's your favorite flavor ice cream?"; "What present would you like to get for your next birthday?"; "What's your favorite smell?" "Make believe you're blowing out the candles on your birthday cake."; and "Make a funny sound with your mouth. If you spit, you don't get a chip."

The remaining questions and directions are far richer psychologically and are at the "heart" of the game. These are not as anxiety provoking as a request to make up a story that will reveal free fantasies; however, they provide highly meaningful therapeutic material. Some typical cards: "All the girls in the class were invited to a birthday party except one. How did she feel? Why wasn't she invited?''; ''Everybody in the class was laughing at a girl. What had happened?''; ''A boy has something on his mind that he's afraid to tell his father. What is it that he's scared to talk about?''; ''What's the worst thing a boy can say to his mother?''; ''Suppose two people were talking about you, and they didn't know you were listening. What do you think you would hear them saying?''; ''What things come into your mind when you can't fall asleep?''; ''If the walls of your house could talk, what would they say about your family?''; ''Tell about something you did that made you proud.''; and ''What's the worst thing that ever happened to you in your whole life?''.

The child's responses are usually revealing of the psychological issues that are most relevant to him or her at that point. The questions and instructions cover the wide range of human experiences. The material elicited is likely to be relevant to the etiology of the child's disturbance. The questions are designed to direct the child's attention to the basic life conflicts which are being resolved in inappropriate and maladaptive ways by the symptomology. They direct the child's attention to the issues that I referred to previously, that is, the basic life conflicts that are at the foundation of psychopathological processes. As mentioned, each response serves as a point of departure for therapeutic interchanges. The therapist does not merely provide the child with a chip and then race on with the game to see who can reach FINISH first. Rather, the therapist tries to get ''as much mileage'' as possible from each response, using his or her discretion in deciding how much discussion is warranted for each patient. Highly defensive and resistant children will not be able to tolerate the kind of in-depth discussion in which the healthier child can readily participate.

The therapist answers the same questions as the child. The greater the therapist's knowledge of the child's problems, the more judicious will be his or her responses. Obviously, it is not the therapist's role to provide answers relevant to his or her *own* life problems. Rather the responses should be designed to provide therapeutic messages pertinent to the child's difficulties. I always respond honestly. Often I will provide a response that will relate to an experience of mine in childhood that is relevant to the patient's problems. Children generally enjoy hearing about the events of their parent's lives that occurred at that time in the parent's childhood that corresponds to the age of the child at the time of the conversation. Such discussions draw children closer to their parents. The same principle holds in therapy. Such revelations, then, can contribute to a deepening of the therapist-patient relationship. As mentioned, a good relationship is crucial if therapy is to be successful. Without it, there will be little receptivity to the therapist's messages and practically no identification with him or her.

Many therapists, especially those with a classical psychoanalytic orientation, may take issue with the freedom with which I reveal myself. They would argue that I am contaminating terribly the therapeutic field and making the patient's free associations practically useless. I am in full agreement that such revelations contaminate the patient's free associations. I am not in agreement, however, that the classical approach is without its drawbacks. It does indeed provide the so-called "blank screen" for the purest projections. However, the acquisition of such information is done in a setting which, I believe, is antitherapeutic. It creates a distance between the therapist and the patient that compromises the development of a good therapist-patient relationship. The patient's thoughts and feelings about the therapist become distorted and divorced from reality. The situation increases the likelihood that the patient will develop delusions about the therapist and will idealize him or her. It will widen the gap between them as the patient comes to view the therapist as perfect. We can love most those whom we know nothing about—but such love is more delusional than real, based as it is on a paucity of information. What is gained in the way of pure free associations is more than counterbalanced, I believe, by the losses of a compromised therapist-patient relationship and the antitherapeutic experience of the patient comparing him- or herself negatively with the therapist. *The Talking, Feeling, and Doing Game* provides the therapist with the opportunity to reveal defects in a noncontrived and nonartificial setting. He or she thereby becomes more human to the patient, and this is generally salutary for the therapist-patient relationship. In addition, my revelations are not those that would compromise my own privacy and that of my family. Even with these restrictions, there is enough that has gone on in my life to provide me with a wealth of potential information for revelation.

I uniformly answer all questions. Some highly defensive children, however, may find it difficult to do so. Sometimes, I will inform such children that failure to answer the question will result in their not getting a reward chip, and this will lessen the likelihood that they will win the game. Some children are motivated by this "threat" and try to respond to the card. On occasion, a child will refrain from answering most cards but still involve him- or herself in the game. Many of these children listen attentively to my responses and, I believe, gain thereby from the game. Although I am working here in a partial vacuum because I am not getting as much information from the child as is desirable, my knowledge of the child's history and background provides me with enough information to give responses to the cards that are meaningful to the child and pertinent to his or her problems.

The question is sometimes raised about winning and losing when playing therapeutic games with children. *The Talking, Feeling, and Doing Game* obviates this problem. It may not be immediately apparent to the therapist that the main determinant as to who wins the game is *luck*. If each player answers each card, the determinant as to who wins the game is the dice. If a player obtains many high thows, then he or she will reach FINISH earlier and thereby acquire fewer chips. If a player obtains a larger number of low throws, more chips will be acquired when going from START to FINISH. Because low and high throws average out for each player, the number of wins and losses also average out over the course of treatment.

Although *The Talking, Feeling, and Doing Game* was originally devised to engage resistant children in therapy, it has proved useful for less defended children as well. In fact, it has proved to be the favorite therapeutic activity of the children in my practice. Many other therapists have informed me that this has been their experience as well. This therapeutic boon is not without its drawbacks, however. One danger of the game is that it will lure the child (and, unfortunately, the therapist) away from utilizing techniques that are more likely to elicit "deeper" psychodynamic material. Dealing with this material is also important in therapy. Accordingly, the therapist should not injudiciously "respect" the child's wishes to devote the entire therapeutic experience to this technique. The game is generally useful for children over the age of five or six, the age at which they begin to appreciate the give and take structure of board games. At that age, of course, the therapist may have to read the cards to the child (or read along with the child), but this is not an impediment. Whereas the mutual storytelling technique and its derivative games are generally not useful above the age of 11, one can get a few more years mileage from *The Talking, Feeling, and Doing Game*. My experience has been that it can be useful up to the age of 14 or 15.

Although primarily designed to be used in the one-to-one therapeutic situation, the game can be used in child group therapy as well (preferably for small groups of three to five children). When so utilized the therapist can use a child's response as a point of departure for group discussion. The game is particularly useful in child group therapy because it provides intrinsic structure in a situation that traditionally tends to become unstructured (the children tend to become playful, rambunctious, distracted, etc.). In addition, it facilitates discussion of problems in a setting in which such conversations are usually difficult to accomplish because of the reticence of most children to engage in them.

Generally, the material elicited when utilizing the Mutual Storytelling Technique is closer to pure dream and free fantasy than that revealed in *The Talking, Feeling, and Doing Game*. The "Make-up-a-Story Television Program" is so structured that there are no specific stimuli around which the stories are told. Traditional play materials such as dolls and puppets, although valuable and frequently effective catalysts for story elicitation, do contaminate the story and tend to "draw" the child's projections into specific directions. The cards in *The Talking, Feeling, and Doing Game* are similarly contaminating. However, I believe that the "push" of the unconscious material to be released in a form specific for the child's needs at that particular time is far stronger than the "pull" of the evoking stimulus and its power to significantly alter the projected material. Accordingly, the "channeling" of the projections is not very significant.

First, I will describe some common responses I provide for each of the three categories of cards. Then I will present some clinical vignettes in which I demonstrate my utilization of the game in the treatment of children.

EXAMPLES OF CARD RESPONSES

Talking Cards

Human behavior lends itself well to being divided into thoughts, feelings, and actions. It was from this observation that I decided to name this game *The Talking, Feeling, and Doing Game*. Furthermore, the sequence here is also important. Thoughts generally precede feelings, and feelings precede actions. Certainly, the sequence is applicable for fight-flight reactions. One sees a danger. A possible emotional reaction is fear. In response to the fear one flees. Another possible emotional reaction is anger. Then, one fights and the anger enhances one's efficiency in protecting oneself from the attacker. For emotions such as sexual arousal and hunger, feelings may precede thoughts. One feels hungry, then one experiences thoughts related to food acquisition. Then one takes action and attempts to obtain food. Because therapy is more likely to deal with fight-flight emotions then those related to eating and sexual arousal (not that these aren't involved in treatment at all), I decided to place *talking* before *feeling* in the name of the game.

The Talking Cards encourage the child to speak about his or her opinions on a wide variety of subjects. The questions are designed to elicit information related to the fundamental problems of life with which all children are confronted. As discussed in Chapter Three the solutions to these problems can either be adaptive or maladaptive. We refer to a maladaptive solution as *symptomatic*. The game is designed to elicit discussion of these issues in the hope that the child will learn how to deal better with these problems of life and thereby not have to resort as frequently to the pathological adaptations.

It is vital for the therapist to appreciate that *there are no standard answers for the therapist to provide*. Rather, each response must be tailored to the particular child with whom the therapist is playing the game. Accordingly, it would be an error for the therapist to use the responses I provide here in the models I have created for the therapist's answers. Rather, they should be viewed as selected examples of the *kinds* of responses that I might provide and as guidelines for the therapist's own responses. Just as the therapist's responding story in the mutual storytelling game is tailored to the patient's story, the therapist's answers in this game are also designed to fit the patient's needs.

Question: What sport are you worst at?

Response: I never really was *very* good at sports. So there are a lot of sports I am pretty bad at. Of the sports that were commonly played in my neighborhood when I was kid, I would say that the one that I was worst at was basketball. I guess that I didn't try hard enough. It's not that I was born a klutz; I just think that I didn't work at it enough. I used to feel pretty bad when kids would choose up sides and I was the last one to be chosen. Had I worked harder at it, it probably wouldn't have happened to me.

The card "What sport are you worst at?" essentially forces the therapist to reveal an area of weakness. Even if the therapist were an olympic decathalon champion, he or she would still be provided with the opportunity to talk about a sport in which there is weakness. Besides providing the aforementioned benefits of such revelation, I use the response to put in a plug for the work ethic. The response also provides the child with the knowledge that I too had my rejections and that I too was not chosen for involvement in various activities when I was a child. This is a universal phenomenon, and it is helpful for the child to know that the therapist too suffered such rejections. It contributes to a sense of communion with the therapist and this cannot but be therapeutic.

* * *

Question: What things come into your mind when you can't fall asleep?

Response: If I had let someone take advantage of me during the day and didn't do anything about it, it would tend to linger on my mind. I would keep thinking about what I should have done and how I didn't do it. This might interfere with my falling asleep. I would keep thinking of the thing over and over again—especially how I might have said something or done something, but I didn't say or do anything at the time. I'm sorry then that I didn't speak up or do something. But later, it was too late. And there may be nothing that I can then do about it. So I have trouble falling asleep because I keep thinking about what I should have done. Sometimes however, there is something I can do about it and then I do it at the time. Then I get it off my chest. Then I feel better. Then I can fall asleep more easily. I did the thing that I was supposed to do.

For example, something happened when I was a young kid that caused me to lose a lot of sleep for a few nights. I was in junior high school at the time. I was walking out of a classroom. Some kids in the class made some kind of a smoke bomb and threw it into one of the desks. The teacher wasn't there and as they left the room the smoke started to pour out of the desk. I was scared that the desk would catch on fire. I wanted to run over and pull everything out of the desk because I was so scared that the whole school might burn down, but I was afraid that the other kids would call me "chicken." So I walked out of the classroom with the others. About five minutes later I heard a fire alarm bell and I wasn't surprised. It was a big school with almost 1000 kids. And we all quickly left the building. As we got outside I could see the smoke coming out of the classroom. The fire engines came and put out the fire. Fortunately, it was caught in time and no one was hurt. Also, the fire didn't spread too far. The kids who lit the smoke bomb were kicked out of school.

I was really sorry that I hadn't had the guts to pull the stuff out of that desk and stomp on it. I think there were other kids in the classroom that wanted to do the same thing, but none of us had the guts. For the next three nights I kept thinking about how much trouble I would have saved everybody—especially those boys—if only I had done what I knew was the right thing. I know some kids probably would have laughed at me, but I would have known I was doing the right thing. It was a big mistake. And I still remember it after all these years, even though I only lost some sleep for a few nights.

Although my response at the beginning is designed to be general, the example I give makes particular reference to self-assertion. In particular, I focus on the importance of doing what one considers to be "right" even though it may be the unpopular thing. I try thereby to encourage self-assertion. Such comments are especially helpful to children with self-assertion problems. The pent-up resentments that such children cause themselves can distract them from learning in school. It also contributes to their becoming targets for bullies and scapegoaters. And this too can interfere with learning as the child comes to dread school attendance.

* * *

Question: What's the best story you ever heard or read? Why?

Response: Of all the books that I ever read when I was young, the one that I remember to have been the best was the one describing the life of Thomas A. Edison. As you probably know, Thomas A. Edison was one of the greatest inventors who ever lived. Although he wasn't the only man to work on these things, his inventions were important—giving us the electric light bulb, the phonograph, and the moving picture camera. He was a poor boy who lived in Ohio. He was a very hard worker and was an extremely curious person. He was immensely interested in how things work.

He had a laboratory near his home and it is said that he would sometimes work most of the night on his inventions. He loved learning about how things work, and he loved trying to figure out better ways of doing things. To this day, people all over the world use his inventions. To this day, he is remembered as having given mankind some of its greatest inventions. He must have really felt great about himself because of all the good he did for mankind. It is mainly his curiosity and hard work that did these things both for himself and for others. It was Thomas A. Edison who said: "Genius is 1 percent inspiration and 99 percent perspiration." Do you know what that means?

Edison epitomizes the gratification and fame that can come to someone who is strongly committed to the work ethic. I emphasize here the great benefit that can come to others from the efforts of a strongly motivated person. My aim here is to engender some desire on the child's part to view Edison as an admirable figure worthy of emulation and inspiration. Obviously, one such message is not going to achieve this goal. However, the seed is planted and with reiteration over time it is quite possible that Edison will become incorporated into the child's psychic structure and join with other introjects to serve as a model for identification and emulation. Younger children, obviously, will not understand the quotation about genius and perspiration. However, even they can be engaged in a discussion of it if the words they do not understand are explained.

* * *

Question: Suppose two people you knew were talking about you and they didn't know you were listening. What do you think you would hear them saying?

Response: I might hear the people saying that I'm the kind of a person who is direct and honest. Although people might disagree, at times, with what I've said, they would agree that I am direct about what my opinions are and don't pussyfoot about them. They know that when they ask me a question, they'll get an honest and direct answer with no hedging, beating-around-the-bush, or saying things that aren't true. I am not saying that they would say that I never lied in my whole life and that I never will, only that they are pretty confident that I'll be honest with them. You see, I believe that there is truth and wisdom to the old saying that "honesty is the best policy." If you tell a lie, you have to go around worrying that people will find out that you've lied. Also, lots of people feel bad about themselves when they lie, they feel guilty about it. And when people find out that you've lied, then they don't trust you even when you've told the truth. So these are the main reasons why I find it better to tell the truth, rather than to lie. What's your opinion on this subject?

Identification with the therapist and modeling oneself after him or her is an important part of the therapeutic process. This is very similar to the educational model in which the child learns, in part, because of identification with the teacher and the desire to gain the same gratifications that the teacher enjoys from learning. The therapist not only serves as a model for learning, but should be serving as a model for other desirable attributes as well, for example, healthy self-assertion, sensitivity to the feelings of others, feelings of benevolence toward those who are in pain, handling oneself with dignity, and honesty. This card enables the therapist to provide examples of such traits. However, the therapist should select traits that are particularly relevant to the child's problems. Furthermore, the therapist must avoid presenting these with a flaunting or holier-than-thou attitude.

* * *

Question: Make believe that you're looking into a crystal ball that can show anything that is happening anywhere in the whole world. What do you see?

Response: I'm looking into a crystal ball. There's a cloud there, and I can't see anything now. Wait a minute . . . wait a minute . . . it's starting to clear. I think I can see something now. Oh, yes, it's a big auditorium. In the front rows are lots of children, school children. In the back rows are all the parents. There's something happening on the stage. There are teachers sitting up there and, oh yeah, there's the principal. He's standing in the front and he's giving something to a child. It looks like he's giving her an award. She certainly looks proud. Now the principal is shaking her hand and everybody's clapping. Now he's making another announcement. And here comes another child up on to the stage and everybody's clapping. He's then giving her an award and the principal's making a little speech about her. There's a big smile on her face. Obviously she's also won a prize or award. Now she's walking off the stage and everyone's clapping.

My message here is clear. I am trying to help the child gain an appreciation for the rewards of successful school work. I focus on the internal reward, the sense of pride and gratification. I also describe the external rewards: the applause of the audience, the speech of the principal, and the prizes. The dramatic element here serves to enhance the child's interest and increase the chance that my messages will be heard.

* * *

Question: Tell about something you did that you are ashamed about?

Response: I had an experience many years ago, when I was a medical intern, that was very embarrassing. It was so embarrassing that I still remember it clearly to this day. It happened when I was an intern. An intern is a young doctor just out of medical school. Well, one Friday morning the resident, the doctor who was my boss, told me that I should prepare a speech about one of the patients that I was treating. He told me that I was to give it the first thing the following Monday morning. He told me to look over the patient's present and past charts as well as to study all the old X-rays. The patient had been sick for many years, and there was a lot of material to cover. He told me that it was important that I do a good job because this was the biggest conference of the month and that all the doctors in the hospital would be there. The hospital had over 200 doctors and it was a very important conference.

Anyway, Monday morning I got to the hospital and started to work with my patients. I noticed that none of the other doctors were there and wondered where everyone was. Suddenly, the telephone rang and I answered. It was the resident. He was very upset and he asked me why I wasn't at the conference. I was so surprised and shocked that I almost fainted. I realized that I had totally forgotten about the conference. I had prepared nothing! I was sick to my stomach. I immediately grabbed the patient's chart, the two X-rays that I could find, and rushed to the conference room.

What I should have done was to publicly announce that I was unprepared and to express my apologies. However, I tried to get away with it. I tried to go through the chart and give a speech about the patient, when I had very little information. I didn't lie or anything like that. I just tried to take a little information from one place and a little from the next but it didn't hang together. Finally, one of the older doctors who organized the conference interrupted me and suggested that we discontinue the conference. I was humiliated. But I was also relieved. I certainly learned an important lesson that day. And I have never again forgotten to prepare a speech. That event took place many years ago, and although it was painful and embarrassing, I learned an important lesson.

The question "Tell about something you did that you are ashamed about" again requires the therapist to reveal an area of imperfection. In the vignette that I selected, I also provide a message about preparing things in advance, thinking ahead, and thereby protecting oneself from humiliation. This message is likely to be of some relevance to most children in treatment.

* * *

Question: If you became mayor of your city, what would you do to change things?

Response: If I became mayor of my city, I would do everything in my power to bring about the passage of two laws. One would prohibit smoking in public places and the other would fine people large amounts of money for letting their dogs crap in the streets. Let me tell you my reasons for saying this. I, personally, find cigarette smoking disgusting. I'm not saying this because smoking causes cancer of the lungs. I'd say this even if smoking *cured* cancer of the lungs. I'm just saying it because I find smoking nauseating. I think that if anyone is stupid enough to smoke, that person should be required to do it privately, in his or her own home. Many people who smoke don't care about other people's feelings. As far as they're concerned, other people can choke or even croak on their smoke. They don't think about the feelings of the people who are suffering because of their smoking. Unfortunately, a lot of people don't speak up and say how the smoke bothers them. But more and more people are doing this.

The other law, about there being big fines for people who let their dogs crap on the streets, would be for the same purposes. People who let their dogs do this don't think about how disgusted others feel when they step in the dog shit. It's really a disgusting thing to have to wipe dog shit off your shoes. It's too bad there are so many people in this world who don't think about other people's feelings. What do you think about people who smoke and people who let their dogs crap on the streets?"

The major thrust of my responses here is to help an insensitive child appreciate how one's acts can affect others and that those who don't think about how they are affecting others are generally scorned. Included also in my response was a message about self-assertion regarding nonsmokers in their relationships with smokers.

* * *

Question: What was the worst punishment you ever got in your whole life? What had you done wrong?

Response: I remember my worst punishment quite well. I was about seven or eight years old at the time. My brother and I had gone off and were playing in an empty lot a couple of blocks from my home. I lived in an apartment house in the Bronx, in New York City. One of the things we liked to do was to make bonfires. We would gather some wood and papers and build a fire. We built them in safe places, not in buildings. We didn't want to burn anything, we just wanted to have some fun building the fire and then throwing garbage and other things into it and watch the stuff burn. Anyway, on this day, we got so involved with the fun of the fire that we didn't realize how late it was. In fact, it was getting dark and we thought that was even greater fun because we could then watch the fire during the night. We were having so much fun that we completely forgot about our parents and how worried and upset they might be because we hadn't come home.

Well, anyway, at about 8 o'clock at night we finally got home. We were supposed to be home about 5:30 or 6 o'clock. Although our parents were very happy to see us, they were also very angry. They were very worried; so much so that they had already called the police to look for us. The police hadn't started to look for us yet; they just said wait a little while longer.

Anyway, my father hit us both with a strap to help us remember never to do such a terrible thing again. They were not only upset about our building fires—which was more dangerous than we had realized—but about our not having thought about their feelings and about how worried they were when we didn't come home. They were scared that we might have wandered off and gotten lost. They were also scared that we might have been kidnapped or even been killed. And they were extremely upset that we hadn't thought about their feelings. Do you know what lessons I learned from that experience?

My hope here is that the story will engender some appreciation in the child of the effects of antisocial behavior on other people, how other people might feel who suffer from or who are otherwise inconvenienced by the child's antisocial behavior. In addition, it emphasizes the point that there were personal repercussions for my behavior. I received a severe spanking that I remember to this day and I also risked being burned by the fire.

* * *

Question: What do you think about a boy who curses at his father?

Response: It's perfectly normal to think curse words about a father. In fact, practically every child I have ever seen will, at times, have such thoughts in mind—especially after something happens that gets the child angry at his or her father. However, if instead you *politely* talk about the things that are getting you angry, then your father is more likely to listen and maybe then you'll be able to solve the problem. Maybe your speaking politely will help, and maybe it won't. However, there's a greater chance it will help solve the problem if you don't use curse words than if you do. And the worst thing is to say nothing at all when you're angry. Then, you won't solve anything and things will probably get worse.

* * *

Question: What do you think about a boy who sometimes wished that his brother were dead?

Response: It's perfectly normal to have thoughts once in a while and even wishes that one's brother were dead. This is especially the case in the middle of a fight. But having a thought once in a while and having a wish once in a while and *really wanting* the brother to be dead are two separate things. Most children are comfortable with the idea that they could think it and wish it once in a while and that there is nothing wrong with them. They know that there is a big difference between having a wish once in a while and *really* wanting it to happen.

There are some children who have such thoughts once in a while who believe that they are terrible to have such thoughts. They believe that only the worst kinds of children would have such thoughts about a brother. They feel terrible about themselves for having such thoughts and try to blot them out of their minds when they start thinking about such things. If such children knew that these thoughts, once in a while, are perfectly normal they might feel better about themselves. They might not feel so guilty about these thoughts and then they would be happier people.

There are some children who have these thoughts once in a while who become very frightened of them. They think that the thought can actually make the brother die. That's silly. A thought can't make anything happen. In fact, no matter how hard a child thinks something, the thought itself can't make the thing happen. Even if the brother wished very hard that the other brother would die, that wouldn't make it happen. If such children changed their minds and realized that thoughts can't make things happen, they would become less afraid of the death wishes. They would then become more comfortable with themselves over them.

My aim here is to reduce guilt in children who believe that occasional hostile thoughts and feelings, especially death wishes, are terrible to have. I inform the child that such thoughts and feelings are commonplace. Many children with such guilt harbor the notion that they are alone in the world or that only the most lowly individuals would harbor such heinous thoughts and feelings. I also attempt to dispel the notion that a thought has magic powers and can bring about an event. This notion is often intrinsically associated with excessive guilt over such thoughts and feelings.

* * *

Question: A girl was very angry at her father and wished that he would be hit by a car. Later that day he was hit by a car. How did she feel? What did she think?

Response: The girl felt very sad. She was not only sad because her father was hit by a car and had to go to the hospital, but she was also sad because she thought that her thoughts had actually caused the car to hit her father. She thought that an angry idea could actually make a thing happen. This of course, isn't true. That would be magic and there is no such thing as magic. A thought cannot make anything happen. Things happen by people doing things. The man who drove the car that hit her father was the one who was responsible for the father's being hurt. Probably it was an accident. If anyone was at fault it was he, not the girl who had the thought and wished that her father would get hit by a car.

The girl didn't realize that everyone has thoughts like that once in a while. She was very angry at her father and, at that time, she had the wish that he would die. It isn't that she *really* wanted her father dead. It's just that when she was very angry, such wishes came into her mind. Fortunately, this girl discussed the whole thing with her father after he came out of the hospital. He told her that he wasn't angry at her for the accident. He told her that her thoughts were normal and to have them once in a while, when a person is angry, is normal. He told her that he didn't blame her for his having been hit by the car. He didn't even blame the man who drove the car.

He did blame the man who fixed the car, because he had done a poor job. Her father had gotten a lawyer and he was going to sue the mechanic, the man who fixed the car, for the hospital bills as well as the money he lost from work when he was in the hospital. Her father discussed with her her feelings that her thoughts might have made the man in the car drive into her father. He told her that this was not the case. He told her that her thoughts could not make the thing happen. It was the car mechanic's fault and not hers. He told her also that her thoughts could not make the car mechanic make his mistake. After that, she didn't feel so bad. After that she realized that thoughts can't make things happen. Then she felt better about herself.

I deal here in detail with the issue of thoughts having magic power as a central element in guilt over anger. It is important to note that this factor is much more likely to be operative in children under the age of five or six. Prior to that time it is normal for children to believe in the magic of their thoughts. The sicker the child the greater the likelihood this notion will persist beyond the age when it should no longer be believed.

Sometimes I will enhance the efficacy of this message by bringing out the play dolls. I may take the little girl doll and the father doll and play act that the little girl is wishing very hard that her father will die. The dialogue may go something like this:

And the little girl wished very, very hard that her father would die. But no matter how hard she wished, her father just didn't die. She was very angry at him because he had done such terrible things to her. She hoped that if he would die then he would no longer abuse and hurt her. So she kept wishing and wishing that he would die. But it just didn't work. He just went on living. (I then move the father doll around as if he was carrying out various activities—demonstrating thereby that he is still alive.) No matter how hard she wished, he just didn't die.

I might then bring into the story a teenage brother (or some other powerful authority figure) who asks the little girl what she's wishing for. In the ensuing discussion the teen-ager also emphasizes the theme that her wishes cannot bring about her father's death. He may, however, enter into a discussion with her about what else she might do to improve her situation.

* * *

Question: If a fly followed you around for a day and could then talk about you, what would it say?

Response: I followed Dr. Gardner around all day and I noticed that the people he is with hardly ever have any doubt in their minds about what he thinks. He's not afraid to tell people what's on his mind and to express his thoughts and feelings. He avoids a lot of trouble this way. If people had to wonder what he thought, there would be a lot of confusion and trouble. He also gets many things accomplished that he wouldn't have if he didn't speak up.

For example, during his lunch break one day, he went to a restaurant with a friend. He asked to be seated in the *No Smoking* section. After they were there awhile, a man sat down at the next table and started to smoke. Dr. Gardner immediately complained to the waiter and the man was asked to either put out the cigarette or sit in the *Smoking* section. He quickly apologized and put out the cigarette. Some people probably would have sat there and said nothing. However, Dr. Gardner didn't. By speaking up, he stopped a person from doing something that was making him uncomfortable.

During the evening he went to the movies with his wife. The sound was on much too loud and lots of people were bothered. However, no one was doing anything about it. Dr. Gardner got up, went out to the lobby and asked for the manager. He asked the manager to lower the volume of the sound. At first, the manager didn't believe him, so he asked the manager to go into the theater and hear for himself. The manager did so and realized that Dr. Gardner was right. He then lowered the volume and then everyone was more comfortable. Again, he saved himself and other people a lot of trouble by politely and firmly expressing his thoughts and feelings. Of course, every once in a while, he may not express his thoughts and feelings and this usually causes some trouble. This helps him remember that the best thing, most often, is to tell people about things that bother you—but to do so in a polite way.

This is another example of my view that it is useful for therapy to help the patient learn important principles in living which can be applied to specific situations as they arise. Clearly, my hope here is that this description will impress upon the child the value of self-assertion. My hope also is that my own ways of dealing with these problems will serve as a model for the child.

Feeling Cards

The Feeling Cards, as their name indicates, encourage primarily the expression of feelings. Many therapists view such expression to be the primary goal of the therapeutic process. These therapists will frequently ask such questions as: "How did you feel about that?" and "That must have made you feel very angry (sad, happy, etc.)." Others speak of therapy primarily as a place where the child can let out or get in touch with his or her feelings. Some pride themselves on their skill when a boy, for example, expresses the anger he feels toward his father by hitting the head of the father doll with a toy hammer. I believe that this view of therapy is naive. I consider the expression of feelings to be a first step toward the alleviation of difficulties. Feelings serve in part to enhance one's efficiency in reaching a goal. When we are frightened, we run faster; when we are angry, we fight harder and more effectively. When sexually excited we make love more ardently. When hungry we eat, sometimes voraciously. And when tired we sleep more deeply.

The therapist's goals should be that of helping patients express their thoughts and feelings at the earliest possible time that is reasonable and appropriate. At such times, the feelings are generally at a low level and can be used most effectively. When feelings build up to high levels they are likely to interfere with their effective utilization. When we are irritated we can use our irritation to attempt to remove the noxious stimulus that is evoking our frustration. If, however, we do not express ourselves early, the angry feelings build up to levels of rage and even fury. When expressed under these circumstances the anger is not likely to be focused on the particular source of frustration. When expressed in a wild and even chaotic fashion, we are not likely to remove expediently the source of irritation. Furthermore, when feelings reach an extremely high level their gratification may become an end in itself, with little further purpose. A murderer, for example, will generally accomplish his or her goal with one or two stabs in the chest. The murderer who continues to stab the victim is no longer using the anger in the service of killing the victim. The same phenomenon applies to sexual gratification, eating, sleeping, and drinking.

As is true of the other cards, the child's reactions should serve as a point of departure for therapeutic interchanges. The examples given here do not present such discussions. Later in this chapter I will provide clinical examples in which sample interchanges are presented. Again, there are no "right" answers to the questions and instructions on the Feeling Cards. Rather, my responses presented here may serve as guidelines for the therapist's responses when playing the game.

* * *

Question: What do you think happens to people after they die?

Response: No one knows for sure. Some people think that there is some kind of life or existence after death. Some believe that there is a soul or ghost that remains after we die. Some people believe that we actually come back to life in another form. And some people believe that there is absolutely nothing that happens after you're dead. They believe that your body just rots away in the ground and that there is no such thing as a soul or ghost or spirit or anything else. They believe that that's just the end of it all forever. That's my personal opinion as well. I don't believe that there is any kind of life or existence after you die. I'm not 100 percent sure, but it's the theory that seems most reasonable to me.

Therefore, because I believe that I only have one life, I try to make it the best life possible. I try not to do things that will foul me up. I work hard so that I'll be able to get the things I want in life. This doesn't mean that I don't take out time to have fun. I do that as well. I try to balance them out and spend time both at work and at fun. However, some of my work is also fun. And some of my fun is also work. The two tend to get mixed up at times. For example, writing books is work, but it's also fun for me. Hiking is fun for me, but it also involves some effort and work.

I think one of the worst things that can happen to a person is to reach the end of his or her life and look back and realize that most of it has been wasted. To avoid this, it is important for people to do those things each day that make life as good as possible. No matter what people believe about what happens after death, most of them agree that it's important to make the one life they have the best possible one. Do you think you're doing this for yourself?

Like many of the questions, the brighter the child, the greater the likelihood the post-response discussion will be rich and meaningful. Although we may enter into a somewhat philosophical discussion, my main purpose here is to help the child gain a sense of the sanctity of life and the importance of doing the best one can for oneself at any point along the way. I believe that people who have a greater appreciation of this unhappy fact are more likely to be motivated to make the most of the relatively short time we have here.

* * *

Question: What's the happiest thing that ever happened to you?

Response: I've had many happy days in my life. Three of the happiest were the three days on which each of my children were born. Of course, that happened many years ago, but I still remember the days clearly. I was so happy on each of those days that I cried. They were tears of joy. I still have those warm feelings when I see little babies. It's hard for me not to touch them and sometimes I'll even ask the mother to let me hold the baby so I can cuddle and kiss the child. Although my children, like all children, may give me trouble at times, they also give me great pleasures. And the pleasures are certainly greater than the pains.

We speak often of the importance of the therapist-patient relationship in therapy. However, the factors that contribute to the development of a good relationship in this area have not been well delineated. This question can be used to help foster a good patient-therapist relationship. My hope here is that the child's relationship with me might improve (admittedly in a small way) by the recognition that children produce warm responses in me. The response conveys the notion that I have the capacity for such pleasure with children in general and this response is not simply confined to my own children.

* * *

Question: What's something you could say that could make a person feel good?

Response: One thing you could say that could make a person feel good is to compliment the person on an accomplishment, that is, on something he or she did very well. For example, if a boy worked very hard making a model airplane, and it turned out very well and looked very good, then I'd say to him, "That's a beautiful job you did!" That would make him feel very good about himself. Or, for example, if a girl started the school year as a very poor student and then improved significantly, she would also feel very good if someone complimented her on her accomplishment. If, for example, she was spending a lot of time in the early part of the year goofing off and fooling around, then she wouldn't feel very good about herself. Let's say that she then begins to study much harder. After a lot of work over a period of time the teacher might say on her report card: "Congratulations, Sarah, you have really improved. Whereas you were once a pain in the neck because you never tried or did your homework, now it's a pleasure to have you in the classroom. It's a pleasure to be your teacher. You've really come a long way. Keep up the good work." Now that's the kind of thing that would make the girl feel good about herself. What do you think about what I've said?

When I congratulate a child on an accomplishment, I generally focus my attention primarily on the deed or the act and direct the child's attention to the good feeling he or she must experience over the accomplishment. I secondarily mention other people who may be pleased over the child's accomplishment and/or external rewards such as high grades, certificates, awards, and so on. Also included here is the notion that hard work is necessary if one is to enjoy these benefits.

*   *   *

Question: Say three curse words. What do you think of people who use these words?

Response: Shit. Crap. Fuck. I think these words are okay to use if you're having a fight with someone outside your home. They serve a useful purpose. They get out anger without *actually* hurting the other person. However, it's a bad idea to use these words in front of parents, teachers, and other adults. They usually get very upset and angry and will tell you that it's not proper to use these words in front of others. So, it's often best to use words that are *more polite* than these if you want to get something accomplished, especially with an adult. There are times when these words are the best words to use. If another kid speaks to you with such words, it can often be useful to use similar words back. There's an old saying, "Sticks and stones may break my bones, but names will never hurt me." This tells very well what I said before about dirty words helping you use anger without actually hurting anyone.

This card is designed for the child who is inhibited in the proper use of profanity in socially acceptable ways and situations. The child may be initially astounded to hear me use such words—believing that it is inappropriate for a doctor to utilize profanity. Obviously, this is not the response I would provide for the child who has an antisocial behavior disorder and uses such words indiscriminately. Rather, I would provide a response that attempts to induce guilt and/or embarrassment over the use of such words.

* * *

Question: What is the best kind of job a person can have? Why? Make believe you're doing that job.

Response: I think the best job a person can have is one in which that person earns money doing something that he or she finds enjoyable. Normally, the more education a person has, the greater the likelihood he or she will have such a job. People who don't have much education, or who drop out of school early, are not likely to have such jobs. It's more likely that they'll have a miserable or lousy job that they hate.

Less important than the fact that they'll earn less money than the more educated person, is the fact that they hate what they're doing. And this is a bad way to spend one's life. It's much better to get education and training. Then, it's more likely that the person will be able to earn money doing something that he or she enjoys. Therefore, my answer to this question is that there is no one best job. My answer then is that it's any job that the person enjoys doing. And there are hundreds of different kinds of jobs different people can enjoy doing. What kind of thing would you like to do when you grow up?

My hope is that my response will contribute to the child's appreciation that what he or she is doing now is going to play an important role in his or her future life. In addition, my hope is that the response will contribute (admittedly in a small way) to the child's motivation to think about the future and be willing to spend some effort toward gaining greater knowledge and skill.

* * *

Question: What do you think is the most beautiful thing in the whole world?

Response: Watching a beautiful sunset, whether it be from the top of a mountain or at the seashore, is to me one of the most beautiful things in the world. It makes me feel relaxed and happy to be alive. Sometimes I read poetry while watching such a scene. And the poems also make me think of beautiful things that help me appreciate how beautiful the world can be if one is willing to stop and enjoy them. Sometimes I will bring along a tape recorder and play a tape of some calm, beautiful music while watching such a scene. This is indeed one of the great pleasures of life.

* * *

Healthy pleasure is well viewed to be a general antidote for just about all forms of psychogenic psychopathology. When one is enjoying oneself in a healthy way, one is at that time not suffering the psychological pain attendant to psychiatric disorder. In addition, the pleasurable feelings are esteem enhancing. Because feelings of low self-worth are often involved in bringing about psychopathological reactions, any experience that can enhance self-worth can be salutary. And aesthetic pleasures are in this category. Accordingly, anything a therapist can do to enhance a child's appreciation of beauty is likely to be therapeutic.

* * *

Question: What do you think about a boy who sometimes plays with his penis when he's alone?

Response: I think that it's perfectly normal—as long as he does it when he's alone. Of course, there would be something wrong with him if he did that in the open, in public; but as a private thing I think it's normal. In fact most teenage boys do it a lot, and many kids play with their penises when they're younger as well. There are some kids, however, who think that playing with their penises is a terrible thing. They think it's sinful, or wrong, or dirty. I completely disagree. Those kids are the ones that have a problem, and not the ones who play with their penises once in a while in private. What's your opinion on what I've just said?

* * *

Question: What do you think about a girl who sometimes plays with or rubs her vagina when she's alone?

Response: I think it's perfectly normal for her to do that when she's alone. Of course, that's not the kind of thing that one would generally do in front of other people. It's a private matter. What do you think?

For the sexually inhibited child these responses enable the examiner to approach a forbidden subject in a noncontrived way. Discussing the subject is in itself therapeutic in that it provides the child with the living experience that such discussions do not result in dire consequences. That which is unmentionable is far more anxiety and guilt provoking than that which is spoken about. The child whose parents never speak about sex will generally become far more inhibited than the parent who preaches often about the sins and evils of sex. Of course, the latter approach is likely to produce guilt as well, but probably not as much as the guilt produced by the situation in which the subject is unmentionable. For the child who is excessively guilty, I might add:

> There are some children who think that touching themselves is a terrible sin or crime. They think it's the worst thing a person can do. This is a strange idea because touching oneself is perfectly natural and normal. It only becomes a problem if the person does it most of the time and then doesn't do other things, or if the person feels very bad or guilty about it. Feeling that it's a terrible sin or crime is then the problem, not doing it. What are your opinions on this subject?

* * *

Question: A boy's friend leaves him to play with someone else. How does the boy feel? Why did the friend leave?

Response: Bob invited Frank to play with him at his house. But Bob was selfish. He wouldn't share. Frank was his guest. He should have known that it's important to be courteous to a guest. He should have known that it's important to be nice to a guest. Anyway, Frank wanted to share Bob's toys with him and Bob refused. Also, Bob always wanted to decide which game they would play. Finally Frank said that if Bob wouldn't play nicely with him and share, he would leave and go play with someone else. Bob's mother overheard the boys talking and took Bob aside into another room. She didn't want to embarrass Bob in front of his friend Frank. She told Bob, while they were alone, that he wasn't playing nicely with his friend and that he wasn't thinking about how his friend felt. She told him that Frank would go home soon if he didn't start to share with him. She told him that Frank had another good friend, George, whom he could go play with if he wanted. What do you think happened? Do you think that Bob listened to his mother? Do you think that his mother was right or wrong in this case?

Some children have great difficulty sharing. They have difficulty putting themselves in the position of their peers and fail to recognize that the child with whom they refuse to share is likely to be alienated. Some of these children have neurologically based learning disabilities that interfere, on a cognitive level, with their capacity to project themselves into other people's position. Other children may have reached the developmental level where this is possible, but have psychological problems in the realm of egocentricism and narcissism that interfere with healthy functioning in this realm. For children in both of these categories, certain Talking, Feeling, and Doing Cards can be useful.

* * *

Question: Make believe you're reading a magazine showing pictures of nude ladies. What do you think about such magazines?

Response: Boy, there really are some exciting looking women in some of those magazines. I think they're great to look at once in a while. They have some of the most beautiful and luscious women in those magazines. Some people are ashamed to admit that they're interested in looking at those women. I don't think there's anything wrong, bad, or sinful to look at those pictures. I don't agree with those people. I think it's natural and healthy. It's only a problem if the person doesn't want to have anything to do with real people and wants to spend a lot of time looking at those pictures. What is your opinion on the subject?

This response is the one I provide for boys who are uncomfortable expressing sexual interest. Obviously, I attempt here to convey some of the excitement that most boys and men have when looking at pictures of nude women. I also attempt to lessen any guilt the child may have over such interest. My hope is that the child will be receptive to my opinions on the subject and will identify with my attitude.

* * *

Question: A boy was laughing. What was he laughing about?

Response: This boy was not only laughing, but he was cheering. He was just jumping up and down with joy. He had just gotten his eighth grade report card and learned that he had gotten into three honors classes in the ninth grade. He was very happy. He had worked very hard in order to make the honor classes and had hoped that he might make one or two of them. But he didn't think that he would get into all three. He was very proud of himself and couldn't wait to get home and tell his parents. His teacher had written a note on the report card that said, "Robert, I am very proud of you. Good luck in high school." He was also very happy because he knew that, when he applied to college, having been in three honors classes would look very good on his record and this would help him get into the college of his choice. And so he ran home from school laughing and singing all the way. It was really a happy day for him. What do you think about what I said about that boy?

This is the kind of response I provide for children with low academic motivation. My purpose here is to enhance their school interest by demonstrating the joys and ego-enhancement that are the potential benefits of such commitment to the educational process.

* * *

Question: Tell about an act of kindness.

Response: A good example of an act of kindness would be visiting someone who is sick in the hospital and giving up a fun thing that you'd prefer to do. Let's say that a boy in a class was in an automobile accident, injured his leg, and had to be in the hospital for six weeks. Even though his mother and father visited him often, he was still very lonely. His really good friends were those who were willing to give up fun things like playing baseball, or watching their favorite television programs, or just hanging around and relaxing, and instead went to visit him in the hospital. He was very grateful when they came to see him. And they felt good about themselves for their sacrifices. Visiting the friend was an act of kindness. Do you know what the word sacrifice means?

This is the type of response I provide self-centered children, those who have difficulty putting themselves in the position of others. In the ensuing discussion, I would try to help the egocentric child appreciate the feelings of loneliness suffered by the hospitalized child. I would also try to engender in the child the feelings of self-satisfaction and enhanced self-worth that comes from benevolent acts.

* * *

Question: Was there ever a person whom you wished to be dead? If so, who was that person? Why did you wish that person to be dead?

Response: During my childhood and early teens there lived a man in Germany named Adolph Hitler. He was a madman. He was insane. He was the leader of Germany during World War II and was personally responsible for the deaths of millions of people. He was one of the greatest criminals in the history of the world. He used to murder people whose opinions, skin color, or religion differed from his. He not only had them shot but he gassed them to death and burned their bodies in ovens. Millions of people died this way. When I was a boy, I used to wish that he would die. I wished that someone would kill him. I hoped then that maybe all this crazy murdering would stop. To this day, I and many other people in the world feel sorry for the millions of people he killed and all the millions of friends and relatives that also suffered because of his murders. Even though the war ended in 1945, there are still millions of people who are suffering because of the terrible things Adolph Hitler did. These are the people who were put in his prisons and concentration camps and escaped, or were fortunate enough not to have been killed. And these are also the people who are the friends, relatives, children, and grandchildren of those who died there. He was a very cruel man. I really hated him, and I often wished he would die or be killed. Finally, in 1945, he committed suicide. If he hadn't killed himself he would have been captured and executed for his terrible crimes.

This question can be particularly useful for children with antisocial behavior disorders who have little sensitivity to the pains they inflict on others. My hope here, by elaborating on Hitler's atrocities, is to engender in the antisocial child a feeling for the pain that criminal behavior causes others. It is important for the reader to appreciate that when responding to Feeling Cards the therapist does well to try to dramatize as much as possible his or her responses in order to bring about a kind of resonating emotional response in the patient. To engender these feelings in the child who is out of touch with them or who has not experienced them to a significant degree is one of the goals of treatment.

* * *

Question: Say something funny.
Response: Okay, I heard a funny riddle. "What's invisible and smells like worms?" (Generally, the patient does not know the answer. In such cases I will give it.) "A bird's fart!" (This joke generally goes over quite well, except among the most inhibited. Incidently, it

is a statement of the low levels to which the child's therapist may have to stoop in the service of his or her calling.)

The joke may be useful for the child with sexual-inhibition problems as an icebreaker. Sexual and scatological issues often get fused and inhibitions in the sexual area often extend to this area as well. By telling the joke the therapist serves as a model for what I consider to be healthy, normal sublimation. It may contribute to the lessening of sexual inhibitions. The child may reason: "If it's okay for him to talk this way, it's okay for me." In addition, the introduction of some levity into the therapeutic experience is also useful. It lightens the session, makes the therapist more human, and increases the likelihood that the child will become involved. It is part of the seductive process, so important in child therapy.

Doing Cards

The Doing Cards involve physical activity in association with the child's responses. These cards, more than the Talking Cards and Feeling Cards, involve a fun element, and this serves to make the session more enjoyable. My purpose here is to counterbalance some of the less pleasurable aspects of treatment that are likely to reduce the motivation for treatment of even the most highly involved child. Some of the Doing Cards involve modeling and this can also be therapeutic. There are some therapists who consider role modeling and physical activity to be a central part of therapeutic process. I am not in agreement. Often, there is an artificial quality to role modeling, and this makes it less therapeutic than actual experiences or imitations that are spontaneously derived from a situation. Accordingly, I most often use the Doing Cards as a point of departure for direct discussion. My hope is that in the course of such discussions the child will have emotional reactions and experiences that will contribute directly to therapeutic change.

* * *

Question: What is the most selfish thing you ever did? Make believe you're doing that thing now.

Response: Well, the most selfish thing I ever did was a long time ago—it was right after the Second World War—it was in 1946 or 1947. I was looking for a way to earn money to pay for my education in college. It was very hard to get jobs after the Second World War. All the war factories were closing down, and people were fired from their jobs. They didn't need them anymore to make tanks, and guns, and things like that. And all the soldiers were getting out of the Army. And everybody was also getting out of the Navy and Air Force. There were millions of people trying to get jobs. And I finally got a job selling magazines to the wives and mothers of the soldiers who had been in the war. I told the people how important it was to buy the magazine because it would help the veterans, the people who fought in the war. After working a few days I found out that this magazine was kind of phoney. A lot of people weren't getting the subscriptions they were paying for, and I felt very guilty about what I was doing.

I was preying on people's sympathy. I was saying that this was very important for the parents and the wives of the soldiers who were killed or who had fought in the war, and it was a kind of phoney organization. I didn't realize it when I got the job, but after I started working I realized it, and I soon quit. But I felt very guilty, and I think I worked a day or two too much because I needed the money. Do you know what I mean? I should have quit as soon as I realized it. There was so much money to be made, and I needed the money so badly that I stuck with it awhile, but then my guilt overcame me and I quit the job. It was a selfish thing to do. Sometimes when people are hungry, when they need money a lot, then they do things that they would never want to do. I was ashamed of myself when I did that. Do you want to say anything about that?

As mentioned, *The Talking, Feeling, and Doing Game* provides therapists with the opportunity to reveal their own deficiencies in a noncontrived and natural way. This lessens the likelihood that the patient will idealize the therapist. It makes the therapist a more real human being. It lessens the likelihood of the development of the unfavorable comparison in which the patient views the therapist as perfect, and views him- or herself as a bundle of psychopathology. The particular incident was chosen because it demonstrates how guilt can be useful in preventing a person from engaging in antisocial behavior. This is the kind of response I provide for patients who do not have enough guilt over their antisocial behavior. My hope is that the vignette will contribute to the development of a slightly stronger superego.

* * *

Question: You're standing in line to buy something and a child pushes in front of you. Show what you would do.

Response: Let's say I'm a kid and I'm standing here in line and some kid pushes himself in front of me. A part of me might want to push him away and even hit him. But another part of me knows that that wouldn't be such a good idea. I might get into trouble or he might hit me back and then I might get hurt. So the first thing I would do would be to say something to him like, "Hey, I was here first. Why don't you go back to the end of the line and wait your turn like everybody else." If that didn't work I might threaten to call some person like a parent, teacher, or someone else around who is in charge. But sometimes there are no other people around to call, so I might just say that it's not worth all the trouble and that all it's causing me is the loss of another minute or two. If, however, the person starts to push me, then I might fight back. But that would be the last thing I would try. Some people might think that I'm "chicken" for not hitting him in the first place. I don't agree with them. I think that hitting should be the last thing you should do, not the first. I don't think that people who hit first are particularly wise or brave; rather, I think they're kind of stupid.

This is the type of response I am likely to provide the antisocial child. As is obvious here, I am trying to educate the antisocial child to the more civilized option that individuals have learned to use in order to bring about a more relaxed and less threatening society. These options may not have been part of the antisocial child's repetoire. Whatever the underlying factors there are in such a child's antisocial behavior (and these, of course, must be dealt with in the treatment), such education is also a part of the therapy.

* * *

Question: You're standing in line to buy something and an adult pushes in front of you. Show what you would do.

Response: I would tell the person that this is my place in line and that I would appreciate his going to the back of the line and waiting his turn like everyone else. If the person looks like he's crazy, someone who might do dangerous things, I wouldn't make a big deal out of it. There are times when it's smart not to speak up and fight for your rights, but most often it's wise to do so. The important thing is to size up the situation, and get a lot more information before acting. Otherwise, you may find yourself in a lot of trouble.

Obviously, the response to this card should be different from the previous one. It is unreasonable and even injudicious to encourage a child to respond in the same manner to both a child and an adult who pushes him- or herself in line in front of a child. My main point here is that there are times when it is appropriate to assert oneself and other times when it is judicious not to.

* * *

Question: Make believe you're doing something that makes you feel good about yourself. Why does that thing make you feel so good?

Response: As you know, I like to write books. I have already given you one of the children's books that I've written. As I'm sure you can appreciate, writing a book takes a lot of work. It's a very hard job. Sometimes I may work over many years on one single book. However, when I finally finish, I really feel good about myself. I feel that I've accomplished a lot. Although I may be very tired over all the work I've put in to it, I'm very proud of what I've done. And then, when the final printed book comes out, that really makes me feel good about myself. I have what is called a "sense of achievement." Do you know what I mean when I say "sense of achievement"?

I use this response for children who are academic underachievers. After clarification of the meaning of the term "sense of achievement," I might ask the child to tell me things that he or she has done that have provided him or her with similar feelings of accomplishment. My hope here, obviously, is to provide the child with some appreciation of the ego-enhancing feelings that one can enjoy after diligent commitment to a task.

* * *

Question: Make believe you're smoking a cigarette. What do you think about people who smoke?

Response: First of all, I want to say that I have not once in my whole life ever smoked a single cigarette. I remember when I was about 14 years old I went to a party. Some of the kids there were smoking. One kid gave me a cigarette. I really didn't want to smoke it, but I felt that if I didn't take it, all the kids would think that I was "chicken." So I took the cigarette, and I lit it, and I took one puff. I then gasped and started to choke. It really made me sick to my stomach. I then put out the cigarette and said to the guy that had given it to me, "I can't really believe that anybody can like this shit. The only reason that you guys are smoking is because you want to look like big shots. It must take a long time to get used to smoking this filthy weed." And that was the first and last time I smoked a cigarette in my whole life.

Now, if I'm to get a chip, I've got to make believe that I'm smoking a cigarette. Okay, here I go! (imitates cigarette smoking) Egh, is this terrible. (starts coughing heavily) This is disgusting. This is nauseating. (more heavy coughing) Egh, I can't stand this any longer. I hope I've done enough of this to get my chip. It's a heavy price to pay for a chip. People who smoke cigarettes must be crazy. Not only is it a disgusting habit but it can give you all kinds of terrible diseases like lung cancer, heart disease, and diseases of your blood vessels.

I think kids start to smoke because they want to act like big shots. It makes them feel like adults. Then they get hooked on cigarettes and they can't stop. When they get older, and begin to appreciate how really terrible it is, they still can't stop. It's a heavy price to pay for looking like a big shot. Also, it's no great stunt to smoke. If you really want to feel big you have to *do things*, over a period, that makes you feel good about yourself. Thinking that you're going to feel good about yourself by putting a cigarette in your mouth is simple minded. It just doesn't work that way. What do you think about what I've just said?

The response, of course, touches on the most common pathological mechanisms that contribute to children's beginning to smoke. It is quite likely that the antisocial child subscribes strongly and somewhat blindly to these sick values. Not having basic competence in meaningful areas, he or she is likely to embrace quick and superficial methods for enhancing self-esteem. Of course, the utilization of smoking in this regard is strongly promulgated by the advertising of the cigarette industry. Cigarette manufacturers know well that they will increase sales if they associate cigarette smoking with sexual attractiveness and adult "maturity." My response also directs itself to the peer pressure element in the initiation of cigarette smoking. As mentioned, I do not create stories when responding to the cards in *The Talking, Feeling, and Doing Game*. The experiences I relate in my response actually occurred and my reasons for not smoking are those that I genuinely hold.

* * *

Question: Make believe someone grabbed something of yours. Show what you would do.

Response: I would first try to use talk before using action. I'd tell the child to give it back and threaten to grab it back if he or she doesn't return it. If the child was my size or a little taller, I'd try to grab it back, providing it wasn't something that could break. If it was something that could break and/or the person was bigger, I would threaten to call the teacher or my parent(s) if it wasn't given back immediately. I might ask a friend or two to help me get it back. But I wouldn't just stand there, say nothing, and let the person get away with it.

* * *

Question: Make believe you've just met a bully. Show what you would do.

Response: If he were my size I'd let him know that I'm not going to let him get away with taking advantage of me. Even though I might be a little scared, I would fight back. If he called me names, I would call him names back. And if he threatened to hit me, I would threaten to report him to the teacher or to his parents. Or, I would tell him that I'll hit him back twice as hard.

Most bullies are usually frightened kids, and they usually try to pick on kids who won't fight back. The best way to get rid of a bully is to fight back. If you keep letting him take advantage of you then he'll keep picking on you.

These cards are especially useful for children with self-assertion problems. My response provides advice regarding the sequence of steps one does well to follow when one's rights are being infringed upon.

* * *

Question: Make believe you're speaking to someone on the phone. Whom are you speaking to? What are you saying?

Response: I'm speaking to the principal of a school. He's asking me whether I think that a certain girl, let's call her Ruthie, should be promoted. He's telling me that she got Fs in most of her subjects, but that he fears that she'll feel very bad about herself if she's left back, that is, if she has to repeat the grade. He fears that she'll be very embarrassed and humiliated. He's telling me that if she has to repeat the grade, she'll be the oldest one in the class and bigger than anybody else in the class and this will make her feel very bad about herself. He's calling to ask my advice regarding what he should do.

Now this is the answer I'm going to give him. "I think that she should be left back. She really isn't ready to go on to the next grade.

She's failed most of her subjects. She'll feel embarrassed if you leave her back. But if you promote her, she'll feel embarrassed in her new class anyway. If you leave her back, she'll be ashamed for a few days or for a few weeks and then she'll probably get over it and get used to her new class. If you promote her, she'll not only be embarrassed all year but will continue to be ashamed as long as you continue to promote her. In addition, she might end up a drop-out because she'll get so far behind that she'll never be able to catch up. It's a choice between feeling bad now for a short period or feeling bad for many years, or possibly even the rest of her life. That's why I'm telling you that I think she should be left back." What do you think about the advice I gave the principal?

There are schools that give the parents veto power over a decision to have a child repeat a grade. This is a terrible disservice to the child. The reasons for my saying this are basically presented to the child in the aforementioned response. The advantage of retention far outweigh its disadvantages, the embarrassed feelings the child suffers notwithstanding. My main purpose here, of course, is to help the child appreciate that there can be consequences if one does not fulfill one's academic obligations, and one of these consequences is being required to repeat the grade and suffer the attendant embarrassment associated with such repeat. In addition, I point out that even if the child does not repeat the grade, there will be humiliations associated with continually being in a classroom where he or she is behind the other students.

* * *

Question: Make believe you're playing a dirty trick on someone.

Response: I don't think I'm going to get a chip on this one. I don't like playing dirty tricks on people. I remember when I was a kid how badly I felt if someone played a dirty trick on me. And I used to feel sorry for those kids who had dirty tricks played on them. I remember once a kid in my class used to like stealing other children's books and hiding them. He thought it was very funny. Actually, it was cruel. Then the kid whose book was stolen would go home and not have a book to do his or her homework. He or she would have to go to a lot of trouble to borrow someone else's book or go over to someone else's house. Sometimes the kid wouldn't even find the book and then he or she would have to pay for it.

Sometimes dirty tricks can be dangerous. I remember once a boy in my class thought it was funny to trip another kid in the classroom.

Well the boy that was tripped fell down and banged his head against the desk. He hit his head right above his eye and his eye almost got knocked out. He got a big cut over his eye and it was bleeding terribly. I really felt sorry for him and everybody was angry at the kid who tripped him. That kid, of course, got into a lot of trouble. The kid who got hurt had to go to the hospital for stitches and for treatment of his eye. His parents threatened to sue the parents of the kid who tripped their son. However, the parents of the boy who tripped the kid agreed to pay for all the medical expenses. So at least they both didn't have to pay for lawyers. These are just some of the reasons why I don't like playing dirty tricks on anyone. How do you feel about playing dirty tricks on people?"

In the attempt to strengthen the antisocial child's superego I elaborate upon the pains that can be caused by those who hurt others. Children with superego deficiencies, who act out hostilely, generally do not think about the discomforts and pains they cause others.

EXAMPLES OF THERAPIST-PATIENT INTERCHANGES

The examples given above are sample responses to individual cards that I provide when playing *The Talking, Feeling, and Doing Game*. Patient responses have thus far not been provided. In this section I present therapist-patient interchanges in which both the patients' and my own responses are provided. In addition, I comment throughout the transcripts on many aspects of the therapy that emerge from the interchanges.

The Case of Frank (Dealing with a Psychopathic Partner)

Frank, an eleven-year-old boy, was brought to treatment because of moderately severe antisocial behavior. He was disruptive in the classroom, a constant thorn in his teacher's side, and had little appreciation of the fact that he was interfering with the education of his classmates. His general sensitivity to the feelings of those who suffered because of his psychopathic tendencies was practically nil. In addition, he suffered with a severe impulsivity problem. He basically lived by the dictum: "I'll do what I want when I want it." Frank's parents were divorced. However, five years after the separation they were still litigating over a wide variety of issues. Often, Frank was embroiled in the divorce conflicts. Some of his psychopathic behavior was derived from identification with his warring parents, both of whom had little sympathy or respect for one another's feelings. In addition, the anger he felt toward them was being displaced onto school authorities. During his third month of treatment we had this interchange:

> *Therapist:* My question says, "If you could live your life all over again, what things would you do differently?" Well, one thing I would do differently was I made a big mistake about 12 or 13 years ago. You see this building we are in right now?
> *Patient:* Uh huh.
> *Therapist:* I like this office very much. This is an office building that my wife and I built with a third person. That person became our partner.
> *Patient:* You built this whole building?
> *Therapist:* Not myself. An architect built it, but I worked with the architect in planning it, and told him exactly what I wanted in the various parts of the building. I am not an architect and I don't know how to build a building, but I can tell him what kinds of things I want.
> *Patient:* Uh huh.
> *Therapist:* And he was the one who actually designed it, and, of course, builders then came and built it.
> *Patient:* What was the mistake?
> *Therapist:* The mistake was that the man I became a partner with was someone I hardly knew. I knew him a little bit. He was a psychiatrist, and that was a big mistake because he turned out to be the kind of person who had many qualities that I didn't like. He wasn't honest. He didn't want to do his share of the work. And he didn't pay his money when it was due. He wasn't a true partner. He didn't think he had to keep promises that he had made or do the things he promised to do in contracts he had signed. And because we had signed papers and because we were locked in here together in the ownership of this building, I couldn't get rid of him so easily. It was a very messy situation.
> And *I* was partly to blame—not that I was doing anything wrong, in my opinion, and nobody was critical of me—because I didn't get to know the man better before I became his partner. I didn't think in advance of the consequences of what I was doing, and I acted so

impulsively and quickly. Had I taken time and gotten to know the person better, I might have been able to avoid the trouble. I might have learned things about his personality which would have warned me that this would be a bad idea that he was a bad-news person.

And for seven years he was my partner, and it was a lot of grief until finally I gave him—it was worth it—and I gave him a lot of money and bought him out. We bought him out, and he left the building, and I was glad to get rid of him. Then my wife and I sold the building afterwards to other people and I am a tenant here now. But that is not the point. The main point is that I shouldn't have acted so quickly. I should have thought in advance about the consequences of what I was doing.

Patient: You were partners?

Therapist: Yeah, right. So then when the guy left, my wife and I were 50/50 partners. What's my main point in saying this? What's the main point I am trying . . .

Patient: Think before you act.

Therapist: Right! Think before you act. And the second point is: If a person is dishonest, if a person doesn't pull his share of the load, then he's disliked by everybody around him. My wife and I had no respect for him. We couldn't stand him, but we were kind of locked in for a number of years until it became possible for us to get up enough money to buy him out and get rid of him. And so that's the other . . .

Patient: You got all that money back?

Therapist: Well, we sold the building to another person, and now we just rent it like any other tenant. But no. It was a loss of money to buy him out, but it was worth it to us. Although it was painful to give him all that money, it was so bad being with him that it was worth it to buy him out. Understand?

Patient: Yeah.

Therapist: He was such an obnoxious individual, and people who do those things really turn others off and produce a lot of resentment in others. Do you want to say anything else about that?

Patient: Yes.

Therapist: Yeah. What do you want to say?

Patient: You made a mistake to take him as a partner in the first place, but you got rid of him so that's really what counts.

Therapist: Right. Let me tell you an interesting story. You've heard of Japan, haven't you?

Patient: Yeah.

Therapist: Well, let me tell you something.

Patient: Okay. (mumbles) . . .

Therapist: Pardon me?

Patient: The Wall of China.

Therapist: Well, Japan is not China. They are two different countries. They are both in Asia.

Patient: Oh, yeah. That's right.

Therapist: Japan is closer to us, but it's off the coast of Asia. It's part of Asia. Anyway, what I want to tell you is that different people have different customs, and the Japanese are very good businessmen, and Americans . . .

Patient: They are?

Therapist: Oh, yeah. Very good businessmen.

Patient: Wow!

Therapist: Yeah. They're one of the richest countries in the world. Even though they are small. They are very good businessmen, very smart. Anyway, uh, years ago when Americans first went to Japan, American businessmen did not know their customs, and they wanted to make business arrangements with them. They sent some Americans to Japan to talk to the Japanese about business, and the men would come there and they'd say to the Japanese, "Okay, let's start talking about this deal. We want to buy. You want to sell."

And they would say, "No. Let's hold off for a while." And they'd say, "Let's go to dinner." They would go out to dinner, and the next day the Japanese would say, "How about playing golf tomorrow?" And they'd play golf. And then the third day they'd say, "Oh, let's, go sailing, or let's go boating, or let's go to some restaurants."

And the people back in the United States would call, or wire, or write to their friends, you know, their associates and say: "Hey, what are you guys doing over there? Why don't you start signing a contract there and working out business arrangements?"

And the Americans in Japan would say, "We can't talk to them about business. All they want to do is sit around and talk, relax, recreation, golf, and they won't talk business yet. They keep holding off." Anyway, this would go on for five, six, seven days, and the Americans would get upset. And finally one day the Japanese would sit down and they'd say one of two things. Are you listening?

Patient: Yeah.

Therapist: They would say, "Okay, let's talk business," and they would very quickly negotiate and very quickly come to a decision. Or they would say, "We're very sorry. We've decided we don't want to sell you anything, or buy anything from you or work out some business arrangement." And they would very politely say, "Goodbye."

Now the Americans couldn't understand that kind of a practice, this custom. And if they did make an arrangement, they'd have a very small contract. They wouldn't have a lot of lawyers, and it would only be a very small contract. In the United States contracts might be almost a book or two with many pages. Do you know why the Japanese did that?

Patient: Why?

Therapist: They felt that the most important thing in a business relationship is the people that you're working with—whether they are honest, whether they are friendly, whether they're nice, whether you can trust them. They felt if they were trustworthy, then they would enter into a business arrangement. And if they didn't like

. . .

Patient: Why, weren't the Americans trustworthy?

Therapist: Sometimes they were. Sometimes they weren't. Some Japanese businessmen are trustworthy and some aren't. But you don't want to have a contract or a business arrangement with someone you don't like. Someone you can't trust. Someone who lies. Someone who is going to steal. You know?

Patient: Yeah.

Therapist: So they decided that since these people came from the United States, and they were in Japan, it was so far away, it was the other side of the earth, they figured let's get to know the person better, and let's see if we like him, if we can trust him, and if we can, then we will sign, and if we can't, we'll say goodbye. What's my main point?

Patient: American don't trust. I mean to trust people.

Therapist: Good try. You're on the right track.

Patient: To, uh, work with the people you know and trust.

Therapist: Yeah. And if you don't know them too well?

Patient: Forget it.

Therapist: Yeah. Or wait. Don't forget it so quickly. Give them a chance, you know. Get to know them well. See if they are trustworthy and honest, and if they are, then you become friendly with them and then you can become friends with them and then you can become business partners or something like that. Okay. Anything else you want to say?

Patient: No.

As the reader can see, I got a lot of mileage out of this card. I first focused on my own impulsivity in making what soon turned out to be an ill-conceived partnership arrangement. My purpose here was to demonstrate to the patient the untoward consequences of impulsivity. My hope was that it would help him become less impulsive. In addition, in the process I was revealing a deficit, and I have discussed the therapeutic benefits to be derived from such revelations. Then, I pointed out how psychopathic individuals invite the ridicule and scorn of those about them. My hope here was that the patient would consider this repercussion with regard to his own antisocial behavior. As mentioned, I do not consider it necessary to switch to a discussion of the patient's behavior in such circumstances. I believe that getting the principle across may be all that is necessary.

The patient was interested in the story and so I decided to get even further mileage out of the card. I then discussed the situation that American businessmen faced when they first started doing business with the Japanese after World War II. My main point, of course, was that honorable and ethical individuals are more likely to be successful in life than those who are dishonorable. Had this message been given in a straightforward manner, it is not likely that it would have "sunk in." However, presented in the format of the Japanese businessmen, the mesage was more likely to be palatable.

The patient was absorbed in what I was saying. I believe that he got the general gist of my message. I believe that relating stories and experiences in this way is one of the most efficacious mediums for transmitting important therapeutic messages. As mentioned, it is an ancient tradition and the therapist does well to utilize it whenever possible.

> *Therapist:* Okay. Okay. What does your card say?
> *Patient:* "Make believe you are giving a gift to someone. What's that gift?" Here. (Patient makes believe he is giving the therapist a gift.)
> *Therapist:* Uh huh. Thank you. What is the gift?
> *Patient:* It's a thing you put on your desk, and it says, it's your name, Dr. Richard A. Gardner, M.D.
> *Therapist:* What is it? Something for my desk? You mean a desk sign? It gives my name? Okay. Thank you very much. That's very nice. I'll put this on my desk, and when I see it, it will make me think of you. You know? It's not just something that's there. When you give someone a gift, and they like you, your gift will remind them of you when they look at the gift and it will give them a nice feeling. It makes you feel good about the person who gave you the gift. And it makes the giver feel good when he knows that the person who got the gift thinks of him nicely and likes him. Okay. Now your chip. You take a chip.

One of Frank's problems was that he did not put himself into the position of those who were victims of his antisocial behavior. My hope here was to help him appreciate other people's feelings via a description of my reactions to a benevolent act on his part. In addition, I hoped that the interchange might contribute to the strengthening of our relationship. It was a description of pleasant and benevolent feelings that can transpire between people, and my hope was that it would contribute to such benevolent feelings between him and me. My basic feeling at the end of the session was that it did contribute to a strengthening of our relationship.

The Case of Andy
[The Boy with Hypospadias]

Andy entered treatment at the age of nine when he was in the fourth grade. The presenting problems were temper outbursts in school, low frustration tolerance, and a significant degree of self-denigration. Andy was an extremely bright boy who was so advanced in mathematics that he was receiving special tutoring at the ninth- and tenth-grade levels in that subject. In spite of his advanced mathematical competence, he was getting B and C grades because of his temper outbursts in the classroom.

Andy was born with hypospadias, a congenital abnormality in which the urethral opening is to be found at some point along the ventral aspect of the penis, rather than at the tip of the glans. During the first five years of his life he was hospitalized on four occasions for operative repair of his congenital defect. During these hospitalizations it was necessary to tie his hands to the bed rails in order to prevent him from tampering with the dressings. Accordingly, Andy not only suffered with the physical pain associated with his operations but with the psychological stress related to his lack of understanding as to why he was suffering.

Andy had an identical twin brother who was completely normal physically. Furthermore, the brother was also extremely bright and the two of them took their math tutoring together. The brother, however, did not exhibit any of the psychological problems with which Andy suffered and was getting extremely high grades. Nor did he exhibit the self-denigration problem and feelings of low self-worth. The boys had a younger sister who did not manifest any difficulties either. The parents had an excellent relationship both between themselves and among the members of the family. I believed that Andy's symptoms were related to the traumas he had experienced in the first four years of his life and that had he been born physically normal he would not have needed psychiatric attention.

Andy's therapy went quite well. From the outset we had an excellent relationship. I was immediately attracted to him, mainly because of the warmth of his personality and his strong desire to be helped. His high intelligence, I believe, also contributed to his therapeutic progress. There are some who hold that brighter people do not necessarily do better in treatment. Although it is certainly true that there are many highly intelligent people who are also so sick that they cannot profit significantly from therapy, I believe it is also true that the more intelligent the person is the greater the likelihood he or she will be successful in whatever endeavor the person chooses to be involved in—and therapy is one such endeavor. In the course of his treatment Andy learned to handle his anger more effectively and to deal with issues very early, before he suffered significant frustrations and pent-up anger—that would ultimately result in temper outbursts. He learned to become more respectful of himself, and this was associated with a reduction in his tendency to berate himself for the most minor errors. The vignettes from *The Talking, Feeling, and Doing Game* that are presented here are from a session that occurred in his sixth month of treatment, about a month before it terminated.

Therapist: Good afternoon, boys and girls, ladies and gentlemen. Today is Tuesday, December 2nd, 1980, and I'm happy to welcome you once again to Dr. Gardner's program. Our guest and I are playing *The Talking, Feeling, and Doing Game* and we'll be back with you when it's time for someone to answer a question. Okay, you go.

Patient: My card says, "A girl was listening through the keyhole of the closed door of her parents bedroom. They didn't know she was listening. What did she hear them saying?" Now she heard them saying that she, she had a temper tantrum, and they were talking about how to punish her.

Therapist: What were they saying exactly?

Patient: The father said to cut off her allowance for a week, but her mother said not to go to the skating rink Saturday.

Therapist: Uh huh. So it was decided . . .

Patient: It was decided, uh, to cut off her allowance for a week.

Therapist: Uh huh. Did that help? Did that help her to remember not to have temper tantrums?

Patient: Yes.

Therapist: But the big question is what did she have a temper tantrum *about?*

Patient: Well, she, she wanted to ride her two-wheeler, but the fender was all broken up. And her father said, "Yeah, we'll have to fix it, but it will be at least a week."

Therapist: Oh, so she was . . .

Patient: She wanted, she wanted to ride it badly.

Therapist: So she was upset that she had to wait so long. Was that it?

Patient: Yes.

Therapist: What could she have done instead of having a temper tantrum?

Patient: She could just have accepted it.

Therapist: Okay. Any other things she could have done? I think that's part of it.

Patient: . . . (big sighs). . . . I don't know.

Therapist: Anything else? There she was. . . . She wanted to go bike riding . . . and her bike was broken . . . and it would take her father a week to fix it. . . . What else could she have done?

Patient: She could . . . she could have just forgot about it.

Therapist: Well, that's also accepting it. Another thing she could have done is to think about another way she could have some fun. For instance, maybe she could borrow a bicycle from somebody.

Patient: Yeah.

Therapist: Like a neighbor. Or if she had a brother or sister. Then let's say she couldn't borrow a bike from somebody. What else could she have done?

Patient: She could have roller skated.

Therapist: Roller skated. She could have done something else that would be fun. Right? Okay, you get a chip for that. Okay. Now I go.

When answering the card about what the girl heard through the closed door of her parent's bedroom, Andy immediately spoke about his temper tantrums. This is an excellent example of how the cards in *The Talking, Feeling, and Doing Game* will often result in the child's focusing on the basic symptoms for which he or she has come to therapy. The parents are arguing about how to punish a girl who had a temper tantrum. The father suggests cutting off her allowance and the mother prefers that she not be allowed to go to the skating rink the following Saturday. The parents are basically utilizing behavior therapy techniques, that is, negative reinforcement. Of course, there is a place for such disciplinary measures, but they do not get to the heart of the problem. As a therapist, I want to go beyond that and not merely foster a method of dealing with temper tantrums that involves suppression and conscious control of them because of the threat of negative reinforcement.

Accordingly, as a point of departure for more extensive psychotherapeutic inquiry, I asked the patient what the girl had the temper tantrums *about*. In this way, I hoped to obtain a specific example which would serve as a point of departure for a discussion into the causes of the temper tantrum. As mentioned earlier in this book, (especially in Chapter Three), the therapist does well to use *concrete examples* rather than *abstractions* when discussing therapeutic issues. In response, the patient gave as an example the girl's broken bike. She was not only upset that she could not ride it but that it would take a week to have it fixed. At this point, I ask the patient, "What could she have done instead of having a temper tantrum?" In this way I introduce an alternative mode of adaptation to the problem. As mentioned, one of the purposes of therapy is to expand the patient's repertoire of options available for utilization when dealing with life's problems. A broken bicycle presents most children with one of the basic problems of life. In this case, the girl was dealing with it with a temper tantrum—clearly an inappropriate and maladaptive way of responding to the situation. Rather than suggesting immediately to the patient what I would consider to be a preferable mode of adaptation, I tried to elicit his contribution to the solution of this problem.

His response, was "She could just have accepted it." This is certainly a mode of adaptation that can be useful. However, I would not consider it high on the hierarchy of solutions. Rather, I would only recommend such resignation after all others have failed. There are certainly times in life when we have to resign ourselves to the fact that there is nothing we can do about a problem. However, I do not generally recommend that solution as the first. Rather, it should be the last, after all others have failed. Accordingly, I asked the patient if there were any *other* things she could have done. The patient had difficulty coming up with another solution. Accordingly, in order to facilitate his coming up with another solution I slowly repeated the problem: "There she was. . . . She wanted to go bike riding . . . and her bike was broken. . . . and it would take her father a week to fix it. . . . What else could she have done?" My hope here was that my restatement of the problem might catalyze the formulation of another solution by the patient.

Finally, Andy said, "She could . . . she could have just forgot

about it." This response, although somewhat different from the resignation response, is still low on the hierarchy of optimal adaptations. Relegating a problem to the unconscious is certainly a way
of adjusting to it. However, it is not a solution that generally involves any gratification, and so the frustrations that generate the
forgetting reaction are likely still to be operative. At this point, I
considered the patient to have exhausted all of his possibilities and
therefore considered it proper for me to suggest an adaptation myself. And this, too, is an important therapeutic principle. As mentioned in Chapter Three, it is only after the therapist has given the
patient every opportunity to find solutions him- or herself that he
or she should suggest modes of adaptation. Accordingly, I suggested that the girl might *borrow* a bicycle from someone (introducing thereby the principle of *substitute gratification*). The patient
immediately responded well to this suggestion. However, I did not
stop there and again invited the patient to consider what options
the girl might have if she could not borrow a bike from someone.
He responded, "She could have roller skated." This is certainly a
reasonable alternative and allowed the patient himself to contribute
to a solution to the problem.

> *Patient:* "What's the best kind of job a person can have? Why?
> Make believe you are doing that job." I think the best job a person
> can have is working for a charity drive, like UNICEF, or The Amer-
> ican Cancer Society or something like that.
> *Therapist:* Okay. Why is that?
> *Patient:* Because it can help other people who need the help.
> *Therapist:* Uh huh. Right! Right! So you can help other people
> through the Cancer Society and UNICEF.
> *Patient:* Uh. Try to raise money for treatment for cancer.
> *Therapist:* Right. And UNICEF?
> *Patient:* To raise money for poor people around the world.
> *Therapist:* Uh huh.
> *Patient:* For people who don't have enough food.
> *Therapist:* Do you know what that answer tells me about you?
> *Patient:* What?
> *Therapist:* It tells me that you're the kind of person who's very
> sensitive to other people's suffering, and who cares a lot about peo-
> ple who are sick, or who are starving, and that's a fine quality to
> have. And that tells me something about you that's a very admirable
> trait. Do you know what an admirable trait is?
> *Patient:* No. I don't know what it is.

Therapist: Admirable is something you admire in somebody. You know?

Patient: Yeah.

Therapist: It shows me that you're a thoughtful person who thinks about other people and feels sorry for those who are sick or in pain, and those who are hungry. That's what it tells me about you. Anything you want to say about that?

Patient: I . . . Thank you.

Therapist: You're welcome. Okay. You get a chip for that.

The patient's response was clearly an unusual one for a child of nine and a half. In fact, I cannot recall having had a response to that card which demonstrated so much sensitivity to and sympathy for the sick and the starving. I considered the response to reflect very healthy values, values that can only enhance the self-esteem of the person who has them. Furthermore, I praised Andy for his sensitivity, and he was genuinely touched by my comment. I believe this was an esteem-enhancing experience for him also.

Therapist: My card says, "Say something about your mother that gets you angry." Well, I remember when I was a kid, about nine years old or so. Those were the days that we had radios, but no TV, if you can imagine such a world. There was absolutely no television, which they had invented already, but it wasn't around in everybody's house. And I used to listen to the radio.

My favorite program was *The Lone Ranger.* Have you ever heard of *The Lone Ranger?* (The patient nods affirmatively.) The Lone Ranger and his Indian friend, Tonto. And I used to love listening to that at night. And I remember on a few occasions that my mother would say to me that I couldn't listen to it until I had finished my job. I had some jobs to do around the house, and I had this homework, and then after I finished that I'd be able to listen to *The Lone Ranger,* and I used to get angry at her for that because . . .

Patient (interrupting): because it was your favorite program.

Therapist: It was my favorite program. Right. And then once I got very angry and I remember, uh, screaming and yelling and using bad language at her, and really having a fit, and then she punished me. She wouldn't let me watch it(sic) at all for a couple of days, and I really felt bad about that, and was very angry . . .

Patient: Did you have TV in your home?

Therapist: No, I said there was no TV in most people's homes then.

Patient: Then how come you said you "watch it"?

Therapist: Did I say "watch it"?

Patient: Yeah.

Therapist: Yeah? Did I say watch it?

Patient: Yeah.

Therapist: No, I *listened* to it.

Patient: Oh.

Therapist: That was my mistake. I guess I would have *wished* that I could have watched it, in my thinking back now as a kid, seeing it was really . . .

Patient: Did you have that when you finally got a TV? Or did you never get one?

Therapist: Oh, we have TVs now when I got older. But TV sets didn't come, weren't in people's homes, I believe, until the late 1940s, the early 1950s I think. It was after the Second World War. Then they had lots of TV sets around. At any rate, that was one of the things that I was angry at my mother about, her not letting me watch *The Lone Ranger.* But I guess it taught me some lessons about being angry about something. That you don't accomplish much by having a fit. That just makes it . . .

Patient: I know.

Therapist: That just makes it worse.

Patient: I know. I usually have a . . . before I came here, I usually had a lot of them.

Therapist: Uh huh. Do you . . .

Patient: And I got punished for them.

Therapist: Uh huh.

Patient: Usually I got sent up to my room, but I got really angry just for that.

Therapist: Uh huh.

Patient: I wanted to play with my brother and sister and I couldn't because I was upstairs.

Therapist: Oh, I see. You were being punished for a fit?

Patient: Uh huh.

Therapist: And what have you learned here about those fits?

Patient: They couldn't help anything!

Therapist: Uh huh. What's a better way? What's a better thing to do when you're angry?

Patient: Just to, just to . . .

Therapist: What's a better thing to do if you are angry about something?

Patient: Just to think about . . . like . . . I could be angry. I could watch what I want to watch afterwards, after the punishment.

Therapist: Uh huh.

Patient: Besides, it would be on again.

Therapist: Uh huh. But what if you are angry about something, before you get the punishment, before you have the fit? What's a good way to handle something that bothers you?

Patient: Don't handle it in that way.

Therapist: Uh huh. What's a better way?

Patient: Uh . . . a better way is to talk about why you are angry.

Therapist: Right. Right! And by talking about it, what do you try to do?

Patient: You . . . you try to let out your anger but by not having any fits and talking about it.

Therapist: Right! And then what's the purpose in talking, besides letting out your anger? What else does it do?

Patient: It helps you understand . . .

Therapist: It helps you understand, and anything else?

Patient: Let's see . . .

Therapist: It helps you *solve* the problem. It helps you do something about the problem without having a fit.

Patient: That's right.

As mentioned, I always give an honest answer to the cards in *The Talking, Feeling, and Doing Game.* I usually have some ambivalence when I get a card that instructs me to make comments about members of my family. I believe that the therapist has an obligation to selectively and judiciously reveal things about him- or herself for the purposes of the therapy. However, one has an obligation to one's family members not to reveal things to others (patients or non-patients) that are private family matters. What one decides to reveal about oneself is a personal decision; what one reveals about one's family members must take into consideration their needs and right to privacy as well. I have also mentioned how useful I have found the response that relates to some childhood event of mine—an event that occurred when I was at approximately the age of my patient at the time of therapy. This helps strengthen the relationship and can enhance the likelihood that the child will become involved in the therapist's response.

Both of these principles were applied in response to the card. My "criticism" of my mother here really said nothing particularly critical about her. Rather, it describes a "deficiency" within me. In addition, I related an event that occurred during my childhood, an event that I suspected the patient could relate to. And he definitely did. He was interested in hearing about my childhood experience. Just as children's hearing about their parent's experiences strengthens the parent-child bond, a child's hearing about a therapist's childhood experiences (when appropriate) can strengthen the therapist-patient relationship.

Andy picked up my error regarding "watching" *The Lone Ranger* on radio and this in itself can be therapeutic. It makes me human and lessens the likelihood that the patient will idealize me. It can be ego-enhancing for him to benevolently correct an error of mine. It is important for the reader to appreciate that something very important happened here when the patient corrected me. My responding to it in a nonchalant manner provided the patient with a therapeutically beneficial experience. Were he to have been in my position he would have reacted with self-denigration ("How stupid can I be"). By my responding in a relaxed and nonself-deprecatory way, I served as a model for such behavior for the patient. He was also provided with the *living experience* that one can make a mistake and not necessarily castigate oneself for it.

The patient then spontaneously began talking about his *own* fits. This switch provided an opportunity to discuss what he learned about dealing with his anger. We spoke about the measures to take that would reduce the likelihood of his anger building up to such a level that he would have a temper outburst. We spoke about dealing with problems in the earliest phase by expressing one's resentment at the outset. As mentioned, the patient was very bright and was able to learn these lessons well. He clearly was able to use his intelligence therapeutically.

> *Patient:* My card says, "What is the worst thing a person can do? Show someone doing that thing." Waste their life away. That's what I think.
> *Therapist:* Uh huh. Give me an example, like somebody who would be wasting his or her life away.
> *Patient:* Let's say there were two boys. Their father died, and each got half the will. One boy . . .
> *Therapist (interrupts):* What's a will?
> *Patient:* The *will*.
> *Therapist:* The will . . . the will. Oh, the will when someone dies? Yeah. Yeah.
> *Patient (nods affirmatively):* Each got a thousand dollars.
> *Therapist:* This is a made-up story of yours?
> *Patient:* Yes.
> *Therapist:* Right.

Patient: One person, actually it's a different version of a story from the Bible.

Therapist: Okay.

Patient: The one that Jesus told.

Therapist: Okay.

Patient: Well, one person used it wisely and went and got a job, but the other one just wasted his life away with it, and wasted most of the money having a good time.

Therapist: Uh huh. Then what happened?

Patient: He did a lot of things. But when the money was gone, he lost his friends and had no more friends.

Therapist: Uh huh.

Patient: So he had to turn to be a bad guy.

Therapist: That was a real waste of his life.

Patient: But the other one continued, continued to prosper, and he still used his money wisely.

Therapist: Uh huh.

Patient: To get food . . .

Therapist: Uh huh.

Patient: Clothing.

Therapist: How did he get all that money?

Patient: Put it in a bank, and got interest on it.

Therapist: Is that how he . . . ? That was in the Bible?

Patient: No, it wasn't in the Bible.

Therapist (smiling): What was the interest rate in those days?

Patient (laughs): No, I said this is sort of like a modern-day fable.

Therapist: All right. I see. But besides putting the money in the bank and getting interest, did he do anything else?

Patient: Yes, he continued his job.

Therapist: Continued his job. That sounds more like the Bible to me. (therapist laughs)

Patient: Yes. (patient laughs)

Therapist: Uh, anyway, uh, now, so what do we learn from that story?

Patient: That you have only one life to live, and if you waste it, that's it!

Therapist: But some people would say that the second guy really had a great time. He just spent the money and really enjoyed himself while the first guy went to work. And what's so great about going to work? Some would say that this guy was the wise one. What would you say about that?

Patient: I think they're wrong.

Therapist: Why do you say they're wrong?

Patient: Because if you lose all your money, how can you have a good time when you lose all your money?

Therapist: Let's compare the two guys when they got older. See there was one guy, the first guy, he put his money in the bank—at a good interest we assume—and therefore didn't have much fun when he was young because he wanted to work and he put all his extra money in the bank. Then when he was old, he had a lot of money, but was too old to enjoy it. The second guy, the one who pissed all his money away when he was younger, ends up badly, but so does the first. What about those two guys? During that period of their lives?

Patient: They both were not living their lives wisely. Well, you put it that way I'm not really sure now.

Therapist: Uh huh.

Patient: Think it was about equal because . . .

Therapist: Why?

Patient: Because that person, the one who saved his money and stuff had a lot of fun when he retired and stuff.

Therapist: I see. So the one who worked was planning for the future. Was that it?

Patient: That's it.

Therapist: Okay. So that he was the smarter guy.

Patient: Uh huh.

Therapist: That's what you are saying?

Patient: Yes.

Therapist: Because he was taking care of his future. He just wasn't only thinking of the present. Is that what you are saying?

Patient: Yes.

Therapist: I would say that there is something else too. Depends upon the kind of job he had. Some people like their work, and some people don't. What about the guy in your story?

Patient: That guy liked his work.

Therapist: Uh huh. What kind of work did he do? What was he doing?

Patient: He was a founder for the ASPCA.

Therapist: A founder? What's a founder? Oh, you mean he started the organization?

Patient: Yes.

Therapist: I assume that this was not what happened in the Bible.

Patient: (patient laughs)

Therapist: Very good. So he was involved in an organization that took care of animals?

Patient: Yes.

Therapist: I see. Well, that's a very nice thing . . .

Patient: The American Society for the Prevention of Cruelty to Animals.

Therapist: Right. So he did a very noble thing.

Patient: Yes.

Therapist: Do you know what noble means?

Patient: I know what it means but I can't put it into words.

Therapist: Okay. It's very good and kind, and things like that.

Patient: That's what it usually means. Usually I know what it means, but I just can't put it into words.

Therapist: Yes. Sometimes it is hard to define the word that you know what it means. So, actually, though you are comparing the lives of these two guys in different phases of their lives. The guy who was working was still enjoying himself in a different way from the guy who was just splurging his money. Right? What happened to the guy who splurged his money?

Patient: He was dead in a couple of years.

Therapist: What about your guy who's working? Did he have any fun at all?

Patient: Yes he had fun.

Therapist: What did he do for fun?

Patient: Well, he had a pet of his own.

Therapist: Uh huh.

Patient: And, and he wanted a dog.

Therapist: Uh huh.

Patient: And since he took pretty good care of it, in the hunting season the dog returned his gratefulness.

Therapist: By?

Patient: Digging out rabbits out of his hole in the ground so he could shoot them.

Therapist: I see. So he was very helpful. But he had a good time with his dog? Is that what you are saying?

Patient: Yes.

Therapist: I see. So he wasn't just an all work kind of guy. He recognized that life required a balance of having fun and working at the same time. Is that right?

Patient: He was very smart.

Therapist: It sounds like that. Okay. Very good. You get a chip. That was a good one. Here's a chip for you.

The patient's response to the question about the worst thing a person could do revealed healthy values on the one hand and, in my opinion, a somewhat stringent value system on the other. His story, obviously based on biblical themes, revealed his appreciation that there is a price to be paid for the self-indulgent life. However, I considered his values to be somewhat rigid and self-abnegating. Accordingly, I introduced a little more flexibility in our conversation about his story. I helped the patient appreciate that a more balanced lifestyle might be the more judicious—a life style in which there was room for both work and play. I also reinforced the patient's selection of a benevolent career for the wise brother, namely, the ASPCA. This is another example of the patient's healthy values with regard to giving.

Therapist: Okay, now it's my turn. Mine says, "Make believe you're drinking a glass of water." Glugh, glugh, glugh, glugh. You know what?

Patient: What?

Therapist: I have to drink a lot of water.

Patient: How come?

Therapist: A couple of years ago, I had a very painful illness.

Patient: What is it?

Therapist: It's called a kidney stone. Do you know what a kidney is?

Patient: No.

Therapist: Well, I'll tell you. I was in the office here with a patient, with a boy and his mother really. In the middle of the session I started to get terrible cramps. And they were so bad that I had to interrupt the session, and I told the people that I can't go on, I had such pain. And we would have to stop the session, and I became . . .

Patient: Did they understand?

Therapist: Yes. They saw that I couldn't work. It was too painful for me. I was in such pain, and I didn't know what was going on. I had never had any pain like that before, and it was really terrible. And then finally, after about two hours, I thought about the various possibilities what it was. And I punched myself lightly over here (therapist points to his back over the kidney area) and I really leaped. And I knew *then* that I probably had a kidney stone.

Patient: How did you know?

Therapist: You see I'm a psychiatrist and I'm also a doctor. A regular doctor. And I figured when that happened . . . I remember from medical school that that means that I probably had a kidney stone. I didn't know. But certainly it sounded like it. Anyway, I called my doctor and went to the hospital and it was a very painful experience. Uh . . . but it finally passed out. And . . .

Patient: What is a kidney stone anyway?

Therapist: Well, you know the kidneys are up here? (Therapist points to kidney area on his back.)

Patient: Yes.

Therapist: Kidneys. And what the kidney does is take the waste from the blood.

Patient: What . . . it's all blocked up?

Therapist: It filters out waste. You know, your kidney makes your urine.

Patient: Yes.

Therapist: Urine is waste.

Patient: Yes.

Therapist: And waste goes out of your body in your urine when you urinate and go to the bathroom for a bowel movement. That's waste products. The things your body doesn't need.

Patient: Yes.

Therapist: Okay. Now the kidney manufactures the urine, and look what it does. It goes from here in the kidney, which is a round thing like that. (Therapist points to his fist.) And the urine goes down this tube called the ureter. (Therapist draws line with finger over anterior surface of his abdomen which follows the path of the ureter.) Then it goes into this thing called the bladder, which is like a ball or sac.

Patient: It's concentrated.

Therapist: Yes, it's concentrated. Very good! The kidney stores it there. It concentrates it and passes it down into the bladder.

Patient: You know what is done with it? When the bladder gets too full, you have to let it out.

Therapist: You let it out. Right! Now the kidney stone is from the kidney. The urine stagnates—it stands there—in certain little places in the kidney. And when that happens it forms stones, which are like little rocks. And then when that rock has to come out, it's very, very painful. It has to go down through the tube called the ureter. And that is very painful. Then the stone goes into the bladder.

Patient: Will I have to have those stones some day?

Therapist: I don't see any reason why.

Patient: Does everyone get them?

Therapist: No. No. I have a special problem with my kidney that makes my kidney make the stones. I mean it's more likely that I'm going to get them than other people. I have that problem. One of the things I have to do is to drink a lot of water; because if I drink a lot of water, then it will lessen the chances that I will get a stone.

Patient: Oh. That's why you have to drink a lot of water.

Therapist: Yeah. Right. That's for me. That's for my kidney. Now let's see. You had a problem too in that same area. Right?

Patient: Yes.

Therapist: Yep.

Patient: I know what it is.

Therapist: Well, what am I talking about?

Patient: Well, my kidneys . . .

Therapist: Not your kidney. Where was your problem?

Patient: In the bladder I think.

Therapist: No . . . no . . . what are you saying?

Patient: I am saying . . . ask my mom.

Therapist: You know. You know what you had.

Patient: No I don't.

Therapist: You had a problem in that your urine wouldn't come out the right way?

Patient: Uhm.

Therapist: Do you remember that problem?

Patient: Yes.

Therapist: Uh huh. How do things stand with that problem now?

Patient: I didn't like it one bit!

Therapist: What happened with that problem?

Patient: Well, after the operation, they got it back to normal.

Therapist: How is it now?

Patient: Okay.

Therapist: Uh huh. What do you remember about those operations?

Patient (big sigh): The four of them I had in Englewood. The fifth one, the last one, I was in New York.

Therapist: Uh hmm. And what do you remember about the operations?

Patient: What do I remember of it?

Therapist: Uh huh.

Patient: Not much because they were four years ago.

Therapist: Uh huh. How old were you then?

Patient: Five.

Therapist: Uh huh. I see. Do you remember anything about them?

Patient: Uh . . . hmm.

Therapist: Do you remember anything about them?

Patient: Yes, it was really painful.

Therapist: Uh huh. Very upsetting, huh?

Patient: Yes.

Therapist: Do you still think you are upset about that now?

Patient: No.

Therapist: Do you think about it any more?

Patient: No.

Therapist: Did we talk about . . . did we talk about those operations here?

Patient: Yes.

Therapist: Did you learn anything here about them that was useful? Here? About those operations?

Patient: I don't really think so.

Therapist: You don't really think so. Uh huh. Did you feel worse about it before you came?

Patient: I felt worse about it before I came.

Therapist: Uh huh. Is there anything about anything that happened here to you that made you feel less worse about the operations?

Patient: Yes. When it was over.

Therapist: What?

Patient: When it was over.

Therapist: I don't know what you mean.

Patient: The operations were . . .

Therapist: No, no. I mean about coming here that made you feel less bad about the operations.

Patient: Yes. I remember everybody has to get sick once in a while, so I don't feel so bad about my operations.

Therapist: That's one thing. Right! Another thing is to talk about it. You know, not to be ashamed about it. It's no sin. It's no crime. You know?

Patient: I know.

Therapist: It's not . . . but you're right. I agree with you. Everybody has something. Everybody has some kind of sickness and things that happen to them, but it doesn't make you a terrible person or anything else. You know?

Patient: I know.

Therapist: Do you think less of me because I had this kidney stone. Do you think I was a terrible person for having it?

Patient: No.

Therapist: No? Anything to laugh about, or people to think it's funny or something?

Patient: No.

Therapist: Uh huh. Do you think I think less of you because you had that trouble?

Patient: No.

Therapist: No. Not at all. In fact, I admire you very much. I think you're a very fine young man.

Patient: Thank you.

Therapist: And I always think well of and respect you.

Patient (smiling): Thank you.

Therapist: Okay, I'll tell you. Our time is almost up. We want to watch a little bit of this. Okay?

Patient: Okay.

Therapist: So let's see who wins the game. Let's see. How many chips do you have?

Patient: Five.

Therapist: Five? I have three, so you are the winner. Congratulations. (Therapist and patient shake hands.) Okay. Let's watch this.

I used the relatively innocuous card "Make believe you're drinking a glass of water" as a point of departure for talking about a problem of mine that was similar to a problem of the patient's. I suspected that this was a good way of getting him to talk about his hypospadias, and my suspicion proved to be true. Talking about my kidney stone provided me with the opportunity to reveal a physical problem of my own and this, I believe, served the patient well. He and I had something in common. I too knew about pains in that area of the body. I had suffered as had he.

I believe that a factor in the patient's presenting complaint of self-denigration related to his feelings that he was less worthy an individual than others because of his hypospadias and the operative procedures he had suffered in association with its repair. The patient had the experience that I did not look upon him as less worthy a human being because of this problem. Furthermore, my telling him about my kidney stone provided him with the opportunity to see that he himself did not look down upon me for having had this disorder. And this added to my credibility when I said that I did not look down upon him and that others were not likely to disparage him because of his hypospadias.

Andy's treatment progressed quite well. The interchange transcribed here took place about one month prior to termination. He enjoyed a marked reduction of his temper outbursts as well as significant alleviation of his tendency to deprecate himself. His grades improved and he became much more acceptable to friends. I believe the primary factors in his therapeutic improvement were his high intelligence and his winning personality. These attracted me to him and this resulted in his liking me. I also admired his healthy values and I believe my reinforcement of them served to enhance his self-esteem. This enhancement of his feelings of self-worth was another significant factor in his improvement.

The Case of Morton
[Therapists Also Get Rejected]

Morton entered treatment at the age of nine because of disruptive behavior in the classroom. Although there was a mild neurological problem present (he was hyperactive, impulsive, and distractable), his primary problem centered on his relationship with his father. Morton's parents were separated and his father often did not show up for planned visits, or when he did he was often late. In addition, he was not the kind of man who basically enjoyed being with his children. Morton's anger was intense, but it was displaced onto his mother, teacher, and peers because he was fearful of revealing it to his father. While playing *The Talking, Feeling, and Doing Game*, the following conversation took place.

Therapist: My question is "What's the worst thing that ever happened to you?"
Well, I would say that one of the worst things that ever happened to me occurred when I was a teenager. There was a girl in my class in high school who I liked very much. I guess at that time I would say that I loved her. And I thought about nothing else but this girl, and I kept thinking about her and I stopped studying. All I could do was walk around and think about her and I don't think she cared for me too much. She wanted to be friendly with me, but she didn't like me anywhere near as much as I liked her. And I met her around June or so or May. I really got hooked on her and started thinking about her all the time, and she didn't treat me very nicely. And it wasn't until the end of August when she sent me a very painful letter in which she spoke about how much she didn't like me. And I discussed this with a friend of mine and he kind of knocked sense into my head and told me that I was crazy if I answered that letter. And after that, it was hard, but I didn't answer it and I stopped seeing her and I gradually got over it. But it was very painful to me and it was too bad that I didn't realize that it was a foolish thing . . .
Patient (interrupting): I got the message.
Therapist: What's the message?
Patient: Like you loved the girl so much, but she didn't love you!
Therapist: Right. And so what do you do in such a situation?
Patient: Just ignore her. That's all I can think of. Other things? I don't know.
Therapist: Well, what should you do?
Patient: Don't let it bother you.

> *Therapist:* Uh huh. Try to get wise, not trying to get something
> . . .
>
> *Patient* (interrupts): Yeah, yeah, yeah, yeah, yeah! (throws dice)
> *Therapist:* Okay. Good.

I believe that my responding revelation about the incident that occurred when I was a teenager was of therapeutic benefit to the patient. While talking about my own experience, I was really encouraging him to take a more realistic attitude toward his father. By my relating the course of events that led to my own resolution to discontinue trying to get affection from someone who was not going to provide it, I was encouraging him to act similarly with his father. At the same time, I revealed to him that I too am susceptible to similar rejections and I hoped thereby to lessen the antitherapeutic idolization that so often occurs in treatment.

Some readers may have wondered at this point whether I was really being candid with the patient when I stated that being jilted by a teenage girl was the "worst thing that ever happened to me in my whole life." I can easily envision a reader saying, "Is that *really* true, Gardner? That was the *worst* thing that ever happened to you in your whole life?" My response is simply that 20 years ago, when this interchange took place, I still recalled the incident as *one* of the most painful of my life. It was selected because it lent itself well to therapeutic utilization. Had I to answer that question now, I would select from some more recent and certainly more formidable tragedies (such as the murder of my brother in 1985) that would more reasonably qualify for being considered the *worst*.

A subsequent interchange:

> *Therapist:* Okay, my card says, "Make believe a piece of paper just blew in the window. Something is written on it. Make up what is said on the paper."
>
> It says on the paper, "If at first you don't succeed, try, try again. If after that you still don't succeed, forget it. Don't make a big fool of yourself." That's what it says on the paper. What do you think of that?
> *Patient* (laughing): That's a good one.
> *Therapist:* Okay.

My response is a quote from W. C. Fields who is alleged to have made the statement. In my *The Boys and Girls Book About*

Divorce (1970a, 1971b) I have elaborated on this message and made it into a chapter entitled "Fields' Rule." The message here is essentially a reiteration of my previously described experience with my teenage girlfriend. This time, however, the patient did not resist the message and stated with enthusiasm, "That's a good one."

The Case of Harry [Getting Therapeutic Mileage from an Auto Mechanic]

Harry's background history was presented in Chapter Eight (Valentine's Day Candy from a Loving Mother). The interchange recorded below took place while playing *The Talking, Feeling, and Doing Game*.

Patient: "What do you think about a boy who lets his dog make a mess in the house? What should his parents do?" His parents should not let him do what he wants and tell him that if he wants a dog, he's going to have to take care of his messes and everything.

Therapist: And suppose he still doesn't listen?

Patient: Then if he doesn't listen, he's not going to have a dog.

Therapist: Right. And that would be a sad thing. Do you know any other way to do it?

Patient: No.

Therapist: I can't think of one. If he wants to have the fun of a dog, he has to have . . . what's the word?

Patient: . . . the fun of the dog, then he has to take care of the dog.

Therapist: Right!

Patient: If he does not want the fun of the dog, then he is not going to get it.

Therapist: Right! He has to have the responsibility, and he has to do things sometimes he doesn't like. That's how most things are in life. They're a mixture. If you want to get a certain amount of fun, you have to do certain things you don't like sometimes. Do you know anything that's not like that?

Patient: (nods negatively)

Therapist: Well, it's hard to think of something that isn't like that. There's always a mixture of these things.

Okay, my card says, "Of all the things you learn in school, what do you like learning about least? Why?" Well, I don't go to school anymore, but I remember when I was in school the subject that I didn't like very much was economics. Do you know what economics is? What is economics?

Patient: Sort of like a job.

Therapist: Well, it's something like that. It's about money, and buying, and selling, and prices, and things like that. It didn't interest me very much, but I knew I had to take that subject if I wanted to pass in high school and in college. You know?

Patient: Yeah.

Therapist: They just required it. Because I wanted to get my diploma and finish up and because I wanted to take the other courses, I knew I had to take it. I had to take the bad with the good. Do you understand?

Patient: Yes.

Therapist: That's something like we were talking about before, that nothing is perfect and everything is a mixture. What do you think about that?

Patient: (nods negatively)

Therapist: You don't like that idea too much?

Patient (without much conviction): It's okay.

Therapist: It's okay. Is there anything like that in your life? Accepting the bad with the good? Do you know of anything in your life that's like that? I do. Do you have to accept bad things with the good things in any part of your life?

Patient: Yeah, I do.

Therapist: Can you give an example from your life of that?

Patient: No.

Therapist: I can think of one.

Patient: What?

Therapist: Your parent's divorce. There are things there where you have to accept the bad with the good. There are things with your parents' divorce that has to do with accepting the bad with the good.

Patient: No.

Therapist: Oh come on, you can think of something.

Patient: I don't want to say it.

Therapist: You don't want to say it. Well, okay. That's too bad. In this game you get chips for answering. Right? Do you feel like playing this game? Okay, because part of the game is to answer the questions. So if you want to get a chip, you have to say something about your parents'.

Patient (interrupts): Well, you've got to answer your questions, I don't.

Therapist: I answered already. I answered with economics. But I'm giving you a chance to get an extra chip if you can say something about your parents.

Patient: No, I don't want an extra chip.

Therapist: You don't want it. Okay.

One of Harry's problems was that he refused to accept responsibility. He did not want to suffer any discomfort or inconvenience. He fit well into the category of the boy whom I described earlier—the deprived child who lives by the pleasure principle because he was never rewarded with love and affection for self-restraint. I tried to use the examples of the dog and the subject of economics to get across the point that toleration of discomfort is often necessary if one is to enjoy certain benefits. On an intellectual basis the patient appeared to be somewhat receptive. I then tried to shift into a discussion of the advantages and disadvantages of parental divorce. However, Harry would have no part of the discussion. The lure of the chip reward did not serve as an incentive. Accordingly, I did not pressure him any further and we proceeded with the game.

The interchange with Harry here raises an important technical point in the treatment of patients. Some therapists take a very passive position regarding any pressures on the patient to speak about a specific subject. They consider this not only respectful of the patient's wishes, but believe that to do otherwise is to invite further resistance to the treatment. They also believe that such urging can be anxiety provoking and that it is per se antitherapeutic. I generally do not pull back so quickly when a patient exhibits manifestations of resistance and/or anxiety when discussing a "touchy subject." I believe to do so might deprive the patient of an important therapeutic experience. Some patients need a little urging and are better off afterwards for having experienced the thoughts and feelings attendant to dwelling on the sensitive subject. The therapist cannot know beforehand how much anxiety and resistance will be engendered by suggesting further inquiry into a given area. He or she should be exquisitely sensitive to whether or not the therapist's pressure is producing undue anxiety and/or resistance. If such appears to be the case, it is time to "pull back." Here, I believed that Harry was approaching that point when he adamantly refused to pursue this subject—even after being informed that he would thereby deprive himself of a further chip. He firmly stated, "No, I don't want an extra chip." I got the message, and we proceeded with the game.

Therapist: Let's go on then. (throws dice) My question is, "What do you think your life will be like 20 years from now?" Well, 20 years from now I will . . .

Patient (interrupts): You might be dead in 20 years.

Therapist: Well, how old do you think I am?

Patient: Forty-two.

Therapist: Thank you very much. I appreciate the compliment. No, I'm going to be 50 next month. What do you think of that?

Patient: I thought you were 40 something.

Therapist: I am 40 something. I am 49, I am 49 and 11/12. So twenty years from now I will be 50. (Therapist laughs as he immediately recognizes the slip and its obvious significance.) I really wish I would be fifty. Twenty years from now I will be 70. Do you think I'll be dead?

Patient: Yes.

Therapist: You think so?

Patient: Yes, because my uncle was in the hospital and he died.

Therapist: There are a lot of people who die before 70, and there are a lot of people who don't. I certainly hope that I'm still alive.

Patient (speaking with warmth and conviction): So do I.

Therapist: Anyway, if I am alive, and I think I probably will be, I can't be 100 percent sure, I will probably still be a psychiatrist and will be trying to help kids.

Patient: But you will not have me as a subject(sic) because I will be 30 years old.

Therapist: You will be 30 years old? What will you be doing then? I will be doing psychiatry.

Patient: I will be an auto mechanic.

Therapist: An auto mechanic.

Patient: Do I get a chip for that?

Therapist: Okay, you get a chip for that. I hope you will be a good auto mechanic, and I hope you have a very good business.

Patient: Yeah, so do I. Lots of money!

Therapist: But you have to work very hard at it you know. Whatever you do, if you're going to goof off, if you're an auto mechanic and you goof off, you're not going to have any customers. People are not going to come back. But if you do a good job, then you'll have many customers. Right?

Patient: (nods affirmatively)

Therapist: Okay. Very good.

One could argue that Harry's thinking I might be dead 20 years from now was definitely a manifestation of hostility. Although I admit this is certainly a possibility (especially because it was preceded by my strongly encouraging him to talk about the touchy subject of his parents' divorce), his comment may have had nothing to do with hostility. It is important to appreciate that Harry was 10 years old, and I was mid-to-late middle aged. Children's appreciation of adult's ages is often limited. Furthermore, his appreciation of the significance of a 20-year advance in my age is also likely to be somewhat distorted. I did not automatically assume that his interjected response reflected hostility. (I do not doubt the possibility either; I only consider it unlikely.)

I did, in the true analytic spirit, ask Harry to guess my age rather than blurt it out. However, in Harry's case, I did not consider it a fruitful area of inquiry to delve into his erroneous speculation any further. His guess that I was 42 instead of 49 was not, in my opinion, conclusive evidence for some kind of psychodynamically determined error. To have done so, in my opinion, could have been antitherapeutic in that it would have involved us in an inquiry into a subject that might or might not have had psychological significance. I was content to leave the issue alone and reveal my actual age. As mentioned, I believe there is often an important benefit to be derived in treatment from such revelations. They bring the patient and therapist closer, and this may be more important than an analytic inquiry. Even though the therapist may be depriving the patient of some important psychoanalytic insight, this may be more than compensated for by the strengthening of the therapist-patient relationship that such divulgences bring about.

I answered the question by informing Harry that I fully intended to be continuing to do psychiatry in 20 years. I wanted to get across the notion that I find my work interesting and enjoyable, and that the prospect of retiring completely is not only distasteful to me, but would be completely out of character for me. My hope was that some of this attitude toward productive endeavors might filter down to Harry.

Harry then answered the question and offered that he would be an auto mechanic. I generally follow through with such interruptions because they often provide useful therapeutic material. Unless the interruption is obviously a resistance maneuver, I "milk it for all it's worth." It would be completely outside of the philosophy of the game for me to say to the patient: "Hey, wait a minute now. This is my question. You wait your turn." Such a response would totally defeat the purpose of the game—which is to elicit psychodynamically meaningful material from the patient.

The patient emphasized the material benefits to be derived from being an auto mechanic. I took this opportunity to introduce a comment about the work ethic and the importance of doing a good job and establishing a good reputation. I do not believe at that point that the statement "hit him in the guts." However, it behooves the therapist to transmit his or her therapeutically important messages and hope that they will ultimately be received. In no way did I consider Harry's switching the subject to his future life as an auto mechanic to be a resistance maneuver. Rather, I welcomed it from the realization that school and work are analogous and that anything I could say about his work as an auto mechanic would be likely to have applicability to his school work. Furthermore, because Harry was extremely unreceptive to discussing his school work directly, I viewed discussions about the principles of being an auto mechanic to be a potential vehicle for talking symbolically about Harry's school difficulties in a way that Harry would welcome.

> *Patient:* My card says, "What would you do if you found $10,000?" If I found $10,000, first I would return it to the police station to see if it is anybody's. Then, if it is not anybody's, I would know in 30 days that I would get to keep it. If I get to keep it, then I am going to buy my own auto mechanic shop.
> *Therapist:* That's a good purpose.
> *Patient:* So my store will be nice, and many people will come. So it will be a nice clean place to get your car fixed, and washed, and everything, and take every bit of advice to make people's cars look nice. It will be a real, nice, clean place.
> *Therapist:* To create a good impression. Right?
> *Patient:* Yeah, to create a good impression.
> *Therapist:* That's important. It's important to create a good impression. It shows you have pride in your place; but it's also important that you do good work, you know. There are some places that look flashy and nice, but the work is no good.
> *Patient:* Mine is going to look flashy and do the best work.
> *Therapist:* Okay. I think that the important thing is the work. The second important thing is how it looks.

Here, the patient again focused on external appearances and made no mention of the quality of work that his auto mechanic shop would provide. I praised him on his interest in a clean shop that made a good appearance. But, I also emphasized the importance of high-quality work. This was especially important for this boy whose commitment to the work ethic in school left much to be desired.

These interchanges on the subject of the auto mechanic shop represent what I consider to be among the most efficacious forms of child psychotherapeutic interchange. To the casual observer the patient and I are involved in a relaxed discussion on the somewhat neutral and even banal subject of auto mechanic shops. There is almost a "folksy" quality to the conversation. However, from the patient's point of view it is probably just that: simply a conversation. From my point of view, however, much more is going on. At every point I am actively concerned with two processes: 1) the ostensible conversation and 2) the underlying psychodynamic meaning of what is going on. What may appear to be a relaxed conversation is, for me, almost a façade. The wheels are ever going around in my head. I am ever concerned with both of these processes simultaneously. I am ever trying to relate my comments to the patient's basic difficulties and how they are reflecting themselves in what he is saying. This is the way I transmit my most important therapeutic communications. I cannot emphasize this point strongly enough.

Freud referred to dreams as "the royal road to the unconscious." I am in full agreement. And I would consider stories and conversations of this kind to be the royal road to therapeutic change in children. And even with adults the process has merit. Quite often I will in the course of the session with an adult patient relate an anecdote or an event that has relevance to his or her problems. It is a way of getting home a point with a vehicle that is extremely powerful; far more powerful, I believe, than a therapeutic approach that relies upon gaining insight into unconscious processes. Lastly, it is an approach that has history to recommend it. It is an ancient method that has survived to the present day because of the universal recognition of its efficacy.

> *Therapist:* "Of all the things you own what do you enjoy the most? Make believe you are doing something with that thing." I would say that one of the most important things I own is my typewriter. (therapist imitates typing)
>
> *Patient* (interrupts): Isn't that your favorite thing? What about that? (patient points to mounted video camera)
>
> *Therapist:* You like that too?
>
> *Patient:* Yeah!
>
> *Therapist:* Why do you think I would choose that?
>
> *Patient:* Because you could make movies.

Therapist: That is a lot of fun. I think that's a good answer too. That is also one of my favorite things. I like the TV because I can see myself on television anytime I want.

Patient: You can say "hello," and you can look at the television, and see yourself say hello.

Therapist: Yes, but more important than that it helps me be a better psychiatrist.

Patient: It does?

Therapist: Yeah, because we are playing this game here and people see themselves on television, and it helps them see themselves better, and it helps me be a better psychiatrist in this way.

Patient: Uh-oh!

Therapist: What is uh-oh?

Patient: You're supposed to have two of these chips.

Therapist: Oh, did I forget? Okay, I guess I forgot. (therapist takes chip) Okay. Let's get back to the question. You were close when you guessed the TV camera, but I was not going to say that. I was going to say *typewriter* because with the typewriter I write books, and stories, and things like that. It makes me feel very good because when I write a book—and especially when it comes out—it makes me feel good that I created something.

I began responding to the question about my favorite possession by mentioning the typewriter. I planned to use it as a point of departure for discussing the gratifications I enjoy from writing. My hope was that this would engender in Harry greater motivation in his academic pursuits. However, he interrupted me and pointed to the video camera that was recording the program that we were making. As mentioned, I generally welcome such interruptions because they usually relate to issues that may be more relevant to the child than those that I may be focusing on at that point. (Of course, when the interruption is a reflection of resistance, then I do not permit it and insist upon my right to return to my card and answer my question.)

I allowed the digression and got as much mileage as I could out of a discussion of the video camera and the closed-circuit television system. I got in the message that it was useful for helping people see themselves and this, of course, is a crucial aspect of treatment. I did not get very far with this explanation when the patient noted that I had failed to collect one of my reward chips. When the game is being played at its best, both the therapist and the patient may forget whose turn it is and may forget to collect the reward chips. Following the rectification of this error, I returned to the typewriter theme and focused on the good feeling I have when a book of mine comes out. At that point Harry interrupted me, and the following interchange took place.

> *Patient* (interrupts): What's that over there? (Patient points to a pile of just-published books, *Dr. Gardner's Fables for Our Times* [1981b].)
> *Therapist:* That's my new book. It just came out.
> *Patient:* When?
> *Therapist:* The book came out yesterday. Would you like to borrow a copy?
> *Patient* (very enthusiastically): Yeah!

The psychological significance of this interchange concerning the new book as well as the subsequent conversation, will be more meaningful with the following background information. I routinely give a complimentary copy of my book *Stories About the Real World* (1972a) to every new patient. These stories cover a wide variety of conflict situations of childhood, and it is a rare patient who does not relate to at least one of the stories. I use the child's reactions as a point of departure for therapeutic interchanges. Accordingly, Harry had been given a copy of this book during my initial consultation. Subsequently, I lent him a copy of my *Dorothy and the Lizard of Oz* (1980d). Unfortunately, he lost the book. When he told me of the loss, it was with a complete absence of embarrassment, guilt, remorse, or a desire to make restitution. Because of this I told him that I would lend him another book with the understanding that if he lost this one, he would have to pay for it. I considered this requirement to provide Harry with a useful therapeutic experience. Not to have made some attempt to require responsibility on his part would have been, in my opinion, antitherapeutic. This is just the kind of *living experience* that I consider important in therapy. The therapist should seize upon every opportunity he or she can to provide patients with such experiences. The interchange over the lost book is an excellent example. Harry absolutely refused to accept the book with that proviso. We discussed it for a few minutes at that time, and I tried to impress upon him that I felt bad that the book was lost and that I wanted to protect myself from further losses. I also tried to help him appreciate his own lack of remorse over the loss, but this fell on deaf ears. In the conversation I knew that he wished to borrow the book, but I knew also that he did not wish to assume responsibility for its loss. I believed that my refusal to lend him the book without "protecting myself" might have been a more valuable therapeutic experience than any discussions we did have or might have had on the subject.

This is what I was thinking when Harry pointed to the new book. It was not placed there to attract his attention. (I do not set up artificial situations like this in therapy. No matter what items are present in the therapist's office, the pressure of the unconscious is going to invest them with special meaning in accordance with the psychological processes of the patient.) Harry immediately expressed interest in the book, and I thought this would be a wonderful opportunity to offer to lend him a copy. He responded with enthusiasm.

> *Therapist:* I'll let you borrow a copy, but let me ask you something. If you were in my place, would you be hesitant to lend the book? Should I be hesitant to lend you a book?
>
> *Patient:* I think you should give me the book just like you gave the *The Real World Stories.*
>
> *Therapist:* Okay, but what about lending you a book? You don't think I should lend you the book?
>
> *Patient:* No.
>
> *Therapist:* Why not?
>
> *Patient:* I don't know.
>
> *Therapist:* I had an experience with you that made me hesitate to lend you a book. Do you remember that experience? What was the experience?
>
> *Patient:* The last . . . book you lent me I lost.
>
> *Therapist:* Yeah, I lent you a book and you lost it.
>
> *Patient* (angrily): So don't give me the book; I don't really care.
>
> *Therapist:* But if I just give it to you, that won't help you remember not to lose things.
>
> *Patient:* Ah, I don't want your book . . . just forget it!
>
> *Therapist:* It's a new book of fables called *Dr. Gardner's Fables for Our Times.*
>
> *Patient:* I don't really care about it; you can keep it for yourself.
>
> *Therapist:* I just want to say something. If I lend it to you now . . . I would like to lend it to you and give you a second chance. I never condemn a person for one mistake. Do you know what I mean? You're entitled to a mistake; everybody makes mistakes. But it makes me hesitant; it makes me a little concerned. How about this? I'll lend you the book?

Patient (interrupts): No, I don't want it!

Therapist: Let me tell you what I'm suggesting.

Patient: I don't want it!

Therapist: I'll tell you what. I'll lend you the book, but if you lose it, you have to pay for it.

Patient: No, I'm not going to do it.

Therapist: Why not?

Patient: Because I don't *need* the book.

Therapist: Okay, that's up to you, but I would have liked you to have borrowed it, but I'm not going to lend it to you just like that, because I'm afraid you might lose it or not take good care of it. But maybe you'll change your mind. If you change your mind, let me know.

Patient: Okay. Did you answer your question?

Therapist: I think I did.

Patient: Wait . . . what was that question?

Therapist: "What are my favorite things?" I said my typewriter because it makes me feel good when I write books and the books help other people. Books help other people with their problems. They teach them things and lots of people say they learn a lot from them. And that makes me feel good too. You feel good when you do something that helps other people. Do you do things that make you feel good? What do you do that makes you feel good?

Patient: I'm nice to people.

Therapist: That's right, it makes you feel good when you're nice to people, right?

Patient: Yeah.

Therapist: Right. You get a chip for that answer, because it was a very good answer. And I get a chip for my answer.

It was quite clear that Harry really wanted to borrow the book. However, he absolutely refused to assume any responsibility for its loss. I tried to seduce him into making a commitment by continuing the conversation in the hope that it would intensify his craving for the book. Although I was unsuccessful in getting him to make the commitment to provide restitution if the book were lost, I do believe that he had a therapeutic experience. There were indeed repercussions for his casual attitude over the loss of my book, and he had the living experience that book owners under such circumstances are likely to be reluctant to lend him additional books. He suffered the frustration of not being able to borrow the book. This, I hoped, would be a useful therapeutic experience. There was no analytic inquiry here; there was little if any insight gained by Harry. However, something therapeutic was accomplished—the lack of insight on Harry's part notwithstanding.

Many therapists are far less enthusiastic than I about interchanges such as these. They are deeply committed to the notion that without insight there cannot be therapeutic change. They subscribe deeply to Freud's dictum: "Where there was unconscious, there let conscious be." I am not as enthusiastic as Freud was over the therapeutic benefit of insight. I am much more impressed with the therapeutic changes that occur from experiences as well as messages that are imparted at the symbolic level. For therapists who are deeply committed to the insight route to change, I often provide the analogy of my scuba-diving experience. My instructor repeatedly advised the class that it was vital for all of us to learn ways of dealing with emergency situations while under water. The worst thing that one can do in such situations is to hold one's breath and get to the top as rapidly as possible. It is one of the quickest ways of killing oneself. It is one of the quickest ways of bursting one's lungs. Accordingly, we were repeatedly advised to fight the impulse to rise to the top when we were in trouble. We were meticulously taught the various ways of dealing with underwater emergencies. I can tell the reader from personal experience that the urge to hold one's breath and rise to the top under such circumstances is immense. It seemed that every force and reflex in my body was dictating such a course of action. It was only with formidable self-control that I fought these urges on two occasions when I had difficulty. Of course, my knowledge of the consequences of submitting to them was of help in my suppressing them.

I mention the scuba experience because it relates directly to those therapists who are deeply committed to insight as the primary mode for helping their patients. Just as my scuba instructor urged me to fight my impulse to hold my breath and rise to the top, I suggest that therapists fight their impulses to pursue the insight route. I suggest that they consider the alternatives discussed in this book. I do not view insight as totally meaningless in the therapeutic process, but I generally view it as less significant for children than it is for adults, and even for adults it is a low-priority therapeutic modality. It is frosting on the cake. I am in agreement with Frieda Fromm-Reichmann who said, "The patient needs an experience far more than an insight."

CONCLUDING COMMENTS

The popularity of *The Talking, Feeling, and Doing Game* has been a great source of gratification. It has become standard equipment for the child psychotherapist, and many therapists consider it vital in their work with children. Over the years I have received many letters in which the therapist has expressed gratitude for my introduction of the game. I have even had the dubious compliment on a few occasions of plagiarized versions being introduced. These, to the best of my knowledge, have never enjoyed similar popularity. (One such plagiarizer lost motivation to continue marketing the game after a letter from my attorney "reminding him" of the consequences if he did not cease and desist.)

Although the game was originally devised in an attempt to engage children who were not free enough to provide self-created stories when utilizing the mutual storytelling technique and its derivative games, it has proven useful for more cooperative and insightful children as well. In fact, I would say that it is a rare child who will not get involved in the game.

I have also found it useful in the therapy of small groups of children in the five to twelve age range. Children in this age bracket are traditionally poor candidates for group therapy because of their age-appropriate rambunctiousness. Often, the therapist finds him- or herself serving more as a disciplinarian than a therapist. *The Talking, Feeling, and Doing Game* provides an organization and a structure that is often so powerful that children of this age are diverted from the horseplay that often compromises significantly the group therapy. One can use it for this purpose in a number of ways. One way I have found useful is to have the first child respond to a card and then get input from each of the other players on the first player's response. Each of the other participants, of course, receives a chip for his or her contribution. The second child may now answer the same question or choose one of his or her own. In this way I go around the board, engaging each child in the responses of the others. When utilizing the game in this manner the therapist can choose whether or not to participate as a player. I generally prefer to play as one who takes the card him- or herself for the sake of "egalitarianism" as well as the desire to gain the therapeutic benefits to be derived from my revelations about myself.

The game can also be useful in selected family therapy situations. Generally, unsophisticated and/or uneducated parents may welcome the game as a catalyst for family discussion; more sophisticated and/or educated parents will generally not need such assistance in their family therapy work.

The Talking, Feeling, and Doing Game is not without its disadvantages. All good drugs have their side effects. In fact, it is often the case that the more powerful the drug the greater the side effects. One of the main drawbacks of *The Talking, Feeling, and Doing Game* is that it may be *too* enticing to both the patient and the therapist. It is seemingly an easy therapeutic modality. Many therapists, I am certain, play it without fully appreciating its complexities and how difficult it can often be to utilize it properly for therapeutic purposes. The child, too, may find it attractive because it seemingly protects him or her from talking about more painful subjects directly. It should not be used as the only therapeutic modality because it will deprive the therapist of some of the deeper unconscious material that can more readily be obtained from projective play and storytelling. In short, therapists should not be tempted into using the game throughout every session; they should do their utmost to balance the therapeutic activities with other modalities.

I have also found the game particularly useful in the treatment of children with neurologically based learning disabilities. Its utilization for this purpose is described elsewhere (1973g; 1974e; 1975c,d,e; 1979e; 1980b,c). For further articles on the game's general utilization I refer the reader to book chapters of mine on the subject (1983d, 1986d).

TWELVE

Bibliotherapy

In the best books, great men talk to us, give us their most precious thoughts, and pour their souls into ours. God be thanked for books. They are the voices of the distant and the dead, and make us heirs of the spiritual life of past ages. Books are true levelers. They give to all, who will faithfully use them, the society, the spiritual presence of the best and greatest of our race.

William Ellery Channing

INTRODUCTION

I use the term *bibliotherapy* to refer to the use of books in the therapeutic process. I believe that this therapeutic modality has not been given the attention it deserves. My experience has been that this area is underrepresented in the psychotherapeutic literature, although one does occasionally come across articles on this subject. Psychoanalysts, especially classical psychoanalysts, generally frown upon therapists' recommending specific books to their patients, lest the "blank screen" be contaminated. I am in agreement that suggesting specific reading material to a patient may indeed bring about such compromise, but I also believe that this drawback may be more than compensated for by the advantages to the patient of such reading material.

As I have mentioned on numerous occasions throughout this book (especially in Chapter Three), I consider the educational element to be central to the psychotherapeutic process. And even in the most passive therapeutic approaches, the patient generally learns from the therapist about how better to cope with and adapt to life. There is deep wisdom in the aphorism "knowledge is power." Hans Strupp (1975), who has devoted himself extensively to delineating the elements in psychoanalytic psychotherapy that are of therapeutic value, considers a most important element to be what he calls "lessons in constructive living". The more knowledgeable one is about the world, the greater will be one's ability to cope with its inevitable problems, the greater will be one's capacity to adapt to it, and the less will be the likelihood that one will have to resort to pathological ways of dealing with life. Knowledge about the world may contribute not only to preventing the formation of psychological disturbances but to reducing them as well.

One of the most popular and ancient sources of such knowledge is books. Children often enjoy reading books and being read to from them. Books therefore provide a multisensory (visual and auditory) vehicle for the communication of therapeutic messages. They provide a mode of communication that might not be possible through simple discussion. Pictures and colors attract the child and enable the messages to be delivered "in an attractive package."

Books have been written to help prepare children for specific traumatic experiences, such as hospitalization (M. Pyne, 1962). There have been books written for adopted children (C. Livingston, 1978; F. Rondell and R. Michaels, 1951). Dozens (and probably hundreds) of books have been written for children on the subject of sex. Some of the most well known are by E.W. Johnson (1967), W.B. Pomeroy (1968, 1969), and P. Mayle (1973). Although these books can provide therapeutic benefit in a palatable format, it is important that therapists and parents select books that are appropriate to the child's intellectual and maturational levels. Goldings and Goldings (1972) have written an excellent article describing the various ways in which books can serve as a therapeutic modality.

My own contributions in this area generally fall into four categories: 1) expository, 2) reality-oriented, 3) fables, and 4) fairy tales. Although there are certainly other categories of children's literature, these are the four in which I have written. Furthermore, I have placed these categories in such an order that they represent a continuum from the most didactic to the most fantastic. This sequence may also be viewed as representing a continuum from the most to the least anxiety provoking, from those that may be the least interesting to children to those that are predictably the most attractive. Each type can be useful in therapy and all can be made attractive to children, especially if they deal with issues of psychological relevance to the child at the time he or she is reading the story.

THE EXPOSITORY BOOK

In expository books, the child is told directly the particular therapeutic information which the author wishes to convey. Of the four types of bibliotherapy discussed here, expository books are likely to be the ones to which children are least receptive because they do not contain any of the fanciful elaboration that is so predictably attractive to children. They may be more successful, however, if they deal with themes that are particularly relevant to problems that the reader is dealing with at the time the book is read. The child's interest, then, stems not so much from the desire for entertainment, but from the need for solutions to problems that are causing pain and stress.

It may be of interest to the reader to learn that the first book I ever wrote was in this category. In fact, it was not until 1964 that I first thought about writing a book. And the idea did not originate with me, rather it came from the father of a child in treatment. The child, then twelve, was known to be "brain injured" (the term used for what we presently call minimal brain dysfunction). During the three years prior to my consultation, he developed a series of superimposed symptoms that are generally considered psychotic: arm flapping, sitting on the floor, dropping blocks, and preoccupation with dinosaurs. In the initial screening interview the parents were particularly cautious about discussing the child's difficulties in his presence as they had been repeatedly warned by various authorities that they should never reveal to him that he was brain injured.

My evaluation confirmed the basic neurological impairments and revealed that the child was overwhelmed by anxiety. One of the primary sources of his anxiety was related to his ignorance of what was wrong with him. Accordingly, I advised the parents to tell the child what was wrong with him and to describe the nature of his problems and its causes. They flatly refused, quoting the various authorities who had warned them never to reveal to the child the nature of his illness. In the ensuing discussions I presented to the parents my various reasons for recommending that the information be revealed and managed to convey to them the judiciousness of such revelation. I explained to them how such withholding of information could cause distrust of the parents, how it was increasing the child's anxiety, and how it could make the child feel that his illness was worse than it really was. In one self-created story the child spoke of the dinosaurs as being stupid and as having small brains. I tried to impress upon the parents my belief that the dinosaur preoccupation was related to the child's view of himself as stupid, which was really not the case in that he was of average intelligence. I reassured the parents that I would schedule follow-up appointments and be available to help them and the child work through any possible untoward reactions he might have following the revelation.

Reluctantly, they went home and followed my advice. Within a few weeks there was a dramatic reduction (in fact, almost a disappearance) of the secondary psychogenic symptoms. The primary neurological manifestations, of course, still remained. The parents were most gratified over the results. In our closing session the father thanked me again for my help and suggested, "Doctor, you ought to write a book about brain injury for children. It really helped my boy and a book on this subject should certainly help others." Two years later, the New York Association for Brain-Injured Children published my *The Child's Book About Brain Injury* and my career as a writer was launched.

MBD: The Family Book About Minimal Brain Dysfunction

In 1973 this book was updated, expanded, and republished as *MBD: The Family Book About Minimal Brain Dysfunction* (1973a). The first half of the book is devoted to parents and provides them with advice that might prove useful to them in handling the special problems of the MBD child. The second half is written for MBD children and helps them understand the various manifestations of their disorder. Advice is provided in a concrete fashion to help them deal more effectively with their difficulties. The book is based on the principle that discussing the "undiscussable" makes the taboo subject less anxiety provoking. It is also based on the assumption that the more information one has about a disorder, the better the likelihood one will be able to deal with it as effectively as possible. In both the parents' and the children's sections, the importance of using the book as a point of departure for parent-child communication is emphasized. I have found the children's section especially useful in therapy. Reading the book along with the child can bring up a variety of issues that are useful to discuss in the therapeutic situation.

The Boys and Girls Book About Divorce

The Boys and Girls Book About Divorce (1970a, 1971b) has thus far been my most popular book. It is a source of deep gratification that it has undergone many printings, in both hard cover and paperback, and there have been a number of foreign translations as well. It may be of interest to the reader to learn that the book was originally rejected by sixteen major publishers. Finally, in 1970, it was published by Science House (now Jason Aronson, Inc.), a publisher of psychiatry and psychology books. But it was the Bantam paperback, which came out a year later, that enjoyed widespread popularity.

When writing the book, I faced the conflict of whether to write it in a novel or expository form. With regard to the novel, I wondered whether it might be more appealing because it would be closer to the type of story that is traditionally enjoyed by children. However, the primary drawback of using this format would be that I could not possibly create any story that would be specifically relevant to the experiences of more than a fraction of all children of divorce. For example, if the story was about a girl, it might be less likely that boys would identify with her. If a child's father left the home, the story would not be appealing to those children whose mothers had left. No matter how much I might try to relate common divorce experiences, the story could only be similar to what a small percentage of the target audience had actually experienced.

The expository form, I suspected, would have the advantage of enabling me to include a wider variety of experiences to which children of divorce were commonly exposed. There need be no limit on the number of possible situations I could cover. There was the risk, however, that the didacticism of such a presentation might be boring to the child. In considering the advantages and disadvantages of the alternatives, I decided to take my chances with the expository form. The success of the book suggests that my choice was a judicious one.

The book on divorce was written because I had observed that many parents were not being appropriately honest with their children regarding the major issues of the divorce. Such secretiveness was contributing, in a variety of ways, to the psychological problems with which these children often suffered. For example, a mother might complain that her son kept blaming himself for the divorce. Often a contributing factor (but by no means the only cause of such a preoccupation) was the fact that the child was not told anything about the reasons for the separation. In such situations, it was not surprising that the boy would tend to blame himself in his search for a possible explanation. The book encourages such children to ask important questions and it encourages parents to answer them. Another common problem that children of divorce suffer is that of anger inhibition. They may fear expressing anger toward the "abandoning" parent lest they see even less of that parent. And they may fear expressing anger toward the custodial parent, lest that parent "abandon" them as well—abandonment now being very much in the child's scheme of things. The book helps children deal with these, as well as a wide variety of other problems that are likely to arise in the lives of children of divorce.

After making the decision to write the book, I spent the next two years gathering data. I scribbled on scraps of paper any issue arising in my practice that I thought might be useful to include. Journal articles became a further source of information. And experiences of supervisees, colleagues, and friends provided further data. After two years of such data gathering, I organized my collection of scrap papers and notes. I found that they naturally fell into a number of discrete categories. Each pile of slips (representing a category) became a chapter in the book. And each pile was further subdivided with the result that these smaller piles became subsections of the chapters. It was from such pieces of paper that the book was written over a period of a few weeks.

During the next year the manuscript was lent to a series of children, for both parents and children's comments and reactions.

In this way, deletions were made and further material added. I was fortunate in meeting Alfred Lowenheim, a most talented artist, who did the illustrations. Of the many artists who submitted renditions, Al's were clearly the best. His capacity to draw a wide variety of children's facial expressions was unique. And more important was his ability to introduce a note of hope and optimism into the most morbid situations. Because the divorce issue is such a painful one, such qualities in the children's facial expressions were particularly important. Al's contributions to the book's success was formidable and my debt to him is great.

Down the years I have continued to receive letters from children. Invariably, they tell me how useful the book has been to them. In addition, many describe the difficulties they are having over their parents' divorce and will often ask me for advice. Every letter has been answered. Although attempts have always been made to provide advice, this obviously, at times, has had to be limited.

Particularly gratifying have been the foreign translations (Japanese, 1972f, 1980f; Spanish, 1972g; Dutch, 1972h, 1980e; Hebrew, 1977d; French, 1981d). The Japanese translation (1972f) contributed to my being invited in 1974 to present a lecture series in Tokyo, Kyoto, Kobe, and Hiroshima. The Dutch translation (1972h) played a role in my invitation to serve as a visiting professor at the University of Louvain in Brussels in 1980 and 1981. The popularity of the Japanese translation has always been somewhat puzzling to me in that cultural patterns would, I suspect, make it quite difficult for the average Japanese child to follow some of the recommendations made in the book. For example, it is hard for me to imagine a Japanese child telling his father that he is angry at him for being late at the time of his visits. Also, it is difficult for me to imagine a Japanese child taking my advice not to take seriously those who would ridicule him because of his parents' divorce. The Japanese are a shame-oriented people and are exquisitely sensitive to the feelings of others. In spite of these apparent problems that I suspect the book presents to the Japanese child, the book appears to have enjoyed considerable popularity there.

The book is written at a level understandable to the average six-to-seven year old when it is read to him or her. Most eight year olds can read the book with little or no help from parents. However, the book is also written for the parents, the third-to-fourth grade level notwithstanding. Most parents appreciate this and have found the book useful to read. Teenagers will often refuse initially to read it because they consider it beneath them with its obvious cartoon-like illustrations, large print, and elementary-grade reading level. Once they have overcome these initial hesitations, they have often found it very useful.

In a sense the book is a psychiatry primer, written for children. This is not, in principle, an inappropriate thing to do. There is no concept in all of psychiatry, in my opinion, that cannot be understood by the average 11 year old. Our terminology is often merely jargon that is designed to impress. It attempts to give a scientific ring to the commonplace. Accordingly, it often produces more confusion than elucidation, in that the psychiatric term becomes less well defined than the concept it was designed to describe.

As every writer of children's book knows well, it is the parents, not the children, who buy the book. They screen and censor and are not likely to buy a book that they would consider detrimental or offensive to their children. *The Boys and Girls Book About Divorce* certainly contains material that is considered such by many parents. A book that raises the question as to whether a parent loves a child is not one that some parents would consider proper reading material for their children, let alone something they would spend their money on. A book that encourages children to express their anger at their parents (albeit using words more polite than the ones that enter their minds) is also one that would make many parents hesitate.

Even in the introduction there are possible parental "turn-offs." Telling parents that they *should* tell the child that an absent parent does not love him or her (when such is really the case) is not considered the popular thing to do. And telling parents that they *should* criticize the absent parent to the child (in a balanced way in which assets are also presented), goes against traditional advice. Accordingly, I am sure that many parents put the book down as soon as they read my comments in the introduction. In spite of the presence of this somewhat unpopular material, the book has continued to grow in popularity—attesting to the fact that there are thousands who are willing to look at unpleasant truths and recognize that more euphemistic books, although less painful to read, are not as likely to be useful to children in such serious situations as divorce.

I think one of the book's appeals lies in the fact that I attempt to provide practical and concrete advice for every problem pre-

sented. The child is told what he or she can do to try to help him-
or herself. Unrealistic solutions are discouraged and the possibility
of both success and failure is presented.

In 1968, when the book was originally written, I called it *The
Child's Book About Divorce*. An editor suggested that some children
might consider the word *child* demeaning, and suggested *The Boys
and Girls Book About Divorce* as a safer title. Recently (in the late
1970s), the use of the words *boys* and *girls* has come under attack.
Making a distinction about sex, when such distinction is irrelevant,
is considered "sexist." Such critics might consider the title *The Boys
and Girls Book About Divorce* to be objectionable because it refers
to the sex of the reader for no apparent purpose. Although I have
not seen any children (yet) who have been offended by the title, I
have to admit that the distinction is not particularly necessary for
the purposes of the title or even the bulk of the contents of the book.

To rectify this "error" might bring me back to the original title,
with the risk of using that. Of other options, each seems to have its
drawbacks. *The Youngsters Book About Divorce* seems too stilted,
The Kids Book About Divorce, too folksy and slangy. The word *kids*
is also considered by some to be intrinsically demeaning because
the word can connote young sheep. (Pedantic grade school teachers
are particularly enthusiastic about this distinction.) Perhaps in the
future my "error" will become ever more obvious and my title will
invariably date the book. Although the title may, after 15 years, be
on the verge of becoming dated, the book's contents, to the best of
my knowledge, have not yet become so.

The Boys and Girls Book About One-Parent Families

On a number of occasions, I have received a telephone call from a
distraught parent (usually a stranger) asking me for advice regarding a child's attending a parent's funeral. Usually my advice is requested to help resolve a family argument over whether or not the
children should attend a parent's funeral. Often it is the grandparents who hold that the children's presence would be psychologically detrimental to them, while the surviving parent believes that
it might be useful and/or desirable. Often the parent does not have
the psychological strength or maturity to withstand and/or refute
the grandparents' arguments and wants my support for his or her

position. Feelings run strong on this issue and I cannot say that my advice that the children be invited (but not required) to attend is always heeded. Usually I provide some of the important reasons (Gardner, 1976b, 1976c, 1977e, 1979f), but these are not compelling to those who have been so deeply engrained with the notion that having children attend a funeral (like other exposures to death) cannot but be psychologically detrimental.

Because of such experiences with parents, I decided to write a book for children that could be useful to them in dealing with parental death. Thus my *The Boys and Girls Book About One-Parent Families* (1978b, 1983c). Although optimally useful prior to the death of the parent, the book has not, to be the best of my knowledge, been commonly used during this period. It has been more frequently used at the time of death to help parents make such decisions as to what to tell the children, whether or not to take them to the funeral, and to help them work through their reactions. Like my *The Boys and Girls Book About Divorce* (1970a, 1971b), the book, although written for children, is written for the parents' guidance as well. The material not only provides the child with information that should prove of interest and use, but is also designed to serve as a point of departure for communication with the surviving parent and other adults. Such communication serves as a vehicle for the release of pent-up feelings—a release that is central to the mourning process. Such communication is also likely to provide the child with information that can be useful in facilitating the mourning process and information that could correct distortions that might contribute to the development of psychopathology. Furthermore the communication entrenches the child's relationship with the surviving parent—so vital a process at this unfortunate period in the child's life.

In addition, I provide information to children living in two other types of one-parent families, namely, divorced families and families in which a parent (usually a mother) has never been married. Although the unwed mother is far less the pariah today that she was in past years, children of such mothers still suffer some stigma as well as other difficulties specific to their situation. Overcoming old taboos and open communication are the best solutions to dealing with these problems. The material on divorce is a partial update of material previously presented in *The Boys and Girls Book About Divorce*. This book was also translated into Japanese (1981e).

The Boys and Girls Book About Stepfamilies

Considering my other books for children in the divorce situation, it was only natural that I write *The Boys and Girls Book About Step-families* (1981c). It too is a book in the expository vein. Again, it is most likely to be of interest to children in this situation or children anticipating entering into stepfamily life. It covers a wide variety of issues with which stepfamilies are commonly confronted: what to call a stepparent, the love between stepparents and stepchildren, loyalty conflicts, adjusting to new lifestyles, relationships between stepsiblings, and adoption by a stepparent. The issues raised are designed to serve as points of departure between the children and parents living under in what is often a difficult situation.

The Parents Book About Divorce

Each of my children's books is also written for parents. The parents are advised to read the book along with the child and to use the material therein as a point of departure for a wide variety of interchanges. Furthermore, the parents have always been in mind as I write the children's books. I view them as reading these books as well. And many parents have confirmed my anticipations that they would find these books useful for themselves, even though they are written at the child's level. My *MBD: The Family Book About Minimal Brain Dysfunction* (1973a) has a section for the parents. *The Boys and Girls Book About Divorce*, however, has only an introductory chapter for them. Because I had so much more to say to parents, I decided to write a special book for them. Doubleday invited me to write *The Parents Book About Divorce* (1977b, 1979a), anticipating a book of about 200 pages. When I submitted my manuscript they were originally upset because they anticipated that my material would require a book of 350 to 400 pages and so they asked me to resubmit a smaller book with a substantial amount of material deleted. Considering practically *all* of it to be important and recognizing possible lack of objectivity regarding this conclusion, I requested that *they* review the manuscript and decide themselves what material they thought should be deleted, but requested that they discuss with me first any material they wished to omit. About a month later they informed me that they had carefully reviewed the book, with an eye toward omitting material, and could find nothing that would warrant omission. Although I recognized that some parents would be turned off by the book's length I consider it to contain only the minimal material necessary for parents to read in the divorce situation.

When I submitted the original manuscript to Doubleday I informed them that I was including an extremely important passage in the introduction and that I would omit this passage only with great reluctance. The passage:

> I believe that it (the book) provides an in-depth coverage of the most common problems that parents are confronted with when dealing with children's reactions to separation and divorce. It does not provide any simple answers. The problems dealt with here are complex. Those who would give simple answers to these complicated problems may initially attract a wide audience; however, their solutions are doomed to failure and those who rely on them are bound to become disappointed and disillusioned. This book, therefore, is for those who are suspicious of or fed up with simple solutions and are willing to expend the effort of dealing with these problems more realistically.

Clearly, this is not the kind of introduction that sells books in an age when people seem to be much more attracted to simple and quick solutions to complex problems. The fact that the book has gone through multiple printings over the last nine years is testimony to the fact that there are still many people who recognize that complex problems can only be dealt with with complex answers. This book has also gone into a French translation (1979g).

Understanding Children—A Parents Guide to Child Rearing

Mountains of books have been written on child rearing. There is not a year in which we don't see at least a few more added to the ever-growing heap. Generally, the most popular of these books are those that provide simple answers. Those who propose complex solutions are not likely to sell many books. The best way to write such a best seller is to take a few (at most) simple ideas and expand them into a book by repeating them over and over and then fattening the text with clinical examples (real or invented). By using large print, wide margins, and "filler" pages, the publishers can be relied upon to make the whole thing look like a book.

The next step is for the author to peddle the book on television. A few exposures is not likely to do much. A nationwide campaign is much more likely (but is in no way guaranteed) to be effective. The worst things that an author can say on such television programs are: "That's a very complex subject . . . ," "There's really no simple solution to that problem . . . ," or "I cannot really say why that particular child acted in the way that he did. . . . " Few today would buy a book written by someone who has no simple solutions. Few want to burden themselves with complex answers that may not even apply to one's own child. Success is much more likely if one provides a snappy answer to every question—no matter how complicated. In addition, if the responses are sprinkled with humor, and even slapstick, Mr. Funny is likely to sell even more books. Last, if the author has show-biz talent and can ham it up, he or she may become a TV celebrity—someone invited by the most popular talk shows. If the author feels that such appearances involve no compromise of professional dignity, if every remark made is used by the "M.C." as a taking off point for a joke, then he or she may be even more successful. And his book will make him a bundle.

My contribution to this "mountain of books" on child rearing is *Understanding Children—A Parents Guide to Child Rearing* (1973c). As might be expected from what I have said previously, the book has no simple answers or quick solutions. In fact, some of my explanations have turned off those readers who would have been much happier with shorter discussions. Where possible I have used in headings such traditional child-rearing clichés as: "My Joey would never do such a thing," "All I want is that my children should be happy," "We keep a united front," et cetera. Although this book is yet another addition to the sea of child-rearing volumes, I would like to believe that it is better than the majority of them. Although many parents have found it useful (it has gone through multiple editions), I have resigned myself to the fact that it will probably never enjoy widespread popularity because of its complexity. It too has undergone a Dutch translation (1975f).

REALITY-ORIENTED STORIES

As mentioned, the didacticism of the expository presentation has the drawback of increasing the risk that the child will lose interest. Children are more predictably attracted to stories that involve fanciful elaborations around their central messages. Accordingly, reality-oriented stories are generally less appealing (especially for younger children) than fables and fairy tales. Children, however, are likely to be attracted to reality-oriented stories if others, rather than the readers themselves, are the ones to whom the unpleasant things are happening or the ones who think and do the "bad" things. In addition, children are likely to be more involved if the story deals with issues that relate to the problems and conflicts with which they are directly dealing at the time. The "lessons in constructive living" are thereby assimilated in a way that is generally less confronting than the expository presentation, but more than in the fanciful categories described below.

We do well to appreciate that to view reality with perfect clarity all the time may be too painful for anyone. A certain amount of fantasy is pleasurable and may even be necessary to preserve our sanity. However, excessive involvement with fantasy may ill-equip us to deal with reality. Some balance, then, must be arrived at. This balance should be definitely weighted on the reality side of the scale, if one is to function most adequately in life.

At the time in the lives of our children when we are most concerned with teaching them about reality, we simultaneously expose them to a world of unreality—a world of fairy tale, fancy, and myth. Although the child certainly derives many benefits from fantasy, such exposure at the same time often engenders unreal expectations about living which may contribute to life-long feelings of dissatisfaction and frustration.

In the attempt to provide a contribution on the reality side of the balance, I wrote *Dr. Gardner's Stories About the Real World*, (1972a). These stories do not begin with *once upon a time* because they did not take place a long time ago in some mythical land, but are occurring now, everywhere around us. They are not stories about beautiful princesses, handsome knights, fairy godmothers, sorcerers, and wizards. They are not about perfect people and they do not offer perfect solutions. Rather, the problems which the children face in these stories are not quickly resolved and, in the process of solving them, the children suffer certain discomforts and inconveniences. The people with whom the children in these stories deal are genuinely human. They have their assets and their liabilities, their strengths and their weaknesses. They are often inconsistent and misguided. They lie, curse and exhibit the host of human frailties. But they are also benevolent, intelligent, fair and possess other human qualities which we all admire. This is the way people really are and children must come to appreciate this if they are to deal adequately with life.

These stories, then, are about actual things which have happened, and will continue to happen, to real children. Stories about reality, like stories about unreality, can capture the imaginations of our children and provide them with meaningful gratifications. Lastly, these stories do not end with *and they lived happily ever after*. No one lives ever after; we are all mortal. And no one is always happy. Life is a mixture, and unhappiness is an inevitable part of it.

Our hope, therefore, lies in achieving whatever satisfactions we may reasonably expect in the short time allotted to each of us. The likelihood of our gaining such gratifications depends, in part, upon how accurately we perceive the truths of life. Unreal fantasy, its gratifications notwithstanding, does not equip us to pursue our goals. These stories then enhance, rather than detract, from our children's chances for happy experiences in life—and this is their purpose.

When utilizing the mutual storytelling technique, my stories are designed to provide specific information that is directly relevant to issues that are important for the child patient at the very time we are involved with one another during the therapeutic session. The stories presented here are less specific. They deal with issues that are common, if not universal. However, their drawback is that they are not as likely to be as exquisitely relevant to the child at the time of presentation as those provided when engaging in mutual storytelling.

One could argue that reading children's stories such as these is like putting Penicillin in the drinking water. A small percentage of the population, those suffering at that particular time with certain types of infectious diseases, will profit from drinking such water. For the overwhelming majority of the rest, the Penicillin will have been wasted in that it will pass right out of the body and have little, if any, effect on the individual. And there will be a small percentage who will suffer some untoward reaction because of a special sensitivity to the drug. Or one could argue that reading such stories to children is like feeding a sick child every drug in the medicine cabinet, in the hope that one will get him or her better. I cannot disagree with such criticisms of bibliotherapy. However, my experience has been that the themes dealt with in my *Stories About the Real World* (1972a) are so common, again if not universal, that children have been drawn to them with a surprising and gratifying degree of consistency. I recognize my immodesty here, but that is what has happened with these stories. There are many children who have quoted them to other children and their parents. Others have put the book under their pillows at night. Others have carried it along for special guidance in tense situations. And others have asked parents to repeatedly read to them specific stories. There is no question that such utilization has been useful for these children. Not only does it help prevent the kind of distorted thinking that contributes to the formation of psychopathology and other forms of maladaption, but can contribute to the alleviation of such disorders as well.

The book contains six stories. *Oliver and the Ostrich* deals with the issues of avoidance and denial. ("There are some people who have a very strange idea. They believe that the ostrich hides his head in the sand when something dangerous is about to happen—such as when another animal is going to attack. This isn't true. The ostrich wouldn't do such a foolish thing.") *Say You're Sorry* focuses on the common utilization (by children as well as adults) of the "I'm sorry" manipulation to avoid facing up to or suffering the consequences of one's maltreatment of others. ("Eric did not want to be sent to his room and so he grumbled to Carol, 'O.K., I'm sorry.' But he really didn't mean it. He was lying. He just said he was sorry so he wouldn't be punished.") In *Peter and the Dog* I attempt to help children deal with frustration via the utilization of substitutive gratification. ("Peter loved his new pets and he played with them every day. He was no longer sad that he didn't have a dog.") *The Girl Who Wouldn't Try* encourages the use of conscious control, and toleration of anxiety as a method of desensitization to the inevitable fears that all must learn to accept in new situations if one is to gain the benefits to be derived from such involvement. In addition, it focuses on the "nothing ventured, nothing gained" theme. ("She knew it was going to be scary to try, but she also realized that you can feel pretty bad about yourself if you don't.") *Jerry and the Bullies* was originally entitled *Dirty Words*. The original publishers, however, decided that some of the expletives should be deleted and so the expurgated version is the one that was published. The story encourages healthy expression of anger, in a manner appropriate to the situation, in a way that is not simply cathartic but attempts to remove the noxious stimulus that is causing the anger to generate. ("It may surprise you but bad words can be very useful. They can help a person show his anger or disappointment in a way that really doesn't harm anyone.") Lastly, *The Hundred-Dollar Lie* deals with the injudiciousness of lying. It does not focus on the ethical or moral reasons for not lying as much as the practical and more mundane: the fear of disclosure, the lowered feeling of self-worth, the social rejection one suffers with the reputation of being a liar, etc. ("He was scared. He kept worrying about all the children finding out about his lie. He was afraid that they would all call him liar and that he wouldn't have any friends anymore.")

This book has also enjoyed foreign translations (Dutch, 1974f, and Italian, 1976d). In addition, the interest in this book was so great that I subsequently published a second volume, *Stories About the Real World, Volume II* (1983b). The stories in this second volume deal with such issues as the work ethic, the differentiating between things one can control from things one cannot control, cigarette smoking, toleration of the unpleasant, looking at naked children, and lying.

FABLES

Storytelling has proved to be one of the most powerful techniques that mankind has ever devised for molding human behavior. By telling stories about things that happened to *others*, unpleasant messages were found to be far more palatable than those pertaining to "present company." And the farther away and the more remote the "others" were, the less threatening the story was to the listeners. The important principle, however, could be retained. The lessons that were learned could still be transmitted as long as it was others, rather than present company, who had learned them. The essential precondition for such stories to be useful was that the leaders had to take the position: "Of course, no one here would do such things—or even think such things—but it is interesting to hear about others who have engaged in such nefarious practices and what they have learned from their experiences and misdeeds." And the farther away the story's characters lived, the more remote they appeared to be from the audience, the less threatened the listeners were. Last, making the men handsome, the women beautiful, and introducing adventure, humor, sex, violence, and dramatization, added to the attractiveness of the vehicle and insured greater receptivity to the messages, even those that were particularly anxiety provoking. The central philosophy of the method is well stated in a refrain from a song sung by Jack Point, the jester, in Gilbert and Sullivan's operetta *Yoeman of the Guard:*

> When they're offered to the world in merry guise
> Unpleasant truths are swallowed with a will—
> For he who'd make his fellow, fellow, fellow creatures wise
> Should always gild the philosophic pill!

The story can be attractive and nonthreatening. It allows for the imparting of important principles and guidelines without the listener experiencing personal guilt or fear of incrimination. The listeners are usually not even consciously aware that their interest is determined primarily by the fact that they harbor the same impulses (however unacceptable) as the story's protagonists, that they are grappling with the exact same conflicts as those who lived far away, long ago, in distant lands. The method is so powerful and useful that I would hazard the guess that it was crucial for the survival of the earliest civilizations and that those societies that did not utilize the method did not survive. Every society that I know of has its heritage of such stories. These were transmitted first by the spoken and then by the written word down the generations: the Bible, the Koran, various legends, myths, fairy tales, parables, and other traditional tales.

The fable is one such vehicle. Like the others it utilizes symbolization in order to disguise. Like the others, it uses allegory to transmit its messages. Allegory, by definition, involves the representation of an abstraction via a concrete or material form. It is a symbolic narrative. The fable is one of the purest forms of allegory. But the *sine qua non* of the fable is that its protagonists be animals. Without the animal, the story cannot justifiably be called a fable. An occasional human being may be found but, if there are too many, the story will no longer be a fable. But the animals in the fable are typically human, with all the human foibles: avarice, lust, jealousy, arrogance, false pride, and so on. Finally, the fable, if it is to be worthy of the name, has one or more morals or lessons. Too many lessons may reduce a fable's effectiveness. Burdening the mind of the listener with too many lessons is likely to reduce the impact of a single moral.

The use of the animal symbol for stories or other purposes dates back to the earliest civilizations. Animal drawings on cave walls probably antedated human figures. Anthropomorphization of animals is ubiquitous in primitive religions, animal worship being one manifestation of such anthropomorphization. (Anthropomorphization still persists in modified form in most modern and more sophisticated religions.) Children, who have much in common with primitives with regard to their thinking processes, are traditional lovers of animals. I am referring not only to the actual pleasure that children derive from animals in reality (from pets and visits to the zoo, for example), but to the use of animals as symbols in their fantasies. The animal appears to be the child's natural choice for allegorical symbolization.

Child therapists have known, since the second decade of this century, that children will tell them much about themselves if encouraged to relate self-created stories about animals. But if one tries to get the children to appreciate that they are really talking about themselves (i.e., "gain insight"), they are likely to become resistive and inattentive. This valuable source of information about their underlying psychodynamics may thereby be lost to the therapist. But discuss the animals as animals, and lengthy therapeutic conversations are possible. One seven-year-old child once said to me, upon being asked to make up a story about the animal figurines I provided him, "Remember, this story has nothing to do with me or anyone in my family. It's only about animals!" I agreed not to challenge him on this statement, and he was thereby allowed to provide me with a wealth of information about himself that was therapeutically useful. Had I tried to analyze his resistance to coming to terms with the fact that he was really talking about himself, I probably would not have been able to be of much help to him in the areas revealed by this story.

Without knowing that they have been doing it, children have been telling fables to therapists for years. Children are probably the best fabulists of us all. My experience as a fabulist comes through the mutual storytelling technique. It was through experience with the mutual storytelling technique, more than from any other source, that I came to create fables of my own.

Modern psychoanalytic theory provides us with a powerful tool for understanding the underlying meaning of children's stories, be they self-created fables or other symbolic narratives. It provides a depth of understanding far more profound than that which is generally appreciated by the listener. The same theoretical principles can be used in the creation of stories such as the fables I relate in my *Dr. Gardner's Fables for Our Times* (1981b).

In this book I present thirteen fables, each of which portrays the ways in which certain animals have dealt with a wide variety of "human" problems. *The Show-Off-Peacock* deals with exhibitionism. The problem of dependency is dealt with in *The Kangaroos and Their Pouch*. The problem of blind mimicry and submission to the opinions of others is dealt with in *The Parrot and the People*. In *The Squirrels and the Skunk* the squirrels learn that one should use concrete evidence rather than reputation before deciding about a person's (the skunk's) personality attributes. The problem of self-assessment as related to one's own opinion versus the opinions of others is dealt with in *The Pussycat and the Owl*. The *Wise-Guy Seal* learns that honest effort is more likely to produce results than dreamy procrastination. In *The Dogs and the Thieves* we learn about dogs whose barks are worse than their bites and the respect that is engendered in "dogs" who "speak softly and carry a big stick." In *The Ant and the Grasshopper* we learn about the efficacy of cooperative group effort in contrast to what an individual alone can do. *The Dolphin and the Shark* deals with the issue of sensitivity to other people's feelings. In *The Squirrel and the Nuts* we learn about the value of advanced planning. *The Ostrich and the Lion* deals with the denial mechanism. *The Beaver and the Owl* deals with the value of fortitude, knowing when to give up, and the respect one engenders in others when one is strong enough to admit mistakes. Last, in *The Fox and the Big Lie* we learn about the alienation one suffers from others by lying.

As I am sure the reader can appreciate these stories deal with central problems of life from which symptoms are often derived. As is most often the case when I utilize the mutual storytelling technique, each of these stories ends with a moral. And this, of course, is very much in the tradition of the fable. However, I have often found more than one moral to a story and have had no hesitation listing them. (It is nowhere written that a story must have only one moral.) In fact, in one story (*The Pussycat and the Owl*) I found no less than twelve (yes twelve!) lessons. The moral serves an important function. It "nails down" the story's main theme and increases the likelihood that the listener will "get the message."

FAIRY TALES

Introduction

The fairy tale has traditionally been one of the most attractive forms of children's literature. The fairy tale tradition is ancient and its appeal universal. Children's enjoyment of and widespread fascination with these stories is strong testimony to the fact that they provide important psychological gratifications. These tales have been passed down from generation to generation. However, over the years countless variations have been introduced. It is most likely that each modification satisfied the particular psychological needs and motivations of the individuals who introduced them. Many of these changes were probably not consciously made; rather, they were more likely the result of unconscious processes. It is reasonable to speculate that listeners repressed or suppressed from conscious awareness those aspects that were personally less significant and retained the more psychologically meaningful components. The story that was thereby "heard" was different from that which was then retold. The resultant version experienced similar modifications as each new generation of storytellers introduced its own alterations. The invention of the printing press in the fifteenth century brought about a certain stabilization to this process. However, no systematic publication of fairy tales was done on a large scale until the seventeenth century when Charles Perrault published his collection of such tales. In the early nineteenth century Jakob and Wilhelm Grimm, in Germany, and Hans Christian Andersen, in Denmark, published collections of known fairy tales as well as those of their own. These publications brought about even further standardization of the stories, but many versions of each story are still to be found.

Psychoanalytic theory provides us with a valuable instrument for understanding the underlying psychological meaning of many of these stories. There are certainly many schools of thought among psychoanalysts and their interpretation of fairy tales would certainly not be consistent. I believe, however, that most analysts would not take issue with most of the interpretations that I will propose below. Some of the stories have one or two basic themes that are consistently dealt with throughout. Other stories appear to be no more than a potpourri of many elements which do not lend themselves to any unified or consistent psychological interpretation. Psychoanalytic theory not only provides us with a tool for understanding the meaning of each individual fairy tale but, in addition, can provide us with insights as to why the fairy tale, in general, is so attractive to the child.

Reasons Why Fairy Tales Are Extremely Attractive to Children (of All Ages)

I believe that many factors contribute to the fairy tale's universal attraction to children. First, fairy tales allow the child to satisfy, in fantasy, wishes that would be impossible to gratify in reality. The child is small and weak in a world of adults, whom he or she views as giants. By identifying with the characters in the fairy tale the child can gain a sense of power that he or she does not actually possess. And with such power the child can acquire whatever one's heart desires may be—riches, wisdom, strength, etc. In *Jack and the Beanstalk*, *Jack*, on the brink of poverty and starvation, procures the giant's riches—enabling him thereby to support his mother in the style to which she had previously been accustomed prior to the death of his father. Similarly, *Hansel and Gretel* use the witch's jewels to provide their father and stepmother with enough financial stability to insure that the children will not once again be driven out of the house because of food privation. The *Ugly Duckling* becomes a beautiful swan. *Beast*, in *Beauty and the Beast*, becomes a handsome prince. Poor wretched *Cinderella* marries the rich handsome prince and lives happily ever after. *Thumbelina* and *Tom Thumb*, although miniscule, are able to enjoy the excitement of adult adventure, during which experiences they are magically protected from the inevitable dangers of the world of grownups. As enjoyable and appealing as these themes are, the methods by which the gratifications are achieved are usually magical, with little or no effort on the part of the story's protagonist. Although such fantasies provide solace and hope, they are clearly maladaptive ways for adjusting to the real world.

It is probable that those who are less deprived have less need for such tales. The pauper can enjoy a story in which a poor man becomes king; but a king is likely to have little interest because he already reigns. Similarly, adults have less need for fairy tales than children. Adults are more capable of providing themselves with what a child is unable to acquire. To children, the world is populated by giants. No matter how filled with love and material possessions their lives may be, they still envy the power and prerogatives of the adults around them. Therefore a child can be greatly inspired by a story in which the underdog magically triumphs over the powerful. The possible danger of such tales, however, is that they may encourage the child to hope for magic solutions to life's problems rather than to strive for the rewards that may be had by a more realistic approach.

Fairy tales simplify the world, making it easier to understand. This is especially attractive and comforting to children who, by virtue of their immaturity, inexperience, and naiveté cannot but find the world confusing and at times incomprehensible. In fairy tales everyone is stereotyped. There is no such thing as people with mixtures of assets and liabilities, with desirable and undesirable traits. People are clearly either good or bad. Things are either right or wrong. And one can tell from the outset the category into which the person or act will fall. In *Beauty and the Beast*, Beauty is pure beauty and *Beast* is ugliness incarnate. *Snow White's* queen mother is bad and is consistently so throughout. Stepmothers, like those of *Cinderella* and *Hansel and Gretel*, are perennially wicked. Such simplification of the world is appealing and is one factor in the fairy tale's attraction.

Unfortunately, simplifying a complex problem is not likely to be of help in solving it. And seeing people as simply all good or all bad ill equips us to deal adequately with real people who are inevitably a mixture of both. Believing that there are people who are all good cannot but be disillusioning as everyone will invariably reveal imperfections. And anticipating some people to be all bad will rob us of the gratifications of what might have been extremely satisfying relationships.

Fairy tales not only allow for the fantasized gratification of wishes for beauty, riches, power, etc., but allow for the release of hostile impulses as well. Children, like the rest of us, are frequently frustrated by the world around them. None of us can have more than an infinitesimal fraction of all the things we may want. So frustration is inevitable and frustration ultimately produces anger. However, survival of civilized society depends upon the repression and/or suppression of anger and its diversion into useful and/or innocuous channels. Long before written history, mankind must have appreciated that the proper control of anger was central to the viability of a civilized and productive society. With no restraints on the expression of anger there would be perpetual fear and chaos, a totally predatory and destructive world. But too much suppression of anger produced various kinds of personality problems that made such individuals ill-equipped to function adequately in society. Some middle path for anger expression had to be found.

One such method of innocuous release is provided by fairy tales. By identifying with characters who act out their anger the child can vicariously release hostility in ways that cause no actual harm to anyone. *Jack* kills the giant. *Hansel* and *Gretel's* stepmother abandons the children in the woods as her solution to the domestic food privation problem. The witch in turn would resort to starvation and cannibalistic devouring of the children for which, in retaliation, she is boiled to death in her own pot. *Snow White's* stepmother dances to her death on hot stones. Such innocuous release of anger notwithstanding, the fairy tale teaches violent solutions to interpersonal problems rather than more civilized methods. People in them rarely sit down and try to resolve their differences in humane and civilized ways. Killing off an adversary is suggested as the first, quickest, and cleanest way to solve a conflict.

In fairy tales the heroes and heroines traditionally live happily ever after. *Cinderella* marries the handsome prince and lives happily ever after. So do *Jack* and his mother and *Thumbelina* and her little prince, and *Hansel* and *Gretel*, and *Beauty* and *Beast* (the latter no longer as a beast, of course, but as a handsome prince), and so do countless others.

Life is a constant struggle for happiness, a state that somehow always seems to elude us. The best that most of us can hope for are intermittent states of happiness. Most recognize that life, at best, is a mixture of both happiness and unhappiness. One of the fairy tale's appeals, therefore, is that it provides fantasy gratification of the desire to live in a state of perpetual happiness and provides hope that such constant euphoria can indeed be obtained. As satisfying as such fantasies and hopes are, they have the drawback of lulling the individual into believing that such states of perpetual ecstasy can really be achieved. One of the reasons people marry is that they believe that it is a step not only to being happy, but to living happily ever after. And it is the *Cinderella* stories of our childhood and others like it that contribute to the inevitable disillusionment with marriage that results when one finds that it's just not producing the continued state of happiness that our childhood fairy tales promised.

A significant aspect of the fairy tale's appeal lies in the symbolic presentation of its messages. Long ago mankind must have realized that it was crucial to the survival of civilization to get as many members of society as possible to adhere to certain rules and regulations. It was also realized quite early that messages transmitting such rules, when presented directly, in undisguised fashion, were far less attractive than those conveyed in the form of exciting stories with appealing characters. Sermons can be dull and dry. Bible stories are more likely to attract the congregation's attention. Reading a list of rules of behavior is not likely to capture a large and enthusiastic audience. Legends, myths, and fables— which convey the same messages in symbolic form—are much more likely to be attended to and remembered. And fairy tales are in the latter tradition. Not only do they present their messages in an attractive package, but the characters utilized are from distant lands and lived long ago. Learning lessons from the experiences of such characters is far less anxiety provoking than hearing about the consequences of unacceptable acts performed by oneself or those close by. The audience can relax and listen with receptivity when hearing about the misdeeds of others because none of the listeners need reveal his or her own participation in similar behavior or need admit similar inclinations or desires. But the messages nevertheless sink in and the lessons are learned.

In the fairy tale such lessons are quite dramatically portrayed, again in simple and often stereotyped fashion. Good ultimately triumphs over evil. Hardworking and loyal *Cinderella* wins the hand of the handsome prince, while her self-indulgent and haughty stepsisters are left frustrated and enraged. *Hansel* and *Gretel* acquire the witch's jewels, implicitly as a reward for their continued loyalty to their father and stepmother. *Beauty*, although revolted by *Beast's* ugliness, agrees to marry him because of feelings of compassion, pity, and guilt. As the reward for her high principles and self-sacrificial decision, *Beast* is transformed back into the handsome prince he was before being bewitched. Via a series of harrowing experiences *Tom Thumb* learns how injudicious it is to run away from home.

What Should We Do with Fairy Tales?

What then should we do with these stories? On the one hand, they are an extremely effective method of communication and among the most powerful vehicles for attracting the attention of children and transmitting messages to them. On the other hand, fairy tales are filled with many elements that are sick and maladaptive. Because of these detrimental factors there are some who would dispose of them altogether. I believe that we should try to retain those elements of the fairy tale that have proved useful and discard that which appears to be harmful. One can create stories in which the rich visual imagery and dramatic qualities of the fairy tale are retained and healthy messages substituted for the unhealthy.

As discussed throughout this book, I am a strong believer in the therapeutic value of a storytelling mode of communication—especially when dramatization, allegory, and metaphor (elements invariably found in the fairy tale) are utilized. Messages so communicated are much more palatable and much more likely to be appreciated and retained than those directly stated. Sterile facts are not as likely to be remembered as those which are provided in an attractive package. And fanciful elaboration, so typical of the fairy tale, provides such packaging. The fairy tale is a proven vehicle for evoking the kind of visual imagery that enhances the impact of a communication. For example, one can use judiciously the magic element of the fairy tale. Children enjoy magic as a source of drama and excitement. And if the magic is *not* used to solve a character's central problem, it can add to the reader's pleasure and not foster unreal expectations. The same is true for the element of triumph. We all need to win once in a while, but winning in the real world involves effort, trial, and error. If our children are exposed to stories that demonstrate these processes, they can be helped to mature. The hostility in fairy tales can also be useful. However, it must be channeled into healthy directions. By confining themselves to self-defense and not indulging in sadistic gratification, the heroes can serve as models for the civilized release of anger.

Modern psychoanalytic theory has provided us with valuable tools to accomplish these goals. Psychodynamic insights have enabled us to understand more deeply than ever before the nature of the unhealthy elements in the fairy tale. And such knowledge has enabled us, as well, to create stories with more salutary themes.

Fairy Tales for Today's Children

In my *Fairy Tales for Today's Children* (1974a) I have taken four popular fairy-tale themes, dispensed with or revised elements that I consider pathological, and replaced them with what I consider to be healthier resolutions of the problems confronting the protagonists. My favorite is *Cinderelma*.

The terms *Cinderella* and *they lived happily ever after* have become almost synonymous. The story is one of many that children are exposed to at the most impressionistic time of their lives. Stories such as these contribute to the notion that marriage per se can provide not only happiness, but eternal happiness (or at least happiness until the end of one's days). The theme is multiplied many times over during a child's formative years and even later. Believing it cannot but produce frustration in one's real relationships with members of the opposite sex. It is a contributing factor to disillusionment in marriage and divorce. It is a contributing factor to general dissatisfaction in life, as one is led to believe that there are indeed individuals who live continual euphoric existences. Although all know of beautiful movie stars with multiple marriages and others who kill themselves (either quickly or slowly), the myth does not seem to be dispelled by these confrontations with reality.

In my story, *Cinderelma*, the heroine, is not rescued by a prince. Nor is she magically transformed by a fairy godmother. Her attempts to seek easy, quick, and magic solutions to her problems prove futile. But ultimately, via her own efforts (coupled with a little bit of luck and some craft), she is able to led a productive and gratifying life—not forever, but "until the end of her days."

In *The Princess and the Three Tasks*, I have borrowed elements from stories written in the chivalric tradition in which the suitor must prove his worth and affection by exposing himself to significant travail and suffering on behalf of the loved one. My hope here is to communicate in the allegorical mode just how irrational this common masochistic mechanism is for the suitor and insensitive and egocentric for the lady so courted.

In *Hans and Greta*, I use the universally absorbing theme of parent-child hostility and conflict, but have modified it. The children's problems are not solved by killing the witch and by the step-mother's convenient death. These are clearly unrealistic and unsuitable solutions. We can not so readily murder those who mal-treat us; nor do they so conveniently die. (In fact, they often appear to have a greater longevity than those who treat us kindly.) In my story the children's hostilities are confined to self-defense. In ad-dition, the stepmother is depicted somewhat less stereotypically. She is occasionally fun to be with. Also, the children do not come to the family's rescue by bringing home the witch's treasure. Chil-dren are rarely able to solve a family's problems and it is unfair to suggest that this is possible.

In *The Ugly Duck*, I do not accept the attractive solution that those who are scapegoated because of inborn differences may wake up someday with their liabilities turned into assets. The little duck in my story doesn't discover he's really a swan. But, with the help of the wise old owl, he manages to work out a reasonable solution to the social alienation he suffers.

Modern Fairy Tales

My second book of modified fairy tales, *Modern Fairy Tales* (1977a), provides four more stories in which I have removed what I con-sider detrimental in traditional fairy-tale themes and substituted what I consider to be more salutary. My favorite in this collection is *Mack and the Beanstalk*.

Jack and the Beanstalk is one of the "purer" fairy tales. It does not appear to contain the multiplicity of psychoanalytic themes so often seen in the fairy tale which, as mentioned, is often a potpourri of many elements contributed by a long succession of individuals down the generations. I believe that its purity, in part, is related to the fact that it is such a powerful oedipal statement. The story is basically one in which Jack accomplishes all his oedipal desires. The giant in the sky represents Jack's father. From the psycholog-ical point of view, he has already been ejected from the household and can be considered to be dead in that he resides in the sky, that is, in heaven where dead people supposedly go. Although Jack has, thereby, gratified his oedipal wishes, he does not have the where-withal to support his mother in the style to which she had been accustomed prior to the death (or perhaps more correctly, murder) of his father. In order to provide himself with the funds that would enable Jack to support his mother in the style to which she had been accustomed, *Jack* makes three trips up to heaven in order to acquire from his father possessions that would be of use to *Jack* in gratifying his oedipal desires. *Jack's* father appears to have accomplished the enviable feat of "having died and taken it (his money) with him." Interestingly, the little old lady who resides in the giant's castle exhibits amazing disloyalty to the giant. She, of course, is an alter ego of *Jack's* mother and serves to help him in the acquisition of the giant's possessions. The trading of the cow for the beans and the growing of the beanstalk are merely mechanisms that serve to provide *Jack* with a route (the beanstalk) to his father in heaven.

First, the giant's treasure of gold coins is stolen. This provides *Jack* with the wherewithal to support his mother in grand style. However, monetary sources have a way of being depleted and before long *Jack* is once again in want of funds. And so he returns to heaven, this time to steal the giant's goose that lays the golden eggs. Like the legendary money tree, funds are now provided by a living form and so the supply is richer and seemingly endless. In addition, an egg-laying goose is an excellent representation of the mature female, that is, *Jack's* mother. The eggs, as the product of the mother's procreative endeavors, readily symbolizes *Jack* himself. The fact that the eggs are golden serves to gratify *Jack's* wish that he be precious and desirable.

One would think that *Jack* would now be satisfied. The golden eggs supply him with an endless source of funding for his oedipal gratifications. But *Jack* is not an easily satisfiable young man. He once again returns to the giant's home, this time to steal his most treasured possession, the golden harp. This curvaceous, sweet-music producing instrument, on which one plays with one's hands, lends itself well to symbolizing the sexual female—in *Jack's* case, again his mother. The sexual element here is more overtly symbolized. Now that *Jack* has everything that he has wished to obtain from his father, he kills him by chopping down the beanstalk. This act may also serve as a symbolic castration of his father in retaliation for possible unconscious fears that his father will castrate him for his oedipal wishes.

As mentioned, *Jack and the Beanstalk* is one of the purer fairy tales from the psychoanalytic point of view. However, its attraction, in part, lies in the unrealistic and usually unattainable oedipal gratification that *Jack* enjoys. *Jack's* counterpart in my version of the story, *Mack and the Beanstalk*, has no such luck. Other than Sophocles' Oedipus in the original Greek tragedy, and possibly a few others whom I do not personally know, most boys do not have the opportunity to gratify their unrealistic and impractical oedipal fantasies. My story provides what I consider to be a more realistic solution for Jack's oedipal desires, while retaining much of the richness of the original tale. I believe that my story, if read to boys at the three-to-five-year age level, can be useful in helping them resolve in a more realistic way any oedipal conflicts they may have. I have not conducted any formal studies to ascertain whether it has indeed been useful in this regard. I have, however, learned of a few boys (through their parents) who have been very moved by this story, have repeatedly asked that it be reread to them, and who have demonstrated their appreciation of the sharing element in their relationship with their fathers.

Draco the Dragon is not derived from any particular fairy tale; rather it utilizes the common fairy tale theme of the fire-breathing dragon for the purpose of dealing with the common problem of hostility expression. The theme of hostility in fairy tales is ubiquitous. The most gory and sadistic kinds of torture and murder are depicted. There are many who would "clean them up" by omitting the hostility. I believe that this is not only naive but also a disservice to children. Anger is part of our psychological repertoire. It enhances our efficiency in protecting ourselves. Without it mankind would probably not have survived. One of the greatest problems we have in the world today is that of learning how to use our anger most effectively and advantageously. Like electricity and atomic power, although potentially lethal, it can also be an immensely useful servant. My story attempts to portray some of the valuable uses of anger through the experience of Draco, the fire-breathing dragon.

In The Adventures of Sir Galalad of King Arthur's Court, I have taken some well-known themes from Arthurian legend and modified them in ways that I consider salutary. The issues of magic acquisition of power and blind fealty are especially focused upon. However, there are some more subtle messages as well that should be appreciated by most adults.

There is probably no one who ever lived who has not at one time or another wished that he or she had been born someone else, or wished that he or she could change places with someone considered more fortunate. The Prince and the Pauper tells of the outcome of one such transformation. My story of The Prince and the Poor Boy also deals with this wish. The theme of searching for a better home elsewhere is an ancient one and appears in stories as far removed from one another as L. Frank Baum's *The Wizard of Oz* and Voltaire's *Candide*. My rendition throws in for good measure a few elements from *Aladdin's Lamp, Dick Whittington and His Cat*, and *The Elves and the Shoemaker*—all modified, of course, along the lines of the principles mentioned above.

Dorothy and the Lizard of Oz

The Wizard of Oz, written by L. Frank Baum and first published in 1900, is probably the most popular fairy tale of the twentieth century. The book enjoyed widespread popularity even before its MGM movie version appeared in 1939. The movie rendition significantly enhanced its popularity, and its exposure on television each year has become a tradition that has ensured its transmission to further generations of children. The story certainly satisfies the major criteria for being considered a fairy tale. There are the magic solutions that instantaneously solve the most complex problems. Rich fantasy and dramatization, so characteristic of the fairy tale, enhance the story's attractiveness. There is the satisfaction of wishes that cannot be gratified in reality. There is the stereotyped world in which all people and things are immediately recognized as either good or bad, right or wrong. And all consistently remain in the assigned role throughout the story. And, of course, like all good fairy tales, it ends with everyone presumably living happily ever after. Unless something comes along to replace or surpass it in the next fourteen years, future generations will probably come to consider *The Wizard of Oz* to be the twentieth century's major contribution to the fairy tale genre.

When a story enjoys such widespread popularity, it usually provides important psychological gratifications. Modern psychoanalytic theory provides us with a tool for understanding these to a degree not previously possible. Let us see what such an inquiry can teach us about *The Wizard of Oz*. Let us start with *Dorothy's* three friends, as their stories are easier to analyze than *Dorothy's*. The *Strawman* does not have a brain, that is, he feels that he is stupid. In the original book the *Wizard* gives the *Strawman* a brain of bran and nails, "a bran new brain" with nails to make him "sharp." In the movie version, the *Strawman* is given a diploma. This is not only designed to give the *Strawman* and everyone else the impression that he is now smart (*Dorothy*, the *Tin Woodman*, and the *Cowardly Lion* are certainly convinced), but somehow gives the *Strawman* actual knowledge as well. (Immediately after receiving the diploma he suddenly spouts the Pythagorean theorem as applied to an isosceles triangle.) There is no one, no matter how well educated and/or brilliant (the two do not necessarily go together) who does not feel, at times, intellectually inadequate. At best, even the most gifted and dedicated scholar can only grasp and feel competent with an infinitesimal fraction of all there is to know. And the child cannot but feel even more inadequate with regard to the knowledge of and capacity to deal with the vast world. By identification with the *Strawman*, one gratifies the wish for feelings of intellectual competence. And better yet, little effort is required. Whereas others have to attend universities for four or more years before being granted their diplomas, the *Strawman* earns his university degree in less than a minute. In the short time it takes the *Wizard* to bestow the diploma upon the *Strawman*, he becomes "smart"—an appealing shortcut, especially to the child who faces what may appear to be an endless educational process.

Now to the *Tin Woodman*. His problem is that he doesn't have a heart, only an empty tin chest. His problem is ostensibly solved when the *Wizard* gives him a heart. In the original Baum version, the heart is made of stuffed silk. In the MGM version, it is a red, ticking clock-heart. Wearing this around his neck and listening to the ticking sounds convinces the *Woodman* and others around him that he now can love. Again, little effort is required to enjoy the benefits of being capable of loving. Presumably, one of these benefits is that one will be loved in return. Although not elaborated upon in the story, the main drawback to being unable to love is that one is not likely to engender loving feelings in others. However, some reference is made to this by the MGM *Wizard* who, when giving the *Tin Woodman* the clock-heart, states, " . . . a heart is not judged by how much you love, but by how much you are loved by others." It is not, then, that altruistic needs are being thwarted here but self-serving gratifications. The *Tin Woodman's* grief here is not only that he is being deprived of the good feelings that come when one loves another, but of the pleasures derived from being loved as well. Giving love is the most predictable way to get love. When one doesn't give love, one is not likely to get it. The heart, then, is to provide the *Tin Woodman* with both—the capacity to give love and the hope of receiving it. However, no work, no effort is expended in order to get his heart. None of the traditional factors that we consider indispensable to the loving relationship seems to be necessary. No giving, no sacrifice, no sympathy, empathy, toleration, admiration, respect, sexual attraction, or sharing of experiences are warranted. This capacity to love and be loved is suddenly acquired, merely by wearing a little ticking clock.

Everyone wants to be loved and everyone wants the pleasure of loving. The infant's need to be loved is vital. Without the love of parents and/or other significant figures in his environment the infant will be deprived of the necessities vital to life, and he or she may even die. All of us, no matter how independent of others we may come to be, still crave for the love, affection, and attention of others. And all of us, once we have known the feeling of giving love, seek to enjoy that emotion again, no matter how elusive and transient it may be. Part of the appeal of *The Wizard of Oz* is that it enables us, via identification with the *Tin Woodman*, to gratify vicariously our need to be loving people, capable of both giving and receiving love.

Now to the *Cowardly Lion*. All of us are afraid at times. The younger we are the more fears we are likely to have. The infant finds himself helpless in a world of giants, some of whom he depends upon for his very existence. And no matter how old we get, no matter how competent we may become, we still live in fear of many things. If we are to achieve many of our goals in life and if we are to fight off those who may threaten us, we need the stamina to tolerate these inevitable fears, to suffer them rather than to avoid them. This is what we call courage. Such willingness to suffer these uncomfortable fearful feelings is crucial if we are to fight off those who would endanger us or if we are to acquire what is frightening or dangerous.

Intimately associated with courage is potency. It is difficult to imagine courage without power. We do not speak of courage alone, but courage to do something: courage to fight, courage to stand up, courage to strive. The *Cowardly Lion*, then, is not simply looking for courage, he is also looking for the power that comes with courage. Courage is the prerequisite for the more important gratification of power. The *Wizard* provides these in the medal for bravery that he gives the *Lion*. The *Lion* does earn his medal (a "triple cross") in that it is awarded for "bravery against wicked witches." However, this one act and its reward produce a total conversion from cowardice to bravery. The cowardice problem is instantly cured, and the cure, presumably, is lifelong.

In infancy we are fearful and weak. As we grow older, we

become less fearful and less impotent. But no matter how old and competent we become, we all at times become fearful. All of us, at times, wish for greater courage to sustain us during our fearful periods. And all of us look for the power to help us overcome the fearful situation. Such courage and power only come with time, experience, and endurance. The *Wizard of Oz* provides courage (and presumably power) in as much time as it takes him to pin the medal on the *Cowardly Lion's* chest. Not only is the *Lion* convinced that he is brave, but his friends are convinced as well.

The attraction of the *Strawman*, the *Tin Woodman*, and the *Cowardly Lion* is that they provide children (and, to a lesser extent, adults) with vicarious gratification of needs that are central to their well-being, if not their very existence. By identification with these figures, children gain intellectual competence in compensation for feelings of ignorance of how to deal with the world. They are provided with the capacity to love and thereby are provided with the most powerful and predictable tool for gaining the love of others. And they gain courage, the prerequisite of power, in compensation for the sense of impotence that is intrinsic to childhood. There are few needs that are more important to children. No surprise then that the *Strawman*, the *Tin Woodman*, and the *Cowardly Lion* are so universally loved.

And now for *Dorothy*. Her main problem is that Miss Gulch, the mean woman from the town near her aunt and uncle's farm, has an order from the sheriff empowering her to take *Dorothy's* dog *Toto*. It seems that *Toto* got into Miss Gulch's garden. She threatened him in such a frightening way that he bit her, thereby providing her with the justification for taking him away from *Dorothy*. We presume he will be put in such a place or state (the story is not clear about his exact disposition) that there will be no further danger that he will ever bite anyone again. Unfortunately, her aunt and uncle (law-abiding citizens that they are) do not support *Dorothy* in her attempts to thwart Miss Gulch, and they tell *Dorothy* to hand the dog over to her. The story deals with this problem by the mechanism of escape. In the land of Oz *Dorothy* and *Toto* are supposedly safe from Miss Gulch, the sheriff, and anyone else who would want to take *Toto* away from her.

The Oz solution, however, is not without its drawbacks. Not only is *Dorothy* exposed to a whole new host of problems (a realistic element in an otherwise unrealistic tale), but she sorely misses her aunt and uncle (their disloyalty to her in the Gulch incident not-withstanding). The *Wizard* does get *Dorothy* back to Kansas, thereby removing her from the dangers she is exposed to in Oz and grat-ifying her desire to return once again to her loved ones. Also, she learns an important lesson in Oz (again in the MGM version): " . . . if I ever go looking for my heart's desire again, I won't look any further than my own backyard. Because if it isn't there, I never really lost it to begin with." This, of course, is an ancient wisdom. However, although *Dorothy* does finally return to Kansas, the prob-lem with Miss Gulch is not dealt with at the end of the story. *Dor-othy* fled Kansas, and then flees Oz. The problem that originally caused her flight from Kansas is not solved. This flaw in the tale notwithstanding, *Dorothy* is still a beloved figure for children and adults as well. I believe that the atttraction comes from another factor in the story, one that is far larger than the lesson that *Dorothy* learns. In fact, I believe that most children (or adults) cannot say what the lesson is that *Dorothy* learned, so small a role does it play in the movie. I would go further and say that most younger children (under seven or eight) do not even know what *Dorothy* is talking about when she relates the lesson she has learned.

Dorothy's main attraction is that she visits the "land over the rainbow." She gratifies our desire to go to a land where "bluebirds fly," the land where "the dreams that we dare to dream really do come true," the land where "troubles melt like lemon drops, away above the chimney tops." In short, *Dorothy* gratifies our desire to go to paradise. Although Oz is not continual pleasure for *Dorothy*, by the end of the story she manages to clear the place of its only flaws: the two wicked witches. The story implies that after she has left, the Munchkins and other denizens of the land will now lead the life of eternal peace and bliss that Oz was designed to provide.

Life is, at best, a continual struggle, and the desire for a par-adise is universal. Dreaming of a land over the rainbow can provide us with just the kind of narcosis that can make life more bearable and at times more pleasurable. To recognize that this is only an unrealistic dream can enable us to enjoy the gratifications of such fantasies without being too swept up by them. To believe that one can really find such bliss in life, on an ongoing basis, may produce grave disappointment and disillusionment. Judy Garland, the ac-tress who played *Dorothy*, was ever associated with the song "Over the Rainbow." Throughout her career, audiences repeatedly asked her to sing the song. A performance was rarely considered complete without it. Her name became inextricably bound to the song and its myth of a paradise land over the rainbow. It is public knowledge that Judy Garland's life was anything but happy. To the best of my knowledge she found little gratification in her marriages and for many years fought, but never overcame, a drinking problem. In her later years people did not attend her performances primarily to hear a beautiful voice (so much had it deteriorated), but many came out of pity, to help her make a comeback. She probably appreciated this, but such awareness must have been extremely distressing and debasing. One could speculate that she, like so many others in Hollywood, got swept up in their screen fantasies. They, like their audiences, come to believe that paradise can be found on earth and they will never be satisfied until they find it. People whose lives are a constant quest for such "happiness" are doomed to deep frustration. The main attraction of *The Wizard of Oz*, then, is that it fosters the hope for such a paradise on earth. It gratifies vicariously our desire to live in such a world. Its main drawback, of course, is that it contributes to the disillusionment that inevitably must come to those who believe in and pursue such fantasies.

In *Dorothy and the Lizard of Oz* (1980d), I have tried to retain what is healthy in the Baum and MGM versions and to omit what I consider to be unhealthy and contributory to inappropriate and maladaptive ways of looking at and dealing with life. Although I have taken away some of the attractiveness of the original, my hope is that I have provided even more attractive substitutes. And if they are not as attractive, they will at least ultimately be more gratifying because they are based on reality and real possibilities for living in the real world.

CONCLUDING COMMENTS

It is my hope that the reader will agree with me that child therapists do not utilize frequently enough bibliotherapeutic techniques. This is unfortunate because both attempts to do just those things that we are trying to do in psychotherapy, namely, to change the way people think about the world and the methods they use to deal with it. I believe that these offerings have not only proved useful for children whom I have seen in therapy, but for others as well. Writing books such as these has given me the feeling that I have been able to use what I have learned from my patients to bring about therapeutic change in a large audience of other people whom I have never personally met. Unlike the surgeon who can see within minutes the products of his labors, we in psychiatry must patiently hope that a small fraction of our efforts will prove useful. Writing books such as these has enhanced my ability to gain, as a psychiatrist, this important gratification.

THIRTEEN

Psychoanalytically Oriented Child Psychotherapy

Psychoanalysis is a field in which one man's fantasy becomes another man's reality.

Author of this wisdom unknown to the author of this book

THE SO-CALLED DISCIPLINE OF CHILD PSYCHOANALYSIS

There is no chapter on child psychoanalysis in this book. My main reason for excluding such a chapter is that I do not believe that a field with this name is justifiable. The number of children who are bona fide candidates for this kind of treatment is so small that I do not believe a whole discipline is justified for their treatment. To me, having a field called child psychoanalysis is like having a field called pediatric gerontology. What kind of child would a pediatric gerontologist treat? It would have to be a person who is chonologically very young but who is physically very old. Now, what kind of a disease could a child have that should warrant treatment by such a specialist? I recall from medical school learning about a disease called *progeria*, an endocrinological disorder that is seen in

722

children. Here, the endocrine glands so malfunction that signs and symptoms develop that result in the child's looking like a little old person. If there are other such diseases I do not know of them. Do we start a field called pediatric gerontology for the treatment of the rare case of progeria? I say no. Similarly, I do not believe that we should have a field called child psychoanalysis for the small fraction of child patients who are candidates for such therapy.

I basically view child psychoanalysis to be a field in which attempts have been made to apply adult psychoanalytic treatment to children. The attempt on the part of those who do this is so strong that they often lose sight of the fact that only a small percentage of the children whom they are treating are basically truly candidates for this kind of treatment. They have to deny the obvious fact that the vast majority of the patients they are treating are not cognitively capable of availing themselves of the kind of therapy they are offering. As mentioned, I do not believe that most children are capable of involving themselves in meaningful psychoanalytic inquiry until the age of ten or eleven, when they reach what Piaget referred to as the level of *formal operations*. It is at this phase that the child of average intelligence first exhibits the capacity to separate an entity from the symbol used to denote it and cognitively move back and forth between the entity and the symbol. Under proper training and exposure, some children of average intelligence may be taught to do this earlier. Of course, by two or three years of age children will dream, and the creation of dreams involves the formation of symbols (manifest content) to denote specific unconscious entities (latent content). But the unconscious *formation* of dream symbols is not the same as the conscious cognitive capacity to appreciate the relationship between the dream's manifest and latent contents. I am not claiming that *no* capacity for such analysis is possible before the age of ten or eleven. I am only claiming that the average child has limited capacity for such prior to that time, and the younger the child is, the less the likelihood that a significant amount of time spent in such endeavors is possible. Of course, a seven year old with an extremely high IQ might be able to function intellectually as an eleven year old and then have the cognitive capacity for psychoanalytic inquiry.

Another factor that contributes to the paucity of child candidates for psychoanalytic treatment is the environmental one. There are some families in which the members routinely try to understand the underlying meaning of what they are doing. But these families are rare. Often, they are people who themselves have a strong commitment to psychoanalytic treatment. In the vast majority of families, however, people are not thinking much about the underlying reasons for the things they are doing. The child who grows up in an atmosphere where such inquiry is routine is more likely to be a candidate for psychoanalytic treatment.

Over the years I have had colleagues who have gone beyond their psychoanalytic training into the so-called subspecialty of child psychoanalysis. Quite often, I have been approached by such trainees with the request that I refer them patients who might be suitable candidates for child psychoanalytic treatment. Frequently, I am told that the ability to pay will not be a consideration in that the child will be treated at a minimal fee, and even for nothing, if found suitable for psychoanalytic therapy. The offer to treat at such low cost comes not generally from the altruistic desire to aid the needy; rather, it derives from the fact that candidates in these programs routinely have significant difficulty finding suitable child patients. The main reason for this is that the vast majority of parents absolutely refuse to involve their children in a treatment program four times a week over a span of three, four, or even more years. The typical child analytic patient, then, would start at age five or six and end at ten or eleven, spanning thereby most of the so-called latency period.

There is something psychopathic about those who make such a recommendation. I am not claiming that all therapists who involve themselves in such programs are psychopaths, only that it requires some kind of superego deficiency to recommend such a treatment program to parents. The patient's childhood has to be compromised significantly if a parent is stupid or gullible enough to involve a child in such a treatment program. To go to an analyst four times a week involves giving up four days a week of after-school activities. Playing with friends, recreational activities, sports, after-school extra-curricular activities, homework, television viewing (not necessarily 100 percent detrimental), and even relaxing and doing nothing must all be compromised for the allegedly higher purpose of the psychoanalytic treatment. The theory here is that the losses that result from such privations are more than counterbalanced by the benefits derived from the therapy. Although I believe that the treatment I provide is efficacious for many of the children I see, I do not believe that any child would derive more benefit from seeing me four times a week than from engaging in the aforementioned activities. Once or twice a week, maybe; four times a week, never!

It is not only the frequency of the treatment that deprives candidates of suitable patients. It is also the criterion that the child be analyzable. I see an average of one such child every two or three years. These colleagues have a long and hard search. What ultimately happens, however, is that they rarely find their patients. Rather, they somehow convince the parents of children with severe psychiatric disturbances to involve their children in such a program. They are so pleased to have finally found a parent who is willing to make such a commitment that they look less carefully at the nature of the child's problems—especially with regard to whether he or she has the capacity for introspection, self-inquiry, and analytic thinking. My experience has been that many of the patients who are receiving such treatment under the aegis of a formal child psychoanalytic training program are children with significant learning disabilities who in addition have formidable superimposed psychogenic problems. And such children are among the least likely to have the cognitive capacity for psychoanalytic inquiry. Others are children who could justifiably be classified as borderline psychotic. Here too, the disorder is so severe that the parents are willing to commit the child to such extensive treatment in the hope (not likely to be realized) that this more intensive form of therapy will bring about improvement and even cure of the child's disorder. However, such children are least likely to be able to form the kind of deep relationship that serves as the foundation for psychotherapeutic treatment (psychoanalysis being one branch of psychotherapy). Accordingly, we have many therapists graduating from such programs who have never basically analyzed a child.

For these reasons I have never pursued an educational program that would involve, either immediately or ultimately, training in child psychoanalysis. I consider myself to be an *adult* psychoanalyst and a child psychiatrist, but not a child psychoanalyst. If I had control over the use of the term *child psychiatrist*, however, I would refer to myself as a *pediatric psychiatrist*. The term child psychiatrist can easily connote an individual who is a child and yet is also a psychiatrist.

REASONS WHY ADULT PSYCHOANALYTIC TECHNIQUES CANNOT GENERALLY BE APPLIED TO CHILDREN

The cognitive incapability of children to involve themselves in psychoanalysis is only one of a variety of reasons why I consider such treatment to be inappropriate and inapplicable for children under the age of eleven or so. Here I will discuss some of the technical aspects of the therapy per se that make it extremely difficult, if not impossible in many cases, to apply this treatment modality to children.

"Where There Is Unconscious, There Shall Conscious Be"

Psychoanalytic treatment is based on the theory that certain psychogenic problems are the result of attempts on the part of the individual to deal with suppressed and repressed unconscious material. The primary way in which analytic treatment helps individuals with such problems is to assist in the process of bringing into conscious awareness those unconscious processes that have contributed to the development of the symptoms. In fact, most psychoanalysts would hold that a psychotherapeutic program that does not have this as one of its primary goals cannot justifiably be called psychoanalysis. Most such analysts would not say that the alternative treatment modality cannot possibly be useful; rather, they would hold that it cannot justifiably be called psychoanalysis. However, the same individuals also generally believe that psychoanalysis is the most definitive, "deep," and thorough treatment for psychogenic disorders in which the suppression and repression of unconscious processes are playing an important etiological role.

There are literally thousands of articles written describing how the process of bringing unconscious material into conscious awareness has resulted in significant alleviation and even cure of psychogenic symptoms. Many of these articles describe rapid alleviation of symptoms immediately after the patient has gained such awareness. After reading these articles I often refer to the treatment success as one in which there has been a "great leap forward into mental health." Other factors that may have been operative in bringing about the described change are often not described. The assumption is made that merely by bringing unconscious material into conscious awareness, the patient has improved markedly and has even been cured. I suspect that many of these reports are fabrications. I suspect that others are genuine, but that the patient has provided the therapist what he or she wanted to hear and the therapist has been quick to report the "cure" before the patient had the opportunity once again to exhibit the same symptoms or possibly others. These therapists are so desirous of confirming their theory and obtaining cures by their methods, and so eager to get their happy results into print, that they must selectively blind themselves to certain realities that are taking place with their patients and/or themselves.

Basically, then I do not believe that this aspect of treatment, whether it be for adults or children, is the central therapeutic modality. I am not denying that such insights can often be helpful. However, as described in Chapter One, as far back as my residency days I came to appreciate that much more had to happen in treatment—things unrelated to the gaining of insight—before therapeutic change could be brought about. I am not claiming that insight into unconscious processes is of *no* value. In fact, I routinely encourage such inquiry with my adult patients. I am only claiming that it is a small part of the therapeutic process and that other factors, many *more* important (see Chapter Three), are operative. Even if I am wrong here and insight into unconscious processes is indeed the central factor in the alleviation of certain types of psychogenic problems, I do not believe that the vast majority of children have the cognitive capacity to avail themselves of this route to the alleviation of their difficulties.

The Denial Mechanism

There is another factor that also makes it extremely difficult, if not impossible, to engage children in analytic treatment. I am referring here to the utilization of denial mechanisms. Denial may very well be the most commonly used defense mechanism. And children use it so frequently that it can be considered normal. Most if not all child therapists see boys who have behavioral problems in school. Typically, they tease, scapegoat, provoke, and involve themselves in a wide variety of alienating behaviors with peers. Invariably, the boy denies that he is the initiator and insists that it is always the other children who are the provocateurs. Generally, the patient describes himself as having been minding his own business when some wise guy came over and tried to knock the halo off his head. When the child is confronted with reports from his teacher in which the patient is described as having been observed to be the initiator dozens of times, the teacher is described as a "liar." Or, the child will describe *himself* as the one who was being scapegoated. If the examiner incredulously asks such a youngster, "Are you telling me that you have *never* once—in your whole life—started the fight," the child may sheepishly admit that he might have. When, however, the examiner asks the child to provide a specific example of such a time, the child will usually respond, "I can't remember" or "I forgot." The child described here is *normal*. If this is abnormal, then 99.9 percent of all children are abnormal. Has a boy been born who says, "I started it" when mother reprimands siblings for fighting? What mother ever says to her children, "Raise your hand if you stole the cookie?"

I recognize that the denial described here in children has both conscious and unconscious contributions. In some cases, I believe that unconscious processes are primarily operative, in other children conscious elements predominate. However, I do not believe it really matters what the balance is between these two factors. Whatever their balance, the net result is that the denial mechanism interferes significantly with the capacity of children to analyze meaningfully their behavior. In order to involve oneself in an analysis one must first view the behavior as undesirable. Then one must be motivated to remove it. And then one must be capable of analyzing the unconscious contributing factors if one believes that such a procedure is the best way to remove the symptoms. Denial mechanisms interfere with the child's reaching the first step. One could use the metaphor of the baseball diamond here. The denying child is still on home plate and has not progressed one millimeter toward first base.

Transference and the Resolution of the Transference Neurosis

In Chapter Three I discussed the classical psychoanalytic theory of the transference and the resolution of the transference neurosis. I describe there how these factors are considered central in analytic cure. Specifically, in psychoanalytic theory the term *transference* refers to the transfer of thoughts and feelings from significant figures in one's life (especially people who were influential in early childhood) onto the analyst. As a result of such transfer the patient attempts to involve the analyst in the same kinds of psychopathological interactions that were utilized when relating to parents and other significant figures. Such a pathological reaction is referred to as the *transference neurosis*. When the term *transference neurosis* is used, however, it refers to a compulsive and repetitious pattern. It refers to a situation in which the patient consistently attempts to involve the therapist in the neurotic relationship. The resolution of the transference neurosis involves not only the development of insight into what is occurring but experiences over time that the interactions that worked successfully with others will not succeed with the analyst. One factor (among many) that motivates the patient to give up the pathological mode of interaction is the fear of loss of the therapist's affection if the patient persists in the attempts to so involve the therapist. Implicit in this theory is that children will develop a transference neurosis, that is, they will attempt to involve the analyst in the same pathological patterns that they have utilized with parents and/or parental surrogates.

Anna Freud and Melanie Klein differed with regard to their views on whether or not a child could develop a transference neurosis. Melanie Klein held that the child could do so and believed also that the analysis of such a neurotic pattern was central to successful psychoanalytic treatment. Anna Freud was more cautious and most often took the position that children's transferential reactions were weaker than adults'. My own experience has been that the vast majority of children do not develop strong transferential reactions with their therapists. I believe that this relates primarily to the fact that their investment in their parents is so great that there is little "left over" for the analyst. Children are deeply wrapped up in their home lives and the most of their emotional commitment is to their parents. When one thinks about it, it cannot be otherwise. The parents are the providers of food, clothing, shelter, protection, guidance, and a wide variety of other services. So enmeshed are children in their home lives, they are not likely to develop significant involvement with others. The younger the child the more this principle holds. Of course, children can become involved with their teachers, but rarely does such involvement come close to that which exists with a parent. Even when a child's involvement with a teacher is unusually strong, it does not generally last significantly into the summer vaction. A child may have spent five to seven hours a day with a teacher, more than 180 days of a year. And such involvement is far greater than that which any child has with an analyst, even a child who sees an analyst four sessions a week. Yet even the strongest involvements with teachers do not generally result in deep attachments.

In the therapeutic situation children rarely develop the depth of involvement that can serve, I believe, as a foundation for the development of a bona fide transference neurosis. I could envision an extremely deprived child developing such involvement, but this is rare. Such deprived children are rarely brought for intensive on-going treatment. The same disinterest and neglect results in the parents not being willing to take the time, trouble, and most often incur the expense to bring the child for therapy. The deprived child embraces strangers who come to the door; the child who has a good relationship with a parent is likely to be cautious and only slowly gets involved. One could compare these two children with two women of 28, both of whom are patients of the same 35-year-old male analyst. One is married, has three young children, and comes to treatment because of marital difficulties. The other is single, lives alone, and comes for therapy because she is approaching 30, sus-pects that she may have difficulties relating to men, and fears she may not marry and have children (things she wishes very much to do). The first woman may view the analytic sessions as an intrusion that just stretches her out more and adds to her already formidable burden of taking care of her house and children and involving her-self with her husband. The second may live from session to session and may become deeply absorbed with strong thoughts and feel-ings about the analyst. The first may have never thought about whether or not he is married. The second may be obsessed with the question. The first may welcome the therapist's vacations as a respite from the hassles of her daily living. The second may dread their occurrence and may become obsessed with where he is va-cationing and what he is doing. And now I ask the reader: "Which woman will develop a stronger transferential reaction to the ana-lyst?" The answer is obvious.

Accordingly, I do not believe then that the vast majority of chil-dren develop the strong kind of transferential reaction that classi-cal analysts consider to be crucial for the development of the transference neurosis. This is not to say that the therapist should not refrain from involving him- or herself in attempts on the child's part to involve the therapist in psychopathological interactions. I am only saying that the restraints that the therapist makes in this area are not likely to cause as much frustration as they would in an adult who has a strong transferential reaction. The reason here is basically that the child doesn't care very much about whether the therapist withdraws affection in response to alienating behavior: there was little love in the first place and so there is little love lost.

Free Association and the Blank Screen

Another central element in the psychoanalytic process is based on the theory that the analyst obtains the best information about the unconscious processes that underly the patient's symptoms by encouraging the patient to free associate, that is to verbalize his or her thoughts as they enter conscious awareness without any censoring, altering, or placement in logical sequence. One of the best atmospheres for facilitating free association is said to be the one in which the patient lies on a couch in order to remove him- or herself from environmental stimuli that might "contaminate" the free associations and direct them into particular channels. And the most important of these potentially contaminating stimuli are those that may emanate directly from the therapist via facial expressions, gestures, comments, and even his or her existence. The method came to be described as one in which the patient talks to a "blank screen." This procedure stemmed from Freud's original work with hypnotherapy. Although he abandoned the technique from the recognition that it had significant limitations in bringing about the alleviation and cure of psychoneurotic problems, he retained the basic practice of the patient's remaining in the supine postion, removed from the ability to visualize the therapist. Freud stated that one of his reasons for retaining this aspect of hypnotherapy was that he felt uncomfortable with a face-to-face relationship with a patient seven days a week. (Originally, psychoanalytic treatment was given seven days a week. When Freud's wife complained that she and the children hardly ever saw him, he dropped the frequency down to six times a week. Efficiencies necessitated during World War II dropped the frequency down to five.) This pathological reason for Freud's retaining the couch, after recognizing that hypnotherapy had serious limitations, is not given the attention it deserves by classical analysts. I believe that many of them have the same reason for retaining the couch, that is, they too are uncomfortable with ongoing face-to-face involvement with their patients. Of course, other reasons are given for retaining the couch, such as the fact that it lessens the likelihood that the patient's associations will be contaminated. As mentioned earlier in this book, I believe that this advantage of the couch is far outweighed by the disadvantages associated with the unreal interactions and often pathological relationship it produces between the patient and the therapist.

Even Freud did not believe that it was appropriate to put children on the couch and have them free associate to a "blank screen." But he did believe that the child's bringing unconscious processes into conscious awareness was extremely important if one were to psychoanalyze a child. As mentioned earlier in this book, H. Von Hug-Hellmuth, A. Freud, and M. Klein all held that the child's self-created stories were analogous to the free associations of the adult and could provide similar information for psychoanalytic utilization. Just as the adult analyst helps a patient analyze his or her free associations, the child analyst is supposed to help the child analyze self-created stories. I am in agreement that self-created stories are often a rich source of information about unconscious processes and can justifiably be compared to (but are not identical with) the free associations of an adult. I am somewhat dubious, however, about the ease with which child analysts claim they are able to get children to analyze their stories. I have had far less success than they, and I do not believe that it relates to any particular therapeutic impairments on my part; rather, I believe it relates more to the child's cognitive immaturity and other factors discussed in this chapter.

Another disadvantage of the blank screen—and this may be its most important—is that it lessons the likelihood that an optimally beneficial therapist-patient relationship will emerge. Rather, it tends to produce idealization of the therapist, that is, a view that the therapist is perfect or close to it. It also contributes to idolization of the therapist, that is, a view that the therapist is somewhat God-like. These thoughts and feelings about the therapist are definitely antitherapeutic. Many therapists welcome such reactions by their patients. I believe the most likely cause of this desire to be aggrandized is that it helps them compensate for feelings of inadequacy. The optimum kind of therapist-patient relationship is one in which the patient comes to see the therapist as a *real* human being, with both assets and liabilities. Viewing the therapist as perfect is going to make it difficult for the patient to relate to others who are merely human and who will inevitably reveal qualities that will be alienating to the patient. Just as viewing one's parents as perfect can interfere with the ultimate development of healthy human relationships, viewing one's therapist as perfect can also have this detrimental effect.

Analysis of the Childhood Roots of the Symptoms

Psychoanalytic treatment is also based on the theory that if patients are to enjoy permanent alleviation of symptoms, then they must go back and understand their childhood roots. Most analysts hold that such understanding is best arrived at via free association and analytic inquiry. Such insight, they believe, is an important factor in psychoanalytic cure. Others believe that simple understanding is not enough and that patients must reexperience certain early childhood experiences (especially psychological deprivations and traumas), particularly if such reliving is followed by movement along healthier paths. Others hold that important contributing factors to the development of symptoms are suppressed and repressed feelings that were not exhibited at the time of early traumas and that the belated expression of these pent-up feelings is central to psychoanalytic cure. I have significant reservations about both of these theories.

First, with regard to the issue of going back to childhood roots, the child patient is already back there. Accordingly, child analysts would say that when one treats children one has the opportunity to deal with the problem *before* or *at the time* it originates and can thereby "nip the problem in the bud." Others would say that the fact that the child exhibits a symptom indicates that there have been *earlier* traumas which must be understood if there is to be a cure. Accordingly, if a six- or seven-year-old child comes for treatment, one tries to go back to earlier ages, perhaps two and three, when the problems began. Although a child might be able to recall a few events from that earlier period, I cannot imagine the overwhelming majority of children utilizing such fragmentary recollections in a meaningful way over time. I certainly have never seen a child who is interested in or capable of doing this. Of course, it could be argued that my own lack of conviction for the approach might be sensed by the child and I would thereby be squelching a procedure that might be useful. I cannot deny that this might be the case, but I consider it unlikely.

With regard to the theory that the patient must go back and relive past experiences and thereby channel them into new directions, I also have little conviction for this approach. My general view is that one's past experiences certainly contribute to the development of present behavior, both normal and pathological. However, I also consider past experiences to be like "water under the bridge." One can remember the past, one can learn from it, but one cannot relive it. Reliving is artificial and is not, in my opinion, going to bring about therapeutic change.

With regard to the theory that expressing past, buried emotions that were previously unexpressed is important in the therapeutic process, the notion here is that these pent-up feelings are like a well-encased pocket of pus in an abscess. The analogy goes further and compares the analyst to the surgeon who lances the abscess in order to release the pus. This too I consider extremely unlikely. Although I believe that there may be some therapeutic value derived from belated reactions of this kind ("better late then never"), I believe that the longer the time between the trauma and the analytic treatment, the more diffuse the "abscess" is going to become and the more enmeshed the unresolved feelings will become fused and entwined with other unconscious material. Simple expression ("lancing") then is not likely to work. To alleviate problems related to longstanding supression and repression, one must deal with the factors that produced the original suppressions and repressions and which may still be operative at the present time. Accordingly, one avoids a repetition of the same suppression in the future by learning from the past and present.

The Freudian Stages of Psychosexual Development

Classical psychoanalytic treatment is not simply based on the theory that neurotic problems have their roots in childhood. The theory gets more specific and relates the childhood difficulties to problems related to Freudian stages of psychosexual development: oral, anal, phallic, and genital. Freud's theory of the childhood stages of psychosexual development was based on the analysis of adults many years after these events allegedly took place. Freud never treated a child. Little Hans' treatment was conducted by his father under Freud's supervision. What to me is amazing about the theory is that so many people have believed it, although it is becoming less popular these days. As I have discussed in detail elsewhere (Gardner, 1973c) I have little conviction for Freud's theory of childhood development. Accordingly, I am not likely to explain symptoms in accordance with its prescriptions and so would not be providing children with an important element in their psychoanalysis, namely, relating their difficulties to fixations, regressions, and so forth, at the oedipal and the so-called pre-oedipal levels of development.

The Superego and Intrapsychic Conflict

Psychoanalytic treatment was designed to alleviate and cure neurotic problems. Neurotic problems, according to classical theory, are considered to be the result of intrapsychic conflicts. Specifically, there may be conflicts between the *id* (unconscious primitive impulses) and the *superego* (the conscience and the ego-ideal). Or there may be conflicts between the superego and the *ego* (a variety of ideas that are either in or readily accessible to conscious awareness). I will not discuss here my areas of agreement and disagreement about this fundamental concept. What I wish to focus on here is the issue of superego development. To have a neurosis one must have a superego. Furthermore, one must have a strongly developed superego to have a neurotic conflict. All would agree that there are stages in superego development and that the progression goes from a very weak to almost nonexistant superego in infancy to the potential for very strong superego functioning as one gets older. And this progression develops from birth to death. All would agree, as well, that children have more poorly developed superegos than adults. Psychoanalysis is designed primarily for psychoneurotic problems, those in which there is some kind of intrapsychic conflict, especially one that involves the superego.

Classical Freudians generally consider children's superegos to be more developed than I view them to be. Most children below the age of 11 or 12 do not have such strong superego development that intrapsychic conflicts are set up. And when I do see such children they are generally in the upper age levels of childhood, 10 to

12. The paucity of children with intrapsychic conflicts at younger ages reduces even further the potential population of children who are candidates for psychoanalysis. Even Freud appreciated the fact that people who act out their impulses, rather than internalize and cogitate over them, are not likely to be candidates for psychoanalysis. Accordingly, he did not consider juvenile delinquents and those with psychopathic tendencies to be candidates for psychoanalytic treatment. The vast majority of children I see act out rather than dwell over and introspect about their thoughts, feelings, and impulses. They need more guilt, not less. Again, the rarity of intrapsychic conflict in children (especially younger ones) is another reason why they are generally poor candidates for psychoanalysis.

PSYCHOANALYTICALLY ORIENTED CHILD PSYCHOTHERAPY

My criticisms of psychoanalysis notwithstanding, I still consider myself a psychoanalyst. I still believe that unconscious processes play an important role in the development of the majority of psychogenic problems. I believe that the defense mechanisms described by S. Freud and A. Freud are for the most part valid and that they play an important role in the development of symptoms. They help us understand the linkages (discussed in Chapter Three) between the fundamental problems of life and the symptoms that are derived in an attempt to deal with them. In short, they help us understand *psychodynamics*. I believe that dream analysis (discussed later in this chapter) is a therapeutically useful procedure. And even free association—in selected situations—can be a valuable therapeutic tool.

Accordingly, I have not discarded entirely psychoanalytic theory. Rather, I believe that we do well to take from the theory and the techniques that have been devised to utilize it those elements that appear to be useful and to discard those that we suspect will be of little value. Here I describe how I use those aspects of the theory and technique that I have found useful in my work, specifically those techniques that are derived from and are modifications of traditional psychoanalytic procedure. For the purposes of this discussion, I refer to this approach as *psychoanalytically oriented child psychotherapy*.

The Development and Utilization of Insight

First, as mentioned, the approach here is based on the theory that unconscious processes play a role in symptom formation. However, I do not believe that it is necessary (and certainly not crucial) for patients to gain conscious awareness of their unconscious processes in order to derive therapeutic benefit. This not only holds true for adults (who are often resistant to doing so, even though they may profess receptivity to the process), but to children who, as mentioned, are often cognitively incapable of such an endeavor. If the patient does gain such insight, I am certainly pleased. In fact, I welcome such insight but I do not pressure patients, especially children, into deriving it. I do not consider insight to be a crucial factor in bringing about therapeutic change. Rather, I view it as "frosting on the cake." It is an additional and potentially useful therapeutic modality which is nice to have when one can get it, but I do not pressure patients into deriving it. What is crucial is that the *therapist* make every attempt to learn as much as possible about the child's unconscious processes. If the therapist doesn't learn about these factors, then no one is equipped to help the child (at least by psychotherapeutic methods). The therapist utilizes such knowledge in the child's treatment. And the therapist's knowledge is gained by the analysis of the child's stories, pictures, verbal productions, etc.

The next question relates to what the therapist does with such information. If the therapist uses the information to provide a responding story, then the technique cannot justifiably be called analytically oriented therapy because basic issues are *not* being brought into conscious awareness. Rather, I would call the procedure *utilization of the mutual storytelling technique*. If the therapist uses the information to involve the child in a discussion at the symbolic level ("Why did the cat bite the dog?"), this also cannot justifiably be called analytically oriented child psychotherapy. I would refer to this procedure as *discussion at the symbolic level*. Here again, nothing is being brought to conscious awareness. It is when the therapist attempts to use the information so gained in the attempt to help the child gain insight that the procedure might justifiably be called analytically oriented psychotherapy. In pure psychoanalysis every reasonable attempt is made to get the patient him- or herself to derive the insight, with only catalytic comments by the analyst. In the form of treatment I am discussing here *the analyst surmises the psychodynamic meaning of the patient's productions and then attempts to impart information to the patient and/ or the parents.* The purpose here is for them to utilize this information in bringing about symptom alleviation.

One can say that there is a continuum between pure psychoanalysis and analytically oriented therapy. To the degree that the patient him-or herself derives the insights, to that degree could the procedure justifiably be called psychoanalysis. In contrast, to the degree that the therapist provides back the information learned from the child's unconscious, to that degree should the procedure be referred to as analytically oriented child psychotherapy. Of course, the patient's own guesses, hunches, and "associations" could also be useful for the therapist in helping him or her surmise the underlying meaning of the presented material. To the degree that the child's contribution to the understanding of the underlying psychodynamics have been operative, to that degree can the procedure be justifiably called psychoanalysis. And to the degree that the therapist's contribution to insight has been operative, to that degree can the procedure be considered analytically oriented psychotherapy.

What Psychoanalytically Oriented Child Therapy Is, and What It Is Not

When I use this term *analytically oriented psychotherapy,* I am referring to a procedure that does not rely upon the analysis of resistances in order to remove them. I do not expect the child to do so. This is not only the result of the ubiquitous use of the denial mechanism by children, but the wide variety of other mechanisms that children might utilize to protect themselves from conscious awareness of their unconscious processes, for example, reaction formation, compensation, and projection. It does not rely upon the development of the transferential reaction or transference neurosis. It utilizes free association of the type to be found when the child is asked to provide a self-created story. It does not rely upon insight into earlier childhood roots of the symptoms; rather, it focuses on the immediate past and the present to provide guidelines for future behavior. It is not based on Freud's theory of childhood psychosexual development. In fact, it is not based on any single particular theory of development. Rather, it is based on the specific developmental issues that are applicable to that particular child at that time. Accordingly, there might be children who are having trouble with toilet training and others who are masturbating. In both cases, I would address myself to individual and family factors that might be causing trouble. Others exhibit age-appropriate sibling rivalry problems, difficulties in adjusting to new situations, separation fears, and so on, and each of these is dealt with with some understanding of the developmental norm but without any need to fit the behavioral manifestation into a particular developmental theory or therapeutic approach. I am not claiming here that developmental theories have no validity. Nor am I claiming that one cannot learn some useful things from them (some more than others, however, and one of the very least being the Freudian theory of psychosexual development). I am only stating that one should avoid the trap of trying to put a particular child into a particular theoretical Procrustean bed.

Some Common Ways in Which the Therapist Uses Psychodynamic Information

The information that the therapist gains can be used for a wide variety of psychotherapeutic purposes. It can be used to help the patient assert him- or herself more appropriately (at the age-appropriate level). It can be used to increase or decrease guilt, depending upon what is appropriate for the patient. S. Freud considered it necessary to attempt to reduce the guilt of his hysterical women who were too inhibited in the expression of their sexual feelings. This has resulted in many therapists' believing that they should uniformly try to reduce patients' guilt and *never* do anything to increase it. This is an error. Some patients need *more* guilt and some *less*. Most of the children I see need more guilt, not less. They have behavior disorders, they act out, and many exhibit manifestations of the ever-increasing psychopathy of our society.

The therapist may use the information to help patients express their resentment in appropriate ways. It can be used to help people with low self-esteem involve themselves in maneuvers that are likely to enhance feelings of self-worth. The information can be used to help the child correct cognitive distortions, for example: "It's wrong to have angry thoughts toward a parent," "If someone calls me a bad name that person must be right," and "It's okay to cheat on tests." It can be used to help a child gain a more accurate view of his or her parents—both their assets and their liabilities—and to respond more appropriately to this knowledge. It can be used to help a child alter pathological emulation and identification. It can help to reduce overdemanding ego-ideals, for example, " A grade of B is a perfectly acceptable grade. As long as you think that you're a failure if you don't get an A, you're going to be miserable." And it can be used to help a child expose him- or herself to anxiety-provoking situations in order to facilitate the desensitization process. In short, the information obtained from the child by the therapist can be used for a wide variety of therapeutic procedures. The case of Tara, described in Chapter Seven, is an excellent example of how the therapist's insight into the unconscious factors that were causing symptoms proved useful in bringing about therapeutic alleviation. In fact, this is one case in which the term "cure" might be applicable.

THE USE OF THE TALKING, FEELING, AND DOING GAME IN FACILITATING PSYCHOANALYTIC INQUIRY

As mentioned, there are rare children who can make use of analytic inquiry. I am not against children's doing so. I am only against the attempt to apply the technique to the vast majority of children. In this section I will discuss the value of *The Talking, Feeling, and Doing Game* in facilitating inquiry in children who are possible candidates for such an introspective approach to the alleviation of their problems.

* * *

Question: Of all the things you own, what do you enjoy the most? Make believe you're doing something with that thing.

Response: Of all the things I own, one of the things I enjoy the most is my video cassette recorder and camera. I like making television programs of myself and the children whom I treat. It's even better now since I bought a color TV system, because now we can see it in color rather than black and white. It not only helps me learn things about the children who come to see me, but it helps me learn things about myself. The TV system gives people a chance to see themselves the way others see them. It's very hard for most people to look at themselves clearly. The TV system helps people do this.

Even though some of the things that people learn from it may not be pleasant, the information can be useful. I'm very interested in understanding why people do the things they do, and the television system helps me learn these things. This is a subject that interests me very much. I'm very curious about how the human mind works and why people do the things they do. I find it an interesting and fascinating subject to learn about. And that information can help me be of help to other people, and the television set helps me to learn these things.

My hope here is that some of my own enthusiasm for psychological inquiry will engender a similar interest in the child.

* * *

Question: What is one of the stupidest things a person can do? Show someone doing that thing.

Response: One of the stupidest things a person can do is to make believe there is no problem when there really is. The person who does that is not going to do anything to solve the problem. So it's going to continue to exist and may even get worse.

At this point I might ask the child if he or she can think of an example of someone who does this, that is, someone who has a problem and makes believe that there is no problem. It is hoped that the child will provide an example that relates to his or her own situation. If not, I might provide the following example for the child who is unmotivated in school and denies the problem.

Response: Well, one example would be of a girl who is doing very poorly in school and is making believe that she has no problem. She just thinks about other things. When others try to tell her that she's having a problem in school, she doesn't want to listen. Then she doesn't do anything to correct the problem or to solve it. Then things will probably just get worse and at the end of the year she may find that she'll have to repeat the grade. Or, even if she gets promoted, she may find that she gets very embarrassed in school because most of the other children know the answers and she doesn't.

I might at this point discuss with the child my story "Oliver and the Ostrich" from *Dr. Gardner's Stories About the Real World* (1972a). The story deals with the issue of the denial mechanism in the context of a discussion of the ostrich. In the story it becomes apparent that the ostrich does *not* hide its head in the sand in times of danger ("The ostrich wouldn't do such a foolish thing"). It focuses on the adaptive mechanisms (primarily involved in flight or fight) that ostriches utilize in dangerous situations. (They do not differ from the rest of the animal kingdom in this regard.) This story has proven popular among my patients, and it can contribute, I believe, to a reduction in the utilization of the denial mechanisms.

* * *

Question: What is the worst problem a person can have?

Response: I think one of the worst problems a person can have is to make believe that there are no problems when there really are. Such people don't do anything about the problems they have. By making believe there are no problems, they continue to ignore them; but problems don't go away. Because they make believe there are no problems, they don't do anything to solve their problems.

A boy, for example, might be doing very poorly in school, but might not wish to think about it. When his parents try to tell him about the trouble, he might stick his fingers in his ears so that he can't hear them, or he might close his eyes so that he can't see them waving his poor report card at him. This may make him feel better at the time because he then doesn't have to think about his terrible report card. However, he might end up with having to repeat the grade. By then it would have been too late to do anything about the problem. Perhaps then he'll learn his lesson. That's why I say that making believe there's no problem when there really is can be one of the worst problems a person can have.

* * *

Question: Who was the best teacher you ever had? Why?

Response: The best teacher I ever had was a man named Dr. Geoffrey Osler. He was a neurologist. A neurologist is a kind of doctor who specializes in diseases of the nerves. He really loved being a teacher. He was very excited about what he taught. When he taught, everybody in the class got excited about the subject matter as well. Enthusiasm spread throughout the whole class. In his class, learning was fun. In addition, he had a tremendous amount of knowledge and everyone respected him for it. Although it's been over twenty years since I took his course, I still remember many of the things he said. In addition, he started me thinking about a lot of things I hadn't thought about before and I still find myself trying to learn more about those things. He increased my curiosity. He increased my desire to find out the answers to interesting questions. I feel very lucky to have had such a teacher.

Dr. Osler was also interested in understanding how the human mind worked. He was also a psychiatrist, but he was primarily a neurologist. He liked to understand why people did the things they did. I, of course, am a psychiatrist, and I want to learn even more about the reasons why people do the things they do. And I try to get my patients to be curious about that as well. It's sometimes amazing to find out the reasons why a person does what he or she does. Often, people don't understand why they do something and, when they come to understand why they do things, they are really amazed. Also, when they do understand these things, it can often help them prevent or avoid trouble.

My aim here, clearly, is to sweep the child up in the same enthusiasm that I had, and still have, about Dr. Geoffrey Osler. My hope here also is that the child may develop some curiosity about finding out about the inner workings of his or her own mind.

* * *

Question: What turns you on, that is, what excites you?

Response: One of the things that excites me is puzzles and games in which you have to try to figure out answers. I remember when I was a kid I used to love playing checkers and chess. I also used to like doing puzzles in children's books. Later on I used to like doing crossword puzzles in newspapers. When I was in Junior High School, and started to learn algebra, I used to love to figure out mathematical problems, especially those that were very hard to figure out the answer. I remember when I was a teenager there was a program on the radio called "The Quiz Kids." They used to take the best students from the various high schools and ask them very hard questions. I wasn't smart enough to be a quiz kid, but I used to love listening to that program. I used to love trying to figure out the answers to the questions and once or twice I even got an answer when none of the quiz kids did. I really felt good about myself then. But, more important, I found it a lot of fun to try to figure out the answers to difficult questions. That's the kind of thing that really turns me on. It also turns me on to understand why people do the things they do. That can help people stop doing those things.

My hope here, obviously, is to engender in the child the same kind of excitement I have about learning. Perhaps, by getting a feeling for such gratification, there may be some enhancement of the child's curiosity and motivation to learn as well, both about things in general and about his or her own inner mental processes.

* * *

Question: Make believe you've just opened a letter you've received from someone. What does this letter say?

Response: Let's say it's a letter from a former patient. I'll read the letter:

Dear Dr. Gardner:

I am writing you from this college where I'm now going. I appreciate very much your therapy. Before I came to treatment I was not doing very well in school, and I learned some of the reasons why I was having trouble in school and I solved some of those problems so that I now have been able to go to college. I didn't want to think about the reasons why I was doing certain things at first. But after I started thinking about them I realized that I could learn some important things about myself.

Your friend,

Bob

Anything you want to say about that?

My hope here is that the child might be motivated for self-inquiry in order to enjoy the benefits derived by Bob.

DREAM PSYCHOANALYSIS

The best way to demonstrate psychoanalytic technique is via the analysis of dreams. I am in full agreement with Freud who held that the dream is the "royal road to the unconscious." Accordingly, I present here dream analyses of a few child patients (as stated, they are relatively rare) who were interested in and receptive to the analysis of their dreams. Because the same principles are applicable to the analysis of other material as well, I will use dream analysis to present my views on this treatment modality. Before proceeding to the clinical vignettes, I will present my views (not unique) regarding the meaning of dreams and then some basic principles applicable to helping children analyze their dreams. The same principles that I utilize with adults are applicable to children; however, as will be seen, I must modify these when working with children.

The Purposes of Dreams

It is reasonable to speculate that human beings have wondered about the meaning of dreams as far back as there were people dreaming. Wise men and seers have often been viewed as particularly astute in ascertaining the meaning of dreams. Joseph's dream in the Bible is well known. Although I have many criticisms of psychoanalytic theory and technique, I still consider certain elements in psychoanalysis to be extremely useful. One of these is its contribution to dream analysis. Although I am not in agreement with the reflex way in which many analysts see oral, anal, and oedipal themes in them, I am in agreement with some of the basic theories of Sigmund Freud regarding the meaning of dreams. Particularly, I believe that the emergence of unconscious material is more likely to take place at night. During the day the necessary involvements and distractions of real living do not allow us much time to attend to unconscious material that may be pressuring for eruption into conscious awareness. At night, when these external stimuli are reduced significantly, unconscious material becomes freer to pass into conscious awareness. However, because of guilt and/or anxiety attendant to the emergence of such material, the individual disguises the material. The dream is a product of such emerged material. I consider it to be one of the richest (if not the most rich) source of information about unconscious processes. It is also a testimony to the creativity of the human being (even that of a child) because of the ingenuity that is sometimes utilized in its formation. I present here what I consider to be some of the most reasonable theories regarding the meaning of dreams. I do not claim that this is an exhaustive statement, only that these theories appear most reasonable to me. Our paucity of knowledge about the meaning of dreams also compromises our ability to provide a comprehensive statement about their meaning at this point.

The Dream as a Vehicle for Wish Fulfillment   The theory that the dream serves the purpose of wish fulfillment is ancient. Many dreams are obvious examples of this mechanism. The hungry person dreams of food. The thirsty individual dreams of drink. The sexually frustrated person dreams of sexual gratification. And the angry person dreams of wreaking vengeance. Freud too considered wish fulfillment to be one of the dream's primary purposes. Freud went further, however. He described dreams to have a *latent* and a *manifest* content. The latent material resides within the unconscious because its emergence into conscious awareness produces guilt and/or anxiety. However, so strong are the forces pressing for release of unconscious material that its emergence into conscious awareness cannot be long prevented. Accordingly, an internal psychological compromise is devised in which the repressed material is permitted access to conscious awareness, but in a disguised form. By using such disguise mechanisms as *symbolization* and *condensation*, the individual essentially fools him- or herself into not recognizing the true nature of the material that has now entered conscious awareness. It is as if the right hand has fooled the left hand. In addition, the individual utilizes the mechanism of *secondary elaboration* in which the dream is given an organization that it does not intrinsically possess. Such organization enables the individual to feel more comfortable with the dream because it now follows some traditional sequence. Secondary elaboration also serves the purposes of self-deception, in that the reorganization process disguises the dream even more.

Freud believed that one of the dream's primary purposes was to preserve sleep. For example, a hungry person might be awakened by hunger pangs that threaten to interrupt the vital sleep process. By dreaming of eating, the individual again "fools" the hunger pangs, fantasizes satiety, and thereby preserves sleep. Another example provided by Freud of the dream's sleep-preserving function is that of the person who, while dreaming, hears loud environmental noise. In order to prevent the noise from awakening the dreamer, the fracas is incorporated into the dream. In this way, the dream satisfies its sleep-preservation function. However, Freud had difficulty fitting the nightmare into this theory, in that this kind of dream usually ends with the person's awakening. This exception did not cause him to abandon the general theory of sleep preservation; rather, he concluded that the nightmare was an exception to this principle and when an individual had a nightmare the dream process was considered to have broken down and failed in its primary function of sleep preservation. Although I am in agreement with Freud that *one* of the purposes of the dream is to provide wish fulfillment, I believe Freud put too much emphasis on this dream function, to the neglect of others. I consider the wish-fulfillment function to apply only to one possible category of dream. As I will discuss, I consider there to be other functions unrelated to wish fulfillment. And the nightmare, which I will discuss below, is an example of one of these functions.

Freud ascribed many sexual meanings to dreams, meanings that I would be less prone to consider sexual. In particular, many of the symbols found in dreams were considered by him to be phallic or vaginal. However, Freud also emphasized the importance of utilizing the patient's own free associations in order to ascertain what the symbols meant for that particular patient. He presents, thereby, a somewhat contradictory theory about the symbols. He considered certain symbols to be universal, especially in the phallic/vaginal realm. Yet he viewed other symbols to be idiosyncratic and devised by the patient. I have little conviction for the notion of universal symbols that are somehow inherited from the unconscious minds of one's parents and ancestors. (Carl Jung was especially committed to this notion.) Rather, I believe that environmental influences (familial, social, and cultural) are the most important (if not exclusive) determinants of what a symbol (dream or otherwise) will mean. In addition, I am far less likely to ascribe sexual meanings to many of the symbols that Freud and his followers so quickly assumed to have such significance. These criticisms notwithstanding, I consider Freud's *The Interpretation of Dreams* (1900) to be a monumental contribution and recommend it to all those who are interested in learning about the classical psychoanalytic theory of dreams.

There are some dreams in which there is simple release of pent-up thoughts and feelings which might also be considered a kind of wish-fulfillment dream. I am referring here to sexual dreams in which the individual gains sexual gratification as a way of providing release for pent-up and frustrated sexual feelings. The adolescent boy's "wet dream" would be an example of this kind of dream. As the youngster grows older, and has greater opportunities for sexual fulfillment, he experiences a diminution in the frequency of such dreams. The association of the dream with ejaculation raises some interesting questions. Does the dream fantasy precede the sexual excitation and resultant ejaculation, or does the hormonally induced genital arousal stimulate the production of the dream fantasy? Another type of simple release dream would be one in which an individual fantasizes harm befalling some individual toward whom intense angry feelings are felt. In these simple release types of wish-fulfillment dreams, there is little if any disguise. The individual is generally quite clear about the basic function of the dream. However, if there is guilt and/or anxiety over the release of these feelings, then some disguise elements may be introduced, such as substituting the identity of the object of the sexual or hostile feelings.

The Dream as a Vehicle for Alerting the Individual to Danger
This is an extremely important function of the dream which I believe was not given proper attention by Freud. In fact, I believe that the dream may more commonly serve the alerting role than the role of simple wish-fulfillment. Most dangers are not repressed. The individual looks at them squarely and then reacts appropriately, generally either by fight or flight. However, there are certain situations in which an individual may wish to ignore the fact that a danger exists because to appreciate it might result in guilt, anxiety, or other untoward reactions. Under such circumstances the information about the danger is relegated to unconscious awareness. An internal psychological conflict then arises. On the one hand, thoughts of the danger press for release into conscious awareness in order to alert the individual to its existence. On the other hand, such appreciation may result in a variety of unpleasant and even painful psychological reactions. Again, the dream compromise is brought into play. The danger emerges into conscious awareness in disguised form, satisfying thereby both arms of the conflict.

Let us take as a theoretical example of this kind of dream a situation in which a personnel manager in a large corporation has an appointment with a prospective employee. About an hour prior to the interview with the job candidate he receives a call from a senior official in his organization telling him that the interviewee is a relative of his wife's and that he should be given special consideration. During the interview the personnel manager scans briefly the man's application, but does not give it the detailed perusal that he normally does. Following the interview the personnel manager decides that he is going to recommend the applicant for a position and hopes that this decision will place him in a favorable position with the senior official who recommended that he give the man every opportunity. That night the personnel manager has a dream in which the applicant that he saw that day, now an employee in the company, stealthily enters the company vault and successfully absconds with a huge sum of money. Then, after the theft is discovered, the personnel manager finds himself under serious criticism—even to the point where his job is in jeopardy—because he has hired the man. He wakes up, horrified over the prospect of losing his job.

Let us carry the example further and place this man in psychoanalytic treatment. The analyst encourages the patient to think about any possible clues he was given that the man might have had criminal tendencies, or even a record. The patient states that he had absolutely no awareness of such. However, when reviewing carefully the details of the interview, the analyst learns that the patient rapidly looked over the application. Recognizing this as atypical behavior, the analyst suggests that the patient review again— but this time very carefully—the applicant's application. The patient then returns to his office, reviews the application very carefully, and notes that there was a two-year period which appears to be completely unaccounted for. This occurred when the interviewee was between 19 and 21 years of age. Immediately he calls back the applicant and, in the course of the interview, asks him about the gap in his school and work history. At this point, the applicant, somewhat apologetically, states that he was in jail during that period, but dismisses it as the result of a series of "adolescent indiscretions" that were not even worth mentioning. He goes on to reassure the personnel manager that these incidents are "water under the bridge," that he has learned his lesson, "paid his debt to society," and can be relied upon to be a "solid citizen." The personnel manager returns to his next analytic session and, in the discussion of what has transpired, comes to the realization that the applicant is *still* somewhat psychopathic, in that he withheld the information from the application rather than disclose it, and that such deceptive tendencies not only existed in the past but exist at the present time as well.

He now finds himself presented with a new problem. Does he hire the man in order to keep himself in favor with the senior company official or does he reject the applicant and risk thereby the disfavor of his superior? As a result of further analytic work he decides that this dilemma is not a burden he need assume himself; rather, he can present the information to the senior official and let *him* decide what to do. This is not an option that he had previously considered, but it emerged from the analytic interchange. It is an example of the way in which therapy opens up new options, options that may not have previously been considered by the patient, options that are often preferable to those already operating in the patient's repertoire. If he follows this course, he need not feel responsible for any untoward consequences of hiring this individual. Now it becomes the senior official's responsibility if the applicant does not prove trustworthy.

This example has been presented because it demonstrates well how the dream can serve to alert an individual to a danger that he or she might not previously have been aware of. In this case, the man had to repress from conscious awareness his recognition of the gap in the application to avoid risking the displeasure of a senior company official. There was a danger, however, and it pressed for release into conscious awareness. A dream compromise was made, one that satisfied both unconscious and conscious processes. Had the man not been in treatment he might not have appreciated the significance of the dream and might thereby have suffered significant untoward repercussions of his oversight. Furthermore, and unrelated to this discussion of dreams, the vignette demonstrates how therapy, by opening up new options, can help individuals deal better with the fundamental problems of life in ways that they might not have previously considered.

At this point, I will present a dream that I myself had about a patient. It serves as an excellent example of the dream's value as an alerting mechanism. Many years ago a man of 25 requested treatment for homosexual difficulties. He considered his homosexuality to be psychogenic and hoped that therapy would help him achieve a heterosexual life pattern. The patient was born and raised in New England and had attended a prestigious boarding school and Ivy League college. His father had died when he was three and he had absolutely no recollection of him. He was raised with his mother and three older sisters, all of whom doted over him. His mother often undressed in front of him, even into the teen period. He first began having homosexual experiences in boarding school, but did describe some successful heterosexual experiences as well. However, his homosexual experiences were much more gratifying to him. In his early twenties he married in the hope that this might bring about a heterosexual orientation. He had not told his wife about his homosexuality at the time of his marriage. After about a year she became aware of his activities and at first hoped that she might be able to salvage the marriage. When I saw him, she had decided upon divorce and he went into therapy, hoping that he could avoid future similar consequences of his homosexuality. At the time he entered treatment, he was also in difficulty in the firm where he worked. He was employed by an investment banking firm, and it was becoming increasingly clear to him that he was being passed over for promotions because of suspicions of his homosexual lifestyle.

During the first two months of treatment, the patient appeared to be involving himself well in the therapy. He was a mild-mannered man who was quite polite and formal. His relationships, however, were invariably tempestuous, especially his homosexual relationships, in which there was significant jealous rivalry. In association with the stresses of these relationships, he would often drink heavily and sometimes became quite depressed. Consciously, I did not consider the patient to be significantly different from other patients I was seeing with regard to any particular thoughts and/or emotional reactions that I might be having about them. One night, however, after about two months of treatment, I had a dream in which the patient was pursuing me with a knife in an attempt to murder me. Although I fled in terror, he was gaining on me and I awakened just at the point where he was about to stab me. When I awakened, it was with a sigh of relief that I appreciated that it was only a dream. I was in analytic training at the time and so I began to think seriously about what the possible meaning of the dream could be. I had to consider the most obvious explanation, namely, that my dream was a reflection of unconscious homosexual desires toward my patient. Because I had never previously had any particular inclinations in this direction (and none since, I might say), I found it difficult to accept this as a possible explanation. However, I also had to accept reluctantly the latent homosexual explanation because of the way unconscious processes operate. I was also taught in analytic training that when a therapist has a dream about a patient, it invariably indicates inappropriate countertransferential reactions. I was not too comfortable with this unflattering explanation either. I could not recall having had any dreams previously about my patients (nor have I had any since), but I did, on occasion, exhibit what I had to accept were inappropriate countertransferential reactions. Accordingly, I was left with the feeling that the dream was important but without any particular explanation for its meaning. (At that time, I was not appreciative of the alerting value of dreams.)

About two weeks after the dream, the patient entered the session in an agitated state. Although I do not have verbatim notes on the interchange that ensued during that session, the following is essentially what took place:

Patient (quite tense):   I'm very upset. I can't take it any longer. I can't continue this way.

Therapist: Tell me.

Patient: This is very difficult to talk about.

Therapist: I suspect that it will be, but I know you appreciate that it's important for you to discuss those things here that you are hesitant to speak about.

Patient: Yes, I know I have to tell you but it's difficult.

Therapist: I'm listening.

Patient: I can't stand it any longer. I've got to tell you. I'm in love with you. And I've been in love with you since the first session. I can't stand it any longer. While I'm talking to you about my problems, I keep thinking about how much I love you.

Therapist: You know, the word *love* can mean many things. It would be helpful to us if you could tell me the *exact* kinds of thoughts and feelings you've been having when you say that you love me.

Patient: That's even harder.

Therapist: I can appreciate that; however, if we're to fully understand what's happening, it's important that you try to tell me.

Patient: If you really want to know, I want to have sex with you.

Therapist: Even there, having sex with someone is a statement that covers a lot of ground. I'd like you to try to be more specific about the particular kinds of thoughts and feelings you're having when you say that you want to have sex with me.

Patient: Well, I just wouldn't want to start having sex right away. I'd want there to be some overtures on your part, some advances by you.

Therapist: I'm starting to get the picture. Now what specifically would you want me to say and do.

Patient: Well, I just wouldn't want you to simply ask me. I'd want you to plead.

Therapist: What would you want me to say specifically?

Patient: I'd want you to beg me. I'd want you to get down on your knees and beg me to have sex with you. (Patient now becoming agitated.) I'd want you to be extremely frustrated, to be very horny. I'd want you to be on the floor kissing my feet, begging me over and over again to have sex with me.

Therapist: What then?

Patient: Well, I wouldn't just have sex with you then. I'd want you to beg more. I'd want you to kiss my feet. I'd want you to promise to do anything at all to get me to have sex with you. You'd be on the floor crying and pleading. But I still wouldn't gratify you. I'd let you squirm. I'd let you plead. (Patient now becoming enraged.)

Therapist: What then?

Patient: Finally, when I felt you had enough punishment, I'd make you get undressed and then I'd make you lie down on the ground on your belly. Then I'd fuck you in the asshole and reduce you to my level. I'd humiliate you and gratify you at the same time.

Therapist: Is that the end of the fantasy or is there more?

Patient: Oh, there's more; I just wouldn't stop at that. First, I'd call your wife. I know you're married; you have that ring on your finger. And I saw those pictures on your desk; I assume those are your kids. Anyway, what I'd do then would be to call your wife. I'd tell her that you're a fag. And I'd tell her that you have sex with your patients.

Therapist: What do you think would happen then?

Patient: Then she'd divorce you. What woman would want to live with a fag?

Therapist: Anything else?

Patient: Yeah, I wouldn't stop there. I'd call the people who are in charge at the Columbia Medical School, the dean or whoever it is. I'd tell him that they have someone on the faculty there who fucks his patients. I'd also tell them you're gay. And I'd tell them that you had sex with me. Then they'd kick you off the faculty.

Therapist: Anything else?

Patient: Yeah, one more thing. I'd call the medical society and tell them what you really are, a fag, a gay doctor who fucks with patients. And they'd take away your license.

Therapist: Anything else?

Patient: No, that's it.

Therapist: You know, you started this session by telling me that you "love" me. Is this your concept of love?

Patient: Well, maybe it's not love, but it's the way I feel. Maybe it's the way I feel because I know that you don't love me the way I love you.

Therapist: Here you tell me you love me and then you tell me how you want to humiliate me, expose me as a doctor who has sex with patients. Then you tell me that you would like to have my wife divorce me and then I'd be kicked off the faculty at the medical school and then lose my medical license. It sounds to me like you want to destroy me. It doesn't sound very much like love to me. It sounds to me like the opposite, like hate.

In the ensuing discussion, the patient was too upset to really be able to gain any insight into what was going on. His treatment did not last much longer. He left about two weeks later, claiming that I really did not have very much affection for him. If I really wanted to show my affection, I would have sex with him. Although the vignette demonstrates well an important psychodynamic mechanism operative in some patients with male homosexuality, namely, the use of love as a reaction formation to hate, it is not presented here for that purpose. Rather, it is presented as an example of an alerting dream. It is reasonable to speculate that at the time of the dream I was already receiving subtle signals of the patient's hostility. I was not aware of these consciously and may have been threatened by them. However, the awareness of the hostility built up in my unconscious and finally erupted into conscious awareness via the alerting dream. Had the man continued in therapy I would have used the dream to help me make decisions regarding hospitalization. The dream suggested that this was indeed a dangerous man. Of course, one would not and should not use one's own dream as an important criterion for deciding whether or not to hospitalize a patient. The clinical behavior must be paramount; however, the dream should not be ignored either. As I hope the reader agrees, the dream can be a powerful source of information about dimly sensed but not overtly recognized dangers.

The Dream as a Method of Desensitization to a Trauma   This is another function of the dream that has nothing to do with wish fulfillment. Here the individual has been exposed to a severe psychological trauma and the dream serves the process of desensitization. Following the trauma the individual is not only consciously preoccupied with thoughts and feelings associated with the trauma but is so overwhelmed by it that many of the psychological reactions associated with it become relegated to unconscious awareness as well. This is not specifically related to the fact that the individual feels guilt and/or anxiety over thinking about the trauma; rather, the trauma is so overwhelming that sleep time must also be ultilzed if one is to effectively accomplish the purposes of desensitization. The principle of desensitization is basically this: Each time the individual reexperiences the trauma it becomes a little more bearable. And, over time, with repeated reliving of the trauma, even though only in fantasy, the individual adjusts to it.

A situation in which desensitization dreams are common is the one in which a soldier has been exposed to uninterrupted battlefield conditions over an extended period. He may have been injured and observed friends to have been injured and even killed. Under these circumstances he may have suffered a severe enough stress reaction to the combat that hospitalization may prove necessary because he has become ineffective in his capacity to function adequately on the battlefield. In the hospital the soldier has repetitious dreams in which the battlefield conditions are being reexperienced. In the dream he may hear shells blasting around him and even may respond with the same fright reaction that was present during combat. So powerful may be the need to relive the experience that the dreams themselves may not appear to be enough and he may actually hallucinate the same experiences, again in the service of desensitization. Whereas the dreams occur at night, the hallucinations take place in the waking state. The dream and hallucination may not be the only vehicles for desensitization. The soldier becomes obsessed as well with thoughts of the battlefield conditions. And each time they are relived mentally, some adjustment takes place. Last, he is likely to be talking about his experiences frequently and such discussions serve as a desensitization mechanism as well.

The Nightmare   In the typical nightmare the child is fearful that some malevolent figure will cause him or her terrible harm. Typically, the figure is a monster, frightening creature, and sometimes even a nebulous blob or point that is approaching the child menacingly. Usually, the figure comes into the child's room from a window, or out of a closet, or out from under the child's bed. The closer the malevolent fantasy gets to the child, the more frightened the child becomes. And the child generally awakens just at the point when the malevolent creature is about to touch or envelop the child. At the point of awakening, the child is generally quite frightened, is often crying, and is usually consoled by parents who reassure the child that there are no such things as monsters, creatures, et cetera. The creatures in nightmares have a way of evaporating completely when lights are turned on and do not appear in broad daylight. Like vampires, they abhor the rays of the sun.

In my residency days I was taught that the malevolent figures in a child's nightmare represent one or both parents. In order to ascertain whether the creature is symbolic of mother or father, the examiner was advised to question the child in order to elicit information about the sex of the interloper. If male, then father was viewed to be the hostile parent and, if female, then mother got accused. The child who dreamed of witches was to be viewed as one whose mother was inordinately hostile to him or her, and the child who dreamed of monsters (usually identified as male) had the misfortune of being brought up in a home where father was hostile. Even then, I was uncomfortable with this explanation and suspected that I was falsely accusing parents of being hostile when there was no significant evidence for more than the normal amount of irritation and impatience that any parent will exhibit from time to time in the child-rearing process.

It was with these considerations that I began to formulate another concept of the meaning of the nightmare. Specifically, I believe that the interloper is better understood as the incarnation of the child's own unacceptable angry impulses that have been relegated to the unconscious. Nightmares begin when children are about two to three years of age. This is a time when they are continually being frustrated by parents who must—if they are worthy of the name *parents*—inhibit and restrict the child continually throughout the course of the day: "Don't go into that cabinet," "Don't stick your hand up on top of the stove," "Stay away from the baby," "Big boys don't wet their pants," "Don't run out in the street," et cetera. There is hardly a five-minute period when children of this age are not restrained, constricted, and warned about some catastrophe that will befall them if they're allowed to go their merry way. The resentments engendered by such frustrations are enormous, yet they cannot be expressed overtly for fear the children may lose the affection of significant figures who are vital for their well-being and even survival. Also, there are many other stimuli impinging upon the child during the day that distract him or her from the pent-up anger. At night, when these other distracting stimuli are removed, the pent-up hostilities of the day, which are continually pressing for expression, are allowed release. Daytime activities such as sports, sibling fights, and television—which have provided some release of hostility—are no longer available. At night, residual hostility from unresolved daytime frustrations is then freer to press for release.

In the nightmare, the symbolic derivatives of the child's anger (the robber, monster, terrible creature, etc.) press for expression into the child's conscious awareness (symbolized, I believe, by the child's room). The child disowns the angry feelings that are his or her own by projecting them outward. They are viewed as coming from outside the house, the closet, or from under the bed. Accordingly, the child utilizes two mechanisms for reducing guilt and/or anxiety over the expression of anger: symbolization and projection. Via symbolization, the anger is not viewed as anger; rather, it is viewed as some malevolent creature. And via projection, the anger is not viewed as the child's own; rather, it is projected outward in the form of a creature that comes toward the child from some distance. The child wakes when the anger is about to enter the child's own space, at the point where there is the risk that it will be recognized as coming from within. The malevolent figure may (as I was taught in residency) symbolize hostile elements within significant figures (such as parents). I believe, however, that this explanation should not be given first priority. When the frightening figures threaten to abduct or kidnap the child, then the dream may reflect separation anxieties.

With this theory of the meaning of a child's nightmares, I generally do not consider them to be an abnormal phenomenon between the ages of two and seven or eight, unless they occur with a frequency greater than three or four times a week. I consider them to be a normal way of dealing with the inevitable frustrations and resentments that arise during the course of the child's life in this phase of development. If they are occurring more frequently than a few times a week, then one must look for some problems in the child's life that may be contributing to their intensification. Generally, this would involve looking for abnormal degrees of anger-engendering experiences, such as harsh treatment by parents, neglect, and rigid, and/or punitive teachers.

Last, it is important that the examiner differentiate the nightmare from the *sleep terror disorder*. I generally view the former as a psychological phenomenon which may reach pathological proportions. Most psychiatrists today agree that the latter is a physiological disorder associated with very specific EEG changes. Phenomenologically the sleep terror disorder is quite different from the nightmare in that during the nightmare the child is lying in bed with eyes closed and some restlessness may be observed. In the sleep terror disorder the child's eyes are open and the child may even be running around the house—even though in an altered state of consciousness. In addition, when the nightmare is over the child generally remembers most if not all of what he or she has dreamt. When the child is awakened or wakes up spontaneously from the sleep terror disorder, there is generally amnesia for the event.

The Panic Dream   On occasion I have seen patients who have dreams in which there is no recollection at all of any cognitive material. They wake up panicky and, as hard as they try, they cannot think of any associated fantasies. Many psychoanalysts hold that such dreams are a manifestation of the threatened eruption into conscious awareness of unconscious thoughts and feelings over which the individual feels guilt and/or anxiety. Whereas some individuals are able to allow themselves release of such material via symbolization, condensation, projection, and a variety of other disguise mechanisms, these individuals are so fearful of release of these thoughts and feelings that even the disguised representations are not permitted eruption into conscious awareness.

A number of years ago I had such a patient, a young woman of about 21. She was clearly a very tense and inhibited individual who not only did not allow herself to enjoy sexual experiences, but even denied having sexual urges. I suspected that her panic dreams related to the threatened eruption into conscious awareness of sexual feelings over which she was so guilty that she could not even allow their expression through dreams at night. I theorized that her dreams produced awakening just at the point where some kind of symbolic release might materialize. A friend and colleague of mine at the time was actively involved in sleep research and we both agreed that she might be a good candidate for study. Specifically, the plan was that we would monitor her sleep in the sleep lab, awaken her immediately after she had dreamt, and then learn the nature of her dream fantasies.

Although this occurred over 20 years ago, I still remember the evening quite clearly. The patient went to sleep in one room and was wired up to my friend's equipment in the adjacent room where my colleague and I could observe her and review the recordings of her sleep patterns. Because of his sleep research, my friend had already adjusted well to being a night person. Because I was very much a traditional day person, it was decided that I would sleep as much as possible, only to be awakened when my patient showed evidence of dreaming. There being no bed in the monitoring room, I had to sleep on the floor. On five or six occasions throughout the course of the night my friend awakened me and whispered excitedly that my patient was now dreaming. However, after a few seconds, she would spontaneously awaken—at which point she denied any recall of any dreams. This was not surprising because there were only a few seconds of dream activity recorded. Finally, around six in the morning, my colleague informed me that she was now having what appeared to be a lengthy dream. At the end of this dream we awakened her to have her record her dream verbally on an audio tape recorder. Her response: "I dreamed that I was with these two men. I don't know who they were. They were strangers. They kept asking me to go on a picnic with them, but I wouldn't. They kept asking me to go on the picnic and I kept telling them no. That's all I can remember, but I know that I never went to a picnic with them." The only conclusion that one can definitely draw from this experience is that a patient's resistances can be so formidable that they can prevent the revelation of anything the patient really doesn't want to reveal, no matter how intrusive the examiner's tools of investigation. I cannot say whether the "picnic" the patient envisioned my friend and I to be taking her to involved sexual activities. I could only say that whatever its purpose, she was going to have no part of it.

In recent years, most psychiatrists would consider this kind of dream to be the nighttime equivalent of the panic attack. It would be interpreted simply as some kind of cerebral discharge, analogous to a seizure. I believe that this explanation has some merit. I believe that there are some people with very low threshholds for flight reactions with the result that such reactions may be triggered off by inconsequential stimuli. The panic attack, then, may be a manifestation of such a reaction. I would not, however, completely discount the psychoanalytic explanation as being totally inapplicable to all patients. I still hold that the aforementioned patient's attacks were more likely related to the threatened eruption into conscious awareness of unconscious material (in this case sexual) over which she felt guilty. She never had any similar attacks during the day. This, of course, does not disprove my explanation but it certainly may lend some support to it. At night, without the distracting stimuli of the day, the repressed sexual urges were more likely to pressure for release and attention and produce the panic (anxiety) attack (dream).

The Dream as a Mechanism for Providing Brain Cell Stimulation I do not believe that the aforementioned categories cover all the different types of dreams. They cover the main kinds of dreams that I have had experience with in my work with patients. There are many dreams that I do not understand. Even after eliciting the patient's associations, I am still left without the faintest idea about the dream's meaning. I suspect that for some of these dreams, there may not be a meaning and that they may simply be a manifestation of nocturnal cerebral activity. Just as muscle cells need to be constantly stimulated to remain strong and viable, so do nerve cells. Tonic contractions of muscle cells keep them "in shape"; perhaps nerve cells in the brain need cognitive stimulation to keep them in shape. Such nerve cell stimulation may be provided in the daytime by cognitive rambling and daydreams, and during the nighttime by dreams that may have no additional meaning other than to provide such stimulation. This notion, of course, is one that many psychoanalysts would have difficulty with in that they would argue that the contents of a dream are selected from a universe of possible combinations of thoughts, feelings, and imagery, and that it must be highly meaningful. Although I approach dream work with the goal of analyzing and with the belief that most are analyzable, I am still left with the lingering feeling that my failure to analyze some (but not all) of them has less to do with analyzing inadequacies on my part (certainly possible) and more to do with the fact that the dream may not be analyzable. And the reason it is not analyzable is that there is nothing to analyze. The dream is merely a manifestation of some kind of cognitive brain activity that is taking place throughout the course of the night. Last, I recognize that there may be other categories of dreams that I am not appreciative of, and so I do not consider these additional possible explanations when attempting to understand a patient's dream.

Teaching Children How to Psychoanalyze Dreams

Children Who Are Candidates for Dream Analysis   The older the child the greater the likelihood he or she will be able to profit from a psychoanalytic inquiry into a dream's meaning. Also, the more intelligent the child the more receptive will he or she be to the therapist's suggestion to try to understand the meaning of the dream. Introspective children are more likely to be receptive to such endeavors than those who tend to act out their thoughts and feelings. Children whose parents are introspective, especially if they have had psychoanalytic experiences themselves, are more likely to involve themselves in the endeavor of analyzing a dream. Another factor is intellectual curiosity. Children who are good students are more likely to be good dream analyzers. They are interested in expanding their horizons and learning new things. They enjoy learning for learning's sake. And learning about the meaning of a dream is just another example of an opportunity to satisfy one's intellectual curiosity.

If the therapist has had a successful dream experience with the child, then the likelihood of the child's involving him- or herself meaningfully and enthusiastically in further dream analysis is enhanced. Such a successful analytic experience would be one in which the child and the therapist together have successfully analyzed a dream with the result that the child has had the experience that such inquiries provide interesting and useful information. This experience is hard to define. It is one in which the patient essentially says "Ah ha, now it all fits together," or "That's right," or "What do you know?". There is a kind of "eureka" response. Not only is there an intellectual understanding in which everything seems to fall into place, but an associated emotional reaction of having made a wonderful discovery. This is an important goal to be worked toward. If this aim is realized, then one is more likely to have a patient who will be receptive to dream analysis (regardless of age); and if one does not reach this goal, then one is not likely to have a patient who will commit him- or herself in a meaningful way to dream analysis (again regardless of age). Obviously, the older the patient, the greater the possibility that the therapist will be successful in reaching this goal.

If, during my initial two-hour consultation, I consider a child to be a possible candidate for dream analysis, I will recommend that the child tell a parent each morning whether or not he or she has had a dream. If so, I recommend that the child tell the parent the dream and have the parent write it down at that point. I emphasize that there is no dream that is so short, silly, or embarrassing that it doesn't warrant my attention. I advise shy children, or those who show evidence for hesitation, to reveal their dreams to their parents; that if they don't wish to tell a parent the dream, then they should write it down themselves. My first suggestion, that the dream be told to the parents, is consistent with my general therapeutic philosophy that one should attempt to establish an open pool of communication among family members about the child's problems and that the parents should be working actively along with the child in the treatment. This does not preclude certain privacies.

It is only a statement that the general thrust of my approach is to "put things out on the table." The child whose mother asks each morning about a dream and who is attentive to writing it down is more likely to stimulate interest in and cooperation by the child in the dream analysis endeavor.

Fundamental Principles of Dream Analysis   As a foundation for my subsequent discussion on teaching children how to understand the formation of dreams and techniques for analyzing them, I present here what I consider to be the basic theory of dream formation by unconscious processes. I do not claim that I am presenting here a comprehensive theory of dream formation. As the reader can already appreciate, my discussion above of the various types of dreams can only lead one to the conclusion that they are quite complex and that there is still much that we have to learn. These qualifications notwithstanding, I believe that the principles outlined here can serve well to help children analyze their dreams. Children's dreams tend to be easier to analyze than those of adults. Their repertoire of knowledge is smaller than adults', and the information they can draw upon to form dreams is less comprehensive. In addition, the processes of symbolization, condensation, and projection tend to be less complex and sophisticated than those utilized by adults.

One does well to view the dream setting as a theatrical production. The dreamer not only writes the script, but is also the choreographer and dictates the movements, gestures, and behavior of all the protagonists. The dreamer also sets the stage and decides what props shall be brought in, where they shall be placed on the stage, and when they shall be utilized. The individuals who appear in the dream may be drawn from the whole gamut of humanity: real and fictional, past and present, well-known and unknown. The props can be selected from the infinite variety of things, scenes, and objects. Animals may be used and even composites of a wide variety of animate and inanimate objects. Traditional rules of logic, movement, and sequence need not be respected.

The protagonists of the dream generally represent the dreamer and/or individuals who are of significance to the dreamer at that time. An individual may divide him- or herself into two or more parts, with each part representing one or more aspects of the dreamer's personality. For example, a very religious adolescent girl, who is guilty over her emerging sexual feelings, may have a dream in which she is observing the Virgin Mary reprimanding a prostitute. It is not unreasonable to conclude that the girl is symbolizing herself here in three separate forms: 1) the Virgin Mary, a symbol of her desire to be pure, 2) the prostitute, who symbolizes her emerging sexual inclinations, and 3) the observer, the girl herself who is witness to her conflict. The dream also is a demonstration of her guilt over sex and her view that people who do not engage in such activities are pure and innocent and those who do are no better than whores.

Another rule that is useful to follow in understanding dreams is that individuals who appear in the dream who are ostensibly of trivial or inconseqential significance are generally not so. If, for example, an adult women of 50 has a dream in which she is walking with another woman whom she has not seen since childhood, then one does well to conclude that the friend is being brought into the dream as a symbol of some quality that exists in the dreamer herself. They were both childhood friends and therefore the two lend themselves well to serving as alter egos of one another. The examiner does well to ask the woman what thoughts comes to mind regarding the old friend whom she has not seen for many years. With rare exception, the qualities that she recalls the friend to have had during childhood are likely to be qualities of her own that are of some concern to her (the dreamer) at the time of the dream. The old friend is not being brought in for the friend's benefit. Rather, she is being brought in for the dreamer's benefit. Our dreams are very egotistical, and we do not waste our valuable dream time for the benefit of others, especially people we haven't seen in 40 years.

It is also reasonable to assume that the dream is dealing with issues that are related to events that occurred within the day or two prior to the dream's occurrence. Each night, the dream deals with the "unfinished business" of the day. Most people's lives are so filled with various kinds of recent "unfinished business" that we do not dip back in time to weeks or months before the dream to work through older problems that may not have been resolved. Generally, the unresolved problems of the day are dealt with the same night or the next night. Then, even though older business may be "unfinished," there are newer events that take priority over older unresolved issues. The "old stuff" appears to pass into oblivion and is superseded by material that now commands our attention. We cannot go around endlessly nursing old wounds or continually trying to resolve every problem that we are confronted with. Our minds tend to work on the same principle as that used by the administrator who files away problems and never has the need to resolve them. The difference, however, is that the administrator may never deal with any problem and files them all away. We try to deal with each problem each day and try to deal, as well, with problems that may have taken place the day before, but we continually have to deal with new problems that confront us and command our more immediate attention. It is hoped that the dreams will at least solve some of these problems so that our minds do not end up like the administrator who routinely files away every problem without any resolution at all of any of them. It would be an error for the reader to conclude that the older material *never* is dealt with in dreams. If the older material relates to severe psychological traumas, especially those that have persisted over time, then the dream may be utilized in the service of dealing with these. An example of this would be the desensitization kind of dream that is used to deal with the psychological traumas attendant to prolonged exposure to military combat. Under these circumstances, the older material takes priority over newer; however, it does so because it has remained a present-day concern as well.

Consistent with this notion of the higher priority that dreams give recent material, the props that have been brought in are more likely to be related to recent events, especially the previous days' experiences. Whatever the object that the patient selects to put on the stage—and these are selected from a universe of possible objects—it generally has some relevance to things that were going on in the day or two prior to the dream's occurrence. Also, one must consider the general ambiance of the dream. Does it take place in the frozen snow or the warm jungle? Are there grey clouds or bright sunshine and a clear sky? Is it underground in a cave or above ground on top of a mountain? All these aspects of the environment are of meaning in the dream because they have been selected from the infinite variety of possible milieus.

As mentioned, I do not believe that a particular symbol necessarily has the same meaning for everyone. Freud was especially prone to ascribe sexual meaning to many dream symbols. A snake, for example, may very well symbolize a penis. But it can also symbolize feelings of low self-worth and surreptitiousness. Snakes crawl on the ground and are quite "sneaky" in the way they sneak up upon us. However, snakes are also poisonous and they may therefore symbolize hostility and murderous wishes. One cannot know what the snake means to any particular person unless one elicits that individual's free associations to it. There are individuals for whom a snake may have some special significance, unrelated to the aforementioned possible meanings. The examiner who starts off with the assumption that the snake has some particular meaning is likely to lead the patient into incorrect interpretations of the dream. Furthermore, even traditional sexual symbols may stand for other things. A phallic symbol may not simply stand for a penis but for power and strength—traditional associations to the penis in our society. A vaginal symbol may not simply stand for the vagina but for femininity, passivity, and child rearing. These, too, are traditional associations to the female in our society. (I am making no statements here as to whether or not these associations are "good" or "bad." I am merely stating that they are common associations in our society at this time, although things may be changing somewhat.) A common dream experience is the one in which the individual feels like he or she is being overwhelmed by bugs, insects, or other noxious vermin. These often represent threatened eruption into conscious awareness of a variety of unacceptable thoughts, feelings, and impulses. One must try to ascertain from the dreamer what these noxious intruders might symbolize for him or her.

Explaining the Theory of Dream Formation and Analysis to a Child   With the aforementioned principles as background, the examiner is in a better position to explain the principles of dream formation and interpretation to the child who is a potential candidate for dream analysis. I generally begin in the following way with the potentially receptive child: "Did you know that the mind has two parts, a conscious part and an unconscious part?" (The reader may wonder here whether I have forgotten about the superego. Of course, I have not. I simply use this oversimplified dichotomy for the purposes of helping a child learn the basic principles of dream analysis.) I then try to get the child to appreciate that in the *conscious mind* are facts that people are generally aware of, for example, age, address, name of school, name of teacher, favorite flavor ice cream, etc. I will then discuss the kinds of things that are to be found in the *unconscious mind*. Here are thoughts and feelings which the child may feel guilty about and may think are wrong. For example, a child may think that it is very bad to have an occasional wish that a brother or sister might get hit by a car. To such a child I might say, "That child doesn't realize that to have a thought like that *once in a while* is normal and that it doesn't really mean that the person wishes the brother or sister *really* to be hit by a car. It only means that the child is angry at that brother or sister at that point. Anyway, if the person feels very bad about such a thought and thinks that only the worst kinds of children have such a thought, then that person is going to push that thought out of his or her mind and push it into the unconscious part of the mind so that he or she doesn't have to think about it at all."

I then engage the child in a discussion of the kinds of thoughts and feelings that might be relegated to the unconscious and those that a person might comfortably accept as conscious. When the child provides examples of thoughts and feelings that might be relegated to the unconcious, I may learn something about the things that that particular child is guilty about.

Once the concept of conscious/unconscious has been understood, I proceed to a discussion of the process of dream symbolism. One technique that I have found useful in helping children understand this concept is that of the "secret code." I ask the child if he or she has ever seen a James Bond movie. I generally receive an answer in the affirmative. I try to help the child recall some secret agent therein who used a secret code. We then discuss the formation of secret codes, for example, a code in which the number 1 stands for A, 2 for B, 3 for C, etc. When one "cracks" the code, one merely tries to figure out which letter stands for which number. In this way the code is "decoded." I will generally use the terms "crack the code" or "decode the code" to refer to the process of analyzing the symbol. Once this concept is understood, I explain to the child that dreams also make up their own codes. I explain that the unconscious mind changes information into code form before it goes into the conscious mind. In this way the person may not feel so bad or ashamed about the stuff that comes out of the unconscious mind into the conscious mind.

I will then ask the child to see if he or she can decode or crack the code of a dream that I will now present. I have found this example to be useful:

> A little girl is walking down the street. She sees a boy her own age making wee-wee. In her home she was taught that it's naughty to look at a little boy doing that. She wanted to look at the boy, but she felt very bad and guilty because she wanted to look at him. So

she turned away and didn't look. But she was still very curious to see what his penis looked like. That night she had a dream. In that dream she saw that very same little boy watering the grass with a hose. He was holding the hose in his hands and a stream of water was coming out of the hose. The water curved out from the hose down to the grass. What do you think the hose stands for? What do you think the water stands for? Do you think that dream had anything to do with what happened that afternoon when she saw the boy making wee-wee and wished that she could see his penis?

The overwhelming majority of children will generally "figure out" the meaning of this dream. When they do, I try to emphasize the point that the dream satisfies a wish: "The little girl wished that she could see the boy make wee-wee, but felt that it was wrong or bad and so could not satisfy her wish. At night, she gratified the wish to see his penis. However, because she felt this was the wrong thing to do she had to put it into a code form."

I also try to emphasize the wish-fulfillment function of the dream. In order to do this I will generally provide other questions to the child that provide practice with the use of the dream for this purpose. For example, I might give this question:

A boy's father comes home one day and tells him that he has tickets for the circus that weekend. He is very happy. He is very excited about the fact that he will be going to the circus in a few days. In fact, he tells all his friends about the fact that that Saturday he's going to the circus. Unfortunately, on Friday the boy gets sick. He is so sick that he has to stay in bed and he can't go to school. He has high fever and a headache and he's nauseated and he vomits. The doctor says that he'll have to stay home and will have to remain in bed for at least three days. The boy is very sad. He wishes that he could go to the circus. What do you think he dreams of that night?

Again, it is a rare child who does not get the correct answer to this question. I then take the wish fulfillment issue further. I may discuss the kinds of dreams a poor boy may have, a boy who has no money. Or the kinds of dreams a very hungry girl might have, a girl who hasn't eaten or drunk anything for many days. I will then follow these relatively simple dreams with dreams in which there is a combination of both wish fulfillment and symbol formation. For example:

A boy named Tom started a fight with his younger brother Bill, and Bill went crying to their father and told him what Tom had done. The father got very angry and punished Tom. He told him that he could not watch his favorite television program that night. Tom was *very sad* that he couldn't watch his television program. He was also *very angry*, so angry that he felt like doing something very mean and cruel to his father. But he quickly put that thought out of his mind because he realized that if he were to do something mean or cruel to his father that he might even get a worse punishment. That night Tom had a dream about his father in which the angry feelings came out. Can you make up a dream showing how the angry feelings came out?

If the child tells a dream in which the anger is acted out overtly, I may accept that as an answer. However, I may also say, "Well, that's one possible dream. However, this particular boy felt very bad about such angry thoughts. He felt so bad and guilty about having such thoughts that he could not let them into his conscious mind. He had to make up a code. He had to disguise the angry thoughts before he could let them come into his conscious mind." I will then ask the child to make up a dream in which the anger is released in coded form. If the child cannot do so I may suggest a dream in which the boy's *friend* hits the father with a baseball bat. Or, the child might have a dream in which he is hitting a policeman. Or the father, while driving his car, has an accident. In this way I help the child appreciate the concept of wish fulfillment by symbolic processes.

With this introduction into the theory of dream formation and analysis, I may then turn to the child's dream and ask him or her to try to figure out what it means. A good principle to follow is that the element that is most likely to produce useful information is the idiosyncratic or atypical one. These are the more highly individualized symbols and are more likely to provide useful leads regarding the dream's meaning. The therapist must keep in mind the fact that his or her suggestions regarding the meaning of a particular element in the dream are always speculations. The therapist should do everything to get the patient to present his or her guesses and hunches regarding a symbol's meaning before offering his or her speculations. Even the patient's "wild guesses" may be more on point than the therapist's carefully considered explanations. The patient's guesses are more likely to be related to the issues that have brought about the dream's formation.

One device that I have found useful in getting children to free associate to a dream entity is to utilize what I call the "foreign boy" question. Let us say, for example, a child has a dream in which a shoe appears. One could simply ask the child what comes to mind in association with the word *shoe*. If a child appears to have difficulty providing associations I might ask this question: "Suppose a foreign boy moved into your neighborhood and he didn't know very much English. Suppose he asked you what the word *shoe* means. What would you say?" I have found this question provides a much higher percentage of useful associations than the more general question "What comes to mind about the word *shoe*?"

It is only after the patient has exhausted all possible associations and explanations that the therapist should offer his or her interpretations or hunches for the patient's consideration. The hope here is that the patient will latch on to the explanation and have the aforementioned feeling that "It fits," "You're right," or "That's it." When the therapist has this response, then he or she knows that the interpretation is likely to be valid. But if the patient just merely says, "Yes, that sounds right," without the feeling that the explanation "clicks" or is on target, then one cannot be sure that the interpretation was indeed valid. Last, one does not merely analyze dreams as an intellectual game. The purpose is to utilize what is learned in the service of the therapeutic goals. Here I will present some sample dream analyses of patients who were unusually gifted in this regard.

Clinical Examples

The Case of Sean (The Monks, the Spanish Inquisitors, and the Lions)   Sean, a ten-year-old boy, was referred because of marked anxiety, feelings of inadequacy, and poor school performance in spite of high intelligence. He was an extremely "uptight" and tense youngster. He sucked his thumb and his tension interfered with his falling asleep. His massive feelings of inadequacy and insecurity interfered with his properly asserting himself. He spoke in a low voice, to the point where he was sometimes almost inaudible. He was easily scapegoated by peers because of his fear of self-assertion. His mother's overprotectiveness played an important role in bringing about these symptoms. Her indulgence did not provide him with the opportunities to gain the feelings of self-confidence that come with competence. She was particularly fearful of exposing him to any unpleasant experiences and this played a role in his having a "thin skin." Furthermore, she was afraid to do anything that might evoke anger in Sean, fearing that such expressions on his part would be a reflection of parental deficiency in her. Sean's father was a busy businessman who left much of the care of the children to the mother. Even on weekends, he was so engrossed in his business that there was little time left for Sean and his older sister. Sean was basically quite angry over his father's withdrawal, but was afraid to express it.

During his third month in therapy, Sean's mother informed me at the beginning of the session that he was not doing his homework. In subsequent discussion it became apparent that my previous advice to the mother that Sean not be permitted to watch television until he had completed his homework assignments was not being implemented. Although the mother stated that she thought my recommendation was a good one, she claimed that she was hesitant to follow through with it. It became apparent that the mother was hesitant to implement my recommendation because the patient would consider her "mean." This was just another example of the mother's intolerance of any resentment on Sean's part toward her. In the ensuing discussion I learned that, from an early age, Sean had found that he could manipulate his mother into not instituting appropriate restrictions and punishments by accusing her of being mean to him. As a result of our discussion, the mother stated that she was going to be firmer in her determination not to allow herself to be so manipulated. Then I asked the patient how he felt about his mother's new determination. He stated that he was pleased with the outcome of the discussion because now he would probably get more homework done. Recognizing that Sean might be suppressing and repressing the inevitable anger I suspected he felt over his mother's resolution, I tried to encourage his expression of such. I expressed incredulity that he was reacting in such a calm way with comments such as "Are you sure that this doesn't bother you at all?" and "I can't believe, that somewhere deep down, there aren't at least some thoughts and feelings of resentment over your mother's saying that she's going to come down harder on you from now on."

In the next session the patient stated that he was more diligent in doing his homework and was pleased about the discussion of the previous session. He then presented the following dream:

There was a group of men. They were old and they had beards. The beards were long and hung way down. They wore grey robes which covered their whole bodies. They looked like Monks from the Spanish Inquisition. They were in a dark castle and they were chasing me around the castle.

Then they chased me to a trap where there were lions. I managed to escape through a trap door and I got out of there. I got away from the lions and the men in the grey robes. I was in the bright sun.

When analyzing this dream the patient was first asked what an inquisitor was. He said they were judges from the Middle Ages who had torture chambers and dungeons, and they would put prisoners in there. On further inquiry he stated that they asked prisoners lots of questions. He was then asked who these inquisitors could stand for—a person who is a judge, who asks a lot of questions, and who is capable of punishing. He responded in a surprised fashion that they might stand for the therapist whom he saw as a judge and as someone who asked him many questions. He denied, however, that he felt that my recommendation to his mother that she firmly uphold the homework-television policy was seen by him as punishment.

Following this I asked him who the lions might represent and he replied that they were probably his parents who were also pressuring him to fulfill his obligations, but against whom he denied any anger.

I pointed out to him that although he professed compliance with my recommendation and pleasure with its implementation, his dream suggested that he looked upon both his parents and me as being punitive and that we were people to be avoided and escaped from. I therefore informed him that I was somewhat dubious about his commitment to the new homework program because his dream reflected his view that it was oppressive and his desire to avoid its implementation.

The analysis of this dream enabled me to avoid unwittingly supporting the patient's resistances. To have praised the patient for his compliance would have gone along with him in his denial of his anger and his devious avoidance of his responsibilities. The session ended with the attitude on my part that he would really have to show me his good intentions and that I, at the present time, was somewhat incredulous that he would follow through with conviction. Having been overprotected so long and having so skillfully manipulated his mother into being extremely "soft" with him, this boy needed a "hard line," and the dream offered me good justification for such.

About three months later, by which time there had been moderate diminution of Sean's tension and anxiety, there was little change in his school performance. Because of the improvement in his anxiety symptoms, Sean began to talk about leaving treatment. He was no longer feeling much discomfort over his tension and, as far as he was concerned, he could live quite well without doing much homework. His request to stop came near the end of the session and so it was decided to discuss the matter further in the next session.

When he arrived for his next session, Sean told me that he had a dream. For the purposes of understanding this dream, the reader should appreciate that the patient's treatment took place in 1964 and 1965, a few years after President Kennedy's assassination. This was the dream:

> We were on a class trip to the junior high school. It was Kennedy's birthday and there were exhibits on Kennedy's life. First, we went to the Kennedy exhibit. Then we went to the gym and we were playing basketball. Then we saw some drunken janitor stumbling about in the gym. Then I was at Kevin's house and I was playing the organ. Then I woke up.

When analyzing the dream, the patient was first asked about John Kennedy. He said that Kennedy was an Irish Catholic just like himself. He was then asked what Kennedy could stand for in his own life and he replied, "studying, school, and success." He was then asked what the drunken janitor could stand for and he replied, "failure." He was then asked to tell me about his friend, Kevin. He said that Kevin was a "smart kid who does well without doing very much work." He then described how he would like to be like Kevin and also be able to get good grades without working very hard. He interpreted his being at Kevin's house as implying that he would like to be like Kevin. When asked about the organ he said, "That stands for playing games just like the gymnasium period." The patient was then asked what the whole dream meant. He responded that it stood for the three choices he had regarding what he could do with his life. First, he could work hard and try to be like John

Kennedy. Or he could spend his time playing and end up a drunken bum. His third option was to be like his friend Kevin who does well without working too hard.

I then asked him what the dream meant in view of the fact that the was considering leaving treatment. He replied that it was probably telling him that his leaving treatment was dangerous in that he might end up a drunken bum if he did. I then asked him if the dream might lead him to change his mind and he replied that it did not. I asked him if he had an emotional reaction to the dream, if it "grabbed him," and he said no.

This dream is a good example of how a patient can provide an accurate intellectual analysis of a dream without a resulting effect on the patient's clinical behavior. One reason for the failure of such linkage in Sean's case was that the forces encouraging him to leave treatment were strong. His mother, at the time of this dream, was exhibiting marked resistance to Sean's therapy, and he was no doubt responding to and complying with her attitudes toward the treatment.

Sean's treatment could not justifiably be called psychoanalysis. Most of the sessions were spent playing the mutual storytelling and derivative games. There was, of course, some discussion. There were times, however, when Sean actively participated in dream analysis and the dreams just presented are representative samples. Accordingly there were times when his therapy could justifiably be called *psychoanalytically oriented psychotherapy*. Timothy, the next patient to be presented, spent much more time involved in analytic work. Accordingly, his treatment could more justifiably be considered closer to pure *psychoanalytic therapy*. However, I would not even consider Timothy's treatment to justify the label *psychoanalysis* because much of the time was still spent in nonanalytic work because he was disinclined to involve himself in such inquiry on an ongoing basis.

The Case of Timothy ("A Boy Eats His Belt and His Mother Gets Angry") Timothy entered treatment at the age of eight because of generalized tension. He was an extremely "uptight" boy who was best described as a "worry wart." Although very serious minded, he was not attending properly to his studies. It was obvious from the first interview that he was identifying strongly with his mother who had similar characteristics. She was an English teacher who constantly had a sad look on her face and always appeared as if the weight of the world was on her shoulders. Timothy's father was a successful businessman. Timothy and his older brother were both in classes for the intellectually gifted, even though Timothy was doing poorly in school. Both parents had had extensive psychoanalytic treatment, and both were continually talking about the underlying meaning of many of the things that were said and done in the household. It was not surprising, then, that Timothy approached the world from that vantage point, and his high intelligence enabled him to profit from psychoanalytic inquiry. I would not consider his treatment to be justifiably called psychoanalysis because he was still unreceptive to spending most of his sessions talking directly about the underlying meaning of what he was doing and saying. Furthermore, when the topic got difficult for him he preferred to play the mutual storytelling game. But even there, at times, he would try to analyze directly his stories.

From the first weeks in treatment it became quite apparent that Timothy suffered with an anger inhibition problem and this, I believed, was a factor in his chronic state of tension and seriousness. During his sixth month of treatment Timothy reported this dream:

A boy eats his belt and his mother gets angry.

Timothy's mother wrote down every dream and the slip of paper on which this dream was written had nothing else recorded. When I asked Timothy if there was anything more in the dream he replied that there wasn't. The following interchange then took place:

Therapist: What do you think this dream means?
Patient: I don't know.
Therapist: I'd like you to try to guess what you think the dream means.
Patient: I'm trying to guess, Dr. Gardner, but I really don't know.
Therapist: Okay, let's try to do it this way. Suppose a foreign boy moved into your neighborhood and he didn't know too much English. Suppose he asked you what the word *belt* means, what would you say?
Patient: It's something that holds up your pants.
Therapist: So if you eat your belt what happens?
Patient: My pants would fall down.
Therapist: And what would happen then?

Patient (somewhat ashamed): Everybody could see my underwear.

Therapist: Okay, so now what do you think the dream means?

Patient: I don't know.

Therapist: Well, your mother is in the dream too. Isn't she?

Patient: Yes.

Therapist: What did you say happened with her in the dream?

Patient: Well, she got angry.

Therapist: So, what could that mean that your mother gets angry if you pull down your pants.

Patient: She'd get angry if I pull down my pants and she saw my underwear.

Therapist: Okay, but what does all that stand for? What could all that mean?

Patient: It means that if I show her my underwear she'll get angry.

Therapist: Yeah, but as you know, things in dreams stand for other things. What could her being angry when you show her your underpants mean? What could that stand for? How would you decode that?

Patient: Well, maybe it means that if I take off the outside clothing and show her what's inside me I think she'll be angry.

Therapist: What do you mean when you say that if you show her what's inside you?

Patient: Well, maybe it means that I think she'll get angry at me if I tell her about the thoughts and feelings that I have that are underneath. Maybe my angry feelings.

Therapist: So what you are saying, then, is if you show her your angry feelings you think she'll get angry at you? Is that it?

Patient: Yes, that's it. I'm always scared that she'll get angry at me.

Therapist: Well, what kinds of things might you say that would get her angry at you, especially things that you're afraid to talk about?

Patient: She's always on my back all the time. She's always asking me a lot of questions. When I tell her that she bothers me too much, she gets even angrier at me.

Therapist: Well, I think that we should talk about that with your mother and father in our next family meeting.

Patient: Okay. But I still think she'll get angry at me.

Therapist: Well, we'll see.

I believe that many classical psychoanalysts would consider me to have missed entirely the purpose of this dream. They would have considered it an excellent example of an oedipal dream. They would consider the boy's exposing his underpants to his mother to be the first step toward his exposing his penis for the purposes of oedipal gratification. There are two possibilities here, namely, that the oedipal explanation is valid or it is not. The patient's associations certainly did not suggest directly sexual-oedipal themes. Rather, his associations suggested fear of revealing his underlying thoughts and feelings. The argument that these are merely cover-ups for underlying sexual-oedipal thoughts and feelings may very well be valid, but they are not substantiated directly by the patient's associations. Furthermore, one of the most humiliating things that can happen to a boy in the latency period is that his genital area be seen by the girls in his class. This has nothing to do with sex, but more to do with embarrassment. Accordingly, I consider embarrassment over genital exposure to be a far more likely explanation for this dream than the oedipal-sexual theory.

When a child has difficulty expressing anger to parents, one cannot simply recommend that the anger be expressed. After all, the child is a child and the parent is an adult and has much more power than the child. We are not dealing here with an egalitarian situation. Accordingly, the therapist must be somewhat cautious when encouraging children to express their anger toward their parents. One has to have a thorough knowledge of the parents, especially with regard to how reasonable they will be about accepting benevolently the child's civilized expression of resentment. If the therapist believes that the child can handle the situation him- or herself, and if the parents can be relied upon to listen with receptivity to the child's complaints (especially when presented in a civilized way), then it is in the best interests of the child's treatment for him or her to express the resentment *without* the therapist being present. However, when one expects irrational and/or inappropriate responses from the parents—especially excessively punitive ones—then it is best that the anger be expressed in a family session. In the office setting there is an implied protection by the therapist because he or she is in a position to monitor the parents' responses. And this was my decision in Timothy's case because of his parents' (especially his mother's) difficulty in handling his angry expressions in a completely rational way.

One month later, Timothy came in with this dream:

> My grandfather said that he was going to take me and my brother to the circus. At one o'clock we asked him to take us and he said he

was too busy. At two o'clock he said he was busy. At three o'clock he said he was going to kill me. I was scared and then I woke up.

As mentioned, the patient's father was a businessman. He was deeply involved in his business and often came home quite late. On weekends, as well, he was so often engrossed in his work that he had little meaningful time for his children. At times he would interrupt his weekend work to be with his sons; at other times he was unreceptive to their requests. This is the interchange that took place in association with the analysis of this dream.

Therapist: So, Timothy, what do you think this dream means?

Patient: I don't know. This isn't circus season. Nothing was said about the circus in my house.

Therapist: Well, what could *circus* stand for? See if you can figure out the meaning of circus. What comes to mind about the circus?

Patient: Well, the circus is a lot of fun. I really have a good time when I go.

Therapist: Well, maybe then the circus means fun things. What do you think?

Patient: Okay, maybe it means fun things. But my grandfather's never taken me to the circus.

Therapist: Yeah, but also your grandfather doesn't live here. Doesn't he live in San Francisco?

Patient: Yeah, he does. I hardly ever see him.

Therapist: So maybe it's not your grandfather in the dream. Remember what we said about people sometimes standing for other people in dreams?

Patient: Yes. Maybe he stands for my father because my father took us to the circus last year and the year before that.

Therapist: That seems reasonable to me. So what is the dream saying when it talks about your grandfather and the circus?

Patient: It's something about doing fun things with my father.

Therapist: I agree. So, now what could the dream mean? What's all the rest of it about?

Patient: Well, it says that I keep asking my father to do fun things with me and he keeps saying that he's too busy. He's always busy with his work. He works in his den at home. And he's always up there working.

Therapist: Is he always up there? Doesn't he come down at all?

Patient: Yeah, he comes down.

Therapist: Will he come down if you ask him?

Patient: Sometimes he will and sometimes he won't.

> *Therapist:*   Does he get very angry at you when you ask him?
> *Patient:*   Sometimes he gets angry, and sometimes he doesn't.
> *Therapist:*   What does the dream say about how angry he'll get?
> *Patient:*   The dream says that he'll kill me.
> *Therapist:*   Do you think he'll *really* kill you?
> *Patient:*   No, he wouldn't do that.
> *Therapist:*   Do you think maybe you're seeing it as worse than it really is? Do you think he would really be as angry at you as the dream says?
> *Patient:*   No, I guess not. I guess I'm worrying too much about that, like you always say that I worry too much about things.
> *Therapist:*   So what can you do about this now?
> *Patient:*   I think I should talk to him more.
> *Therapist:*   I think so too. I don't think he'll be as mean as you expect him to be.

In the first dream, I recommended a family session when Timothy expressed his fears of telling his mother how angry he was. In the second, I suggested that he tell his father directly. My reasons for this were that, as mentioned, I did not believe that Timothy's *mother* would respond properly to his expressions of resentment. However, I did anticipate that his *father* would be more receptive to such expression and that Timothy did not need my help on this issue. This is an extremely important point therapeutically and one that some family therapists do not fully appreciate. Routinely conducting family therapy may deprive patients of independent self-assertion because every session involves a certain amount of implied protection by the therapist.

In his ninth month of treatment Timothy related this dream:

> I was telling jokes and trying to make some people laugh. Then Alfred E. Newman, the guy from *Mad* comics, came in. He was funny and made everyone laugh. He chased me for fun until they got to my house where there was very good cake and jam that was very bitter. I poured the jam on Alfred's cake. My mother scolded me and gave Alfred a fresh piece of cake. Then I woke up.

The following interchange took place in association with the analysis of this dream:

> *Therapist:*   So, lets hear. What do you think about this dream?
> *Patient:*   I love *Mad* comics. It's my favorite magazine. It's really very funny.

Therapist: Okay, but who does Alfred E. Newman stand for? Do you remember what I said about the people in a dream and how strangers usually stand for other people or parts of yourself?

Patient: Alfred E. Newman's ears stick out, just like my brother's. Sometimes I tease him and I call him Alfred E. Newman.

Therapist: So do you think Alfred E. Newman in the dream stands for your brother?

Patient: Yeah, I guess so. I can't think of anybody else who he might stand for.

Therapist: So what's happening there in the dream between you and your brother?

Patient: Well I'm starting to tell jokes and then he comes in and tells better jokes. He knows more jokes than I do. That gets me angry when he tells better jokes.

Therapist: But you know, he's older than you and I'm sure that when you're as old as he is you'll be able to tell as many good jokes as he can. What do you think about that?

Patient: Well maybe. I hope so.

Therapist: Okay, let's go on with the dream. So what else is it saying?

Patient: I guess I'm getting back at him by pouring that lousy jam on his cake. And then my mother gets angry at me because I did that. She's always getting angry at me when I fight with him.

Therapist: But it sounds like here you're starting up. In the dream he wasn't doing anything to you and you just poured that bitter jam on his cake. Isn't that right?

Patient: Yeah.

Therapist: So what this dream tells me is that one way of getting your mother to be less angry at you is for you not to start up with your brother so much. Wouldn't you agree?

Patient: Yes.

I considered this dream to be a normal sibling rivalry dream. My advice that Timothy not start up with his brother was not likely to be complied with to a significant degree. I consider sibling rivalry normally to be fierce and advice by parents and therapists that siblings squelch the expression of their rivalrous feelings are not likely to be complied with to a significant degree. In fact, if they did comply with such advice I would suspect one or both children to have anger inhibition problems. The predictable failure of such advice notwithstanding, it still behooves therapists and parents to recommend that the children "cool it."

One month later, during his tenth month of treatment, Timothy related this dream:

My friend Robert had a contest. The winner was to get his house. The family that won moved into the house. After the family moved in Robert sent me to the house to remind them about some lights in the basement. I went into the basement. There I got a needle in my eye. A voice told me that I would have to catch a lion in order to get the needle out.

As mentioned, the therapist does well to focus on the most idiosyncratic element in a dream. It is the most highly individualized aspect of the dream and is generally going to provide the richest amount of information about the dream's meaning. I am not recommending, however, that the therapist automatically encourage the patient to focus on that element first. One must still sit back and let the patient select those elements that he or she considers important to focus on. However, at some point the therapist must direct attention to that element in the dream if the patient has not. Otherwise, the most meaningful and revealing part of the dream may be bypassed. This is the interchange that took place in association with the analysis of this dream:

> *Therapist:* That sounds like a very good dream, Timothy. Let's hear what you think about it.
> *Patient:* I think that's a hard dream to figure out. I don't know what it means.
> *Therapist:* Did anything happen in your life in the last day or two that's anything like anything in the dream?
> *Patient:* I can't remember anything.
> *Therapist:* Are you sure? Was there anything that happened that was like in the dream?
> *Patient:* Well, Michael (the patient's brother) is scared to go down into the basement of my house. He's going to be 11 and he's still scared to go down in the basement. Yesterday my mother asked him to get some light bulbs that we have down there, and he didn't want to go. He was scared. So they asked me to go and I went.
> *Therapist:* Are you scared at all to go down into the basement?
> *Patient:* Well, sometimes a little bit, especially at night. But I'm not as scared as he is. He's *really* scared and won't even go.
> *Therapist:* Do you think any of this has to do with the dream?
> *Patient:* Maybe it does, but I don't know how.
> *Therapist:* Well, the house is divided into two parts. The light part and the dark part. Isn't that so?
> *Patient:* I guess it is that way. There's the part that you see and the part that you can't see.

Therapist: Does that sound like anything we've been talking about?

Patient: Do you think it has something to do with the two parts of the mind, the conscious part that we know about and the unconscious part that we don't know about?

Therapist: That's right! That's *very good!* You really remembered that very well. I'm very proud of you. You're really a smart boy. I've told you that before, and I'm telling you that again. Most kids wouldn't have been able to figure that out.

Patient: Thank you.

Therapist: You're welcome. Now let's go on and see if we can figure out more about the dream. Now what are you doing in the basement?

Patient: Well, I'm taking the lights out of the basement.

Therapist: What could that mean?

Patient: If you take the lights out of a place then you can't light it up. Then it stays dark.

Therapist: Right. So what does that mean in your dream?

Patient: I guess I don't want to see what's in the dark place, in my unconscious mind.

Therapist: I would agree. I think that's what that means. You'd rather not look at certain things. Now let's try to figure out more about the dream. What happens in the basement?

Patient: While I was down there I got a needle in my eye, and a voice said that I would have to catch a lion in order to get the needle out.

Therapist: What do you think that's all about?

Patient: I don't know. That's a funny thing.

Therapist: That sure is. I never heard of anything like that in a dream before. I think it's a very important thing to try to understand. Let's take one part at a time. I think it might be a good idea to start with the needle. What do you think that needle stands for? What did the needle look like?

Patient: It looked like one of those needles that doctors use when they give you an injection.

Therapist: I think that's giving us very important information. You say it's a doctor's needle. What could that mean?

Patient: Well, maybe it has something to do with you. You're a doctor.

Therapist: I agree. I think it probably does have something to do with me. What could it mean that I'm putting a needle in your eye?

Patient: I don't know.

Therapist: Well, why does a doctor put a needle in you. Why do doctors give shots?

Patient: To make you better. When you're sick they give you shots to make you better.

Therapist: So what does that mean in your dream?

Patient: It means that you're putting a needle in my eye to make me better.

Therapist: But why in your eye?

Patient: The eye is where I see. Maybe you're trying to make my eyes better. Maybe you're trying to help me see better.

Therapist: Very good! I thought that too. Here I try to help you see things more clearly. So the needle in your eye has something to do with your therapy. Is that right?

Patient: Yes. That's right.

Therapist: Now what else is happening there?

Patient: Well the dream says that in order to get the needle out I would have to catch a lion.

Therapist: That's an interesting thought. I wonder what that means? Do you have any idea?

Patient: I don't know.

Therapist: Well, it says something about the needle staying in there and then something has to happen before it comes out. If putting the needle in and keeping it there stands for your treatment, what does taking the needle out stand for?

Patient: The end of treatment. It has something to with the time I can stop treatment.

Therapist: That's the thought that I had, that is has something to do with your stopping treatment. Then the needle would come out. But it says something else. It says something about your having to catch a lion before you can stop treatment. What could that be all about?

Patient: It's about a lion. I don't know.

Therapist: Well, what does a lion stand for? What comes to mind about a lion?

Patient: They roar. They're the king of the beasts. They're the strongest animal in the jungle. Lots of people are scared of them. They can eat a lot of other animals.

Therapist: Okay, so what does the lion stand for?

Patient: The lion is scary. It's something that I'm scared of. I think the lion stands for my anger.

Therapist: I agree with you. It sounds to me like a good guess. Now let's go further with that. The dream says you have to catch a lion before the needle can come out of your eye. Is that right?

Patient: Yes. Maybe catching a lion means looking at my anger.

Therapist: Tell me more about that. I think you're on the right track.

Patient: Well, maybe it means that I have to talk more about my anger and do more things with my anger before I can stop treatment.

Therapist: I *agree! I agree 100 percent.* I want to congratulate you on your figuring out the meaning of this dream. I think you did a great job. I'm really *proud* of you. We really did it together. Without your ideas, we could never have figured out the meaning of the dream. Most kids your age could never have done such a good job with a dream.

Patient: Thank you.

Therapist: You're welcome.

There is nothing else to say here; I believe everything in the interchange is self-explanatory. The vignette certainly demonstrates well the power of the analytic inquiry for those rare patients who can avail themselves of this form of treatment. However, it is important for the reader to appreciate that, as I have said so many times in this book, insight is only one step toward alleviation of psychopathology. Unless it is translated into experience and ongoing changes in thinking it is not likely to be effective.

During his tenth month in treatment the patient related this dream:

I was playing with my chemistry set and I was going to light a candle with a match. I looked down and I saw a wasp's nest on the floor. It was very big. My mother asked me to do something and I stepped on the wasp's nest and I was stung. I didn't step on it on purpose; I stepped on it by mistake.

The following interchange then took place:

Therapist: So, Timothy, what do you think about this dream?

Patient (providing his usual first response):   I don't know. I don't know what to think.

Therapist: Is there anything in this dream that's like anything that happened in any of the other dreams we talked about recently?

Patient: Well, it has something to do with lighting up a place or a room. And I had that other dream in which I took the light bulbs out of the basement.

Therapist: Yes, I had that thought too. What did it mean in the other dream, about the lights?

Patient: Well in that dream I was taking the bulbs out of the cellar, which meant that I didn't want to look at the things in my unconscious mind.

Therapist: Yes, that's right. You have a good memory for such things. And that's very useful. It helps us figure out the meaning of dreams when you have a good memory. You're lucky to have such a good memory. Okay now, that's what it meant in the other dream. Now what's happening here?

Patient: Well, here I'm lighting a candle. I'm making it light.

Therapist: So what does that mean?

Patient: It means that I want to look at things. In the other dream I didn't.

Therapist: But do you actually look at things here? Did you actually light the candle with the match in this dream?

Patient: No, I was going to but I didn't because I saw the wasp's nest on the floor.

Therapist: Let's hold off with the wasp's nest for just a minute. What is this dream telling us then about your desire to light up your unconscious mind?

Patient: It tells me that I'm not sure, that I have mixed feelings about it.

Therapist: Right! That's right. I like to use those words *mixed feelings.* So a part of you wants to light it up and a part of you doesn't. Is that right?

Patient: Yes.

Therapist: This also tells me that you're getting closer to doing it, to putting on the lights in your unconscious mind. In the other dream you just took the bulbs out of the cellar. In this dream you're thinking about lighting the candle, but you don't get to do it. You have mixed feelings about it. I guess you're still scared.

Patient: I guess so. But I was going to, but then I saw the wasp's nest on the floor.

Therapist: Okay, let's talk about that. What could the wasp's nest stand for?

Patient: I think that's like my anger again. Wasps sting and they're mean and they can hurt you.

Therapist: Okay, that sounds reasonable. That sounds like a good explanation. Then what?

Patient: Well I stepped on them.

Therapist: So what does that mean?

Patient: Maybe it's like catching a lion from the other dream. I'm less scared of touching angry things.

Therapist: I think that's a good explanation.

Patient: That was a good dream.

Therapist: Yes, you did a very good job so far, but there's still another part that we have to try to figure out.

Patient: What's that? I thought we're all finished with this dream.

Therapist: No, I think there's one other part that may be hard for you to understand, but I think it's important for us to discuss it.

Patient: What's that?

Therapist: Well, at first you said that you stepped on the wasp's nest and then you said that you did it by mistake.

Patient: Is that important?

Therapist: Yes, it's important. Why do you think I think it is important?

Patient: I don't know.

Therapist: Can you try to figure out why I think that's important?

Patient: I can't think of the reason. I just said that I did it and then I said it was a mistake.

Therapist: Well, I think that shows me that you had mixed feelings about stepping on the wasp's nest. It may also mean that you felt bad or guilty about it, and that's why you had to say that you did it by mistake. When somebody does something by mistake you can't blame them for it. It says to me that maybe you thought you might get punished or something if you stepped on the wasp's nest on purpose, that is, if you touched your anger or let your anger come out.

Patient: I don't understand what you're saying.

Therapist: Let me try it again. When you say that you did something by mistake, you hope that you won't get punished. Isn't that right?

Patient: Right.

Therapist: You just could have dreamed that you stepped on the wasp's nest, but then you had to tell me that you did it by mistake. I think from that that you probably feel that there's something wrong about doing it and you had to apologize in advance. Saying you made a mistake is a way of protecting yourself from getting punished for doing something.

Patient: Do you mean that I was scared that something would happen to me if I did it on purpose and that saying it was a mistake was an excuse so I wouldn't get punished?

Therapist: Yes, that's it. I'm glad you understand that.

Patient: I think I do.

Therapist: Why don't you tell it to me again so I'm sure you understand?

Patient: It means that I don't want to say that I wanted to do it but that I am scared to say I want to do it so I said it was a mistake so I wouldn't get punished!

Therapist: That's right! You certainly are a smart boy. Most kids your age would not have been able to understand that. Now, the important question is what do you think would happen if you were to show your anger?

>   *Patient:*   I guess my mother and father would get very angry at
> me.
>   *Therapist:*   Have you learned anythng here about that?
>   *Patient:*   Yes, I learned that they won't get as angry as I think they
> will. I make them mean sometimes when they aren't. But my mother
> is pretty mean sometimes.
>   *Therapist:*   Yes, but not all the time. And you make her worse
> than she really is. I think the more practice you have talking about
> your anger, the easier it will be for you to let it out and the more
> practice you have letting it out in a nice good way with your mother
> and father the less scared you'll be about it.

Again, little need be said about the analysis of this dream. It
shows therapeutic progress with regard to the patient's comfort
with gaining insight into his unconscious processes as well as increasing comfort with the expression of anger. However, in both
cases there was ambivalence, but this was still a step forward. Timothy had some difficulty understanding the significance of his
statement that he had stepped on the wasp's nest "by mistake." I
believe he finally did come to understand the meaning of this statement. However, I did not stop there and tried to relate his understanding to the reality of his situation with his parents. There is no
point to gaining a psychoanalytic insight if it is not translated into
clinical behavior.

Timothy's treatment lasted about a year and a half. By the time
we discontinued therapy he had enjoyed significant improvement
in his ability to assert himself and express resentment in appropriate ways. He was far less tense and worrisome. His relationships
with his parents had improved significantly, and he was generally
a much happier boy. However, there was still residua of his serious
attitude, and at times he would become inhibited in expressing
himself.

A follow-up. Timothy and I lived in the same community. Our
families were members of the same community swim club. One
day, as I was basking in the sun, Timothy came over to me and
said, "Excuse me Dr. Gardner, I know you're not on duty now, but
I had a dream last night and I was wondering if you could help me
analyze it. I don't have much money, but I can pay you fifty cents."
I informed Timothy that post-treatment dream analyses were free
and I would be happy to discuss the dream with him. I cannot recall at this point what the dream was, but I do know that he handled

himself with amazing facility regarding its analysis. I mention this here for two reasons. First, it is a demonstration of how the patient's facility with analysis remained with him following the therapy and probably has held him in good stead ever since. In addition, it is a statement of the good relationship that I had with him that he was able to approach me a year later in the way he did.

CONCLUDING COMMENTS

Throughout this book I have been critical of many aspects of psychoanalytic theory and its application to treatment. It would have been an error for the reader to conclude that I am completely critical of *all* aspects of psychoanalysis. Rather, I consider myself to have been selective and have retained and utilized what I consider to be valuable contributions and have rejected that which I consider to be of little or no value. It is also important for the reader to appreciate that my criticisms of psychoanalysis (both as a theory and as a method of treatment) do not stem from a book I once read on the subject. Rather, I went through a full six-year program of psychoanalytic training at the William A. White Psychoanalytic Institute in New York City. There I was schooled not only in the classical Freudian tradition but in the modifications introduced by others, especially Harry Stack Sullivan, Erich Fromm, and Frieda Fromm-Reichmann.

In addition, in medical school, in residency, and again during my psychoanalytic training I underwent personal psychoanalysis with analysts of three different persuasions (one classical and two culturally oriented). Furthermore, I believe that most of the techniques described in this book are within the psychoanalytic tradition. They are based on the belief that there does exist a mental compartment that is justifiably referred to as *the unconscious part of the mind.* Also, I believe that unconscious processes play an important role in the development of psychogenic symptoms. I believe also that knowledge of these processes is an important factor in bringing about therapeutic change. However, my approach does not rely heavily on the patient's (especially children's) conscious awareness of these unconscious processes. Rather, I believe that the therapist's awareness is crucial, as is the therapist's utilization of such information in bringing about therapeutic change for the patient.

It is my hope that, after reading this chapter, the reader will come away with the conclusion that I do indeed have some talents in understanding and utilizing psychoanalytic techniques and that this will lend greater credibility to my criticisms for those who are dubious about my areas of disagreement with the traditional psychoanalytic model, both as a theory and as a treatment modality.

FOURTEEN
Family Therapy

Happy families are all alike; every unhappy family is unhappy in its own way.

Leo Tolstoy

There is nothing really new in the alternative life-styles that are being given so much publicity these days. There is no pattern that has not been tried many times over, somewhere, someplace, in mankind's long history. There are just so many possible arrangements that one can devise between two sexes. The number of possible combinations between males and females is not that great, and we have had ample opportunity to try them all. Group marriages, communal living, polygymy, polyandry, homosexual marriage, and single parenthood have all been tried many times over. To the best of my knowledge, no society utilizing any of these lifestyles—as a primary arrangement for a majority of the population—has become a predominant force in human civilization. Children do best when they grow up in a home where there is one recognized father and one identifiable mother—each of whom has established a close relationship with their children from the time of their birth. Such children are most likely to perpetuate their heritage and build upon it. I am not presenting monogamy as the perfect arrangement. There is no question that it imposes more restrictions

*and frustrations than most other institutions and relationships, but
of the various possible parental arrangements for the upbringing of
children, it is the one that will most predictably produce
psychologically healthy children and thereby is the arrangement
most likely to perpetuate successfully the human species.*

R.A. Gardner

In Chapter One I mentioned that as early as my residency days I
was impressed with the value of family therapy as a therapeutic
modality. During the two years of my military service the limitations placed upon me by my commanding officer necessitated my
doing family consultations if I were to provide any kinds of services
at all to the large number of people who were seeking treatment.
Although utilized as a stop-gap measure to provide "the greatest
good for the greatest number," I recognized the value of this therapeutic modality in its own right and have used it extensively since
then, even in situations where there were no constraints on my
time or demands for "super-efficiency" in providing services for
large numbers of people. In my analytic training I became even
more appreciative of the interpersonal factors in bringing about
psychopathology. Although adjunctive family therapy was not permitted for psychoanalytic control patients, the interpersonal emphasis contributed to my respect for this treatment modality.

THEORETICAL CONSIDERATIONS

What Is the Normal Family?

When doing family therapy one must ask the basic questions: "What
is the normal family?" "Are there really happy, smooth-running
families?" "Is the 'normal' family a family in which there is a significant amount of hostility, friction, scapegoatism, jealousy, and
the utilization of one another as vehicles for the gratification of a
variety of pathological needs?" Certainly the latter kind of family
outnumbers the former. As a therapist, I recognize that I may not
be getting an accurate view of what the "normal family" is because
those who seek my services are likely to have significant family
difficulties. However, I could also argue that the sickest families

never come my way because their pathology interferes with their seeking the services of mental health professionals. My general view is that the family is most often *not* the warm, friendly, supporting entity that it is often idealized to be on television. As J.L. Framo (1982) states: ". . . Family living can also paradoxically provide the context for tragedy and anguish of endless variety—the cruel rejections, marital discord or emptiness, murderous hostility, the child unloved or discriminated against, 'parentification' of the child, jealousy, hatred, unrealized fulfillments, and outrages against the human spirit."

The family, of course, begins with the marital unit. And the basic reasons why two people involve themselves in a marriage are generally both healthy and pathologic. I have often said that if I were to have had the opportunity to rewrite the words to the song *Some Enchanted Evening*, I would write, "Some enchanted evening, across a crowded room you shall see a stranger, whose needs both healthy and neurotic will dovetail with yours. Then, you'll make a beeline for one another, stomping over people in between, and read life's meaning in one another's eyes." Although this variation may not sell many tapes, and although it may be difficult to put these new words to a tune, I believe that they reflect more accurately the reality of the marital bond. The good marriage, then, is one in which the healthy involvements far outweigh the pathological and in the pathological realm there is a relative balance in equilibrium that also has a stabilizing influence on the relationship. Examples of the healthier elements would be mutual respect, admiration, sharing, respect for each other's rights and interests, sexual attraction, a reasonable degree of romantic feelings (I didn't say pathological degree), and a desire to share certain creative endeavors (of which child rearing would be a good example). Examples of some of the coexisting pathological patterns might be: sado-masochism, independence/dependence, mutual symbiosis, and healer-patient relationships. With this kind of a relationship as its nucleus, it is likely that parent-child relationships, as well, are likely to be combinations of both healthy and pathological patterns.

My personal belief, then, is that there are indeed some very good, tight, and smooth-running families; but these are rare and still have their problems and their frictions. My goal then is to help families achieve this ideal. However, this ideal may not be attainable for the vast majority of families. Therapists who believe that the norm is indeed the smooth-running family, may be setting up an unrealistic goal for their patients. It is also important for the therapist to appreciate that there are some families that appear to be smooth running in which there is a significant degree of repression of anger. In such families a heavy price is being paid for "peace," and it is definitely a pathological situation.

The Family Psychiatrist

I believe the ideal arrangement in a clinical practice is that the psychiatrist (or qualified mental health professional) be in the position of the old-time family doctor who saw all members of the family as the need arose. Carrying this analogy over into psychiatry, the psychiatrist over time would become increasingly familiar with the various members of the family and see one or more in varying combinations (any imaginable combination) as warranted. There would be no such concept as termination. When problems were a great source of stress, the individual family member would come into treatment willing to tolerate the discomforts and privations associated with that treatment because of the hope of alleviating the symptoms. If therapy progressed well, the balance would tip in the direction in which the discomforts of attending therapy outweighed the psychological pains attendant to the symptomatology. Then treatment would be interrupted and the patient invited to return if and when the balance tipped back. There would be no sense of failure under such circumstances because both patient and therapist would recognize that life is such that new situations are likely to arise which might once again warrant therapy.

On occasion, however, the family psychiatrist might want to refer someone for individual therapy or another kind of treatment from another person. At present, in many (if not most) training centers (with the exception of family therapy centers), each member of the family is assigned a different therapist, in a different section (adult therapy, adolescent therapy, child therapy), and the treatment of the family is piecemeal. Most clinics that I know of work in this disjointed and divisive way. Some do, however, have "adjunctive" family therapy programs, and these vary from rarely used facilities to reputable aspects of the program. Family therapy centers, however, although working within this context, can narrow themselves in the opposite direction by doing too much family therapy and not providing enough individual work or other combinations of treatment.

The Procrustean Bed

Many family therapists reason in this way: Because a child's psychogenic pathology begins and is perpetuated in the family, and because the child's pathology can only be understood in the family context, one must treat the whole family if one is to conduct adequate therapy. I believe wholeheartedly that the first two aspects of this statement are true. But I do not believe that the third necessarily follows. Because a child's pathology arises from and can only be understood within the context of the family does not mean necessarily that the therapeutic program should involve all members of the family. What arose in the family might be primarily intrapsychic by the time the child comes for treatment, and thus much more individual work may be necessary. Or, other family members may not be motivated to attend, and bringing them in by coercion and guilt evocation is not likely to prove efficacious therapeutically. One must be *selective*. Some children need to be seen alone, some need to be seen alone on occasion and with other family members in a flexible arrangement at other times, and some need family therapy. Many readers, I am sure, are familiar with the Greek legend about the giant Procrustes, who put those who fell into his hands upon an iron bed. If they were longer than the bed, he cut off the overhanging parts. If shorter, he stretched them until they fit in it. Family therapy should not be a *Procrustean* bed in which all families are forced to fit, regardless of the nature of the problems and regardless of the interest and availability of the family members.

"Life Is a Rorschach Test"

In Chapter Six, in my discussion of the extended evaluation, I described how family interviews are an excellent way of learning about what is going on in a family when one is presented with diametrically opposed opinions by different family members when seen individually. I emphasized there that it is important for the therapist to appreciate that one is not only interested in what really happened but in the thoughts and feelings *about* what happened as well. In a sense, life is a Rorschach Test. First, there is the actual inkblot, which is a reality in itself. And then there is the projection onto the inkblot that is also a reality. The total reality, then, is the combination of the two. Family therapists should be concerned with both realities. I discussed also in Chapter Six the fact that family interviews allow the therapist to observe interactions that are not likely to be understood or even known about when the various individuals are seen alone. I discussed, as well, the fact that in such interviews we can genuinely say that the whole is often greater than the sum of its parts. New things come out that may not have become apparent, and may never become apparent, when the individuals are seen alone. Their interactions evoke responses in each other that may lay dormant and hidden in the individual sessions.

Now to carry the projective test analogy further. When one administers a projective instrument to an individual, one obtains only a part of the information necessary for a valid assessment. One needs clinical data as well. The two sources of information complement one another. Some psychologists place very heavy emphasis on the psychological test data, believing that this taps the unconscious processes which are more important to understand than conscious and behavioral material. Others go to the other extreme and are dubious about the value of projective materials, claiming that all of us have psychodynamics, and all of us can be considered pathological when projective material alone is reviewed. Their argument is that these interpretations have not and cannot be standardized reasonably well, and therefore conclusions emerging from them must be highly speculative and may even be dangerous. I view myself as being somewhere in the middle with regard to this conflict and, as someone who takes information from both sources, recognizing the drawbacks of each.

But this analogy can be carried further. Evaluating an individual with clinical interviews and projective tests is still only an evaluation of a small part of the "problem." For children, especially, the problem cannot be well understood unless one has evaluated the family. Seeing the child alone provides information only about one piece of the puzzle. It is for this reason that I conduct the relatively extensive and exhaustive evaluation described in Chapter Six, an evaluation that includes other family members, both individually and jointly.

Providing Experiences

In Chapter Three I discussed the importance of providing patients with *experiences* in the course of the treatment. Although many of these experiences can take place in the context of the therapist-patient relationship, family therapy provides many opportunities for experiences with the people "out there" with whom the patient is relating far more significantly and extensively than with the therapist. A girl, for example, may fear telling her parents about certain resentments she has, because she anticipates horrible retaliation. The therapist, after extensive evaluation of the parents, is convinced that the girl's fears are exaggerated. However, merely telling the youngster that this is the case is not likely to prove useful. Urging the child to have experiences outside the office that may help alter this concern may also prove futile, in that the girl may be too fearful to risk the anticipated repercussions of expressing her resentment. Encouraging such self-assertion in the family therapy session may be the best way to accomplish this goal. In the presence of the therapist, the child may be reassured that the anticipated consequences are less likely to take place because of the implied protection by the therapist. Then, having had the experience in the therapeutic setting that the feared repercussions did not materialize, the child is in a better position to take the risks of such self-assertion outside of the therapist's presence. As discussed in Chapter Seven, this is what I believed occurred with Freud and little Hans.

Hospitalization

One must also be selective with regard to the hospitalization of children because of the risk that it will compromise the opportunities for family therapy. Plucking the person out of a family context, putting the individual in the hospital, and then treating that person in isolation from the family in the hope that such treatment will help the individual reintegrate him- or herself into the family is often naive. I generally view hospitalization to be warranted primarily for people who are homicidal, suicidal, or who cannot be relied upon to care for themselves regarding drug management. Otherwise, I rarely hospitalize. This concept of removing the person out of the family to help the individual reintegrate into it is often naive to the point of being absurd. Unless one has decided before hospitalization that transfer to another location is going to take place, it is rarely the indicated form of treatment. I agree that on occasion a certain amount of decompression may be necessary, but this indication applies only to a small fraction of all those who are removed from their families for psychiatric hospitalization. I believe that this system is anachronistic and is based on the medical model that an illness exists within the individual him- or herself only.

Is Family Therapy Only Marital Counseling with the Children Observing?

Some critics of family therapy claim that family therapy often ends up being psychotherapy of the parents with the children being present as observers. Although such an outcome may certainly take place, I do not believe that this criticism is warranted as a generalization. Children create their own scenarios that warrant attention, either individually or within the family therapy context. A good example of this is the disorder that I have termed the *parental alienation syndrome* (Gardner, 1985, and 1986b). In this disorder, in response to the terrible loyalty conflicts associated with protracted custody litigation, children, in an attempt to ingratiate themselves to a brainwashing parent, will develop their own scenarios of denigration of the "hated" parent that go significantly beyond the programming parent's indoctrinations. One of the indicated treatments of this disorder is family therapy wherein focus on the child and both parents is crucial.

COMMON SITUATIONS IN WHICH FAMILY THERAPY IS INDICATED

Basic Requirements

There are certain provisions which must be satisfied for meaningful family therapy. Family therapy is primarily a talking kind of therapy. For the sessions to be useful *all* the participants must be willing and capable of involving themselves meaningfully in the discussion. Because children under the age of eight or nine are not likely to satisfy this criterion to a significant degree, I generally do not utilize family therapy when the designated patient is a child under this age. I am not claiming that nothing at all can be accomplished if children below eight or nine are brought into family therapy sessions; I am only saying that it is a therapeutic approach with a low degree of efficiency. The child is not likely to sustain for long involvement in the discussions and then may become disruptive and distracting. Also, one must differentiate between an occasional family interview and ongoing family treatment. Younger children may very well contribute to an occasional family meeting, but they are not likely to sustain their interest and meaningful involvement over the course of a prolonged therapeutic program. The more advanced beyond this age level the children are, the greater the likelihood they will be candidates for family therapy. Children at the adolescent level are generally the best candidates.

Another provision that must be satisfied for family therapy to be successful is that the participants be genuinely motivated to attend. Many family therapists use various kinds of coercive and guilt-evoking maneuvers to engage reluctant children and adolescents. A youngster may not wish to attend the family sessions (beyond the initial consultative family session) to be of assistance to his or her younger sibling. The youngster may be much more interested in his or her own after-school activities, watching television, or just hanging around doing nothing. Family therapists have been known to say to such youngsters: "If you really love your brother and really cared for him, you'd be willing to come here." This maneuver may be successful in getting the "body" of this youngster into the room, but it is not likely to bring his or her "soul" into the treatment. Another youngster says, "I don't see why I have to come, I don't have any problems." Some family therapists will respond, "*That's your problem. You'll be halfway cured when you see that you have problems.*" This is an asinine statement to make to a youngster. No person ever gained insight from a statement like that. It's a definite "turnoff" and serves no useful purpose. I can't imagine youngsters going into family therapy with an invitation like that.

Communication Problems

Family therapy is indicated for people who have trouble communicating. It can be particularly useful in this regard. If a good relationship is established between the family members and the therapist, then he or she can serve as a good model for effective communication. Of course, therapists who are strictly adherent to the classical psychoanalytic model may not serve well as family therapists. Most do not involve themselves in this form of treatment. But if those who are so trained decide to involve themselves in this therapeutic modality, they do well to recognize that their training may serve as an impediment because of the verbal passivity that it engenders. Once things are "out on the table," the individuals may have the experience that the terrible repercussions they anticipated are not forthcoming. It then becomes easier to communicate. As mentioned, sometimes "breakthroughs" occur, and the individuals then continue on the new level of communication for the rest of their lives. It is not uncommon for people to discover new dimensions in other parties that they never knew existed. The whole nature of a relationship may change as a result of a few sessions in which people may have opened up for the first time in years, if ever.

Family therapy, when successful, is likely to open up communication and enable people to become comfortable communicating when they previously were not. It is reasonable to say that a significant contributing factor in the formation of psychogenic symptoms is the repression and suppression of thoughts and feelings that the individuals would rather not attend to. The therapist must take these skeletons out of the closet, open Pandora's boxes, and put out on the table issues that were previously hidden under it. Family therapy can often accomplish this in a relatively short period, sometimes within a session or two. Generally, it takes much longer to accomplish these same ends when the individuals are seen separately or, even worse, when only one of the involved parties is seen. Sometimes, the family therapy sessions can indeed be considered a "breakthrough" in that the new pattern of open communication may last for the rest of the lives of all the involved individuals, even after the original family has become extended, and even after the children have grown up and left the household.

Antisocial Behavior

The primary kinds of problems for which family therapy is indicated are, obviously, those problems in which all the family members are embroiled. One example would be an acting-out adolescent whose parents have found futile all attempts to reason with the youngster or get him or her to conform more reasonably. The therapy not only involves exploration and treatment of the youngster's sources of anger, but dealing with the antisocial behavior on the disciplinary level as well. The youngster's active observation of and participation in these discussions may be the best way to deal with the antisocial behavior. The parents have to be helped at the counseling level, wherein they may have to come to appreciate what is normal antagonism toward parents and what is pathological. They may need counseling regarding their disciplinary measures, which may be too stringent (and even sadistic) or too lenient. They have to be helped to know when to pull back and accept their impotence in situations they cannot control and when they have to step forward and intervene.

Separation Anxiety Disorder

Another example of a situation in which family therapy would be indicated is the one in which a child with a separation anxiety disorder is involved with an overprotective mother, but whose father passively and sometimes actively supports the mother's overprotectiveness. Although such a child certainly needs individual work in order to assist in the reduction of the symbiotic tie between the child and the mother, family therapy may also be useful in helping the mother gain insight into her overprotectiveness. Because she is often so defended against such insights, the assistance of the father might be useful. In some cases his blindness to the problem may make him useless as an adjunct in the treatment; in other cases he has some dim appreciation of what is going on between his wife and child and with the therapist's assistance may then serve as an important participant in the treatment (Gardner, 1984).

Marital Conflict

Family therapy may be particularly useful in situations in which a marital conflict is embroiling the children. In such situations it is common for the children to be used as weapons. Loyalty conflicts may ensue, antisocial behavior against one or both parents may result, psychosomatic complaints may be exhibited, and a variety of other symptoms may emerge when the children are so utilized. If the parents then separate, there is an even greater likelihood that family therapy will be indicated. The separation increases the likelihood that the children will be used as spies, weapons, and/or saboteurs. The parents no longer have access to one another's homes, the children do. In addition, the children are welcomed with open arms into each domicile, making them excellent subjects for such utilization. And this situation may prevail beyond the divorce. In fact, I believe that families involved in separation and divorce conflicts are among the best candidates for family therapy. Many parents are astonished when I make this recommendation. A common reply: "But Doctor, we're no longer married, so we shouldn't be in therapy together." Such parents have to be helped to appreciate that although legally divorced, they may be still psychologically married and that a psychological divorce may only be accomplished through treatment. And, if their residual psychological marriage involves a pathological embroilment of their children in their conflicts, then family therapy is the primary form of therapy that is indicated.

A mother may call me to make an initial appointment for her daughter. I advise her that my usual procedure is to see both parents and the child at a two-hour consultation. I make no mention of any relevance of the invitation to the marital status of the parents, whether they are married, separated, or divorced. The mother may respond, "But my husband and I are divorced." The implication here is that because of their divorced status I will not want him to attend the meeting. I will then ask her if her former husband still involves himself with her daughter. She will generally respond affirmatively. I will tell her then that my experience has been that it is preferable that both parents attend this meeting, regardless of their marital status. A common response: "But Doctor, we'll only fight the minute we get in there." To which I will often respond: "We've only been speaking a few minutes, and I know very little about your daughter. But this I can tell you, the likelihood of my being of help to your daughter without some kind of family work is extremely small. I can't imagine helping your daughter while she remains living in a situation in which the two of you automatically fight within minutes of the time you're in the same room together. Because one of my therapeutic aims will be to alleviate this situation, why don't we start working toward this goal as soon as possible. Now I'm not telling you that my aim is to reconcile you with your former husband, nor is my goal to get you to fight. I recognize that fighting is unpleasant. However, the fighting will provide me with some information, and my hope is that my observing the fighting will provide me with the tools to help you alleviate or even discontinue it." Therapists who allow themselves to be talked out of doing indicated family therapy because the people fight too much would be equivalent to doctors who don't provide treatment for pharyngitis patients because the patients have sore throats and will have trouble swallowing the pills.

Post-Marital Conflict

Now to carry this even further. When third (and fourth) partners or stepparents appear on the scene, post-divorce animosities may become even stronger. A stepmother, for example, may continually support her new husband's hostility toward his former wife. The two women, therefore, are actively involved in the pathological difficulties that the children are exposed to and embroiled in. The mother and the stepmother may never have met one another, yet have come to view each other as the incarnation of all evil. In such situations it is extremely common for the children to "butter up" each of the parties, saying only that which they know each party wants to hear and strictly refraining from making any comments that would risk alienation. This results in even further polarization of the parties. When I have recommended that the parents and stepparents involve themselves in a joint counseling arrangement, I am often responded to with incredulity. However, it is clear that this is the indicated form of treatment. Just putting the parties in the room together provides them with an experience that may alter their misconceptions far more effectively than years of individual therapy. They may come to appreciate that they are not the ogres they viewed one another to be and that the children's fabrications have contributed to a worsening of the situation. Also, lines of communications may be opened that can also be therapeutic. Subsequently in this chapter I will present an example that demonstrates these points quite well. Accordingly, I consider family problems in which there are difficulties between stepparents, natural parents, and former spouses to be among the primary situations for which family therapy is indicated.

SITUATIONS IN WHICH FAMILY THERAPY IS CONTRAINDICATED

Those "Identified Patients" Who Do Indeed Need "Individual Attention"

Family therapists often use the term "identified patient" with the connotation that other members of the family have inappropriately identified the individual as *the* patient in order to remove themselves from that role. I think many family therapists go too far on this point. In order to justify this position they often look for psychopathology in all of the members of the family and claim that this covert psychopathology may be just as virulent as the symptomatic psychopathology of the identified patient. An example of this is their frequent reference to the family as "the patient." They push this too far. There are times when the *identified patient is truly the patient and the family psychopathology is not that significant.* Sometimes giving each member of the family a diagnosis serves to justify bringing them all into the therapist's Procrustean bed, but it is detrimental to the family members. It provides healthy family members with the label of psychopathology. There are definite times when the so-called identified patient is truly the only person needing treatment.

In Chapter Three I compared the therapeutic model to the educational. Just as many children can learn best in a classroom, there are some who *need* "individual attention." There are some who need to be taken out of the classroom for special individual tutoring, either alone or in small groups. This analogy holds in the therapeutic situation as well. I have also stated in Chapter Three my belief that psychotherapy is essentially a "brainwashing" experience. Some children need "individual attention," that is, individual brainwashing. And some children need brainwashing in association with other members of their family, that is, "family brainwashing." Children who need primarily individual brainwashing may still require family sessions in which information is obtained and some therapy is done. However, these children need primarily concentrated individual attention. There is group brainwashing and there is individual brainwashing. Both play a role. In this section I describe children for whom the individual approach is the optimum and for whom family therapy, as the primary therapeutic modality, is contraindicated.

The Mutual Storytelling Technique and Derivative Games
Certain child psychotherapeutic techniques, devised by the author, are not utilized optimally in the family therapy setting. The mutual storytelling technique (Chapters Eight and Nine) and its derivative games (Chapter Ten) are best used when the child is being seen alone. In fact, the family's presence is likely to compromise the child's freedom to create and tell revealing stories and/or their presence may serve as a distraction, especially if younger siblings are present. Furthermore, these treatment modalities involve immediate responding stories and comments by the therapist. The family,

under such circumstances, would merely be observers. Although something might be learned by them from such observation, it is an inefficient utilization of their time in that they might conceivably spend the whole session merely observing what is going on (and this is especially true of the derivative games). Of course, one could argue that the therapist might modify the technique and use the interchanges between the child and therapist as points of departure for family involvement. To the degree that one does this, to that degree the family should be present. However, to the degree that the therapist does this, to that degree is time devoted to this special mode of communication reduced. These techniques were devised to enable the examiner to provide communications at the primary process level. Family discussions are at the secondary process level. One can't have it both ways. Both levels of communication have a place in therapy. Accordingly, my final conclusion on this point is that to the degree that the therapist wishes to use primary process communications in his or her work, to that degree will family therapy interfere. Last, if the examiner tries to use these techniques with siblings during the family interview, he or she will quickly find that the second child's story will be significantly contaminated by the first child's. This is the main reason why these techniques are contraindicated in group therapy with children, and it is an important reason for their contraindication in family therapy in which children are involved.

Separation Anxiety Disorder I have mentioned children with a separation anxiety disorder. They certainly need individual therapy in order to help them break the symbiotic tie with their mothers. This does not preclude some family therapy entirely, but there must be some individual work as well if the child is to be helped (Gardner, 1984).

Antisocial Adolescents Family therapy may be an important aspect of the treatment of adolescents with antisocial behavior (as well as other forms of adolescent psychopathology). However, adolescents also need an individual separate relationship with their therapists in order to help them separate and gain independence from the family. This is one of the main reasons why one would not want to have a total family therapy approach for many adolescents. This does not preclude, however, some family therapy sessions in both the evaluative and therapeutic aspects of treatment.

The Intellectually Normal Child with a Very Bright Sibling(s)   Let us consider the situation in which the youngest child is in the normal to above-average range intellectually and has one or more extremely bright older siblings. As a result, the youngest suffers with profound feelings of low self-worth, loses interest in school, and develops temper outbursts. There is absolutely no pathology necessarily present here in the older siblings or the parents. Or, the parents may be sports oriented and the siblings who are born with high talent potential in this area do well, whereas the sibling who does not have such talents may suffer greviously. Although one could argue that the parents' emphasis on sports is psychopathological, it may not be. To say this is the same as saying that parents who emphasize education are necessary pathological. There may be no indoctrination or excessive pressures; the child just cannot live up to normal parental expectations.

Exaggerated Reaction to the Birth of a Sibling   There are children who react excessively to the birth of a younger sibling. And, if instead of one younger sibling, twins, triplets, or quadruplets appear (I have in therapy now a child in the last category), the older siblings may develop symptoms that stem from inordinate jealous rivalry. There may have been no particular psychopathology in the family prior to the birth of the multiple siblings. The birth of a single sibling may be a formidable trauma to the first-born child. It can well be compared to the situation in which a husband, for example, comes home with another woman, introduces her to his wife, and tells her, "Dear, I want you to meet Jane. She's a wonderful person—both in and out of bed—and she's going to be living with us. I'm sure you two women will get along quite well." Imagine then a child's being greeted not with one but multiple siblings simultaneously. The shock can be formidable and the residual psychological effects profound. One can justifiably classify a child's reactions to multiple births as a post-traumatic stress reaction without necessarily attributing any particular psychopathology to other members of the family. In fact, one can make the generalization that post-traumatic stress reactions and various situational reactions may not necessarily be related to psychopathology in the family. A child exhibiting untoward reactions to parental death may not be doing so because of family psychopathology. Even reactions to parental divorce may not necessarily be related to parental psychopathology, although it may be easier to assign such pathology in these cases. I am not claiming that some kind of family counseling may not prove useful in the treatment of post-traumatic stress reactions, only that it is not indicated as the primary and exclusive therapeutic approach.

The Child with a Sibling Who Suffers with a Neurologically Based Learning Disability   Another situation in which family pathology may not be operative in bringing about a child's problems is the one in which a normal sibling suffers from the fact that there is a child with a neurologically based learning disability in the family. The normal child suffers many indignities because of the presence of the LD sibling. The LD sibling intrudes when the normal child brings friends. The LD child is a continued source of embarrassment to the normal child. The LD child, having few if any friends, frequently imposes him- or herself on the normal child and plays with his or her friends. The normal child's friends may even refuse to come to the house because of this situation. Furthermore the normal child suffers with special problems concerning sibling rivalry. There is increased jealousy because the LD child needs and requires special and more attention from the parents. The normal child may be made to feel excessively guilty over the expression of the usual hostility that is present in the sibling rivalry situation, but here the hostility is greater because of the frustrations and privations the normal child suffers and so the guilt may also be greater. The parents' inducing guilty feelings in the normal child because of the hostility may not be a pathological manifestation on their part. It may be necessary for the protection of the handicapped child. The normal child's need for treatment in such a situation may be real, and he or she may be designated as the patient without particular psychopathology in the parents. Again, I am not claiming that absolutely no counseling is warranted, only that the primary therapeutic approach is generally individual treatment.

A Child Dealing with the Impending Death of a Parent   Another situation in which family therapy is contraindicated is the one in which a child is reacting to the impending death of a parent. The dying parent may be utilizing denial mechanisms in the attempt to deal with his or her forthcoming demise, and this must be respected by family members. Under such circumstances it would be cruel and inhumane to involve such a parent in family therapy. However, there are circumstances in which the parent may be dealing more directly with the death and then, of course, family therapy may be strongly indicated. But here again, it would be a grievous error to place pressure on any family members to attend, whether it be the dying parent or any of the other individuals. The others, as well, may wish to avoid discussions of the forthcoming tragedy and this must be respected.

Borderline or Psychotic Family Members

There are families in which a member may be so fragile that psychotic decompensation would take place as a result of the confrontations that emerge in the course of family therapy. Such a member may have to be excluded. However, if such a person is absent from the family meetings we cannot say that meaningful family therapy is taking place. To place such a parent in the family session may also result in hospitalization. Then the child may be worse off than he or she was when the parent was in the home.

Fixed and Unchangeable Family Subsystems

Another situation in which family therapy may be contraindicated is the one in which the parents are involved in a psychopathological pattern that can be best viewed as a "fixed constant." The child, however, is suffering symptoms. For example, a strongly masochistic mother may be married to a man who treats her sadistically. The child is continually exposed to their sadomasochistic conflicts. Neither is particularly motivated for treatment, and neither has insight into the fact that he or she is suffering from psychopathological difficulties. Both point a finger to the other as the source of the problems in their relationship. Family therapy is a waste of time because each of the parents spends the session time complaining about the other. And comments and confrontations by the children are also of no value in alleviating this form of bondage. Marital counseling is futile for the same reason, that is, the parents spend the complete session accusing each other of causing their difficulties. All attempts on the therapist's part to help either of the parents gain insight into his or her role in the perpetuation of the marital difficulties proves futile. Under such circumstances the therapist does best to see the child alone and help him or her adjust to the reality of the situation. The aims of therapy here would be to help the child avoid identifying with the parental characteristics, to appreciate its pathological elements, and to alleviate other psychological difficulties that may result from being exposed to and sometimes embroiled in the parental animosity.

EVALUATING AND PREPARING FAMILIES FOR FAMILY THERAPY

Assessment in the Evaluative Sessions

As discussed in Chapter Five, I routinely see the child and both parents in the initial two-hour consultation. One of my purposes here is to get across the message that active parental involvement will be expected. As discussed in Chapter Six, I usually conduct a family interview as part of my extended evaluation. Some family therapists suggest that the family interview be required for all children's initial interview in order to get across the message at the outset that the *total* family will be involved in the treatment. I am not in agreement with this position because I do not routinely involve the whole family in the treatment of children who are brought for treatment.

The first interview often establishes important precedents. The very fact that I invite both parents in at the outset is a statement that the participation of both is going to be warranted in the child's treatment. I generally do not invite the stepparents to attend the first two-hour consultative interview. However, there are certain situations in which such an invitation is extended. For example, I recall receiving a telephone call from a mother who requested that I see her daughter. I informed her that my usual procedure is to see both parents and the child in a two-hour consulation, during which time I see the parent and the child in varying combinations, as warranted. She informed me that she was divorced and remarried and that she and her child were living with her new husband; her former husband was not remarried. I asked her then about the relationships between the child, her father, and her stepfather. She stated that the relationships the girl had with both father and stepfather were good. I then asked her about the nature of the relationship between the father and stepfather, and she claimed that they had a cordial relationship without significant hostility.

She then asked me which of the two I thought should properly attend the first meeting. I responded that three possibilities come to mind with regard to who should join the mother and child in the initial interview: 1) the natural father, 2) the stepfather, and 3) both the father and the stepfather. I told her that I thought that she might be able to give a better answer to that question than I, because she was much more familiar with these individuals than I and that I, as a stranger, might not be able to make the most judicious decision. She immediately opted for the third arrangement, namely, the one in which both father and stepfather would be present together. I told her that that was fine with me and that that was really my first choice but that I preferred that the family members attend in this way because of their own conviction for it rather than from some demand or command coming from me. In this case, I was pleased with the way things went in that I got important information from both father and stepfather in the initial joint interview. And, throughout the course of the child's therapy, both men contributed, both singly and jointly.

In the course of the extended evaluation I will see each of the parents once or twice alone and then conduct a joint session. This provides me with important background information about the child's problems and can be useful in helping me ascertain whether or not the parent might be a candidate for family therapy. For example, in the joint evaluative session, one might consider an inhibited and "uptight" father theoretically to be a candidate for family therapy (even though he has brought the child for treatment), but he may be so threatened by open communication that he is basically not a candidate for family therapy. It might be offered on a trial basis, but with many such people optimism for involvement is unwarranted. In the joint evaluative session one might find that the marital problems are so formidable that family therapy is likely to degenerate into a situation in which the children become mere observers to the parental counseling. In the individual interview one may learn that father, for example, is having an affair which he believes his wife is unaware of. In the interview with the wife one learns that she is utilizing denial mechanisms to protect her from admitting to herself what is going on. Therapists must be extremely cautious about upsetting such an equilibrium. At some level, the mother may prefer to suffer the indignities of the affair over the privations and frustrations attendant to the matter being brought to surface and the possibility of divorce. In such cases the therapist might consider it preferable to "let sleeping dogs lie" and *not* recommend family therapy where the risks of disclosure might be great.

Who Shall Be Prepared for Involvement in Family Therapy

When considering the question of who shall be prepared for family therapy, I generally do not think seriously about engaging children under the age of four or five. As mentioned, with rare exception, they are more disruptive and distracting than contributory. Between the ages of six and eleven, the older the child, the more likely I am going to engage him or her. But here again, I generally do not view latency-aged children to be good candidates for family therapy. It is only at about the age of 11 or so that most children are capable of involving themselves meaningfully in this therapeutic modality.

Although adolescents may certainly be involved in the treatment, one should not try to coerce a youngster who shows significant resistance to involvement. I have already mentioned the inappropriateness of therapists' trying to involve youngsters with comments such as, "If you really loved your brother you would join the treatment" or "You're wrong, you do have problems. Your problem is that you don't see you have problems. When you see that you have problems, that will be your first step to a cure." Such a reluctant adolescent could be invited, however, to join intermittently when he or she considers there to be a problem for which the therapist's assistance is considered warranted.

With regard to the parents, one often sees a situation in which one parent is significantly more motivated for treatment than the other. (My experience has been that mothers are generally much more motivated than fathers for the treatment of their children as well as for family therapy.) Again, I would not use "arm twisting" maneuvers to engage a father. I might say, "I believe that active involvement on your part in your child's treatment is important. My experience has been that the more involvement I have on the part of both parents, the greater the likelihood of therapeutic success. If you feel strongly that you don't wish to involve yourself, I will proceed as best I can. However, you must know that I will be working under compromised conditions." (Once again I use my old friend "the-ball-is-in-your-court-baby" principle.) When I make this statement I do not convey the feeling that I will be terribly disappointed if the reluctant parent rejects my offer. I will not lose sleep that night. I did not create the child's pathology and it is not my job to cure the child. Rather, it is my job to try to use every reasonable attempt to alleviate his or her difficulties. One of my roles is to help clarify issues so that people will know the consequences of their actions. Because there is no personal harm that will befall me if the reluctant parent refuses to involve him- or herself, there is no significant pressure on my part to coerce that parent into involvement. This does not preclude my benevolently pointing out the benefits that might be derived from such involvement, but this can be done without coercion or guilt evocation.

Separated and Divorced Parents

Separated and/or divorced people are traditionally reluctant to involve themselves together in the initial interview and the joint meetings that are conducted as part of the extended evaluation. In order to engage divorced parents who express initial reluctance to involve themselves in the consultation I emphasize the point that their ongoing animosity indicates to me that they are psychologically married, even though legally divorced. I point out that a bond of animosity is nevertheless a bond. I try to help them appreciate that as long as they are not psychologically divorced, their child is likely to suffer as will they. Considering the reluctance of divorced parents to involve themselves in the initial evaluation, it is often more difficult to involve them in the ongoing process of the child's therapy. But even then, their level of involvement is usually at the counseling level, that is, to help them deal with the child. The recommendation of ongoing family therapy to such individuals often comes as quite a shock. And yet I believe that family therapy is often warranted in divorced families.

When I help divorced parents gain conviction for family therapy, I reassure them that it is not my goal to effect a reconciliation. I impress upon them the fact that their child's psychopathology is not likely to be resolved as long as he or she is continually exposed to or embroiled in their ongoing conflicts. My goals are to clarify issues and to reduce psychopathology. On occasion, the new friend or spouse of one of the parents may be significantly threatened by the therapy of the original family, fearing a reconciliation will come about.

Let us take the example of a woman whose new husband has now been invited into family therapy with his former wife. When she first learns of my proposal from her husband, she reacts with incredulity and rage, claiming that she fears that the counseling might result in a reconciliation between her new husband and his former wife. I will invite this woman to my office and say: "As I see it, at the present time, your husband is a bigamist! Although legally he is divorced from his first wife and married to you, from the psychological point of view he is married to *two* women. In fact, I would go further and state my belief that, from the psychological point of view, he is more married to her than he is to you. If one were to have a printout of all of his thoughts each day, and one were to count the number of thoughts devoted to you and compare them to the number of thoughts devoted to her, it is likely that she would be ahead. I am in agreement that the thoughts pertaining to her would be more hateful ones and those pertaining to you would be more loving ones; however, hateful thoughts are still thoughts and a definite manifestation of ongoing involvement.

Your husband has stated emphatically that he has no intention of divorcing you and remarrying his first wife. And she, as well, has insisted that she has no desire to remarry your husband. Because all three of you are in agreement on this point, I cannot have as my goal your husband's divorcing you and remarrying his former wife. My goal will be to help him obtain a psychological divorce from his first wife. If I am successful in this regard I believe your relationship will be *freer* to become a deeper one. Also, I don't want you to feel that you have to just sit on the sidelines worrying about what's going to happen. I would like you to become an active participant because you're living at times with your husband's children and are playing an important role in their growth and development. [In some cases I may recommend ongoing involvement on the part of this stepmother, in other cases intermittent participation.] Because you'll be actively involved, you'll be able to see for yourself what's happening and, if anything comes up which suggests that your fears may be realized, you'll be there to deal with the situation when it arises and not learn about it after matters have gone too far. But, as I have said, I think that such an eventuality is extremely unlikely." My experiences have been that such reassurances do work and enable the initially reluctant third party to involve him- or herself in a meaningful way.

Family Therapy with Stepfamilies

Again, I think the stepfamily situation is one of the most common and important situations in which family therapy is warranted. When parents are newly divorced, and still embroiled in the post-divorce conflicts, there are only two adults who are actively involved in the perpetuation of the child's syptomatology. When one or more stepparents (or "significant others,"—I will use the terms synonymously) appear on the scene, additional adults are added who may be playing an active role in a child patient's difficulties. The child then can best be viewed as being part of a network of individuals all of whom are involved in bringing about and perpetuating the psychiatric disturbance.

Let us take the example of two remarried parents who are still involved in ongoing litigation. Father gains psychological support from his new wife and mother gains support from her new husband. The opposing armies then are lined up, with the child in the middle of a no man's land—available for the two sides to utilize in the service of their causes. The child may be used as a rope in a tug of war, as each side tugs for the child to be an ally. The child may also be used as a weapon by one side against the other. Or, the child may be used as a saboteur. The child's loyalty conflicts may be formidable and it becomes highly likely that the child will lie and say to each side what *that* party wants to hear. The two stepparents may never have met one another, yet they soon come to hate each other. They accept as valid the criticisms provided by their spouses and may not give serious consideration to the possibility that exaggerations and distortions may be operative. The stepparents serve then to polarize the child's parents even further.

Under such circumstances, it is naive and foolhardy on the part of the therapist to think that he or she can help such a child without active work with all four parties involved. Here again, formidable preparation by the therapist may be necessary. The parents and stepparents have to be helped to appreciate that they are actively contributing to the perpetuation of the child's difficulties and that the likelihood of the child's improving without a change in their situation is small.

Of course, the parents' lawyers may be working to sabotage the treatment. Each may advise the clients not to reveal certian information, so as not to compromise the parent's position in litigation. Under these circumstances, I generally will comment to the parents along these lines: "Your lawyer may get an A+ from his law school professor for advising you not to reveal anything that might compromise your position in court; however, he gets an F− from the psychiatry professor because his advice is likely to perpetuate your child's psychological problems as well as your own. You have a choice to make. To the degree that you reveal yourselves here, to that degree, I can be of help to your child and you. However, the price you may pay may be a compromise of your legal situation. In contrast, to the degree that you withhold information here, you compromise my ability to be of help to you and your family. However, such withholding may very well improve your situation in court. You have to decide what you want to do." As mentioned previously in this book, I refer to this as the "the-ball-in-your-court-baby" principle. The information is provided, the advantages and disadvantages of each step outlined, and the patient is left to decide what he or she wants to do with the information.

Involvement of Other Parties in the Family's Treatment

I usually confine myself to the child, parents, and stepparents (when warranted) in my family therapy. I generally do not bring in other parties on an ongoing basis. I may, however, bring other individuals in on an occasional basis, as warranted. Grandparents, for example, may become involved. A mother, for example, may expand to his parents the hostility she feels toward her former husband. In situations such as these the mother may remove the children from the grandparents or make it extremely difficult for them to have ongoing contact with them. Under these circumstances, the children's only contact with the grandparents may be during visitations with the father. In some cases this compromise may work; in others it may not in that the visitations may not provide the optimum involvement on the children's part with the grandparents. The mother may not permit them to call the grandparents or the grandparents to communicate with the children when they are in the mother's home. This is most often a serious error on the mother's part. It deprives the children of important grandparental input, which can be a very valuable and healthy aspect of their psychological development. The love and adoration of grandparents for grandchildren can often serve as a buffer for the unwarranted criticisms and other frustrations of life to which all humans are inevitably exposed. At times, the therapist can help the mother appreciate this and assist her in steps towards a rapprochement between herself and the grandparents. On occasion, bringing the grandparents in, for joint interviews with the mother and father, can facilitate this reconciliation process.

People in divorce situations tend to use what I call "clumping." They expand their animosity to innocent individuals and thereby add to their grief. The children tend to see the departed parent as having abandoned "us" rather than the custodial parent. Mothers tend to clump their former husbands with their parents, and fathers tend to clump their former wives with their parents. The animosity spreads and the disruption of the children's lives intensifies. Some grandparents go along with the request of their children to join forces with them against a separated spouse. Others, more judiciously, refuse to serve in this capacity. It is the therapist's role to do everything possible, both in individual and joint interviews, to prevent this unnecessary extension and expansion of the divorce difficulties.

COMMON PSYCHODYNAMIC PATTERNS IN FAMILY PSYCHOPATHOLOGY

Volumes have been written on the many types of family psychopathology. Here, I will describe some that I have found to be most common, but I do not claim an exhaustive presentation of this area.

Complementary Psychopathology in the Marital Dyad

It is crucial that the therapist appreciate that the personality patterns that we exhibit in any situation are, in part, based on the individuals with whom we are involved. The lieutenant assumes one role in his relationships with privates and a very different one in his relationships with generals. The boss is a different person to his secretary than he is to his wife and children. In the family, often the most immature part of one's personality emerges. In Chapter Five, in my discussion of the criteria I utilize to ascertain whether therapy is warranted, I pointed out how the home environment is the least useful for determining whether children need therapy. I stated there that the home environment (when compared to school and neighborhood) is the most flexible one and the most tolerant of atypical behavior. My discussion in that chapter related to children; however, the same principles apply to adults. With our family we can "get away with" much more than we can with peers, co-workers, supervisors, and even those who may work under us. After all, the repercussions for exhibiting immature and pathological behavior are far less in the home than anywhere else. The most powerful business moguls may become pussycats in their relationships with their wives. Feared executives may be used as scapegoats by their children at home. Leaders of countries, who exhibit significant proficiency in command, may be inept in their homes.

J.L. Framo (1982) points out how roles are accepted in the family context: "Whenever two or more persons are in close relationship, they collusively carry psychic functions for each other. The collusion can be benign: If you are scared I can afford to be brave; if you are responsible I can allow myself to be irresponsible; if you take the hard line, I can take the soft line. The collusion can be more serious and unconscious: I will be your bad self and act out your impulses if you will never leave me." A pact or a bargain is unconciously made between and among the various individuals in the family which serves to allow the gratification of both healthy and pathological interactions.

Therapists do well to appreciate that people marry for both conscious and unconscious reasons. They consciously seek someone who has certain qualities that they admire and respect. However, they also unconsciously seek individuals who have pathological and ostensibly undesirable qualities that they also inwardly crave. In the marital situation, especially after the romantic love denial mechanism wears off, they may involve themselves more overtly in the psychopathological interactions. These seemingly undesirable modes of relationships emerge from longstanding personality patterns which are still a source of attraction/alienation. A man, for example, states that he wants a wife and the woman he marries states that she wants a husband. In actuality, however, he may unconsciously want a mother and she unconsciously wants a child. What is presented as a husband-wife relationship is in actuality a parent-child mode of interaction. An uptight, verbally inhibited man who is ill at ease in social situations marries a woman who is very talkative and can be relied upon to fill his vacuum in social situations. Although he says he wants a wife and she says she wants a husband, what we actually have is a man with verbal constipation married to a woman with verbal diarrhea. Wife says she wants a husband and husband says he wants a wife. She really wants a sadist and he really wants a masochist. Some in this category actually reach orgasms by being beaten; others flagellate each other verbally, but the gratifications are similar.

L. Kubie (1956) considers extremely important the marital pathological interactions in which the parties utilize each other to "wipe out old pains" or to "pay off an old score." For example, a man might want to make his bad mother (now equals wife) good or use her as a target for the present expression of past resentments originally felt toward his mother. For individuals to do this they must marry people who have the very same alienating qualities that they claim they never want to have in a spouse. These qualities exist as internal bad objects in the individuals themselves, and these are then projected out onto the spouse, even when they don't exist. The spouse is then viewed as a "bad internal object representation." The distorted view of the spouse, then, results from two processes: 1) a transference onto the spouse of feelings originally felt toward one's own parents in childhood and 2) a projection of one's own internal bad object parental representations that have been incorporated. The real personality of the family member then hardly exists because the individual is seen primarily, if not exclusively, as a bad object representation and/or as someone who is distorted by one's own transferences. According to Kubie these two processes contribute significantly to the individual's desire to use the spouse to "settle old scores" and/or to "right old wrongs."

J.L. Framo (1982) also considers a central problem in family pathology to relate to the fact that family members are still reacting to parental introjects that persist from childhood. He considers parents to be reenacting with their spouses early problems with their own parents that have not been worked through. The husband who treats his wife as if she were his mother tends to perpetuate or master old conflicts with mother through his wife.

Use of the Child to Fulfill
Pathological Parental Expectations

Parents commonly identify and label their children in accordance with their own anticipations and expectations. And the various children in the family may acquire different designations. One is considered "bright," another "a good business man." This child is "a little devil" and another will "never amount to anything." One little toddler will "end up promiscuous, I can tell by the look in her eyes." Another newborn infant will "end up a star football player, he already has the muscles for it." Whether the qualities are desirable or undesirable, the child is likely to fulfill the family prophecy.

Many years ago, while serving as a psychiatrist in the military, a colonel once came to me, quite depressed, claiming that this was the most painful and humiliating day of his life. The story, he stated, began seventeen years previously at the time when his wife gave birth to their oldest, a boy: "The obstetrician came out of the delivery room and told me that my wife had just given birth to a boy and that both she and the child were doing fine. The first thought that came to my mind was, 'The one thing I fear most is that this boy will grow up to be a homosexual. I hope I never live to see that day.' And so, in order to prevent that terrible thing from happening, I bought him these porno books when he was three and four years old. I bought both homosexual and heterosexual porno books. I showed him the pictures in each and explained to him how the things that the men were doing to each other were *bad* and how the things these men and women were doing together were *good.* When he was thirteen years old, and started to mature physically, I told him that he never has to worry about sexual frustration because I was going to take him to a 'nice lady' who was going to teach him about sex. So I took him to a house of prostitution where he had his first experience with a woman. I told him that anytime he wanted money to go back I would give it to him. And last night, doctor, the thing I was most terrified of, occurred. The military police came and informed me that they had found him in bed with a sergeant engaged in homosexual activities."

This boy was almost doomed to become homosexual, so great were the father's unconscious pressures on him to go in this direction. His compliance was in part related to the boy's recognition, at some level, that a homosexual was exactly what his father wanted him to be. In the 1940s, during the author's teenage period, there was a song entitled "Your Lips Tell Me No No, But There's Yes Yes In Your Eyes." It is quite likely that this mechanism was one factor operative in this boy's compliance with his father's basic wishes. Some verification of this in this case was obtained by me subsequently when I learned that the father wanted exact details about the nature of the boy's homosexual involvement. It was clear that he was gaining vicarious gratification from these explanations.

M. Bowen (1978) describes the "family projection process" in

which one member of the family (usually a parent) will project onto
a child his or her own problems and bring the child for treatment
for that problem. A mother, for example, may project onto the child
fears and worries about herself. The child accepts the projection
in order to accommodate the mother. An excellent example of this
phenomenon is to be found in the separation anxiety disorder
wherein the child takes on the mother's fears of the world and views
it as similarly anxiety provoking. The child goes further, however,
and actually acquires the mother's complex psychodynamic patterns that are utilized to deal with anger, namely, reaction formation, projection, and withdrawal (Gardner, 1984). These examples
of the projection process in understanding the psychodynamics of
family pathology are strong testamonies to the author's previously
mentioned aphorism that "Life Is a Rorschach Test." There are the
external realities and the projections that we place on them. Both
elements are real. And the final reality is the sum of both factors.
Family treatment must help all parties separate the external physical reality from the projections that are placed on them. Parents
must be helped to see their children as being a combination of what
they really are and what they view them to be. Similarly, children
must be helped to isolate these components in their views of their
parents. In the process of such treatment all individuals develop
more accurate and individual definitions of themselves, which are
quite different from those roles that they were originally viewed to
have in the family.

The Constructive and Cohesive Factors
in Pathological Interactions

It is important for the reader to appreciate that pathological modes
of interaction between and among family members are not 100%
detrimental. They are derived in an attempt to establish some kind
of an equilibrium and generally provide benefits in spite of the pains
and discomforts attendant to their perpetuation. Once again, an example from my military experience demonstrates this point quite
well. An elderly couple once came to me for consultation, at the
initiation of the wife. He was 86 and she 83, and they had been
married 63 years. They lived near a central military hospital in
Frankfurt am Main, Germany, where I was stationed. (Retired military people often choose to live near military hospitals where they
can receive free medical care and live close to other military reti-

rees.) The wife described things as having gone well during the first 61 years or so of the marriage, stating that her husband was a good man, and did not gamble, drink, or run around with other women. Furthermore, he was a devoted husband, father, grandfather, and great-grandfather. Accordingly, they had never sought counseling before. (I always like a "fresh case," so that I don't have to deal with statements like, "Well, doctor so and so said . . . " and "You know, doctor, the other person we saw has a very different opinion.")

The wife then went on to tell me that during the previous two years her husband had become progressively more preoccupied with accusations of infidelity. It was not simply that he was perpetually accusing her of being unfaithful, but he was accusing her of having a special attraction for young recruits, ages 18 to 20. His suspicions reached the point where he would hardly leave her alone and when with her his allegations were continual. When she would go shopping at the PX, for example, on her return he would confront her: "Well, as I figure it, it should have taken you an hour and a half. It should have taken you a half hour to get there, a half hour to shop, and a half hour to get back. It's taken you an hour and three-quarters. I know you had a 'quickie' in the alley with one of those young soldiers." No amount of reasoning on the wife's part was successful in dispelling her husband's delusion. Her argument that she had no such inclinations proved futile. Her attempts to prove that her absences did not take longer than necessary were again resonded to with incredulity and accusations that she was lying.

By the end of the interview it became apparent to me that if I had a pill that could magically dispel this old man's delusions, I would have done both him and his wife a disservice. Both of them were deriving important psychological gratifications from the symptom, their ostensible complaints notwithstanding. From the husband's point of view, it was not that he had a wife who was old and less attractive than she was 63 years previously. Rather, his wife was still so attractive that young men in their late teens would choose her over far younger women who were clearly available. The symptom, therefore, enabled him to deny the unpleasant reality of his wife's aging. It also provided him with the enhanced self-worth associated with his belief that at his age he had such an attractive wife. And there were similar gratifications for the wife. Her protestations notwithstanding, she was flattered by her husband's belief that she was still so pretty that young men would prefer her over peers. And both of them utilized the discussions over the delusion as a way of filling up the vacuum of their empty lives. Accordingly, as mentioned, if I indeed had a pill to dispel this delusion I would have deprived them both of valuable psychological benefits. It was from this recognition that I advised them to try to fill their lives more meaningfully by taking advantage of the many services that the military had available for such individuals. Furthermore, I advised them to involve themselves in various programs for the elderly back in the United States where they were soon planning to move.

In addition to recognizing the positive benefits that family members may derive from psychopathological processes, the therapist must appreciate how deep-seated the psychopathological interpersonal patterns can be and that they are often generations in the making. In fact, they may be so formidable that their alleviation or cure might result in the individual's becoming a pariah from the family, so different will the person become. I do not believe that therapists give proper appreciation to this factor in explaining therapeutic failure. If, as a result of the treatment, the individual becomes entirely different from his or her extended family, it is not likely that the therapy will be successful. The so-called "cure" is too heavy a price to pay—entailing, as it will, total removal and isolation from one's family.

This phenomenon was well demonstrated by a 22-year-old young woman I saw a number of years ago. Her presenting complaint was that she found herself gravitating toward young men who would maltreat her; when treated more benevolently, she became tense, anxious, and even found herself provoking her dates into treating her hostiley. She suspected that something might be wrong with her, but wasn't sure. The girl grew up in a blue-collar home in northern New Jersey (pertinent to this discussion). When she was 14 years old, she told her parents that she wanted to go to college. Her father responded by beating her, while accusing her of trying to be superior to the rest of her family. He claimed that no one in their extended family had ever gone to college and there was no reason why she should do so. Over the next few years she continually prevailed upon her parents to let her go to college and, finally, with some minimal assistance from her mother, her father agreed to let her go with very stringent provisions. The most important of these was that she would have to pay her entire school expenses by working in his gasoline station, which was on the West

Side of Manhattan (across the river from New Jersey) in an extremely rough and dangerous neighborhood. Furthermore, she would have to begin work at 5:00 in the morning, when he opened the gas station, and work there until about 8:00 A.M., when she then went off to school. He always paid her minimum wages and this was the source of the financing of her education. There was hardly a day when she was not propositioned, physically mauled in a sexual way, and even exposed to a few attempted rapes. When she would complain to her father about these indignities, he invariably scoffed and told her that it was her imagination, even though the advances were often made in situations when her father could easily have overheard or even seen what was happening. At the time that I saw her, the girl had graduated from college and was working as a secretary in a typical white-collar position.

It is my usual practice to invite the nearest of kin of all of my patients for a family interview, regardless of the age of my patient. In this case, as she was their only child, I invited her parents to join us in one of our early sessions. Her mother accepted the invitation but her father rejected it, claiming that he did not "believe in" psychiatry. Besides, he is reported to have said that he did not think his daughter had any psychiatric problems anyway. Accordingly, I saw the girl and her mother. Early in the interview I asked the mother what problems she considered her daughter to have. She replied, "Doctor, my daughter is perfectly fine. She doesn't have any problems, I don't know why she's coming here." When I asked her what her daughter had told her about the reasons for her visits, she replied, "I know that she thinks she has a problem with boys. She says that she often finds herself trying to get them to treat her badly, and even to hit her. I don't know why she's talking about that as if it was a problem. All men hit their wives. That's normal."

I then asked the mother if she was quite sure that "all" men hit their wives and that there were no exceptions. She replied, "Doctor, my husband's always hit me, all my sisters are beaten by their husbands, and all my brothers beat their wives. My father beat my mother, all my uncles beat my aunts, and all my aunts were beaten by their husbands. My grandfather beat my grandmother, etc., etc." I then asked her if she could conceive of the possibility that there might be marriages in which husbands did not beat their wives. She responded that she would not believe any man who claimed that he didn't beat his wife, nor would she believe any woman who claimed that she wasn't hit by her husband.

With this family background it is not difficult to see what was happening with this girl. When she went to college, she found herself in an entirely unique environment—different from any she had ever experienced. She found herself with young men who treated her benevolently. With them she was like a "fish out of water." And, when she went into the business world, she found herself in a similar situation. In order to make her relationships with boys more familiar, she would provoke them in the hope that they would treat her badly and even hit her. This is what she knew, this is what she was used to, and this was familiar. What is strange is often very anxiety provoking.

This girl's situation reminded me of the comment of Tevya, the father in the movie and play *Fiddler on the Roof*. In one of his moving soliloquies, dealing with his shock on learning that his daughter is going to marry a Gentile young man, he looks up to the heavens and says, "I could understand, God, how a bird might fall in love with a fish. But where would they live?" This girl was basically a masochist. All known females in her extended family, back as many generations as one could go, were masochists. And all of them found sadists for husbands. One could almost predict at the time of her birth that she too would become a masochist. Certainly, other factors were probably operative in bringing about her masochism. However, what I have described above was, I believe, the most formidable and significant component.

I describe this patient's situation here because it demonstrates so well my point that a patient's symptomatology, although presented as an individual problem, may be deeply rooted in family processes—processes that may go back many generations. With such a heritage, with such powerful contributing factors, the therapist must have very modest goals in the treatment of such symptoms. And even when close work with the family is possible, the chances of alleviation may be minimal.

The Family of the Schizophrenic Patient

During my residency days in the late 1950s, when the influence of the psychoanalytic movement was very strong, many therapists viewed schizophrenia to be primarily psychogenic in etiology. There was much talk about the so-called "schizophrenigenic mother." Theories abounded about how such mothers would create schizphrenia in their children through their rejection and especially by their "double bind" communications. These were messages in which their words basically said one thing and their intonations and gestures another. In line with this belief, many therapists considered family therapy to offer the best hope for schizophrenic patients.

Most psychiatrists and psychologists these days tend to view schizophrenia as primarily, if not exclusively, a manifestation of organic disease of the brain. My own view is that there are some individuals whose genetic loading for the development of schizophrenia is so high that they are born psychotic. There are others whose high genetic loading results in schizophrenic symptomatology exhibiting itself in the early years of life. In such cases the usual frustrations of life are enough to bring them over the threshold of illness. Moving along the continuum, there is a whole range of individuals from those who have a high to those with a low predisposition for developing the disorder. The latter, at the low predisposition end of the continuum, will only develop psychotic symptomatology under conditions of extreme and/or prolonged psychological trauma, for example, uninterrupted exposure to battlefield conditions or involvement in massive catastrophies such as volcano eruptions, earthquakes, plagues, and similar catastrophic events. With this view, I am not in agreement with those family therapists who utilize family therapy as a primary therapeutic modality for schizophrenic patients. By their own admission, they will agree that it is, at best, a long and arduous process with limited possibilities of success. I believe that family therapy may be helpful to such individuals by reducing additional pathological processes as well as helping families cope with having to live with the handicapped family member. But this is a far different goal from that of family therapists who believe that the illness is primarily if not exclusively psychogenic.

TECHNICAL CONSIDERATIONS WHEN CONDUCTING FAMILY THERAPY

Conducting the Treatment in the Home

It is of interest that H. Von Hug-Hellmuth (1913, 1921) suggested that the child's psychoanalyst see the child in his or her own home setting. She recognized that the child would be more likely to be comfortable at home and that the therapist might be able to make observations and gain information that might not so readily become available in the office setting. As a pioneer, her recommendation might have resulted in this practice becoming a standard pattern. However, this is rarely done. I suspect an important factor relates to time that would be lost by the therapist with such travel, time that could be spent with one or two other patients. In addition, for most patients, having the therapist come to the home would add an additional expense to treatment. Although I have no personal experience with doing family therapy in homes, I have conducted home visits on some occasions and from these experiences my views were derived. I believe that the aforementioned principles hold with family therapy. The parents might be more relaxed and spontaneous in their own home and provide information that might not become available so readily in the office setting. The children especially are more likely to be spontaneous. I suspect, however, that these advantages are very soon outweighed by the disadvantages. The time expenditure and cost probably soon negate the benefits to be derived from doing the treatment in the home. Furthermore, I believe that the pressure of the pathological forms of interaction are so formidable that they will generally exhibit themselves in any setting.

Team Therapists

Many hold that when doing family therapy it is better to have a male-female team serving as therapists rather than a single therapist. Those who propose the team approach almost invariably recommend that it be a male-female team, rather than two therapists of the same sex. Like all other things in life, there are advantages and disadvantages to the arrangement. One advantage is that the therapists are likely to emerge as mother and father figures and the family then will have a set of "parents" upon whom they can project and transfer various feelings. In such an arrangement it may be that the "parents" will be split into a "good" and a "bad" parent. Such "splitting" may be used therapeutically, but it may contribute to rivalrous feelings between the therapists. This is not as likely to take place with a single male or female therapist. Other kinds of parentification may take place between family members and the co-therapists, involvements that are not as likely to arise with a single therapist.

In order for this arrangement to work, it is extremely important that the team members have a good relationship, in their private and personal lives as well as in their group experiences. If their interaction is significantly pathological it is likely to contaminate significantly the family's treatment. In all human relationships there is likely to be some competition. If, in the family therapy situation, the family starts exhibiting preferences for one therapist over the other (no matter how pathological such preferences may be), it may be difficult for the therapists not to exhibit some competitive/rivalrous feelings themselves. If the competition so engendered is mild and can be considered within the normal range, then it might be openly discussed with the family and dealt with properly. However, if it becomes accentuated and pathological components enter, then this competition might be detrimental to the family's treatment. Time spent on working through the pathological rivalry between the co-therapists diverts focus away from the family—compromising significantly the family's treatment—notwithstanding the possible benefits to be gained from observing such working through. And, if time is not spent on this pathological competitiveness, then it will surreptitiously interfere with the family's treatment.

Another risk of co-therapists treating a family is that a covert sexual/amorous relationship may evolve, if it was not present prior to the family's involvement with the therapists. A man and a woman working closely together on the same project, especially if they are deeply committed to it, are likely to find other feelings emerging as they work together. If these are mild and are dealt with in an ongoing stable relationship, then there should be no problems with the family's treatment. If, however, the relationship is a tempestuous one, then this is likely to contaminate the therapy. Or, if one of the therapists becomes involved with a third party, an involvement that induces feelings of jealous rivalry, then this too is likely to contaminate the family's treatment in that the therapists are not likely then to have a good working relationship. These kinds of problems are rarely discussed, but I believe they are quite common. The ideal arrangement, then, for co-therapists is that they be involved in their own relationships, which are stable and gratifying, so that there is little temptation to involve themselves in a sexual/amorous relationship with one another. If this is not the case, family therapy can still be viable if their relationship is strictly a professional one, with so little inclination for sexual/romantic involvement that the occasional urges in this area that may arise are easily contained.

The Utilization of Other Parties in the Family's Treatment

In the previous section, I have discussed the theoretical aspects of bringing other people into the family's treatment. Here I focus more on the technical aspects. I believe that it behooves therapists to take a flexible approach with regard to inviting other parties into the treatment. A crucial determinant should be how valuable the other party can be, both as a source of information and as a person who should justifiably be involved in the ongoing treatment. My experience has been that a housekeeper can provide valuable information in that she lives in the home and is generally party to many of the pathological involvements that the therapist wishes to focus on. However, an obvious drawback to her involvement is that she may fear compromising herself in at least two ways. First, her divulgences might alienate one or more family members and this might contribute to a compromise of her relationship with such a party(ies). There may even be the risk that she may lose her job if she alienates significantly a powerful individual in the family, someone who could be instrumental in forcing her to leave her position. When I meet with a housekeeper, I generally do so in the presence of the other members of the family. In this way, I do not provide opportunities to be given "secrets" that might compromise my position with the family. (Having pertinent information that one is not free to reveal to patients is a serious compromise of treatment.) Under these circumstances the therapist must recognize that the housekeeper may be withholding information (for the aforementioned reasons). Nevertheless, she can still be a valuable source of information in the data-collection process. However, I have not yet seen fit to involve her in ongoing treatment. I suspect, however, that there may be situations in which such involvement may be warranted and even useful.

A grandparent, as well, can be a valuable source of information and I have occasionally brought in the grandparent(s) during the data-collection process. On occasion, I have seen fit to invite the grandparent(s) for occasional follow-up meetings with the family. Although I can theoretically envision a situation in which one or more grandparents might be involved in ongoing treatment, I have not yet had the occasion for such treatment. I suspect that a situation in which it would be indicated would be one in which the grandparent lives in the home and then is indeed a member of the psychological nuclear family. J.L. Framo (1982) brings in the family of origin in consultation (not on an ongoing basis) as part of the initial evaluation. In these sessions each of the parents is seen alone with his or her own parents, but the grandchildren are not present. The purpose here is to observe the kinds of interaction each of the parents have with their own parents, because such modes of interaction are likely to reproduce themselves in the marriage and in the family therapy. Gaining this information is accomplished best by focusing on each parent's life as a child in the home of the grandparents, rather than on the marriage itself. Of course, this does not preclude the therapist's gaining information from the grandparents about their observations of the parents and their grandchildren.

The way in which a grandmother's involvement proved useful in the therapy of a child was well demonstrated by a six-year-old boy whose mother brought him to treatment with the chief complaints that he was not paying attention in school and not responsive to the teacher's warnings that if he did not "shape up" he would not be promoted. He seemed to be oblivious to these threats. He did little homework and hardly concentrated in the classroom. The child's father was in jail for embezzling money from the bank where he had worked. I saw the child while his father was in jail and he was then living with his mother and paternal grandmother (who had moved into the house to help her daughter-in-law while her son was in jail).

In the family interview (mother, patient, and maternal grandmother) it emerged that the paternal grandmother was extremely indulgent and hardly ever provided the child with consequences for inappropriate behavior. She had to be the all-giving mother and could not tolerate the possibility of the child's being angry at her. In fact, although in her mid-sixties, her life-long pattern had been to avoid whenever possible people's becoming angry at her, and this was extended to her grandchildren. Having grown up in a household where there were rarely consequences for his noncompliance, it was not surprising that the patient was similarly noncompliant in the classroom. Although I only saw the grandmother

once, the information so gained proved valuable in this boy's subsequent therapy and played an important role in alleviation of his
symptoms.

Changing the Family's Concept
of the "Designated Patient"

As mentioned, there are situations in which individual work is warranted. I discuss here the situation in which the designated patient
serves to help the rest of the family members avoid looking at their
problems. When conducting family therapy there is the risk that
the therapist will go along with the family and agree that the *designated patient* is the only one who has problems and that other
family members are the healthy ones. This may work well as a starting point, in getting a handle on the problems, but one must expand
the pathology concept quickly into the total family network and
delineate the role that each member plays in the so-called patient's
difficulties. The therapist may not be successful in this regard in
that in order to achieve this goal it is necessary to convince all family members that they are involved in the development and perpetuation of the patient's psychopathology. If the therapist is not
successful in convincing all members, then he or she does best to
treat only those members who are committed. As mentioned, using
guilt and/or coercion as maneuvers for enlisting the involvement
of the noncommitted is likely to work against the goals of the treatment. Such parties will balk and add new problems that may not
previously have been present.

The Therapeutic Ally

In the evaluative process it is important that the therapist ascertain
whether or not there are individuals who can serve as a *therapeutic
ally*. Generally, this will be an individual who is healthier than the
others or, at least, is healthier than others with regard to the major
area of pathology. An example of this would be a father who is
aware of the fact that his son, who is suffering with a separation
anxiety disorder, is involved with a mother who is overprotective.
Often fathers in such families are passive and dependent in their
relationships with their wives, view the overprotection as an asset,
and will go along with the mother's view of herself as a super-
mother, as someone who cares for her child more than other moth-

ers who are considered to be neglectful. If, however, the father has been complaining about the symbiotic relationship for years, then he may be a valuable therapeutic ally. Such an ally has firsthand information which can be extremely useful in the therapy.

Not only is the therapeutic ally an important source of information, but his or her confrontations may very well result in less defensiveness by other family members than the same confrontations provided by the therapist. In addition, the presence of such a person increases the likelihood that the treatment will be successful, in that one has an "inside" person working along with the therapist. The presence of such an individual can also decrease the likelihood that the family will quit treatment. If there is no one in the family who recognizes the psychopathology, all may "close ranks" in response to the anxiety-provoking confrontations that arise inevitably in the treatment—and then the family may leave en masse. A family member might be able to rationalize quitting therapy in response to an unpleasant confrontation provided by the therapist, but it is far more difficult to justify leaving when one's husband or wife has provided the confrontation.

Another advantage of the therapeutic ally is that the therapist can prevent or reduce the likelihood of denial and rationalization. For the therapist to say, "I view you as a person who is . . . " may be responded to with, "Well, Doctor, that 's your opinion. It tells me that you don't know me very well." However, when a family member says the same thing, one cannot so readily use this form of refutation. In addition, it gives the therapist the opportunity to say, "Your husband says . . . What do you think about this?" When three or four family members say the same thing, then it is even more difficult for one party to refute the validity of the confrontation. Confrontation by "insiders" is more likely to be "heard" than confrontation from the therapist, who is an "outsider." But even then, the party who is being confronted may respond with, "There's a conspiracy going on here. All of you are going along with him(her) and are afraid to say what you really think." There are two possibilities here. The first is that this indeed is a rationalization and the confronting parties have a valid point. The second is that there *is* a conspiracy and that the "accused" person's statement is valid, namely, that everyone is falling into line with a dominant accuser. It behooves a therapist to contribute his or her own opinions on this and, whichever turns out to be the case, to pursue the issue therapeutically.

"Letting It All Hang Out"

From what has just been described, the reader might conclude that family therapy is excessively confrontational, and little if any respect is given to defense mechanisms or to the need of people not to discuss certain issues. *This is not the case.* The skilled family therapist does not subscribe to the rule of "letting it all hang out." This can be used sadistically and antitherapeutically. In fact, even in the best marriages, it is preferable that certain things not be spoken about. The purpose of a revelation is not merely to reveal it for it's own sake. Its purpose is to do something constructive with it. To use a revelation in this way, it must be made benevolently. We are not dealing here with individual psychoanalysis—that is, family members are not being exposed to the free associations. There are some naive individuals (sometimes supported by therapists) who indiscriminately utilize, in marriage or family therapy, principles applicable to the analytic situation. This can be extremely destructive. The rule that one must tell all to the psychoanalyst still holds. This should not be carried over to a rule that one must tell all to all members of one's family. Some material is justifiably the individual's own personal business, and the revelation of such information may be detrimental to other family members. For example, all human relationships are ambivalent and the relationships between family members are no exception. In fact, it is in the family that the strongest feelings, both loving and hateful, are likely to arise. And some of the hateful feelings may be quite sadistic at times, even in the normal family. Furthermore, there may be certain information that may be of concern to certain family subsystems, but not to the entire family. An example of this would be a sexual problem that exists between the parents. In our society, we generally do not consider it judicious for parents to discuss the details of their sex life with their children, although the personality patterns that have contributed to and result from the sexual problem are of interest to the children who are and/or have been exposed to these patterns. The details of the sexual act need not be exposed, whereas the personality patterns related to the sexual problems might very well be. In such situations the therapist does well to set aside special times for the treatment of the subsystems, with all family members being aware that such separate subsystem treatment is taking place.

Transferential Reactions

There are some family therapists who hold that transferential reactions are not as likely to emerge in the family therapy setting as
they are in the individual psychoanalytic situation. The argument
here is that the transference tends to get diffused by the presence
of other people and that the absence of free associations may also
reduce the likelihood of transferential reactions occurring. I am not
in agreement with this position. I believe that the tendency to transfer feelings from one's own parents (or other significant caretakers
of childhood) to other individuals in one's life, a therapist or members of one's own present family, is extremely powerful. In fact, I
believe the pressure for such transference is so powerful that it is
not significantly reduced by the presence of other parties in the
room. The pressure for expression of these thoughts and feelings
and the need to involve oneself in these kinds of relationships is
formidable. Individuals who are likely to fit in with the psychopathological pattern are identified quite early, and attempts to involve them in these relationships are likely to appear regardless of
the number of the people in the room and in spite of the failure to
have the opportunity to free associate. I believe classical pychoan-
alysts are somewhat grandiose here with regard to their view of the
exclusivity of the analytic transferential reaction. The analyst is just
one among many others with whom the pathological transferential
reaction is likely to exhibit itself. I admit that the analytic situation
is unique with regard to what one can do with such reactions, but
this is a separate issue from that of the likelihood of their appearance.

There are some who argue that the family therapy situation
does not permit the kind of depth relationship that serves optimally
as the foundation for therapy. As discussed in Chapter Seven, I do
not consider the depth of the therapist-patient relationship to be
determined significantly by the number of people in the room;
rather, it is determined by the personality qualities of the individuals involved in the relationship. In a sense, one can view the family therapy situation as being one in which there is now a new
member in the family (or members if there are co-therapists). Although the therapist is certainly different from other family members, there are certain similarities with regard to the possibility of
a deep relationship forming. The notion that family therapy nec-

essarily dilutes this possibility is similar to the idea that a parent who has two or three children is less likely to provide each of them with the optimum kind of love that a parent with an only child can give. This quantification theory of affection is not consistent with the reality of the human personality. We have it within our power to have affectionate relationships with a number of people. I am not saying hundreds of people, only a number of people. I am particularly vague regarding my use of the word "number" because it would be simpleminded to try to ascertain what that particular number could be. It varies with each individual, and it varies with the nature and the depth of the various kinds of relationships in which the person is involved. However, that number is certainly greater than the number of people in the overwhelming majority of nuclear families.

The Family Therapy–Individual Therapy Combination

Family therapy sometimes involves what can be best described as *individual therapy in the presence of other family members.* There are times when material will emerge from one participant that warrants individual focus by the therapist. At such times impromptu individual work with that person may be warranted, even though other family members are present. Ideally, such interactions should not comprise a significant percentage of the family sessions. If they do, then one must consider whether individual therapy of one or more of the participating parties may be the more efficient therapeutic modality. To require people to come every session to just sit and observe the individual treatment of one or two other parties is not likely to prove very useful and may be wasteful. I am not claiming that it is of no value at all, it is just that the benefits derived by the observers may be so little that they are far outweighed by the disadvantages of their attending every session. Furthermore, when conducting such therapy, the therapist must use his or her judgment regarding revelations that might prove detrimental to the observers. My general experience has been that when it is the child who requires such focus, there is little danger of anything deleterious coming out. When it is one of the parents, however, revelations may be detrimental, and the therapist has to attempt then to detect when the individual work is becoming risky. Under such circumstances it may be advisable to conduct an individual session, with the full awareness on the part of the family that such an interview is taking place. There is no problem setting up such an appointment if, early in the treatment, the provision for such individual counseling is discussed and the justification for private interviews agreed upon by all family members. However, and this point is important, when conducting such interviews they must be done with the understanding that the interviewee will allow the therapist to use his or her judgment in deciding whether or not and what to reveal of the information so provided. Without such license, the family therapy is likely to be jeopardized significantly, if not compromised completely. It is during the evaluative sessions that the therapist should be able to obtain enough information to ascertain whether or not a significant number of secrets are present, and if so, not recommend family treatment. There are some family therapists who rigidly oppose any individual sessions. I believe they are making a mistake. They are preventing the working through of certain problems which are best discussed individually. Strict exclusion of individual sessions only drives underground information that is likely to be extremely important to disclose.

The Talking, Feeling, and Doing Game in Family Therapy

I first began using *The Talking, Feeling, and Doing Game* (Gardner, 1973b) in 1970. It was only published after about three years of my working intensively with this instrument. On occasion, a child would ask me if his or her mother could play along with us. Without any preconceived notions as to whether or not this would be a good idea, I invited the mother to join us. Most often, I found the idea to be a bad one. The mother would play only hesitantly, recognizing that she was revealing personal material that she did not want disclosed to the child. Accordingly, she would censor her answers. But even then, what did come out was often more related to her own situation than to the child's. Accordingly, I found myself like a surgeon who has patients in two separate operating rooms and is trying to operate simultaneously on both of them. As a result of these experiences I discouraged participating parents from playing the game during the children's individual therapeutic sessions. However, over the years conference participants would often tell me about how valuable they found the game in family therapy. I was initially confused by these reports because this was the opposite of my own experience. Furthermore, I felt uncomfortable proposing the game to the vast majority of the parents whom I was seeing in association with their children.

I subsequently realized that many of the conference participants were working with families with low educational levels and/or psychological sophistication. Often these were people who had difficulty expressing their inner-most thoughts and feelings. They needed *The Talking, Feeling, and Doing Game* as a vehicle for such expression. In contrast, the parents I was seeing in my practice were mainly upper-middle-class people who generally were more educated, more psychologically sophisticated, and more appreciative of the introspective process. They didn't need *The Talking, Feeling, and Doing Game* to help them talk about what was on their minds. In short, if the reader is working with families who are less educated and sophisticated, then *The Talking, Feeling, and Doing Game* may prove valuable, but my own direct experience with this utilization in family therapy has been limited.

Clinical Example

Bob and Sally were five and three years old respectively when their parents separated. The family lived in a large Eastern city. Their mother remained in the apartment with the children, and the father took an apartment in a nearby neighborhood. He was reliable, attentive, and provided the children with meaningful parental input. About a year later the father met another woman and a year after that moved to a suburban community. He still remained loyal and dutiful to the children and would take them to his suburban home during his weekend visitations. One day, when the children were about eight and six, the mother appeared at the father's doorstep with the children and announced that she had met a man who lived 200 miles away, she was going to live with him, and he could now have permanent and complete custody of the children. The mother explained that the father now had a full family with a suburban home and that he could provide the children with a much better life than she. She said she thought it would be in the children's best interests that she have limited if any contact with them again. And so the children moved in with their father and stepmother. The father's new wife had not previously been married, had married the children's father during her mid-thirties, and welcomed the opportunity to have a "whole family" at this relatively late period in her life.

During the next five years the children did not see their mother at all, but did occasionally receive a Christmas present. Then, she suddenly appeared at the father's home and announced that she wished to visit with the children once again on an ongoing basis. The father's response was to permit the mother to visit the children, but he absolutely refused to finance their air transportation (which he could well afford) or even involve himself in any transportation to airports if the mother were to pay for flights (which he knew she was ill-equipped to do). Rather, he insisted that if the mother wished to see the children she would have to pick them up herself and return them to her home. For each weekend visitation she would have to leave her home early Saturday morning, drive four to five hours, pick the children up, and then return home with them. If she was lucky with regard to the traffic, this took all day. She would spend Saturday evening and Sunday morning with the children. Then, on Sunday afternoon, she would drive them back (usually hitting Sunday evening traffic), and then return back to her home. Thus a weekend of visitation would generally involve 16 to 18 hours of driving. The father was so intent on punishing his former wife for what she had done that he had blinded himself to the fact that he was also causing his children to suffer the discomforts of such unnecessary travel.

There had never been anything but an extremely strained relationship between the mother and stepmother. When the mother would call the home to arrange for visitations, the stepmother would not even engage in innocuous amenities, but would immediately turn the phone over to her husband saying, "It's her." When the mother would arrive to pick up the children she was not permitted in the home; rather, she was required to honk the horn outside and the children would be sent out. And this situation prevailed during the seven-year period of "rapprochement," at the end of which my services were enlisted. At that point the mother was planning to litigate for more money in order to get some relief from this oppressive visitation program. However, all had decided to try to avoid litigation and seek a consultation outside of the legal process.

During my initial evaluation it became apparent that the children were contributing significantly to the polarization of the mother from her former husband and his wife. Although now in their teens, they were still saying to each parent what they believed that parent wanted to hear. Accordingly, each parent was brought to believe that the other was the incarnation of all the evil that existed on earth. After a visit with their mother, the children would tell their stepmother and father what a terrible time they had and how many indignities they suffered at her hands. Similarly, when with their mother they would describe the terrible conditions under which they lived in their father's home. Having no direct communication with one another, the parents were in no position to appreciate that they each were being "buttered up" in order to gain affection. This is one of the important ways in which the litigious process enhances and perpetuates alienation. Without having the opportunity to have direct contact with the other side, the worst distortions become entrenched and delusions of malevolence are likely to persist. And this is especially the case when the children, from the fear of rejection, feed into the process by their fabrications.

After seeing the suburban family in varying combinations, and after seeing the mother alone (she travelled the 200 miles to my office for the purpose of the interview), I recommended an interview in which the three adults, the two children, and myself would be present. The father and stepmother were horrified at this suggestion and initially refused to discuss it further. The mother, although reluctant, was more receptive. Finally, I was able to prevail upon the father and stepmother to try one such interview and to use experience rather than speculation to make their decision regarding whether or not they wished to participate. Accordingly, an open-ended interview was set up.

When the interview began it was quite clear that all the parties were quite tense. I believe that the parents were tense because they anticipated the worst kinds of treatment from each other. And the children were tense, I suspected, because they realized that their lying would be disclosed. Within about a half hour everyone became more relaxed and the adults began to appreciate that they were not indeed the ogres that they had viewed one another to be. In the ten years that the stepmother and mother knew one another they had never really had one civil conversation. The actual experience for each one of being in the same room with and seeing that the other was a human being, without horns, without fire or poison spitting from her mouth, was successful in correcting their distortions. Years of separate psychotherapy would not have accomplished this. They next came to appreciate that they had been "buttered up" by the children. Interestingly, as is often the case, the children showed little regret over the troubles their fabrications had caused.

In the ensuing discussion the father came to understand that he was so enraged at his former wife that he had blinded himself to the fact that he was causing his children unnecessary distress by insisting that the mother assume all the travel obligations of visitation. Accordingly, he agreed to drop the children off at the airport and to pick them up there on their return, as well as contribute to the financing of the air travel. As the meeting drew to a close the father stated that he thought it had been quite useful and invited his former wife to join him, his wife, and the children at his home for further discussion. All agreed that this could prove useful. The result was a resolution of the primary problems without resorting to adversary litigation. I am convinced that had this family not chosen this more judicious course they would have involved themselves in extremely expensive and psychologically draining litigation which would have been far less likely to have solved their difficulties.

There is another important principle demonstrated here. It relates to a phenomenon that may initially appear to the reader to be totally unrelated, but is very much applicable. I am referring to the appreciation by airport officials that when hijackers have seized a plane and threaten destruction of the passengers if their demands are not complied with, it behooves the airport officials to stall the hijackers as much as possible. They recognize that the longer they are successful in keeping the hijackers on the ground, the less the likelihood they will murder the hostages. They know that, at the time that the plane is seized, the passengers are generally viewed as subhuman creatures, as people of a different race, religion, or creed—whose lives are not worth very much. If the hijackers and the passengers are required to remain together for long periods, it is likely that they will get to speak with one another and that the hijackers will see similarities between the hostages and their loved ones at home. They are likely to compare the passengers with relatives and friends and find that all human beings, all over the world, regardless of race, religion, or creed, basically want very similar things for themselves and their families. Specifically, they want their children to grow up physically healthy, reasonably educated, with the opportunity to become self-sufficient, independent human beings capable of supporting themselves and their families with a reasonable degree of comfort and freedom from fear and disease. They come to appreciate that everyone has aspirations and disappointments, hopes realized and hopes dashed. Once such familiarity has been experienced, the hostages are no longer viewed as vile and worthless creatures, and it becomes far less probable that they will be slaughtered. The same phenomenon was operative in the group family session described above and is one of the ways in which family therapy can achieve results that may be difficult—if not impossible—to obtain in individual treatment.

CONCLUDING COMMENTS

I have said previously that doing child psychotherapy is like juggling three greasy balls, any one of which may slip—resulting in a failure of the whole performance. This analogy holds even more in family therapy. Here, one may have five or six greasy balls. When one or two is lost from the act there is still enough to continue, but the treatment then becomes compromised. A husband and wife, for example, may have a fight, and one of them may try to hurt the other by refusing to attend the sessions. Similarly, a child may act out and refuse to attend as a hostile retaliatory maneuver. Sessions may be very anxiety provoking and resistant and individuals, who are too defensive to tolerate the confrontations, may leave with flimsy rationalizations: "Everything is okay now, we don't have any more problems," "My wife and I can't take off so much time from work," or "We're quitting. Nothing's happening. We've come six times and our child is no better." We are not dealing here with an analytic patient who is oriented toward analyzing resistances. Rather, we are dealing with a whole family equilibrium that may be threatened by the therapeutic process. Accordingly, people who do family therapy must have a high tolerance for premature removal from treatment.

In recent years, family therapists have attempted to formulate *transactional diagnoses*, rather than diagnoses based on symptoms. As discussed in detail in Chapter Three, psychogenic symptoms represent the most superficial manifestations of the underlying psychodynamic patterns. Similarly, the primary symptoms of family pathology are superficial manifestations of the underlying intrafamilial psychodynamic patterns. Although I believe that the shift in diagnostic focus is admirable, I believe also that it presents formidable difficulties. The underlying psychodynamic patterns (whether they are in the individual or in the family) are multiple, complex, and interrelate with one another as a network. It is difficult enough to delineate these in an individual; it is a far more formidable task to do this with a family. The question then becomes one of which of these multiple patterns should be selected when one is making a family transactional diagnosis. Perhaps one solution to this problem is to list the primary pathological interactional patterns that are applicable to a particular family.

Furthermore, although there may be some similarity between the diagnoses of individuals, there is much greater variability with regard to family patterns. One could say that no two people are alike; but there are at least some people who are similar enough to warrant the same diagnosis, such as elective mutism, paranoia, separation anxiety disorder, and so on. Because there is much greater variability among families, family diagnoses are likely to have far less inter-rater reliability than individual diagnoses. As a result, the communicative value of these transactional diagnoses would probably be even less than that of individual diagnoses. Furthermore, so great is the variability among families that it would be very difficult to find large numbers of families warranting the same diagnosis. Accordingly, I believe we do better at this point to describe the interactional patterns that exist among the various family members, both the total group and the various subgroups. For example, one might say that the husband and wife have a sado-masochistic relationship, and that the son and the mother are involved in a symbiotic relationship in which the son is passively dependent upon an overprotective mother.

In earlier years I was quite reluctant to accept court-ordered patients because they were generally so poorly motivated for treatment that the likelihood of a successful outcome was extremely small. However, I began accepting court-ordered custody evaluations as an impartial examiner, even though one of the parties might have been initially reluctant. I found that I was still able to work effectively under these circumstances and provide the court with useful evaluations. Because both parties were lying anyway, it made no difference whether they came voluntarily or involuntarily (Gardner, 1982, 1986b). More recently, I have also been accepting patients under court-ordered family therapy. Most often, these have been families who have been involved in protracted litigation without full resolution of their conflicts, especially custody conflicts. These have been people whose animosity has been so great that they could not agree to enter treatment voluntarily. Here again, I have met with some success. The situations were ones in which there would have been no possibility for therapy without the court order and the court's power to require such treatment has proved useful. Sometimes the parties have been told that if they do not resolve their differences through treatment, there will be repercussions such as a court decision regarding custody that will definitely be a source of grief to at least one of them. In some states judges have been ordering families, especially parents, into marathon sessions of mediation, with their lawyers present, in order to resolve custody/visitation disputes. There are still formidable problems with such court-ordered treatment. If the parties are strenuously resistant to the idea, then they may go through the motions, but little if anything will be accomplished. Others may overcome initial reluctance and profit immensely from the procedure.

As discussed in detail elsewhere (Gardner, 1982, 1986b), it is injudicious, if not foolhardy, for a person who has served as an impartial examiner in custody litigation to serve subsequently as a family therapist. The parent who has not been supported in the custody conflict is likely to harbor significant animosity toward the evaluator, and this cannot but compromise significantly the family treatment.

FIFTEEN

Concluding Comments

The love of money is the root of all evil.

Bible: I *Timothy, vi,* 10

A penny will hide the biggest star in the universe if you hold it close enough to your eye.

Samuel Grafton

The lust for money breeds corruption—even among psychiatrists.

R.A. Gardner

In this final chapter I will comment on three areas that I believe are justifiably placed at the end of this book. First, this book is based on the *theory* that child psychotherapy can be effective. I will comment here on my views on that issue. Second, I will discuss my views on termination of therapy. Third, I will comment on the field of child psychotherapy at this point and the direction I consider us to be headed in the future.

THE EFFICACY OF CHILD PSYCHOTHERAPY

Most would agree that it is extremely difficult to assess objectively the efficacy of psychotherapy. It is impossible to use control groups because even identical twins do not respond similarly to psychotherapeutic techniques. Even the same therapist could not say that he or she was treating identically each member of such a pair. In addition, there are no two therapists who work the same way. Research projects in which groups receiving "psychotherapy" are compared to groups receiving no treatment or other forms of therapy invariably suffer from the intrinsic weakness of defining exactly what kind of treatment the "psychotherapy" group has received. Often there are a number of therapists, of varying degrees of experience, who had administered the psychotherapy. And what has gone on in the room alone with the patient is basically unknown to the researcher. Even when detailed studies are made of the exact therapeutic transactions, only a small fraction of what has gone on can possibly be known. Even verbatim transcripts and videotapes provide limited information—such is the complexity of the process and so vast is our ignorance of exactly what is happening.

Another factor that makes it difficult to assess psychotherapeutic efficacy is the improvement that often occurs with all patients over the passage of time. Most of us become more judicious in our actions as we grow older, and most of us learn from our experiences. As mentioned, Hans Strupp (1975), who has studied in depth the elements in psychoanalytic psychotherapy that contribute to therapeutic change, considers what he refers to as "lessons in constructive living" to be central to psychotherapeutic improvement. As I have emphasized throughout this book, the more we learn about how to deal better with the inevitable problems and conflicts of life, the less the likelihood we will have to resort to psychopathological ways of adjusting. Psychotherapy helps patients deal more wisely with the inevitable conflicts and frustrations of life.

The child therapist observes such improvement even more dramatically. If a 40-year-old person spends two years in treatment, approximately 5% of his or her life has been devoted to therapy. However, if a seven-year-old child remains in treatment until the age of nine, more than 28% of the child's life has been spent in therapy. The changes that will naturally occur from ages seven to nine are much greater than those that will naturally occur from ages 40 to 42. Nine year olds are generally much more integrated than seven year olds; they are much more predictable in their actions, and are much more receptive to the requests and demands of significant adults in their lives. They are also able to deal better with the problems of life with which they are continually confronted. It is difficult, if not impossible, to know whether the changes that occur during the period from seven to nine are related to treatment or would have occurred anyway. Although I am convinced that the therapeutic experience does modify behavior, this belief is based more on faith than on proof. It is not simply blind faith, however. It is based on experiences that suggest strongly a cause-and-effect relationship between the changes that therapy attempts to effect and the changes that occur in the child's life. In this book I have presented a detailed account of the techniques that I believe can be effective in bringing about such changes.

TERMINATION

For many years I have been dissatisfied with the concept of termination as it is viewed by most psychoanalysts. The criteria for making the decision as to whether or not a patient should leave treatment are usually based on two considerations: 1) the degree of alleviation of symptoms and 2) the degree to which projective material (dreams, projective tests, play fantasies) reveals freedom from psychopathology. Psychoanalysts, especially, are often less concerned with improvements in the first area than they are in the second. When there is symptomatic improvement and the second category reveals pathological processes, a patient may be encouraged to remain in treatment in order to be certain that the problem has been completely "worked through." In adult analysis, especially, one looks for a "termination dream"—a dream that suggests strongly that the problems have not only been worked through (both at the conscious and unconscious levels), but that the patient is ready to leave treatment.

I believe that the primary criteria for deciding whether or not therapy should terminate should be the patient's symptoms. Information obtained from projective material may be highly revealing with regard to underlying psychodynamics, but it is often of little value in providing information as to whether or not a symptom is indeed present. If a symptom is present then one points to the psychodynamics for the explanation. In such cases things seem to fit together. But there are times when projectives suggest the presence of symptoms, and there are no symptoms that correspond directly to the pathologic psychodynamic pattern. We all have psychodynamics and all psychodynamics reveal a certain degree of inappropriate and maladaptive ways of dealing with life situations. When there are no particular symptoms, what does one do with the psychodynamics? I say do nothing. One should treat symptoms, not psychodynamics. I believe that many psychoanalysts do not fully appreciate the implication of what I have just said. What ultimately happens is that the patient provides (often unconsciously) that projective material which will justify to both the analyst and the patient that termination is indeed appropriate. It is at that point that the patient had better "get out quickly"—before new dreams appear that will inevitably reveal psychopathological processes! It is at that point that the analyst had better write his or her article if it is to demonstrate a "complete" analysis.

The whole concept of termination is, I believe, artificial. Life is filled with problems and there will always be new difficulties arising in anyone's life. The vast majority of projectives include resolutions that could be considered inappropriate, maladaptive, or pathological. It is only in extreme cases that we can say with certainty that a particular dream is pathological. It is very difficult to differentiate the dreams of psychotics from those of neurotics and those of so-called "normal" people. Accordingly, the use of projective material for determining when therapy should end is artificial and could result in people being retained in treatment unnecessarily (and indefinitely).

I believe the best position for the therapist to take is one that is similar to that of the general medical practitioner. The patient comes when there is difficulty and continues treatment until the problems are alleviated to a significant degree. At that point the physician tells the patient not to hesitate to return if there is any further trouble, either with that particular difficulty or with others. In such cases the patient does not feel humiliated or embarrassed when there is a continuation of the problem or when new problems arise. People who have had their analyses "terminated" are less likely to return with such comfort. In addition, the analyst who has considered the therapy "terminated" may be similarly reluctant to reinstitute treatment because to do so suggests that the previous analytic work was somehow deficient.

Psychotherapy (of which psychoanalysis is one type) is a life experience that, if successful, enriches and expands one's horizons. It is one of many life experiences that can provide such growth and these can punctuate our lives. When someone asks me *when* the therapy of most of my patients terminates with certainty, I usually say: "When one of us dies." But even then the therapy may not truly be terminated. If it turns out that I am the one to die first (and this is more likely because I am older than most of my patients), the treatment may still continue in that the patient may from time to time think about what went on in the therapy and find useful the things that have been said. So the true answer to that question is: "After both of us have died one can say that the therapy will have truly been terminated." But even then, it may not terminate for the survivors who have profited from the patient's treatment. Henry Brooks Adams said of teachers, "A teacher affects eternity; he can never tell where his influence stops," and this can be true for us therapists, as well.

THE FUTURE OF THE FIELD OF CHILD PSYCHOTHERAPY

Unfortunately, at the present time, I have a pessimistic view about the future of child psychotherapy as a discipline. Many changes are taking place in the world at large, and in medicine in particular, that do not bode well for the future of child psychotherapy. I will first discuss the situation in the world at large, then in medicine, then in child psychiatry, and finally the implications of these changes for child psychotherapists in other disciplines.

The Ever-Burgeoning Psychopathy in American Society

I believe that American society (and many other societies as well) has become increasingly psychopathic in the last 15 to 20 years. This is not only reflected by increasing rates of homicide, rape, arson, and theft, but by more subtle manifestations of self-serving behavior on the part of people in general. Its manifestations are ubiquitous. Children are being sexually abused with increasing frequency, not only by their parents but by their teachers. Anyone willing to pay $25,000 can get a forged medical degree with associated counterfeit credentials. There was a time when London policemen did not carry guns because even the lowest criminals could be relied upon to refrain from shooting an unarmed person. This is no longer the case. With increasing frequency scientists in academic life are submitting falsified data in order to enhance their reputation and chances for promotion. The U.S. government is facing increasing difficulties getting repayment for student loans. In New York City, census collectors in 1980 were filmed sitting in or standing around their cars filling out batches of census forms while listening to rock music. In the same city construction inspectors have refused to accept promotions because they will then be removed from the more lucrative payoffs to be gained on the street. I could continue and I am sure the reader can supply his or her own examples of the increasing psychopathy of our society.

Payment of Fees

When I was in medical school, a physician who required patients to pay his or her fee at the time services were rendered would have been considered materialistic, "money hungry," and "grubby." Bills were sent and it was expected that the vast majority of patients in treatment would have a sense of responsibility with regard to their payments. Any physician now who trusts the vast majority of patients to pay for his or her services in the future is not going to remain in practice very long. Most physicians now unabashedly and unashamedly request that their patients pay at the time services are rendered. In fact, there are many physicians who will not admit a patient to the hospital unless payment is made in advance. This change may not affect significantly practice in other branches of medicine, but it can compromise psychiatric treatment. Implicit in the demand that payment be made at the time services are rendered is the notion of distrust. There is no way to separate the two. The patient is basically being told: "I want you to pay *now*, because I don't trust you to pay me *in the future*." Increasingly, psychiatrists are coming to appreciate that the traditional monthly bill is becoming an anachronism, applicable in simpler times, but no longer consistent with survival in the more cutthroat world of the late 20th century.

At this point I still allow my adult patients to pay me at the end of each month. I take the position that it is better to lose a certain percentage of my billings than to say uniformly to all adult patients that I distrust them. If, however, a patient begins to renege, I am quick to bring this up in treatment and to provide therapeutic justification for more frequent payments or even payment every session. In this situation, distrust cannot be viewed as an inappropriate generalization in which an innocent party is being distrusted because others act in a distrustful way. Rather, my distrust of the patient stems from untrustworthy behavior exhibited by him or her. With my child patients, however, I ask the parents to pay at the time of each session. I am not completely happy with this practice, but it is better than the traditional method because of the high parental default rate I was experiencing increasingly in recent years. The default rate of childrens' parents was higher than that of adult patients who were being seen directly because there was less direct monitoring and surveillance of the parents. Unfortunate as it is, that is the reality of the situation. This practice has not affected my relationship with my child patients because it it not *they* I am distrusting, but their parents. One could argue here that I am compromising my relationship with parents and, therefore, as one who has spoken so much about the importance of the therapist's relationship with parents, I am compromising indirectly my child patients' treatment. I admit to this compromise. My only answer is that I too have to earn a living.

Malpractice Suits

The ever-burgeoning rate of malpractice suits has also had its effect on medicine. At the time of this writing there are neurosurgeons in the greater New York City area who pay a malpractice insurance premium of $105,000 per year. Although this is almost unimaginable, it is true. Young people cannot enter a field in which they have to pay such astronomical premiums starting on the first day they open their offices. Judicious physicians practice what has come to be called "defensive medicine." Here, they must always be thinking about the potential malpractice suit that may be brought in the course of conducting day-to-day medical practice. Tests are ordered which would not previously have been requested because of the remote possibility that they may be accused of being sloppy or negligent. The chances of the test being positive may be one in 100,000, but the spectre of being cross-examined on a witness stand because they failed to order a particular test results in this extra expense to the patient. It appears that there are no longer any such things as naturally occurring birth defects. If a child is born with a congenital anomaly, the parents see nothing inappropriate about suing the obstetrician. The situation has gotten so bad that many OB-GYN practitioners have stopped delivering babies entirely and confine themselves solely to gynecological practice. There are thousands of parents of children with neurologically based learning disabilities who are suing obstetricians. The child may have nothing more wrong with him or her than the fact that the IQ is at the 20th percentile level. Accordingly, a normal variation is given a diagnostic label—a disease—and an innocent obstetrician is then sued for malpractice. Psychiatrists practice with the fear that their reports will be used as evidence in malpractice litigation. Accordingly, they are becoming increasingly cautious about what they say in their reports, and the result is that these are becoming progressively less useful.

I believe that we in medicine should certainly be accountable for our errors and that we should not be immune from malpractice suits. However, we have a malpractice situation here in the United States that is unconscionable. At the present time, there is approximately one lawyer for every 850 people in the population, and the ratio is increasing. There are many hungry lawyers and many doctors who are viewed as being "rich." (Remember the bumper sticker: "Become a doctor and support a lawyer.") Furthermore, we have the despicable practice of the contingency arrangement. Under this program a patient need not put down a cent to institute malpractice litigation. The attorney works for nothing in the hope that he or she will win and thereby receive anywhere from 33 to 50% of the award. Most countries in the world consider this an unsavory practice and it is outlawed. But it cannot be so easily outlawed in the United States because the state legislatures are largely populated by attorneys, the friends and relatives of the malpractice lawyers. The malpractice situation is another example of the general psychopathy of our society—the psychopathy that is compromising the clinical practice of psychiatry.

The Craze for Quick Cures

Another manifestation of the psychopathy in our society that is affecting psychiatric practice is the desire for quick solutions and rapid cures. I believe that the vast majority of patients who interrupt treatment prematurely do so because they are dissatisfied with a therapeutic program that involves effort over a long period. Psychodynamic therapies of the kinds described in this book generally take time, and sometimes a long time. The factors that have contributed to the development of the child's symptoms may have been generations in the making. The child patient may have been exposed to the detrimental environmental influences from the day of birth. It is unreasonable to expect the therapist to undo all these contributing factors in a short period. Yet, most patients want just that. And, as the old law of supply and demand dictates, when there is a demand for something, there will be a supply. When people are willing to pay for the things they are demanding, there will be people who will supply what is being demanded and accept payment for the services they are providing. It matters little whether the product being supplied is of any value. What matters primarily is whether people are willing to pay money for it.

Accordingly, there is an ever-burgeoning supply of practitioners who promise quick solutions. The most influential of these in the field of psychiatry are the so-called "biological psychiatrists." Although there is a wide range of opinions regarding the role of nature vs. nurture among people who espouse this position, their general view is that nature (genes, constitution, metabolic processes, et cetera) is the primary determinant of psychiatric disorder. Theirs is certainly an attractive position. Rather than spend long periods going into background history, rather than undergoing the tedious process of trying to understand underlying psychodynamics, all one has to do is provide a medicine that presumably will correct the biological abnormality that is theorized to be the cause of the disorder. When it comes to asking for grants, these people are obviously at an advantage over those of us who want to investigate the longer and presumably less predictably successful kinds of treatment. Those who fund such research (whether it be the government or other institutions) are more likely to be attracted to these presumably more "cost-effective" forms of treatment.

A parallel situation exists in psychology. Psychodynamically oriented psychologists, who believe that prolonged and intensive psychotherapies are likely to be the most efficacious, are not being viewed benevolently by those who provide money for research, training, and teaching. Rather, behavior therapists who believe that inquiry into the unconscious is a waste of time and money, are more likely to obtain grants. They are more attractive, as well, to schools and institutions, where large numbers of patients are provided services. There was a time when we spoke of doctors providing treatment to patients. Now the lingo calls us "providers" and our treatment "delivery of services." The word *delivery* connotes to me someone in a truck delivering a product. We have not reached that point yet, but I would not be surprised if very soon we start referring to our patients as "the customers."

Training in Child Psychiatry

As a result of this situation there has been a dramatic shift in the type of training young child psychiatrists now receive. Most of the medical school training programs in the United States began in the 1940s and 1950s when psychoanalytic theory reigned supreme. During that period there was hardly a department that was not chaired by a classically oriented psychoanalyst. In the late 1960s and early 1970s the pendulum began to shift in favor of the biological psychiatrists. This occurred at a time when hospitals became increasingly pressured to support ever more complex and sophisticated forms of medical treatment. Furthermore, the hospitals could no longer rely on the relatively inexpensive care provided by paraprofessionals such as nurses, attendants, laboratory technicians, et cetera. People could no longer be relied upon to dedicate themselves to the treatment of the ill with little financial remuneration. On the one hand, one could say that the shrinkage of such dedicated individuals was related to a psychopathic society in which fewer individuals were willing to make sacrifices in compliance with noble principles such as self-sacrifice, sympathy for the underprivileged, and dedication to the needs of the poor. On the other hand, one could argue that people decided that they no longer wanted to be exploited by hospital administrators. I believe that both factors operated here with the net result that there are fewer people who are working in hospitals because of high and noble principles, and there are also fewer people who are being exploited. Unions became stronger, wage demands more stringent, and hospitals had to cut back in every possible way in order to survive.

They became increasingly dependent on their outside funding. Up to the 1970s a departmental chairperson (there were mainly chairmen in those days) was chosen primarily on the basis of medical expertise and dedication, and only secondarily on administrative capabilities and funding sources. Hospitals now find themselves in the position of having to use the latter criteria for selection much more than the former. We are living in a time when a person who is a candidate for a departmental chair is judged primarily on his or her "track record" in acquiring funding, and medical expertise is of only secondary consideration. The effect of this on psychiatry has been to place psychodynamically oriented people at a tremendous disadvantage with regard to chairing departments. This has reached a point where there is hardly a child psychiatry department in the United States today that is chaired by a dynamically oriented child psychiatrist. As is to be expected, the chairpersons themselves not only hire people who think the way they do but also favor individuals who themselves have good "track records" regarding funding for their work.

As a result of this situation, the young child psychiatrist in training may have little if any psychodynamically oriented therapeutic experience. In many of these departments the primary therapeutic modalities are determined by what is short, seemingly quick, and "cost effective." Drug therapy, obviously, satisfies this proviso. To a lesser extent, behavior therapy is attractive for the same reasons. Cognitive therapies, whose primary aim is to change relatively quickly distorted thinking, are also very much in vogue. Many people in these programs see no need to get background history about the patient's family or to investigate into underlying psychodynamics. The symptom is viewed as the disease and symptom alleviation or removal is considered the only goal of treatment. Even the manual of psychiatric diagnoses (DSM-III) reflects this philosophy. It is basically antipsychodynamic. The selection of a disorder's name is based primarily, if not exclusively, on the manifest symptoms.

One of the most unfortunate outcomes of all this is the diagnostic category known as *attention deficit disorder* (ADD). If one looks at the charts of child patients in hospitals, clinics, and the offices of child psychiatrists, child neurologists, pediatricians, child psychologists, and school guidance counselors, the "disease" is indeed epidemic. It has become the rubber-stamp diagnosis of the 1980s. Any child who does not listen to his or her parents or teachers is quickly labeled "ADD." If one is to believe these reports, we are experiencing an epidemic greater than we ever had with any other disorder known to medicine.

The implication is that these children are suffering with a neurophysiological derangement which may or may not be associated with hyperactivity (also presumed to be neurophysiologic in etiology). With this assumption, the next step is to provide a convenient drug: enter psychostimulant medication. At this time it is reasonable to say that psychostimulant medication is being prescribed by the ton—literally by the ton. All this is quick and slick, but a terrible disservice to patients. I believe that the vast majority of children who are diagnosed as having ADD have problems that have nothing to do with their attentional capacity, but are more likely to have difficulties related to psychogenic rather than neurophysiological factors. Their difficulties, I believe, are more readily explained by family and other environmental influences that have resulted in psychological problems for these children. Most children who are considered to have ADD are diagnosed on a purely empirical or observational basis. When objective criteria for attentional capacity are utilized (such as the Digit Span, Arithmetic, and Coding subtests of the *WISC-R*) the diagnosis cannot be justified.

In my forthcoming book, *Psychotherapy of Psychogenic Learning Disabilities* (1987), I will discuss in detail my own studies that support my position that the ADD label (not the hyperactivity label) is a myth that exists in the brains of those who make the diagnosis and not in the brains of those who are being so diagnosed. I do believe, however, that *some* hyperactive children are indeed so on a neurophysiological basis and will be helped by psychostimulant medication. My main point here is that the popularity of the ADD and hyperactivity labels and the ubiquitous use of psychostimulant medication is another manifestation of the search for quick and simple cures for complicated problems, the worship of cost-effectiveness, the anxieties engendered by introspective psychotherapeutic approaches, the prevailing psychopathy of our society, and the resulting dehumanization of psychiatry.

Prepaid Treatment Plans

Another phenomenon that has compromised significantly the quality of psychiatric care and threatens to do so even more in the immediate future is the increasing popularity of prepaid treatment plans. Their main purpose has been to provide patients with lower cost treatment. One can argue that the present medical system leaves much to be desired. Rich patients clearly receive far better care than the poor. They have the opportunity to select their doctors freely and have the wherewithal to pay their fees, no matter how high. On the other end of the scale, the indigent generally attend hospital clinics, have no choice of physicians, and are often treated by those in training. As is usually the case, those in the middle class get something in between. Prepaid insurance plans provide such care, especially for the middle class. There is no question that many physicians have exploited the public with their unconscionable fees. If a person has a brain tumor and all the neurosurgeons in private practice are charging $15,000 for its removal, the patient has little choice but to pay. There is no question that this is a form of exploitation. There is no question that some kind of backlash was predictable. There is no question also that people in clinics have been getting inadequate treatment and that some kind of retaliatory reaction was also foreseeable. However, indigents are less likely to involve themselves effectively in movements for their rights than those who are better educated and in a better financial position. Some of the prepaid plans are manifestations of this backlash. I discuss here some of the most well known, those that do not provide free choice of physician within the plan.

A development that has grown in recent years, now at an ever increasing rate, is the establishment of *health maintenance organizations* (HMOs). Many large companies have traditionally provided their workers with the opportunity to select their physicians. Under a typical program the worker would be reimbursed a significant percentage of the cost of medical care. The basic philosophy was that an individual should be free to choose any physician he or she wished to, without any external restrictions. In recent years companies have found that it is more "cost-effective" to engage the services of and even to build their own clinics and hospitals and to give their workers a choice. If one chooses the company's medical facilities, one may pay nothing or very little. One is still free to go to receive treatment from an outside physician, but one will get little if any reimbursement for doing so. Obviously, under such a program, very few people are going to select the latter course. Large companies have not only set up their own clinics but even their own hospitals. Those who have not set up their own have contracted with private hospitals that were established for this purpose. Insurance companies, as well, have found it an attractive program. The physicians in these organizations are often employees. They are paid specific salaries and their work is monitored, again with regard to whether or not it is "cost-effective." One result of this trend has been a progressive shrinkage of private practice. Young physicians today cannot generally look forward to the autonomy of individual practice because an increasing percentage of their potential patient population is now receiving care from HMOs. They too must become salaried employees if they are to make a living in the field of medicine.

There are four specialties in medicine that have been particularly hurt by HMOs, specifically dermatology, allergy, plastic surgery, and psychiatry. The general consensus among administrators of HMOs is that these specialties often provide frivolous treatment and the therapy is frequently prolonged unnecessarily for the financial benefit of the physician. Accordingly, the funds allotted for treatment in these four categories is generally a much smaller fraction of the traditional than in other medical specialties. Although one might argue that much of the "bread and butter" of plastic surgery is unnecessary cosmetic surgery, one cannot as easily give a convincing argument that much of psychiatric therapy is equally frivolous. The result is that physicians and patients under HMO plans are told that they must accomplish their treatment in a fixed number of sessions. Therapists who claim that therapy takes much longer are not likely to remain employed very long. Those who subscribe to a theory that short-term therapy is as good as the long-term variation will be viewed with favor. This is a ripoff on the public. As mentioned so frequently throughout this book, psychotherapy can only be meaningful in the context of an ongoing relationship, and one cannot put a fixed number of hours on the development, evolution, and therapeutic benefit of this relationship. And the next step has already taken place. Therapists in private practice, suffering from the emigration of their patient population to HMOs, are now taking jobs in HMOs. And they are going along with the philosophy that treatment can indeed be accomplished in a predetermined number of sessions.

A related development is the establishment of *preferred-provider organizations* (PPOs). Here, private practitioners, in an attempt to compete with HMOs for patients, group together and bid for service contracts with insurance companies, industries, et cetera. These organizations do comparative shopping in the medical marketplace and contract with a group of providers who agree on a predetermined list of charges. These practitioners, then, are charging higher rates to patients who are not members of these plans than they are to subscribers. Again, it is unreasonable to assume that patients who are receiving care at the lower fee are going to get the same quality of care and attention as those who are paying more. And this is especially the case in psychiatric treatment where the fixed charges are likely to limit the number of sessions available to the patient.

Another arrangement is the *independent practice association* (IPA). IPAs were also established to compete with HMOs for patients. Here, a group of physicians gets together and forms its own service plan. Whereas in HMOs and PPOs an outside organization, such as an industry or an insurance company, sets up the plan, in the IPA the doctors themselves organize and administer the program. They therefore save the costs of paying outside administrators. As is true for PPOs, doctors seeing patients under the IPA plan generally charge two fees, a higher fee for their genuinely private patients and a lower fee for those who come under the service contract. Again, I have the same reservations about IPAs as I do about HMOs and PPOs, namely, that psychiatric care has got to be compromised by the limited amount of time available under these fixed fee service plans.

Another development that is compromising significantly the quality of care in the field of psychiatry is the growth of the diagnostic related groups (DRGs). Again, in order to improve the cost-effectiveness of medical care and to increase the efficiency of such treatment (especially with regard to paperwork), many of the payers of medical care (insurance companies, Blue Cross/Blue Shield, Medicare, Medicaid, et cetera) have made up a list of hundreds of disorders for which hospitals provide treatment. The hospital is given a fixed amount of money for the treatment of patients suffering with one or more of these disorders—regardless of the number of days in the hospital and regardless of the kinds of medicines, procedures, operations, et cetera that are required. The amount of payment is based on the average cost for the treatment of the particular condition in the recent past. Although this approach certainly saves much paperwork and perhaps even reduces the number of days a patient will remain in the hospital, it cannot but compromise psychiatric treatment. It behooves hospitals to discharge patients at the earliest possible time, and this is likely to result in patients not being allowed to stay the optimum amount of time. Doctors who keep their patients in longer than the average may find that their treatment is becoming "cost ineffective." They will be advised by hospital administrators to shorten the duration of their patients' stays or risk the displeasure of those who pay their salaries and/or determine their suitability for enjoying the benefits of hospital privileges.

I consider all of these prepayment plans to pose the risk of curtailed treatment for patients. To me plans like these, when applied to psychiatry, can be compared to restricting marriages to 7.3 years, because that is the average duration of the marriages in the community in which the couple is marrying. The analogy is applicable because the therapeutic relationship, if a good one, has similarities to the good marriage with regard to the intimacy and closeness that emerges. The other drawback of these prepaid plans is that physicians on salary are not as likely to work as enthusiastically and with as high motivation as those who enjoy the promise of higher earnings for enhanced competence and the establishment for themselves of a reputation for excellence. Most human beings (including doctors) are not so saint-like that they will work as assiduously for a fixed income as they will in a situation where there is the promise of greater rewards. In some ideal world of perfect people, such differentiations may not be made. In our real world, however, real doctors are not going to give as much attention and commitment to their prepaid patients as they will to those who provide promise of greater remuneration. And this difference is especially true in psychiatry when one compares the remuneration for a few sessions under a fixed-fee program and that which is possible from a private patient in an ongoing therapeutic program.

The Dehumanization of Psychiatric Care

If the reader detects a note of pessimism in the above, he or she is correct. I have little reason to feel confident about the future of the field of child psychiatry, whether practiced in the hospital, clinic, or in a private setting. The hospitals and clinics are training automatons who provide a dehumanized kind of treatment. In recent years I am seeing with increasing frequency reports that are completely devoid of information about family background, developmental history, and underlying psychodynamics. The patients are "processed" and the care "delivered." The clinic administrators pride themselves on the total number of people they can process in a given period and gloat over comparisons between their own turnover rates and those of previous administrators who worked when traditional psychotherapeutic techniques were being utilized. Patients come to the clinic and, while waiting to see their doctors, fill out symptom checklists. These are then fed into a computer and compared with previous symptom checklists. By the time the patient is seen, the therapist has the up-to-date data in hand and is allegedly in a position to assess the patient's "progress." The whole session may take five to ten minutes, during which time the primary purpose is to adjust medication and write prescriptions. There is little if any time for any discussion of the human problems that may be contributing significantly to the patient's problems. But even if there were, the doctor has not been trained adequately in psychodynamic therapy and may have little if any conviction for it.

The young physician who is thinking of entering the field of child psychiatry and who recognizes how unconscionable the system is, has great difficulty finding training in a more humane setting. If the physician were to find more humanistic therapy being provided in a nonmedical training program, such as psychology for example, he or she would still be faced with formidable problems. Certainly, such training would not be recognized toward certification in a medical specialty and psychologists might not even recognize the physician's training as being adequate for admission to the program. If the individual decides to go through one of the dehumanized medical programs and tolerate its deficiencies in the hope of rectifying them later, he or she will have had little training to serve as a basis for the subsequent more humane type of psychiatric treatment.

Those who recognize how unconscionably inadequate are our present training programs in child psychiatry have little place to turn. When young people ask my advice about where in child psychiatry they can train, I tell them I know of no center within the field of medicine. I suspect that there may be a few programs in which psychodynamically oriented therapy is still the prevailing approach. However, I have no optimism that such programs will remain long in effect. In every program that I am familiar with, the process has been the same: a psychodynamically oriented chairperson has been replaced by someone with a deep commitment to the biological approach. Dynamically oriented chairpersons have been fired, prematurely retired, eased out, forced out, or thrown out! In short, what we are witnessing is the corruption of a field by lust for money. The aforementioned influences that are eroding the field at a frighteningly rapid rate are formidable, and I see little evidence that things will change in the near future.

CHILD PSYCHOTHERAPY IN NONMEDICAL DISCIPLINES

Now to other disciplines that are providing psychotherapy. There was a time, less than ten years ago, when psychologists were warring with psychiatrists with regard to who has the right to do psychotherapy. That war is over. There was no truce; there was no armistice. Rather, psychiatry just walked away from the battlefield. Psychiatry views itself as having "returned to medicine." The recent attitude of psychiatry has been: "Leave psychotherapy to the psychologists and the social workers; they can hold the hands of people who need that sort of thing." The general public has similarly come to view psychiatrists almost exclusively as the purveyors of drugs and as therapists for psychotics, severe depressives, and others who have physical disorders that require shock therapy and/ or medication. Psychologists are now viewed by the general public as the providers of psychotherapy. This may be a good thing considering the deplorable state of present-day residency programs. It is now the psychologists who are fighting with the social workers over who should have the right to do psychotherapy. And others have quickly entered the arena: pastoral counselors, nurse practitioners, family counselors, marital counselors, and a large assortment of others with varying degrees of training and expertise. There is likely to be a Pyrrhic victory in the end because if these people are fighting over patients for private practice, as the HMOs, PPOs, and IPAs continue to grow there will be very few patients left, if any. They will end up finding that what they have "won" will be jobs that will confine them to "cost-effective" therapeutic programs with a specific number of hours allotted to each patient.

FINAL COMMENTS

It would be an error for the reader to conclude that I am white-washing completely psychodynamic child psychotherapy in this section of my book. Biological psychiatry, in part, enjoyed popularity as a justifiable backlash against the widespread enthusiasm for classical psychoanalysis and its derivative techniques. There was a grandiosity to some of these practitioners that bordered on the delusional. They considered themselves to have had in the palm of their hands the definitive and the most effective form of psychotherapeutic treatment ever devised in the history of humankind. Those who disagreed with them were viewed as having psychological problems that have not been properly analyzed. Furthermore, the length of the treatment programs they were utilizing was inordinately long, even if there was the funding available for such prolonged treatment. The idea that most patients be treated four or five times a week was patently absurd.

And there are those who were (and still are) providing worthless treatment that is referred to as "play therapy." I have come across numerous child therapists who actually believe that play therapy is nothing more than playing with a child. They have little if any insight into the fact that the play, if it is to justifiably warrant the name *play therapy,* must be more therapy than play and that the play should only be a vehicle for the transmission of therapeutic messages and experiences. These practitioners also may have contributed to the backlash as it has been applied to child therapy. Hundreds of thousands of hours have been wasted while therapists have been taking children to soda fountains, baseball games, circuses, et cetera, under the aegis of child therapy.

So there was much housecleaning that had to be done (and still has to be done) among those who do child therapy. I recognize that this is an extremely pessimistic note on which to end a book. However, it is the reality of the world in which we are living and to deny it would be foolish and self-destructive. If all that I predict here regarding child psychotherapy comes to pass (and much of it has already happened), then a book like this might not prove very useful—because very few people will be in a position to provide the kind of therapy described herein. I have recognized this while writing this book, but I still felt that it had to be written. I felt that I had to write a compendium of my contributions and pull together my ideas. There are still enough people at this point who have the autonomy and flexibility to practice the kind of child therapy described in it. Perhaps one day there will be some kind of a backlash against the recent depravities, and more people will come to appreciate how unconscionable many present therapeutic programs are. My hope is that they will work toward bringing us once again into an atmosphere in which more humane therapeutic approaches will prevail. Perhaps this book may serve (admittedly in a small way) to inspire others like myself who are still striving to maintain what was good in the past and to contribute to its reflowering in the future.

References

Aichorn, A. (1925), *Wayward Youth*. New York: The World Publishing Co., 1954.

Alexander, F. (1950), Analysis of the therapeutic factors in psychoanalytic treatment. *Psychoanalytic Quarterly,* 19:482–500.

Alexander, F. and French, T. (1946), The principle of corrective emotional experience. In *Psychoanalytic Therapy: Principles and Application,* pp. 66–70. New York: The Ronald Press.

Allen, F.H. (1972), *Psychotherapy with Children*. New York: W.W. Norton.

The American Psychiatric Association (1980), *Diagnostic and Statistical Manual, Third Edition (DSM-III)*. Washington, D.C.: American Psychiatric Association.

Axline, V.M. (1947), *Play Therapy*. Boston: Houghton Mifflin Co.

—— (1964), *Dibs in Search of Self*. Boston: Houghton Mifflin Co.

Baldock, E.C. (1974), *The Therapeutic Relationship and Its Ramifications in Child Psychotherapy*. San Jose, California: The Family Service Association of Santa Clara County Monograph.

Beery, K.E. and Buktenica, N.A. (1982), *Developmental Test of Visual-Motor Integration*. Chicago: Follett Publishing Co.

Bellak, L. and Bellak, S.S. (1949), *Children's Apperception Test*. Larchmont, New York: C.P.S. Co.

Bender, L. (1952), *Child Psychiatric Techniques*. Springfield, Ill: Charles C. Thomas.

Bowen, M. (1978), *Family Therapy in Clinical Practice.* New York: Jason Aronson, Inc.

Buck, J.N. (1948), The H-T-P technique: A qualitative and quantitative scoring manual. *Journal of Clinical Psychology,* 4(5):317–396.

Burns, R.C. and Kaufman, S.H. (1970), *Kinetic Family Drawings.* New York: Brunner/Mazel.

Conn, J.H. (1939), The child reveals himself through play. *Mental Hygiene,* 23(1):1–21.

—— (1941a), The timid, dependent child. *Journal of Pediatrics,* 19(1):1–2.

—— (1941b), The treatment of fearful children. *American Journal of Orthopsychiatry,* 11(4):744–751.

—— (1948), The play-interview as an investigative and therapeutic procedure. *The Nervous Child,* 7(3):257–286.

—— (1954), Play interview therapy of castration fears. *American Journal of Orthopsychiatry,* 25(4):747–754.

Dickens, C. (1850), *The Personal History of David Copperfield,* p. 13. New York: Dodd, Mead, and Co., Inc., 1943.

Dunn, L.M. (1965), *Peabody Picture Vocabulary Test.* Circle Pines, Minnesota: American Guidance Service, Inc.

Dunn, L.M. and Dunn, L.M. (1981), *Peabody Picture Vocabulary Test—Revised.* Circle Pines, Minnesota: American Guidance Service, Inc.

Elkisch, P. (1960), Free art expression. In *Projective Techniques in Children,* ed. A.I. Rabin and M.R. Haworth, pp. 273–288. New York: Grune & Stratton.

Ellis, A. (1963), *Reason and Emotion in Psychotherapy.* New York: Lyle Stuart.

Erikson, E.H. (1950), *Childhood and Society.* New York: W.W. Norton.

Framo, J.L. (1982), *Explorations in Marital and Family Therapy.* New York: Springer Publishing Co.

Freud, A. (1946), *The Psychoanalytical Treatment of Children.* London: Imago Publishing Co.

—— (1965), *Normality and Pathology in Childhood.* New York: International Universities Press.

Freud, S. (1900), The Interpretation of Dreams. In *The Basic Writings of Sigmund Freud,* ed. A.A. Brill, pp. 183–549. New York: Random House, Inc. (The Modern Library), 1938.

—— (1908), The relation of the poet to daydreaming. In *Collected Papers,* Vol. 4, pp. 173–183. New York: Basic Books, Inc., 1959.

—— (1909), A phobia in a five-year-old boy. In *Collected Papers,* Vol. 3, pp. 149–209. New York: Basic Books, Inc., 1959.

—— (1924), The passing of the Oedipus complex. In *Collected Papers,* Vol. 2, pp. 269–276. New York: Basic Books, Inc., 1959.

Freud, S. and Breuer, J. (1895), *Studies in Hysteria*. New York: Basic Books, Inc., 1957.

Gardner, R.A. (1966), *The Child's Book About Brain Injury*. New York: New York Association for Brain-Injured Children.

—— (1968a), The mutual storytelling technique: Use in alleviating childhood oedipal problems. *Contemporary Psychoanalysis*, 4:161–177.

—— (1968b), Book Review, Ginott, H.G. (1965), *Between Parent and Child*. New York: The Macmillan Co. Reviewed in *Psychology Today*, 1(12):15–17.

—— (1969a), The game of checkers as a diagnostic and therapeutic tool in child psychotherapy. *Acta Paedopsychiatrica*, 36(5):142–152.

—— (1969b), The guilt reaction of parents of children with severe physical diseases. *American Journal of Psychiatry*, 126:636–644.

—— (1969c), Mutual storytelling as a technique in child psychotherapy and psychoanalysis. In *Science and Psychoanalysis*, ed. J. Masserman, Vol. XIV, pp. 123–135. New York: Grune and Stratton.

—— (1970a), *The Boys and Girls Book About Divorce*. New York: Jason Aronson, Inc.

—— (1970b), The use of guilt as a defense against anxiety. *The Psychoanalytic Review*, 57:124–136.

—— (1970c), Die Technik des wechselseitigen Geschichtenerzahlens bei der Behandlung eines Kindes mit psychogenem Husten. In *Fortschritte der Weiterentwicklung der Psychoanalyse*, ed. C.J. Hogrefe, Vol. 4, pp. 159–173. Göttingen: Verlag für Psychologie.

—— (1970d), The mutual storytelling technique: Use in the treatment of a child with post-traumatic neurosis. *American Journal of Psychotherapy*, 24:419–439.

—— (1971a), *Therapeutic Communication with Children: The Mutual Storytelling Technique*. New York: Jason Aronson, Inc.

—— (1971b), *The Boys and Girls Book About Divorce* (Paperback edition). New York: Bantam Books, Inc.

—— (1971c), Mutual storytelling: A technique in child psychotherapy. *Acta Paedopsychiatrica*, 38(9):253–262.

—— (1972a), *Dr. Gardner's Stories About the Real World*, Vol. I. Cresskill, New Jersey: Creative Therapeutics.

—— (1972b), Little Hans—the most famous boy in the child psychotherapy literature. *International Journal of Child Psychotherapy*, 1(4):27–32.

—— (1972c), On D.W. Winnicott and some as yet undefined qualities of the child therapist. *International Journal of Child Psychotherapy*, 1(2):7–12.

—— (1972d), "Once upon a time there was a doorknob and everybody used to make him all dirty with fingerprints . . . " *Psychology Today*, 5(10):67–92.

—— (1972e), The mutual storytelling technique in the treatment of anger inhibition problems. *International Journal of Child Psychotherapy*, 1(1):34–64.

—— (1972f), *The Boys and Girls Book About Divorce* (Japanese edition). Tokyo, Japan: Mikasa-Shobo, Ltd.

—— (1972g), *The Boys and Girls Book About Divorce* (Spanish edition). Buenos Aires, Argentina: Editorial Galerna. Cresskill, New Jersey: Creative Therapeutics (1986).

—— (1972h), *The Boys and Girls Book About Divorce* (Dutch edition). Wageningen, Holland: L.J. Veen's Vitgeversmaatschappij N.V.

—— (1973a), *MBD: The Family Book About Minimal Brain Dysfunction.* New York: Jason Aronson, Inc.

—— (1973b), *The Talking, Feeling, and Doing Game.* Cresskill, New Jersey: Creative Therapeutics.

—— (1973c), *Understanding Children—A Parents Guide to Child Rearing.* Cresskill, New Jersey: Creative Therapeutics.

—— (1973d), Treatment of the projected self. *International Journal of Child Psychotherapy.* 2(1):7–12.

—— (1973e), Book Reviews: Winnicott, D.W. (1971), *Playing and Reality.* New York: Basic Books, Inc.; and Winnicott, D.W. (1971), *Therapeutic Consultations in Child Psychiatry.* New York: Basic Books, Inc. Reviewed in *Contemporary Psychoanalysis*, 9(3):392–400.

—— (1973f), *The Mutual Storytelling Technique* (12 one-hour audio cassette tapes). Cresskill, New Jersey: Creative Therapeutics.

—— (1973g), Psychotherapy of the psychogenic problems secondary to minimal brain dysfunction. *International Journal of Child Psychotherapy*, 2(2):224–256.

—— (1974a), *Dr. Gardner's Fairy Tales for Today's Children.* Cresskill, New Jersey: Creative Therapeutics.

—— (1974b), La technique de la narration mutuelle d'historettes. *Médecine et Hygiène* (Geneva), 32:1180–1181.

—— (1974c), Dramatized storytelling in child psychotherapy. *Acta Paedopsychiatrica*, 41(3):110–116.

—— (1974d), The mutual storytelling technique in the treatment of psychogenic problems secondary to minimal brain dysfunction. *Journal of Learning Disabilities*, 7:135–143.

—— (1974e), Psychotherapy of minimal brain dysfunction. In *Current Psychiatric Therapies*, ed. J. Masserman, Vol. XIV, pp. 15–21. New York: Grune & Stratton.

—— (1974f), *Dr. Gardner's Stories About the Real World* (Dutch edition). The Hague, Holland: Vitgeverij Bert Bakker BZ.

—— (1975a), *Psychotherapeutic Approaches to the Resistant Child* (2 one-hour audio cassette tapes). Cresskill, New Jersey: Creative Therapeutics.

—— (1975b), Techniques for involving the child with MBD in meaningful psychotherapy. *Journal of Learning Disabilities,* 8(5):16–26.

—— (1975c), Psychotherapy in minimal brain dysfunction. In *Current Psychiatric Therapies,* ed. J. Masserman, Vol. XV, pp. 25–38. New York: Grune & Stratton.

—— (1975d), Dr. Gardner talks to children with minimal brain dysfunction (one-hour audio cassette tape). Cresskill, New Jersey: Creative Therapeutics.

—— (1975e), Dr. Gardner talks to parents of children with MBD (one-hour audio cassette tape). Cresskill, New Jersey: Creative Therapeutics.

—— (1975f), *Understanding Children—A Parents Guide to Child Rearing* (Dutch edition). Bilthoven, Holland: Vitgeverij Amboboken B.V.

—— (1976a), *Psychotherapy with Children of Divorce.* New York: Jason Aronson, Inc.

—— (1976b), Helping children deal with parental death (two 1-1/2 hour cassette tapes). Cresskill, New Jersey: Creative Therapeutics.

—— (1976c), Easing the damage of divorce and death. *Blue Print for Health,* Vol. XXVI, No. 1, pp. 49–56. Chicago: Blue Cross Association.

—— (1976d), *Dr. Gardner's Stories About the Real World* (Italian edition). Rome, Italy: Editore Armando Armando.

—— (1977a), *Dr. Gardner's Modern Fairy Tales.* Cresskill, New Jersey: Creative Therapeutics.

—— (1977b), *The Parents Book About Divorce.* New York: Doubleday and Co., Inc.

—— (1977c), *Dr. Gardner's Modern Fairy Tales.* Cresskill, New Jersey: Creative Therapeutics.

—— (1977d), *The Boys and Girls Book About Divorce* (Hebrew edition). Tel Aviv, Israel: Sadan Publishing House, Ltd.

—— (1977e), Children's guilt reactions to parental death: Psychodynamics and therapeutic management. *Hiroshima Journal of Psychology,* 4:45–57.

—— (1978a), *The Reversals Frequency Test.* Cresskill, New Jersey: Creative Therapeutics.

—— (1978b), *The Boys and Girls Book About One-Parent Families.* New York: G.P. Putnam's Sons.

—— (1979a), *The Parents Book About Divorce* (Paperback edition). New York: Bantam Books, Inc.

—— (1979b), Intergenerational sexual tensions in second marriages. *Medical Aspects of Human Sexuality,* 13(8):77ff.

—— (1979c), *The Objective Diagnosis of Minimal Brain Dysfunction.* Cresskill, New Jersey: Creative Therapeutics.

—— (1979d), Helping children cooperate in therapy. In *Basic Handbook of Child Psychiatry*, ed. J. Noshpitz, Vol. III, pp. 414–433. New York: Basic Books, Inc.

—— (1979e), Psychogenic difficulties secondary to MBD. In *Basic Handbook of Child Psychiatry*, ed. J. Noshpitz, Vol. III, pp. 614–628. New York: Basic Books, Inc.

—— (1979f), Death of a parent. In *Basic Handbook of Child Psychiatry*, ed. J. Noshpitz, Vol. IV, pp. 270–283. New York: Basic Books, Inc.

—— (1979g), *The Parents Book About Divorce* (French Edition). Paris, France: Ramsay "image."

—— (1980a), The mutual storytelling technique. In *The Psychotherapy Handbook*, ed. R. Herink, pp. 408–411. New York: New American Library.

—— (1980b), Minimal brain dysfunction. In *Child in Normality and Psychopathology*, ed. J. Bemporad, pp. 269–304. New York: Brunner/Mazel, Inc.

—— (1980c), What every psychoanalyst should know about minimal brain dysfunction. *Journal of the American Academy of Psychoanalysis*, 8(3):403–426.

—— (1980d), *Dorothy and the Lizard of Oz.* Cresskill, New Jersey: Creative Therapeutics.

—— (1980e), *The Boys and Girls Book About Divorce* (Dutch edition). Deventer, The Netherlands: Van Loghum Slaterus B.V.

—— (1980f), *The Boys and Girls Book About Divorce* (Japanese edition). Tokyo: Shakai Shisa Sha Ltd.

—— (1981a), The mutual storytelling technique and dramatization of the therapeutic communication. In *Drama in Therapy*, ed. G. Schattner and R. Courtney, pp. 211–235. New York: Drama Book Specialists.

—— (1981b), *Dr. Gardner's Fables for Our Times.* Cresskill, New Jersey: Creative Therapeutics.

—— (1981c), *The Boys and Girls Book About Stepfamilies.* Cresskill, New Jersey: Creative Therapeutics.

—— (1981d), *The Boys and Girls Book About Divorce* (French edition). Montreal, Canada: Presses Sélect Ltée.

—— (1981e), *The Boys and Girls Book About One-Parent Families* (Japanese edition). Tokyo, Japan: Kitaoji Shobo.

—— (1982), *Family Evaluation in Child Custody Litigation.* Cresskill, New Jersey: Creative Therapeutics.

—— (1983a), Treating oedipal problems with the mutual storytelling technique. In *Handbook of Play Therapy*, ed. C.E. Schaefer and K.J. O'Connor, pp. 355–368. New York: John Wiley & Sons, Inc.

—— (1983b), *Dr. Gardner's Stories About the Real World*, Volume II. Cresskill, New Jersey: Creative Therapeutics.

—— (1983c), *The Boys and Girls Book About One-Parent Families*. New York: Bantam Books, Inc.

—— (1983d), The Talking, Feeling, and Doing Game. In *Handbook of Play Therapy*, ed. C.E. Schaefer and K.J. O'Connor, pp. 259–273. New York: John Wiley & Sons, Inc.

—— (1984), *Separation Anxiety Disorder: Psychodynamics and Psychotherapy*. Cresskill, New Jersey: Creative Therapeutics.

—— (1985), Recent developments in child custody litigation. *The Academy Forum*, 29(2):3–7. New York: The American Academy of Psychoanalysis.

—— (1986a), The game of checkers in child therapy. In *Game Play: Therapeutic Uses of Childhood Games*, ed. C.E. Schaefer and S. Reid, New York: John Wiley and Sons. (in press)

—— (1986b), *Child Custody Litigation: A Guide for Parents and Mental Health Professionals*. Cresskill, New Jersey: Creative Therapeutics.

—— (1986c), Child Custody. In *Basic Handbook of Child Psychiatry*, ed. J. Noshpitz, Vol. V, Chap. 73. New York: Basic Books, Inc. (in press)

—— (1986d), The Talking, Feeling, and Doing Game. In *Game Play: Therapeutic Uses of Childhood Games*, ed. C.E. Schaefer and S. Reid. New York: John Wiley & Sons. (in press)

—— (1987), *Psychotherapy of Psychogenic Learning Disabilities*. Cresskill, New Jersey: Creative Therapeutics. (in press)

Gardner, R.A. and Gardner, A.K. (1978), *A Steadiness Tester for Objectively Diagnosing Hyperactivity and/or Attention Sustaining Impairment*. Lafayette, Indiana: Lafayette Instruments, Inc.

Gardner, R.A., Gardner, A.K., Caemmerer, A. and Broman, M. (1979), An instrument for measuring hyperactivity and other signs of minimal brain dysfunction. *Journal of Clinical Psychology*, 8(3):146–152.

Gardner, R.A. and Broman, M. (1979), Letter reversal frequency in normal and learning-disabled children. *Journal of Clinical Child Psychology*, 8(3):146–152.

Goldings, R. and Goldings, H. (1972), Books in the playroom: A dimension of child psychiatric technique. *Journal of the American Academy of Child Psychiatry*, 12(1):52–65.

Goodenough, F. (1926), *Measurement of Intelligence by Drawings*. New York: World Book Co.

Group for the Advancement of Psychiatry (1957), *The Diagnostic Process in Child Psychiatry, Report No. 38*. Washington, D.C.: American Psychiatric Association.

Haas, R.B. and Moreno, J.L. (1951), Psychodrama as a projective technique. In *An Introduction to Projective Techniques*, ed. H.H. Anderson and G.L. Anderson, pp. 662–675. Englewood Cliffs, New Jersey: Prentice-Hall, Inc.

Haley, J. (1973), *Uncommon Therapy: The Psychiatric Techniques of Milton H. Erickson, M.D.* New York: W.W. Norton and Co.

Hammer, E.F. (1960), The House-Tree-Person (H-T-P) drawings as a projective technique with children. In *Projective Techniques in Children,* ed. A.I. Rabin and M.R. Haworth, pp. 258–272. New York: Grune & Stratton.

Harris, D.B. (1963), *Children's Drawings as Measures of Intellectual Maturity.* New York: Harcourt, Brace and World, Inc.

Hartley, R.E., Frank, L.K., and Goldenson, R.M. (1952), *Understanding Children's Play.* New York: Columbia University Press.

—— (1964), The benefits of water play. In *Child Psychotherapy,* ed. M.R. Haworth, pp. 364–368. New York: Basic Books.

Haworth, M.R. and Keller, M.J. (1964), The use of food in therapy. In *Child Psychotherapy,* ed. M.R. Haworth, pp. 330–338. New York: Basic Books, Inc.

Haworth, M.R. and Rabin, A.I. (1960), *Projective Techniques in Children.* New York: Grune & Stratton.

Heimlich, E.P. (1965), The use of music as a mode of communication in the treatment of disturbed children. *Journal of the American Academy of Child Psychiatry,* 4(1):86–122.

—— (1972), Paraverbal techniques in the therapy of childhood communication disorders. *International Journal of Child Psychotherapy,* 1(1):65–83.

—— (1973), Using a patient as "assistant therapist" in paraverbal therapy. *International Journal of Child Psychotherapy,* 2(1):13–52.

Hug-Hellmuth, H. von (1913), *Aus dem Seelenleben des Kindes.* Leipzig: Deuticke.

—— (1921), On the technique of child analysis. *International Journal of Psychoanalysis,* 2(3/4):287–305.

Johnson, A.M. (1949), Sanctions for superego lacunae of adolescents. In *Searchlights on Delinquency,* ed. K.R. Eissler, pp. 225–245. New York: International Universities Press.

—— (1959), Juvenile delinquency. In *American Handbook of Psychiatry,* Vol. I, ed. S. Arieti, pp. 844–849. New York: Basic Books, Inc.

Johnson, E.W. (1967), *Love and Sex in Plain Language.* Philadelphia: Lippincott.

Kanner, L. (1940), Play investigation and play treatment of children's behavior disorders. *Journal of Pediatrics,* 17(4):533–546.

—— (1957), *Child Psychiatry.* Springfield, Ill: Charles C. Thomas.

Kellogg, R. and O'Dell, S. (1967), *The Psychology of Children's Art.* New York: CRM Random House.

Kessler, J.W. (1966), *Psychopathology of Childhood*. Englewood Cliffs, New Jersey: Prentice-Hall, Inc.

Khan, M.M.R. (1972), On D.W. Winnicott. *International Journal of Child Psychotherapy*, 1(2):13–18.

Klein, M. (1932), *The Psychoanalysis of Children*. London: Hogarth Press.

Kritzberg, N.I. (1966), A new verbal projective test for the expansion of the projective aspects of the clinical interview. *Acta Paedopsychiatrica*, 33(2):48–62.

Kubie, L. (1956), Psychoanalysis and marriage: Practical and theoretical issues. In *Neurotic Interaction in Marriage*, ed. V.W. Eisenstein, pp. 10–43. New York: Basic Books, Inc.

Levy, D.M. (1939), Release therapy. *The American Journal of Orthopsychiatry*, 9(4):713–736.

—— (1940), Psychotherapy and childhood. *The American Journal of Orthopsychiatry*, 10(4):905–910.

Lippman, H.S. (1962), *Treatment of the Child in Emotional Conflict*. New York: McGraw-Hill.

Livingston, C. (1978), *"Why Was I Adopted?"* Secaucus, New Jersey: Lyle Stuart, Inc.

Machover, K. (1949), *Personality Projection in the Drawing of the Human Figure*. Springfield, Ill: Charles C. Thomas.

—— (1951), Drawing of the human figure: a method of personality investigation. In *An Introduction to Projective Techniques*, ed. H.H. Anderson and G.L. Anderson, pp. 341–370. Englewood Cliffs, N.J.: Prentice-Hall, Inc.

—— (1960), Sex differences in the developmental pattern of children as seen in human figure drawings. In *Projective Techniques in Children*, ed. A.I. Rabin and M.R. Haworth, pp. 230–257. New York: Grune & Stratton.

MacLeish, A. (1956), *J.B.* Boston: Houghton-Mifflin Co.

Marcus, I.M. (1966), Costume play therapy. *Journal of the American Academy of Child Psychiatry*, 5(3):441–451.

Mayle, P. (1973), *Where Did I Come From?* Secaucus, New Jersey: Lyle Stuart.

Moskowitz, J.A. (1973), The sorcerer's apprentice, or the use of magic in child psychotherapy. *International Journal of Child Psychotherapy*, 2(2):138–162.

Mullahy, P. (1970), *Psychoanalysis and Interpersonal Psychiatry*. New York: Jason Aronson, Inc.

Murray, H. (1936), *The Thematic Apperception Test*. New York: The Psychological Corp.

Napoli, P.J. (1951), Finger painting. In *An Introduction to Projective Techniques*, ed. H.H. Anderson and G.L. Anderson, pp. 386–415. Englewood Cliffs, N.J.: Prentice-Hall, Inc.

Pomeroy, W.B. (1968), *Boys and Sex*. New York: Delacorte Press.

—— (1969), *Girls and Sex*. New York: Delacorte Press.

Pyne, M. (1962), *The Hospital*. Boston: Houghton Mifflin Co.

Rambert, M.L. (1964), The use of drawings as a method of child psychoanalysis. In *Child Psychotherapy*, ed. M.R. Haworth, pp. 340–349. New York: Basic Books, Inc.

Rogers, C.R. (1951), *Client Centered Therapy*. Boston: Houghton-Mifflin.

—— (1967), Client-centered psychotherapy. In *Comprehensive Textbook of Psychiatry*, ed. A.M. Freedman and H.I. Kaplan, pp. 1225–1228. Baltimore: Williams & Wilkins.

Rondell, F. and Michaels, R. (1951), *The Family That Grew*. New York: Crown Publishers, Inc.

Schneidman, E.J. (1947), *The Make-A-Picture Story Test*. New York: The Psychological Corp.

Solomon, J.C. (1938), Active play therapy. *American Journal of Orthopsychiatry*, 8(3):479–498.

—— (1940), Active play therapy: further experiences. *American Journal of Orthopsychiatry*, 10(4):763–781.

—— (1951), Therapeutic use of play. In *An Introduction to Projective Techniques*, ed. H.H. Anderson and G.L. Anderson, pp. 639–661. Englewood Cliffs, N.J.: Prentice-Hall, Inc.

—— (1955), Play technique and the integrative process. *American Journal of Orthopsychiatry*, 25(3):591–600.

Stone, I. (1971), *The Passions of the Mind*, pp. 624–627. New York: Signet (New American Library, Inc.).

Strupp, H.H. (1975), Psychoanalysis, "focal psychotherapy," and the nature of the therapeutic influence. *Archives of General Psychiatry*, 32:127–135.

Stubblefield, R.L. (1967), Sociopathic personality disorders I: Antisocial and dyssocial reactions. In *Comprehensive Textbook of Psychiatry*, ed. A.M. Freedman and H.I. Kaplan, pp. 1420–1424. Baltimore: Williams & Wilkins.

Sullivan, H.S. (1953), *The Interpersonal Theory of Psychiatry*. New York: W.W. Norton and Co.

Thomas, A., Chess, S. et al. (1963), *Behavioral Individuality in Early Childhood*. New York: New York University Press.

Waelder, R. (1933), The psychoanalytic theory of play. *Psychoanalytic Quarterly*, 2(2):208–224.

Wechsler, D. (1974), *Wechsler Intelligence Scale for Children-Revised (WISC-R)*. New York: The Psychological Corporation.

Winnicott, D.W. (1968), The value of the therapeutic consultation. In *Foundations of Child Psychiatry*, ed. E. Miller, pp. 593–608. London: Pergamon Press.

—— (1971), *Therapeutic Consultations in Child Psychiatry*. New York: Basic Books, Inc.

Woltmann, A.G. (1951), The use of puppetry as a projective method in therapy. In *An Introduction to Projective Techniques*, ed. H.H. Anderson and G.I. Anderson, pp. 606–638. Englewood Cliffs, N.J.: Prentice-Hall, Inc.

—— (1964a), Mud and clay, their functions as developmental aids and as media of projection. In *Child Psychotherapy*, ed. M.R. Haworth, pp. 349–363. New York: Basic Books, Inc.

—— (1964b), Diagnostic and therapeutic considerations of nonverbal projective activities with children. In *Child Psychotherapy*, ed. M.R. Haworth, pp. 322–330. New York: Basic Books, Inc.

—— (1972), Puppetry as a tool in child psychotherapy. *International Journal of Child Psychotherapy*, 1(1):84–96.

Index

ABO incompatibility, jaundice due to, 173
Abortion, mother's experience of, 187, 189
Abstractions, use of, 87, 299
Abuse, sex, 454
Academic performance
  determining need for treatment and, 224
  initial evaluation of, 181
  See also School
Accomplishment(s)
  developing sense of, 631–32, 642
  initial evaluation of, 183–84
  opportunity in initial interview to present, 204–5
Ackerman, Nathan, 9
Acting, play, 61–62. *See also* Dramatized storytelling
Acting-out behavior, mutual storytelling technique in case of, 444–51. *See also* Antisocial behavior
Active play therapy, 42–43
Adams, Henry Brooks, 66
Adaptation, expanding repertoire of options for, 73–74, 126, 436–37, 641, 655–56, 749–50

ADD, 851–52
Adolescents
  confidentiality in therapy of, 368–69
  in family therapy, 803, 809
  in initial screening interview, 157
Adult therapy, confidentiality in, 366–67
Adventures of Sir Galalad of King Arthur's Court, 714
Affection
  for patient, 107–9
  quantification theory of, 832
  See also Therapist-patient relationship
Age
  -appropriate pictures, 212–13
  of candidates for therapy, 379–80
  family therapy use and, 796–97, 809
  gestational, 168, 170–71
  for mutual storytelling and derivative games, 408–9, 607
  of patient, parental involvement and, 380
  of speech onset, 177–78
  for *Talking, Feeling, and Doing Game,* 683

Aichhorn, August, 109
Alerting mechanism, dream as, 748–54
Alexander, F., 117, 204
Allen, F. H., 44–45
Allen, Woody, 81, 343
Alphabet Soup Game, 577–89
Ambivalence
  introduction through mutual story-telling of, 428
  parental, over treatment, 372–75
American society, increasing psy-chopathy in, 845–46
"Amotivational syndrome," 144–45
Analytically oriented psychotherapy. *See* Psychoanalytically oriented child psychotherapy
Andersen, Hans Christian, 75
Anger
  over birth of sibling, case of, 470–99
  blocks used in expression of, 57–58
  displaced, 565, 669–71
  fairy tales and release of, 707–8
  guilt over, 305–6, 390, 626–27
  of passive-aggressive child, 145–46
  profanity used in, 632–33
  water play for release of, 58–59
Anger inhibition problem
  during divorce, 690
  dream analysis in case of, 774–87
  mutual storytelling technique in case of, 430–37
  nightmares as result of, 756–57
  story about healthy expression of anger, 701
  stuttering related to, 391–93
Animal symbols in fables, 702–5
Animal transformation questions, re-sponses to
  of children, 320–34
  of fathers, 287–90
  need for specificity in, 330
  normal, 322–23
Annie Hall (movie), 81, 343
Anorexia in males, 11
Antisocial behavior, 646–52
  attempt on therapist's life, 139–41
  Doing Card response to lessen, 639–40, 645–46
  family therapy for, 798–99, 803
  Feeling Card response focusing on pain of, 637

  due to feelings about competent sibling, 470–99
  Talking Card response focusing on effects of, 624–25
Anxiety
  -alleviating factor in hostility, 140
  dream analysis in case of, 769–73
  from ignorance, 687–88
  in initial interview, 28, 156, 196–97, 199–200
  panic dream caused by, 758–59
  See also Separation anxiety disor-der
Apathy, mutual storytelling tech-nique in case of, 415–17, 430–37
Aristotle, 86
Assets, opportunity in initial inter-view to present, 204–5. *See also* Accomplishment(s)
Assistant therapists, parents as. *See* Parental involvement in child's treatment
Association, free, 731–33, 769, 830
Atmosphere of story, analyzing, 413–14
Attempt on therapist's life, 139–41
Attention deficit disorder (ADD), 851–52
Atypicality as criteria for ascertain-ing psychopathology, 331
Audio tape recorder, use of, 31, 409–10
Axline, V., 15, 49

"Baby talk," 111
Background information
  from father, 277–96
  from mother, 250–75
  See also Screening evaluation, ini-tial
Bacon, Francis, 239
Bag of Things Game, The, 543–50
Bag of Toys Game, The, 532–43
Bag of Words Game, The, 550–58
Baldock, Edgar, 100
Baum, L. Frank, 715
Beauty and the Beast, 706, 707
Beery, K. E., 218
Bellak, L., 597
Bellak, S. S., 597
Bender, L., 51, 60–61, 62

Bibliotherapy, 34, 685–721
  expository books, 687–97
    Boys and Girls Book About Divorce, The, 32, 34, 151, 671, 689–93
    Boys and Girls Book About One-Parent Families, The, 693–94
    Boys and Girls Book About Stepfamilies, The, 695
    MBD: The Family Book About Minimal Brain Dysfunction, 32, 688–89
    Parents Book About Divorce, The, 158, 229, 695–96
    Understanding Children—A Parents Guide to Child Rearing, 34, 696–97
  fables, 701–5
  fairy tales, 705–20
    Fairy Tales for Today's Chidren, 34, 711–12
    Modern Fairy Tales, 34, 112–15
    reasons for attraction to, 706–10
    use of, 710–11
    Dorothy and the Lizard of Oz, 715–20
  reality oriented stories, 698–701
Biological psychiatry, 8, 27, 35, 849, 859
Birth
  delivery at, 169–71
  pregnancy, information on mother's, 167–69
  of sibling, 226, 470, 480–83, 804–5
  weight, 168, 170
Blank screen approach, 76, 614, 685, 731–33
Blocks, use of, 57–60
Board games, 34, 63–64. *See also* Mutual storytelling derivative games; *Talking, Feeling, and Doing Game, The*
Board of Objects Game, The, 523–32
Borderline psychotics, 725, 806
Bowen, M., 817
Boys and Girls Book About Divorce, The (Gardner), 32, 34, 151, 671, 689–93
Boys and Girls Book About One-Parent Families, The (Gardner), 693–94
Boys and Girls Book About Stepfamilies, The (Gardner), 695

Brain cell stimulation, dream as mechanism for providing, 759–60
"Brainwashing," psychotherapy as, 802
Brief psychotherapies, 74–75
Broman, M., 218
Bronx High School of Science, The, 2–3
Bruch, Hilda, 10–11
Buck, J. N., 53
Buktenika, N. A., 218
Burns, R. C., 52–53, 125
Butler, Samuel, 1

Caemmerer, A., 218
Cancellation of sessions, 236–37
Candidates for dream analysis, 760–62
Candy, seductive reasoning with, 133–34
Castration threats, 394–95, 453, 455, 456, 458. *See also* Oedipal problems
CAT, 597
Channing, William Ellery, 685
Chess, S., 373
Child psychiatry, residency training in, 12–18, 20–21
Child psychoanalysis
  discipline of, 722–25
  historical considerations of, 36–38
  inapplicability of psychoanalytic techniques, 726–36
  Talking, Feeling, and Doing Game and, 740–44
  See also Psychoanalytically oriented child psychotherapy
Child rearing
  inquiry of mother regarding, 245–48
  joint interview and discussion of, 350–52
  Understanding Children: A Parents Guide to Child Rearing, 34, 696–97
Children's Apperception Test (CAT), 597
Child's Book About Brain Injury, The (Gardner), 32, 688
Child talk, 111–13
Cinderella, 707–9
Cinderelma, 711

Clay, use of, 55–57, 59–60
Client-centered therapy, 15–17, 46–49
Clinical examples
  of Alphabet Soup Game, 579–89
  of *Bag of Things Game*, 544–50
  of *Bag of Toys Game*, 533–43
  of *Bag of Words Game*, 553–58
  of *Board of Objects Game*, 527–32
  of dramatized storytelling, 468–518
  of dream psychoanalysis, 769–87
  of family therapy, 834–38
  of *Feel and Tell* game, 572–77
  of *Make-a-Picture Story Cards*, 598–607
  of mutual storytelling technique, 415–64
  of parental involvement in child's treatment, 384–403
  of *Pick-a-Face Game*, 591–95
  of *Scrabble for Juniors*, 561–70
  of therapist-patient relationships, 138–52
Cognitive capacity for psychoanalytic inquiry, 14–15, 723, 726, 727
Cognitive distortions, correction of, 121–22
Cognitive therapies, 851
Columbia-Presbyterian Medical Center, New York Psychiatric Institute at, 8–18, 20–21, 27
Communication
  child talk, 111–13
  confidential relationship with child and, 370
  "double bind," 822–23
  encouraging open family, 243–44, 370–71
  fostered by initial three person interview, 154
  after parental death, 694
  primary vs. secondary process level, 803
  problems, family therapy for, 797–98
  between stepparents and natural parents, 801, 836–37
  at symbolic level, 41–43
  therapist as educator, 85, 120–26
Competition
  benevolently motivated, 50
  in board games, 63–64

  with father, case of, 321–22
  healthy vs. unhealthy, 522
  in mutual storytelling derivative games, 521–22
  in team therapy approach, 825
Compulsion, touching, 397–98, 579–89
Compulsive laughing problem, 322
Conceptualizations, use of, 87, 299
Concrete examples, effectiveness of, 87, 299–300
Condensation in dreams, 746
Confidentiality
  in adolescent therapy, 368–69
  in adult therapy, 366–67
  in child psychotherapy, 369–72
  in Little Hans case, 386
  parental involvement in child's treatment and, 366–72
Conflicts
  intrapsychic, 478–80, 735–36
  loyalty, 796, 799, 812
  marital, 32–33, 249–50, 799–800
Confrontational process, 125–26, 829
Conjoint therapy of parents, 250. See *also* Marital counseling
Conn, J., 41–42, 406
Conscious awareness of unconscious material, 405, 726–27. See *also* Insight
Conscious material, defined, 67
Conscious mind, explaining to child, 765–66
Consensual validation, 125
Constructive and cohesive factors in pathological family interactions, 818–22
"Constructive living," lessons in, 84, 842
Contingency arrangement in malpractice suits, 848
Convulsions, 185–86
Cooperation
  fable about, 704
  at home, 226–27
  of parents, 389–90
Coordination, initial evaluation of, 178–79
Corporal punishment, 245, 445
Corrective emotional experience, 117–18, 204
Cost-effectiveness, emphasis on, 850–56

Costumes, use of, 61–62
Co-therapists, 824–26
Couch, use of, 76, 731–32. *See also* Blank screen approach
Counseling, marital, 249–50, 360–61, 796
Court-ordered custody evaluation, 839
Court-ordered family therapy, 839–40
Creativity of therapist, 101–3
Cuddling
  direct verbal inquiry with child about, 302
  mother's response to, 245–46
  reaction from birth to, 174–75
Cure
  quick, craze for, 849–50
  time-limited therapy and, 74–75, 239–40, 854
  transference, 115–17
Curse words, use of, 625, 632–33
Custody evaluations, 34–35, 839
Custody litigation, 158–59, 310, 796, 812–13, 835–37, 839–40

Dance, 62
Danger, dream as vehicle for alerting individual to, 748–54
Death
  of parent, 147–49, 693–94, 805–6
  of sibling, 398–401
Decision regarding therapy, inability to make, 230–31
Defense mechanisms, 8–9, 727–28, 736. *See also* Denial mechanisms
"Defensive medicine," 847–48
Deficiencies
  child's reluctance to reveal, 119, 200–201
  direct verbal inquiry with child about, 302
  opportunities to reveal therapist's, 149–50, 621–22, 639–40, 659–60
  Talking Card response focusing on, 617–18
  therapeutic benefits to revealing, 203–4
Dehumanization of psychiatric care, 856–58
Delusions about therapist, 76–77,

128–29, 614, 732–33. *See also* Therapist-patient relationship
Denial mechanisms, 482–83, 488
  child psychoanalysis and, 727–28
  of dying parent, 805
  fable about, 704
  mother's description of marriage and, 248
  Pick-a-Face Game, use in case of, 591–95
  stories dealing with, 313, 314, 380, 700, 741–42
Dependency, 304–5, 704. *See also* Overprotectiveness of mother
Deprivation, cases of, 106–7, 204–5, 257, 279, 304, 306–7, 308, 312, 313, 338, 488, 570, 730
Desensitization, 521, 575–77, 700, 754–55, 764
"Designated patient," 801–6, 828
Development
  Freudian stages of psychosexual, 734–35
  milestones of, initial evaluation of, 175–78
  psychotherapy based on child's particular, 738–39
Diagnostic evaluation, intensive, 239–363
  of child, 296–340
    direct verbal inquiry, 298–304
    Draw-a-Picture and Draw-a-Family tests, 314–18
    dreams, 334–40
    first memory question, 306–9
    free picture, 309–14
    three wishes question, 304–6
    verbal projective questions, 318–34
  family interview, 353–56
  of father, 275–96
  joint interview with parents, 341–52
    correction of distortions and false data, 341–44
    marriage, learning about the, 346, 348–50
    parental dealings with children, 350–52
  of mother, 240–75
    background information, 250–75
    causes of child's difficulties, 244–45

Diagnostic evaluation, intensive (*cont.*)
  of mother
    description of marriage, 248–50
    initial inquiry, 241–44
    parental dealing with child, 245–48
    psychiatric treatment, history of, 250
    presentation of findings, 356–63
    to parents, 358–63
    preparation of, 356–58
Diagnostic related groups (DRGs), 855–56
Dickens, Charles, 96
Direct interpretation of drawing, 53–54
Divorce
  animosity spread to grandparents, 814
  Boys and Girls Book About Divorce, The, 32, 34, 151, 671, 689–93
  Boys and Girls Book About One-Parent Families, The, 693–94
  family therapy and, 810–11, 834–38
  initial consultation and, 160–61
  Parents Book About Divorce, The, 158, 229, 695–96
  parents' use of children in, 799–800
  payment of fees and, 160
  psychopathic behavior derived from conflict in, 647
  teaching reality about parents in, 124–25
  telling child of impending, 229
  See also Marital conflict; Marital counseling; Marriage
Doll play, 41, 42, 43–44, 340, 471–99, 627
Dorothy and the Lizard of Oz, 720
Dr. Gardner's Fables for Our Times (Gardner), 704
Dr. Gardner's Stories About the Real World (Gardner), 126, 698–701, 741
Draco the Dragon, 714
Dramatized storytelling, 61–62, 465–518
  clinical examples, 468–518
    antisocial behavior due to sibling rivalry, 470–99

  in neurologically based learning disability cases, 468–70, 499–518
  as enriching experience, 132
  parental involvement, 467
Draw-a-Family test, responses to
  of children, 314–18
  of fathers, 290–94
  of mothers, 265–70
Draw-a-Person Test, 53–54
  for child
    in initial interview, 213–15
    in intensive diagnostic evaluation, 314–18
  father's responses to, 290–94
  mother's responses to, 265–70
Drawing
  developmental and intellectual assessment from, 54
  direct interpretation, 53–54
  fantasies created around, 50–53
  finger painting, 54–55, 59–60
  freely-drawn picture, 211–13, 309–14
  projective drawing technique, 52–53
Dream psychoanalysis, 744–87
  clinical examples, 769–87
  purposes of dreams, 745–60
    alerting individual to danger, 748–54
    brain cell stimulation, 759–60
    desensitization to trauma, 754–55, 764
    nightmare, 755–58
    panic dream, 758–59
    for wish fulfillment, 745–48, 767–68
  teaching children, 760–69
    fundamental principles of analysis, 762–65
Dreams
  of child, diagnostic evaluation through, 334–40
  of father, 294–96
  formation by unconscious processes, 762–65
  Freud on, 677
  information about underlying psychodynamics in, 335–40
  latent vs. manifest content, 746
  mother's assistance in analysis, 376, 401–3

prior to initial evaluation, 270–71
repetitious, 267, 270, 271–72, 294–96, 334
termination, 843
DRGs, 855–56
Drug therapy, 361, 851, 852
DSM-III, 224, 227–28, 851
Dunn, L. M. and L. M., 138

Educational experience
of author, 2–7
excitement about learning, encouraging, 742–44
therapy as, 84–89, 686
levels of learning, 85–89
therapist as teacher, 85, 120–26
value of, 398–401
Efficacy of child psychotherapy, 842–43
Egocentricism, 94, 470, 637
Elective mutism, 178
Elkisch, P., 53
Ellis, A., 122
Emotional experience, corrective, 117–18, 204
Emulation of therapist, 78–82
Equilibrium
family, 374, 818–22, 838
marital, 346, 350
Erickson, E. H., 58
Erikson, M., 87
Evaluation
custody, 34–35, 839
for family therapy, 807–9
See also Diagnostic evaluation, intensive; Screening evaluation, initial
Expectations
from treatment, drawings revealing, 315–17
use of child to fulfill parental pathological, 816–18
Experience
corrective emotional, 117–18
parental involvement in treatment and, 382–83, 387–88
providing patients with, 88–89, 387–88, 679–82, 794–95
reliving past, 734
Expository books, 689–97
Boys and Girls Book About Divorce, The, 32, 34, 151, 671, 689–93

Boys and Girls Book About One-Parent Families, The, 693–94
Boys and Girls Book About Stepfamilies, The, 695
MBD: The Family Book About Minimal Brain Dysfunction, 32, 688–89
Parents Book About Divorce, The, 158, 229, 695–96
Understanding Children—A Parents Guide to Child Rearing, 34, 696–97

Fables, 701–5
Failure, therapeutic, therapist's comfort with, 104–5
Fairy tales, 705–20
Fairy Tales for Today's Children, 34, 711–12
Modern Fairy Tales, 34, 712–15
reasons for attraction to, 706–10
use of, 710–11
Dorothy and the Lizard of Oz, 715–20
Family
background information
from father, 277–96
from mother, 250–75
drawings of, 215, 290–94
equilibrium, 374, 818–22, 838
history, 187–89
interview, 352–56, 807–9
members, individual therapy of, 28–30
normal, defining, 790–92
"projection process," 817–18
psychiatrist, 792
Family Evaluation in Child Custody Litigation (Gardner), 35, 247
Family therapy, 9, 103, 789–840
clinical example, 834–38
common psychodynamic patterns, 814–23
court-ordered, 839–40
deprivation of self-assertion through routine, 778
evaluating and preparing families for, 807–14
expression of anger in, 776
situations contraindicating, 801–7
situations indicating, 796–801

Family therapy (*cont.*)
  Talking, Feeling, and Doing Game,
    for, 683–84
  technical considerations, 823–38
    "designated patient," changing
      family's concept of, 828
    family-individual therapy combi-
      nation, 832–33
    revelation, purpose of, 830
    Talking, Feeling, and Doing Game
      in, 833–34
    team therapists, 824–26
    therapeutic ally in, 828–29
    transferential reactions, 831–32
    treatment in home, 823–24
    utilization of other parties in
      treatment, 826–28
  theoretical considerations, 790–96
Father
  history of, 189
  intensive diagnostic evaluation of,
    275–96
    background information, 277–96
    initial inquiry, 275–76
    marriage, description of, 276
    psychiatric treatment, history of,
      276–77
  receptivity to "opening up," 240
  relationship with child's maternal
    grandmother, 251
  See also Parent(s)
Fear
  of expressing feelings, 302–3
  of going to psychiatrist, 202, 316
  as symptom, 69–70
Feel and Tell, 570–77
Fees, payment of
  compromised parental commit-
    ment due to, 372–73
  discussion with parents about,
    161–62, 233–37
  by divorced parents, 160
  for missed sessions, 236–37
  prepaid treatment plans, 852–56
  reduction of, 235–36
  trust involved in, 846–47
Fiddler on the Roof (movie), 822
Fields, W. C., 670
"Fields' Rule," 671
Finger paints, 54–55, 59–60
First memory question, responses to
  of child, 306–9

  of fathers, 278–80
  of mothers, 253–55
Five wishes question, responses to,
  258–62, 281–83
Foods, seductive reasoning with,
  133–34
"Foreign boy" question, 769
Formal operations stage, 14, 40, 334,
  405, 723
Framo, J. L., 791, 815, 816, 827
Frank, L. K., 58, 61, 62
Free association, 731–33, 769, 830
Freely-drawn picture, 211–13, 309–
  14
French, T., 117
Frequency of treatment, 724–25
Freud, Anna, 39–40, 115, 121, 130,
  385, 405, 729, 732, 736
Freud, Sigmund, 7, 8–9, 36–38, 39,
  74, 88, 122, 371, 384–91, 451–
  52, 677, 682, 731, 732, 736,
  739, 744–47, 764
Fromm, Erich, 21, 787
Fromm-Reichmann, Frieda, 21, 132,
  787
Frustration
  nightmares as result of pent-up,
    756–57
  tolerance, therapist's, 100–101
Fun, seductive reasoning with, 131–
  32
Funeral, child's attendance of par-
    ent's, 693–94. *See also* Death
Future of field of child psychother-
    apy, 845–58
  craze for quick cures, 849–50
  dehumanization of psychiatric
    care, 856–58
  fees, payment of, 846–47
  increasing psychopathy in Ameri-
    can society and, 845–46
  malpractice suits, 847–48
  prepaid treatment plans, 852–56
  training, 850–52

Games, board, 34, 63–64. *See also*
  Mutual storytelling derivative
  games; *Talking, Feeling, and
  Doing Game, The*
Gardner, A. K., 218
Gardner, R. A., 64, 91, 159, 204, 218,

247, 250, 364, 374, 395, 463, 464, 550, 694, 735, 789–90, 799, 803, 818, 833, 840, 841
Garland, Judy, 719–20
Gasset, Ortega y, 36
Gaudi, Antonio, 404
Gilbert, William S., 519
GMBDS. *See* Group of Minimal Brain Dysfunction Syndromes (GMBDS)
Goldenson, R. M., 58, 61, 62
Goldings, H., 686
Goldings, R., 686
Goodenough, F., 54
Gourevitch, Anna, 22–23
Grab-bag games, 532–58
  Bag of Things Game, 543–50
  Bag of Toys Game, 532–43
  Bag of Words Game, 550–58
Graf, Max, 36, 37, 387
Grafton, Samuel, 841
"Grandma's criteria," 247, 301
Grandparents
  animosity of divorce spread to, 814
  in family therapy, 813–14, 826–28
  influence of, 251–52
  information about, 251–52
Grimm, Jakob and Wilhelm, 705
Group of Minimal Brain Dysfunction Syndromes (GMBDS), 162
  causes during pregnancy of, 167–69
  colic, history of, 175
  complications with delivery and, 170, 171
  comprehension and understanding, evaluation of, 179
  congenital anomalies and, 174
  developmental lags, 175–78
  genetic factors, 189
  home behavior, 183
  MBD: The Family Book About Minimal Brain Dysfunction, 32, 688–89
  medical history evaluation for, 186
  medications as factor in, 187
  peer relationships and, 181–83
  reaction to cuddling and, 174–75
  school performance and, 179–81
  screening battery, 218–21
Group therapy, 10, 23–24, 94, 102–3, 616, 683

Guilt, 122
  over anger, 305–6, 390, 626–27
  Doing Card response focusing on, 639–40
  over hostility, 317, 626, 805
  kinds of, 242
  panic dream caused by, 758–59
  parental, 241–42, 373–74, 377–78
  psychodynamic information used to reduce or increase, 739
  Talking Card response to reduce, 625–26
Gunplay, influence of, 531

Haley, J., 87
Hallucinations as vehicles for desensitization, 755
Hammer, E. F., 53
Hans and Greta, 711–12
Hansel and Gretel, 706, 707, 708
Harris, D. B., 54
Hartley, R. E., 58, 61, 62
Hass, R. B., 62
Hats, play acting with, 62
Haworth, M. R., 56
Health maintenance organizations (HMOs), 853–55
Heimlich, E., 63
Historical considerations in child psychotherapy, 36–65
  Allen's "relationship therapy," 44–45
  blocks, use of, 57–60
  child psychoanalysis, 36–38
  clay, use of, 55–57, 59–60
  communication at symbolic level, 41–43
  doll play, use of, 41, 42, 43–44
  dramatization, 61–62
  drawings
    direct interpretation of, 53–54
    fantasies created around, 50–53
  finger paints, 54–55, 59–60
  "paraverbal therapy," 63
  psychoanalytic play therapy, 39–41
  puppets and marionettes, use of, 60–61
  release therapy, 49–50
  Rogers' "nondirective" or "client-centered therapy," 15–17, 46–49

Historical considerations in child
psychotherapy (*cont.*)
traditional competitive board
games, 34, 63–64
water play, 58–60
HMOs, 853–55
Home behavior
as criterion of psychopathology,
206
direct verbal inquiry with child
about, 301
initial evaluation of, 183
need for treatment and, 225–27
Homosexuality, 339–40, 750–54, 817
Hospitalization, 795–96
Hospitals, funding for, 850–51
Hostility
alerting dream and awareness of,
754
anxiety-alleviating factor in, 140
blocks used in expression of, 57–58
clay used for release of, 56
in fairy tales, 714
guilt over, 317, 626, 805
nightmares as result of, 756–57
parental, 146–47, 381
parental involvement in treatment
and, 381, 383
playing tricks as expression of, 503
therapist's role in releasing, 60
water play for release of, 58–59
Housekeeper, use in family therapy,
826
House-Tree-Person Technique, 53
Hug-Hellmuth, H. von, 39, 404, 405,
732, 823–24
Humor, 107, 132–33
Hypnotherapy, 731

"Ice breakers," 134–38
Idealization of therapist, 76–77, 128–
29, 614
Identification
Talking Card response allowing
for, 620–21
with therapist, 78–82, 118–20
"Identified patient," 801–6, 828
Idiosyncratic elements in dream, fo-
cusing on, 780–86
Idolization of therapist, 76–77, 128–
29, 732–33
Impartiality of therapist, 374, 839–40

Independent practice associations
(IPAs), 855
Individual child psychotherapy with
parental observation and intermittent participation, 365, 378
Individual therapy-family therapy
combination, 832–33
Initial screening evaluation. *See*
Screening evaluation, initial
Insight
development and utilization of,
737–38
effectiveness in therapeutic
change, 40
experience vs., 89
therapeutic benefit of, 682
into unconscious processes, 726–
27
See also Child psychoanalysis; Psychoanalytically oriented child
psychotherapy
Intensive diagnostic evaluation. *See*
Diagnostic evaluation, intensive
Interpretation
of Draw-a-Person test, 213–14
of drawing, direct, 53–54
factors determining, 343
of freely-drawn picture, 212–13
of self-created stories, 213
See also Diagnostic evaluation, intensive; Mutual storytelling derivative games; Mutual
storytelling technique; Psychoanalytically oriented child
psychotherapy; *Talking, Feeling, and Doing Game, The*
Interpretation of Dreams, The
(Freud), 747
Interviews
family, 352–56, 807–9
initial
with child alone, 210–23
with child and parents together,
196–208
with parents alone, 208–10
play, 41–42
See also Diagnostic evaluation, intensive
Intimacy, self-revelation and, 126–29
Introspective children, dream analysis and, 762. *See also* Child
psychoanalysis; Insight; Psy-

choanalytically oriented child psychotherapy

IPAs, 855

J.B. (MacLeish), 26
Jack and the Beanstalk, 706, 708, 712–13
Jealousy of therapist-patient relationship, parental, 373
Johnson, A. M., 123, 374
Johnson, E. W., 686
Joint interview with parents, 341–52
  correction of distortions or false data, 341–44
  information on marriage from, 348–50
  larger perspective from, 341, 345–48
  parental dealing with children, 350–52
Jung, Carl, 747

Kanner, L., 39
Kaufman, S. H., 52–53
Keaton, Diane, 81, 343
Kellogg, R., 53
Kessler, J. W., 373
Khan, M. M. R., 98, 99–100
Kinetic Family Drawings, 52–53
Klein, Melanie, 39, 40, 115, 385, 405, 729, 732
Kolb, Lawrence C., 8
Kritzberg, N. I., 217, 523, 558
Kubie, L., 816

Langford, William, 12–13, 21
Lazarus, Emma, 82
Learning
  academic, initial evaluation of, 181
  encouraging excitement about, 742–44
  from fairy tales, 709–10
  therapeutic, levels of, 85–89
  See also Educational experience; Neurologically based learning disability; School
Length of treatment, 232–33, 360, 724
Levy, D. M., 49–50
Lippman, H. S., 373
Litigation, custody, 158–59, 310, 796, 812–13, 835–37, 839–40

Little Hans case, 36–38, 371–72, 384–91, 451
Living experience, seizing opportunities for, 88–89, 387–88, 660, 679–82, 794–95
Love in *The Wizard of Oz,* 716–17
Low-birth-weight babies, 170
Lowenheim, Alfred, 691
Loyalty conflicts, 796, 799, 812, 836–37. *See also* Custody litigation; Divorce
Lying, 119–20, 347, 423, 701, 704

MacBeth (Shakespeare), 86
Machover, K., 53–54, 214
Mack and the Beanstalk, 712, 713–14
MacLeish, Archibald, 26
Magic
  cure fantasies, 420–28, 499–518, 536, 538–39
  in fairy tales, attraction to, 707, 710
  powers of thought, notion of, 626–27
  tricks, seductive reasoning with, 134–35
Make-a-Picture Story Cards (MAPS), 215–16, 595–607
  advantages over TAT, 216
  diagnostic utilization, 595–97
  therapeutic utilization, 598–607
"Malevolent transformation," 447
Malpractice, 358, 362–63, 367, 847–48
Manifest content of dreams, 746
MAPS. *See Make-a-Picture Story Cards* (MAPS)
Marcus, I., 61–62
Marionettes, 60–61
Marital counseling, 249–50, 360–61, 796
Marital equilibrium, 346, 350
Marriage
  Cinderelma story, 711
  complementary psychopathology in, 814–16
  conscious and unconscious reasons behind, 815–16
  parents description of, 209
    by father, 276
    in joint interview, 346, 348–50
    by mother, 248–50
  residual psychological, 800, 810

Masochism, case of pathological family interaction based on, 820–22

Masturbation, 634–35

Maternal grandparents, information about, 251–52

Mayle, P., 686

MBD. *See* Group of Minimal Brain Dysfunction Syndromes (GMBDS)

MBD: The Family Book About Minimal Brain Dysfunction (Gardner), 32, 688–89

Medical history, initial evaluation of, 185–87

Medication, 187, 361, 851, 852

Meister, Morris, 2

Memory
   first memory question, responses to
   of child, 306–9
   of father, 278–80
   of mother, 253–55
   of therapist's own childhood, 95–96, 613–14, 659–60

Metaphor, value of, 86–87. *See also* Dramatized storytelling; Mutual storytelling technique; Mutual storytelling derivative games; *Talking, Feeling, and Doing Game, The*

Michaels, R., 686

Minimal brain dysfunction. *See* Group of Minimal Brain Dysfunction Syndromes (GMBDS); Neurologically based learning disability

Missed sessions, payment for, 236–37

Modern Fairy Tales (Gardner), 34, 712–15

Morals in fables, 704–5

Moreno, J. L., 62

Moskowitz, J. A., 135

Mother
   assistance in dream analysis, 376, 401–3
   failure, feelings of, 241
   guilt feelings, 241–42
   history of, 187–89
   intensive diagnostic evaluation of, 240–75

background information, 250–75
causes of child's difficulties, 244–45
description of marriage, 248–50
initial inquiry, 241–44
parental dealings with child, 245–48
psychiatric treatment, history of, 250
involvement in school activities, 246
overprotectiveness of, 572–77, 769–70, 799, 828–29
sexual seductivity of, 394–97, 398, 453, 454, 553–58, 579, 589
unwed, 694
See also Parent(s)

Motivation
   family therapy, requirement of, 797
   Feeling Card response encouraging, 633, 636–37
   of therapist, treatment of projected self as, 94–95

Mourning, psychological importance of, 400

Mullahy, P., 126

Multiple births, child's reaction to, 804. *See also* Siblings

Murray, H., 216, 597

Music, therapeutic aspects of, 63

Mutism, elective, 178

Mutual storytelling derivative games, 519–608
   Alphabet Soup Game, 577–89
   Board of Objects Game, 523–32
   competition in, 521–22
   family therapy, use in, 802–3
   Feel and Tell, 570–77
   Grab-bag games, 532–58
      Bag of Things Game, 543–50
      Bag of Toys Game, 533–43
      Bag of Words Game, 550–58
   Make-a-Picture Story Cards, 215–16, 595–607
   Pick-a-Face Game, 589–95
   Scrabble for Juniors, 558–70

Mutual storytelling technique, 21, 43, 62, 150, 404–64
   audio tape recorder use in, 31
   basic technique, 408–10
   clinical examples, 415–64

family therapy, use in, 802–3
fundamentals of story analysis,
    413–15
historical background, 404–8
self-created stories, specific tech-
    nique for eliciting, 410–13
video tape recorder, use in, 33

Napoli, P. J., 55
Need for treatment
    criteria for deciding, 223–28
    recommendation of, 231–33
    recommendation of no, 229–30
Negative reinforcement, 520–21
Neighborhood, peer relationships in,
    225
Neurologically based learning disa-
    bility
    cases of
        animal question responses in,
            320–21
        Bag of Things Game, use in, 548–
            50
        dramatized storytelling used in,
            468–70, 499–518
        first memory response in, 308
    malpractice suits over, 848
    in sibling, 539, 805
Neurosis
    intrapsychic conflicts and, 735–36
    transference, 114, 729
New York Association for Brain In-
    jured Children, 32
New York Psychiatric Institute at
    Columbia-Presbyterian Medical
    Center, 8–18, 20–21
Nightmares, 755–57
Nondirective therapy, 15–17, 46–49
Nonmedical disciplines, child psy-
    chotherapy in, 858
Normal family, defining, 790–92

O'Dell, S., 53
Oedipal interest, 451–52
    family factors and development of,
        589
Oedipal problems
    author's approach to alleviation of,
        454–55
    cases of
        Alphabet Soup Game, use in,
            579–89

Bag of Words Game, use in, 553–
    58
mutual storytelling technique in,
    456–63
tics developed due to, 394–97,
    579
touching compulsion due to,
    397–98, 579–89
fairy tales on, 712–14
family factors and development of,
    589
Oedipus complex
    author's view of, 452–54
    Freud's theory of, 451–52
One-parent families, 693–94. *See also*
    Divorce
Options, expanding patient's reper-
    toire of, 73–74, 126, 436–37,
    641, 655–56, 749–50
Osler, Geoffrey, 742–43
Overloading of messages, 532, 539
Overprotectiveness of mother, 572–
    77, 769–70, 799, 828–29

Paints, finger, 54–55, 59–60. *See also*
    Drawing
Panic attack, 759
Panic dream, 758–59
Paraverbal therapy, 63
Parental alienation syndrome, 796
Parental capacity, 247–48, 301–2
Parental involvement in child's treat-
    ment, 14, 30–31, 233, 360, 364–
    403
    clinical examples, 384–403
    confidentiality issue, 366–72
    disagreement over, 161
    in dramatized storytelling, 467
    Little Hans case, 36–38, 371–72,
        384–91, 451
    parental ambivalence, reasons for,
        372–75
    situations contraindicating paren-
        tal presence, 379–84
    ways for parent to be useful, 375–
        79
Parent-child relationship
    alleviation of oedipal problems
        and, 455
    fairy tales about, 706–7, 711–14
    in initial interview, 207–8

Parent(s)
accepting reality about, 124, 542–43, 570, 670, 806–7
child's telling dreams to, 761–62
communication between stepparents and natural, 836–37
death of, 147–49, 693–94, 805–6
depth of affection for child, 204–5
description of child's assets, 204–5
diagnostic evaluation of. *See under* Diagnostic evaluation, intensive
divulging adolescent's dangerous behaviors to, 369
of father, 277
hostile, 146–47, 381
illness of, 189, 384, 600–607
in initial interview, 28, 154–56
with child, 196–208
with parents alone, 208–10
of mother, relationship between, 252
pathological expectations, use of child to fulfill, 816–18
presence during intensive evaluation of child, 297–98
presentation of diagnostic findings to, 359–63
reactions to child's therapy, 100–101
separation from child-therapist dyad, disadvantages of, 155–57
siblings discussion about, 354–55
taking child's side in conflict with, 109–11
therapist's experience as, 103
therapist's relationship with, 111, 377
time alone with child, 106–7
withholding information from child, 201–2
See also Father; Marriage; Mother
Parents Book About Divorce, The (Gardner), 158, 229, 695–96
Participation, parental. *See* Parental involvement in child's treatment
Passive-aggressive child, 145–46, 222–23, 311, 324–25
Passive role for therapist, problems with, 102. *See also* Blank screen approach

Patient-therapist relationship. *See* Therapist-patient relationship
Peabody Picture Vocabulary Test (PPVT), 135–38
Pediatric psychiatrist, use of term, 725
Peer relationships, 206, 642–43
determining need for treatment and, 225
direct verbal inquiry with child about, 300–301
initial evaluation of, 181–83
Scrabble for Juniors, use in case of difficult, 561–64
Perrault, Charles, 705
Personal History of David Copperfield, The (Dickens), 96
Personality, genetic vs. environmental determination of, 119
Phallic symbols, 268, 764, 765
Phobic child, 124
death of sibling and case of, 398–401
Little Hans case, 36–38, 371–72, 384–91, 451
Piaget, J., 14, 40, 93, 334, 405, 723
Pick-a-Face Game, 589–95
Play
acting, 61–62
doll, 41, 42, 43–44, 340, 471–99, 627
interview, 41–42
therapy, 17
active, 42–43
balance between play and therapy, 64, 98, 107, 131, 377, 859
clay, use of, 55–57, 59–60
competitive board games, 34, 63–64
enriching experiences in, 132
finger painting, 54–55, 59–60
psychoanalytic, 39–41
water play, 58–60
See also Dramatized storytelling
Pleasure in therapist-patient relationship, 108–9
Pomeroy, W. B., 686
Positive regard, "unconditional," 15, 17, 47, 108
Positive reinforcement, 520–21, 610–12
Post-marital conflict, family therapy

for, 801. *See also* Divorce; Step-parents
Post-traumatic stress reaction, 804–5
PPVT, 135–38
Predictability of therapeutic process, 102
Preferred-provider organizations (PPOs), 854–55
Premarital relationship of parents, 257, 281
Prepaid treatment plans, 852–56
Preparation of participants in family therapy, 809–13
Presentation of diagnostic evaluation, 356–63
  to parents, 358–63
  preparation of, 356–58
Pressure of tests on child, 297
Prince and the Pauper, The, 714
Prince and the Poor Boy, The, 714–15
Princess and the Three Tasks, The, 711
Privacy of therapist's family, 659
Private practice of author, 27–35
Procrustes, Greek legend of, 793
Profanity, use of, 625, 632–33
Projection
  clay, use of, 55–57
  "family projection process," 817–18
  in nightmares, 757
  onto spouse, 816
  termination and, determination of, 844
  of therapist into child's position, 93–95
  See also Mutual storytelling derivative games; Mutual storytelling technique; *Talking, Feeling, and Doing Game, The*
Projection Action Test, 62
Projective drawing technique, 52–53
Projective questions, responses to
  of children in diagnostic evaluation, 318–34
  of fathers, 281–90
  of mothers, 257–58, 262–64
Psychoanalysis
  of author, 6–7, 17–18, 21–22
  cognitive capacity for, 14–15, 723, 726, 727
  confidentiality principle, 371–72

  techniques of, inapplicability to children, 726–36
  childhood roots of symptoms, analysis of, 733–34
  denial mechanisms and, 727–28
  free association and blank screen, 731–33
  Freudian stages of psychosexual development, 734–35
  superego and intrapsychic conflict, 735–36
  transference and resolution of transference neurosis, 728–31
  unconscious material, dealing with, 726–27
  training in, 21–27, 787
  See also Freud, Sigmund; Theoretical and developmental foundations of author's techniques
Psychoanalytically oriented child psychotherapy, 722–88
  child psychoanalysis, discipline of, 722–25
  defining, 738–39
  dream psychoanalysis, 744–87
  clinical examples, 769–87
  purposes of dreams, 745–60, 764, 767–68
  teaching children, 760–69
  insight, development and utilization of, 737–38
  Talking, Feeling, and Doing Game, use of, 740–44
  use of psychodynamic information, 739–40
Psychoanalytic play therapy, 39–41
Psychopathy in American society, increase in, 845–46
Psychosexual development, Freudian stages of, 734–35
Psychosis, borderline, 725, 806
Psychostimulant medication, 852
Psychotherapeutic process, central elements in, 66–90
  as educational experience, 84–89, 686
  levels of learning, 85–89
  therapist as teacher, 85, 120–26
  opening up new options, 73–74, 126, 436–37, 641, 655–56, 749–50
  symptoms, origin of, 67–72

Psychotherapeutic process, central
 elements in (*cont.*)
 time-limited therapy, comments
  on, 74–75, 239–40, 854
 See also Therapist-patient relationship
*Psychotherapy of Psychogenic Learn-
 ing Disabilities* (Gardner), 852
Puppets, 60–61
Pyne, M., 686

Questionnaire, screening. *See under*
 Screening evaluation, initial
Quick cures, craze for, 849–50
Quotations, use in diagnostic find-
 ings, 357–58

Rabin, A. I., 56
Rambert, M. L., 53
Rational-emotive psychotherapy, 122
Reality about parents, child's acceptance of, 124, 542–43, 570, 670,
 806–7
Reality-oriented stories, 698–701
Recommendations, presenting initial,
 228–37
 fees, discussion of, 233–37
 lack of decision on therapy, 230–
  31
 need for treatment, 231–33
 no need for treatment, 229–30
 presence of child at, 228–29
"Reflected appraisals," 126
Regression
 clay, use of, 56
 finger painting and, 54–55
 regressive gratifications, value of,
  59–60
Reinforcement, positive and negative, 520–21, 610–12
Relationship therapy, 44–45
Release
 clay use for hostile, 56
 therapy, 49–50
 type of wish-fulfillment dreams,
  747–48
 See also Anger inhibition problem
Repetition in dramatized storytelling,
 509, 513
Repetitious dreams, 267, 270, 271–
 72, 294–96, 334

Residency training of author, 8–18
 child psychiatry, 12–18, 20–21
 general psychiatry, 8–12
Resistance
 with drawings, 50–51
 overlap between symptoms and, 49
 parental, 372–75
 Rogers' view of, 48–49
 sensitivity to seriousness of, 673
 to symbolic representation, 41, 42
 transference cure, 115–17
Resolution of the Oedipus complex,
 Freud's theory of, 452
Resolution of the transference neurosis, 114–15
 inapplicability with children, 728–
 31
Respect, therapist-patient, 76–78
Reversals Frequency Test, The, 218
Rewards
 of benevolent acts, emphasizing,
  637, 651–52
 of school work, demonstrating,
  621–22
Rice, Grantland, 609
Rogerian treatment, 15–17, 46–49
Rogers, Carl, 15, 46–49
Rondell, F., 686
Rorschach test, life as, 793–94

Sado-masochistic tendencies, 347–
 48
Schizophrenic patient, family of,
 822–23
Schneidman, E. J., 215, 595
School
 behavior, 181, 565–70
 mother's involvement in activities
  at, 246–47
 parents' performance in, 256–75,
  280
 performance in, 206
  determining need for treatment
   and, 224–25
  initial evaluation of child's, 179–
   81
  recommendation for therapy from,
   230
  repeating of grade in, 644–45
  written report of findings for, 362–
   63
Scrabble for Juniors, 558–70

Screening evaluation, initial, 153–238
criteria for deciding need for treatment, 223–28
initial telephone call, 157–62
interviewing child alone, 210–22
additional diagnostic instruments, 216–21
Draw-a-Person test, 213–15
freely-drawn picture, 211–13
Make-a-Picture test, 215–16
interviewing child and parents together, 196–208
interviewing parents alone, 208–10
participants in initial consultation, 28, 154–57
presenting initial recommendations, 228–37
questionnaire, topics on, 162–94
basic data, 164–67
comprehension and understanding, 179
coordination, 178–79
delivery at birth, 169–71
developmental milestones, 175–78
family history, 187–89
home behavior, 183
infancy-toddler period, 174–75
interests and accomplishments, 183–84
medical history, 185–87
other professionals consulted, 194
peer relationships, 181–83
post-delivery period, 171–74
pregnancy, 167–69
present medical status, 187
psychological symptoms, 189–94
school, 179–81
siblings, 194, 195
Secondary elaboration, mechanism of, 746
Seduction, role of, 129–38
candy and other foods, 133–34
fun, 131–32
humor, 132–33
magic tricks, 134–35
Peabody Picture Vocabulary Test, 135–38
Self-actualization, 15–17, 46–49, 119
Self-assertion, 71–72
Bag of Things Game focusing on, 544–50

Doing Card response on, 641–44
in family therapy, 795
outside of family therapy, 778
Talking Card response on, 618–19, 623, 624, 628
Self-created stories
around drawings, 50–53
as free associations, 732
interpretation of, 213
specific technique for eliciting, 410–13
See also Mutual storytelling derivative games; Mutual storytelling technique; *Talking, Feeling, and Doing Game, The*
Self-revelation, intimacy and, 126–29
Self-serving behavior, increase in, 845–46
Separation anxiety disorder
family projection process and, 818
family therapy for, 799
Feel and Tell game, use of, 572–77
individual therapy for, 803
initial screening interview and, 28, 156, 196–97
mutual storytelling technique, use of, 437–44
in nightmares, 757
over potential loss of parents, 600–607
Sex abuse, 454
Sexual/amourous relationship between co-therapists, 825–26
Sexual inhibition, Feeling Card response to lessen, 634–35, 638–39
Sexual seductivity of mother, 394–97, 398, 453, 454, 553–58, 579, 589
Sexual symbols, 56, 764–65
Shakespeare, William, 86, 87, 465
Sharing
concept in alleviation of oedipal problems, 455, 460–63, 558, 584
of parental attention with siblings, 481–82, 483, 499
Sheps, Jack, 10
Short-term psychotherapy, 74–75, 239–40, 854
Siblings
antisocial behavior disorder over, 470–99
birth of, 226, 470, 480–83, 804–5

Siblings (*cont.*)
  death of, 398–401
  fighting among, 226
  information about, 194, 195
  information on child's treatment
    for, 353
  with neurologically based learning
    disability, 805
  participation in family interview,
    352–56
  rivalry with, 183, 206, 226, 322,
    325, 778–79
  separation anxiety over loss of,
    437–44
  sharing of parental attention with,
    481–82, 483, 499
  treatment of, 28–29
  very bright, normal child's reac-
    tion to, 804
  view of parents, 354–55
Siding with child in conflict with
    parents, 109–11
Sleep-preservation function of
    dreams, 746
Sleep terror disorder, 757
Snow White, 707, 708
Social workers, 858
Solomon, J. C., 17, 42–43, 406
"Squiggles Game," 52
Statue of Liberty syndrome, 82–84,
    105
Steadiness Tester, The, 218
Stepparents, 34, 695, 801, 807–8,
    812–13
Stereotypes in fairy tales, child's at-
    traction to, 707
Stone, Irving, 387
Stories About the Real World (Gard-
    ner), 34, 151, 237–38, 303–4,
    488, 679
Story analysis, fundamentals of, 413–
    15
Storytelling
  Draw-a-Person test and, 214–15
  as enriching experience, 132
  See also Bibliotherapy; Dramatized
    storytelling; Mutual storytelling
    technique
Stress
  capacity to distort under situations
    of, 341–44
  reaction, post-traumatic, 804–5

Strupp, Hans, 84, 121, 686, 842
Stubblefield, R. L., 374
Stuttering, case of, 391–93
Substitutive gratifications, providing,
    417, 441–42, 455, 558, 604–6,
    656, 700
Sullivan, Harry Stack, 21, 125, 126,
    447, 787
Superego
  development
    intrapsychic conflict and, 478–
      80, 735–36
    in neurologically based learning
      disability case, 468–70
    reiterative process for, 477
  deficiencies, case of, 429–30
  "lacunae," 123
  loosening up of, 122–23
Symbols
  capacity to separate entity denoted
    by, 723
  dream, 746, 757, 762–68
  in fables, 702–5
  sexual, 56, 268, 747, 764–65
  story analysis and significance of,
    413
  universal, 747
  See also Mutual storytelling deriva-
    tive games; Mutual storytelling
    technique; *Talking, Feeling,
    and Doing Game, The*
Sympathy, 82, 93
Symptoms
  analysis of childhood roots of,
    733–34
  initial evaluation of, 189–94
  initial observation for presence of,
    210–11
  insight utilization and alleviation
    of, 378
  of low self-worth, 123–24
  oedipal, 453–54
  origin of, 67–72
  termination based on, 843–44
  transference cure and alleviation
    of, 116–17
  transient, 158, 223–24
  viewed as disease, 851

Tactile projective game, 570–77
Talk, child, 111–13

Talking, Feeling, and Doing Game,
   The, 34, 150, 609–84
  basic format, 610–16
  card responses, 610, 616–46
    Doing Cards, 639–46
    Feeling Cards, 629–39
    Talking Cards, 616–28
  disadvantages, 684
  dramatized storytelling and, 473–
    76
  to facilitate psychoanalytic inquiry,
    740–44
  in family therapy, 683–84, 833–34
  in group therapy, 103, 616, 683
  in initial interview, 217–18
  in intensive diagnostic evaluation,
    340
  positive reinforcement in, 610–12
  reasons for development of, 607–8
  therapist-patient interchanges, ex-
    amples of, 646–82
    hypospadias, boy with, 652–68
    psychopathic partner, dealing
      with, 646–52
    revelation of therapist's deficien-
      cies in, 128, 613–14, 669–71
TAT, 216, 597
Teacher
  child's involvement with, 729–30
  therapist as, 85, 120–26
Teaching children to psychoanalyze
  dreams, 760–69
  candidates for, 760–62
  fundamental principles of, 762–65
Team therapists in family therapy,
  824–26
Technical considerations in family
  therapy. *See under* Family therapy
Teenagers, use as authority in stories, 424, 547. *See also* Adolescents
Telephone call, initial, 157–62
"Tender years presumption," 35
Termination, 843–45
Terror disorder, sleep, 757
Thematic Apperception Test (TAT),
  216, 597
Theoretical and developmental foundations of author's techniques,
  1–35
  educational background, 2–7

internship, 7–8
military service, 18–20
private practice, 27–35
psychoanalytic training, 21–27
residency training, 8–18
  child psychiatry, 12–18, 20–21
  general psychiatry, 8–12
Therapeutic ally in family therapy,
  828–29
*Therapeutic Communication with
  Children* (Gardner), 33, 124
Therapist-parent relationship, 111,
  377
Therapist-patient relationship, 76–84,
  91–152
  blank screen approach and, 76,
    614, 685, 731–33
  child's view of therapist, 110–11
  clinical examples, 138–52
    amotivational syndrome, 144–45
    attempt on therapist's life, 139–
      41
    death of boy's father, 147–49
    hostile parent, 146–47
    passive-aggressive child, 145–46
    rebuking of patient, 141–44
    revelation of therapist's defect,
      149–50
  depth of, 831–32
  factors conducive to therapeutic
    change, 105–38
    affection for patient, 107–9
    child talk, 111–13
    corrective emotional experience,
      117–18, 204
    educator, therapist as, 85, 120–26
    identification with therapist, 78–
      82, 118–20
    intimacy and self-revelation,
      126–29
    resolution of transference neu-
      rosis, 114–15
    seduction, role of, 129–38
    taking child's side vs. parents,
      109–11
    transference cure, 115–17
  Feeling Card response developing
    good, 631
  interchanges in *Talking, Feeling,
    and Doing Game,* 646–82
  hypospadias, dealing with boy
    with, 652–68

Therapist-patient relationship (*cont.*)
  interchanges in *Talking, Feeling, and Doing Game*
  psychopathic partner, dealing with, 646–52
  revelation of therapist's deficiencies in, 128, 613–14, 669–71
  interviewing child and parents together and, 196
  parental jealousy of, 373
  parental participation and, 378
  personality of therapist and, 91–105
    boredom, 104
    childlike characteristics, 98
    comfort with therapeutic failure, 104–5
    excitation, 96–97
    flexibility and creativity, 101–3
    frustration tolerance, 100–101
    inner warmth response, 97–98
    liking children, 93
    memory of own childhood, 95–96, 613–14, 659–60
    parent, therapist as, 103
    parental instinct, strong, 99–100
    projection into child's position, 93–95
    "on the same wavelength," 99
  rapport in, 222–23
  receptivity of therapist's message, 77–78
  respect vs. idealization/idolization of therapist, 76–78, 128–29, 614, 732–33
  trying to help vs. helping, 82–84
Thomas, A., 373
"Threat therapy," 230
Three wishes question, 217, 304–6
Tics, 393–97, 589
Time-limited therapy, 74–75, 239–40, 854
Tolstoy, Leo, 789
Touching compulsion, case of, 397–98, 579–89
Training
  author's experience, 5–18, 20–21
  central problem in, 25–27
  dehumanization of treatment and, 856–58
  medical school, 5–7, 850–52
  model of psychiatric, 12

  in nonmedical program, 857
  psychoanalytic, 21–27, 787
Transactional diagnoses, 838–39
Transference
  cure, 115–17
  in family therapy, 831–32
  inapplicability with children, 728–31
  neurosis, 114, 729
  resolution of, 114–15, 728–31
  onto spouse, 816
Transformation, "malevolent," 447
Transient symptomatology, 158, 223–24
Trapp, Maria, 153
Treatment
  length of, 232–33, 360, 724
  need for, 223–33
    criteria for deciding, 223–28
    recommendation of, 231–33
    recommendation of no, 229–30
  parental ambivalence over, 372–75
  parental involvement. *See* Parental involvement in child's treatment
  prepaid plans, 852–56
  presentation of program to parents, 360–62
  of projected self, 94–95
Trying to help vs. helping, 82–84
Turnover in psychiatric training, effect of, 12

Ugly Duck, The, 712
Ugly Duckling, The, 706, 707
"Unconditional positive regard," 15, 17, 47, 108
Unconscious material and processes
  bringing into conscious awareness, 405, 726–27
  defined, 67
  dream formation and, 762–65
  emergence in dreams, 745
  explaining to child, 765–66
  insight into, development and utilization of, 737–38
  therapist's awareness of, 787
  See also Psychoanalytically-oriented child psychotherapy
Understanding, initial evaluation of child's, 179
Understanding Children: A Parents Guide to Child Rearing (Gardner), 34, 696–97

"Unfinished business" in dreams, 763–64
Universal symbols, notion of, 474

Vaginal symbols, 765
Validation, consensual, 125
Value(s)
    identification with therapist's, 78–82
    imposition, problem of, 80
    judgments, 78–81
    revealed in *Talking, Feeling, and Doing Game* interchange, 656–57, 660–64
Verbal inquiry of child, direct, 298–304
Verbal projective questions, responses to
    of children, 318–34
    of fathers, 283–90
    of mother, 262–64
    preparation of diagnostic findings on, 358
Video tape and cassette recorders, use of, 33, 35, 409–10, 467–68

Waelder, R., 40–41
"War games," influence of childhood, 531

Water play, 58–60
Wavelength, being on same, 99
Wayward Youth (Aichhorn), 109
Wechsler, D., 218
Wechsler Intelligence Scale for Children—Revised (WISC-R), 135, 218, 340
Weight
    birth, 168, 170
    problem, 326, 327
William A. White Psychoanalytic Institute, 21–27, 787
Winnicott, D. W., 52, 96–100
WISC-R, 135, 218, 340
Wish(es)
    five wishes question, parents' responses to, 258–61, 281–83
    fulfillment, dream as vehicle for, 745–48
    guilt over, 626–27
    three wishes question, 217, 304–6
Wizard of Oz, The (Baum), 715–20
Woltmann, A. G., 43, 55, 60, 61
Word processor for preparation of diagnostic findings, 356–57
Wordsworth, William, 1
Work ethic, developing, 550, 619–20, 631–32, 675–77
Work history of parents, 257, 280–81
Written report for parents, 362–63